D0471971

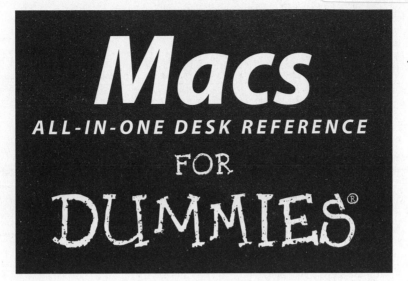

Macs
ALL-IN-ONE DESK REFERENCE
FOR DUMMIES®

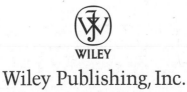

by Wally Wang

WILEY

Wiley Publishing, Inc.

Macs All-in-One Desk Reference For Dummies®

Published by
Wiley Publishing, Inc.
111 River Street
Hoboken, NJ 07030-5774

www.wiley.com

Published by Wiley Publishing, Inc., Indianapolis, Indiana

Published simultaneously in Canada

For general information on our other products and services, please contact our Customer Care Department within the U.S. at 800-762-2974, outside the U.S. at 317-572-3993, or fax 317-572-4002.

For technical support, please visit www.wiley.com/techsupport.

Wiley also publishes its books in a variety of electronic formats. Some content that appears in print may not be available in electronic books.

Library of Congress Control Number: 2008920769

ISBN: 978-0-470-16957-5

Manufactured in the United States of America

10 9 8 7 6 5 4 3 2 1

WILEY

About the Author

I might as well use this space to tell you about myself on the off chance that anyone actually reads it. After suffering through post-traumatic stress disorder after working for General Dynamics for 1.5 years and Cubic Corporation for another 2 years (where I can count my contributions to making the world a better place on one amputated, missing finger), I soon fled the world of Department of Defense contractors to the sanctuary of the personal computer market, where I was fortunate enough to make a living writing computer magazine articles and books.

I've written several dozen computer books, most of which are out of print (unless someone still wants a book teaching them about the joys of Turbo Pascal programming or how to write macros in WordPerfect 5.0 for DOS). While spending most of my adult life covering the rise and fall of the computer industry, I noticed a pattern. Every computer company that was the leader in its field would eventually mess up by failing to update its product for several years and then finally churn out a shoddy update that drove their customers en masse to a rival, thereby turning the rival into the new leader of that particular category.

This happened when WordStar failed to update its word processor for four years and finally cranked out an incompatible version (called WordStar 2000) that everyone hated, thereby causing people to flock to WordPerfect instead. WordPerfect promptly fumbled the ball when it failed to update its product to run on Windows, which let Microsoft Word take over from there.

The same situation occurred again in the database market when dBASE took too long to issue an update and when it did, the update turned out to be the buggy dBASE IV that everyone hated, which caused everyone to switch to Paradox. Like WordPerfect, Paradox fumbled the ball by not creating a Windows version, which allowed Microsoft Access to take over the database market.

That's when I noticed that Microsoft was fumbling the ball in the operating system market. After failing to update its operating system for five years, it promptly issued a buggy (like dBASE IV) and incompatible (like WordStar 2000) version dubbed Vista. One look at Vista made me realize that history was about to repeat itself and Vista would soon be the main reason people would crown a new leader in the operating system category. After ruling out competitors like Linux, I realized that the next leader of the personal computer market could only be Mac OS X.

So that's when I became a complete Mac user, dumping Windows XP (and my free copy of Vista) in favor of learning and mastering the Macintosh. That's who I am today: a devoted Mac user who has realized that the Mac is the future of the personal computer market because the Mac is reliable, easy to use, and most importantly, fun to use as well. Not that anyone cares what I think, though.

Dedication

This book is dedicated to all those long-suffering Windows users who have switched over to the Mac and discovered that it's possible to buy and use a computer that actually works.

Author's Acknowledgments

This book could never have been written without the invention of the printing press, so thank you, Johannes Gutenberg! On a more contemporary level, a big thanks goes out to Bill Gladstone and Margot Hutchison at Waterside Productions. Of course, if they weren't my agents, they would have just gotten someone else to write this book and you'd see a different name plastered across the cover.

Another big round of thanks goes to the whole, happy crew at Wiley Publishing for turning this project into reality: Bob Woerner for entrusting me with the massive Mac tome you have in your hands; Paul Levesque for keeping this whole project together; Dennis Cohen for helping me make the transition from the world of Windows to the much better world of the Mac; and Virginia Sanders for editing, revising, and correcting what I wrote so I don't wind up looking like an idiot.

I also want to acknowledge all the stand-up comedians I've met, who have made those horrible crowds at comedy clubs more bearable: Darrell Joyce (`http://darrelljoyce.com`), Leo "the Man, the Myth, the Legend" Fontaine, Chris Clobber, Bob Zany (`www.bobzany.com`), Russ Rivas (`http://russrivas.com`), Don Learned, Dante, and Dobie "The Uranus King" Maxwell. Another round of thanks goes to Steve Schirripa (who appeared in HBO's hit show The Sopranos) for giving me my break in performing at the Riviera Hotel and Casino in Las Vegas, one of the few old-time casinos left that the demolition crews haven't imploded (yet).

I'd also like to acknowledge the animals in my life who have played such a large role in forcing me to buy paper towels, liquid cleaners, and air fresheners: Bo, Scraps, Tasha, and Nuit (my cats) and Ollie and Loons (two birds who live with my sister because if they lived with me, they would have long ago become meals for Bo, Scraps, Tasha, or Nuit).

Finally, I'd like to acknowledge Cassandra (my wife) and Jordan (my son) for putting up with my long hours and my insistence that everyone dump their Windows XP PCs right away (an easy decision since they never worked right anyway) and migrate completely to the Mac.

Publisher's Acknowledgments

We're proud of this book; please send us your comments through our online registration form located at `www.dummies.com/register/`.

Some of the people who helped bring this book to market include the following:

Acquisitions and Editorial

Senior Project Editor: Paul Levesque

Acquisitions Editor: Bob Woerner

Copy Editor: Virginia Sanders

Technical Editor: Dennis Cohen

Editorial Manager: Leah Cameron

Editorial Assistant: Amanda Foxworth

Sr. Editorial Assistant: Cherie Case

Cartoons: Rich Tennant (`www.the5thwave.com`)

Composition Services

Project Coordinator: Kristie Rees

Layout and Graphics: Claudia Bell, Stacie Brooks, Karl Byers, Reuben W. Davis, Melissa K. Jester, Barbara Moore, Ronald Terry, Christine Williams

Proofreaders: Christopher M. Jones, Jessica Kramer

Indexer: Broccoli Information Management

Anniversary Logo Design: Richard Pacifico

Publishing and Editorial for Technology Dummies

Richard Swadley, Vice President and Executive Group Publisher

Andy Cummings, Vice President and Publisher

Mary Bednarek, Executive Acquisitions Director

Mary C. Corder, Editorial Director

Publishing for Consumer Dummies

Diane Graves Steele, Vice President and Publisher

Joyce Pepple, Acquisitions Director

Composition Services

Gerry Fahey, Vice President of Production Services

Debbie Stailey, Director of Composition Services

Contents at a Glance

Introduction ***1***

Book I: Mac Basics *7*

Chapter 1: Getting to Know Your Mac 9
Chapter 2: Starting Up, Sleeping, and Shutting Down 15
Chapter 3: Getting Acquainted with the Mac User Interface 25
Chapter 4: Running Programs 55
Chapter 5: Installing and Uninstalling Software 77
Chapter 6: Managing Files and Folders 93
Chapter 7: Customizing Your Mac 129
Chapter 8: Accessibility Features of the Macintosh 153
Chapter 9: Maintenance and Troubleshooting 167

Book II: Photos, Music, and Movies *181*

Chapter 1: Playing with Audio 183
Chapter 2: Playing with Pictures 205
Chapter 3: Watching Videos on a Mac 223
Chapter 4: Using Front Row for Movies, Music, and Photos 239

Book III: Browsing the Internet *255*

Chapter 1: Browsing the Internet 257
Chapter 2: Sending and Receiving E-Mail 291
Chapter 3: Chatting in Real Time 319
Chapter 4: Security for Your Mac 335
Chapter 5: Setting Up Your Own Web Site 359

Book IV: Working with iLife and iWork *371*

Chapter 1: Storing Memories with iPhoto 373
Chapter 2: Using iMovie 401
Chapter 3: Using iDVD 425
Chapter 4: Creating Web Sites with iWeb 443
Chapter 5: Using GarageBand 459
Chapter 6: Writing and Publishing with Pages 481
Chapter 7: Making Presentations with Keynote 509
Chapter 8: Doing Calculations with Numbers 535

Book V: Other Mac Programs 565
Chapter 1: Word Processing on the Mac 567
Chapter 2: Office Suites on the Mac 581
Chapter 3: Painting and Drawing on a Mac 597
Chapter 4: Running Windows on a Mac 613
Chapter 5: Having Fun with a Mac 627

Book VI: Time-Saving Tips with a Mac 641
Chapter 1: Protecting Your Data 643
Chapter 2: Managing Your Time with iCal 659
Chapter 3: Storing Contact Information in the Address Book 679
Chapter 4: Using Dashboard 693
Chapter 5: Automating Your Mac 705

Book VII: Mac Networking 723
Chapter 1: Networking Your Macs 725
Chapter 2: Sharing Files and Resources on a Network 739
Chapter 3: Bluetooth Wireless Networking 751

Index 761

Table of Contents

Introduction 1

About This Book..2
How to Use This Book 2
How This Book Is Organized..3
Book I: Mac Basics..3
Book II: Photos, Music, and Movies 3
Book III: Browsing the Internet 3
Book IV: Working with iLife and iWork 3
Book V: Other Mac Programs..4
Book VI: Time-Saving Tips with a Mac..4
Book VII: Mac Networking 4
Icons Used in This Book..4
Where to Go from Here..5

Book I: Mac Basics 7

Chapter 1: Getting to Know Your Mac 9

Different Macintosh Models..9
The iMac 10
The MacBook and MacBook Pro 10
The Mac Mini and Mac Pro..11
Understanding Mac Processors 11
Identifying the Parts of Your Mac 13

Chapter 2: Starting Up, Sleeping, and Shutting Down 15

Starting Your Mac..15
Putting a Mac in Sleep Mode 17
Putting a Mac in Sleep mode manually..17
Putting a Mac in Sleep mode automatically..18
Shutting Down a Mac 22
Restarting a Mac..23

Chapter 3: Getting Acquainted with the Mac User Interface 25

Mastering the Mouse and Keyboard..26
The parts of the mouse 26
The parts of the keyboard..27

Getting to Know the Mac User Interface 33
The menu bar 33
Understanding menu commands 34
Working with dialogs 35
Viewing data in a window 35
Manipulating windows with Exposé 42
Playing with Icons in the Dock and Finder 44
The Desktop 44
The Dock 45
The Finder 48
Getting Help 50
Pointing out commands to use 50
Reading help topics 52

Chapter 4: Running Programs 55

Running a Program from the Dock 55
Adding program icons to the Dock 57
Rearranging program icons in the Dock 58
Removing program icons from the Dock 58
Starting Programs by Double-Clicking Icons 59
Double-clicking a program icon 60
Double-clicking a document icon 61
Using alias icons 62
Switching Between Programs 64
Using the Dock to switch between programs 65
Switching programs with the Application Switcher 66
Using Exposé to switch between programs 66
Switching by clicking different windows 67
Getting Organized on Multiple Desktops with Spaces 68
Turning on Spaces and creating Desktops 69
Configuring Spaces 69
Moving program windows to different Desktops 70
Switching Desktops 71
Increasing (or decreasing) the number of Desktops 72
Turning off Spaces 72
Quitting Programs 73
Closing a document 73
Shutting down a program 73
Force quitting a program 74

Chapter 5: Installing and Uninstalling Software 77

Finding Software 77
Installing Software 80
Installing software from a CD/DVD 80
Installing software off the Internet 83

Uninstalling Software....86
Uninstalling a program....86
Removing program icons from the Dock and Desktop....87
Removing user setting files....89

Chapter 6: Managing Files and Folders 93

Using the Finder....94
Understanding devices....94
Understanding folders....95
Navigating through the Finder....97
Opening a folder....97
Exiting a folder....98
Jumping to a specific folder....98
Jumping back and forth....98
Organizing and Viewing a Folder....99
Selecting items in the Finder....100
Using Icon view....100
Using List view....102
Using Columns view....103
Using Cover Flow view....104
Creating Folders....105
Creating a folder using the Finder menu....106
Creating a folder through the Save As dialog....106
Manipulating Files and Folders....108
Renaming a file or folder....109
Copying a file or folder....111
Moving a file or folder....113
Archiving Files and Folders....114
Creating a ZIP file....114
Creating a DMG file....115
Searching Files....118
Using Spotlight....118
Using Smart Folders....119
Using Smart Folders in the Sidebar....123
Storing Files and Folders in the Dock....123
Storing files in the Dock....123
Creating Stacks in the Dock....124
Opening files stored in a Stack....125
Burning Files and Folders to CD/DVD....125
Creating a Burn Folder....125
Burning the contents of a Burn Folder....126
Deleting a File or Folder....127
Retrieving a file or folder from the Trash....128
Emptying the Trash....128

Chapter 7: Customizing Your Mac 129
Changing the Desktop.....129
Choosing a built-in Desktop image.....129
Choosing an iPhoto image for the Desktop.....130
Choosing your own image for the Desktop.....131
Customizing the Screen Saver.....132
Choosing a screen saver.....132
Defining hot corners.....133
Changing the Display and Appearance.....135
Changing the screen resolution.....135
Changing the color of the user interface.....136
Changing the Date and Time.....137
Adjusting Sounds.....139
Saving Energy.....142
Picking a Printer.....144
Adding (and deleting) a printer.....144
Defining a default printer.....145
Creating Separate Accounts.....145
Types of accounts.....146
Creating an account.....147
Switching between accounts.....149
Deleting an account.....151

Chapter 8: Accessibility Features of the Macintosh 153
Correcting Vision Limitations.....153
Correcting hearing limitations.....155
Correcting keyboard limitations.....156
Correcting mouse limitations.....157
Using Voice Recognition and Speech.....160
Setting up voice recognition.....160
Setting up speech capabilities.....164

Chapter 9: Maintenance and Troubleshooting 167
Handling Startup Troubles.....167
Booting up in Safe Mode.....168
Booting from a CD/DVD.....169
Booting from another Mac through a FireWire cable.....170
Shutting Down Frozen or Hung Up Programs.....171
Removing Jammed CDs/DVDs.....174
Repairing and Maintaining Hard Drives.....175
Verifying a disk.....175
Verifying disk permissions.....178
Preventative Maintenance.....179

Book II: Photos, Music, and Movies 181

Chapter 1: Playing with Audio 183

Understanding Audio File Formats 183
- Lossless audio files 184
- Compressed lossless audio files 184
- Compressed lossy audio files 184

Playing Audio with iTunes 186
- Listening to CDs 186
- Converting an audio disc into digital files 188
- Importing digital audio files 190
- Sorting your digital audio files 191
- Playing digital audio files 194
- Searching for a song 195
- Using a playlist 196
- Creating a Smart Playlist 197
- Deleting a playlist 202

Burning an Audio CD 202

Chapter 2: Playing with Pictures 205

Understanding Digital Photography 205
- Understanding megapixels 205
- Understanding flash memory cards 206
- Understanding digital image file formats 209

Transferring Digital Images to the Mac 209
- Defining a default program for retrieving images 210
- Retrieving images using iPhoto 211
- Retrieving images using Image Capture 211

Capturing Pictures from Other Sources 213
- Capturing pictures with Photo Booth 213
- Capturing pictures off Web sites 215

Editing Digital Images 216
- Selecting all or part of a picture 217
- Changing colors 219
- Adding and removing items in a picture 220

Chapter 3: Watching Videos on a Mac 223

Understanding Video Disc Formats 223

Understanding Digital Video Formats 224

Playing a Digital Video File 225

Playing a DVD 226
Understanding full screen mode and window mode 226
Viewing the DVD and Title menus 229
Skipping through a video 229
Viewing frames in steps and slow motion 230
Skipping by chapters 230
Placing bookmarks in a video 231
Creating video clips 233
Viewing closed captioning 235
Viewing different camera angles 236
Choosing different audio tracks 236
Customizing DVD Player 236

Chapter 4: Using Front Row for Movies, Music, and Photos 239

Using the Apple Remote 239
Making a Mac go to sleep 240
Booting up a Mac 240
Controlling applications 241
Pairing an Apple Remote with a Mac 242
Accessing Front Row 244
Starting Front Row 244
Highlighting an option in Front Row 244
Selecting an option in Front Row 244
Exiting a Front Row submenu 245
Playing Movies and Videos 245
Playing a DVD 246
Playing a digital video file 246
Playing a TV show 247
Playing a music video 248
Playing Music and Other Sounds 250
Playing an audio CD 250
Playing a digital audio file 251
Playing podcasts 252
Playing audiobooks 253
Viewing Pictures 254

Book III: Browsing the Internet 255

Chapter 1: Browsing the Internet 257

Setting Up an Internet Connection 257
Ethernet connection 257
Wireless access 258
Dial-up access 261

Browsing through Web Sites....264
Defining a home page....264
Visiting a Web site....265
Searching for Web sites....267
Searching previously viewed Web sites....267
Using bookmarks....268
Browsing with SnapBack....276
Using tabbed browsing....277
Using Web Clips....279
Search for Text on a Web Page....281
Saving Web Pages....283
Saving a Web page as a file....283
Printing a Web page as a file....284
Sending a Web page by e-mail....285
Sending a Web page as a link....286
Viewing and Playing Multimedia Files....286
Watching video....286
Listening to streaming audio....288
Viewing PDF files....288
Downloading Files....288
Downloading a file....289

Chapter 2: Sending and Receiving E-Mail....291

Setting Up an E-Mail Account....291
Gathering your e-mail account information....292
Configuring your e-mail account....293
Writing E-Mails....296
Creating a new e-mail....296
Replying to a message....297
Forwarding a message....297
Sending a file attachment....298
Sending a message to multiple recipients....299
Using e-mail stationery....300
Spell and grammar checking....303
Receiving and Reading E-Mail....305
Retrieving e-mail....305
Reading e-mail....306
Viewing and saving file attachments....307
Storing e-mail addresses....308
Deleting messages....310
Organizing E-Mail....311
Searching through e-mail....311
Sorting e-mail....311
Organizing e-mail with mailbox folders....313
Automatically organizing e-mail with smart mailboxes....314
Automatically organizing e-mail with rules....316

Chapter 3: Chatting in Real Time 319

Setting Up an iChat Account 319
Storing names in a buddy list 321
Organizing a buddy list 322
Chatting with Someone 325
Initiating a text chat 326
Initiating an audio chat 328
Initiating a video chat 329
Accepting (Or Blocking) a Chat Invitation 330
Changing your status 331
Becoming invisible 332
Accepting (or blocking) chat invitations with privacy levels 332

Chapter 4: Security for Your Mac 335

Locking Down Your Mac 335
Using passwords 336
Configuring a firewall 340
Buying a firewall 342
Creating Multiple Accounts 344
Creating a Managed with Parental Controls account 345
Creating a Guest account 347
Dealing with Junk E-Mail 354
Bouncing junk e-mail 355
Filtering junk e-mail 356

Chapter 5: Setting Up Your Own Web Site 359

Types of Web Sites 360
Free, advertiser-sponsored Web site hosts 360
Free ISP Web site hosts 362
Fee-based Web site hosting service 363
Creating Web Pages 365
Creating a Web page with HTML code 365
Creating Web pages with other programs 366
Creating Web pages with dedicated Web page designers 367
Uploading Web Pages 368
Using .Mac 369

Book IV: Working with iLife and iWork 371

Chapter 1: Storing Memories with iPhoto 373

Importing Pictures 373
Organizing Events in the Library 375
Creating an Event 375
Browsing through an Event 375

Naming an Event 376
Merging Events 377
Splitting an Event 378
Moving pictures from one Event to another 379
Sorting Events 380
Organizing Pictures 381
Viewing pictures stored in a single Event 381
Viewing pictures stored in all Events 382
Naming pictures 383
Rating pictures 384
Adding keywords to a picture 385
Storing pictures in albums and folders 386
Deleting pictures, albums, and folders 389
Editing Pictures 389
Rotating a picture 389
Cropping a picture 390
Straightening a picture 392
Fixing a picture 393
Adding visual effects to a picture 393
Controlling colors in a picture 394
Sharing Pictures 396
Printing pictures 396
E-mailing pictures 397
Saving pictures to a CD/DVD 398
Using pictures in iWeb and iDVD 398
Ordering books, calendars, and cards 399

Chapter 2: Using iMovie 401

How iMovie Works 401
Organizing the Event Library 401
Organizing the Project Library 402
Importing a Video into the Event Library 403
Importing from a digital video camera 403
Importing a digital video file 405
Working with Projects 406
Creating an iMovie project 406
Selecting video clips 408
Deleting video clips 410
Deleting a project 411
Printing a project 412
Editing Video Clips in a Project 412
Rearranging the order of video clips 412
Adjusting the size of a video clip 413
Adding titles 415
Adding transitions 417
Adding audio files 418

Saving a Video 419
Saving a project as a digital video file....................420
Saving (and removing) a video for iTunes 421
Saving (and removing) a project for YouTube....................421
Saving (and removing) a project in the Media Browser 423

Chapter 3: Using iDVD 425

Burning a Video Straight to DVD....................425
Creating a DVD with the Magic iDVD Option....................427
Working with iDVD Projects....................430
Adding photos to a title menu theme 432
Adding options to the title menu 433
Moving and deleting buttons 438
Defining opening content for your DVD 439
Saving your iDVD project 440

Chapter 4: Creating Web Sites with iWeb 443

The Parts of a Web Page....................443
The purpose of text....................444
The purpose of graphics 444
Putting together a Web page....................445
Creating a Web Site in iWeb 445
Picking a theme 446
Adding new pages 447
Deleting Web pages 448
Designing a Web Page....................449
Replacing placeholder text 449
Replacing placeholder graphics 449
Changing the Web page theme 450
Customizing the Parts of a Web Page....................451
Moving an object....................451
Resizing an object 452
Rearranging an object....................453
Deleting objects....................454
Working with text 454
Working with graphics....................457
Publishing Your Web Pages....................458

Chapter 5: Using GarageBand 459

Recording Audio....................459
Recording audio through Magic GarageBand....................460
Creating music with software instruments 463
Playing with a real instrument....................466

Editing Audio 468
Splitting a track....468
Joining a track....469
Moving tracks 470
Arranging tracks by regions....471
Modifying the key and tempo 473
Saving Music 474
Saving a song in iTunes 475
Saving a song to disk....476
Burning a song to CD 476
Recording Podcasts 477
Recording speech....477
Adding jingles and audio effects 478
Adding pictures 479

Chapter 6: Writing and Publishing with Pages 481

Working with Document Templates....481
Replacing placeholder text 483
Replacing placeholder pictures....484
Working with Text 485
Editing text 485
Formatting text 486
Adjusting text spacing and margins....487
Using Formatting Styles....491
Applying styles 491
Creating temporary styles....495
Creating and Placing Text Boxes....496
Creating a text box 496
Moving a text box....497
Resizing a text box 497
Creating linked text boxes....498
Wrapping text around a text box....500
Working with Digital Photographs 501
Adding a picture 502
Moving and resizing a picture....502
Modifying a picture 503
Polishing Your Document....506
Spell checking a document 506
Exporting a document 507

Chapter 7: Making Presentations with Keynote 509

Creating a Presentation....509
Working with Themes....510
Choosing a theme for a new presentation 511
Defining a default theme....511

Changing Presentation Views 512
Working with Slides 514
Adding a slide 514
Rearranging slides 515
Deleting a slide 516
Grouping slides 516
Manipulating Text 518
Editing text on a slide 518
Formatting text 518
Adding Media Files 520
Adding sound 520
Adding iPhoto pictures 521
Adding iMovie videos 522
Editing Pictures and Movies 523
Moving and resizing a picture or movie 523
Modifying a picture 524
Creating Transitions and Effects 527
Creating a slide transition 527
Creating text and graphic effects 528
Making text and graphics move on a slide 529
Polishing Your Presentation 531
Viewing a presentation 531
Rehearsing a presentation 531
Exporting a presentation 532

Chapter 8: Doing Calculations with Numbers 535

Understanding the Parts of a Numbers Spreadsheet 535
Creating a Numbers Spreadsheet 538
Working with Sheets 539
Adding a sheet 540
Deleting a sheet 540
Adding a table or chart 540
Deleting a table or chart 541
Naming sheets, tables, and charts 542
Designing Tables 542
Moving a table 542
Resizing a table 543
Adding a row or column 544
Deleting a row or column 545
Resizing rows and columns 545
Formatting a table 546
Typing Data into Tables 547
Formatting numbers and text 547
Typing formulas 549
Formatting data entry cells 553
Deleting data in cells 556

Making Charts....556
Creating a chart....556
Editing a chart....558
Manipulating a chart....558
Deleting a chart....559
Making Your Spreadsheets Pretty....559
Adding a text box....559
Adding a picture....560
Deleting text boxes, shapes and pictures....561
Sharing Your Spreadsheet....561
Printing a spreadsheet....561
Exporting a spreadsheet....562

Book V: Other Mac Programs....565

Chapter 1: Word Processing on the Mac....567

The Basic Features of Word Processing....567
Creating a document and adding text....567
Copying or cutting text....568
Deleting text....569
Formatting text....569
Formatting pages....570
Choosing a Word Processor....571
TextEdit....571
Microsoft Word....571
Microsoft Word alternatives....572
Specialized word processors....573
Word Processor File Formats....575
The Microsoft Word .doc and .docx format....575
RTF (Rich Text Format) files....575
Text (ASCII) files....576
Open Document (.odf) files....576
Web page (HTML) files....577
Portable Document Format (PDF) files....577
Converting File Formats....578

Chapter 2: Office Suites on the Mac....581

Understanding Spreadsheets....581
The parts of a spreadsheet....582
Calculating results with formulas....583
Formatting text and numbers....584
Making numbers meaningful with charts....585

Understanding Presentation Programs 586
Displaying text 586
Displaying graphics 587
Spicing up presentations with transitions 588
Rearranging slides 588
Comparing Office Suites 589
Microsoft Office 589
ThinkFree Office 590
Google Docs & Spreadsheets 591
NeoOffice and OpenOffice 592
RagTime 594
MarinerPak 594
Office Suite File Formats 595
Spreadsheet file formats 595
Presentation file formats 596

Chapter 3: Painting and Drawing on a Mac 597

Understanding Painting versus Drawing 597
Common Raster Editing Features 599
Selecting an entire picture 600
Selecting an area 600
Selecting an irregular shape 601
Selecting with the Magic Wand 602
Erasing pixels 602
Using the paint brush and paint bucket 603
Common Vector-Editing Features 604
Moving and resizing objects with the Selection tool 604
Reshaping an object with the Direct Selection tool 605
Drawing lines 607
Choosing a Painting and Drawing Program 608
Photoshop alternatives 608
Illustrator alternatives 609
Flash alternatives 610
Graphic File Formats 611
Raster (painting) formats 611
Vector graphics (drawing) formats 612

Chapter 4: Running Windows on a Mac 613

Giving Your Mac a Dual Personality with Boot Camp 614
Making sure you can run Boot Camp 614
Installing Windows 616
Choosing an operating system with Boot Camp 619
Using Virtual Machines 620
Using CrossOver Mac 624

Chapter 5: Having Fun with a Mac 627

¿No Hablas Español? Then Get Crackin'! 627
Tooting Your Own Horn 630
Getting Touchy-Feely with Your Keyboard 631
Taking Your Grey Matter to the Gym 632
Playing Hooky with Your Hobby 633
Bring on the Games! 634
Playing strategically 634
Head on down to the arcade 636
Playing multiplayer, online role-playing games 639

Book VI: Time-Saving Tips with a Mac 641

Chapter 1: Protecting Your Data 643

Understanding Different Backup Options 643
Using your hard drive 644
Backing up to CDs/DVDs 644
Storing backups on USB flash drives 644
Backing up with external hard drives 645
Storing backups off-site 646
Going Back to the Past with Time Machine 646
Setting up Time Machine 647
Defining files to skip 648
Retrieving files and folders 650
Working with Data-Recovery Programs 651
Encrypting with FileVault 654
Setting up FileVault 654
Turning off FileVault 657

Chapter 2: Managing Your Time with iCal 659

Understanding iCal 659
Working with the Calendar List 660
Creating a new calendar 661
Creating a new calendar group 661
Moving a calendar or group 663
Renaming and deleting calendars and groups 663
Using the Mini-Month 664
Creating and Modifying Events 664
Viewing events 664
Creating an event 664
Moving an event 666
Duplicating an event 666
Editing an event 667
Deleting an event 670

Finding Events 670
Color-coding events 670
Selectively hiding events 671
Checking for today's events 671
Checking events for a specific date 671
Searching for an event 672
Making a To Do List 673
Viewing and hiding the To Do list 673
Adding tasks to the To Do list 674
Setting due dates for your To Do list tasks 674
Prioritizing your To Do list 674
Completing, editing, and deleting To Do tasks 675
Managing iCal Files 676
Exporting iCal data 676
Importing iCal data 677
Backing up iCal data and restoring a backup file 677
Printing an iCal file 678

Chapter 3: Storing Contact Information in the Address Book 679

Storing Names 679
Designing a template 679
Storing names 681
Displaying companies and people 682
Editing a card 682
Adding pictures to a name 683
Searching names 685
Deleting a name 685
Creating Groups 685
Creating a group 685
Creating a group from a selection of names 686
Adding names automatically with Smart Groups 686
Creating a Smart Group from search results 688
Deleting a Group 689
Managing Your Address Book Files 689
Printing your Address Book 689
Exporting your Address Book 690
Importing data into your Address Book 691

Chapter 4: Using Dashboard 693

Getting to Know Your Dashboard Widgets 693
Moving a widget 694
Customizing a widget 694
Customizing the Dashboard shortcut key 695

Adding and Removing Widgets 696
Removing a widget from Dashboard 696
Making a widget appear in Dashboard 697
Finding New Widgets 700
Disabling and Deleting Widgets from Dashboard 701
Disabling a widget 701
Deleting a widget 702

Chapter 5: Automating Your Mac 705

Understanding Automator 705
Understanding Actions 707
Creating a workflow 709
Adding, rearranging, and deleting actions 711
Running and testing a workflow 712
Saving a workflow 713
Opening a saved workflow 713
Creating Example Workflows 713
Playing with text 713
Playing with digital photography 716
Playing with files 718
Making your Mac imitate you with the Watch Me Do action 721

Book VII: Mac Networking 723

Chapter 1: Networking Your Macs 725

Creating a Wired Network 725
Creating a Wireless Network 727
Setting Up an Airport Extreme Base Station 729
Connecting a Phone or PDA to a Mac 735
Adding a handheld device to your Mac 736
Synchronizing a handheld device with your Mac 737
Resetting a handheld device with your Mac 737

Chapter 2: Sharing Files and Resources on a Network 739

Sharing Files 739
Turning on file sharing 740
Defining user access to shared folders 741
Accessing shared folders 745
Sharing Printers 747
Sharing an Internet Connection 749

Chapter 3: Bluetooth Wireless Networking 751

Identifying Bluetooth Capabilities 751
Configuring Bluetooth 752
Pairing a Device 754
  Pairing with your Mac 754
  Removing a paired device from your Mac 757
Sharing through Bluetooth 757
  Sharing files 758
  Sharing an Internet connection 759

Index 761

Introduction

Whether you're a beginner, an intermediate user, or a seasoned computer expert, you can find something in *Macs All-in-One Desk Reference For Dummies* for you. This book is divided into several minibooks so you can focus on the topics that interest you and skip over the rest. Eventually, you'll need more detailed explanations on specific topics than this book can provide (that's when you should look into a more specialized *For Dummies* book), but if you need a quick introduction to get you started on a variety of topics related to using a Mac, this book can answer your questions, steer you in the right direction, and lead you gently on your way.

This book focuses on the basics for using all aspects of a Mac, from just turning it on and using the mouse to connecting your Mac in a network to organizing your digital pictures and videos to create photo albums and home movies with fancy Hollywood-style effects to . . . you get the idea.

This book even shows you how to use and take advantage of Apple's new iWork suite, which provides word processing and desktop publishing, presentation software, and a spreadsheet program for calculating formulas and displaying your data as 3-D charts. Whether you need a Mac for work, school, or just for fun, you'll find that, with the right software, your Mac can definitely meet your needs.

If you're migrating to a Mac from another computer — you ex-Windows folks know who you are — this book can show you several ways to run your favorite Windows program on a Mac. By running Windows on a Mac, you can basically get two computers in one.

If you're new to the Mac, you'll find this book introduces you to all the main features of using a Mac. If you're already a Mac user, you're sure to find information on topics you might not know much about. By reading this book, you'll have the foundation and confidence to move on to more advanced books.

You might not become a Mac expert after reading this book, but you will become more familiar and comfortable using a Mac, and you might just pick up a few shortcuts and secrets that can make using your Mac even easier. By using or switching over to the Mac, you're sure to find a computer that's easier to use, just as powerful and productive as its rivals, and more important, more fun to use.

If you already have a Mac, you're already convinced that you're using the best computer in the world. Now use this book to help you turn the best computer in the world into the best computer for you.

About This Book

Don't be afraid of this book because of its hefty bulk. You probably won't need (or want) to read this whole thing from cover to cover, and that's fine. Think of this book more as a reference like an encyclopedia or a dictionary than a step-by-step instruction manual that requires you to read every page.

To help you find just the information you need, this book is divided into several minibooks where each minibook tackles a specific topic independent of the other minibooks. Any time you have questions, just flip to the minibook that covers that particular topic.

Each minibook gives you a quick introduction to a specific topic, and then it teaches you the basics to doing something right away. After you find the answers you need, you can put this hefty book back on your bookshelf to get it out of the way so you can get some work done on your Mac.

How to Use This Book

Given the weight of this book, you can use it both as a reference and a weapon that you can throw at unwanted visitors trying to steal office supplies from your desk. If you're completely new to the Mac (or even computers in general), read this book starting with the first minibook and then pick the next minibook that interests you, such as how to use iLife or how to use the Mac's user interface.

If you're already an experienced Mac user, feel free to browse the minibooks that interest you. If you know nothing about a particular topic, such as networking your Macs, you might want to read that minibook in more detail. If you already know about a particular topic, browse through the minibook that covers that topic anyway. You just might find a shortcut or tip that you never knew about before.

Although the Mac is easy to use, it's also easy to get used to one way of using your Mac and never take the time to explore other ways to accomplish the same task (that might be faster) or other ways to use your Mac that you might never have thought about before.

So use this book as a reference, a brief introduction to different features, and a guide to help you discover different ways you can use your Mac.

How This Book Is Organized

This book is divided into seven separate minibooks. Here's a brief description of what you can find in each minibook:

Book I: Mac Basics

This minibook explains everything you need to know just to use your Mac, such as how to turn it on and off, how to use the mouse and keyboard, and how to use the Mac user interface. Even if you're already familiar with using a Mac, you might want to skim through this minibook just to pick up tidbits of information you might not know about.

Book II: Photos, Music, and Movies

More people are using computers to store more than just numbers and text, so this minibook explains how to use your Mac to store and organize digital photographs, audio files of your favorite songs, and digital movies. This is where you discover not only how to store this information on your Mac, but also how to modify it.

Book III: Browsing the Internet

This minibook explains how to connect your Mac to the Internet and what you can do after you're connected. This minibook will teach you the basics of using the Safari Web browser and using e-mail with the Mail program along with explaining how to use video conferencing, design your own Web pages, and protect your Mac from online security threats such as junk e-mail and malicious software like viruses and Trojan horses.

Book IV: Working with iLife and iWork

Computers are only as useful as the software they can run, so this minibook explains how to use the iLife suite (for having fun with your Mac) and the iWork suite (for doing productive work with your Mac). This minibook is where you find out how to store and organize digital pictures and digital videos. If you want to write reports, create presentations, or crunch numbers, you find out how to do that here too.

Book V: Other Mac Programs

With the right software, your Mac can do practically anything, so this minibook introduces you to the variety of programs (many of which are free) for doing everything from painting and drawing to playing games to creating documents with word processors and desktop publishing programs. This minibook also shows you how to use special software to make your Mac run Windows programs so you'll be able to use practically any program you want.

Book VI: Time-Saving Tips with a Mac

This minibook explains how to make the most of your Mac, from backing up your crucial files to using the variety of free programs on your Mac to organize your thoughts or jot down your ideas. You even discover how to store names and addresses, track appointments, and automate your Mac so it can do your work for you while you're away from your computer.

Book VII: Mac Networking

This minibook explains what you need to know in order to set up a network of Mac computers. This is where you can find out how to share hard drives, folders, and printers with other Mac computers.

Icons Used in This Book

To help emphasize certain information, this book displays different icons in the page margins.

This icon identifies a shortcut that can save you time or make accomplishing a specific task much easier.

This icon highlights interesting information that isn't necessary to know but can help explain why certain things work the way they do on the Mac. Feel free to skip this information if you're in a hurry, but browse through this information when you have time. You might find out something interesting that can help you use your Mac.

Watch out! This icon highlights something that can go terribly wrong if you're not careful, such as wiping out your important files or messing up your Mac. Make sure you read any Warning information before following any instructions.

This icon points out some useful information that isn't quite as important as a Tip, but not as threatening as a Warning. If you ignore this information, you can't hurt your files or your Mac, but you might miss something useful.

Where to Go from Here

If you already know what type of help you need, jump right to that particular minibook and start reading. If you just want to know more about your Mac, feel free to skip around and browse through any minibook that catches your eye.

For starters, you might want to begin with Book I and find out about the basics of using your Mac in detail. This first minibook will likely show you new or different ways to do something and help you fully take control of your Mac.

No matter what your experience is with the Mac, don't be afraid to explore and keep making new discoveries. As you expand your horizons, you'll find out that the capabilities of your Mac expand right along with your own growing knowledge. If you know what you want to do, your Mac can probably help you do it, and this book can show you how.

Book I

Mac Basics

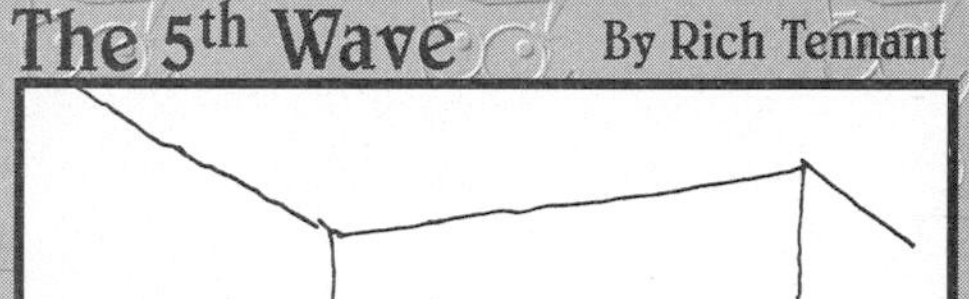

"I'm ordering our new MacBook. Do you want it left-brain or right-brain oriented?"

Contents at a Glance

Chapter 1: Getting to Know Your Mac 9

Chapter 2: Starting Up, Sleeping, and Shutting Down 15

Chapter 3: Getting Acquainted with the Mac User Interface 25

Chapter 4: Running Programs 55

Chapter 5: Installing and Uninstalling Software 77

Chapter 6: Managing Files and Folders 93

Chapter 7: Customizing your Mac 129

Chapter 8: Accessibility Features of the Macintosh 153

Chapter 9: Maintenance and Troubleshooting 167

Chapter 1: Getting to Know Your Mac

In This Chapter

- Identifying your Mac model
- Understanding Mac processors
- Familiarizing yourself with the parts of your Mac

Everyone knows that the Macintosh (Mac, for short) is the easiest computer to use in the world. Just plug in a Mac, turn it on, and you're ready to go, which is the way computers are supposed to work.

Besides being easy to use, the Mac is also dependable and durable. When you use a Mac, you probably won't have to buy a new Mac because you *have* to, but because you *want* to.

Despite the Mac's legendary reputation for being easy to use, you might find the Mac slightly different from other computers you've used before. So to help you understand the way your Mac works, take a few moments to understand the different types of Macs available.

Different Macintosh Models

The Macintosh has been around since 1984, and since that time, Apple has produced a wide variety of Mac models. Although you can still find and use older Macs, chances are good that if you buy a newer Mac, it will fall into one of three categories:

- All-in-one desktop (iMac)
- Laptop (MacBook or MacBook Pro)
- "Headless" Mac (Mac Mini or Mac Pro)

The original Mac came with a built-in screen, which gave the Mac the appearance of a "head." So any Mac model that doesn't come with a built-in screen is often referred to as a "headless" Mac.

By understanding the particular type of Mac you have and its capabilities, you'll have a better idea of what your Mac can do.

No matter what the capabilities of your Mac are, chances are good that it will work reliably for as long as you own it. Remember, things could be worse. You could be stuck using a Windows computer.

The iMac

The all-in-one design of the iMac is an evolutionary extension of the original — 1984-era — Mac design. The iMac combines the computer with a built-in monitor and speakers. (On some iMac models, it's possible to connect a second external monitor if you want.)

The advantage of the all-in-one design of the iMac is that you have everything you need in a single unit. The disadvantage is that if one part of your iMac fails (such as the monitor), you can't easily replace the failed part.

The MacBook and MacBook Pro

The two portable Mac laptop computers, the MacBook and the MacBook Pro, are the most popular Macintosh models. Both models combine the all-in-one design into a compact, lightweight unit that runs off batteries or external power. If you need to take your Mac everywhere you go, you can choose between the consumer MacBook model and the professional MacBook Pro model.

Previous versions of the MacBook were called the iBook, and previous versions of the MacBook Pro were called the PowerBook.

The main difference between the two Mac laptops is price and performance. For the lower price of the MacBook, you get a laptop designed for ordinary uses such as word processing, browsing the Internet, and playing simple games such as chess. For the higher price of the MacBook Pro, you get a faster laptop, larger display, bigger hard drive, and higher performance graphics capabilities designed for professional uses such as video and audio editing or playing the latest 3-D video games.

Another difference is that the MacBook and MacBook Pro include a condensed version of the regular keyboard and use a trackpad instead of a mouse, so you can slide your fingertip across the trackpad to move the cursor on the screen.

If you find the keyboard or trackpad of your laptop Mac too clumsy to use, you can always plug an external keyboard and mouse into your laptop.

The Mac Mini and Mac Pro

The biggest advantages of both the Mac Mini and the Mac Pro are that you can choose the type of monitor to use and you can place them anywhere you want on your desk as long as you have a cable that can reach the monitor. The Mac Mini, in particular, is small enough to hide under your desk or in a corner of your desk.

The Mac Mini is the lower-priced, consumer version designed for people who want an inexpensive Mac for ordinary uses such as word processing and writing and sending e-mail. The Mac Pro is a much higher-priced, professional version with greater graphics and processing capabilities due to its dedicated graphics processor and use of multiple processors.

Understanding Mac Processors

If you're going to write the history of the Mac, you'll probably divide it into three eras. The first Macs used processors from the 68000 series, which served Macs well from 1984 to about 1994. Then came the PowerPC era, which lasted from about 1994 to 2005. Now, fast forward to the present, where Macs use processors made by a company called Intel. If you have an older Mac, it might use a PowerPC or Intel processor. If you just bought a new Mac, it has an Intel processor.

REMEMBER

If you're still using a Mac that uses the 68000 processor, you're using an antique 1980's era computer that might be valuable for historical purposes, but it won't be capable of running any of today's software, including the Mac OS X operating system.

The processor basically acts as the brain of your Mac. A computer is only as powerful as the processor inside it. As a general rule, the newer your computer, the newer its processor and the faster it will run.

Apple stopped using PowerPC processors in 2005 and started using Intel processors, which are the same type of processors used in many Windows PCs. Not only were Intel processors less expensive than PowerPC processors, but they were more powerful as well. As a bonus, using Intel processors also gave the Mac the ability to run the Microsoft Windows operating system (although some people might consider that a drawback).

The type of processor used in your Mac can determine the type of software your Mac can run. The three types of programs available are

- PowerPC programs
- Universal binaries
- Intel programs

Older Mac programs were designed to run only on Mac computers using the PowerPC processor. However, all newer Mac computers that use Intel processors can also run PowerPC programs by using a built-in feature called Rosetta. When you run a PowerPC program on an Intel Mac, Rosetta tricks the program into thinking it's actually running on a PowerPC processor. As a result, all Intel Macs can run nearly all software originally designed for PowerPC Macs.

PowerPC programs tend to run slower on an Intel Mac than on a PowerPC Mac due to the memory and processor resources needed by the Rosetta program.

Most programs now advertise themselves as *universal binaries,* which means they're designed to run on both PowerPC and Intel processors. Before you buy any software, make sure it can run on your computer. If it's a universal binary, it can run equally well on both PowerPC and Intel Macs.

Because Macs are no longer using the PowerPC processor, it's only a matter of time before almost everyone will be using an Intel Mac. That's why some companies are starting to write programs that run only on Intel Macs. If you have a Mac that uses a PowerPC processor, eventually you won't be able to use the latest software available, so you'll be forced to switch to an Intel Mac.

To identify the type of processor used in your Mac, click the Apple menu in the upper-left corner of the screen and choose About This Mac. An About This Mac window appears, listing your processor as either PowerPC or Intel, as shown in Figure 1-1.

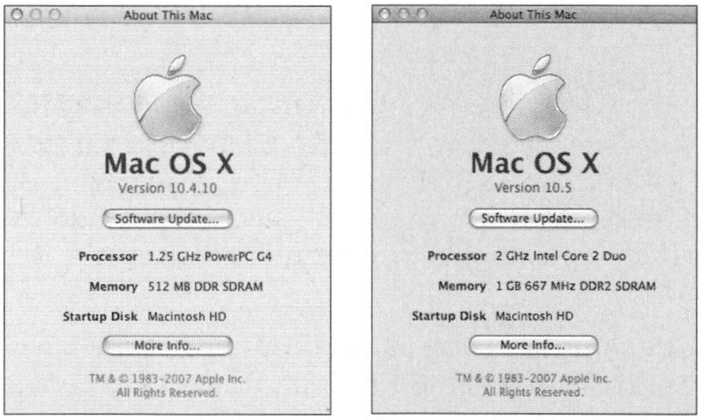

Figure 1-1: The About This Mac window identifies the processor used in your Mac.

PowerPC and Intel processors represent a family of related processors. The PowerPC family of processors includes the G3, G4, and G5 PowerPC processors where the G3 is the slowest and the G5 the fastest. The Intel family of processors includes the Core Solo, Core Duo, Core 2 Duo, and Xeon, where the Core Solo is the slowest and the Xeon is the fastest. Every processor can also run at a specific speed, so a 2.0 gigahertz (GHz) Core 2 Duo processor will be slower than a 2.4 GHz Core 2 Duo processor. If understanding processor types and gigahertz confuses you, just remember that the most expensive computer is usually the fastest.

Identifying the Parts of Your Mac

Just by looking at your Mac, you can tell whether it's an all-in-one design (iMac), a laptop (MacBook or MacBook Pro), or a "headless" unit that lacks a built-in screen (Mac Mini or Mac Pro). However, looking at the outside of your Mac can't tell you the parts used on the inside. To identify the parts and capabilities of your Mac, follow these steps:

1. **Click the Apple menu in the upper-left corner of the screen and choose About This Mac.**

   An About This Mac window appears (refer to Figure 1-1).

2. **Click More Info.**

   A System Profiler window appears.

3. **Click the Hardware option in the Contents category pane on the left to view a list of hardware items.**

   If the list of hardware items (such as Bluetooth, Memory, and USB) already appears under the Hardware category, skip this step.

4. **Click a hardware item such as Memory or Disc Burning.**

   The right pane of the System Profiler window displays the capabilities of your chosen hardware, as shown in Figure 1-2.

   REMEMBER

   Don't worry if the information displayed in the System Profiler window doesn't make much sense to you right now. The main idea here is to figure out a quick way to find out about the capabilities of your Mac. Then you can pick through the technical details to find the parts that you understand and search the Internet to look up the details you don't understand.

5. **When you're done scouting out the contents of the System Profiler window, choose System Profiler➪Quit System Profiler from the main menu to close the window.**

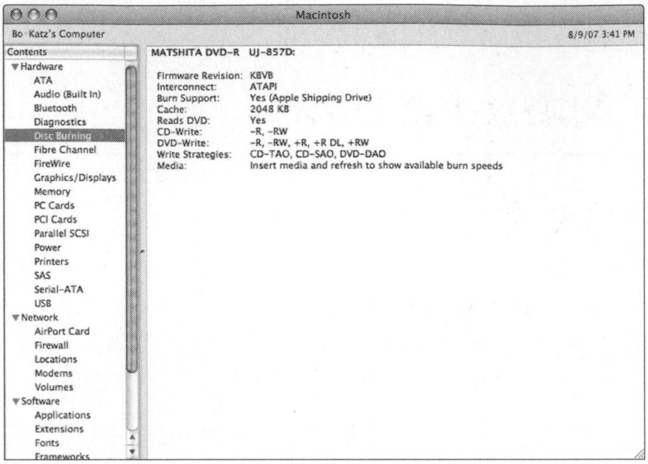

Figure 1-2: The System Profiler window identifies the type and capabilities of the hardware in your Mac.

If you're going to look at anything in System Profiler window, check out Disc Burning and Graphics/Displays under the Hardware option:

- **Disc Burning** tells you all about your DVD/CD–burning hardware, including general info about all the different types of CDs and DVDs that your Mac can read and write to, so you'll know exactly which type to buy.
- **Graphics/Displays** tells you whether your Mac has a separate graphics card, as seen in the VRAM category (Video RAM). If you see the word *shared* in the VRAM category, your Mac doesn't have a separate graphics card and shares the main memory, which means its graphics capabilities will (usually) be slower than a Mac that does have a separate graphics card. If you do not see the word *shared,* the VRAM category simply lists the amount of memory used by the separate graphics card. The more memory, the better your graphics capabilities.

If you have a Mac Pro, you have the option of replacing your graphics card with a better one. If you have any other type of Mac (iMac, MacBook, MacBook Pro, or Mac Mini), you're pretty much stuck with the graphics capabilities built into your Mac.

Chapter 2: Starting Up, Sleeping, and Shutting Down

In This Chapter

- Starting your Mac
- Putting your Mac in Sleep mode
- Shutting down a Mac

Before you can use your Mac, you have to start it up — which makes perfect sense. Now, get ready for the counterintuitive part. After you've got your Mac up and running, you should *just leave it on.* Although you might cringe at the idea of leaving your Mac on when you're not using it, the Mac performs basic housekeeping chores on its hard drive early every morning to keep its files neat and tidy. Don't worry about wasting electricity; the Mac is smart enough to put itself into a low-energy mode — Sleep mode, to be precise — when not in use so it burns up a minimum of energy.

Only if you plan on being away from your Mac for an extended period of time, such as a week or more, should you turn off your Mac completely. If you're going to use your Mac the next morning or Monday after a weekend, leave it on and let it sleep instead.

Starting Your Mac

Here's the simple way to start up your Mac — the way you'll probably use 99 percent of the time:

1. **Press the power button.**

That's it. Depending on the type of Mac you have, the power button might be in back (Mac Mini and some iMacs), front (Mac Pro and some iMacs), or above the keyboard (on laptop models like the MacBook and MacBook Pro).

As soon as you press the power button, your Mac plays a musical chime to let you know that it's starting up. (Techie types say "booting up," a term derived from the phrase "to lift yourself up by the bootstraps.")

The moment electricity starts coursing through your Mac, its electronic brain immediately looks for instructions permanently embedded inside a special Read-Only Memory (or ROM) chip. While your computer is reading these instructions (also known as *firmware*), it displays a big gray Apple logo on the screen to let you know that the computer is working and hasn't forgotten about you.

The firmware instructions tell the computer to check all of its different parts to make sure everything's working. If some part of your computer is physically defective, such as a memory chip, your computer will stop right there. Unless you know something about repairing the physical parts of a Macintosh, this is the time to haul your Mac to the nearest repair shop.

Sometimes a Mac might refuse to start up correctly due to software problems. To fix software problems, check out Book I, Chapter 9, which explains how to perform basic troubleshooting on a Mac.

After your computer determines that all its different parts are working, the last set of instructions on the chip tells the computer, "Now that you know all your parts are working, load an operating system."

When you unpack your Mac and turn it on for the very first time, it will ask that you type your name and make up a password to create an account for using your Mac. To guide you through the process of setting up a Mac for the first time, a special program called the Setup Assistant runs, and it asks for information such as the current time zone, the current date, and whether you want to transfer files and programs from another Mac to your newer one. You also have go through this procedure if you reinstall your operating system. Normally, you need to run through this initial procedure only once. The most important part of this initial procedure is remembering the password you chose because you'll need this password to log into your account or install new software.

An operating system is the program that controls your computer and is usually stored on the computer's hard drive. On the Mac, the operating system is called Mac OS X (which stands for "Macintosh Operating System number ten") followed by a version number such as 10.5.

After the operating system loads, you can start using your computer to run other programs so you can write a letter, browse the Internet, balance your checkbook, or play a game. (You know, all the things you bought your Mac for in the first place.)

Putting a Mac in Sleep Mode

After you've turned on your Mac, don't keep turning it on and off whenever you aren't using it. To save time and prevent wear and tear on your computer, put your Mac into Sleep mode instead. When you put your Mac to sleep, it shuts down every part of your computer, and the computer runs on a bare minimum of power. When you touch the keyboard or click the mouse button, the computer wakes up so you can use it right away.

To put your Mac to sleep, you have a choice of doing it manually or automatically. When you need to be away from your Mac for a short period of time (going to the restroom), you might want to put your Mac to sleep manually. If you suddenly get called to attend a meeting and don't have time to put your Mac to sleep manually, you might want your Mac to put itself to sleep automatically.

Putting a Mac in Sleep mode manually

To put your Mac to sleep manually, choose one of the following two actions:

- Choose ⇨Sleep.
- Press the Control+Eject (or press the power button) and, when a dialog appears as shown in Figure 2-1, click the Sleep button.

The menu appears in the upper-left corner of the screen.

If you have a laptop, a faster way to put your Mac to sleep is just to close its lid. When a laptop is sleeping, you can safely move it.

To wake up a sleeping Mac, just click the mouse button or tap any key. To keep from accidentally typing any characters into any currently running program, press a noncharacter key such as one of the arrow keys.

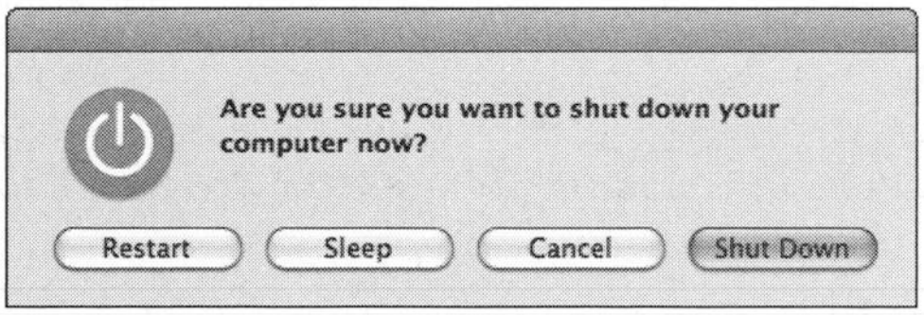

Figure 2-1: If you press the power button, you see a dialog you can use to put your computer in Sleep mode.

Putting a Mac in Sleep mode automatically

Because you can't always plan how long you might be away from your Mac, you can also make your Mac put itself in Sleep mode automatically after a fixed period of time — say, ten minutes or so. That way, if your Mac doesn't detect any keyboard or mouse activity within that fixed period of time, your computer will put itself into Sleep mode automatically.

To make your computer go to sleep automatically, you need to define the following:

✦ The inactivity time

✦ The parts of your computer to put into Sleep mode

The inactivity time defines how long your computer waits before putting itself into Sleep mode. This time can be as short as one minute or as long as three hours. The shorter you define the inactivity period, the more often your Mac might suddenly go to sleep while you're just staring at the screen.

The two main parts of your computer that you can put into Sleep mode are the hard drive and the display (your computer screen). Because the hard drive and the display consume the most power, putting at least one or both of these parts into Sleep mode can dramatically reduce the amount of power your Mac consumes while it's asleep.

To define how your Mac should put itself into Sleep mode automatically, follow these steps:

1. **Choose ⇨System Preferences.**

   A System Preferences window appears, as shown in Figure 2-2.

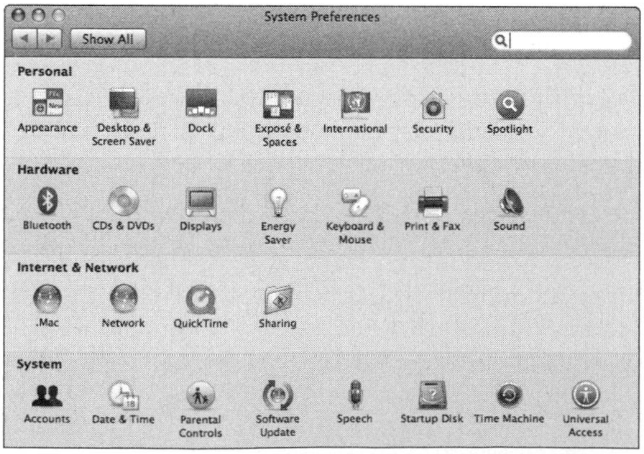

Figure 2-2: The Systems Preferences window lets you modify the behavior of your Mac.

2. **Click the Energy Saver icon (the light bulb) under the Hardware category.**

   An Energy Saver dialog appears, as shown in Figure 2-3. (If you're using a desktop Mac, skip to Step 4.)

   The Settings For pop-up menu lets you choose different energy saver settings on a laptop when running off battery power and when plugged into an electrical outlet. The Optimization pop-up menu lets you customize the energy saver settings or just choose a predefined setting such as Better Energy Savings, Normal, or Better Performance.

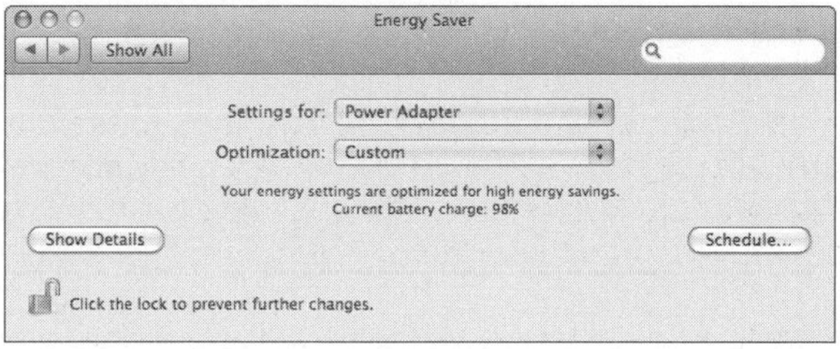

Figure 2-3: The Energy Saver dialog lets you specify how your Mac should go to sleep.

3. **Click the Show Details button.**

   The Energy Saver dialog expands to show you the computer and display sliders, as shown in Figure 2-4.

4. **Drag the Put the Computer to Sleep When It Is Inactive For slider to any value between one minute and three hours.**

   When the computer sleeps, the microprocessor in your Mac goes into a special low-voltage mode. (If you never want your Mac to go to sleep, drag the slider all the way to the right over the Never option.)

5. **Drag the Put the Display to Sleep When the Computer Is Inactive For slider to any value between one minute and three hours.**

   When the display sleeps, the video signal to the monitor is shut off. (If you never want your display to go to sleep, drag the slider all the way to the right over the Never option.)

6. **Select (or deselect) the Put the Hard Disk(s) to Sleep When Possible check box.**

   When you put the hard drive to sleep, the hard drive stops spinning. Because spinning a hard drive burns up energy and wears out your hard drive, putting a hard drive to sleep can help the hard drive last longer.

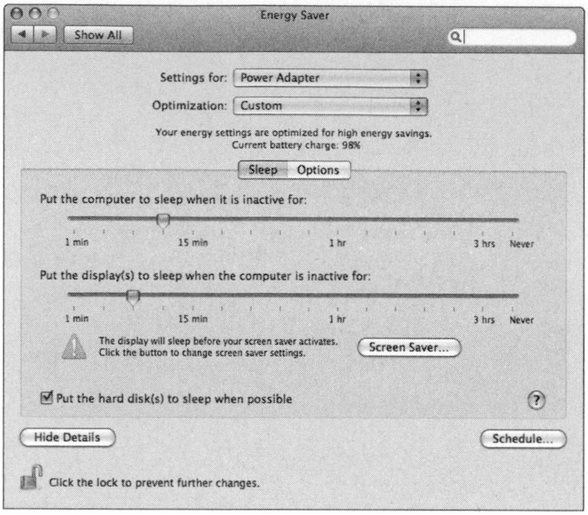

Figure 2-4: The expanded Energy Saver dialog displays sliders for adjusting the time to put your Mac to sleep.

At this point, you can click the Close button of the Energy Saver dialog to save your energy saver changes. (The Close button is the little red button in the upper left of the dialog.) If you want to define additional options for waking up a sleeping Mac, such as remotely over a telephone line or network, follow the remaining steps.

7. **(Optional) Click the Options tab.**

   The Options pane appears.

   If you have a desktop Mac, you see the pane shown in Figure 2-5. If you have a laptop Mac, you see the pane shown in Figure 2-6.

8. **Select (or deselect) one or more of the following check boxes. (Some check boxes won't appear, depending on the type of Mac you have.)**

   - *Wake When the Modem Detects a Ring:* Useful for remotely accessing a Mac over the telephone line. (This option appears only if you have a modem connected to your Mac.)
   - *Wake for Ethernet Network Administrator Access:* Useful for letting a network administrator access and configure a Mac over a network. (Selected by default.)
   - *Allow Power Button to Sleep the Computer:* Lets you put your Mac to sleep by pressing the power button. (Selected by default. This option appears only on desktop Mac computers.)
   - *Restart Automatically after a Power Failure:* Makes your Mac restart if its power gets abruptly cut off. (Deselected by default.)

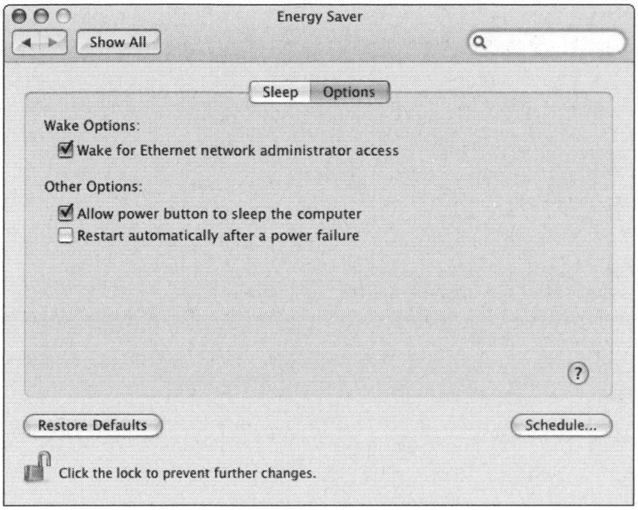

Figure 2-5: The Options dialog for desktop Macs.

- *Show Battery Status in the Menu Bar:* Displays an icon (called a menulet) to show how much charge is left in your laptop's battery. (This option appears only on laptop Mac computers.)

9. **Click the Close button (the red circle in the upper-left corner) of the System Preferences window or choose System Preferences➪Quit System Preferences.**

   Clicking the Close button or quitting System Preferences saves your changes.

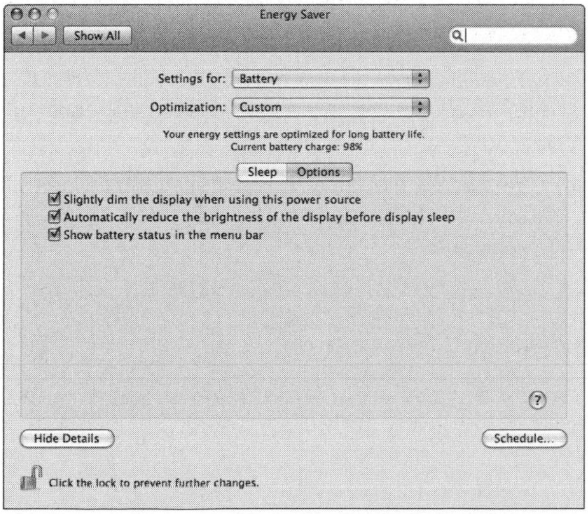

Figure 2-6: The Options pane for laptop Macs.

Shutting Down a Mac

If you won't use your Mac for an extended period of time, you might want to shut it off (although letting it sleep the entire time won't hurt it either). You actually have three ways to shut down a Mac:

- **Choose ➪Shut Down** as shown in Figure 2-7. A dialog appears, asking if you're sure you want to shut down. (Refer to Figure 2-1.) Click Cancel or Shut Down. (If you don't click either option, your Mac will shut down automatically after a few minutes.)
- **Press Control+Eject** (or press the power button) and when a dialog appears — the same one mentioned in the previous bullet point, actually — click the Shut Down button.
- **Press and hold the power button** to force your Mac to shut down.

Figure 2-7: Use this menu to turn off your computer.

The third option, called a *force shutdown,* is used to force all running programs to shut down right away. Generally, a force shutdown is handy if your entire Mac suddenly freezes or hangs, making it unresponsive. If only a single program is freezing or acting flaky, it's usually better to force quit that single program instead of shutting down your entire computer. (See Book I, Chapter 4 for information about how to force quit a single program.)

REMEMBER

Think of a force shutdown like taking a metal pipe and knocking your Mac unconscious, whereas choosing ➪Shut Down or using the Control+ Eject/Power button option is like tucking your Mac into bed with a security \if at all possible.

TIP

You can also force shutdown your Mac by pressing the Control+Option+ ⌘+Eject keystroke combination.

Restarting a Mac

Sometimes the Mac can start acting sluggish, or programs might fail to run. When that happens, you can turn off your computer and start it back up again. This essentially clears your computer's memory and starts it up fresh.

REMEMBER

Restarting a computer isn't the same as turning the computer on and off, which completely resets the computer. If you really want to make sure your computer starts up correctly, turn it off, wait a few seconds, and then turn it on again. If you're in a hurry, try restarting your Mac, and if that doesn't fix the problem, you'll have to turn it off and on again.

To restart your computer, you have three choices:

- Press the power button (or press Control+Eject) and, when a dialog appears, click the Restart button (refer to Figure 2-1).
- Choose ⇨Restart.
- Press Control+⌘+Eject (or Control+⌘+Power button).

TIP

Pressing the Control+⌘+Eject/Power button is the most reliable way to restart a Mac because it doesn't rely on the Mac OS X operating system.

When you restart your computer, your Mac closes all running programs and offers to save any files you're be working on. After you choose to save any files, your Mac will finally boot up again.

Chapter 3: Getting Acquainted with the Mac User Interface

In This Chapter

- **Using the mouse and keyboard**
- **Acquainting yourself with the Mac user interface**
- **Playing with icons in the Dock and Finder**
- **Getting help**

Theoretically, using a computer is simple. In practice, using a computer can cause people to suffer a wide range of emotions from elation to sheer frustration and despair.

The problem with using a computer stems mostly from two causes:

- Not knowing what the computer can do
- Not knowing how to tell the computer what you want it to do

This communication gap between users and computers arises mostly from ordinary people trying to use machines designed by engineers for other engineers. If you don't understand how a computer engineer thinks (or doesn't think), computers can seem nearly impossible to understand.

Fortunately, Apple has solved this problem with the Mac. Instead of designing a computer for other computer engineers, Apple designed a computer for ordinary people. And what do ordinary people want? Here's the list:

- Reliability
- Ease of use

Not a long list, but definitely an important one.

From a technical point of view, what makes the Mac reliable is its operating system, Mac OS X. An operating system is nothing more than a program that makes your computer actually work.

By itself, an operating system works in the background. When you use a computer, you'll rarely see the operating system, but you will see its user interface. The *user interface* is like a clerk at the front desk of a hotel. Instead of talking directly to the maid or the plumber (the operating system), you always talk to the front desk clerk, and the clerk talks to the maid or plumber.

While other companies have been busy designing user interfaces that only computer engineers can understand, Apple designed a user interface that everyone can understand. Dubbed Aqua, Apple's user interface puts the friendly face on the Mac.

Mastering the Mouse and Keyboard

To control your Mac, you need to use the mouse (or trackpad on laptop Macs) and the keyboard. Both the mouse (trackpad) and the keyboard can choose commands, manipulate items on the screen, or create data such as text or pictures.

TECHNICAL STUFF

To modify the mouse and keyboard, click the Apple menu in the upper-left corner of the screen and choose System Preferences. Then click the Keyboard & Mouse icon under the Hardware category.

The parts of the mouse

A typical mouse looks like a smooth bar of soap with one or more buttons and a rubber wheel or ball in the middle. The main purpose of the mouse is to move a pointer on the screen, which tells the computer, "See what I'm pointing at right now? That's what I want to select."

Clicking, double-clicking, and dragging with the left mouse button

A mouse typically has one button on the left and one on the right. To select an item on the screen, you must move the mouse to point at that item and then press and release (click) the left mouse button.

- **Clicking (also called single-clicking):** Moving the mouse and pressing the left mouse button is the most common activity with a mouse.
- **Double-clicking:** If you point at something and click the left mouse button twice in rapid succession (that is, you *double-click* it), you can often select an item and open it at the same time.
- **Dragging:** Another common activity with the mouse is called *dragging*. Dragging means pointing at an item on the screen, holding down the left mouse button, moving the mouse, and then releasing the left mouse button. Dragging is often used to move items on the screen.

If you know how to point and click, double-click, and point and drag the mouse, you've mastered the basics of controlling your Mac with a mouse.

Scrolling with the scroll wheel or ball

Many mice have a rubber wheel or ball embedded in the middle. By rolling this wheel or ball, you can make items (such as text or a picture) scroll up/down or right/left across the screen. Using the scroll wheel or ball can make your Mac just a little bit easier to use.

Pointing and clicking with the right mouse button

Like the scroll wheel or ball, the right mouse button is optional but convenient. Pointing the mouse and pressing the right mouse button is known as *right-clicking.*

Right-clicking is commonly used to display a pop-up menu (often called a contextual or shortcut menu) of commands to do something with the item that the mouse is currently pointing at. For example, if you point at a misspelled word, right-clicking that misspelled word can display a list of properly spelled words to choose from, as shown in Figure 3-1.

Some older mice (as well as some older laptop Mac computers) do not have a right mouse button. To simulate a right-click, hold down the Control key and click the lone mouse button (or hold down the Control key and click the single trackpad button on laptop Mac computers).

If you don't like your mouse, you can always buy a replacement mouse. Some mice are molded to better fit the shape of your hand, so find a mouse that you like and plug it into the USB port of your Mac, or get a wireless mouse that connects to your Mac through the Bluetooth wireless standard.

The parts of the keyboard

The primary use of the keyboard is to type in data. However, the keyboard can also select items and menu commands — although not as easily as using the mouse. The keyboard groups related keys together, as shown in Figure 3-2:

- Function keys
- Typewriter keys
- Numeric keys
- Arrow keys
- Modifier keys

The next few sections cover each kind of key in greater detail.

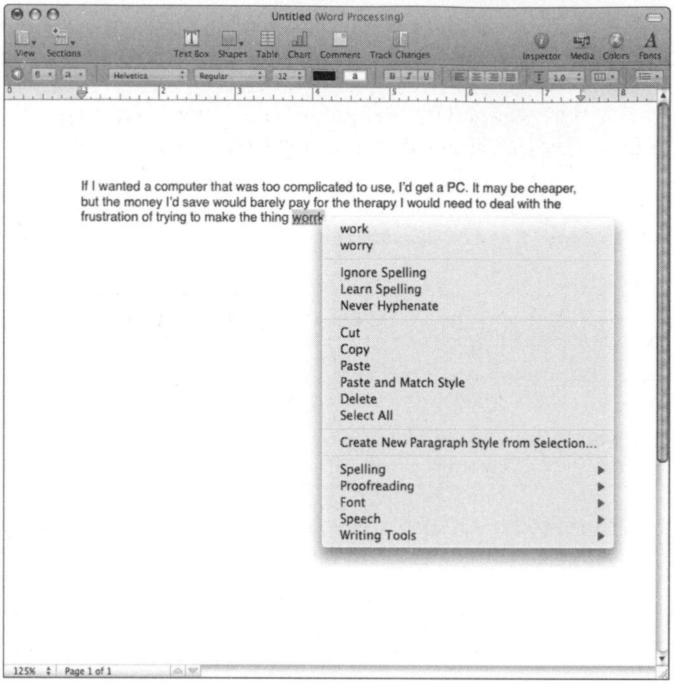

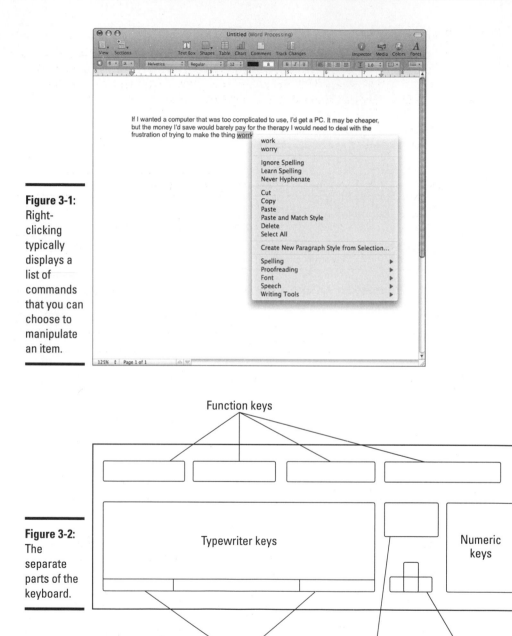

Figure 3-1: Right-clicking typically displays a list of commands that you can choose to manipulate an item.

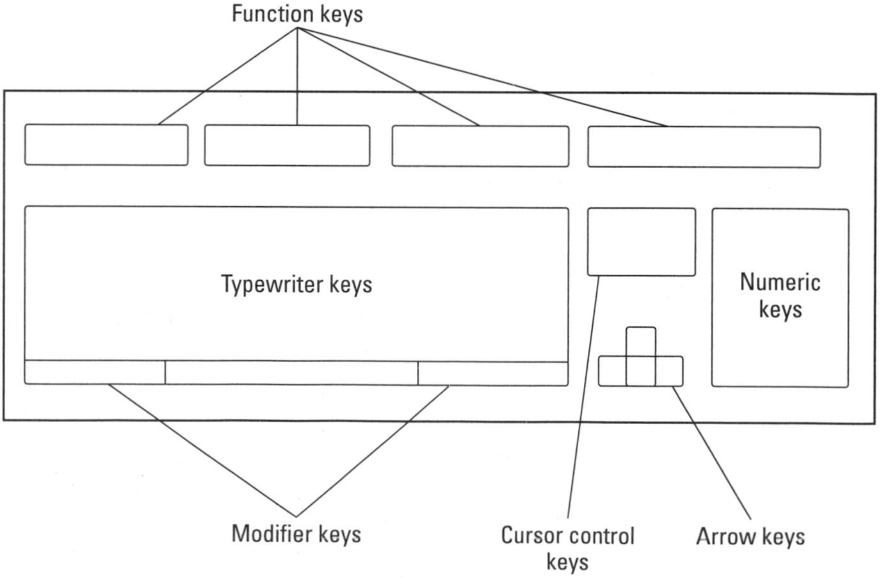

Figure 3-2: The separate parts of the keyboard.

Function keys

Depending on your particular keyboard, you might see 12 to 19 function keys running along the top of the keyboard. These function keys are labeled F1 through F12/F19, along with an Escape key — brilliantly abbreviated "Esc" — and an Eject key that looks like a triangle on top of a horizontal line.

By default, every Mac has already assigned commands to the F8 through F12 function keys, as shown in Table 3-1.

Table 3-1 Mac Assigned Commands

Function Key	*What It Does*
F8	Displays thumbnail images of all workspaces
F9	Displays thumbnail images of all windows in a single workspace
F10	Displays all open windows of the currently active program (the program that has one of its windows on "top" of any other windows).
F11	Displays the Desktop
F12	Displays Dashboard

Pressing the F8 function key displays multiple workspaces defined by the Spaces feature (which you find out more about in Book I, Chapter 4).

The F9 through F11 function keys activate a feature on your Mac called Exposé. Pressing F9 lets you see all the open windows currently running so you can pick the one you want to use right now. Pressing F10 shows you all windows that belong to the currently active program. (You can identify the currently active program by looking for its name on the left side of the menu bar.) Pressing F11 shoves all windows out of the way so you can see the Desktop.

Pressing F12 displays the Dashboard program and its widgets, which are simple programs such as a calculator or calendar. (You find out more about Dashboard in Book VI, Chapter 4.)

As for the other keys — F1 through F7 and (possibly) F13 through F19 — these fellows won't do much of anything in most programs. Because such function keys are about as useful as wisdom teeth, laptop keyboards and the latest Apple keyboards often assign hardware controls to these seldom-used function keys. For example, pressing the F1 and F2 function keys might change the brightness of the screen, whereas pressing other function keys might adjust the volume.

If it turns out that you have a program that actually puts one of these function keys to use meaning you really want to press the function key *as a function key* rather than as a way to control hardware stuff like monitor brightness or speaker volume — you must first hold down the Fn key and then press the function key you want. Holding down the Fn key tells your Mac, "Ignore the hardware controls assigned to that function key and just behave like a normal function key."

TECHNICAL STUFF

Originally, function keys existed because some programs assigned commands to different function keys. Unfortunately, every program assigned different commands to identical function keys, which made function keys more confusing than helpful. You can assign your own commands to different function keys, but just remember that not every Mac will have the same commands assigned to the same function keys. (Not everyone thinks exactly like you, as amazing as that might seem.)

Turning to the two other keys grouped with the function keys, here's what you need to know. The Esc key often works as a "Get out of my way" command. For example, if a pull-down menu appears on the screen and you want it to go away, press the Esc key. The Eject key is used to eject a CD or DVD currently in your Mac.

Typewriter keys

You use the typewriter keys to create *data* — the typing-a-letter-in-a-word-processor stuff or the entering-of-names-and-addresses-into-a-database stuff. When you press a typewriter key, you're telling the Mac which character to type at the current position of the cursor, which often appears as a blinking vertical line on the screen.

TIP

You can move the cursor by pointing to and clicking a new location with the mouse or by pressing the arrow keys as explained later, in the section "Arrow keys."

One typewriter key that doesn't type anything is the big Delete key that appears to the right of the +/= key. This Delete key is used to delete any characters that appear to the left of the cursor. If you hold down this Delete key, your Mac will delete a bunch of characters to the left of the cursor.

Two other typewriter keys that don't type anything are the Tab and Return keys. The Tab key is often used to indent text in a word processor, but it can also highlight different text boxes on the screen.

The Return key moves the cursor to the next line in a word processor, but can also choose a default button (which appears in blue) on the screen. The default button in the Print dialog is labeled Print, and the default button in the Save dialog is labeled Save.

Numeric keys

The numeric keys appear on the right side of the keyboard and arrange the numbers 0 through 9 in rows and columns like a typical calculator keypad. The main use for the numeric keys is to make typing numbers faster and easier than using the numeric keys on the top row of the typewriter keys.

On laptop keyboards, the numeric keys are buried in the normal typewriter keys. To switch the numeric keys on, you have to press the Num Lock key. To switch the numeric keys off, press the Num Lock key again.

Arrow keys

The cursor often appears as a vertical blinking line and acts like a pointer. Wherever the cursor appears, that's where your next character will appear if you press a typewriter key. You can move the cursor with the mouse, or you can move it with the arrow keys.

The up arrow moves the cursor up, the down arrow moves the cursor down, the right arrow moves the cursor right, and the left arrow moves the cursor left. (Could it be any more logical?) Depending on the program you're using, pressing an arrow key might move the cursor in different ways. For example, pressing the right arrow key in a word processor moves the cursor right one character, but pressing that same right arrow key in a spreadsheet might move the cursor to the adjacent cell on the right.

Four additional cursor control keys are labeled Home, End, Page Up, and Page Down. Typically, the Page Up key scrolls up one screen, whereas the Page Down key scrolls down one screen. Many programs ignore the Home and End keys, but some programs let you move the cursor with them. For example, Microsoft programs typically use the Home key to move the cursor to the beginning of a line or row and the End key to move the cursor to the end of a line or row.

To the left of the End key, you might find a smaller Delete key. Like the bigger Delete key, this smaller Delete key also deletes characters one at a time.

REMEMBER

The big Delete key erases characters to the *left* of the cursor. The small Delete key erases characters to the *right* of the cursor.

Modifier keys

The modifier keys are almost never used by themselves. Instead, modifier keys are usually held down while tapping another key. The four modifier keys are Shift, Control (Ctrl), Option, and ⌘ (Command).

If you press the S key, your Mac types the letter "s" on the screen, but if you hold down a modifier key, such as the Command key (⌘) and then press the

S key, the S key is modified to behave differently. In this case, holding down the ⌘ key followed by the S key (abbreviated as ⌘+S) tells your Mac to issue its Save command.

Most modifier keystrokes involve pressing two keys, such as ⌘+Q (the Quit command), but some modifier keystrokes can involve pressing three or four keys such as Shift+⌘+3, which saves the current screen image as a file.

The main use for modifier keys is to help you choose commands quickly without fumbling with the mouse. Every program includes dozens of such keystroke shortcuts, but Table 3-2 lists the common keystroke shortcuts that work in most programs.

Table 3-2 Common Keystroke Shortcuts

Command	*Keystroke Shortcut*
Copy	⌘+C
Cut	⌘+X
Open	⌘+O
New	⌘+N
Paste	⌘+V
Print	⌘+P
Quit	⌘+Q
Save	⌘+S
Select All	⌘+A
Undo	⌘+Z

Many programs display their keystroke shortcuts for different commands directly on their pull-down menus, as shown in Figure 3-3.

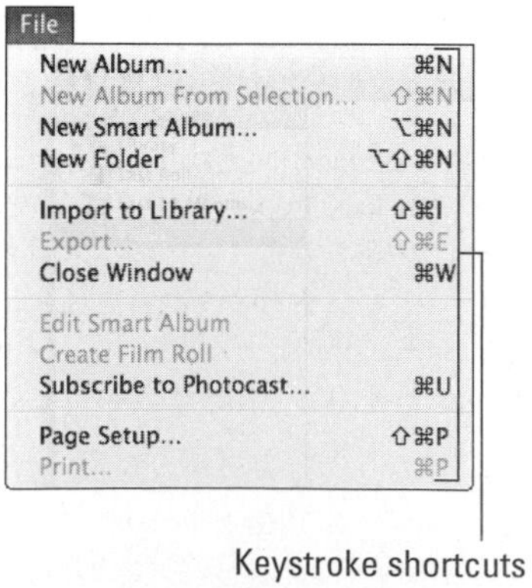

Figure 3-3: Pull-down menus often list shortcut keystrokes for commonly used commands.

Instead of describing the modifier keys to press by name (such as Shift), most keystroke shortcuts displayed on menus use cryptic graphics. Figure 3-4 displays the different symbols you'll find as shortcut commands.

Some people love the keyboard that comes with their Mac, but others feel that it's too soft and squishy, like touching the belly of an animal. If you want a more solid-feeling keyboard that provides more tactile feedback, check out the Tactile Pro 2 keyboard (`www.matias.ca/tactilepro2`).

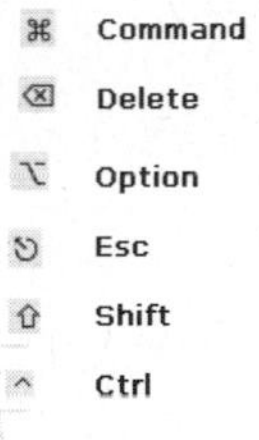

Figure 3-4: A keystroke command symbol guide.

Getting to Know the Mac User Interface

The Mac user interface acts like a communication pathway between you and the operating system and serves three purposes:

- To display all the options that you can choose
- To display information
- To accept commands

One of the most crucial parts of the Mac user interface is a program called the Finder, which displays a window that lets you manipulate files stored on your Mac. You find out more about the Finder later in this chapter.

The menu bar

The menu bar provides a single location where you can find nearly every possible command you might need. Think of the menu bar like the menu of a restaurant. Any time you want to order another dish, you can look at the menu to see what's available. Likewise, when using a Mac, you always know the menu bar will appear at the top of the screen. The menu bar consists of three parts, as shown in Figure 3-5:

- The Apple menu
- The Application menu
- Menulets (Icons)

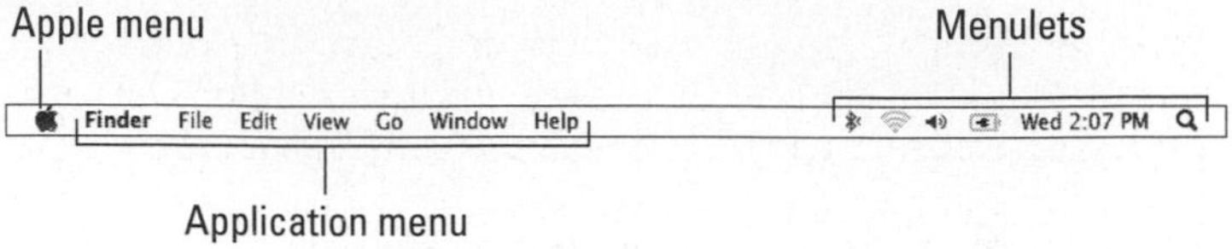

Figure 3-5: The three parts of the menu bar.

The Apple menu always appears on the menu bar and gives you one-click access to commands for controlling or modifying your Mac. The Application menu displays the name of the currently active program along with several menus that contain commands for controlling that particular program and its data. (If you don't run any additional programs, your Mac always runs the Finder program, which you find out more about in this chapter.)

Menulets act like miniature menus that perform a single function, such as adjusting the volume or displaying the current time. Clicking a menulet displays a small pull-down menu or control, as shown in Figure 3-6.

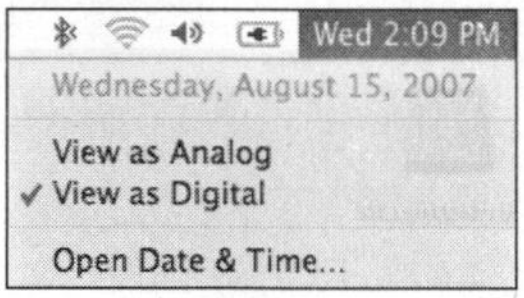

Figure 3-6: Menulets let you control a single function of your Mac.

TIP: If you don't want a menulet cluttering up the menu bar, you can remove it by holding down the ⌘ key, moving the pointer over the menulet you want to remove, dragging (moving) the mouse off the menu bar, and then releasing the mouse button.

Understanding menu commands

Each menu on the menu bar contains a group of related commands. The File menu contains commands for opening, saving, and printing files, whereas the Edit menu contains commands for copying or deleting items. The number and names of different menus depends on the program.

To give a command to the computer, click a menu title in the menu bar (such as File or Edit) to call up a pull-down menu, listing all the commands you can choose. Then just click the command you want the computer to follow (File⇨Save, for example).

Working with dialogs

When your Mac needs extra information from you, it might display a *dialog* — essentially a box that offers a variety of choices. Some common dialogs appear when you choose the Print, Save, and Open commands.

Dialogs often appear in a condensed version, but you can blow them up into an expanded version, as shown in Figure 3-7. To switch between the expanded and the condensed version of the Save dialog, click the Arrow button.

Whether expanded or condensed, every dialog displays buttons that either let you cancel the command or complete it. To cancel a command, you have two choices:

- ✦ Click the Cancel button.
- ✦ Press Esc.

To complete a command, you also have two choices:

- ✦ Click the button that represents the command you want to complete, such as Save or Print.
- ✦ Press Return to choose the default button, which appears in blue.

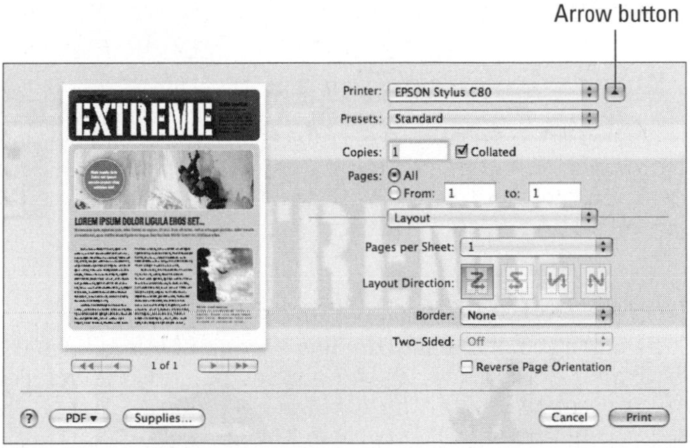

Figure 3-7: When expanded, the Print dialog offers more options.

Viewing data in a window

Every program needs to accept, manipulate, and/or display data. A word processor lets you type and edit text, an accounting program lets you type and edit numbers, and a presentation program lets you display text and pictures.

To help you work with different types of data (text and pictures), every program displays information inside a rectangular area called a *window*, as shown in Figure 3-8.

In the early days of personal computers, a program treated the entire screen as a window for displaying information. This was fine when computers could run only one program at a time, but nowadays you can often run two or more programs at the same time. To give each program a chance to display information on the screen, computers had to divide the screen into windows where each window acts like a miniature screen.

Dividing a screen into multiple windows offers several advantages:

- Two or more programs can display information on the screen simultaneously.
- A single program can open and display information stored in two or more files.
- You can copy (or move) data from one window to another. If each window belongs to a different program, this action transfers data from one program to another.

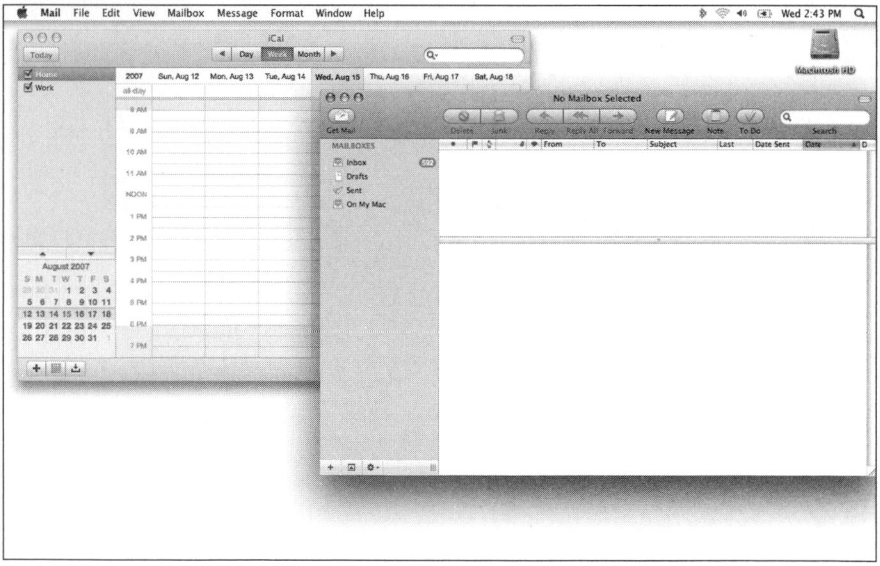

Figure 3-8: Windows allow multiple programs to display information on the screen.

Of course, windows aren't perfect. When a window appears on the screen, it might be too big or too small, in the wrong part of the screen, or displaying the beginning of a file when you want to see the middle or the end. To control the appearance of a window, most windows provide the following built-in controls, as shown in Figure 3-9:

- ✦ Title bar
- ✦ Resize corner
- ✦ Close button
- ✦ Minimize button
- ✦ Zoom button
- ✦ Scroll bars
- ✦ Toolbar button

The following sections show you what you can do with all the fancy controls.

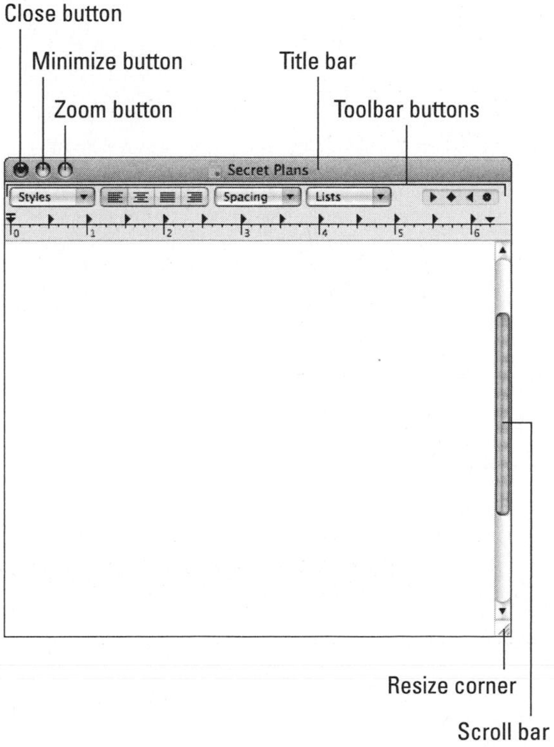

Figure 3-9: Every window provides controls so you can manipulate it.

Moving a window with the title bar

The title bar of every window serves two purposes:

- ✦ It identifies the filename that contains the data displayed in the window.
- ✦ It provides a place to grab hold of when you want to drag (move) the window to a new location on the screen.

If you want to move a window on the screen, you have to drag the title bar by following these steps:

1. **Move the pointer over the title bar of the window you want to move.**
2. **Hold down the left mouse button and drag the mouse.**

   The window moves wherever you drag the mouse.
3. **Release the left mouse button when you're happy with the new location of the window.**

Resizing a window

Sometimes a window might be in the perfect location, but it's too small or too large for what you want to do at that moment. To change the size of a window, follow these steps:

1. **Move the pointer over the resize corner in the bottom-right corner of the window.**
2. **Hold down the left mouse button and drag the mouse.**

   The window grows or shrinks as you drag the mouse.
3. **Release the left mouse button when you're happy with the new size of the window.**

Closing a window

When you're done viewing or editing any information displayed in a window, you might as well close the window to keep it from cluttering the screen. To close a window, follow these steps:

1. **Click the Close button (the little red button) of the window you want to close.**

   If you haven't saved the information inside the window, your Mac displays a dialog that asks whether you want to save it.

2. **In the dialog that appears, click one of the following choices:**
   - *Don't Save:* Closes the window and discards any changes you made to the information inside the window.
   - *Cancel:* Keeps the window open.
   - *Save:* Closes the window but saves the information in a file. If this is the first time you've saved this information, another dialog appears, giving you a chance to name the file to store the information and save it in a specific location on your hard drive.

REMEMBER

Computers typically offer two or more ways to accomplish the same task, so you can choose the way you like best. As an alternative to clicking the Close button, you can also click inside the window you want to close and then choose File➪Close or press ⌘+W.

Minimizing a window

Sometimes you might not want to close a window, but you still want to get it out of the way so it doesn't clutter up your screen. In that case, you can *minimize* a window, which tucks the window as a tiny icon on the right side of the Dock, as shown in Figure 3-10.

Figure 3-10: A minimized window icon on the Dock.

REMEMBER

A minimized window icon on the Dock actually displays the contents of that window. If you squint hard enough (or have a large enough screen), you can see what each minimized window contains.

To minimize a window, choose one of the following:

- ✦ Click the Minimize button of the window you want to tuck out of the way.
- ✦ Click the window you want to minimize and choose Window➪Minimize (or press ⌘+M).
- ✦ Double-click the window's title bar. (This feature can be turned off as explained later in this section.)

To open a minimized window, follow these steps:

1. **Move the mouse over the minimized window on the Dock.**
2. **Click the mouse button.**

   Your minimized window pops back on the screen.

Zooming a window

If a window is too small to display information, you don't have to sit and take it. Just put your Zoom button to use, which appears as a green button in the upper-left corner of every window. (When you move the mouse over the Zoom button, a plus sign appears inside.)

Zooming a window makes it grow larger, as shown in Figure 3-11. With some programs, zooming expands a window to fill most of the screen, but with other programs, zooming expands a window slightly but doesn't fill most of the screen.

The Zoom button is a toggle button, meaning that if you click the button again, you end up shrinking the window back to its smaller size.

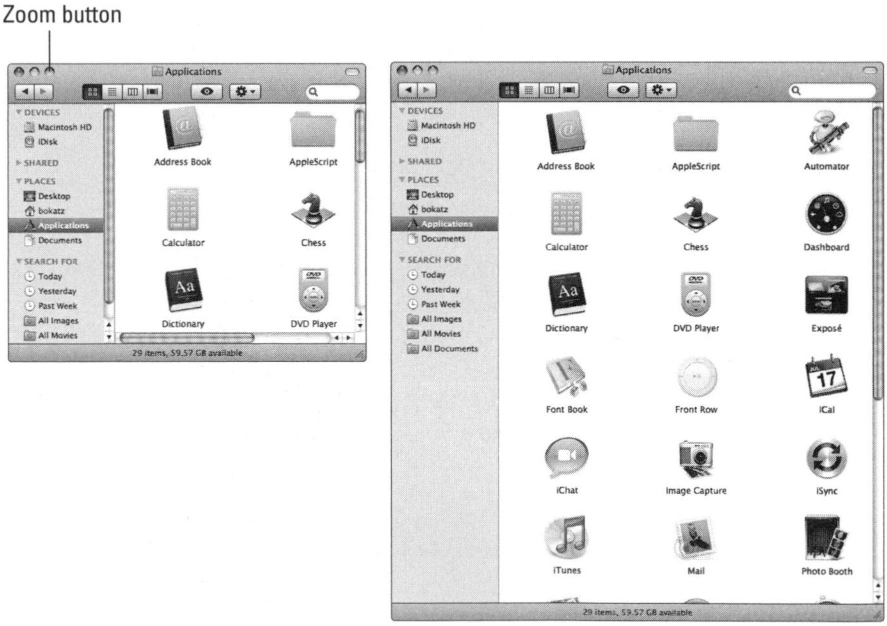

Figure 3-11: The Zoom button expands a window to its maximum size.

Scrolling through a window

No matter how large you make a window, it may still be too small to display the entire contents of its file. Think of a window as a porthole that lets you peek at part, but not all, of a file's contents. If a window isn't large enough to display an entire file, the window will let you know by displaying vertical or horizontal scroll bars.

There are three ways to use the kinds of scroll bars you see in Figure 3-12:

- ✦ **Click the scroll arrows:** Scrolls the window up/down or right/left. If you move the mouse over a scroll arrow and hold down the mouse button, the window will continuously scroll.
- ✦ **Drag the scroll box:** Scrolls through a window faster.
- ✦ **Click in the scroll area:** Scrolls up/down or right/left in large increments.

TIP

Many mice offer a scroll wheel in the middle. By rolling this scroll wheel, you can scroll a window up or down. The Apple Mighty Mouse has a scroll ball in the middle that lets you roll it to scroll up/down or right/left. On a laptop Mac, you can scroll by pressing one fingertip on the trackpad and rubbing a second fingertip up/down or right/left.

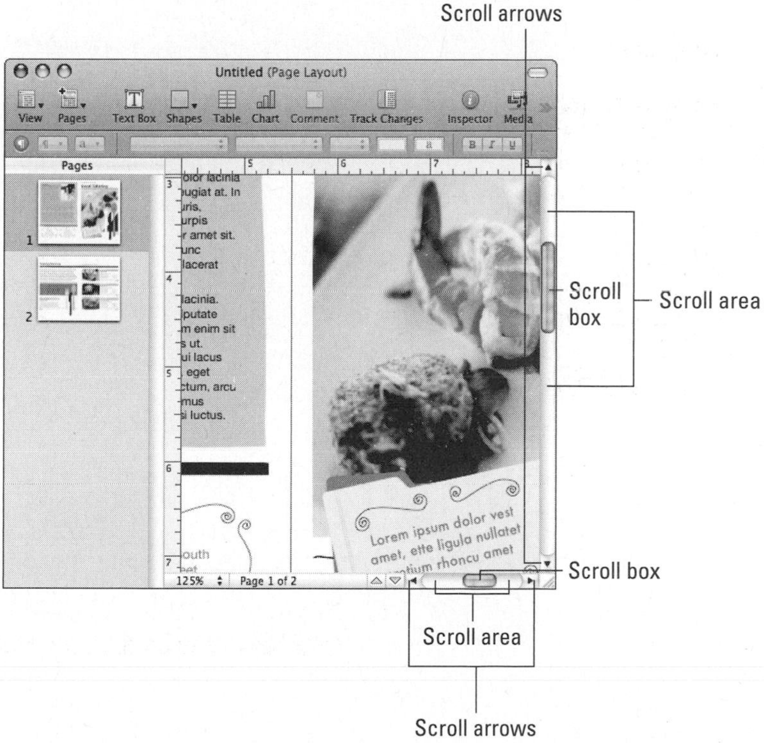

Figure 3-12: The parts of a scroll bar.

Using the Toolbar button

Some windows display a row of icons at the top of the window, known as a *toolbar.* The purpose of a toolbar is to give you one-click access to commonly used commands, such as saving or printing a file. However, these toolbar icons can also clutter up the appearance of a window.

To give you the option of hiding (or viewing) a window's toolbar icons, a window might display a Toolbar button in its upper-right corner, as shown in Figure 3-13.

To toggle between hiding or displaying a toolbar, click the Toolbar button. Some programs might also give you the option of hiding its toolbar another way, such as by choosing View➪Hide Toolbar.

Not all windows have a Toolbar button.

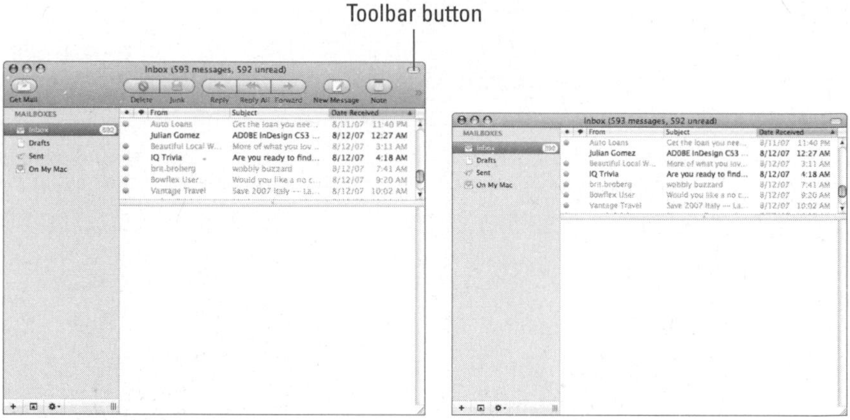

Figure 3-13: The Toolbar button can display (left) or hide (right) a window's toolbar.

Manipulating windows with Exposé

The more windows you open, the more cluttered your screen can appear, much like taking stacks of paper and throwing them all over your desk. To organize your windows, you could move, resize, and minimize each window individually, but that's too tedious and time-consuming. As a faster alternative, you can use a handy feature called Exposé.

The whole idea behind Exposé is to give you these fast, convenient ways to organize your windows:

- Shrinking all windows to the size of thumbnail images so you can see and choose the window you want to use, as shown in Figure 3-14 Pressing the F9 function key does this bit of shrinking for you.
- Showing only those windows that belong to the currently active program, as shown in Figure 3-15. Pressing F10 is the trick here.
- Hiding all windows. Pressing F11 pulls out the old invisibility cloak.

REMEMBER

Pressing the F9, F10, and F11 function keys toggles the display. So pressing F9 initially shrinks all windows as thumbnail images, but pressing F9 a second time reverts all windows back to normal size.

When windows appear as thumbnail images after you press F9 or F10, you can move the pointer over the thumbnail image and view the file name that appears in that particular window.

To switch to a window, click the thumbnail image of that window. Exposé immediately displays your chosen window (at full-size) on the screen.

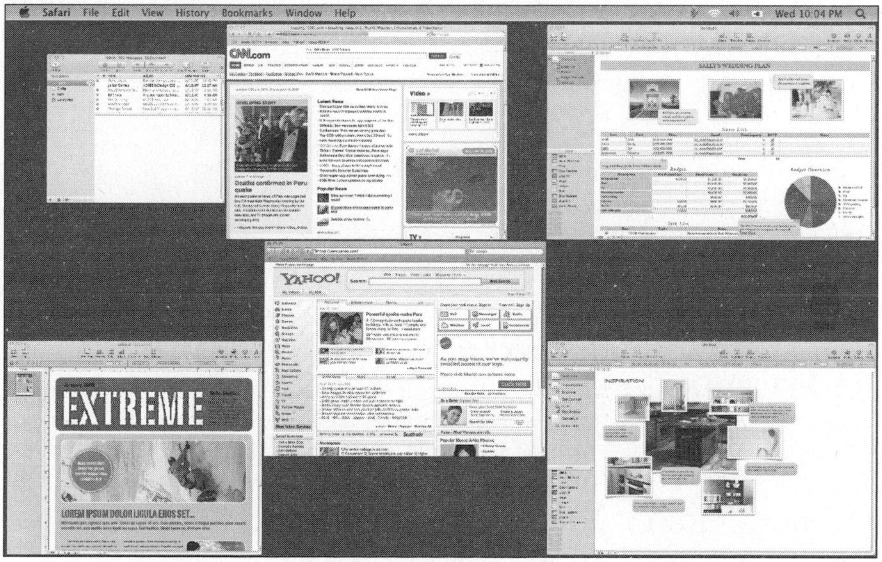

Figure 3-14: Pressing F9 shrinks all open windows into thumbnails.

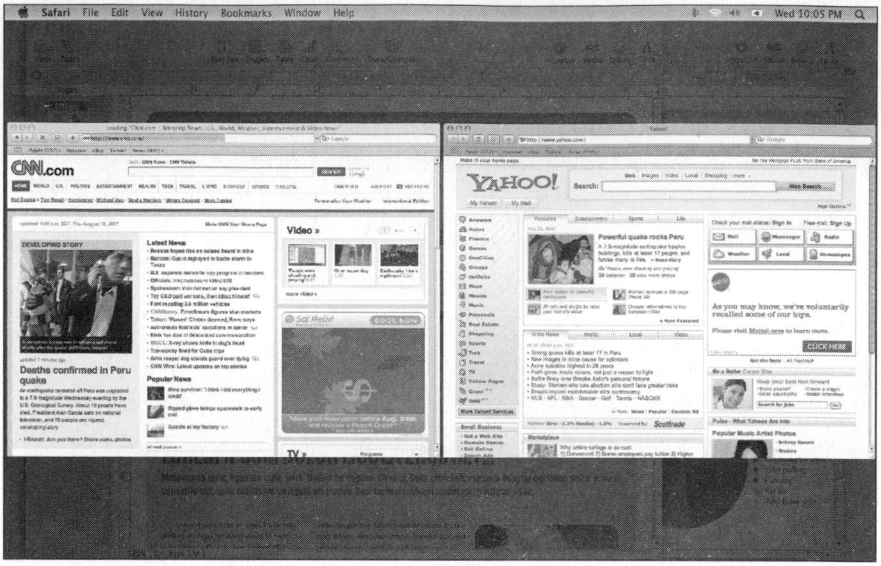

Figure 3-15: Pressing F10 hides all windows except for the currently active program (the name that appears in the Application menu).

Playing with Icons in the Dock and Finder

The Mac shows programs and files as pictures called icons. Program icons act like a visual trademark of the program, such as a Postage Stamp icon that represents the Mail program or the Compass icon that represents the Safari program.

File icons typically contain the filename along with a picture that contains the program that created it. By providing this visual clue, you can see which files were created by specific programs.

Icons commonly appear in three locations, as shown in Figure 3-16:

- ✦ The Desktop
- ✦ The Dock
- ✦ Inside a Finder window

The Desktop

The Desktop appears on the screen when you don't have any open windows covering it up. In the old days, it was common to place program and file icons on the desktop for quick access, much like placing an important book or day planner in one corner of your desk so you can grab it easily.

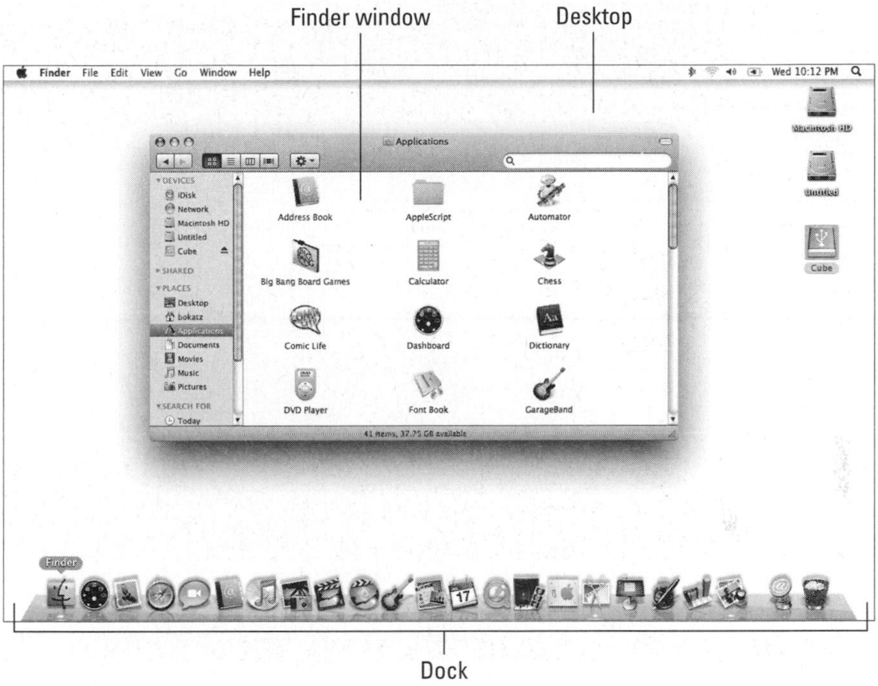

Figure 3-16: The three common locations where you can find icons on the Mac.

Unfortunately, the more icons you store on the Desktop, the more cluttered it appears, making it harder to find anything. Although you can still store program and file icons on the Desktop, it's more common to store program and folder icons on the Dock and program and file icons in the Finder.

REMEMBER

The Desktop always shows an icon that represents your hard drive. If you have any additional storage devices attached to your Mac (such as an external hard drive, a CD or DVD, or a USB flash drive), you see icons for those storage devices on your Desktop, too.

The Dock

The Dock is a rectangular strip that contains both program icons and file icons. To help keep your icons organized, the Dock places Program icons on the left side of a divider and File icons on the right side, as shown in Figure 3-17.

Besides acting as a convenient place to store and find frequently used programs and files, the Dock can also tell you which programs are currently running by displaying a glowing dot under the icon of each running program.

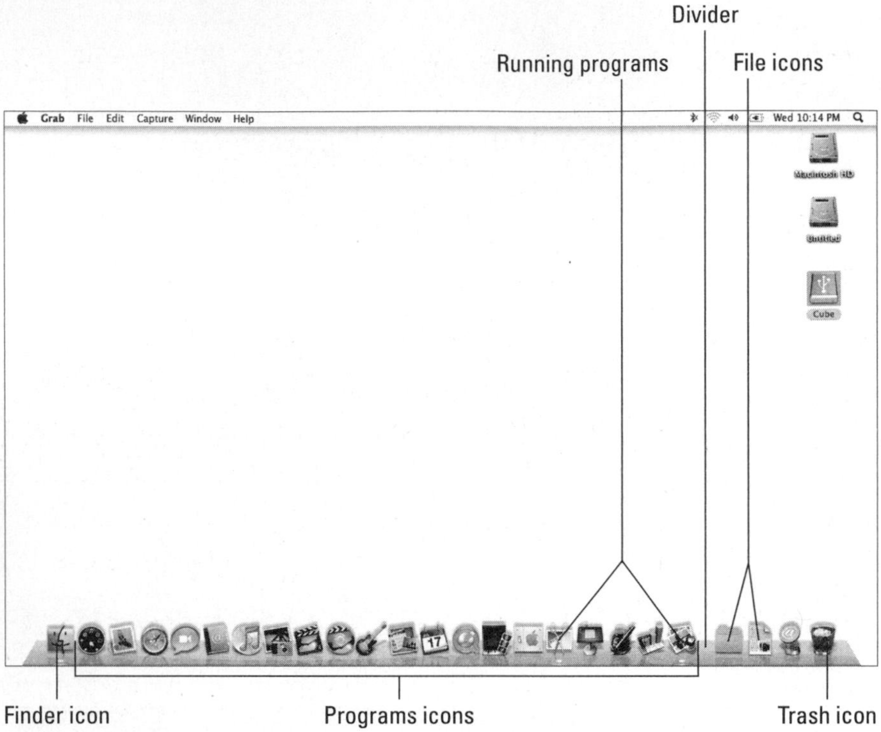

Figure 3-17: The Dock can hold lots of icons.

Moving the Dock

The Dock initially appears at the bottom of the screen, but you can move it to the left or right of the screen. (You can't move the Dock to the top or else it would cover up the menu bar.)

To move the Dock to a new location, follow these steps:

1. **Choose ⇨Dock⇨Dock Preferences.**

   A submenu appears as shown in Figure 3-18.

2. **Click a new position — Left, Bottom, or Right.**

   A check mark appears next to your selection, and the Dock makes its move.

Resizing the Dock

The Dock can grow each time you add more Program or File icons to it. However, you might want to modify the size of icons on the Dock so that the Dock as a whole doesn't appear too small or too large. To resize the Dock, follow these steps:

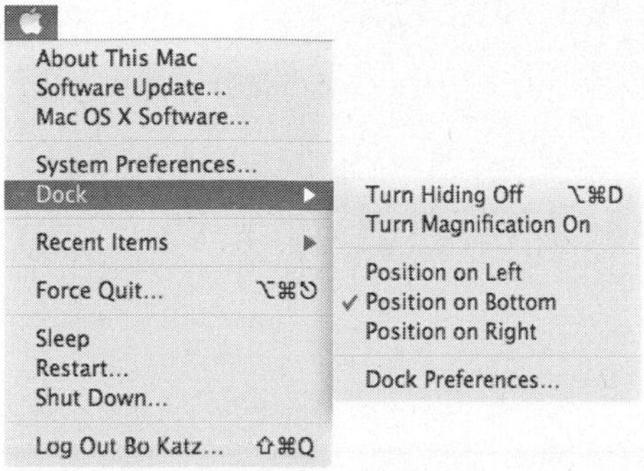

Figure 3-18: The Dock submenu lets you change the position of the Dock on the screen.

1. **Choose ⇨Dock⇨Dock Preferences.**

   The Dock Preferences dialog appears, as shown in Figure 3-19.

2. **Drag the Size slider to adjust the size of all icons on the Dock.**
3. **Click the Close button of the Dock Preferences window.**

   The individual icons on the Dock are resized according to your wishes.

TIP

Another way to resize the Dock is to move the pointer over the Dock divider, hold down the left mouse button, and drag the mouse left or right.

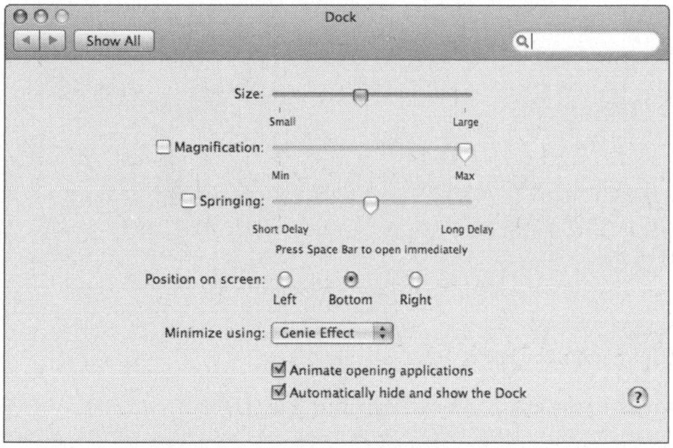

Figure 3-19: The Dock Preferences dialog lets you control the appearance of the Dock.

Magnifying the Dock

The more icons you store on the Dock, the smaller all icons appear as the Dock shrinks to squeeze all icons on the Dock. When icons appear too small, it can be hard to see which icon the mouse is pointing at. To help identify the icon that the pointer is over, you can turn on magnification, which basically pumps up any icon beneath the pointer, as shown in Figure 3-20.

Figure 3-20: Magnification makes an icon on the Dock easier to see.

To turn magnification of the Dock on or off, follow these steps:

1. **Choose ⇨Dock⇨Dock Preferences.**

   The Dock Preferences dialog appears. (Refer to Figure 3-19.)

2. **Select (or clear) the Magnification check box.**
3. **Drag the Magnification slider to adjust the magnification of the Dock.**
4. **Click the Close button of the Dock Preferences dialog.**

TIP

For a fast way to turn magnification on or off, choose ⇨Dock⇨Turn Magnification On (Off).

Hiding the Dock

The Dock might be convenient, but it can clutter up the screen. To get all the advantages of the Dock without the disadvantage of staring at the Dock all the time, you can hide the Dock.

Hiding the Dock means that the Dock tucks itself out of sight, but as soon as you move the mouse near the edge of the screen where the Dock is located (bottom, left, or right), the Dock pops into view.

To hide (or show) the Dock, click the Apple menu and choose ⇨Dock⇨Turn Hiding On (Off).

You find out how to customize the icons on the Dock in Book I, Chapter 4.

The Finder

The Finder is a program that lets you find, copy, move, rename, delete, and open a file on your Mac. You can actually run programs directly from the Finder, but the Dock makes finding and running programs much more convenient.

The Finder runs all the time. To switch to the Finder, click the Finder icon (the smiley face icon on the far left of the Dock) on the Dock.

Sometimes when you switch to the Finder, you might not see a Finder window. To open a Finder window, choose File➪New Finder Window. You can open as many Finder windows as you want, although it's common just to have one or two Finder windows open at a time.

The Finder window looks different than the windows of other programs. Because the Finder helps you manage the files stored on your hard drive, the Finder window consists of two panes, as shown in Figure 3-21.

The left pane, called the Sidebar, displays four different categories:

✦ **Devices:** Lists all the storage devices connected to your Mac, such as hard drives, flash drives, and CD/DVD drives.

✦ **Shared:** Lists all shared storage devices connected on a local area network.

Figure 3-21: The Finder displays two panes to help you navigate to different parts of your hard drive.

✦ **Places:** Lists the Desktop, Home, Applications, and Documents folders, which are the default folders for storing files.

✦ **Search For:** Lists the programs or files you've stored recently such as today, yesterday, or in the past week. This category also lists All Images, All Movies, and All Documents folders where you can view all the images, movies, or documents (files created by word processors, spreadsheets, and so on) stored on your Mac.

The right pane displays the contents of an item selected in the left pane. If you click the hard drive icon in the left pane, the right pane displays the contents of that hard drive. All programs and files displayed in the Finder window appear as icons.

You find out how to use the Finder in more detail in Book I, Chapter 6.

Getting Help

Theoretically, the Mac should be so easy and intuitive that you can teach yourself how to use your computer just by looking at the screen. Realistically, the Mac can still be confusing and complicated. Because most people never read computer manuals anyway, your Mac includes a built-in help system. Any time you're confused using your Mac, try looking for answers in the Mac help system. If you get lucky, you just might find the answer you're looking for.

The Mac help system offers two types of help. First, it can point out specific menu commands to choose for accomplishing a specific task. So if you want to know how to save or print a file, the Mac help system will point out the Save or Print command so you'll always know which command to choose.

Second, the Mac help system can provide brief explanations for how to accomplish a specific task. By skimming through the brief explanations, you can (hopefully) figure out how to do something useful.

Pointing out commands to use

To use the Mac help system to point out the commands you need to use, follow these steps:

1. **Click on the Finder icon on the Dock.**

   The Finder menu bar appears.

2. **Click the Help menu.**

   A Search text box appears, as shown in Figure 3-22.

Figure 3-22: The Search text box.

3. **Click in the Search text box and type a word or phrase.**

   If you want help on printing, for example, type **print**. As you type, a list of possible help topics appears, as shown in Figure 3-23.

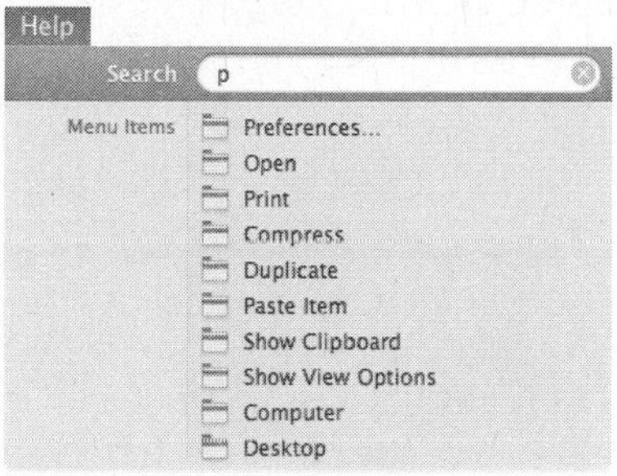

Figure 3-23: As you type, the help system lists help topics.

4. **Click a help topic.**

   A floating arrow points to the command on a menu to show you how to access your chosen help topic, as shown in Figure 3-24.

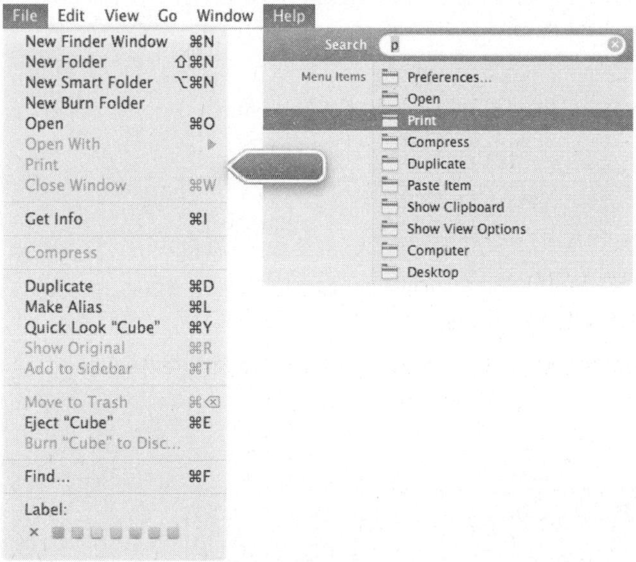

Figure 3-24: The Mac Help System tries to show you how to access a particular command.

When accessing the help system of specific programs, you see a Help System window, as shown in Figure 3-25.

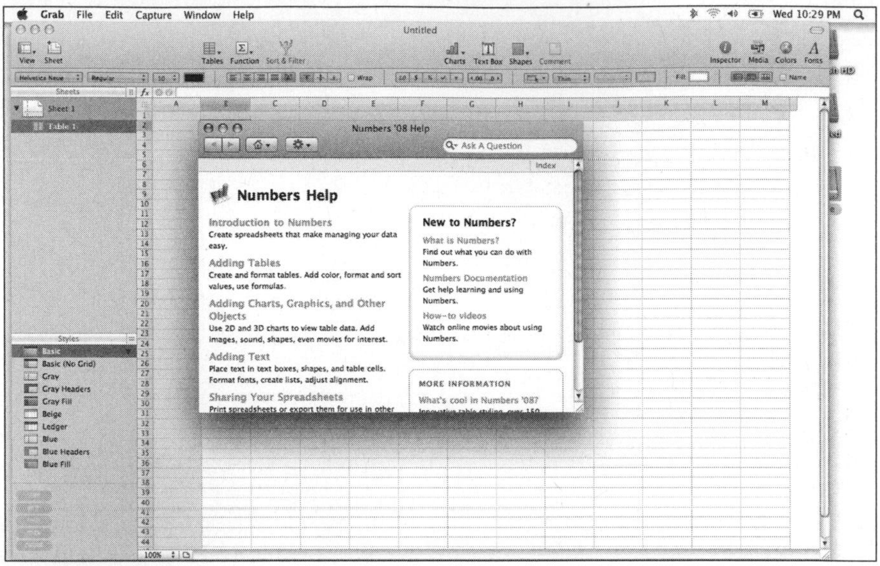

Figure 3-25: The Help System of many programs displays help topics you can click.

Reading help topics

To use the Mac help system to read brief explanations of different help topics, follow these steps:

1. **Click the Finder icon in the Dock.**
2. **Click the Help menu.**

   A help menu appears (refer to Figure 3-22).
3. **Click Mac Help.**

   A Mac Help window appears, as shown in Figure 3-26.
4. **Click a help topic, displayed in blue.**

   The Mac Help window displays additional information about your chosen topic. To jump back (or forward) to a previously viewed help topic
5. **Click the Back (or Forward) button to jump to a previously viewed help topic.**

   You might also want to click the Home button to return back to the original Mac Help Topic window.
6. **Click the Close button of the Mac Help window.**

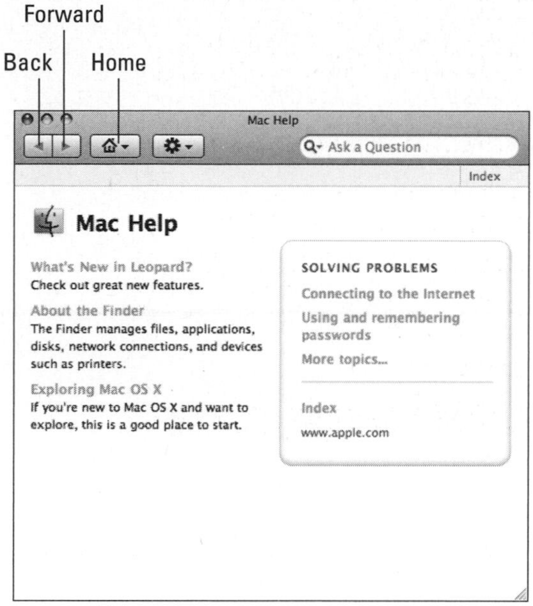

Figure 3-26: The Mac Help window displays topics that you can click.

Chapter 4: Running Programs

In This Chapter

- **Running programs from the Dock**
- **Double-clicking icons**
- **Switching between programs**
- **Using Spaces**
- **Shutting down programs**

After you have the Mac OS X operating system up and running, you can run any additional programs, such as a word processor, a video game, a Web browser, or an e-mail program. The number of programs you can load and run simultaneously is limited only by the amount of hard drive space and memory crammed inside your Mac.

To start up a program, you can choose four different methods:

- Click a program icon in the Dock.
- Double-click a program icon in the Finder.
- Double-click a document icon in the Finder.
- Click a program name from the Recent Items Apple menu.

The next few sections take a closer look at each one of these methods.

Running a Program from the Dock

To run a program from the Dock, just click the program icon that you want to run. (What? Were you expecting something difficult?)

The Dock contains icons that represent some (but not all) of the programs installed on your Mac. When you turn on your Mac for the first time, you see that the Dock already includes a variety of programs that Apple thinks you might want to use right away. However, you can always add or delete program icons from the Dock (more on that later).

When using programs, you can use the Dock in several ways:

- ✦ To gain one-click access to your favorite programs.
- ✦ To see which programs are currently running.
- ✦ To switch between different programs quickly.
- ✦ To see which windows you have minimized. (Minimized windows are tucked out of sight but still open.)
- ✦ To view a specific program window.
- ✦ To hide all windows that belong to a specific program.

Your Mac displays a dot underneath the icon of every running program. By glancing at the Dock, you can identify all running programs at a glance. (See Figure 4-1.)

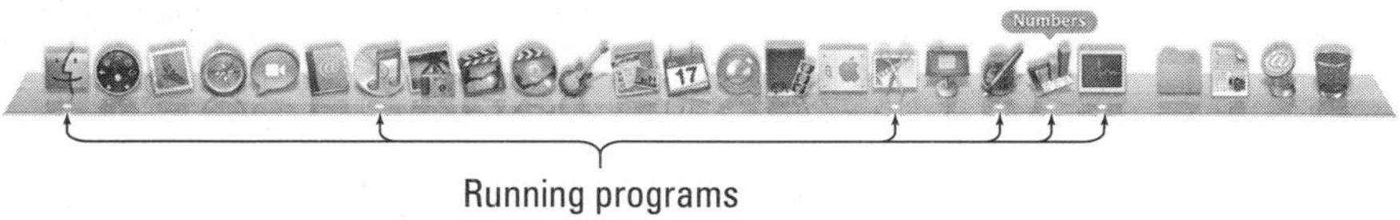

Figure 4-1: The Dock identifies all running programs with a dot.

Knowing which programs are running is a big help, because now you can easily switch between each running program by simply clicking that program icon again. So, if you want to switch to the iTunes program from the GarageBand program, you can just click the iTunes program icon. This would immediately display the iTunes window and display the iTunes program name in the Application menu on the menu bar at the top of the screen. (Clicking the iTunes program icon brings iTunes to the fore, but the GarageBand program doesn't quit on you; it just moseys to the background, waiting for its turn to step into the limelight again.)

The Dock identifies all running programs by displaying a dot underneath the icon of each running program. The Application menu in the menu bar identifies the currently active program. You can have multiple programs running, but you can have only one program that's currently active. (The active program is the one that accepts any data or commands you give it.)

You can add or delete program icons from the Dock so it contains only the programs you use most often, and you can arrange the icons on the Dock to suit yourself and make starting programs even easier. The following sections give you all the dirty details on the relationship between the Dock and its icons.

Adding program icons to the Dock

The Dock includes several programs already installed on your Mac, but if you install more programs, you might want to add those program icons to the Dock as well. One way to add a program icon to the Dock is to click and drag the icon onto the Dock. Here's how that's usually done:

1. **Click the Finder icon in the Dock.**

   The Finder appears.

2. **Click the Applications folder.**

   The Finder displays the contents of the Applications folder.

3. **Move the pointer over a program icon, hold down the mouse button, and drag the pointer where you want to place the icon on the Dock.**

   The existing Dock icons move to the side to make room for the new icon.

   REMEMBER: Make sure you drag program icons in the Dock to the left of the divider, which appears as a gap near the Trash icon. To the left of the divider, you see program icons. To the right of the divider, you can store file or folder icons. (To keep you from dropping programs icons to the right of the divider, your Mac won't let you no matter how hard you might try, so there.)

4. **Release the mouse button to place the program icon in the Dock.**

   REMEMBER: When you drag a program icon in the Dock, you aren't physically moving the program out of the Applications folder onto the Dock; you're just creating a link from the Dock to the actual program (which is still safely stashed in its folder).

You can also add a program icon to the Dock right after you load a program. Remember that the Dock displays the icons of all running programs at all times, but when you exit a program, that program's icon — if it's not one of Apple's Chosen Few and you haven't added it to the Dock — will disappear off the Dock. To keep an icon in the Dock, follow these steps:

1. **Click the Finder icon in the Dock.**

   The Finder appears.

2. **Click the Applications folder.**

   The Finder displays the contents of the Applications folder.

3. **Double-click the program icon you want to load.**

   Your chosen program's icon appears on the Dock with a dot underneath.

4. **Right-click this program icon in the Dock.**

   A shortcut menu appears, as shown in Figure 4-2.

Figure 4-2: Right-clicking a program icon in the Dock displays a shortcut menu.

5. **Choose Keep in Dock from the shortcut menu.**

   Now if you exit from this program, its program icon remains visible in the Dock.

Rearranging program icons in the Dock

After you've placed program icons in the Dock, you might want to rearrange their order. How you arrange your Dock icons is totally up to you. Some people group certain programs on one part of the Dock, and others arrange program icons alphabetically to make them easier to find.

To rearrange program icons in the Dock, follow these steps:

1. **Move the pointer over a program icon that you want to move.**
2. **Hold down the mouse button and drag the mouse sideways.**

   Notice that as you move a program icon, the existing icons move to the side to show you where the icon will appear if you let go of the mouse button.

3. **Release the mouse button when you're happy with the new position of the program icon in the Dock.**

Removing program icons from the Dock

If you keep adding program icons to the Dock, eventually you'll find that you rarely use some of these programs. Rather than let them clutter up your Dock, it's better to get rid of them.

TIP: If you like having a program icon in the Dock but want to make room on the Dock for other programs, you can store programs icons in a folder and then store that folder on the right of the divider in the Dock. Now to load that program, you can click its folder icon in the Dock and then click the program icon.

The only two icons you can never remove from the Dock are the Finder and Trash icons.

To remove a program icon from the Dock, follow these steps:

1. **Move the pointer over a program icon that you want to remove from the Dock.**
2. **Hold down the mouse button and drag the mouse until the program icon no longer appears over the Dock.**
3. **Release the mouse button.**

   Your chosen program icon disappears in an animated puff of smoke.

Another way to remove a program icon from the Dock is to right-click the program icon and, when a menu pops up, choose Remove From Dock.

Removing a program icon from the Dock doesn't remove or delete the actual program.

You can't remove a program icon from the Dock if the program is still running.

Starting Programs by Double-Clicking Icons

The Mac represents files as a graphically descriptive icon with a name. Icons can represent two types of files: programs and documents.

Program files represent software that actually does something, such as play a game of chess or organize your e-mail. *Document files* represent data created by a program, such as a letter created by a word processor, a business report created by a presentation program, or a movie created by a video-editing program.

Program icons are often distinct enough to help you identify the type of program they represent. For example, the iTunes program icon appears as a musical note over a CD, the iPhoto icon appears as a camera over a photograph, and the Mail program icon (for sending and receiving e-mail) appears as a cancelled stamp.

Document icons often appear with the icon of the program that created them or as thumbnail images of their content, as shown in Figure 4-3. So if you saved a Web page in Safari, your file appears as a page with the Safari icon over it.

A third type of icon you might see is called an alias icon, which you find out more about in the "Using alias icons" section later in this chapter. Basically, an alias icon represents a link to a program or document icon.

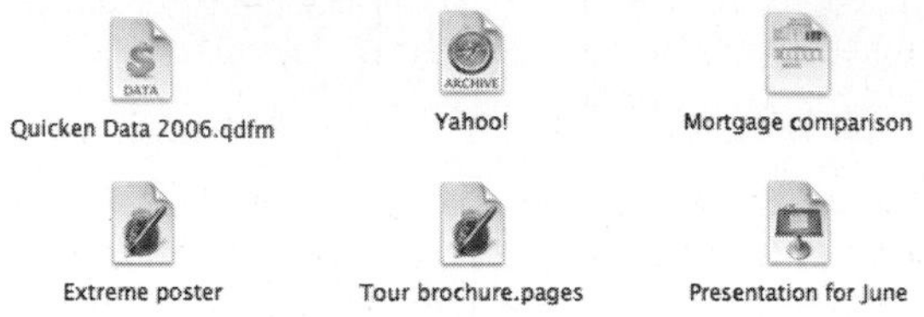

Figure 4-3: Document icons display either thumbnail images of their content or the icon of the program that created them.

Double-clicking a program icon

Because a program's icon might not appear on the Dock, you have to be able to access icons another way. Lucky for you, you can find program icons by looking for them using the Finder. (You can find most programs stored in the Applications folder, but the Finder can help you find any programs that are stored in another folder.)

REMEMBER

It's actually possible to store a program icon in any folder on your hard drive, but you should always store programs in the Applications folder. That way, if you need to find that program again, you just have to look in the Applications folder instead of trying to remember whether you stored it somewhere else.

To run a program by double-clicking its icon, follow these steps:

1. **Click the Finder icon in the Dock.**

   The Finder appears.

2. **Click the Applications folder.**

   The content of the Applications folder appears.

3. **Scroll through this Applications folder window until you see the program icon you want.**

   You might have to double-click a folder that contains a program icon.

4. **Move the pointer over the program icon you want to run and double-click (or click a program icon and choose File⇨Open).**

   Your chosen program appears, typically with a blank window, ready for you to do something programy — such as typing text.

Double-clicking a document icon

When you double-click a program icon, you start that particular program. Unfortunately, if you want to use your newly opened program to work on an existing file, you now have to search for that file and then open it by using the program's File➪Open command.

As an alternative to running a program and then having to find and open the file you want to work with, the Mac gives you the option of just double-clicking the document icon you want to use instead. When you double-click a document icon, your Mac typically opens the program that created that document and then loads that document in the program window.

Sometimes if you double-click a document icon, an entirely different program loads and displays your file. This can occur if you save your file in a different file format. For example, if you save an iMovie project as a QuickTime file, double-clicking the QuickTime file opens the QuickTime Player instead of iMovie.

Think of double-clicking a document icon as equivalent to the two-step process of first opening a program and then opening the document you want to edit.

To double-click a document icon, follow these steps:

1. **Click the Finder icon in the Dock.**

   The Finder comes to the fore.

2. **Click the Documents folder.**

   The Documents window appears.

3. **Scroll through this Documents window until you see the program icon you want.**

   You might need to double-click one or more folders until you find the document you want.

   Although it's possible to store document icons anywhere on your hard drive, it's a good idea to always store documents inside the Documents folder so you'll always know where to start looking first.

4. **Double-click a document icon.**

   Your Mac loads the program that created the document (if it's not already running) and displays your chosen document in a window. If your Mac can't find the program that created the document, it might load another program, or it might ask you to choose an existing program on your Mac that can open the document.

As an alternative to searching for a document manually, you can use your Mac's Spotlight feature to search and (hopefully) find that document for you. To use the Spotlight feature, follow these steps:

1. **Click the Finder icon in the Dock.**

   The Finder appears.

2. **Click in the Spotlight text box, type all or part of a document name, and then press Return.**

   A list of documents matching what you typed appears in the Finder, as shown in Figure 4-4.

3. **Double-click the document you want to open.**

   Your Mac loads a program that displays the contents of your document in a window, ready for you to edit.

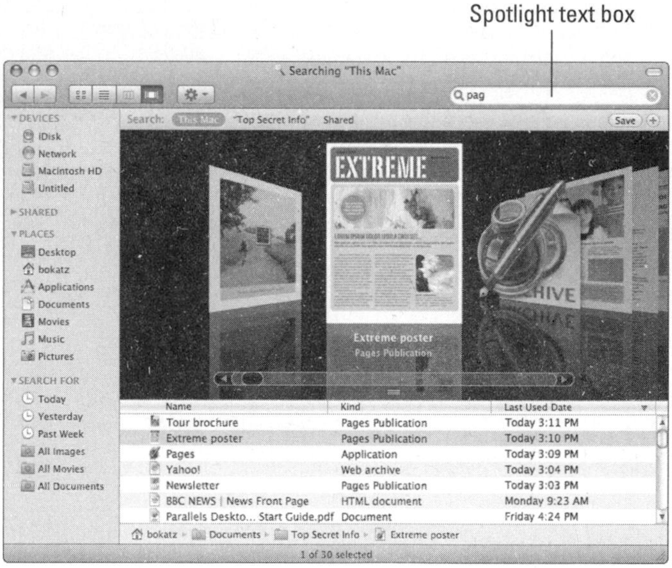

Figure 4-4: The Spotlight text box can help you find a document by name.

Using alias icons

One problem with double-clicking a program or document icon is that you have to *find* that icon first. You can move an icon to a single location, such as on the Desktop, making it more likely that you'll actually be able to find what you want. Unfortunately, moving programs out of the Applications folder or documents out of the Documents folder increases the risk of accidentally deleting an important program or document, or just losing track of where you put it. As an alternative to moving program or document icons, you can create and use alias icons instead.

An alias icon acts like a link to another icon. Double-clicking an alias icon works identically to double-clicking the actual program or document icon. The biggest advantage of alias icons is that you can move and place alias icons anywhere you want without physically moving (and perhaps losing) a program or document icon.

TIP

One way to use alias icons is to create alias icons to your program icons and then store those alias icons in a folder. Now store that folder to the right of the divider in the Dock, and you have easy access to program icons without cluttering up the Dock.

Creating an alias icon

To create an alias icon, follow these steps:

1. **Click the Finder icon in the Dock.**

   The Finder appears and awaits your command.

2. **Click either the Applications or Documents folder.**

   The appropriate window appears on-screen.

3. **Scroll through this window until you see the icon you want.**

   You might have to double-click additional folders until you find the program or document icon you want.

4. **Click to select the icon you want and then choose File➪Make Alias (or press ⌘+L).**

   A copy of your chosen icon appears in the window with an arrow and the word *alias* added to its name, as shown in Figure 4-5.

REMEMBER

An alias icon takes up approximately 100 kilobytes (K) of storage space, which is less than the size of a short letter, so don't worry about alias icons gobbling up hard drive space.

Moving an alias icon

After you create an alias icon, you can place it anywhere. Because it's pointless to store the original icon and the alias icon in the same location, you should store the alias icon in a new location. To move an alias icon, follow these steps:

1. **Move the pointer over the alias icon, hold down the mouse button, and drag the alias icon onto a folder in the left pane of the Finder.**

   The Desktop folder would be a nice choice here.

2. **Release the mouse button.**

   Your alias icon now appears in your chosen folder. Double-clicking this alias icon is equivalent to double-clicking the original icon.

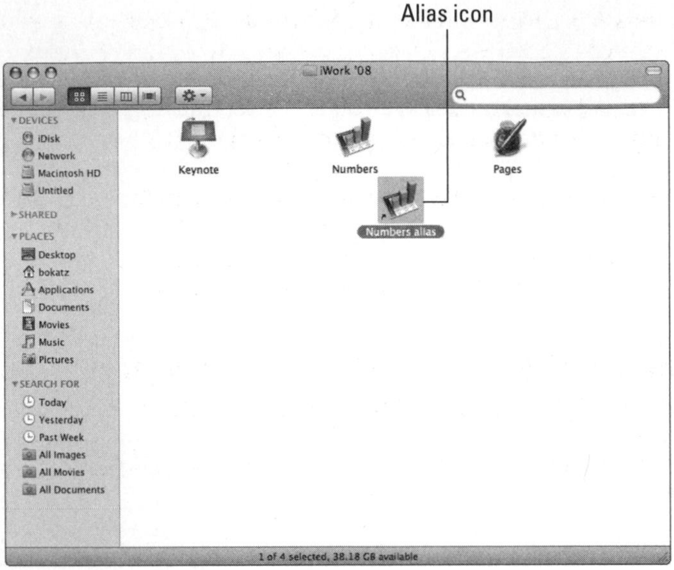

Figure 4-5: A tiny arrow identifies an alias icon.

You can store alias icons on the Desktop for fast access or in specific folders to organize documents without physically moving them to a new location. (Of course, the Dock essentially replaces the need to place alias icons on the Desktop, and Smart Folders basically duplicate the process of creating and storing alias icons in a folder. You find out how to use Smart Folders in Book 1, Chapter 5.)

Deleting an alias icon

After you've created an alias icon, you might decide to delete it. To delete an alias icon, follow these steps:

1. **Right-click the alias icon you want to delete.**

   A shortcut menu appears.

2. **Choose Move to Trash (or press ⌘+Delete).**

   Your alias icon is now an ex-alias icon.

   Deleting an alias icon never deletes the original icon — meaning that if you delete an alias icon that represents a program, you never delete the actual program itself. The only way to delete a program or document is to delete the original program or document icon.

Switching Between Programs

After you start running multiple programs, you'll have multiple windows from different programs cluttering up your screen, much like covering a clean desk with piles of different papers. To help keep your screen organized, you can switch between different programs (such as between a word processor and a game) as well as switch to different windows displayed by the same program (such as a word processor displaying a window containing a business report and a second window containing a letter of resignation).

Your Mac offers quite a few different ways to switch between different programs, including using the Dock, using the Application Switcher, using Exposé, clicking a window of a different program, or by hiding programs or entire desktops (truly an embarrassment of riches).

Using the Dock to switch between programs

To switch to a different (running) program using the Dock, follow these steps:

1. **By looking at the Dock, ascertain which programs are currently running.**

   Dots appear underneath the Dock icons of all currently running programs.

2. **Click a program icon in the Dock that has a dot underneath it.**

   Your chosen program appears on the screen.

If you want to switch to a specific document window opened by a certain program, you can switch to that program and that document window all at once by following these steps:

1. **Check the Dock again to see which programs are currently running.**

   Dots appear underneath the icons of all currently running programs.

2. **Right-click the icon of the program you want to switch to.**

   A shortcut menu appears, listing all documents currently opened by that program, as shown in Figure 4-6.

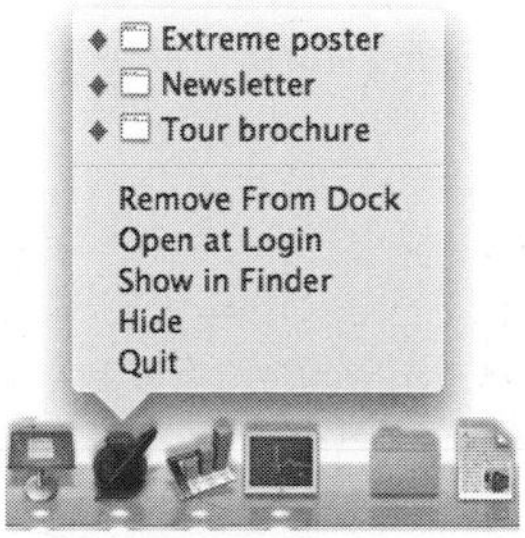

Figure 4-6: The shortcut menu displays a list of all open documents.

3. **Click the name of the document you want to view.**

Switching programs with the Application Switcher

Another way to switch between different programs is to use the Application Switcher, a program that displays icons of all currently running programs. After you open the Application Switcher, you can just choose the icon of the program you want to use. To use the Application Switcher, follow these steps:

1. **Hold down both the ⌘ key and press the Tab key once; then let go of the Tab key (but keep holding down the ⌘ key).**

   The Application Switcher appears, as shown in Figure 4-7.

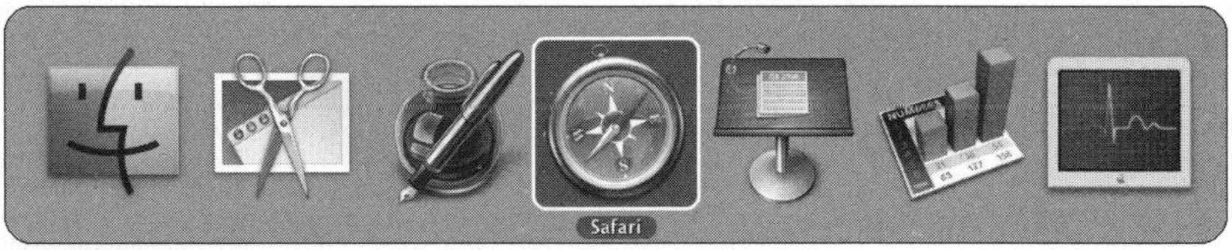

Figure 4-7: The Application Switcher displays icons of all currently running programs.

2. **Press the Tab key (or press the left- and right-arrow keys) to highlight the icon of the program you want to switch to.**
3. **Release the ⌘ key.**

   Your chosen program appears on the screen.

If a program has several files open in different windows, the Application Switcher just switches you to that program, but you still have to find the specific window to view.

Using Exposé to switch between programs

Switching programs using the Dock or the Application Switcher can switch to a specific program, but if that program has several open windows, you need to take time to search for the specific window you want to use. As a faster alternative, Exposé lets you view thumbnail versions of all your open windows from all running programs. Then all you have to do is click the exact window you want to use. To use Exposé, follow these steps:

1. **Press F9.**

   Exposé displays all program windows as thumbnail images.

If you've hidden any windows (which you find out how to do later in this chapter), pressing F9 won't display those hidden windows.

2. **Move the pointer over an open window.**

   Exposé displays the name of the file in that window, as shown in Figure 4-8, so you'll know exactly which window to choose.

3. **Click the thumbnail image of the window you want to use.**

   Your chosen window appears full-size on the screen.

Switching by clicking different windows

A fast, but somewhat clumsier way to switch between programs is to rearrange your windows so you can see two or more windows at once, as shown in Figure 4-9.

To switch between each window, just click anywhere inside that window. The drawback with this method is that you must keep all windows visible at all times, which means you can have a only limited number of windows on the screen at the same time, depending on the size of your computer screen and the size of each window. That means each window can't fill the entire screen, which can make each window too small to use effectively.

Figure 4-8: Exposé shows you all open windows so you can choose the one you want.

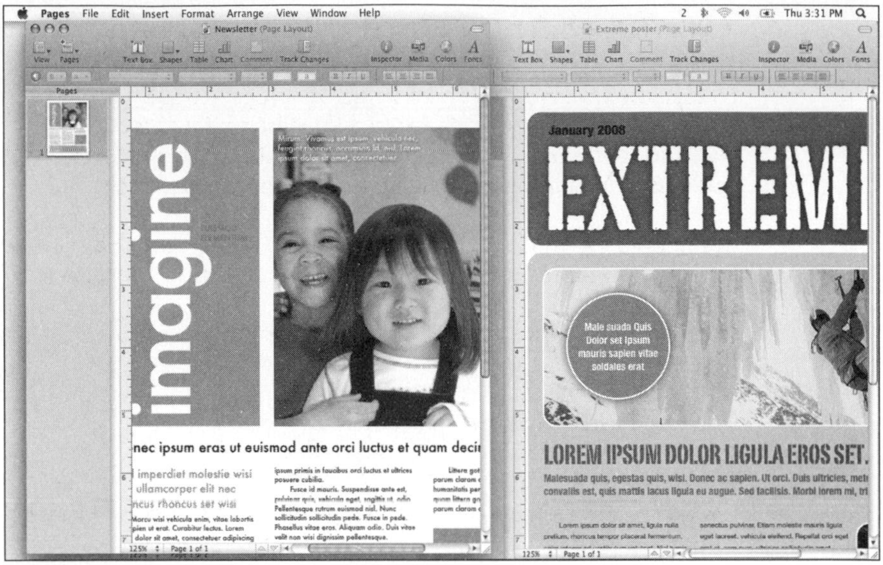

Figure 4-9: Arranging windows side by side lets you view and access each one at the click of the mouse.

Getting Organized on Multiple Desktops with Spaces

Spaces is a handy new feature available since Mac OS X 10.5 Leopard. Spaces essentially divides your Mac into multiple computers by creating up to 16 separate Desktops. The main purpose of Spaces is to help organize multiple programs running at the same time.

Rather than cram multiple program windows on a single screen (Desktop), Spaces lets you store multiple programs in separate Desktops. One Desktop might contain only Internet programs, such as Safari and Mail, whereas a second Desktop might contain only video games.

If one program has multiple windows opened, you can store each program window on a separate Desktop. So if you had a word processor and opened a personal letter and a business letter, you could store the personal letter window on one Desktop and the business letter window on a second Desktop. If you're a busy person who needs to run multiple programs at the same time, Spaces provides one more way to help you stay organized.

REMEMBER

Spaces creates multiple Desktops to create the illusion of multiple computer screens, but each Desktop is actually a single user account. That means any settings you've configured will apply to all Desktops, such as the appearance of the Dock or screensaver.

After you've enabled Spaces and defined the total number of Desktops to create, you can view all your Desktops as thumbnail images. Then you can open and move windows from one Desktop to another.

Turning on Spaces and creating Desktops

Before you can use Spaces to switch between multiple Desktops, you have to turn on Spaces and create some Desktops. Initially, Spaces creates two Desktops, but you can add up to 16 Desktops if you want. The more Desktops you add, the harder it can be to manage them all, so the trick is to pick the number of Desktops you can manage, such as two or three.

Later, if you find out you need more Desktops, you can add more. Likewise, if you find you created too many Desktops, you can delete some.

Turn on Spaces and create your desired number of Desktops by following these steps:

1. **Choose ⇨System Preferences.**

   The System Preferences window appears.
2. **Click the Exposé & Spaces icon under the Personal category.**

   The Exposé & Spaces pane appears.
3. **Click the Spaces tab in the top center of the pane.**

   The Spaces tab appears, as shown in Figure 4-10.
4. **Select the Enable Spaces check box.**

   Selecting this check box turns on Spaces.
5. **Click the Plus or Minus icons in the Rows and Columns fields to change the number of Desktops (between 2 and 16).**

   The number of rows and columns you create simply defines how multiple Desktops are arranged. You could create up to 16 Desktops in a single row or arrange 4 Desktops in a row in four columns. The layout of Desktops matters only when you switch between Desktops using the Control+arrow keys. If you arranged 16 Desktops in a row, switching from Desktop 2 to Desktop 14 would require pressing the Control+right-arrow key 12 times. However, if you arranged 16 Desktops in four rows and columns, switching from Desktop 2 to desktop 14 would require pressing the Control+down-arrow key three times.
6. **Click the Close button of the System Preferences window.**

Configuring Spaces

When you configure Spaces, you can define the number of Desktops to use and the shortcut keys to activate Spaces or switch to a specific Desktop.

From the Spaces tab of the Exposé & Spaces window (shown earlier in Figure 4-10), you can change the following settings to your liking:

- **Using a Spaces menulet:** Select (or clear) the Show Spaces in Menu Bar check box. Selecting this check box displays a Spaces menulet on the right side of the menu bar so you can switch between Desktops.
- **Activating Spaces:** Choose a function key from the To Activate Spaces pop-up menu. The default function key is F8.
- **Switching between Desktops:** Choose a shortcut key from the To Switch Between Spaces pop-up menu. The default is the Control+arrow key combination.
- **Switching to a specific Desktop:** Choose a shortcut key from the Switch Directly to a Space pop-up menu. The default is the Control+number key combination where the number key you press (1, 3, and so on) identifies the number of the Desktop you want to view.

Moving program windows to different Desktops

The first time you use Spaces, all your program windows appear on one Desktop. Now you just need to move them where you want them.

To move program windows to different Desktops, follow these steps:

1. **Press the Spaces function key (F8 unless you changed it).**

   All of your Desktops appear on-screen, as shown in Figure 4-11.

2. **Press F9.**

   Exposé displays every window as a thumbnail within each Desktop image.

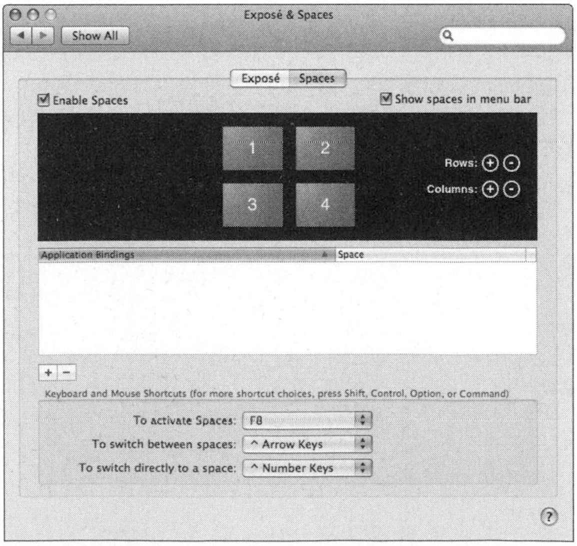

Figure 4-10: The Spaces pane lets you turn on Spaces and define how many desktop to create.

3. **Click and drag a program window onto a different Desktop image and then release the mouse button.**

   Your program window now appears in the other Desktop.

4. **Repeat Step 3 for each program window you want to move to a different Desktop.**

5. **Click the one Desktop image that you want to use right now.**

   Your chosen Desktop image expands to fill the screen.

Switching Desktops

After you've arranged program windows on each Desktop, you can switch to a different Desktop at any time by using one of the following methods:

- Press F8 (or whatever function key you assigned to activate Spaces) and then click on the Desktop thumbnail you want to view.
- Click the Spaces menulet on the menu bar and choose a Desktop number, as shown in Figure 4-12.
- Press the Control+*arrow key* combination until you see the Desktop you want to view. (Press the up/down or left/right arrow keys.)
- Press the Control+*number key* combination. (To view Desktop 1, for example, press Control+1.)

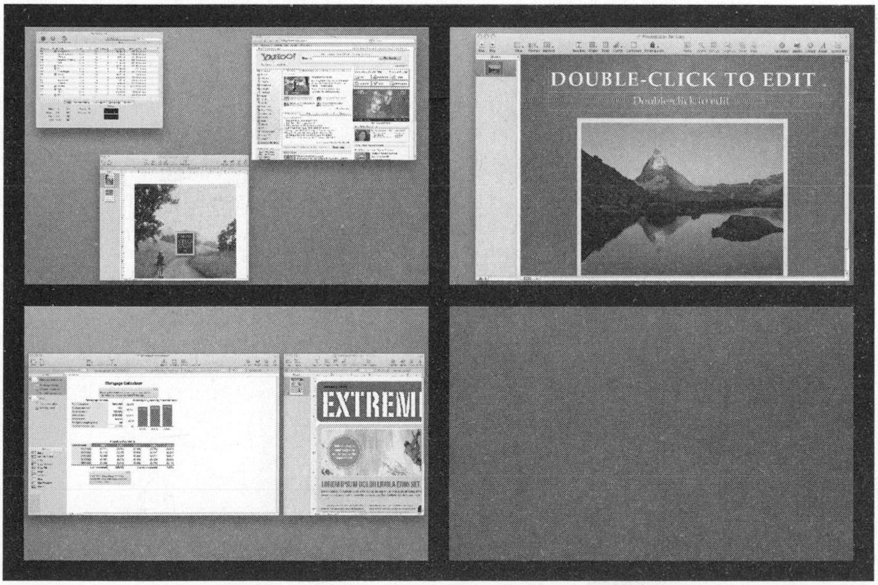

Figure 4-11: Spaces displays thumbnail images of all your separate Desktops.

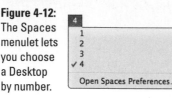

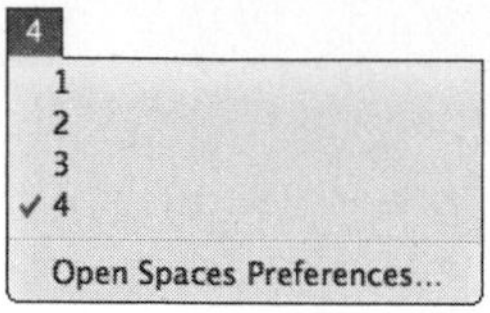

Figure 4-12: The Spaces menulet lets you choose a Desktop by number.

Increasing (or decreasing) the number of Desktops

You can always increase or decrease the number of Desktops available at any time. For example, you might want one Desktop to display your e-mail program and browser and have a second Desktop display your word processor. Then you might suddenly decide you need a third Desktop to display a business presentation. When you're done writing your letter or designing your business presentation, you could decrease the number of Desktops to consolidate the number of Desktops to track.

REMEMBER

If you eliminate any rows or columns of Desktops that already contain program windows, Spaces moves those program windows to another Desktop automatically.

To modify the number of Desktops, follow these steps:

1. **Choose ⌘⇨System Preferences.**

   The System Preferences window appears.

2. **Click the Exposé & Spaces icon under the Personal category.**

   The Exposé & Spaces pane appears.

3. **Click the Spaces tab.**

   The Spaces tab appears.

4. **Click the Plus or Minus icons that appear next to the Row and Column labels to add (or subtract) Desktops.**

   The Spaces pane displays the total number of Desktops you defined.

5. **Click the Close button of the System Preferences window when you're happy with the total number of Desktops you have.**

Turning off Spaces

If you want to turn off Spaces, follow these steps:

1. **Choose ⌘⇨System Preferences.**

   The System Preferences window appears.

2. **Click the Exposé & Spaces icon under the Personal category.**

   The Exposé & Spaces pane appears.

3. **Click the Spaces button.**

   The Spaces pane appears.

4. **Clear the Enable Spaces check box.**
5. **Click the Close button on the System Preferences window.**

When you turn off Spaces, all your program windows return to a single Desktop again. If you turn Spaces back on again, your Mac remembers the number of Desktops you had defined before you turned Spaces off. If you restart your Mac while Spaces is displaying multiple Desktops, your Mac shuts down all windows in all Desktops. When your Mac starts up again, all your Desktops are empty again.

Quitting Programs

No matter how much you love using your, you'll eventually need to shut down a program. When you shut down a program, you also shut down all document windows that program may have open. However, if you only shut down a document in an open application, the program keeps running.

Closing a document

If you want to stop editing or viewing a specific document but still keep a program running, feel free to close just that particular document. You have three different ways to close a document window:

- Choose File⇨Close.
- Press ⌘+W.
- Click the Close button of the document window.

If you try to close a window before saving the file, a dialog appears, asking whether you want to save your file.

Shutting down a program

When you're done using a program, it's a good idea to shut it down so that you free up your Mac's memory to run other programs. The more programs you leave running on your Mac, the slower your Mac could be, so always shut down programs if you don't need them any more.

To shut down a program, you have three choices:

- Choose the menu associated with the application and choose Quit (such as iPhoto⇨Quit iPhoto to shut down the iPhoto program).
- In the Dock, click the program icon that you want to shut down and press ⌘+Q.
- Right-click the program icon in the Dock and choose Quit from the shortcut menu that appears.

If you try to shut down a program that displays a window containing a document that you haven't saved yet, a dialog appears, asking whether you want to save your file.

Force quitting a program

Despite the Mac's reputation for reliability, there's always a chance that a program will crash, freeze, or hang, which are less-than-technical-terms for a program screwing up and not reacting when you click the mouse or type a key. When a program no longer responds to any attempts to work or shut down, you might have to resort to a drastic procedure known as a *force quit.*

As the name implies, force quitting makes a program shut down whether it wants to or not. There are two ways to force quit a program:

- Choose ⌘⇨Force Quit.
- Right-click a program icon in the Dock and choose Force Quit from the shortcut menu that appears. (If Force Quit doesn't appear on the shortcut menu, hold down the Option key and right-click a program icon in the Dock again.)

The next sections give you all the details.

If you force quit a program, you will lose any data you changed right before the program suddenly froze or crashed.

Force quitting through the Apple menu

To force quit a program with the Apple menu, follow these steps:

1. **Choose ⌘⇨Force Quit.**

   A Force Quit dialog appears as shown in Figure 4-13. Frozen or crashed programs might appear in the Force Quit dialog with the phrase `(not responding)` next to its name.

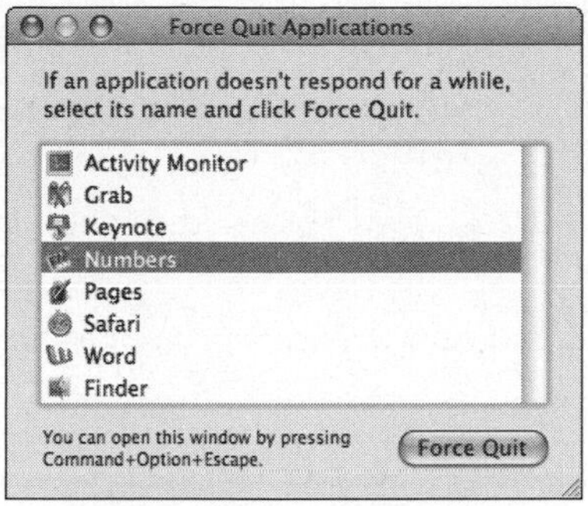

Figure 4-13: The Force Quit dialog shows you the names of all currently running programs.

2. **Click to select the program you want to force quit and then click the Force Quit button.**

Force quitting through the Dock

To force quit a program with the Dock, follow these steps:

1. **Right-click the program icon in the Dock.**

   A shortcut menu appears.

2. **Choose Force Quit from the shortcut menu.**

   If the program hasn't really crashed or if your Mac thinks the program hasn't crashed, you won't see a Force Quit option in this pop-up menu. In that case, you might have to choose the Force Quit option through the Apple menu instead or hold down the Option key, right-click a program icon on the Dock, and then choose Force Quit.

Chapter 5: Installing and Uninstalling Software

In This Chapter

- Finding software
- Installing software
- Uninstalling software

Every Mac comes loaded with plenty of software to get you started, but you'll most likely need to install a few additional programs to do your work. Because you have a physical limit on the amount of software you can install on your Mac, you have two choices. One, you can get another hard drive (an external drive or a larger internal drive) so you can keep installing more programs. Two, you can delete some programs that you don't want or need, which makes room for more programs that you do want and need.

This chapter explains how to install and uninstall software for your Mac. Of course, before you can install any software, you have to know where to find it.

Finding Software

You can find the more popular Mac programs packaged in pretty boxes that typically contain a single CD/DVD, a thin manual, and a lot of empty air. Most of these commercial programs are written and sold by big companies, such as Microsoft, Adobe, or Corel.

Many bargain-priced Mac software sold in stores are designed to run on older Mac computers with PowerPC processors, running the ancient OS 9 operating system. Today's Mac computers with Intel processors, running the Mac OS X operating system, cannot run any software designed for OS 9 without running an additional program such as SheepShaver (`http://gwenole.beauchesne.info/en/projects/sheepshaver`).

No matter how big your local computer store is, it can offer only a fraction of all available Macintosh programs. For a much greater selection of software, you have to browse for Mac programs over the Internet. On the

Internet, you can find three types of software: commercial, shareware, and freeware/open source. The following list spells out how they differ:

- **Commercial software:** Most companies that sell software through stores also sell the same commercial programs over the Internet. Sometimes you can even get a discount if you buy the program directly from the publisher and download it over the Internet. Even better, if you download a program off the Internet, you're assured of getting the latest version of that program. (When you buy a program off the shelf at a local computer store, you have no idea how old that program may be.)

  As a further enticement, commercial programs on the Internet often offer a trial version that you can download and use for a limited amount of time, such as 30 days. After your trial period is over, the program will either stop working or run with many features turned off. If you pay for the software, the publisher will send you a registration key that converts the trial program into a fully functional version. To find trial versions of programs, just visit the Web sites of different software publishers.

- **Shareware software:** Shareware programs are either limited trial versions or fully functional programs, usually written by individuals or smaller companies. The idea is for you to try out the program and if you like it, and then you're supposed to pay for it.

- **Freeware software:** Freeware programs are typically simple utilities or games, although some commercial companies distribute freeware programs as a way to promote their other products. Sometimes companies offer a freeware version of a program and then sell a more advanced version of that same program. As the name implies, freeware programs are available for you to copy and use at no cost.

  A variation of freeware programs is called open source. Like freeware programs, open source programs can be copied and used without paying for them. The main difference is that open source programs let you modify the program yourself if you know the specific programming language that the program was written in.

Table 5-1 lists some popular open source programs and their commercial equivalents.

Table 5-1 Popular Open Source Programs and the Commercial Programs They Can Replace

Open Source Program	*Purpose*	*Commercial Equivalent*
NeoOffice (www.neooffice.org)	Office suite containing a word processor, spreadsheet, presentation program, and database	Microsoft Office

Open Source Program	*Purpose*	*Commercial Equivalent*
OpenOffice.org (`www.openoffice.org`)	Office suite containing a word processor, spreadsheet, presentation program, and database	Microsoft Office
AbiWord (`www.abisource.com`)	Word processor	Microsoft Word
Firefox (`www.mozilla.com`)	Web browser	Safari
Camino (`www.caminobrowser.org`)	Web browser	Safari
Thunderbird (`www.mozilla.com`)	E-mail program	Mail
Tux Paint (`www.tuxpaint.org`)	Children's painting program	Broderbund Kid Pix
Paintbrush (`http://paintbrush.sourceforge.net/`)	Basic image editing	Adobe Photoshop Elements
Nvu (`www.nvu.com`)	Web page designing	Adobe Dreamweaver
Audacity (`http://audacity.sourceforge.net`)	Audio editing	Adobe SoundBooth
ClamXav (`www.clamxav.com`)	Antivirus scanner	Norton AntiVirus
Buddi (`http://buddi.sourceforge.net`)	Money management program	Quicken
celtx (`www.celtx.com`)	Script-writing word processor	Final Draft

Besides being free, many open source programs offer additional features that their commercial rivals lack.

For example, the Safari Web browser comes free with every Mac, but many Web sites are designed to work only when viewed through Internet Explorer or Firefox. So if you use Safari, it's possible that you won't be able to view some Web sites correctly, but you might want to switch to Firefox (or at least keep Firefox on your hard drive) so if you run across a Web site that Safari can't open, just view that Web site in Firefox instead.

To find more shareware, freeware, and open source programs for your Mac, visit the following sites:

- Open Source Mac (www.opensourcemac.org)
- MacShare.com (www.macshare.com)
- Pure-Mac (www.pure-mac.com)
- MacForge (www.macforge.net)
- Tucows (www.tucows.com)

Installing Software

The most common place to install software is inside the Applications folder, so you should specify that folder when installing software. Some programs store their program icon inside the Applications folder plain as day, but others hide their program icons within another folder. (See Figure 5-1 for examples of both ways of dealing with program icons.)

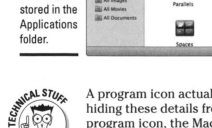

Figure 5-1: Program icons either appear by themselves or inside a folder stored in the Applications folder.

A program icon actually represents a folder containing multiple files. By hiding these details from you and letting you treat a folder of files as a single program icon, the Mac ensures that you can't accidentally delete or move a single crucial file that the entire program needs to work.

Installing software from a CD/DVD

If you buy software from a store, it will probably come on a CD/DVD. When you insert the CD/DVD into your Mac, you might see nothing but a single program icon, along with several other files labeled Read Me or Documentation.

Other times, you might insert a CD/DVD and see an icon labeled Install. When you see an Install icon, you need to run this installation program to install the program on your hard drive.

When installing software, your Mac might ask for your password — the one you set up when you first created you user account. (For more on user accounts, see Book I, Chapter 7.) Forcing you to enter a password ensures that it's really you who wants to install the program, rather than some computer virus or Trojan horse program trying to install itself without your knowledge. Passwords also keep unauthorized people (such as your kids) from installing programs that you don't want, such as video games.

Dragging a program icon off the CD/DVD

If you insert a program's CD/DVD into your computer and just see a program icon, you'll have to install the program by dragging the program icon into your Applications folder. To do this, follow these steps:

1. **Insert the software CD/DVD into your Mac.**

   A window appears, showing the contents of the CD/DVD, as shown in Figure 5-2.

2. **Click the Finder icon in the Dock and then choose File➪New Finder Window.**

   A second Finder shows up, ready to do your bidding.

3. **Move the CD/DVD window and the Finder so they appear side by side.**

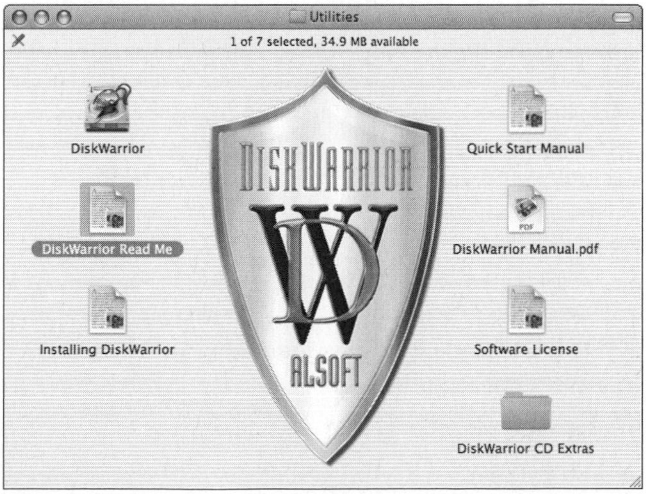

Figure 5-2: A CD/DVD contains a program icon along with other document icons that contain info about the program.

4. **Click and drag the program icon displayed in the CD/DVD window, onto the Applications folder in the Finder Sidebar.**

   Doing so copies the program icon off the CD/DVD and stores it in the Applications folder.

Running an installer program

Instead of displaying the actual program icon, a CD/DVD might display an Install icon, as shown in Figure 5-3. The installer is simply a special program designed to copy a program off the CD/DVD and place it in your Applications folder. Installer programs exist because novices often don't feel comfortable dragging a program icon from the CD/DVD window to the Applications folder in the Finder.

To install software using an installer program on a CD/DVD, follow these steps:

1. **Insert the software CD/DVD into your Mac.**

   A window appears, showing the contents of the CD/DVD.

2. **Look for an icon labeled Install.**

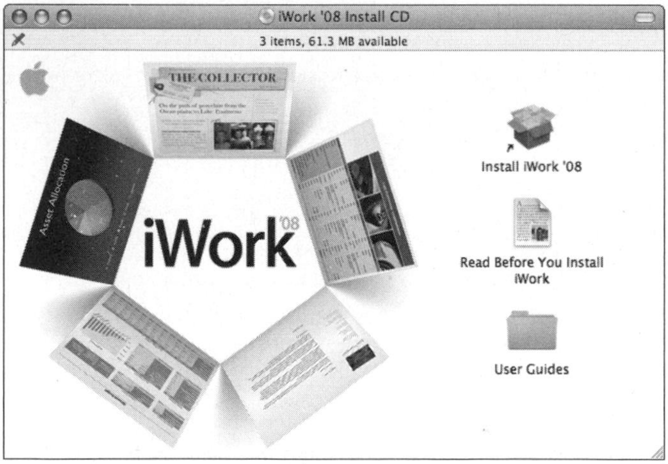

Figure 5-3: A CD/DVD might contain an Install icon that can automatically install a program on your Mac.

   These icons typically look like a cardboard box with its top opened up.

3. **Double-click this Install icon.**

   A dialog appears, asking whether you really want to continue installing.

4. **Click Continue.**

5. **Follow the on-screen instructions.**

   If you have multiple hard drives, the installation program might ask where to install the program. (Generally you should choose your Mac's hard drive unless you have a reason to store the program elsewhere.) Right before the program starts installing, you'll be asked for your password.

TIP

You can often halt the installation process by choosing Installer➪Quit Installer.

Installing software off the Internet

Although you can buy software in a box from your local computer store, it's becoming far more common to buy software directly off the Internet instead. Not only does this save the publisher the time and expense of packaging a program in a fancy box and shipping it to a store, but it also gives you the software to use right away.

When you download a program off the Internet, the program will usually arrive as a DMG (disc image) file. Safari, Mac OS X's default Web browser, stores all downloaded files in a special Downloads folder in your Home folder. The Downloads folder also appears as a Stack right next to the Trash icon in the Dock. (If you're using a different browser, such as Firefox, you might need to define where it stores downloaded files.)

Distributing software as a DMG file is the most common way to compress files for sending over the Internet. A DMG file essentially copies the contents of an entire folder and smashes it into a single file. You can always identify a DMG file because its icon appears with a hard drive icon, and the name includes the three-letter DMG extension, as shown in Figure 5-4.

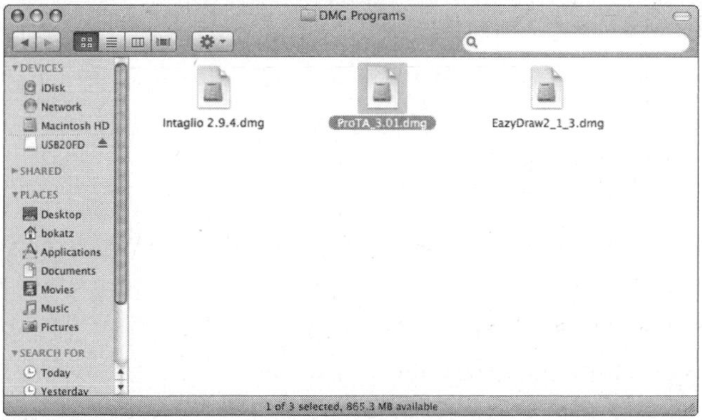

Figure 5-4: DMG files always use the same icon and include the DMG extension at the end of the filename.

After you have a DMG file on your Mac, you're set to install the software inside it. Just follow these steps:

1. **Double-click the DMG file that contains the program you want to install on your Mac.**

   A License Agreement window might appear, as shown in Figure 5-5.

   REMEMBER

   Some DMG files fire right up after you download them off the Internet, so you might be able to skip this step.

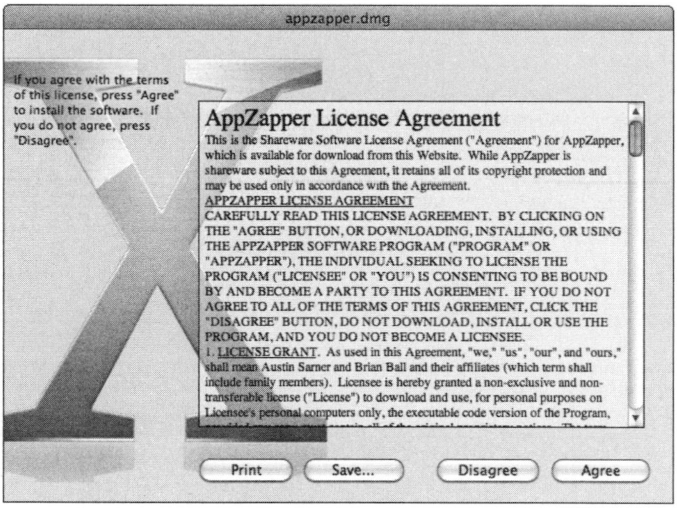

Figure 5-5: A typical license agreement that appears after you double-click a DMG file.

2. **If a License Agreement window appears, click the window's Agree button.**

   If you click the Disagree button, you won't be able to install the program!

   The DMG file displays a device icon on the Desktop and displays a Finder window that contains the program icon stored inside the DMG file, as shown in Figure 5-6.

3. **Click the Finder icon in the Dock and then choose File⇨New Folder Window.**

   A second Finder comes to the fore.

4. **Move this second Finder so it appears side by side with the first Finder that displays the contents of the DMG file.**

5. **Click and drag the program icon in the DMG Finder onto the Applications folder in the second Finder.**

   Doing so installs the program in your Applications folder.

6. **Right-click on the DMG device icon on the Desktop and when a shortcut menu appears, choose Eject.**

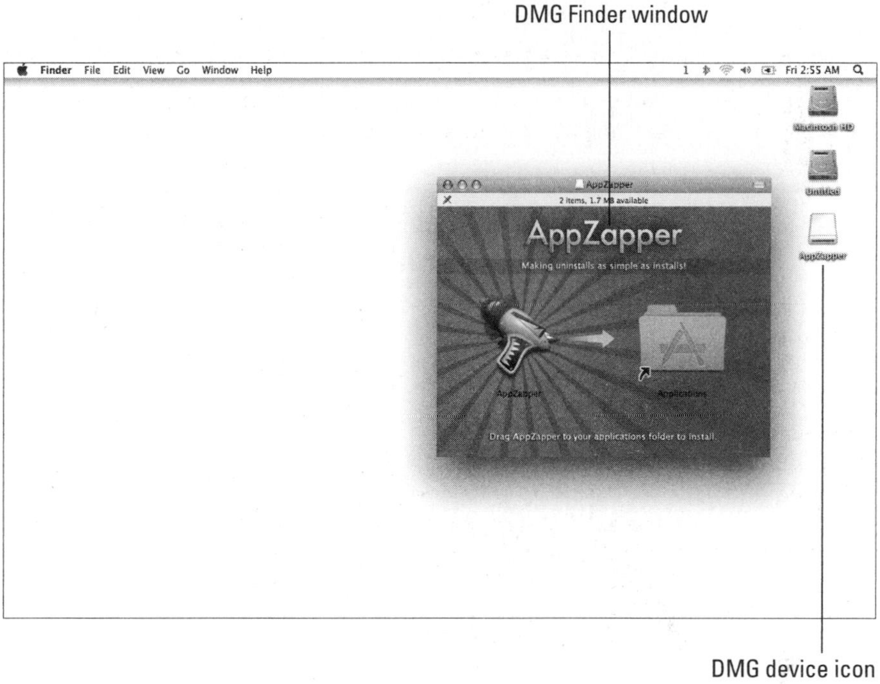

Figure 5-6: Expanding a DMG file displays a program icon that you can drag to the Applications folder.

When you open a DMG file, it creates device icon, which acts like a separate storage device. This device icon acts like a temporary disk so you can copy files off it. After you've installed a program off the DMG file, you might want to eject the DMG device icon just to clear it out of the way. (Leaving it on your Desktop won't hurt anything.)

After you install a program on your Mac, you can always find it again by looking in the folder where you stored it, which is usually the Applications folder. At this point, you might want to add the program icon to the Dock or place an alias icon on the Desktop. (See Book I, Chapter 4 for more information about placing program icons in the Dock and placing alias icons on the Desktop.)

The first time you run a newly installed program, a dialog might pop up (see Figure 5-7), informing you that this is the first time you've tried running this program. To run the program, click Open. This dialog pops up to protect you from malicious programs that might try to install and run by themselves. If you didn't try to run a program and see this dialog pop up, click Cancel.

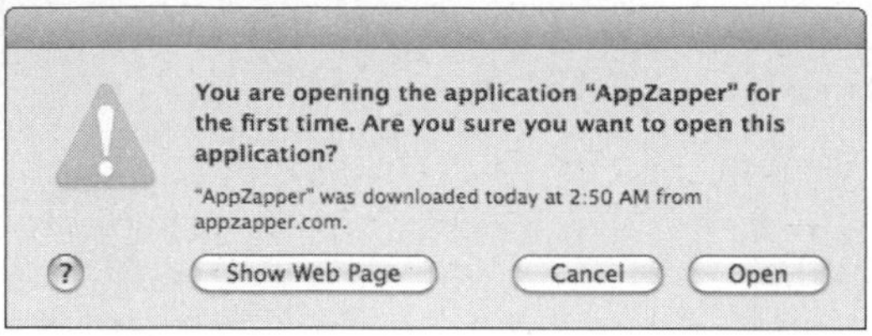
You are opening the application "AppZapper" for the first time. Are you sure you want to open this application?
"AppZapper" was downloaded today at 2:50 AM from appzapper.com.
Show Web Page
Cancel
Open

Figure 5-7: A dialog alerts you when you're running a program for the first time.

Uninstalling Software

If you no longer use or need a program, you can always remove it from your hard drive. By uninstalling a program, you can free up space on your hard drive.

Before uninstalling a program, make sure you don't uninstall a program that you suddenly need after all.

Uninstalling a program can involve three parts:

- **Uninstalling a program:** Uninstalling a program physically removes that program from your hard drive.
- **Deleting program icons/alias icons:** When you delete a program, you don't automatically delete that program's icon from the Dock or any alias icons that you created from that program icon. To delete these additional icons, you must delete them manually.
- **Deleting program settings:** Most programs store user settings in the Library folder, which is buried inside of your Home folder. When you uninstall a program, its user settings files remain on your hard drive. Although not harmful, you might want to wipe these user settings files off your hard drive to free up space for more programs or documents.

The next few sections give you a more detailed look at what's involved when you delete a program.

Uninstalling a program

Because the Mac stores all program files within a single program icon, uninstalling a Mac program is as simple as dragging and dropping that program icon into the Trash.

To uninstall a program, follow these steps:

1. **Make sure the program you want to uninstall isn't running. If it is running, shut it down by choosing the Quit command (by pressing ⌘+Q).**

ZIP, SIT, and other strange files

Occasionally, you might run across files with extensions such as ZIP, SIT, SEA, or RAR. These types of files are all different ways to pack multiple files into a single, compressed file. The Mac can recognize and open ZIP compressed files, but if you need to open a strange file like a TAR or CAB compressed file, you'll want to install and use a free program called StuffIt Expander (`www.stuffit.com`). The StuffIt Expander program can open almost any type of compressed file, even those compressed files originally created on Windows or Linux computers. Your Mac can create ZIP and DMG files (which you find out more about in Book I, Chapter 6), but, if you want to create other types of compressed files, such as SIT or RAR files, you'll have to get another program, such as the commercial version of the StuffIt program.

2. **Click the Finder icon in the Dock.**

   The Finder appears.

3. **Click the Applications folder in the Finder Sidebar.**

   The contents of the Applications folder appear in the window's right pane.

4. **Click to select the program icon or program folder that you want to uninstall.**

5. **Choose File⇨Move to Trash (or drag the program icon or folder over the Trash icon in the Dock).**

   The Trash icon displays an image showing the trash filled with crumpled papers.

   WARNING! Before emptying the Trash, make sure you really want to permanently delete any programs or documents you've placed in the Trash. After you empty the Trash, any files contained therein are permanently deleted from your hard drive.

6. **Choose Finder⇨Empty Trash (or right-click the Trash icon and choose Empty Trash).**

   The program's gone.

Removing program icons from the Dock and Desktop

After you uninstall a program, you should also remove all Dock or alias icons as well because those icons will no longer work. To remove a program icon from the Dock, follow these steps:

1. **Move the pointer over the program icon that you want to remove from the Dock.**

2. **Click and drag the mouse up until the pointer no longer appears over any part of the Dock.**
3. **Release the mouse button.**

   Your chosen program icon disappears in a puff of animated smoke.

If you created multiple alias icons of a program, you'll have to go through your hard drive and find all alias icons and delete them one by one. As a faster way to find and delete alias icons, follow these steps:

1. **Click the Finder icon in the Dock.**

   The Finder comes to the fore.

2. **Click in the Spotlight text box and type the name of the program you uninstalled followed by the word *alias,* such as "PowerPoint alias" or "Camino alias."**

   The Finder displays the location of the specified alias icons, as shown in Figure 5-8.

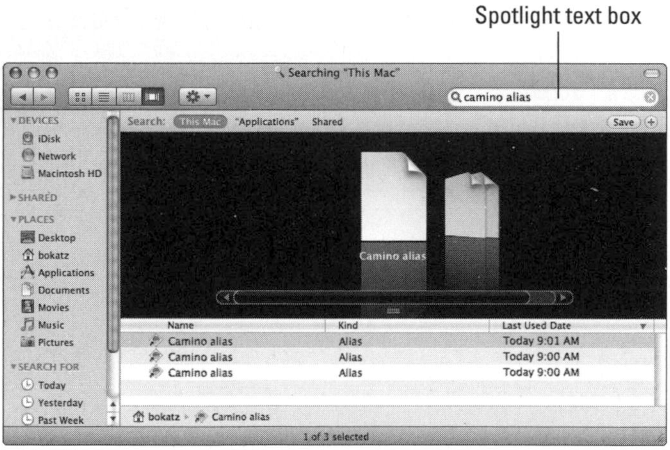

Figure 5-8: Spotlight can help you find all alias icons no matter where you stored them.

3. **Hold down the ⌘ key and click each alias icon you want to delete.**
4. **Choose File⇨Move to Trash.**
5. **Choose Finder⇨Empty Trash (or right-click the Trash icon and choose Empty Trash).**

   Bye-bye, aliases.

Removing user setting files

Almost every program creates special user setting files that contain any custom changes you made to the program, such as changing background colors or modifying icons displayed by the program. When you uninstall a program, its user setting files still remain on your computer.

The more unnecessary files you have cluttering up your hard drive, the slower your Mac will run, because it needs to keep skipping over these unused files to find what it really needs. To keep your Mac in optimum condition, you should delete the user setting files of programs you've uninstalled from your computer.

You have two ways to remove these unnecessary user setting files. First, you can do it manually. Second, you can buy a program to do this for you automatically.

Manually removing user setting files

Manually removing user setting files requires digging into your hard drive and deleting individual files or entire folders. This process isn't difficult, just tedious.

WARNING!

If you feel squeamish about deleting any files that you don't understand, don't delete any files without an expert's help. If you delete the wrong files, you could mess up the way your Mac works.

Many programs store their user setting files in two folders:

- The Application Support folder
- The Preferences folder

To find these two folders, you must look inside the Home folder and then look inside the Library folder.

REMEMBER

Many programs store a user setting file inside the Preferences folder, but not all programs store files in the Application Support folder. So if you open the Application Support folder and can't find any files that include the name of the program you just uninstalled, that means the program never copied any files into this Application Support folder.

To delete program files from the Application Support and/or Preferences folder, follow these steps:

1. **Click the Finder icon in the Dock.**

   The Finder appears.

2. **Click the Home folder that appears in the Finder Sidebar.**

   The contents of your Home folder appear in the right pane of the Finder.

   The Home folder appears in the Finder Sidebar under the username you defined for your account. If your name is Bo Katz, your Home folder might be named bokatz.

3. **Double-click the Library folder.**

   The contents of the Library folder appear in the right pane of the Finder. If you scroll through this window, you'll find the Application Support and the Preferences folders.

4. **Double-click the Preferences folder.**

   The contents of the Preferences folder appear. You'll see files that include different program names as part of their own names, such as `com.plasq.ComicLife.plist` (the user setting files for the Comic Life program).

   If you think you might re-install a program at a later date, keep its user setting files. That way, if you re-install the program, it will use your old user setting files.

5. **Click the user setting file that you want to delete and then choose File⇨Move to Trash.**

6. **Scroll through the Preferences folder and check whether there are any folders that contain the name of the program you uninstalled. If you find a folder that contains such a name, click that folder and then choose File⇨Move to Trash.**

   These folders often contain additional files that the program initially installed on your hard drive.

7. **Choose Go⇨Enclosing Folder.**

   The contents of the Library folder appear again.

8. **Double-click the Application Support folder.**

   The contents of the Application Support folder appear, containing folders used by different programs.

9. **If you find a folder that includes the name of the program you want to uninstall, click that folder and then choose File⇨Move to Trash.**

   Those program files are history.

Automatically removing user setting files

Because manually deleting user setting and preference files might seem scary and intimidating, you might prefer to automatically remove these files instead. To do this, you need to buy and install a special uninstaller program. When you run an uninstaller program, you just tell it which program you want to uninstall, and the uninstaller program identifies all the files used by that program, as shown in Figure 5-9.

Figure 5-9: An uninstaller program such as AppZapper can automatically find and delete all files used by a program.

Some popular uninstaller programs include

- ✦ AppZapper (`www.appzapper.com`), shown at work in Figure 5-9
- ✦ Spring Cleaning (`www.allume.com/mac/springcleaning`)
- ✦ Uninstaller (`http://macmagna.free.fr`)
- ✦ Yank (`www.matterform.com`)

Chapter 6: Managing Files and Folders

In This Chapter

- **Using the Finder**
- **Organizing and viewing folders**
- **Creating folders**
- **Manipulating files and folders**
- **Archiving files and folders**
- **Searching files**
- **Working with Smart Folders**
- **Storing stuff on the Dock**
- **Burning files and folders to CD/DVD**
- **Deleting files and folders**

When you need to organize junk scattered around the house, one strategy would be to just toss everything in the middle of the floor. However, it's probably easier to get a bunch of boxes and store old clothes in one box, old toys in another box, and old books in a third box.

Computers work in a similar way. Although you could dump everything on your hard drive, it's probably easier to divide your hard drive into boxes to help you sort and arrange your stuff. Instead of boxes, the Mac uses something called *folders*.

A folder lets you store and organize related files. The two most commonly used folders on your hard drive are the Applications folder and the Documents folder. The Applications folder contains programs, whereas the Documents folder contains anything you create and save while using a program, such as a letter created by a word processor.

Folders can contain files or even other folders. The whole purpose of folders is to help keep your files organized so you can find them again.

Using the Finder

The main program for managing drives, files, and folders is called the Finder. To access the Finder, just click the Finder icon (the smiley face icon on the far left) in the Dock. The Finder is divided into two parts, as shown in Figure 6-1:

- ✦ A left pane, containing something known as the *Sidebar.* The Sidebar is just a fancy term for a list of all currently connected storage devices as well as all commonly used folders that contain all files used or modified today or yesterday.
- ✦ A right pane, containing the contents of the currently selected drive or folder. If you switch to List, Column, or Cover Flow view, the right pane also shows a hierarchy of files stored inside folders.

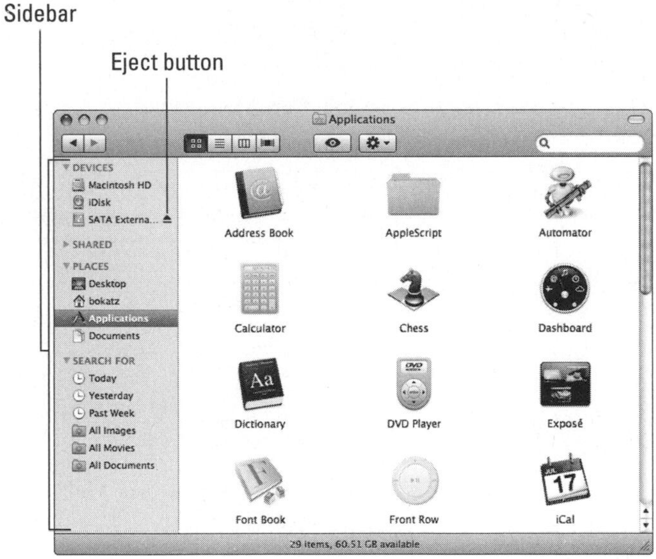

Figure 6-1: The Finder displays the files, folders, and storage devices connected to your Mac.

Understanding devices

The Devices category of the Sidebar lists all removable or non-removable storage devices you can use for saving files. Non-removable devices are always connected to your Mac. Every Mac has one non-removable device, which is the drive that your Mac boots up from; typically, its internal hard drive, which is named Macintosh HD.

A removable drive is any drive that your Mac doesn't boot up from, such as an external hard drive or even its own internal hard drive if you booted up from another drive. You can always eject a removable drive, which simply removes its icon from the Finder, but you can never eject a non-removable drive. After you eject a removable drive, you can physically disconnect it.

WARNING!

If you try to physically disconnect a removable drive before you eject it, your Mac might mess up the data on that drive. Always eject removable drives first before physically removing them.

Removable devices can be attached and disconnected at any time. Common types of removable devices are external hard drives, flash drives, and digital cameras.

To connect a removable device to a Mac, just plug it in using the appropriate FireWire or USB cable.

To remove a removable device from a Mac, follow these steps:

1. **Click the Finder icon in the Dock.**

   The Finder comes to the fore.

2. **In the Finder, click the Eject button next to the removable device you want to remove.**

   If the removable device is a CD/DVD, your Mac ejects it. If the removable device is plugged into a USB (Universal Serial Bus) port on your Mac, you have to physically disconnect the device.

   TIP

   Some other ways to choose the Eject command are

   - Click the device icon on the Desktop and choose File➪Eject.
   - Click the device icon and press ⌘+E.
   - Right-click the device icon and choose Eject from the shortcut menu that appears.

3. **Wait until the device's icon disappears from the Finder.**
4. **Physically disconnect the device from your Mac.**

Understanding folders

All the data you create and save by using a program (such as a database or spreadsheet) gets stored as a file. Although you can store files on any storage device, the more files you store on a single device, the harder it can be to find the one file you want at any given time.

Folders help you divide a storage device into smaller parts. You can even store folders inside other folders. Initially, every Mac hard drive is divided into the following folders:

- **Applications:** Contains all the programs installed on your Mac.
- **Library:** Contains data used by different programs.
- **System:** Contains data used by the Mac OS X operating system.
- **Users:** Contains any files you created and saved.

WARNING!

Never delete, rename, or move any files or folders stored in the Library or System folders, or else you might cause your Mac (or at least some programs on your Mac) to stop working. Files in the Library and System folders are used by your Mac to make your computer work. If you delete or rename files in either folder, your Mac might grind to a halt.

The Users folder contains the Home folder of each account on your Mac, as shown in Figure 6-2. (See Book I, Chapter 7 for more information about Home folders and creating accounts.) Each Home folder consists of additional folders:

- **Desktop folder:** Contains the program and document icons that appear on your desktop.
- **Documents folder:** Contains any files you create and save using different programs. (You'll probably need to divide this folder into multiple folders to keep all your files organized.)
- **Downloads:** Contains any files you've downloaded over the Internet.
- **Library:** Contains folders and files used by any programs installed on your Mac. (Note: There are two Library folders, one stored on your hard drive and one stored inside the Home folder.)
- **Movies:** Contains any video files created by iMovie or other video playing or editing programs such as Final Cut Express or QuickTime Player.
- **Music:** Contains any audio files stored in iTunes or created by GarageBand or any other audio program such as Audacity.
- **Pictures:** Contains digital photographs, such as those stored in iPhoto.
- **Public:** Provides a folder that you can use to share files with other accounts on the same Mac or with other users on a local area network.
- **Sites:** Provides a folder for storing any Web pages, such as those created with iWeb.

Every drive (such as your hard drive) can consist of multiple folders and each folder can contain multiple folders as well. This collection of folders stored inside folders stored inside other folders is called a *hierarchy.* It's important to know how to view and navigate through a folder hierarchy, as shown in Figure 6-2, because that way you'll be able to find specific files.

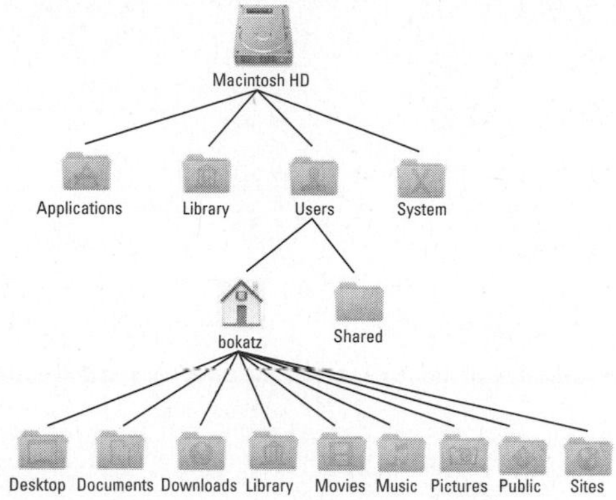

Figure 6-2: The typical hierarchy of folders dividing your Mac's hard drive.

Navigating through the Finder

To get to all the files you've stored somewhere on your Mac, you need to know how to navigate through the different folders and devices by using the Finder. The main navigation tasks are

- ✦ Switching devices
- ✦ Opening a folder (moving down the folder hierarchy)
- ✦ Exiting a folder (moving up a folder hierarchy to view an enclosing folder)
- ✦ Jumping to a specific folder

All are crucial tasks — and all are explained in greater detail in the upcoming sections.

Opening a folder

After you choose a device, the Finder displays all the files and folders stored on that device. To open a folder, you have four choices:

- ✦ Double-click the folder.
- ✦ Click the folder and choose File➪Open.
- ✦ Click the folder and press ⌘+O.
- ✦ Click the folder and press ⌘+down arrow.
- ✦ Right-click the folder and choose Open from the shortcut menu that appears.

Each time you open a folder within a folder, you're essentially moving down the hierarchy of folders stored on that device.

Exiting a folder

After you open a folder, you might want to go back and view the contents of the folder that encloses the current folder. To view the enclosing folder, choose one of the following:

- ✦ Choose Go➪Enclosing Folder.
- ✦ Press ⌘+up arrow.
- ✦ Hold down the ⌘ key and click the title bar of the Finder to display a list of enclosing folders. Then click an enclosing folder.

Jumping to a specific folder

By moving up and down the folder hierarchy on a device, you can view the contents of every file stored on a device. However, you can also jump to a specific folder right away by choosing one of these options:

- ✦ By jumping to a common folder listed in the Go menu — Computer, say, or Network. To jump to your Utilities folder, for example, you would choose Go➪Utilities.
- ✦ By clicking a folder displayed in the Sidebar
- ✦ Using the Go➪Recent Folders command to jump to a recently opened folder. (Using this command sequence displays a submenu of the last ten folders you visited.)

If you display the contents of a folder in List, Column, or Cover Flow views, you can view folder hierarchies directly in the Finder. (You find out more about using the List, Column, and Cover Flow views later in the "Organizing and Viewing a Folder" section.)

Jumping back and forth

As you navigate from one folder to the next, you might suddenly want to return to a folder for a second look. To view a previously viewed folder, you can choose the Back command as follows:

- ✦ Click the Back arrow.
- ✦ Choose Go➪Back.
- ✦ Press ⌘+[.

A command that lets you jump back to a previously opened folder is not the same thing as the Go➪Enclosing Folder command. If you opened an external drive and then switched to Utilities folder on your hard drive, the Back command would return the Finder to the external drive, but the Go➪Enclosing Folder command would open the Applications folder.

After you've used the Back command at least once, you can choose the Forward command. The Forward command basically reverses each Back command you chose. To choose the Forward command, pick one of the following:

- ✦ Click the Forward arrow.
- ✦ Choose Go➪Forward.
- ✦ Press ⌘+].

Organizing and Viewing a Folder

The Finder always shows the contents of a single folder. (A device, such as a hard drive, acts like a giant folder.) However, if a folder contains a large number of files and folders, trying to find a particular file or folder can be frustrating. To organize a folder's contents, the Finder can display the contents of a folder in four views:

- ✦ **Icon view:** Displays files and folders as icons and names.
- ✦ **List view:** Displays files and folders as names, size, and date modified.
- ✦ **Columns view:** Displays files and folders in three columns. Clicking on a folder in the left column displays its contents in the middle column. Clicking on a folder in the middle column displays its contents in the right column.
- ✦ **Cover Flow view:** Displays files and folders like the List view, but also displays files and folders as icons that you can flip through one at a time.

To switch to a different view, choose one of the following within the Finder, as shown in Figure 6-3:

- ✦ Choose View and then choose As Icons, As Lists, As Columns, or As Cover Flow
- ✦ Click the Icon, List, Columns, or Cover Flow icon

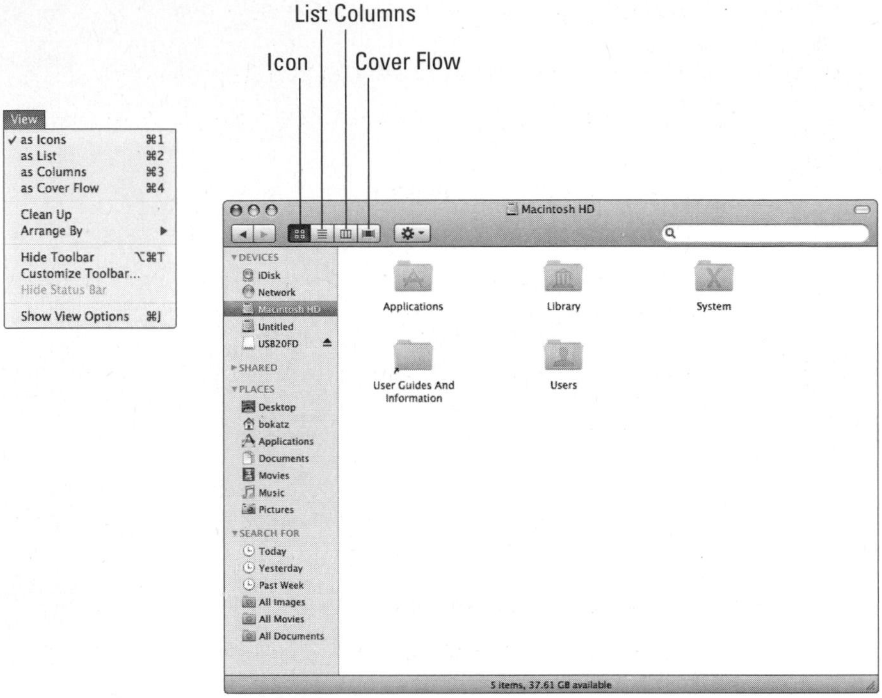

Figure 6-3: The Icon view displays files as descriptive graphics with a name.

Selecting items in the Finder

No matter how you view the contents of a folder, selecting items remains the same. You always have to select an item before you can do anything with it, such as copy or delete it. There are three ways to select items:

- ✦ Select a single item (file or folder) by clicking it.
- ✦ Select multiple items by holding down the ⌘ key and clicking each item.
- ✦ Selecting a range of items by clicking-and dragging the mouse or by using the Shift key.

  REMEMBER

  The Shift key trick only works in List, Columns, or Cover Flow view. Just click the first item you want to select in your particular view, then hold down the Shift key and click the last item in the range that you want to choose. Your desired range is selected, just like that.

Using Icon view

Icon view displays all files and folders as icons. To organize files in Icon view, you can manually drag icons around, or you can have your Mac automatically arrange icons based on certain criteria, such as name or date modified.

To manually arrange icons within Icon view, follow these steps:

1. **Move the pointer over an icon you want to move.**

   You can select two or more icons by holding down the ⌘ key and clicking multiple icons.

2. **Click and drag the mouse.**

   Your selected icon(s) move as you move the mouse.

3. **Release the mouse button when you're happy with the new location of your icon(s).**

When you manually arrange icons, they might not appear aligned with one another. To fix this problem, make sure no items are selected and then choose View➪Clean Up Selection to straighten them up.

Manually arranging icons can get cumbersome if you have dozens of icons you want to arrange. As a faster alternative, you can arrange icons automatically in Icon view by following these steps:

1. **Choose View➪Arrange By.**

   A submenu appears, as shown in Figure 6-4.

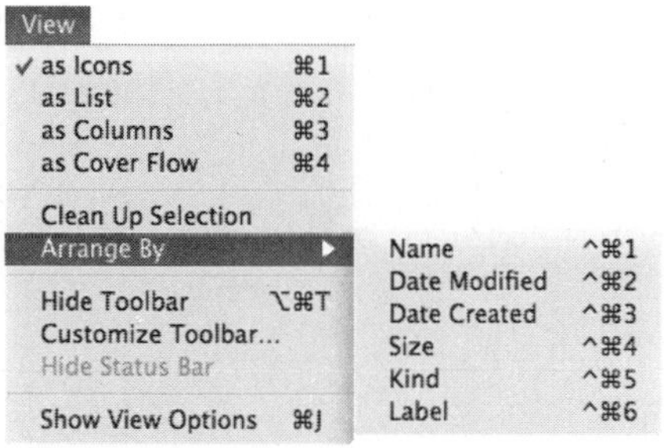

Figure 6-4: The Arrange By submenu lists different ways to organize your icons.

2. **Choose one of the following options:**

   - *Name:* Arranges icons alphabetically.
   - *Date Modified:* Arranges the most recently modified items at the top of the window.
   - *Date Created:* Arranges the most recently created items at the top of the window.
   - *Size:* Arranges the smallest items at the top of the window.

- *Kind:* Arranges items alphabetically by file extension, so JPG files will appear closer to the top of the window than ZIP files.
- *Label:* Arranges icons alphabetically by color. Icons with no color appear near the top of the window followed by icons colored blue, gray, green, orange, purple, red, and yellow.

Using List view

List view displays each item by name, size, date it was last modified, and the kind of item it is such as a folder or a PDF (Portable Document Format) file. The biggest advantages of List view are that it always displays items in alphabetical order, it can display more items in the same amount of space than the Icon view, and it displays hierarchies of folders as indented items, as shown in Figure 6-5.

TIP

Because List view can display the contents of two or more folders at a time, this lets you select files from multiple folders. Also, if you click a column heading in List view (such as Name or Date Modified), the Finder sorts your items in ascending or descending order.

List view identifies folders by a folder icon and a triangle symbol pointing to it. Clicking that triangle symbol expands that folder to display its contents — files, folders, whatever. Clicking the triangle again collapses that folder to hide its contents.

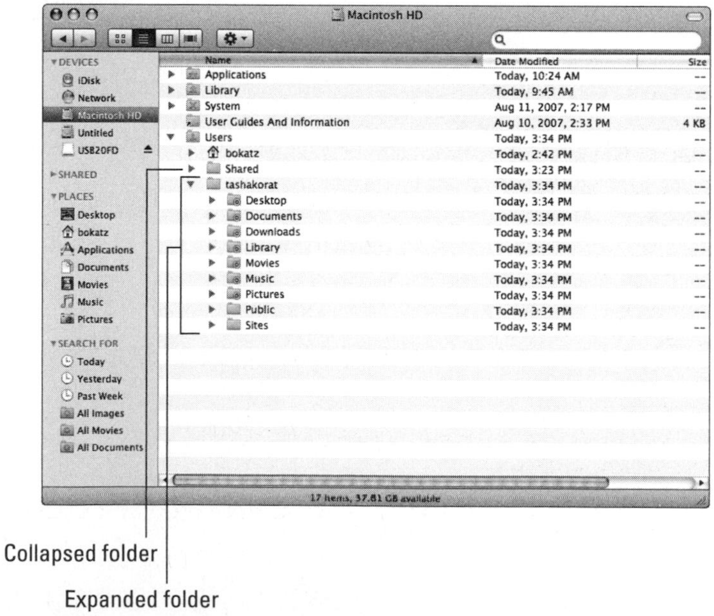

Figure 6-5: List view displays items in rows and folders as hierarchies.

Using Columns view

Columns view initially displays files and folders in a single column. As was the case with List view, all folders display a triangle next to the folder name. (Okay, okay, in List view the triangle is just to the left of the folder name, and Columns view has the triangle at the far right, but you get to the idea.) Clicking a folder displays the contents of that folder in the column to the right, as shown in Figure 6-6.

To arrange items in all columns in the Columns view, follow these steps:

1. **Choose View⇨Show View Options.**

   An Options window appears, as shown in Figure 6-7.

2. **Click the Arrange By pop-up menu (a new addition in Leopard) and choose one of the following options:**

   - *Name:* Arranges icons alphabetically.
   - *Date Modified:* Arranges the most recently modified items at the top of the window.

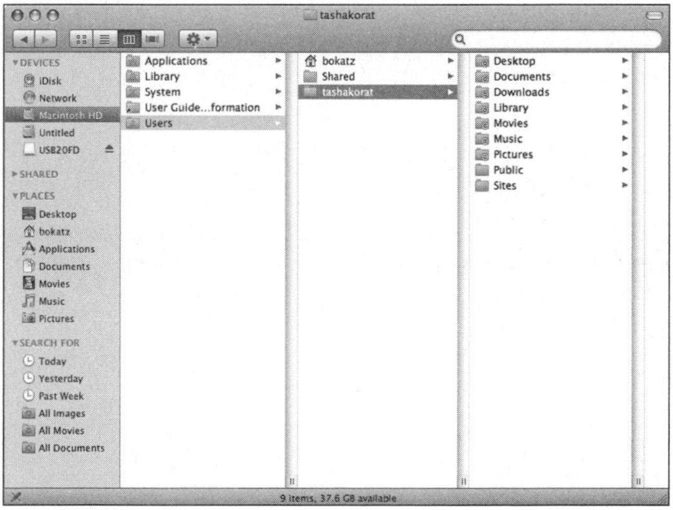

Figure 6-6: Columns view displays the folder contents in adjacent columns.

   - *Date Created:* Arranges the most recently created items at the top of the window.
   - *Size:* Arranges the smallest items at the top of the window.

- *Kind:* Arranges items alphabetically by file extension, so JPG files will appear closer to the top of the window than ZIP files.
- *Label:* Arranges icons alphabetically by the color label. Icons with no label appear near the top of the window followed by icons labeled blue, gray, green, orange, purple, red, and yellow.

3. **(Optional) Use the Text Size drop-down menu to modify the size of text used for folder labels.**
4. **(Optional) Select one or more of the following check boxes:**
   - *Always open in column view:* Forces the folder to display its contents in column view every time you click on that folder.
   - *Show icons:* Displays or hides files and folder icons.
   - *Show icon preview:* Displays or hides thumbnail images of the file contents on the file icon.
   - *Show preview column:* Displays a column that lists additional details about a file or folder such as its size and last date and time it was opened.
5. **Click the Close button of the Options window.**

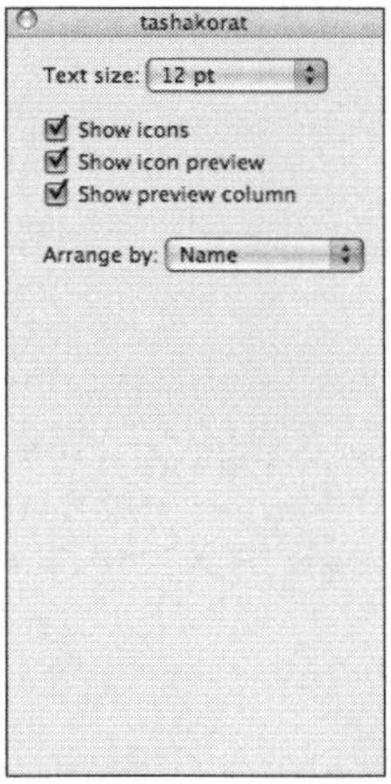

Figure 6-7: The Options window contains an Arrange By pop-up menu so you can sort items.

Using Cover Flow view

Cover Flow view combines List view with the graphic elements of Icon view, as shown in Figure 6-8. Cover Flow originated from jukeboxes that let you pick songs by viewing and flipping through album covers. In the Finder, Cover Flow lets you choose files or folders by flipping through enlarged icons of those files or folders, which can make finding a particular file or folder easier.

Figure 6-8: The Cover Flow view displays both icons and names of items.

To scroll through items in the Cover Flow view, you have a number of choices:

- ✦ Click the left and right scroll arrows on the Cover Flow scroll bar (that appears in the middle of the Finder).
- ✦ Drag the scroll box in the horizontal scroll bar on the Cover Flow scroll bar.
- ✦ Click in the scroll area to the left or right of the scroll box on the Cover Flow scroll bar.
- ✦ Click an icon that appears in the top half of the Cover Flow view.
- ✦ Press the up- and down-arrow keys to select a different file or folder in the list portion of the Cover Flow view. Each time you select a different file or folder, the Cover Flow icon for that file or folder appears.

Creating Folders

In additional to letting you navigate your way through different folders, the Finder also lets you create folders. The main purpose for creating a folder is to organize related files and folders together. You have two ways to create a folder:

- ✦ In the Finder
- ✦ In a Save As dialog

The next sections walk you through both methods.

Creating a folder using the Finder menu

You can create a folder anywhere, although the first place you're likely to create a folder is inside the Documents folder to organize your files. There are an infinite number of ways to divide and organize your Documents folder. You might create multiple folders named Word Processor Files, Spreadsheets, and Databases. Or you might create multiple folders based on topics such as 2012 Tax Info, which might contain a mix of word processor, spreadsheet, and database files. The way you organize your folders is up to you.

To create a folder by using the Finder menu, follow these steps:

1. **Click the Finder icon in the Dock.**

   The Finder appears.
2. **In the Sidebar of the Finder, click the device where you want to create a folder.**
3. **Navigate to and open the folder where you want to store your new folder, such as inside the Documents folder.**
4. **Choose File⇨New Folder.**

   An untitled folder icon appears with its name selected.
5. **Type a descriptive name for your folder.**

   Your new folder is christened and ready for use.

Creating a folder through the Save As dialog

The Finder isn't the only way to create a new folder. When you save a file for the first time or save an existing file under a new name (using the Save As command), you can also create a new folder to store your file at the same time. To create a folder within the Save As dialog, follow these steps:

1. **Create a new document in any program, such as Keynote or Pages.**
2. **Choose File⇨Save As.**

   A Save As dialog appears, as shown in Figure 6-9

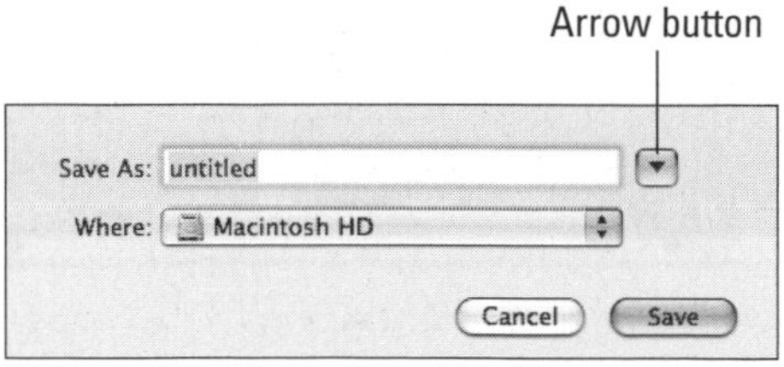

Figure 6-9: The Save As dialog lets you create a new folder while you're saving a file.

3. **Click the Arrow button to the right of the Save As text box.**

   The Save As dialog expands to display a Finder, as shown in Figure 6-10.

4. **In the Sidebar of this Finder, click the device where you want to create a folder and then open the folder where you want to create a new folder.**

5. **Click the New Folder button.**

   A New Folder dialog appears, as shown in Figure 6-11.

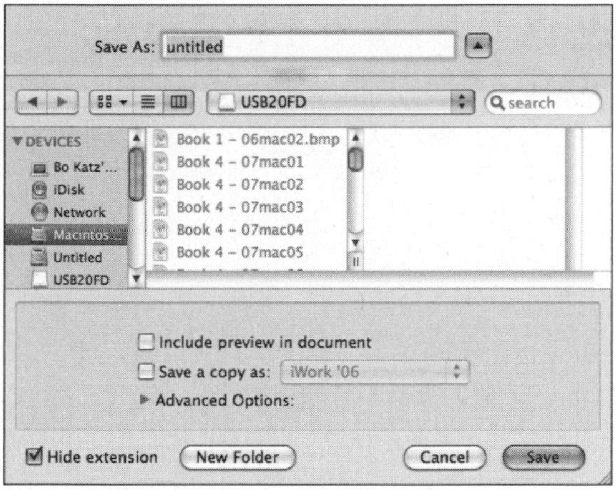

Figure 6-10: The expanded version of the Save As dialog displays a window similar to the Finder.

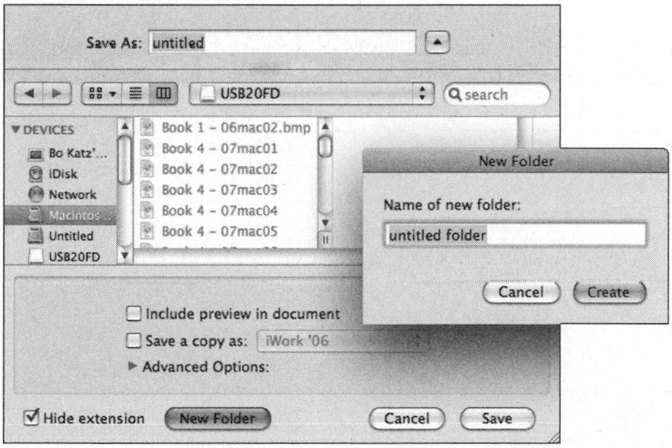

Figure 6-11: The New Folder dialog lets you pick a name for your folder.

6. **Type a name for your folder in the dialog's text field and then click Create.**

A new folder is created in the location you specified.

This name cannot be identical to the name of any existing folder in that location.

7. **Back in the main window of the Save As/Finder dialog, type a name for your document in the Save As text field and then click Save.**

   Your new document is stored in your new folder.

Manipulating Files and Folders

After you've created a file (using a program like a word processor) or a folder (using the Finder or a Save As dialog from a program), you might need to change or edit the name of that file or folder to correct a misspelling or just to change the name altogether. In addition, you might need to move or copy that file or folder to a new location, or delete it altogether.

To make sure you're copying, moving, or changing the right file, you might want to open it first. However, this can take time so a faster way to view the contents of a file is to click that file (in the Icon, List, Columns, or Cover Flow view) and choose File⇨Quick Look or press ⌘+Y, which lets you peek into the file's contents, as shown in Figure 6-12.

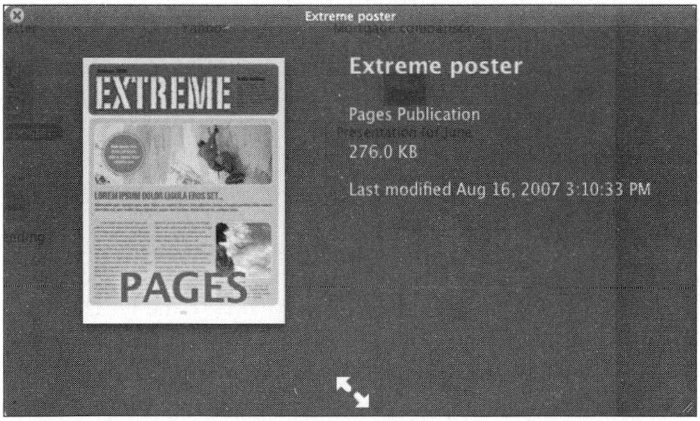

Figure 6-12: The Quick Look command lets you view information about a file.

The Quick Look command behaves differently depending on the type of file you're peeking into:

- ✦ An audio file plays in its entirety so you can hear its contents.
- ✦ A full-size picture file appears in a window so you can see what the picture looks like.

- ✦ A movie file plays in its entirety so you can see and hear its contents.
- ✦ PDF (Portable Document Format) files and HTML files (Web pages) appear in a window so you can scroll through the files and read their contents.
- ✦ A document file (created by other programs such as spreadsheets and word processors) displays the first screen of its contents along with a listing of its name, size, and date of last modification.
- ✦ A folder appears as a graphic icon listing its name, size, and date of last modification.
- ✦ A program file displays its icon along with a name, size, and date of last modification.

Renaming a file or folder

The only limitation on naming a file or folder is that a name can't be longer than 255 characters and the name can't be identical to another file or folder in that same location. For example, you can't have two files or folders named `Tax Info` stored in the same folder (such as the Documents folder). However, you can have two identically named files stored in different folders.

You can't use certain characters when naming files or folders, such as the colon (:). In addition, some programs might not let you use the period (.) or slash (/) characters in a filename either.

Actually, you *can* store identically named files in the same location — as long as a different program created each file. That means you can have a word processor document named `My Resume` and a spreadsheet file also named `My Resume` stored in the same folder.

The reason for this is because a file's complete name consists of two parts: a name and a file extension. The name is any arbitrary descriptive name you choose, but the file extension identifies the type of file. A program file actually consists of the `.app` file extension, a Microsoft Word file consists of the `.doc` file extension, a Pages file consists of the `.pages` file extension, and a Keynote file consists of the `.key` file extension.

So a `My Resume` file created by Microsoft Word is actually named `My Resume.doc`, and the identically named file created by Pages is actually named `My Resume.pages`.

Not all files may have a file extension. It's possible to save a file without a file extension, although this can make it difficult to determine what type of file it is.

To view a file's extension, click that file and choose File➪Get Info (or press ⌘+I). An Info window appears and displays the file extension in the Name & Extension text box. To view file extensions in the Finder, deselect the Hide Extension check box, as shown in Figure 6-13.

Folders don't need file extensions, because file extensions are used to identify the contents of a file, and folders can hold a variety of different types of files.

For a fast way to rename a file or folder, follow these steps:

1. **Click a file or folder that you want to rename.**
2. **Press Return.**

   The file or folder's name appears highlighted.
3. **Type a new name or use the left- and right-arrow keys and the Delete key to edit the existing name.**

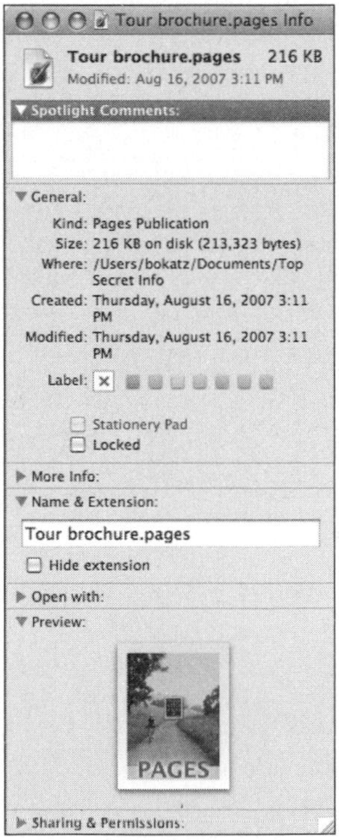

Figure 6-13: You can selectively choose to display file extensions of individual files by using the Info window.

For another way to rename a file or folder, follow these steps:

1. **Click a file or folder that you want to rename.**
2. **Choose File➪Get Info (or press ⌘+I).**

   An Info window appears (refer to Figure 6-13).
3. **Click in the Name & Extension text box and edit or type a new name.**

   When editing or typing a new name for a file, don't change the file extension, or else your Mac won't know which program created that file.
4. **Click the Close button of the Info window to make it disappear.**

   Your selected file or folder appears with its new name.

Copying a file or folder

At any time, you can copy a file or folder and place that duplicate copy in another location. When you copy a folder, you also copy any files and folders stored inside it. To copy a file or folder, you can either use menus or the mouse.

Using menus to copy a file or folder

To copy a file or folder by using menus, follow these steps:

1. **Click the Finder icon in the Dock.**

   The Finder appears.
2. **Navigate to (and open) the folder that contains the files or folders you want to copy.**

   You know the drill by now. Use the Sidebar and the various other search techniques outlined earlier in this chapter to find what you want.
3. **Select one or more files or folders you want to copy.**
4. **Choose Edit➪Copy (or press ⌘+C).**
5. **Navigate to (and open) the folder where you want to store a copy of the file or folder.**
6. **Choose Edit➪Paste (or press ⌘+V).**

   You have your own cloned file or folder right where you want it.

Using the mouse to copy a file or folder

Using the menus to copy a file or folder is simple, but some people find clicking and dragging items with the mouse to be more intuitive. Clicking and dragging works slightly differently, depending on whether you're dragging between two separate devices (such as from a flash drive to a hard drive) or between different folders on the same device.

If you want to use the click-and-drag method to copy a file or folder *from one device to a second device,* follow these steps:

1. **Click the Finder icon in the Dock.**

   The Finder shows its face.
2. **Navigate to (and open) the folder where you want to store your copied files or folders.**
3. **Choose File⇨New Finder Window.**

   A second Finder appears.
4. **In the Sidebar of the new Finder, click a device.**

   This device must be different from the device you chose in Step 2.
5. **In this second Finder, navigate to (and open) the folder containing the file or folder you want to copy.**
6. **Using your mouse, click and drag to select one or more files or folders.**

   If you want to drag a file or folder to a new location on the same device, hold down the Option key while dragging the mouse.
7. **Move the pointer over one of your selected items and then click and drag the selected items into the first Finder and onto the folder you opened in Step 3.**

   Notice that a green plus sign appears near the pointer as you drag the mouse. The green plus sign means you're copying an item, as shown in Figure 6-14.
8. **Release the mouse button.**

   Your selected files and folders appear as copies in the folder you selected.

If you want to use the click-drag-method to copy a file or folder from one folder to another folder *on the same device,* you need to use the Option key. Here's how that works:

1. **Click the Finder icon in the Dock.**

   The Finder obediently appears.
2. **Switch to List, Column, or Cover Flow view.**

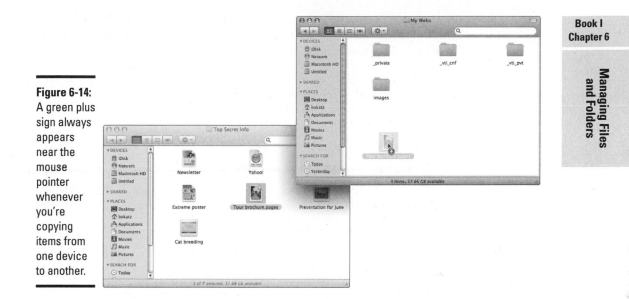

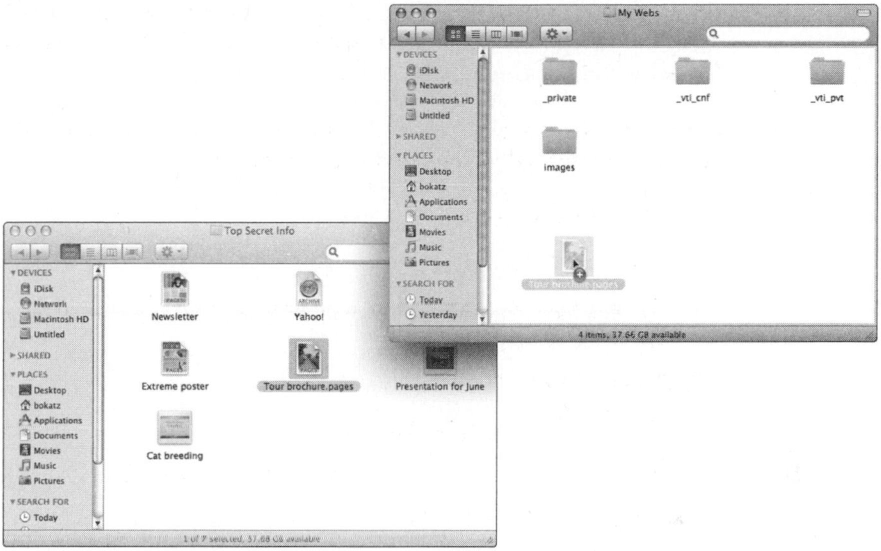

Figure 6-14: A green plus sign always appears near the mouse pointer whenever you're copying items from one device to another.

3. **Click the triangle that appears next to the folder that contains the files or folders you want to copy.**
4. **While holding down the Option key, click and drag to select one or more files or folders.**
5. **Move the pointer over one of your selected items and then click and drag the selected items over a folder.**

   Notice that a green plus sign appears near the pointer as you drag the mouse. This green plus sign means you're copying an item.

   If you don't hold down the Option key in Step 4, you move your selected items rather than copy them.
6. **Release the mouse button.**

   Your selected files and folders appear as copies in their new location.

Moving a file or folder

To move a file or folder by using the menus, you must first copy a file or folder, paste it in a new location, and then go back and erase the original file or folder.

Dragging a file or folder to a new location on the same device (such as from one folder to another on the same hard drive) always moves that file or folder (unless you hold down the Option key, which ensures that the original stays where it is and a copy goes a rovin'). On the other hand, dragging a file or folder from one device to another (such as from a flash drive to a hard drive) always copies a file or folder — unless you use the ⌘ key, which puts a halt to the cloning business and moves the file or folder lock, stock and barrel to a new location.

Archiving Files and Folders

Files and folders take up space. If you have a bunch of files or folders that you never use yet want to save (such as old tax information), you can archive those files instead. *Archiving* basically grabs a bunch of files or folders and smashes them into a single file.

After you've archived a group of files, you can later unarchive that file to retrieve all the files you stuffed into that archive.

There are two common ways to archive files and folders:

- Creating ZIP files
- Creating DMG files

ZIP files represent the standard archiving file format used on Windows computers. (By the way, ZIP isn't an acronym. It just sounds speedy.)

DMG files (which stands for disc image) are meant for archiving files to be shared only with other Mac users. As a general rule, if you want to archive files that Windows and Mac users can use, store them in the ZIP file format. If you want to archive files just for other Mac users, you can use the ZIP or DMG file format.

TECHNICAL STUFF

The ZIP file format is faster and creates smaller archives than the DMG file format. That's why most people use ZIP archives to store data. The most popular use for DMG files is for storing and distributing software.

Creating a ZIP file

A ZIP file can contain just a single file or folder, but it could contain dozens of separate files or folders. To create a ZIP file, follow these steps:

1. **Click the Finder icon in the Dock.**

   The Finder comes to the fore.

2. **Navigate to (and open) the folder that contains the file or folder you want to archive.**
3. **Select one or more items you want archive.**

4. **Choose File⇨Compress.**

   If you selected three items in Step 3, the Compress command will display `Compress 3 items`.

   An archive file named `Archive.zip` appears in the folder that contains the items you selected to compress, as shown in Figure 6-15. (You might want to rename this file to give it a more descriptive name.)

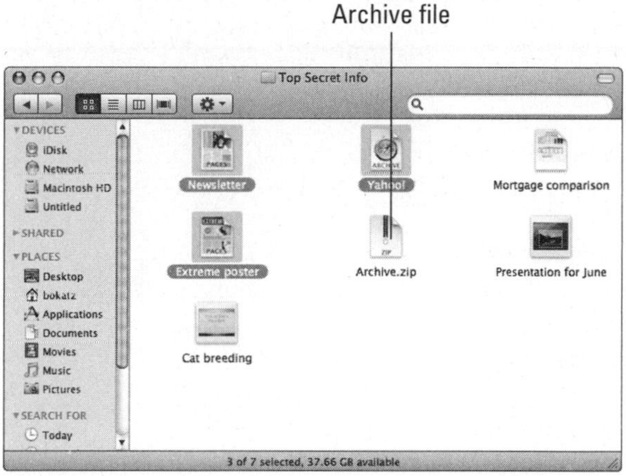

Figure 6-15: ZIP files appear with a zipper icon.

REMEMBER

To open a ZIP file, just double-click it. This creates a folder inside the same folder where the ZIP file is stored. Now you can double-click this newly created folder to view the contents that were stored in the ZIP file.

Creating a DMG file

Although ZIP files are handy for storing files, DMG files are more often used to compress and store large items, such as the contents of an entire folder, CD, or hard drive. To create a DMG file, follow these steps:

1. **Click the Finder icon in the Dock.**

   The Finder appears.

2. **Move or copy the files you want to store in the DMG file into a single folder.**

3. **Choose Go⇨Utilities.**

   The right pane of the Finder refreshes to display the contents of the Utilities folder, as shown in 6-16.

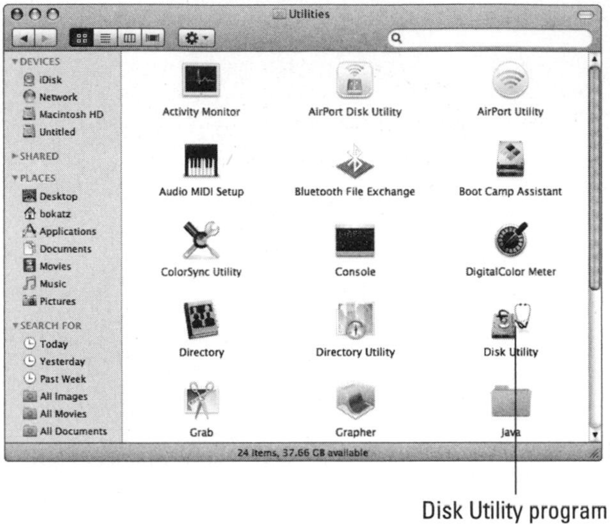

Figure 6-16: The Utilities folder contains the Disk Utility program.

4. **Double-click the Disk Utility program icon.**

   The Disk Utility program loads and displays its window, as shown in Figure 6-17.

5. **Choose File⇨New⇨Disc Image from Folder.**

   The Select Folder to Image dialog appears.

6. **Using the Select Folder to Image dialog, navigate to and then select the folder containing the files you chose in Step 2.**

7. **Click Image.**

   A New Image from Folder dialog appears, as shown in Figure 6-18.

8. **Click in the Save As text box and type a name for your disc image file.**

9. **(Optional) Click the Where pop-up menu and choose a folder or device to store your disc image.**

10. **Click in the Image Format pop-up menu and choose one of the following:**

    - *Read-only:* Saves files in the DMG file just once, but you can never add more files to this DMG file again.
    - *Compressed:* Same as the Read-Only option, except squeezes the size of your DMG file to make it as small as possible.
    - *Read-Write:* Saves files in a DMG file with the option of adding more files to this DMG file later.

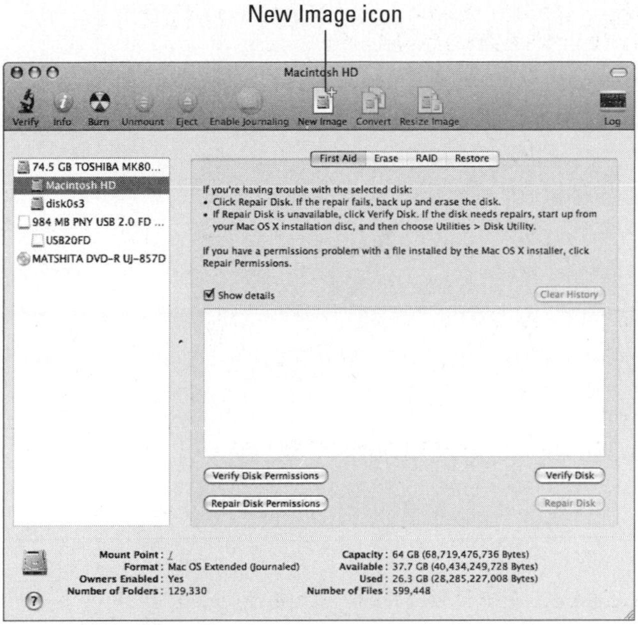

Figure 6-17: The Disk Utility window appears, ready to create a DMG file.

Figure 6-18: A dialog appears where you can name and define the location of your disc image file.

- *DVD/CD master:* Saves files for burning to an audio CD or a video DVD.
- *Hybrid Image (HFS + ISO/UDF):* Saves files in a DMG file designed to be burned to a CD/DVD for use in computers that can recognize the Hierarchical File Structure (HFS), ISO 9660 (International Organization for Standardization), or Universal Disk Format (UDF) for storing data on optical media. (Most modern computers can recognize HFS and UDF discs, but older computers might not.) Also saves files in a DMG file designed to be transferred over the Internet.

11. **(Optional) Click the Encryption pop-up menu and choose None, 128-bit AES, or 256-bit AES encryption.**

    If you choose encryption, you'll have to define a password that can open the DMG file.

    AES stands for Advanced Encryption Standard, which is the latest American government standard algorithm for scrambling data.

12. **Click Save.**

    Disk Utility displays a message showing you the progress as it stores the files in your chosen folder as a DMG file.

13. **When the disk imaging is completed, choose Disk Utility⇨Quit Disk Utility to exit the program.**

Double-clicking a DMG file displays the contents of that DMG file in a Finder.

Searching Files

No matter how organized you try to be, there's a good chance you might forget where you stored a file. To find your wayward files quickly, you can use a feature called Spotlight.

Spotlight lets you type a word or phrase to identify either the name of the file you want or a word or phrase stored inside that file. Then Spotlight displays a list of files that match what you typed. So, if you want to find all the files related to your baseball collection, you could type the word **baseball** and Spotlight would find all files that contain the word *baseball* in the filename or in the file itself.

Using Spotlight

Spotlight searches for text that matches all or part of a filename as well as data stored inside of a file. When using Spotlight, search for distinct words. For example, searching for *A* will be relatively useless because so many files use the letter *A* as part of their file name and inside of most files. However, searching for *ebola* will narrow your search to the files you most likely want.

To use Spotlight, follow these steps:

1. **Click the Finder icon in the Dock.**

    The Finder promptly shows up.

2. **Click in the Spotlight text box, as shown in Figure 6-19.**

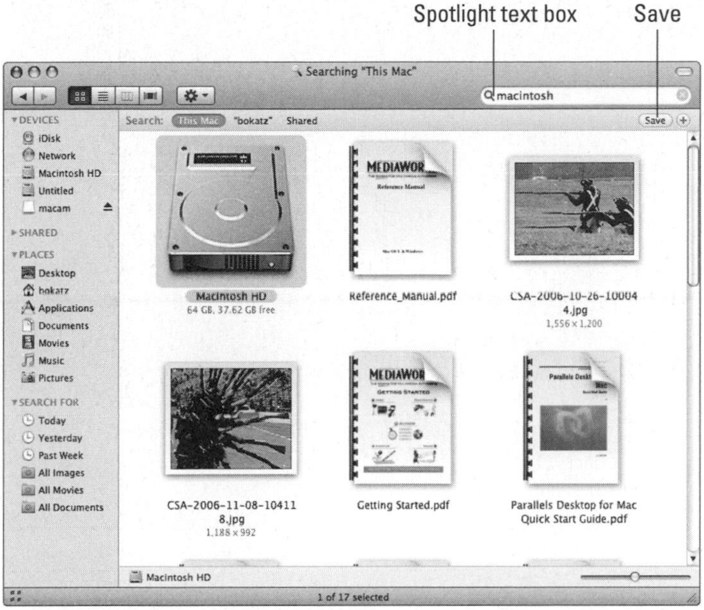

Figure 6-19: The Spotlight text box always appears in the upper-right corner of the Finder.

3. Type a word or phrase.

As you type, Spotlight displays the files that match your text.

At this point you can double-click a file to open it, or you can copy and move it to a new location.

REMEMBER

You can change the way your search results appear by choosing View⇨As Icons, View⇨as List, or View⇨As Cover Flow.

Using Smart Folders

Spotlight can make finding files and folders fast and easy. However, it's possible to find yourself constantly searching for the same types of files over and over again. To solve this problem, you can create a Smart Folder.

A Smart Folder essentially works with Spotlight to keep track of a bunch of files sharing a common characteristic. For example, tell a Smart Folder to store info about only those files that contain the phrase *top secret* in the filename or in the file itself, and from now on, you can always look in that Smart Folder to access all files and folders that match *top secret* without having to type the words in the Spotlight text box all over again.

Think of Smart Folders as a way to make organizing your files automatic. Rather than take the time to physically move and organize files, you can have Spotlight and Smart Folders do the work for you.

A Smart Folder doesn't physically contain any files or folders. Instead, it contains only links to files or folders. This saves space by not duplicating files.

Creating a Smart Folder using Spotlight

To create a Smart Folder, follow these steps:

1. **Click the Finder icon in the Dock.**

   The Finder appears.

2. **Click in the Spotlight text box and type a word or phrase.**

   Spotlight displays a list of files and folders that match your word or phrase.

3. **Click the Save button that appears underneath the Spotlight text box.**

   A Save As dialog appears, as shown in Figure 6-20.

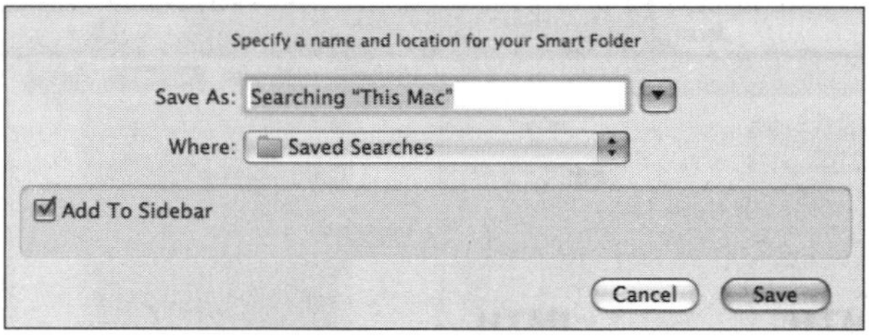

Figure 6-20: The Save As dialog lets you name your Smart Folder and define where to store it.

4. **Click in the Save As text box and type a descriptive name for your Smart Folder.**

5. **Choose a location to store your Smart Folder from the Where pop-up menu.**

6. **(Optional) Deselect the Add To Sidebar check box.**

   If a check mark appears, your Smart Folder will appear in the Sidebar in the Searches section near the bottom. If a check mark doesn't appear, your Smart Folder won't appear in the Sidebar.

7. **Click Save.**

   Your Smart Folder appears in your chosen location. Instead of displaying an ordinary folder icon, Smart Folder icons always contain a gear inside a folder, as shown in Figure 6-21.

Figure 6-21: A Smart Folder icon appears with a gear inside a folder.

After you create a Smart Folder, it automatically keeps your list of files and folders up to date at all times. If you create new files or folders that match the text used to define a Smart Folder, that new file or folder name will appear in the Smart Folder automatically. Delete a file, and the Smart Folder deletes that file as well.

Creating a Smart Folder using other criteria

Besides organizing files and folders using Spotlight, Smart Folders can also list files and folders based on dates, sizes, color labels, and other criteria. To create a Smart Folder using these other criteria, follow these steps:

1. **Click the Finder icon in the Dock.**

   The Finder appears.

2. **Choose File⇨New Smart Folder.**

   A New Smart Folder window appears.

3. **Click the plus sign icon that appears to the right of the Save button.**

   A Kind and Any drop-down menu appear, as shown in Figure 6-22.

   Clicking the plus sign icon adds something to the New Smart Folder window — in this case, a new drop-down menu and a couple check boxes. In other words, it expands the window. After the window expands, though, the plus sign icon changes to a minus sign icon, which you can then use to contract the window back to its original state.

4. **Click the Kind pop-up menu and choose a criterion such as Name or Last opened date.**

5. **Click the Any pop-up menu and choose the type of files you want to find, such as Documents, Movies, or PDF, as shown in Figure 6-23.**

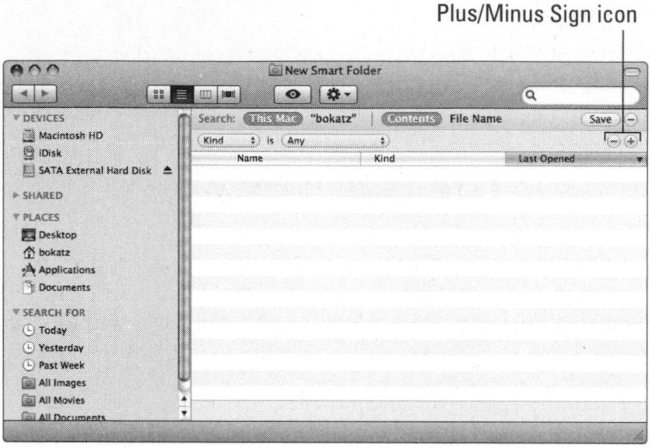

Figure 6-22: Clicking the plus sign icon displays a Kind and Any pop-up menu.

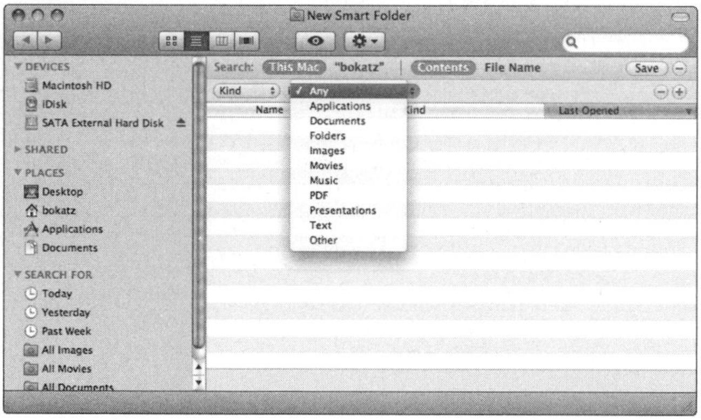

Figure 6-23: Clicking the Any pop-up menu displays a variety of choices for selecting the types of files to appear in the Smart Folder.

6. **Click the Save button that appears underneath the Spotlight text box.**

   A Save As dialog appears (refer to Figure 6-20).

7. **Click in the Save As text box and type a descriptive name for your Smart Folder.**

8. **Choose a location to store your Smart Folder from the Where drop-down menu.**

9. **(Optional) Deselect the Add To Sidebar check box.**

   If a check mark appears, your Smart Folder will appear in the Sidebar. If a check mark does not appear, your Smart Folder won't appear in the Sidebar.

10. **Click Save.**

Your Smart Folder appears in your chosen location. Instead of displaying an ordinary folder icon, Smart Folder icons always contain a gear inside a folder (refer to Figure 6-21).

Using Smart Folders in the Sidebar

To make searching for files easier, the Finder has already created several Smart Folders in the Sidebar. These Smart Folders are named Today, Yesterday, Past Week, All Images, All Movies, and All Documents, and they can be found under the Search For category, as shown in Figure 6-24.

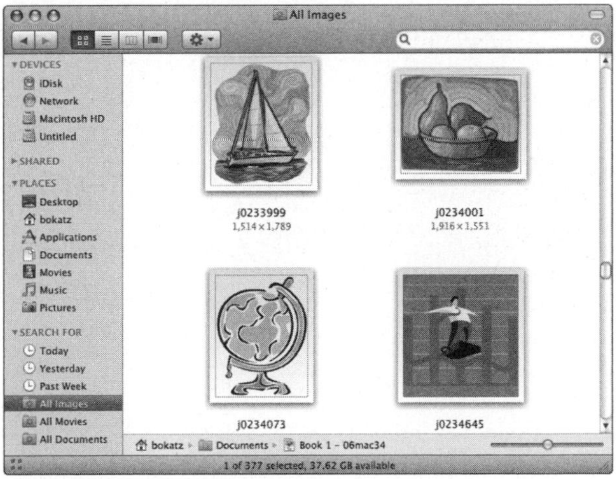

Figure 6-24: The Search For category in the Sidebar contains several Smart Folders you can use right away.

By clicking one of these Smart Folders, you can view certain types of files, such as all files created today (in the Today Smart Folder) or all pictures stored on your hard drive (stored in the All Pictures folder).

Storing Files and Folders in the Dock

You can always find the files and folders you want by using the Finder. However, you might find that loading the Finder constantly just to access the contents of a particular folder can get tedious. As a faster alternative, you can store pointers to files and folders directly in the Dock instead.

Storing files in the Dock

If you have a file that you access regularly, consider placing an icon for that file directly in the Dock. That way, the file icon remains visible at all times (at least as long as the Dock is visible) and gives you one-click access to your frequently used files. To place a file icon on the Dock, follow these steps:

1. **Click the Finder icon in the Dock.**

   The Finder comes to the fore.

2. **Using the Sidebar, navigate to the folder containing a file you use frequently (typically stored somewhere in the Documents folder).**
3. **Click and drag the file onto the right side of the Dock to any space to the left of the Trash icon.**

   The icons in the Dock slide apart to make room for your file icon.

4. **Release the mouse button.**

   Your file icon appears in the Dock. To open this file, just click this file icon.

REMEMBER

A file icon in the Dock is just a link to your actual file. If you drag the file icon off the Dock, your physical file remains untouched.

Creating Stacks in the Dock

Storing files on the Dock can make them convenient to access, but the more file icons you add, the smaller each file icon gets as the Dock shrinks to show all its icons. Rather than clutter the Dock with multiple file icons, consider storing a folder in the Dock instead.

A folder icon when stored in the Dock is called a *Stack.* After you've created a Stack in the Dock, you can view its contents by clicking the Stack.

To store a Stack in the Dock, follow these steps:

1. **Click the Finder icon in the Dock.**

   The Finder appears.

2. **Using the Sidebar, navigate to the folder containing a file you use frequently (typically stored somewhere in the Documents folder).**
3. **Click and drag the folder onto the Dock to any space to the left of the Trash icon.**

   The Dock icons slide apart to make room for your Stack.

4. **Release the mouse button to place your Stack in the Dock.**

REMEMBER

A Stack in the Dock is just a link to your actual folder and files. If you drag the Stack off the Dock, your folder and its file contents remain untouched.

Opening files stored in a Stack

After you've placed a Stack on the Dock, you can view its contents and open a file in that Stack by following these steps:

1. **Click a Stack found in the Dock.**

   If you have less than ten files stored in a Stack, its contents fan out. If you have ten or more files stored in a Stack, its contents are displayed in a grid.

2. **Click the file you want to open in the fan or grid.**

   Your chosen file opens.

Burning Files and Folders to CD/DVD

A simple way to transfer or back up data is to store them on CDs or DVDs. (A CD can store 650–700 megabytes, whereas a DVD can store 4.7 or 8.5 gigabytes.) After you store data on a CD or DVD, you can easily transfer it to another computer, even one running Windows or Linux.

TECHNICAL STUFF

Two types of CDs and DVDs exist: read-only and rewritable. Read-only discs are labeled CD-R or DVD-R, and you can store data on them exactly once. Rewritable discs can store and erase data over and over again. Rewritable discs cost more, but they're reusable so they're more useful. The main advantage of read-only CDs is that some older audio CD players cannot read rewritable CDs but can read read-only CDs. Likewise, some older DVD players cannot read rewritable DVDs, but can read read-only DVDs.

The process of copying data to a CD or DVD is known as "burning a disc." To burn a disc, you must specify which files or folders you want to burn to the disc. If you want to burn files stored in separate folders, you would normally have to copy (or move) all files into a single folder and then burn the contents of that folder to a disc.

Because copying or moving all files to a single folder can be cumbersome, you can create a special folder called a Burn Folder. A Burn Folder doesn't store physical copies of your files or folders. Instead, a Burn Folder contains links to your files and folders. That way, a Burn Folder won't take double the amount of space needed to store your data.

Creating a Burn Folder

To create a Burn Folder, follow these steps:

1. **Click on the Finder icon in the Dock.**

   The Finder appears to do your bidding.

2. **Using the Sidebar, navigate to (and open) the folder where you want to store your Burn Folder.**
3. **Choose File➪New Burn Folder.**

   A Burn Folder appears bearing a circular yellow and black radiation logo, as shown in Figure 6-25.

Figure 6-25: A Burn Folder displays a radiation logo.

4. **Copy and paste the files and folders you want to burn to a disc into the Burn folder.**

Burning the contents of a Burn Folder

After you've stored the links to your various files and folders in a Burn Folder, you can burn the contents of the Burn Folder on to as many discs as you want without having to specify each file and folder to burn each time. To burn the contents of a Burn Folder to a disc, follow these steps:

1. **Click the Finder icon in the Dock.**

   The Finder appears.
2. **Navigate to and open the folder where you stored your Burn Folder.**
3. **Double-click the Burn folder.**

   Your Burn folder opens. (You can also open a Burn folder by selecting it and then choosing File ➪Open.)
4. **Click the Burn button that appears in the upper-right corner of the Finder, or choose File➪Burn *folder name* to Disc, where *folder name* is the name of the folder you've chosen to burn.**

   A dialog appears, asking you to insert a blank disc.
5. **Insert a blank disc in the CD or DVD drive, as appropriate.**

   Sit back and wait for the burning process to complete. (A loud alert sound usually signals the end of a burning session.) If you try to burn more data than the CD or DVD can hold, your Mac won't even try to burn your files. In this case, you have to remove some files from the Burn Folder and try again.

6. **When the burning session is over, eject the finished disc.**

   Some ways to eject a disc are to press the Eject button on the keyboard or right-click the disc icon on the Desktop and choose Eject from the shortcut menu.

Burn Folders are nice for burning files to a CD or DVD, but if you want more than just basic disc-burning capabilities, consider getting a standalone CD/DVD burning program such as Toast Titanium (`www.roxio.com`) or Dragon Burn (`www.ntius.com`). Besides duplicating the basic disc-burning features of Burn Folders, Toast Titanium and Dragon Burn also provide a wealth of features for mixing and editing audio, compressing video, copying entire discs, and burning files on the new Blu-ray disc format.

Deleting a File or Folder

To delete a file or folder, you first have to place that item in the Trash. But putting an item in the Trash doesn't immediately delete it. In fact, you can retrieve any number of files or folders you've "thrown away." Nothing is really gone — permanently deleted — until you empty the Trash.

Deleting a folder also deletes any files or folders stored inside it. So if you delete a single folder, you might really be deleting 200 other folders containing valuable data, so always check the contents of a folder before you delete it, just to make sure it doesn't contain anything important.

To delete a file or folder, follow these steps:

1. **Click the Finder icon in the Dock.**

   The Finder comes to the fore.

2. **Using the Sidebar, navigate to (and open) the folder that contains the file or folder you want to delete.**
3. **Select one or more files or folders.**
4. **Choose one of the following:**
   - Choose File➪Move to Trash.
   - Drag the selected items onto the Trash icon on the Dock.
   - Press ⌘+Delete.
   - Right-click a selected item and choose Move to Trash from the shortcut menu that appears.

Retrieving a file or folder from the Trash

When you move items to the Trash, you can retrieve them again as long as you haven't emptied the Trash since you threw them out. If the Trash icon in the Dock appears filled with a pile of crumbled up paper, that means you can still retrieve files or folders from the Trash. If the Trash icon appears empty, there are no files or folders there you can retrieve.

To retrieve a file or folder from the Trash, follow these steps:

1. **Make sure the Trash icon in the Dock appears full of crumbled up paper.**
2. **Click the Trash icon in the Dock.**

   The Finder appears, showing all the files and folders you deleted since the last time you emptied the Trash.
3. **Select one or more items.**
4. **Click and drag your selected items onto a device or folder where you want to store your retrieved items.**
5. **Release the mouse button.**

Emptying the Trash

Every deleted file or folder gets stored in the Trash. But even files and folders stored in the Trash eat up space on your hard drive. When you're sure that you won't need those items any more, you should empty the Trash to permanently delete the files and free up additional space on your hard drive.

To empty the Trash, follow these steps:

1. **Click the Finder icon on the Dock (or click on the Desktop).**

   The Finder menu appears at the top of the screen.
2. **Choose File➪ Empty Trash.**

   A dialog appears, asking whether you're sure you want to remove the items in the Trash permanently.

   TIP: If you open the Finder and choose Finder➪Secure Empty Trash, your Mac will write over the deleted file with random data to foil any attempt to recover that file later with a special file recovery program. If you want to delete something sensitive that you don't want to risk falling into the wrong hands, choose Finder➪Secure Empty Trash instead.
3. **Click OK (or Cancel).**

TIP: For a faster way of emptying the Trash, right-click the Trash icon in the Dock and choose Empty Trash from the shortcut menu that appears.

Chapter 7: Customizing Your Mac

In This Chapter

- Changing the Desktop
- Customizing the screen saver
- Changing the display and appearance
- Changing the date and time
- Adjusting sounds
- Saving energy
- Picking a printer
- Creating accounts

Every Mac works the same, but that doesn't mean they all have to look the same. To personalize your Mac, you can change the way it looks and even how it behaves. By customizing your Mac, you can stamp it with your personality and truly turn your Mac into a personal computer.

REMEMBER

Don't get too carried away customizing your Mac. The more you customize your own Mac, the harder it might be for you to use a different Mac. In other words, feel free to customize your Mac, but make sure you know how to use a "generic" Mac in case you need to use another one in an emergency.

Changing the Desktop

The Desktop fills the screen in the absence of any program windows. Generally, the Desktop displays a decorative background image, but you can display any image, such as a picture captured with a digital camera or a favorite picture you downloaded off the Internet.

Choosing a built-in Desktop image

Your Mac comes with a variety of images stored and organized into different categories. To choose one of these images as your Desktop image, follow these steps:

1. **Right-click anywhere on the Desktop and choose Change Desktop Background from the contextual menu that appears.**

The Desktop preferences pane appears, as shown in Figure 7-1.

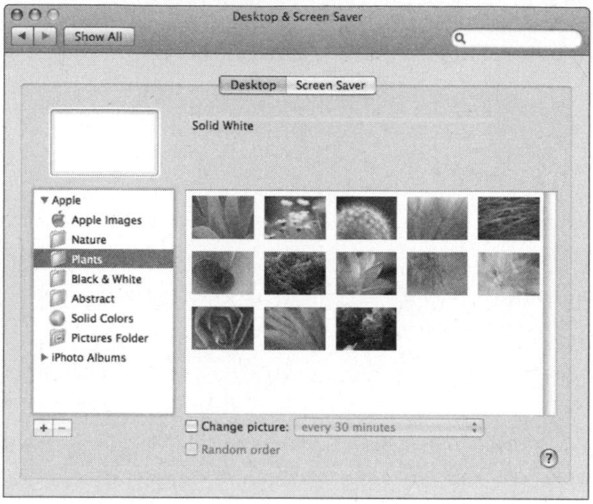

Figure 7-1: The Desktop pane lets you choose a different background image.

2. **In the left part of the pane, click a category such as Nature or Plants.**

   Thumbnail versions of images matching that category appear in the right pane.

3. **Click an image that you like.**

   The Desktop immediately displays your chosen image as its background image.

4. **Click the Close button of the System Preferences window.**

TIP

For variety's sake, select the Change Picture check box on the Desktop tab and click in the Change Picture list box to define how often to change an image, within the category you chose in Step 2, such as every hour. If you select the Random Order check box, your Mac will surprise you by displaying images from all categories in random order.

Choosing an iPhoto image for the Desktop

If you've captured images with a digital camera and stored those images in iPhoto, you can choose one of your iPhoto images to appear on your Desktop. To display an iPhoto image on the Desktop background, follow these steps:

1. **Right-click anywhere on the Desktop and choose Change Desktop Background from the contextual menu that appears.**

   The Desktop preferences pane appears (refer to Figure 7-1).

2. **Click the right-pointing triangle that appears to the left of the iPhoto Albums entry in the left part of the pane.**

   A list of different iPhoto categories, such as Library or Last Roll appears.

3. **Click an iPhoto category, such as Library.**

   The right part of the pane displays all iPhoto pictures contained in your chosen category.

4. **Click an iPhoto image.**

   Your chosen iPhoto image appears on the Desktop as its background image.

5. **Click the pop-up menu that appears underneath the Desktop tab and choose one of the following:**

   - *Fit to Screen:* Blows up the image to cover most of the screen, but might leave edges uncovered depending on the shape of the original image
   - *Fill Screen:* Blows up the image to cover the entire screen
   - *Stretch to Fill Screen:* Stretches a picture to fill the entire screen, which can skewer the image
   - *Center:* Places the image in the middle of the screen at its original size
   - *Tile:* Places the image in rows and columns to fill the screen

6. **Click the Close button of the System Preferences window.**

Choosing your own image for the Desktop

You might have images stored on your hard drive that you never bothered to store in iPhoto, such as pictures of your favorite movie stars or sports heroes that you found on the Internet. To display non-iPhoto images on the Desktop background, follow these steps:

1. **Right-click anywhere on the Desktop and choose Change Desktop Background from the contextual menu that appears.**

   The Desktop preferences pane appears (refer to Figure 7-1).

2. **Choose one of the following:**

   - Click the Pictures Folder under the Apple category.

     This displays all images stored in the Pictures folder. Any images stored in separate folders inside the Pictures folder will not be visible.

   - Click the plus sign icon in the lower-left corner and use the dialog that appears to navigate to the folder that contains the image you want to use.

3. **Click an image that you like.**

   The Desktop immediately displays your chosen image.

   If you select the Change Picture check box and set a time in the Change Picture list box, you can have your Mac display all the images, one at a time, stored in the folder you chose in Step 4.

4. **Click the Close button in the System Preferences window.**

Customizing the Screen Saver

The screen saver is an animated image that appears on the screen after a fixed period of time when your Mac doesn't detect any keyboard or mouse activity. When defining a screen saver, you have to choose an image to display and the amount of time to wait before the screen saver starts up.

Screen savers were important in the old days when most monitors used cathode-ray tubes (CRT). If a CRT monitor displayed the same static image for long periods of time, such images eventually *burned in,* becoming physically etched into the glass. (Look at the screens of really old arcade video games to see these "ghost" images.) If you have a liquid-crystal display (LCD) monitor — standard for modern computers — this won't happen, so screen savers are mostly used for decorative purposes today.

Choosing a screen saver

To choose a screen saver, follow these steps:

1. **Choose ⇨System Preferences from the Finder menu.**

   The System Preferences window appears.

2. **Click the Desktop & Screen Saver icon under the Personal category.**

3. **Click the Screen Saver tab.**

   The Screen Saver preferences pane appears, as shown in Figure 7-2.

4. **Click a screen saver under the Apple or Pictures category.**

   The preview window shows you what your screen saver will look like. (If you select the Use Random Screen Saver check box, your Mac will pick a different screen saver image every time the screen saver starts. After your randomly chosen screen saver starts, that same animated image appears until you press a key to turn off the screen saver.)

   Under the Pictures category, you can choose the Pictures folder, an iPhoto folder, or the Choose Folder option, which lets you pick any folder on your hard drive that contains an image to use.

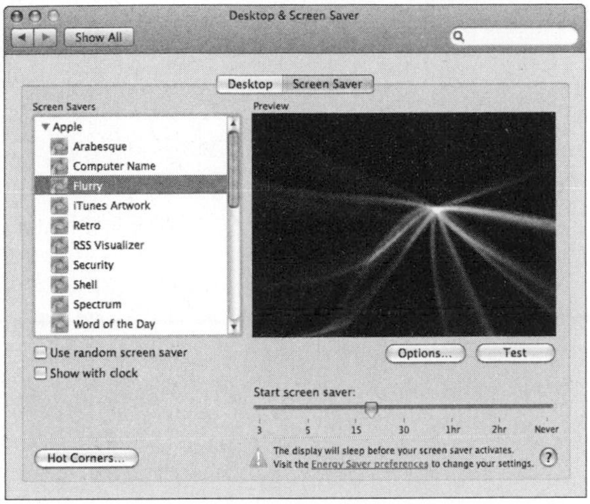

Figure 7-2: The Screen Saver pane lets you define an image and an inactivity time.

5. **Drag the Start Screen Saver slider to specify an amount of time to wait before your screen saver starts ups.**

   A short amount of time can mean the screen saver starts up while you're reading a Web page or document, so you might have to experiment a bit to find the best time for you.

6. **(Optional) Select the Show with Clock check box to display the time with your screen saver.**

7. **(Optional) Click Options.**

   A dialog appears that gives you additional choices for modifying the way your screen saver appears, such as changing the speed that the screen saver image moves.

8. **(Optional) Click Test to view your screen saver in Full Screen mode.**

   Moving the mouse or tapping a key gets you out of test mode.

9. **Click the Close button in the System Preferences window.**

In the early days of the Mac, one of the most popular screen savers displayed pieces of toast and winged chrome toasters flying across the screen. To relive these good old days, download a flying toaster screensaver from Uneasy Silence (`http://uneasysilence.com/toast`).

Defining hot corners

A *hot corner* lets you give a command to your Mac just by moving the pointer into one corner of the screen. Two common uses for a hot corner are to turn on the screen saver and temporarily disable the screen saver.

One reason you might want to turn on your screen saver is if you're going to leave your computer and don't want to wait until the screen saver turns itself on to fill your screen. A reason to temporarily disable your screen saver is to keep it from suddenly running while you're reading something on the screen, such as a news article on the Internet. If you don't disable the screen saver temporarily, it might start up, thinking that the lack of keyboard or mouse activity means that you're gone when you're really just concentrating.

To define a hot corner to start up or disable your screen saver, follow these steps:

1. **Choose ⇨System Preferences from the Finder menu.**

   The System Preferences window appears.

2. **Click the Desktop & Screen Saver icon under the Personal category.**
3. **Click the Screen Saver tab.**

   The Screen Saver preferences pane appears (refer to Figure 7-2).

4. **Click the Hot Corners button.**

   A dialog appears.

5. **Click in the pop-up menu near one of the four corners of the screen image displayed in the dialog, as shown in Figure 7-3, and then choose Start Screen Saver or Disable Screen Saver.**

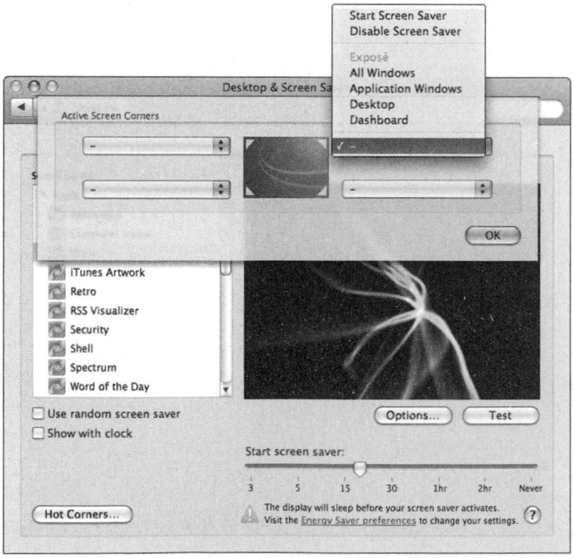

Figure 7-3: Each pop-up menu defines a function for a hot corner.

You can define multiple hot corners to do the same task, such as defining the two top corners to Start Screen Saver and the two bottom corners to Disable Screen Saver.

6. **Click the Close button of the System Preferences window.**

   Now, when you move the mouse into the hot corner defined as Start Screen Saver, you turn on your screen saver. To disable your screen saver, move the mouse into the hot corner defined as Disable Screen Saver.

To turn off a previously defined hot corner, repeat the preceding steps except instead of choosing Start Screen Saver or Disable Screen Saver, choose the dash (-) option — which is the equivalent of assigning no command whatsoever to a hot corner.

Changing the Display and Appearance

Because you'll be staring at your computer screen every time you use your Mac, you might want to modify the way your computer screen displays information. To do that, you'll probably want to mess around a bit with your screen resolution and/or change the color scheme of your various menus, windows, and dialogs. The next sections show how it's done.

Changing the screen resolution

The display defines the screen resolution, measured in *pixels* — the dots that make up an image. The higher the display resolution, the more pixels you have and the sharper the image — but everything on your screen may appear smaller. To change the screen resolution, follow these steps:

1. **Choose ⇨System Preferences from the Finder menu.**

   The System Preferences window appears.

2. **Click the Displays icon under the Hardware category.**

   The Display preferences pane appears, as shown in Figure 7-4.

3. **Choose a screen resolution from the Resolutions list.**

   Your Mac immediately changes the resolution so you can see how it looks. If you don't like the resolution, try again until you find one that's easy on your eyes.

4. **(Optional) Click in the Colors pop-up menu and choose the number of colors to display, such as 256 or Millions.**

   The more colors displayed, the sharper the images will appear on-screen.

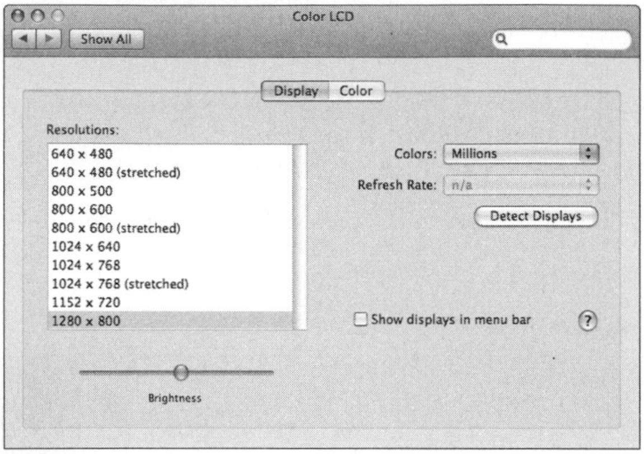

Figure 7-4: The Display preferences pane lets you choose a different screen resolution.

5. **Click the Close button in the System Preferences window when you're happy with the screen resolution.**

Changing the color of the user interface

Another way to change the appearance of the screen is to modify the colors used in windows, menus, and dialogs. To change the color of these user interface items, follow these steps:

1. **Choose ⇨System Preferences from the Finder menu.**

   The System Preferences window appears.

2. **Click the Appearance icon under the Personal category.**

   The Appearance preferences pane appears, as shown in Figure 7-5.

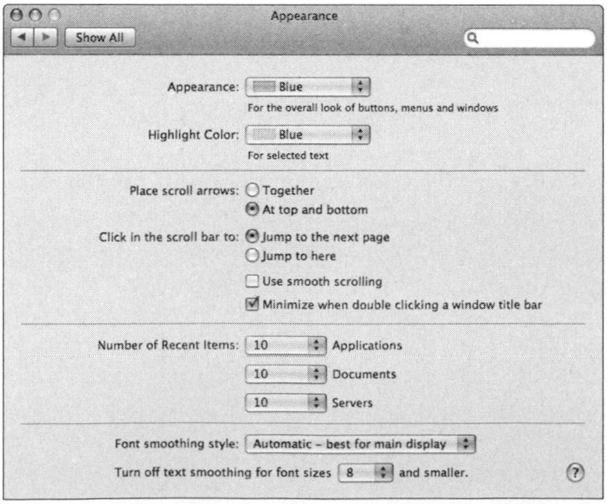

Figure 7-5: The Appearance pane lets you modify colors.

3. **Click in the Appearance and Highlight Color pop-up menus to choose a different color.**

   The Appearance pop-up menu defines the colors that normally show up on windows, buttons, and so on, whereas the Highlight Color pop-up menu defines the color of items that you select.

4. **Click the Close button of the System Preferences window.**

Changing the Date and Time

Although not as impressive as its other functions, your Mac can act like a giant clock. Keeping track of time might seem trivial, but knowing the right time is important so your Mac can determine when you created or modified a particular file as well as keep track of appointments you've made through programs such as iCal.

Of course, keeping track of time is useless if you don't set the right time to begin with, so to set the proper date and time, follow these steps:

1. **Choose ⌘⇨System Preferences from the Finder menu.**

   The System Preferences window appears.

2. **Click the Date & Time icon under the System category.**

3. **Click the Date & Time tab.**

   The Date & Time preferences pane appears, as shown in Figure 7-6.

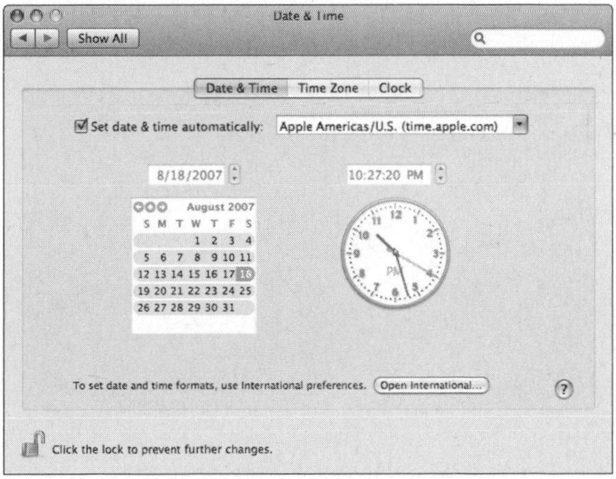

Figure 7-6: The Date & Time pane lets you set the clock in your Mac.

4. **Select (or deselect) the Set Date & Time Automatically check box. If you select this check box, click in the combo box to choose a location.**

   This feature works only if you're connected to the Internet. If you aren't connected to the Internet, click the calendar to pick a date and click the clock to pick a time.

5. **Click the Time Zone tab at the top of the window.**

   The Time Zone preferences pane appears, as shown in Figure 7-7.

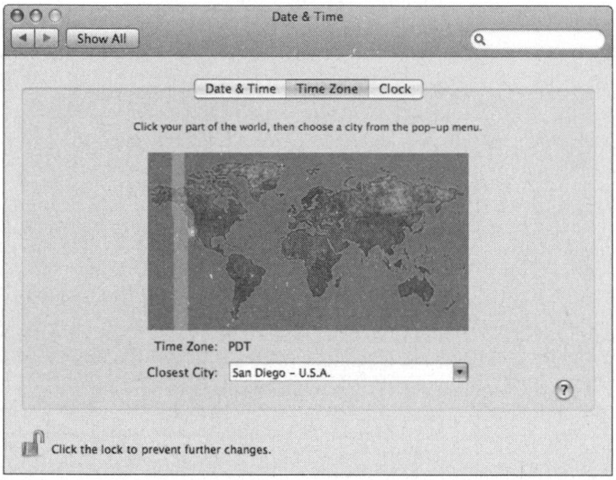

Figure 7-7: The Time Zone pane lets you pick the closest city in your time zone.

6. **Click near your home city on the map.**

   The Time Zone preferences pane displays a vertical strip of light on the map near where you clicked.

7. **Click the Closest City combo box and pick a city in your time zone.**

8. **Click the Clock tab at the top of the window.**

   The Clock preferences pane appears, as shown in Figure 7-8.

9. **Select (or deselect) the Show Date and Time in Menu Bar check box.**

   If selected, this displays the time in the right side of the menu bar. After you make your selection, you can modify the appearance of the clock, such as choosing between a digital or analog clock.

10. **Select (or deselect) the Announce the Time check box.**

    If selected, this makes your Mac recite the time using a synthesized voice every hour, half hour, or quarter hour. (The associated pop-up menus let you specify when announcements are made and what kind of voice is used.)

11. **Click the Close button of the System Preferences window.**

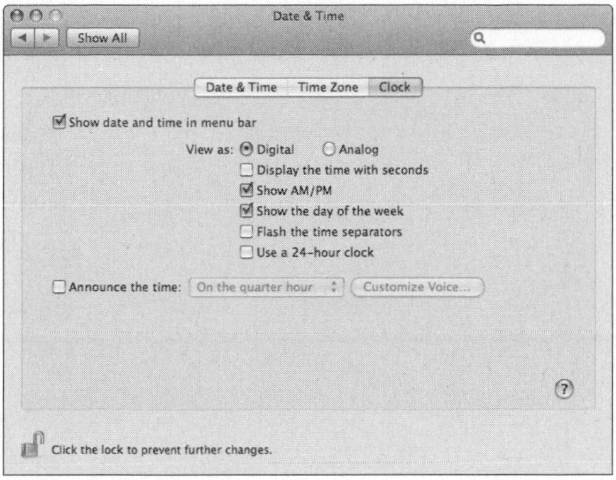

Figure 7-8: The Clock pane lets you pick the type of clock you want.

Adjusting Sounds

Every Mac can play sound through speakers (built-in or external) or headphones, from making the simplest beeping noise to playing audio CDs like a stereo. The three most important ways to modify the sound on your Mac involve volume, balance, and input/output devices.

Volume simply means how loud your Mac plays sound by default. Many programs, such as iTunes, also let you adjust the volume, so you can set the default volume and then adjust the volume within each program as well.

Balance defines how sound plays through the right and left stereo speakers. By adjusting the balance, you can make sound louder coming from one speaker and weaker coming from the other.

Depending on your equipment, it's possible to have multiple input and output devices — speakers and headphones as two distinct output devices, for example. By defining which input and output device to use, you can define which one to use all the time.

To modify the way your Mac accepts and plays sound, follow these steps:

1. **Choose ⇨System Preferences from the Finder menu.**

   The System Preferences window appears.

2. **Click the Sound icon under the Hardware category.**

   The Sound preferences pane appears.

3. **Click the Sound Effects tab.**

   The Sound Effects preferences pane appears, as shown in Figure 7-9.

Figure 7-9: The Sound Effects pane lets you define which sound to use as an alert.

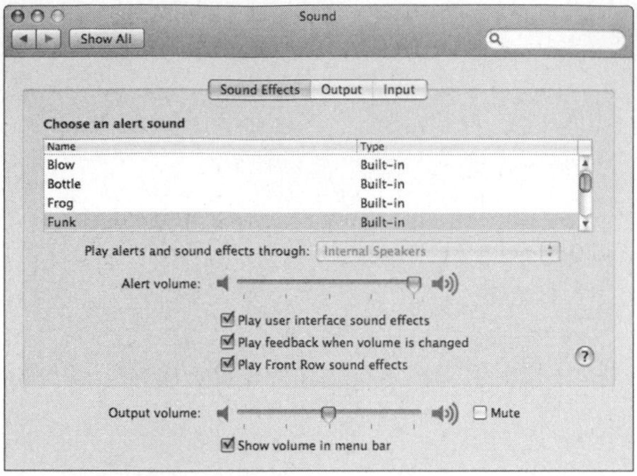

4. **Choose a sound to use for alerts from the displayed list.**

   This sound will play when your Mac needs your attention, such as when you're quitting a program without saving a document.

5. **(Optional) Drag the Alert volume slider to the desired location.**

   The Alert volume defines how loud (or soft) your Mac will beep if it needs to attract your attention.

6. **(Optional) Select (or deselect) any of the following three check boxes:**

   - *Play User Interface Sound Effects:* Lets you hear sounds such as the crinkling of paper when you empty the Trash or a whooshing sound if you remove an icon off the Dock.
   - *Play Feedback When Volume Is Changed:* Beeps to let you know that you've changed the volume and your new volume settings are active right now.
   - *Play Front Row Sound Effects:* Plays sound effects when you're using the Front Row program. (See Book II, Chapter 4 for more information about using Front Row.)

7. **(Optional) Drag the Output volume slider.**

   The Output volume defines how loud (or soft) your Mac plays any type of audio from alert beeps to audio CDs.

8. **Click the Output tab.**

   The Output preferences pane appears as shown in Figure 7-10 and defines where to play audio, such as through speakers or headphones.

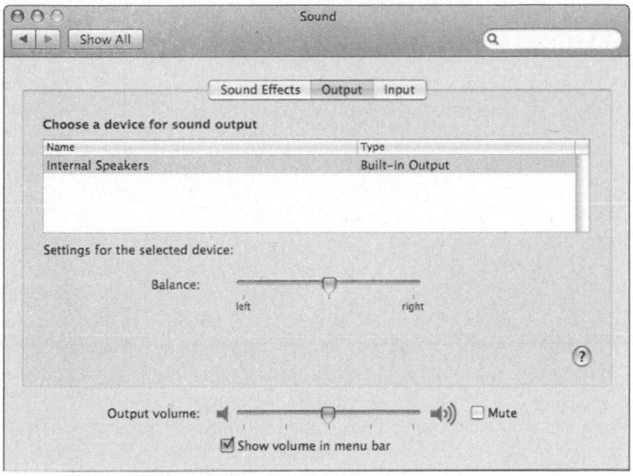

Figure 7-10: The Output preferences pane lets you define how to play sound.

9. **Click the output device you want to use.**

   If you have headphones plugged into your Mac but your Mac also has built-in speakers, you might want to make all sound play through the headphones to avoid annoying anyone around you.

10. **(Optional) Drag the Balance slider to adjust the balance.**

11. **(Optional) Select (or deselect) the Show Volume in Menu Bar check box.**

    If selected, this lets you adjust the volume through a menulet in the menu bar.

12. **Click the Input tab.**

    The Input preferences pane appears, as shown in Figure 7-11. Input defines where your Mac can receive sound, such as through a microphone or through its Line In port, which lets you plug a stereo or TV directly into a Mac to record sound.

13. **Click the input device you want to use.**

    This option lets you choose whether to accept input from a microphone or other device connected through the Line In port. If you want to record your voice, choose microphone. If you plan to record sound from a device plugged into the Line In port, such as a radio or television set, choose Line In.

14. **(Optional) Drag the Input volume slider to adjust the default input volume.**

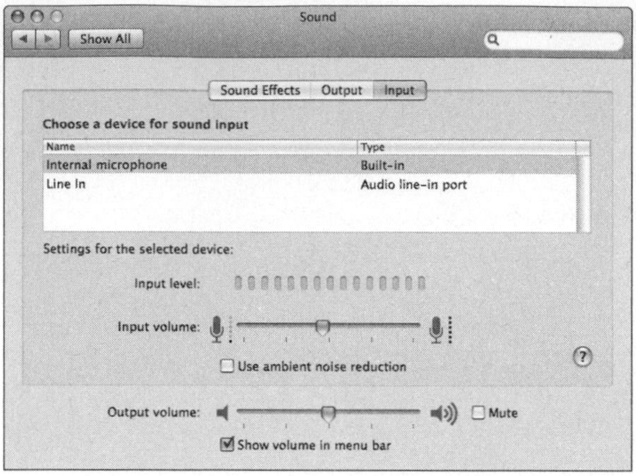

Figure 7-11: The Input preferences pane lets you define how to record sound.

15. **(Optional) Select (or deselect) the Use Ambient Noise Reduction check box.**

    If selected, this feature tries to eliminate background noise but can also accidentally eliminate valid input audio.

16. **Click the Close button of the System Preferences window when you're done.**

Saving Energy

It turns out your Mac can shut off its screen and hard drive if you don't touch the keyboard or mouse after a certain period of time. By reducing its power in this fashion, your Mac can save energy, which can be especially important for a MacBook running on batteries.

To define the energy-conserving features of your Mac, follow these steps:

1. **Choose ⇨System Preferences from the Finder menu.**

   The System Preferences window appears.

2. **Click the Energy Saver icon under the Hardware category.**

   The Energy Saver preferences pane appears.

   Note: If you're using a Mac laptop, you'll see a Settings For pop-up menu and an Optimization pop-up menu so you can define separate settings when your laptop is plugged in and when it's running off batteries. If you're using a desktop Mac, skip to Step 5.

3. **(Optional) Click in the Settings For pop-up menu and choose Power Adapter or Battery.**

4. **Choose an appropriate setting from the Optimization pop-up menu.**

Better Energy Savings would be a good choice. Better Performance makes your Mac run faster but at the cost of consuming more energy, which could drain a laptop Mac's batteries. Normal makes your Mac consume power like a desktop Mac.

5. **Click the Show Details button.**

The Energy Saver preferences pane expands, as shown in Figure 7-12.

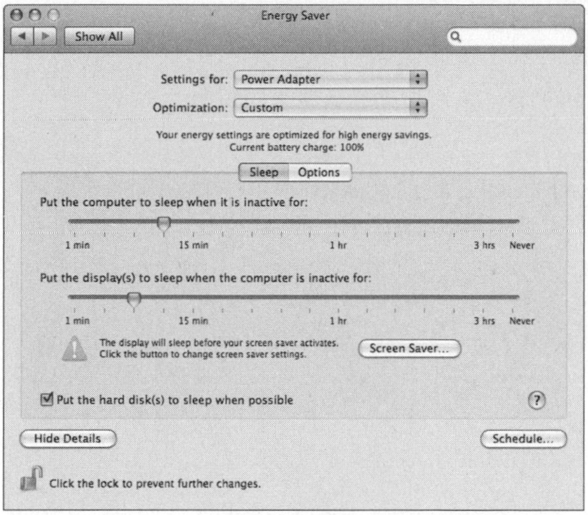

Figure 7-12: The Energy Saver preferences pane lets you define when to put your computer to sleep.

6. **Drag the Put the Computer to Sleep When It Is Inactive For slider to the desired length of time.**

This option uses the term *Computer* to mean the actual microprocessor (such as an Intel Core 2 Duo) used in your Mac. Putting the microprocessor to sleep lowers the amount of energy that the microprocessor consumes.

7. **Drag the Put the Display to Sleep When the Computer Is Inactive For slider.**

The "display" refers to your monitor. Putting the monitor to sleep blanks out the monitor to consume less power.

8. **Select (or deselect) the Put the Hard Disk(s) to Sleep When Possible check box.**

This option reduces power to stop the hard drive from spinning, thus conserving energy.

9. **Click the Close button of the System Preferences window.**

Picking a Printer

To use a printer, your Mac must use a special program called a *printer driver,* which basically tells your Mac how to use your printer. When you buy a new printer, it often comes with a CD that contains a printer driver. If you have an older printer, your Mac might already have a copy of the necessary printer driver.

Making your Mac work with your printer involves a two-step process. First, you must physically connect your printer to your Mac, usually through a USB cable or network connection. Second, you must install the proper printer driver on your Mac. After you have your printer connected to your Mac (with the proper printer driver installed), you can control that printer through your Mac.

TIP

You can download printer drivers (and drivers for other types of hardware such as scanners and pressure-sensitive tablets) directly from Apple's Web site (`www.apple.com/downloads/macosx/drivers`) or from the printer manufacturer's Web site.

Adding (and deleting) a printer

After you've physically connected a printer to your Mac and installed its printer driver, you might need to take one additional step and tell your Mac that this particular printer is connected. To get your Mac to recognize a connected printer, follow these steps:

1. **Choose ⇨System Preferences from the Finder menu.**

   The System Preferences window appears.

2. **Click the Print & Fax icon under the Hardware category.**

   The Print & Fax preferences pane appears.

3. **Click the plus sign icon, as shown in Figure 7-13.**

   A window appears, listing all printers connected to your Mac.

   Note: Your Mac might list local printers (printers directly attached to your Mac) as well as printers linked to your Mac over a network.

4. **Click a printer name in the Printers list and then click the Close button of the System Preferences window.**

   The specified printer is added to the list of available printers.

If you disconnect your printer for any reason, your Mac might still try to use the printer anyway. To prevent this, you need to delete a printer from your Mac's list of printers. To delete a printer, follow the same steps you used to add a printer, but in the Printers list, select the printer to delete and then click the minus sign icon. Then close the window.

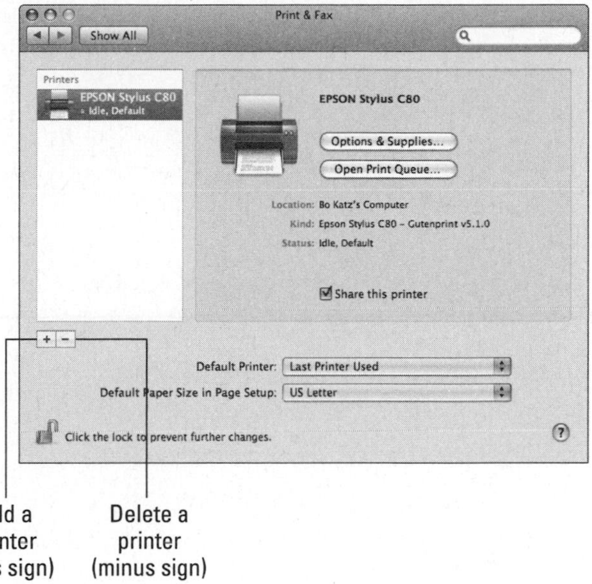

Figure 7-13: The Print & Fax preferences pane lets you add or delete printers.

Defining a default printer

If you have two or more printers hooked up to your Mac, programs won't always know which printer to use. So that's why every Mac always picks a single default printer. This default printer is simply the printer that every Mac program will use unless you specify otherwise.

To define a default printer, follow these steps:

1. **Choose ⇨System Preferences from the Finder menu.**

   The System Preferences window appears.

2. **Click the Print & Fax icon under the Hardware category.**

   The Print & Fax preferences pane appears (refer to Figure 7-13).

3. **Choose a printer name (or just choose Last Printer Used) from the Default Printer pop-up menu.**
4. **Click the Close button of the System Preferences window.**

Creating Separate Accounts

One problem with changing the screen saver or desktop background is that if several people share the same Mac, not everyone will be happy with the same images. Rather than buy separate Mac computers for everyone, you can do the next best thing and divide a single Mac into separate accounts.

An account essentially gives a Mac a split personality. If you create three accounts on your Mac, each account can have its own screen saver and desktop background image. Even better, you can use each account to create and modify files and folders without affecting any other accounts. By using accounts, you can give each person the illusion that they're the sole user of a Mac.

Types of accounts

The first time you turn on your Mac, you have to create an account that consists of a username and password. Multiple people can share a single account, but this increases the risk that someone might delete an important file that belongs to somebody else. It's a better bet to set up multiple accounts on the Mac for multiple users.

You can create four types of accounts:

- **Administrator:** Gives the user access to create, modify, and delete accounts. You should limit the number of Administrator accounts you have to perhaps one or two (one for each parent in a household). Note that when you turned on your Mac for the first time, you created an Administrator account.
- **Standard:** Gives the user access to the Mac but doesn't let the user create, modify, or delete any additional accounts.
- **Managed with Parental Controls:** Gives the user restricted access to the computer, based on the parental controls defined by an Administrator account.
- **Guest:** Gives the user access but doesn't let the user save any files.

Even if you're the only person using your Mac, you might want to consider creating a Standard account. That way you can use the Standard account to browse the Internet or read your e-mail. Now, if some malicious hacker develops a new virus, Trojan horse, or spyware program that can infect Mac computers, the malicious program will be able to infect only the Standard account. Any important files, such as your entire Mac OS X operating system files, will stay isolated in your Administrator account and will remain safe. Think of accounts as dividing a Mac into separate watertight compartments that actually work, unlike those found on the Titanic.

REMEMBER

This section takes a look at how to create accounts in general, but Book III, Chapter 4 specifically explains how to create and manage Guest and Managed with Parental Controls accounts.

WARNING!

The number one reason to have only one Administrator account is to protect yourself. If you create two or more Administrator accounts, anyone using those other Administrator accounts now has full power to erase your Administrator account along with all of your important files. If you have the only Administrator account, no one else can delete your account or files.

Creating an account

Before you create an account, you need to decide the type of account to create as well as come up with the username and password to access that account. To create an account, follow these steps:

1. **Choose ✇System Preferences from the Finder menu.**

   The System Preferences window appears.
2. **Click on the Accounts icon under the System category.**

   The Accounts preferences pane appears, as shown in Figure 7-14.
3. **Click the Lock icon in the bottom-left corner to gain the ability to create accounts.**

   A dialog appears, asking for your password.
4. **Type your password in the Password text box and click OK.**
5. **Click the Add Account (plus sign) icon.**

   A New Account dialog appears, as shown in Figure 7-15.

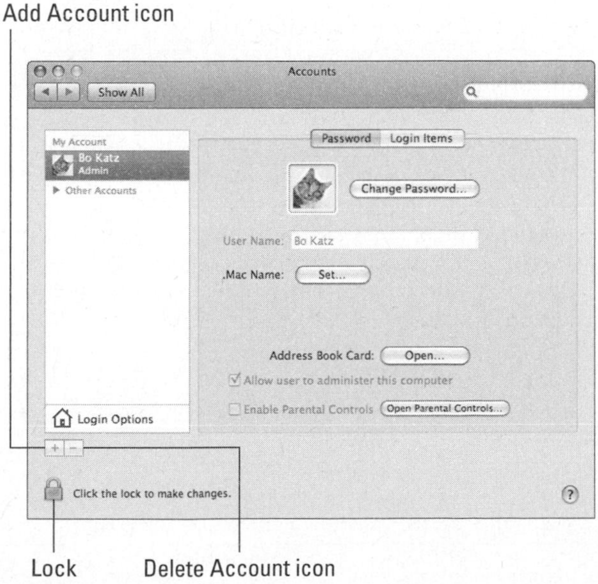

Figure 7-14: The Accounts preferences pane shows you all current accounts created on your Mac.

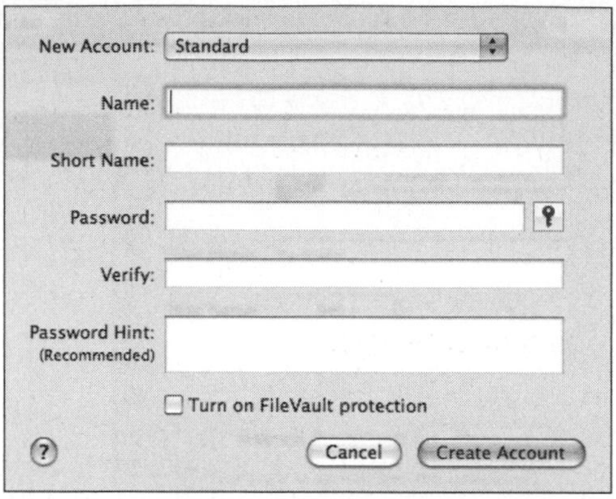

Figure 7-15: The New Account dialog lets you define your new account.

6. **Choose an account type from the New Account pop-up menu.**

   Standard would be a good choice.

7. **Enter the name of the person who'll be using the account into the Name text box.**
8. **(Optional) Click in the Short Name text box and modify the short name for the account that your Mac automatically creates.**
9. **Click in the Password text box and type a password for this account.**
10. **Click in the Verify text box and retype the password you chose in Step 9.**
11. **(Optional) Click in the Password Hint text box and type a descriptive phrase you think will help you remember your password.**
12. **(Optional) Select the Turn On FileVault Protection check box, which will allow the account user to encrypt files.**

    If you allow users to encrypt files, they'll be able to hide the contents of their files even from anyone with an Administrator account. Turning on FileVault protection can also slow down your Mac, since it needs to spend additional time encrypting and decrypting your files.

    If you turn on FileVault encryption and forget your password, your encrypted data is as good as gone because you won't be able to access it.

13. **Click the Create Account button.**

    You are returned to the Accounts preferences pane, which now displays the name of your new account. A dialog appears, asking whether you want to turn automatic log in on or off. (When you had only one account, your Mac would automatically log in to that account. With multiple accounts, your Mac won't know which account to log in to unless you specify an account.)

14. **Click Keep Automatic Login to log in to your Administrator account at startup, or click Turn Off Automatic Login, which requires you to choose an account to use each time you turn on your Mac.**
15. **Click the Close button of the System Preferences window.**

Switching between accounts

The Mac offers several ways to switch between accounts. The most straightforward way is to log out of one account and then log back in to a different account. A faster and more convenient way is to use Fast User Switching, which essentially lets you switch accounts without having to log out of one account first.

To log out of an account, simply choose ⇨Log Out. After you log out, a window appears, listing the names and icons of all accounts. At this time, you can click a different account name to log in to that account.

Before you can log out, you must close any files and shut down any running programs. If you used Fast User Switching, you wouldn't have to bother with any of that, because Fast User Switching temporarily pauses one account while your Mac opens another account.

Intrigued? Read the next section to find out more.

Enabling Fast User Switching

Before you can use Fast User Switching, you have to turn on this feature by following these steps:

1. **Make sure you are logged into your Administrator account.**
2. **Choose ⇨System Preferences from the Finder menu.**

   The System Preferences window appears.
3. **Click the Accounts icon that appears under System category.**

   The Accounts preferences pane appears (refer to Figure 7-14).
4. **Click the Lock icon in the lower-left corner of the Accounts window to allow you to edit your accounts.**

   A dialog appears, asking for your password.
5. **Type your password and then click OK.**
6. **Click the Login Options icon near the bottom-left corner of the Accounts window.**

Your Login Options appear in the right pane, as shown in Figure 7-16.

7. **Select (or deselect) the Enable Fast User Switching check box.**

   If you select this check box, a dialog appears, warning you that Fast User Switching leaves programs running, which could pose a security risk if another account is running a malicious program, such as a program that records keystrokes.

8. **Click OK.**

9. **Click in the View As pop-up menu and choose how you want to display the Faster User Switching menu: Name, Short Name, or Icon.**

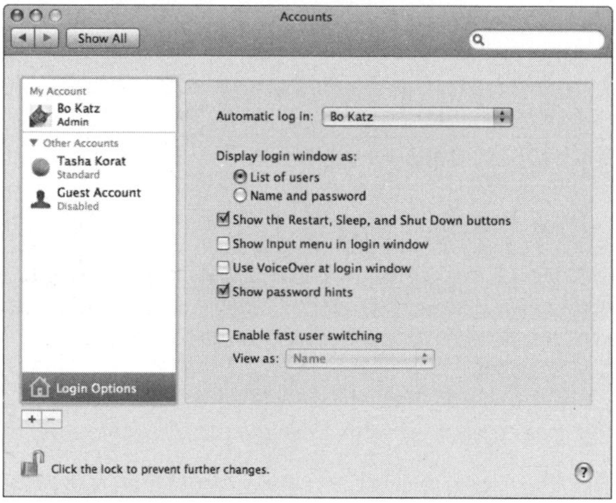

Figure 7-16: The Login Options appear in the right pane.

   These options display what appears on the menulet. Name displays the full account names, Short Name displays abbreviated account names, and Icon displays the icon associated with each account.

10. **Click the Close button of the System Preferences window.**

    The Fast User Switching menulet appears in the right side of the menu bar, as shown in Figure 7-17.

Changing accounts with Fast User Switching

After you enable Fast User Switching, you can switch to a different account at any time by following these steps:

1. **Click the Fast User Switching menulet on the right side of the menu bar.**

   A menu appears (refer to Figure 7-17).

Figure 7-17: The Fast User Switching menulet displays the names of all accounts you can choose.

2. **Click the account name you want to use.**

   A dialog appears, asking for the password to this account.

3. **Type the account password and press Return.**

   Your Mac switches you to your chosen account.

Deleting an account

After you've created one or more accounts, you might want to delete them. When you delete an account, your Mac gives you the option of retaining the account's Home folder, which might contain important files. To delete an account, follow these steps:

1. **Make sure the account you want to delete is logged out.**
2. **Make sure you are logged into your Administrator account.**
3. **Choose ⇨System Preferences from the Finder menu.**

   The System Preferences window appears.

4. **Click the Accounts icon that appears under System category.**

   The Accounts preferences pane appears (refer to Figure 7-14).

5. **Click the Lock icon in the bottom-left corner of the Accounts preferences pane to allow you to edit your accounts.**

   A dialog appears, asking for your password.

6. **Type your password and press Return.**
7. **Select the account you want to delete in the accounts list of the Accounts preferences pane.**
8. **Click the Delete Account icon (the minus sign) in the lower-left corner of the Accounts preferences pane.**

   A dialog appears, asking whether you really want to delete this account and also asking whether you want to save the Home folder of this account, as shown in Figure 7-18.

- *Save the Home Folder in a Disk Image:* Saves the home folder and its contents in a compressed disk image (DMG) file. This keeps the files compressed and out of the way, but they're available in case you need to find them later. This is like stuffing stuff in an attic to get it out of sight, but still keeping it around in case you suddenly need it.
- *Do Not Change the Home Folder:* Keeps the home folder and all its contents so you can browse through the saved files later.
- *Delete the Home Folder:* Wipes out any files the user might have created in the account.

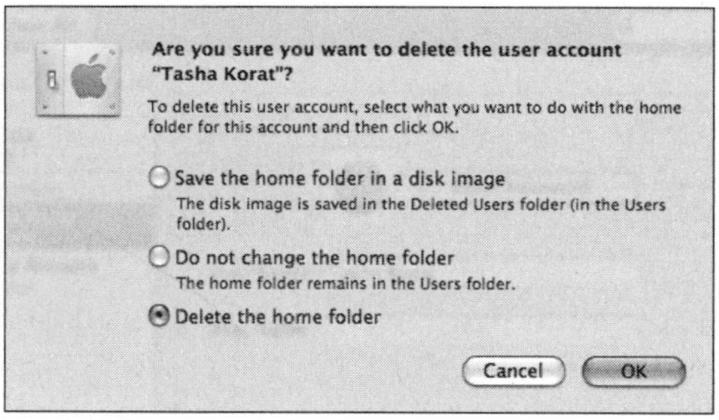
Are you sure you want to delete the user account "Tasha Korat"?
To delete this user account, select what you want to do with the home folder for this account and then click OK.
Save the home folder in a disk image
The disk image is saved in the Deleted Users folder (in the Users folder).
Do not change the home folder
The home folder remains in the Users folder.
Delete the home folder
Cancel
OK

Figure 7-18: Do you really want to delete?

9. **Select a radio button (such as Delete the Home Folder) and click OK.**

   Your Mac deletes the specified account.

Chapter 8: Accessibility Features of the Macintosh

In This Chapter

- Making the Mac accessible
- Recognizing handwriting
- Talking to your Mac

Right out of the box, every Mac behaves exactly the same. This can be a good thing because it means you can use any Mac anywhere and expect it to work the same — whether the Mac is in New Jersey or Norway.

Unfortunately, not everyone has perfect eyesight, hearing, or eye-hand coordination. If you have trouble with your vision, hearing, or movement, using a computer can be difficult. That's why every Mac comes with special universal access features that you can turn on and modify. These universal access features fall under four different categories:

- Seeing
- Hearing
- Keyboard
- Mouse and trackpad

Correcting Vision Limitations

To help the visually impaired, every Mac includes a feature called VoiceOver, which essentially lets your Mac read text, e-mail, and even descriptions of the screen to you in a computer-generated voice. For partially sighted users, the Mac can magnify images on the screen or change the contrast of the screen to make it easier to read. To modify the vision features of your Mac, follow these steps:

1. **Choose ⇨System Preferences.**

   The System Preferences window appears.

2. **Click the Universal Access icon under the System category.**

   The Universal Access preferences pane appears.

3. **Click the Seeing tab.**

   The Seeing preferences pane appears, as shown in Figure 8-1.

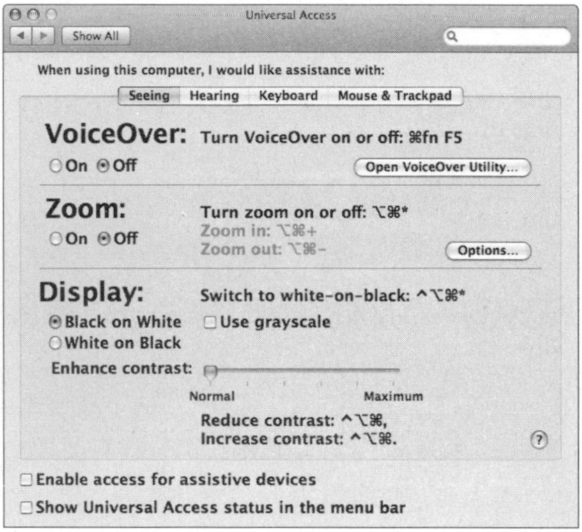

Figure 8-1: The Seeing preferences pane displays options for making the Mac easier to use for the visually impaired.

4. **Click either the On or the Off radio button for the VoiceOver feature.**

   VoiceOver allows your Mac to describe what's on the screen and assist you in using the Macintosh menus.

   TIP: If you also click the Open VoiceOver Utility button, you can customize the way VoiceOver works such as how fast your Mac speaks and the type of computer synthesized voice it uses.

5. **Click either the On or the Off radio button for the Zoom feature.**

   If turned on, the Zoom feature allows you to magnify the screen by pressing Option+⌘+(plus sign) or shrink the screen by pressing Option+⌘+(minus sign).

6. **Under the Display heading, select either the Black on White or White on Black radio button.**

   Some people prefer Black on White (like the pages in this book), but others prefer the greater contrast of White on Black.

7. **Still under the Display heading, drag the Enhance Contrast slider to increase/decrease the screen contrast.**

   Contrast can make the edges of windows and menus easier to see.

8. **Select or deselected the Enable Access for Assistive Devices check box.**

This option allows external devices (such as unique keyboards or mice) to use AppleScript to control the Mac user interface.

9. **Select or deselect the Show Universal Access Status in the Menu Bar check box.**

   If selected, this option displays a Universal Access menulet on the menu bar, allowing you to turn different Universal Access features on or off.

10. **Click the Close button of the System Preferences window, or choose System Preferences⇨Quit System Preferences.**

Correcting hearing limitations

To adjust for hearing impairments, you can increase the volume for your various system alerts or you can have your Mac flash the screen to catch your attention instead. To flash the screen instead of making a beeping noise, follow these steps:

1. **Choose ⇨System Preferences.**

   The System Preferences window appears.

2. **Click the Universal Access icon under the System category.**

   The Universal Access preferences pane appears.

3. **Click the Hearing tab.**

   The Hearing preferences pane appears as shown in Figure 8-2.

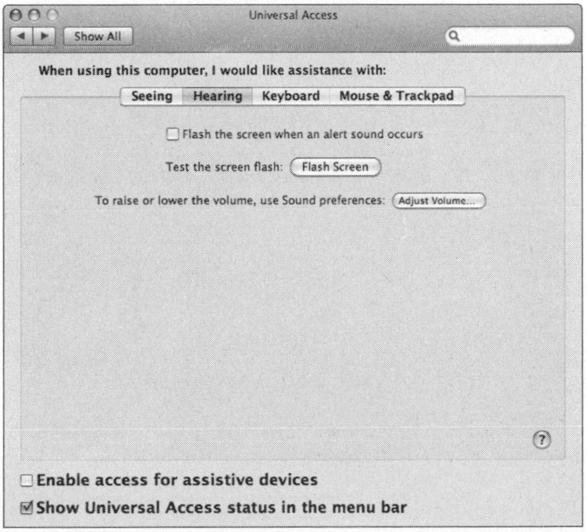

Figure 8-2: The Hearing preferences pane gives you the option of flashing the screen to alert you.

4. **Select (or deselect) the Flash the Screen When an Alert Sound Occurs check box.**
5. **Click the Flash Screen button to see how your Mac will alert you by flashing the screen.**
6. **(Optional) To increase the volume for your various system alerts, click the Adjust Volume button to open the Sound Preferences dialog, where you can then adjust the system volume to your heart's content.**
7. **Choose System Preferences⇨Quit System Preferences.**

Correcting keyboard limitations

If you have physical limitations using the keyboard, the Mac offers two solutions: the Sticky Keys feature and the Slow Keys feature. Sticky Keys can help you use keystroke shortcuts, such as ⌘+P (Print), which usually require pressing two or more keys at the same time. By turning on Sticky Keys feature, you can use keystroke shortcuts by pressing one key at a time. The first key you press, such as the ⌘ key, "sticks" in place and waits until you press a second key to complete the keystroke shortcut.

The Slow Keys feature slows down the reaction time of the Mac every time you press a key. Normally when you press a key, the Mac accepts it right away, but the Slow Key feature can force a Mac to wait a long period of time before accepting the typed key. That way, your Mac will ignore any accidental taps on the keyboard and patiently wait until you hold down a key for a designated period of time before it accepts it as valid.

To turn on the Sticky or Slow Keys features, follow these steps:

1. **Choose ⇨System Preferences.**

   The System Preferences window appears.
2. **Click the Universal Access icon under the System category.**

   The Universal Access preferences pane appears.
3. **Click the Keyboard tab.**

   The Keyboard preferences pane appears, as shown in Figure 8-3.
4. **Select the On radio button for the Sticky Keys feature.**
5. **(Optional) Select the Press the Shift key Five Times to Turn Sticky Keys On or Off check box.**

   This lets you turn thc Sticky Keys feature on or off through the keyboard.

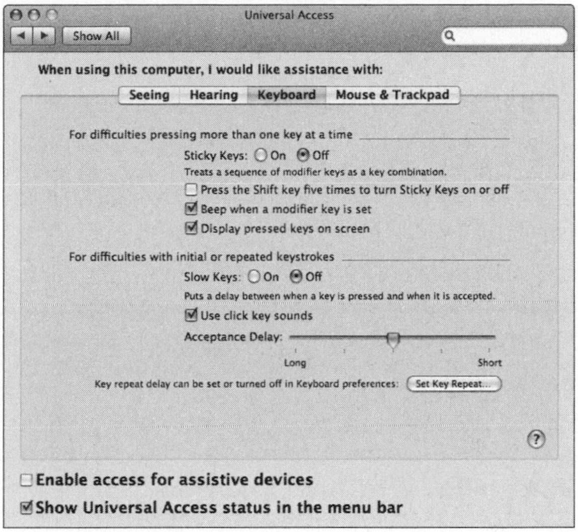

Figure 8-3: The Keyboard preferences pane lets you adjust the behavior of the keyboard.

6. **(Optional) Select the Beep When a Modifier Key Is Set check box.**

   This alerts you when you've pressed a so-called "modifier" key — a key such as Option or ⌘ — which is used in combination with another key to modify how that key works.

7. **Select or deselect the Display Pressed Keys On Screen check box.**

   If this check box is selected, any modifier keys you press (such as the ⌘ or Option key) are displayed on-screen in the upper-right corner of the screen, so you can verify that you've pressed the right key.

8. **Select the On radio button for the Slow Keys feature.**

9. **(Optional) Select the Use Click Key Sounds check box.**

   When selected, this option makes a clicking sound every time you press a key to give you audible feedback when you've typed something.

10. **Drag the Acceptance Delay slider to the desired location.**

    Dragging to the left lengthens the time between pressing the key and computer response, and dragging to the right shortens the time.

11. **Click the Close button of the System Preferences window or choose System Preferences⇨Quit System Preferences.**

Correcting mouse limitations

If you have physical limitations related to using the keyboard, you might also have trouble using the mouse or trackpad. If you have trouble using the mouse, you can turn on the Mouse Keys feature, which lets you control the mouse through the numeric keys, as shown in Table 8-1.

Table 8-1 Mouse Key Commands

Numeric Key	*What It Does*
9	Moves the pointer diagonally up to the right
8	Moves the pointer straight up
7	Moves the pointer diagonally up to the left
6	Moves the pointer to the right
5	"Clicks" the mouse button
4	Moves the pointer to the left
3	Moves the pointer diagonally down to the right
2	Moves the pointer down
1	Moves the pointer diagonally down to the left
0	"Right-clicks" the right mouse button

REMEMBER

The Mouse Keys feature is really designed for keyboards that have a separate numeric keypad. If you're using a laptop or other keyboard that doesn't have a separate numeric keypad, the numeric keys will be embedded in the regular typewriter keys. To control the mouse, you have to turn on the Number Lock key to use the numeric keys to move the mouse. Then you have to press the Number Lock key again to use the keys for typing ordinary letters once more.

The Mouse Keys feature can replace the mouse altogether or just provide you with another way to move the mouse. No matter how you plan to move the mouse, you might still have trouble finding it on the screen. Fortunately, you can enlarge the size of the pointer to make it easy to spot and use.

To turn on the Mouse Keys feature or change the size of the pointer, follow these steps:

1. **Choose ⇨System Preferences.**

   The System Preferences window appears.

2. **Click the Universal Access icon under the System category.**

   The Universal Access preferences pane appears.

3. **Click the Mouse & Trackpad tab.**

   The Mouse & Trackpad preferences pane appears, as shown in Figure 8-4.

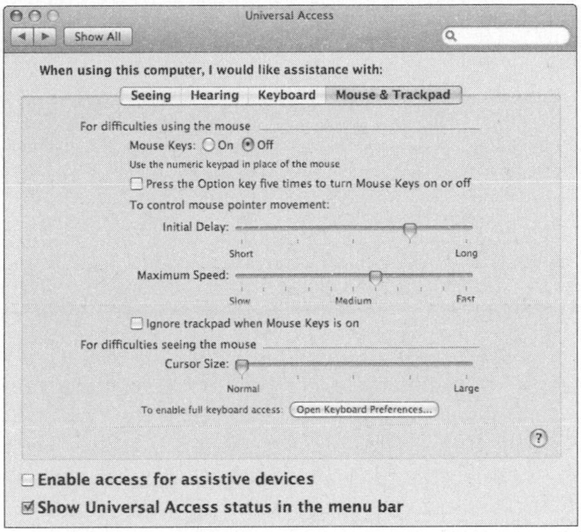

Figure 8-4: The Mouse & Trackpad pane lets you adjust the size of the pointer and determine whether to control the mouse with the keyboard.

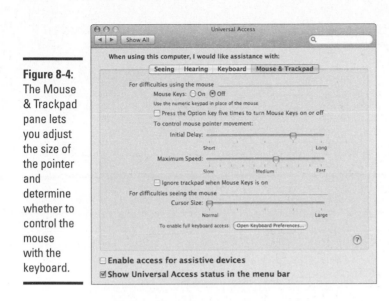

4. **Select the On radio button for the Mouse Keys feature.**
5. **(Optional) Select the Press the Option Key Five Times to Turn Mouse Keys On or Off check box.**

   This lets you turn the Mouse Keys feature on or off from the keyboard.
6. **Drag the Initial Delay slider to define how long the Mac waits before moving the pointer with the numeric key.**

   A short value means the Mac might immediately move the pointer as soon as you press a number key. A long value means you must hold down a numeric key for a longer period of time before it starts moving the pointer.
7. **Drag the Maximum Speed slider to adjust how fast the Mouse Keys feature moves the pointer with the keyboard.**
8. **(Optional) Select the Ignore Trackpad When Mouse Keys Is On check box.**

   Doing so prevents the trackpad from detecting any movement and misinterpreting those movements as mouse commands.
9. **Drag the Cursor Size slider to adjust the size of the pointer on the screen.**

   Again, enlarging the size of the pointer can make it easier to spot and use.
10. **Click the Close button of the Universal Access window or choose System Preferences⇨Quit System Preferences.**

Using Voice Recognition and Speech

For the visually impaired, the Mac offers both voice recognition and speech capabilities. The voice recognition feature lets you control your Mac using spoken commands, and the speech capability lets your Mac read text or beep to alert you when something happens, such as a dialog popping up on the screen.

Setting up voice recognition

To use the Mac's built-in voice recognition software, you have to define its settings and then assign specific types of commands to your voice. Defining the voice recognition settings means choosing how to turn on voice recognition and how your Mac will acknowledge that it received your voice commands correctly. For example, your Mac may wait until you press the Esc key or speak a certain word before it starts listening to voice commands. When it understands your command, it can beep.

To define the voice recognition settings, follow these steps:

1. **Choose ⌘⇨System Preferences.**

   The System Preferences window appears.

2. **Click the Speech icon under the System category.**

   The Speech preferences pane appears.

3. **Click the Speech Recognition tab.**

   The Speech Recognition preferences pane appears, as shown in Figure 8-5.

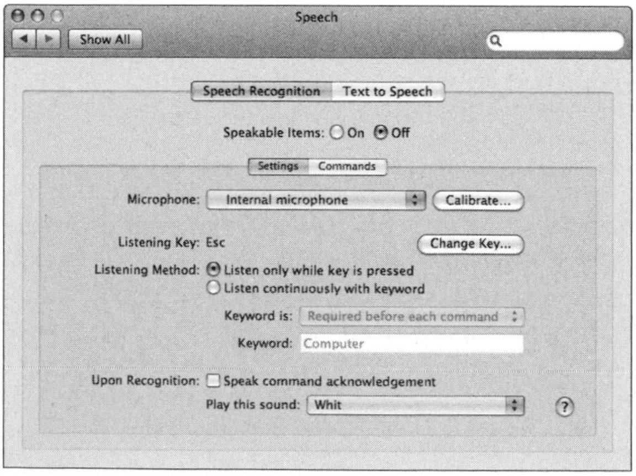

Figure 8-5: The Speech Recognition preferences pane lets you define how to get your Mac to recognize spoken commands.

4. **Click the On radio button for the Speakable Items feature.**

   Turning on this feature lets you control your Mac by giving spoken commands.

5. **Choose an appropriate device for accepting your spoken commands from the Microphone pop-up menu.**

   Internal Microphone would be an obvious choice here unless you happen to have an external microphone connected to your Mac.

6. **Click Calibrate.**

   A Microphone Calibration dialog appears, as shown in Figure 8-6.

7. **Recite the phrases displayed in the Microphone Calibration dialog and adjust the slider until your Mac recognizes your spoken commands.**

   A command phrase in the listing blinks when the computer recognizes your phrasing of the command.

8. **When all phrases are recognized by the computer, click Done.**

   You're returned to the Speech Recognition tab in the Speech dialog.

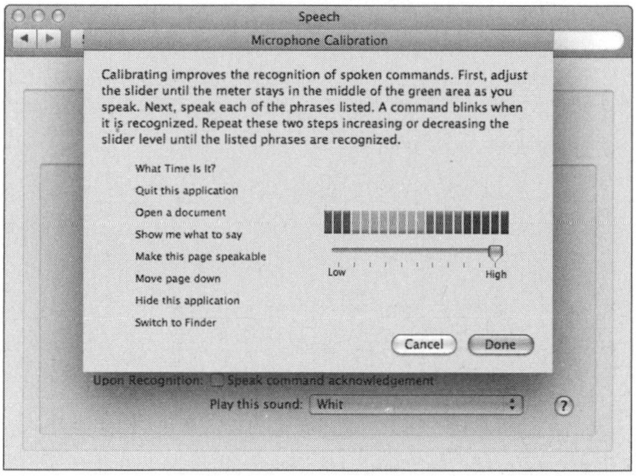

Figure 8-6: The Microphone Calibration dialog lets you train your Mac to your voice.

9. **Click the Change Key button.**

   A dialog appears, as shown in Figure 8-7, asking you to press a key to alert your Mac when you plan to start giving it spoken commands. (The default key is Esc.)

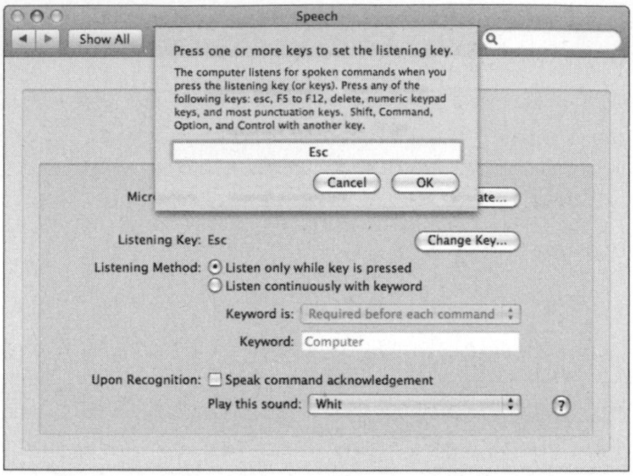

Figure 8-7: A dialog lets you define a listening key to alert your Mac when you'll start giving spoken commands.

10. **Press a key (such as F15 or Esc) and then click OK.**

You're once again returned to the Speech Recognition dialog.

11. **Select one of the following radio buttons in the Listening Method category:**

- *Listen Only while Key Is Pressed:* Your Mac only accepts spoken commands as long as you hold down the listening key defined in step #10.
- *Listen Continuously with Keyword:* Your Mac waits to hear a spoken keyword (such as "Computer" or "Hey, stupid!") before accepting additional spoken commands.

If you chose the Listen Continuously with Keyword radio button, click the Keyword Is pop-up menu and choose one of the following:

- *Optional before Commands:* Your Mac listens for spoken commands all the time. This can make it easier to given spoken commands, but it also means your Mac might misinterpret the radio or background conversations as commands.
- *Required before Each Command:* You must speak the keyword before your Mac will accept spoken commands.
- *Required 15 Seconds after Last Command:* You must repeat the keyword within 15 seconds after each command.
- *Required 30 Seconds after Last Command:* Same as the preceding option except the Mac waits up to 30 seconds for the next spoken commands.

12. **Click in the Keyword text box and type your keyword to speak to the Mac.**

The default keyword is *Computer.*

13. **(Optional) Select the Upon Recognition: Speak Command Acknowledgement check box.**

14. **If you selected the Upon Recognition: Speak Command Acknowledgement check box, choose a sound from the Play This Sound pop-up menu to make your Mac play an acknowledging noise when it recognizes a command.**

15. **Click the Commands subtab.**

    The Commands subtab appears, as shown in Figure 8-8.

16. **Select the check boxes for one or more of the following command sets:**

    - *Address Book:* Listens for names stored in your Address Book.
    - *Global Speakable Items:* Listens for common commands applicable to any situation, such as asking the computer, "What time is it?"

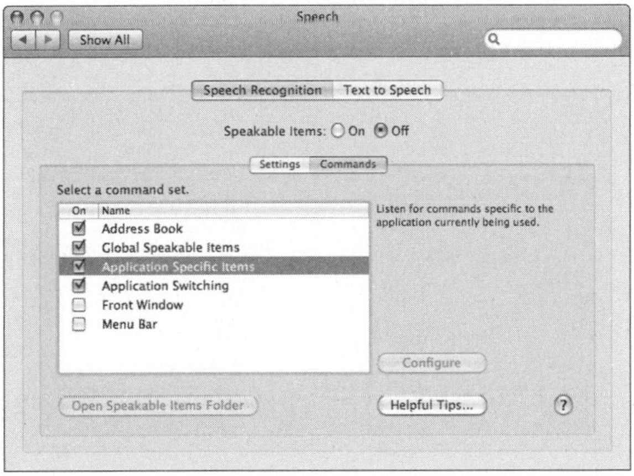

Figure 8-8: The Commands subtab lets you assign different actions to voice commands.

- *Application Specific Items:* Listens for commands specific to each application. A word processor might have a Format menu and commands, but an audio-editing program might not.
- *Application Switching:* Listens for commands to switch between, start, or quit programs.
- *Front Window:* Listens for the commands to control specific items in the currently displayed window, such as telling the computer to click a button or check box.
- *Menu Bar:* Listens for commands to display pull-down menus and choose a command.

17. **Click the Close button of the System Preferences window or choose System Preferences⇨Quit System Preferences.**

If you find the Mac's built-in voice recognition features too clumsy to use, consider buying separate programs that let you control your Mac with your voice. Two popular voice-recognition programs for the Mac are iListen (`www.macspeech.com`) and IBM ViaVoice (`www.nuance.com/viavoice`).

Setting up speech capabilities

Your Mac has a collection of different computer-synthesized voices that can read text to you or alert you when something occurs, such as when you try to quit a program without saving a document. To define the speech capabilities of your Mac, follow these steps:

1. **Choose ⌘⇨System Preferences.**

   The System Preferences window appears.

2. **Click the Speech icon under the System category.**

   The Speech preferences pane appears.

3. **Click the Text to Speech tab.**

   The Text to Speech preferences pane appears, as shown in Figure 8-9.

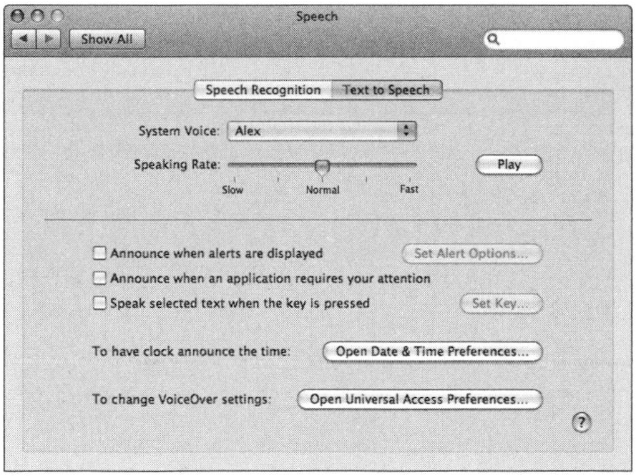

Figure 8-9: The Text to Speech preferences pane lets you define the synthesized voice characteristics of your Mac.

4. **Choose a synthesized voice from the System Voice pop-up menu.**

   There's Alex and Agnes and even Victoria.

5. **Drag the Speaking Rate slider to the desired location (somewhere between Slow, Normal, and Fast) and then click Play to hear your chosen synthesized voice at the specified speaking rate.**

6. **(Optional) Select the Announce When Alerts are Displayed check box.**

This makes your Mac speak when it needs your attention. (You might be given a message saying you don't have enough room on your hard drive to save a file, for example.)

7. **If you chose to select the Announce When Alerts are Displayed check box in Step 6, click the Set Alert Options button.**

   A dialog appears, as shown in Figure 8-10, letting you define how the Mac should speak an alert.

8. **Make any changes you want in the Set Alert Options dialog and then click OK.**

   You are returned to the Text to Speech preferences pane.

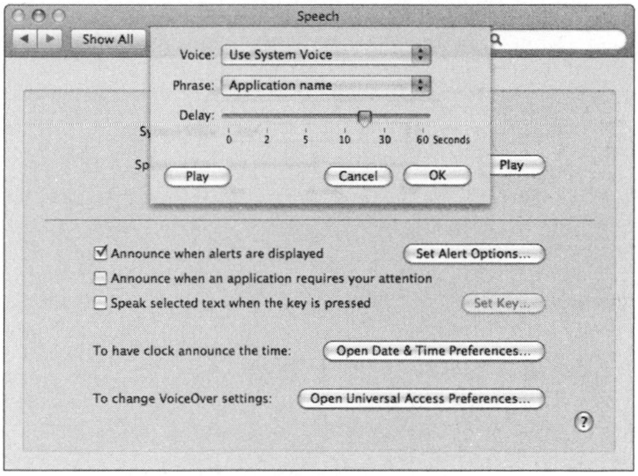

Figure 8-10: This dialog lets you customize which voice and phrase to speak along with a delay time.

8. **(Optional) Select the Announce When an Application Requires Your Attention check box.**

   This makes your Mac speak when a specific program needs additional information from you, such as when you try to close a file without saving it first.

9. **(Optional) Select the Speak Selected Text When the Key Is Pressed check box and then click the Set Key button.**

   A dialog appears, as shown in Figure 8-11, letting you press a key combination (such as ⌘+F16) to tell the Mac when to start reading any text you may have selected.

10. **Press a keystroke combination and then click OK.**

    Once again, you're back at the Text to Speech preferences pane.

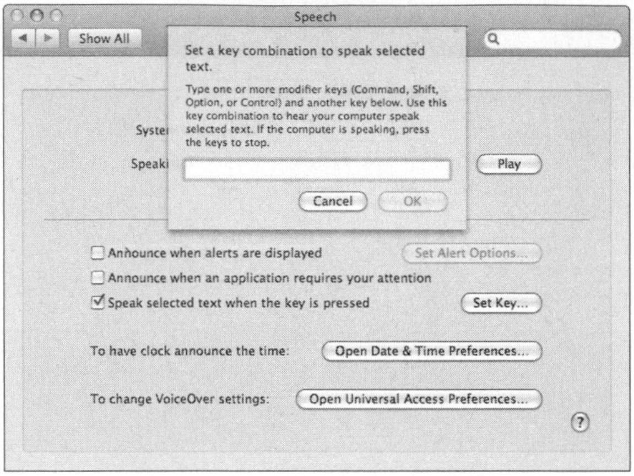

Figure 8-11: A dialog lets you define a keystroke combination to tell the Mac when to start speaking selected text.

11. **Click the Close button of the System Preferences window or choose System Preferences⇨Quit System Preferences.**

TIP

To find different types of keyboards and mice designed to make controlling your computer even more comfortable, search for *"ergonomic input devices"* using your favorite Internet search engine. The search engine will display a list of Web sites selling everything from left-handed keyboards and mice to foot pedals and keyboards designed to type in letters by pressing multiple keys like piano chords.

Ultimately, you don't have to settle for the ordinary keyboard and mouse that comes with your Mac. For a little extra money, you can buy the perfect keyboard and mouse that can make your Mac more comfortable for you to use.

Chapter 9: Maintenance and Troubleshooting

In This Chapter

- Handling startup troubles
- Taking care of program freezes and hang-ups
- Unjamming jammed CDs/DVDs
- Troubleshooting disk problems and repairs
- Performing routine maintenance

No matter how well-designed and well-built a Mac is, it's still a machine, and all machines are liable to break down through no fault of your own. Many times, you can fix minor problems with a little bit of knowledge and willingness to poke and prod around your Mac. However, sometimes your Mac might be in more serious trouble than you can fix, so don't be afraid to take your Mac into your friendly neighborhood computer repair store (one that specializes in repairing Macs, of course).

REMEMBER: If your Mac isn't working correctly, check the obvious things first, like making sure it's plugged in and that any connecting cables to the Mac are plugged in and secure.

WARNING! Only open your Mac if you know what you're doing. If you open the case and start fiddling around with its internal guts, you might damage your Mac.

Handling Startup Troubles

Sometimes you might press the power button to turn on your Mac — and nothing seems to happen. Other times, you might press the power button and see the usual Apple logo on the screen — and then nothing happens from that point on. If you can't start up your Mac, your Mac will be as useless as a broken PC (or one running Vista).

Before you rush your Mac to the emergency room of Mac repairs, do some simple troubleshooting yourself. At the very least, recover your important files so you won't lose them when sending your Mac to the repair shop.

Booting up in Safe Mode

If you turn on your Mac and you can't see the familiar desktop, menu bar, and Dock, don't panic just yet. The first thing to do is try to boot up your Mac in what's called *Safe Mode,* a boot sequence that loads the bare minimum of the Mac OS X operating system, just enough to get your computer running.

Many startup problems occur when nonessential programs, such as appointment reminders, automatically load and wind up interfering with other startup programs, preventing your Mac from booting up correctly. Booting up in Safe Mode cuts all nonessential programs out of the loop, so that only your core programs load. A successful boot in Safe Mode at least tells you that your Mac's core system hasn't been compromised.

By booting up your Mac in Safe Mode, you can remove any programs you recently installed and restart to see if that fixes the boot up problems. If you remove recently installed programs and problems still persist, copy any important files off your hard drive to protect your crucial data in case the hard drive is starting to fail.

To boot up in Safe Mode, follow these steps:

1. **Turn on your Mac.**
2. **Hold down the Shift key.**

You might need to hold down the Shift key until the screen shows you that your Mac is booting up, such as when the Apple logo appears on the screen

TIP

Your Mac comes with a free utility program called Disk Utility, which can repair minor problems. Third-party utility programs, such as DiskWarrior (`www.alsoft.com`), are designed to repair major problems that Disk Utility can't fix.

If the problem isn't due to other programs trying to load when you turn on your Mac, you might have a more serious problem with your hard drive. A minor problem might involve scrambled data on your hard drive that you might be able to repair with a special utility diagnostic program such as DiskWarrior (`www.alsoft.com`). A more serious problem could be physical damage to your hard drive. In that case, the only solution might be to fire up the system in Safe Mode again, copy over any critical files to a backup drive, and then replace the hard drive.

Booting from a CD/DVD

If you can't boot up from your hard drive, even in Safe Mode, and any utility program you run can't fix the problem, you might have to boot from a CD or DVD by using one of the following types of discs:

- ✦ The original Mac OS X CD/DVD
- ✦ Technical troubleshooting CDs/DVDs

Every Mac comes with a special CD/DVD that contains the entire Mac OS X operating system. The purpose of this CD/DVD is to reinstall the operating system and return your Mac to its original condition when you first brought your computer home. There are two reasons why you might want to reinstall the operating system:

- ✦ If your computer becomes so hopelessly fouled up, it might be easier to wipe out everything and start from scratch rather than try to rescue the hard drive.
- ✦ If you plan on selling or giving your Mac away, you'll want to wipe out your data and return the Mac to its original condition so someone else can personalize the Mac for themselves.

WARNING!

Wiping out your hard drive and reinstalling the operating system from scratch will also wipe out any important files stored on your hard drive, so make sure you're willing to accept this before reinstalling the operating system off a CD/DVD. Ideally, you should have all your important files backed up in a separate location, such as an external hard drive or a CD/DVD, before wiping out your hard drive completely.

The second type of CDs/DVDs you can boot from are troubleshooting discs. Apple provides the free Disk Utility program on the original installation DVD that came with your Mac. You can buy a troubleshooting CD/DVD such as DriveGenius (`www.prosofteng.com`), TechTool Pro (`www.micromat.com`), or DiskWarrior (`www.alsoft.com`). By running any of these programs directly off the CD/DVD, you can attempt to resurrect any hard drive that fails to boot up on its own. Sometimes these troubleshooting CDs/DVDs can repair a hard drive, and sometimes they can't, but if you have important files trapped on your hard drive, this option might be your only hope to retrieve your files.

The type of CD/DVD you use depends on what you want to do. Start with a technical troubleshooting CD/DVD to fix your hard drive. If you can't fix your hard drive, you might have to resort to the more drastic step of wiping out your hard drive and reinstalling everything from the original Mac OS X CD/DVD

No matter which CD/DVD you use, you still need to boot off of it. Here's how that's done:

1. **Turn on your Mac.**
2. **Insert a CD/DVD into your Mac.**
3. **Click the Apple menu and choose Restart.**
4. **Hold down the C key.**

   This command tells your Mac to boot off the CD/DVD instead of the hard drive.
5. **Follow the instructions on the screen to either reinstall the operating system (when using the original Mac OS X Install CD/DVD) or repair your hard drive (when using a technical troubleshooting CD/DVD).**

Booting from another Mac through a FireWire cable

As an alternative to booting up from a CD or DVD, you can also boot up from another Mac connected to your computer through a FireWire cable. A FireWire cable simply plugs into the FireWire ports of each Mac, connecting the two Macs together.

After you've connected two Macs through a FireWire cable, you boot up the working Mac normally and boot up the other Mac in FireWire Target Mode. This makes the second Mac's hard drive appear as an external hard drive when viewed through the working Mac's Finder.

By doing this, you can run a utility program (such as Tech Tools Pro, DriveGenius, or DiskWarrior) on the working Mac to rescue the hard drive of the defective Mac, much like jump-starting a car's dead battery by using a second car with a good battery.

To boot up from a second Mac connected by a FireWire cable, follow these steps:

1. **Connect the second Mac to your Mac using a FireWire cable.**
2. **Turn on the working Mac.**
3. **Turn on the defective Mac (the one that's having startup troubles) and hold down the T key.**

   When the defective Mac's hard drive appears as an external drive on the working Mac, you can copy your important files off the hard drive or run a utility program to fix the hard drive on the defective Mac. After copying files or repairing the hard drive, you'll need to disconnect the FireWire cable and restart both Macs.

Shutting Down Frozen or Hung Up Programs

Programs might occasionally run perfectly fine, but suddenly when you try to do anything with them, nothing happens no matter which keys you press or where you click the mouse. Sometimes you might see a spinning wait cursor (also called a "spinning pizza" or a "spinning beach ball of death"), which stays on the screen and never goes away.

If you wait a few minutes, such frozen or hung up programs might eventually recover and allow you to use them again. More often, however, the spinning wait cursor keeps spinning in an oh-so-annoying fashion. To end the torment, you need to *force quit* the frozen or hung up program — basically, you shut it down so that the rest of your Mac can get back to work. To force quit a program, choose one of the following methods:

✦ Right-click the program's icon on the Dock and choose Force Quit from the menu that appears.

✦ Choose ⇨Force Quit to display the Force Quit Applications dialog, as shown in Figure 9-1. Then select the name of the hung-up program and click the Force Quit button.

✦ Press Option+⌘+Esc to display the Force Quit Applications dialog (see Figure 9-1). Then select the name of the hung-up program and click the Force Quit button.

✦ Load the Activity Monitor program (located inside the Utilities folder in the Applications folder), select the program name as shown in Figure 9-2, and then choose View⇨Quit Process. A Quit Process dialog appears. Click Force Quit.

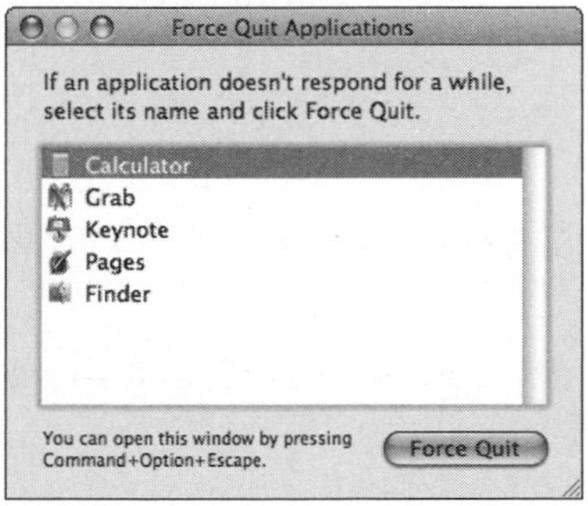

Figure 9-1: The Force Quit Applications dialog lets you choose a program to force quit.

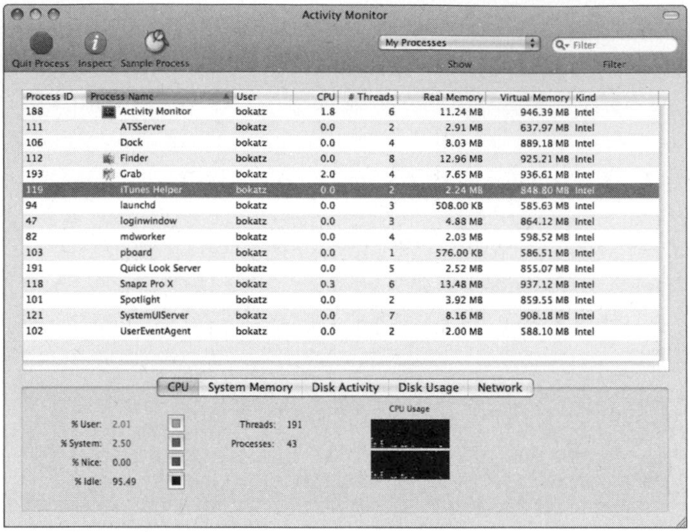

Figure 9-2: The Activity Monitor lets you choose a program to force quit.

Besides using the methods in the preceding list, you can also use the Terminal program to force quit a program. Just follow these steps:

1. **Load the Terminal program (located in the Utilities folder inside the Applications folder).**

   The Terminal window appears, as shown in Figure 9-3.

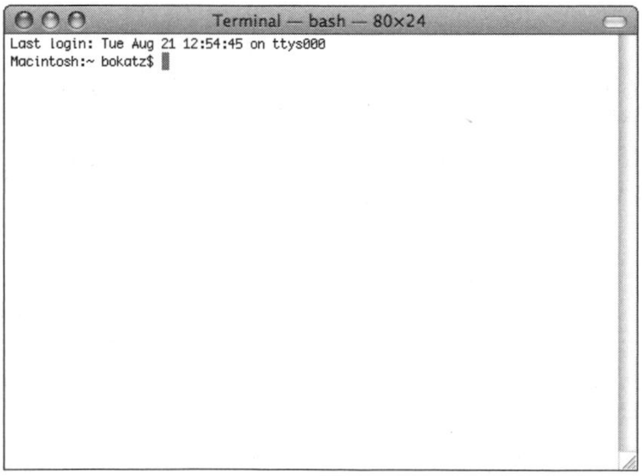

Figure 9-3: The Terminal window lets you control your Mac by typing commands.

2. **Type** top **and press Return.**

   The Terminal window displays a list of all programs currently running, as shown in Figure 9-4.

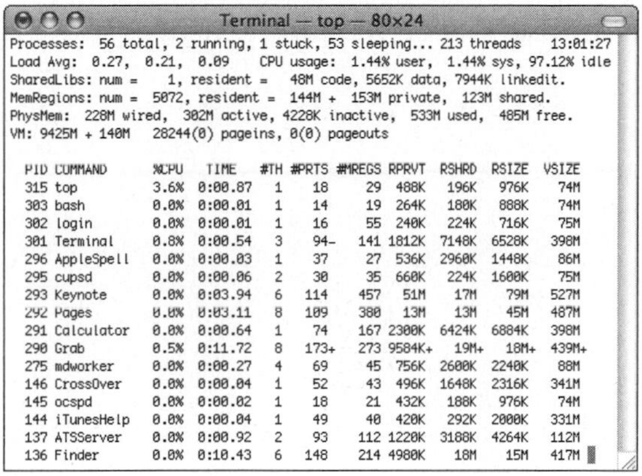

Terminal — top — 80x24
Processes: 56 total, 2 running, 1 stuck, 53 sleeping... 213 threads 13:01:27
Load Avg: 0.27, 0.21, 0.09 CPU usage: 1.44% user, 1.44% sys, 97.12% idle
SharedLibs: num = 1, resident = 48M code, 5652K data, 7944K linkedit.
MemRegions: num = 5072, resident = 144M + 153M private, 123M shared.
PhysMem: 228M wired, 302M active, 4228K inactive, 533M used, 485M free.
VM: 9425M + 140M 28244(0) pageins, 0(0) pageouts
PID COMMAND %CPU TIME #TH #PRTS #MREGS RPRVT RSHRD RSIZE VSIZE
315 top 3.6% 0:00.87 1 18 29 488K 196K 976K 74M
303 bash 0.0% 0:00.01 1 14 19 264K 180K 888K 74M
302 login 0.0% 0:00.01 1 16 55 240K 224K 716K 75M
301 Terminal 0.8% 0:00.54 3 94- 141 1812K 7148K 6528K 398M
296 AppleSpell 0.0% 0:00.03 1 37 27 536K 2960K 1448K 86M
295 cupsd 0.0% 0:00.06 2 30 35 660K 224K 1600K 75M
293 Keynote 0.0% 0:03.94 6 114 457 51M 17M 79M 527M
292 Pages 0.0% 0:03.11 8 109 380 13M 13M 45M 487M
291 Calculator 0.0% 0:00.64 1 74 167 2300K 6424K 6884K 398M
290 Grab 0.5% 0:11.72 8 173+ 273 9584K+ 19M+ 18M+ 439M+
275 mdworker 0.0% 0:00.27 4 69 45 756K 2600K 2240K 88M
146 CrossOver 0.0% 0:00.04 1 52 43 496K 1648K 2316K 341M
145 ocspd 0.0% 0:00.02 1 18 21 432K 188K 976K 74M
144 iTunesHelp 0.0% 0:00.04 1 49 40 420K 292K 2000K 331M
137 ATSServer 0.0% 0:00.92 2 93 112 1220K 3188K 4264K 112M
136 Finder 0.0% 0:10.43 6 148 214 4980K 18M 15M 417M

Figure 9-4: The Terminal window displays information about every running program.

3. **Under the COMMAND column, look for the name of the program you want to force quit.**

   Sometimes only an abbreviated form of the complete program name appears, rather than the full name.

4. **In the PID (Process ID) column, find the number that appears to the left of the program name; write this PID number down.**

5. **Type** q.

   The Terminal window removes the list of running programs and waits for your next command, as shown in Figure 9-5.

6. **Type** kill ### **and press Return, where ### is the PID number of the program you wrote down from Step 4.**

   This force quits your chosen program.

   If you can't kill a program using the normal `kill ###` command, try `kill -9 ###`, where ### represents the PID number of the program you want to kill. This `-9` option can usually kill programs that the ordinary kill command can't.

7. **Choose Terminal➪Quit Terminal.**

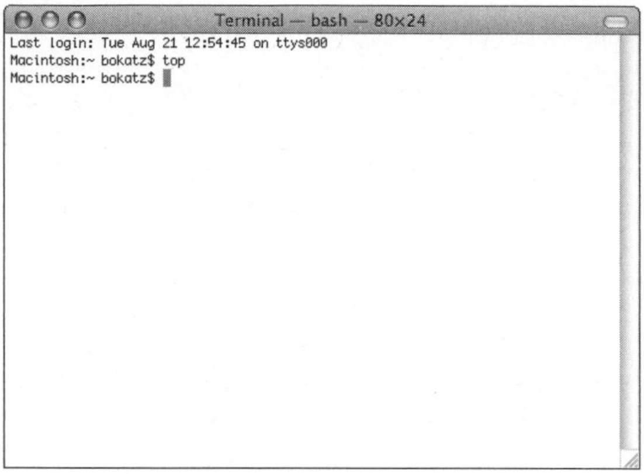
Terminal — bash — 80×24
Last login: Tue Aug 21 12:54:45 on ttys000
Macintosh:~ bokatz$ top
Macintosh:~ bokatz$

Figure 9-5: The Terminal window waits for your next command.

Removing Jammed CDs/DVDs

If a CD/DVD gets jammed into your Mac's CD/DVD drive, you can try one (or more) of the following methods to eject the CD/DVD:

- ✦ Press the Eject key on your keyboard.
- ✦ Drag the CD/DVD icon off the desktop and over the Trash icon on the Dock.
- ✦ Choose ⌘⇨Restart, and hold down the mouse or trackpad button while your Mac boots up.
- ✦ Click the Eject button next to the CD/DVD icon in the Sidebar of a Finder.
- ✦ Click the Eject button next to the CD/DVD icon in iTunes.
- ✦ Choose Controls⇨Eject DVD from inside the DVD Player program.
- ✦ Load the Disk Utility program (located in the Utilities folder inside the Applications folder), click the CD/DVD icon, and click the Eject icon.
- ✦ Click to select the CD/DVD icon on the Desktop and choose File⇨Eject from the main menu.
- ✦ Click to select the CD/DVD icon on the Desktop and press ⌘+E.
- ✦ Right-click the CD/DVD icon on the Desktop and choose Eject from the menu that appears.

WARNING! Although it might be tempting, don't ram tweezers, a flathead screwdriver, or any other object inside your CD/DVD drive to pry a jammed disc out. Not only can this scratch the disc surface, but it can also physically damage the CD/DVD drive.

Repairing and Maintaining Hard Drives

Hard drives can fail in two ways. First, the data could get scrambled on the hard drive, confusing your Mac and making it impossible to read data from it. If data gets scrambled, you can often reorganize your data (using a disk utility program) and get your hard drive back in working condition again.

Second, the surface of your hard drive might be physically damaged. If this occurs, your only option is to copy critical files off the damaged hard drive (if possible) and replace it with a new one. (If you run a disk utility program and it fails to repair any problems on your hard drive, this might be a sign that your hard drive surface is physically damaged.

The Disk Utility program that comes free with every Mac — tucked away in the Utilities folder inside the Applications folder, if you're curious — can examine your hard drive, but to fix any problems it might find, you have to boot your Mac from a different hard drive or from the Disk Utility CD/DVD that came with your Mac.

In the following sections, I show you the tools for figuring out which problem you have and what to do to fix it.

Verifying a disk

If you suspect that your hard drive might be scrambled or physically damaged, you can run the Disk Utility program to verify your suspicions. When using Disk Utility, select a device and choose one of the following:

- **Verify Disk:** Checks to make sure all the files on that device are neatly organized.
- **Verify Disk Permissions:** Checks to make sure all files, installed with each program, maintain the permissions originally assigned. (Permissions apply only to your startup disk.)

The Disk Utility program can verify and repair all types of storage devices, including hard drives, flash drives, and other types of removable storage media such as compact flash cards.

To verify a disk, follow these steps:

1. **Load the Disk Utility program (stored inside the Utilities folder in the Applications folder).**

   The Disk Utility window appears.

2. **Click the device (hard drive, flash drive, and so on) that you want to verify in the left pane of the Disk Utility window. (See Figure 9-6.)**

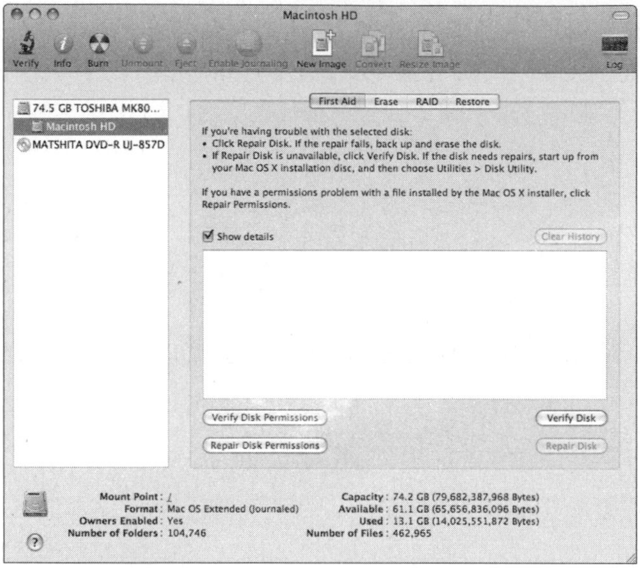

Figure 9-6: The Disk Utility window lets you pick a drive to examine.

3. **Make sure the First Aid pane is visible. (If not, click the First Aid tab to call it up.)**
4. **Click the Verify Disk button.**

   The Disk Utility program examines your chosen device. If Disk Utility can't verify that a device is working, you see a message informing you that First Aid feature of Disk Utility has failed, as shown in Figure 9-7.

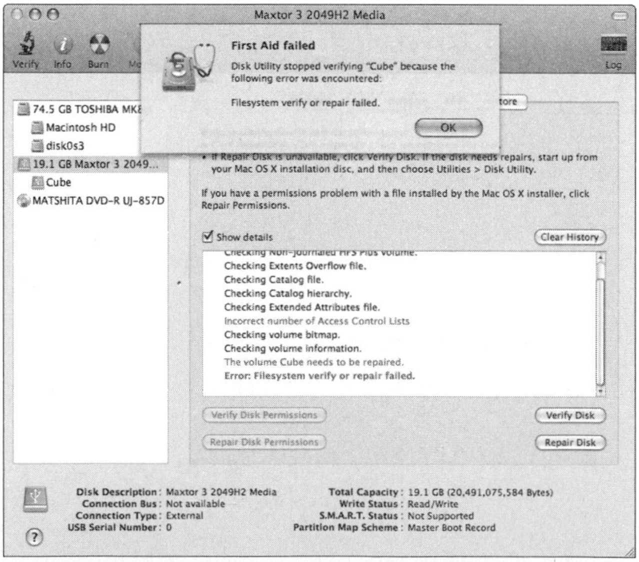

Figure 9-7: The Disk Utility informs you about whether a device might need repairing.

5. **Click OK and then click the Repair Disk button.**

   You can do this step only with a non-startup disk.

   Disk Utility tries to fix your device. If it succeeds, you see a message informing you that the device is now repaired.

You can verify your hard drive to identify any problems, but you cannot repair your startup hard drive using the copy of Disk Utility stored on your startup hard drive. To repair your startup hard drive, you need to follow these steps:

1. **Insert your Mac OS X install disc that came with your Mac.**

   The Mac OS X installation disc contains the Disk Utility program to help you troubleshoot your startup disk.

2. **Restart your Mac by choosing ⇨Restart.**

   The Restart dialog appears.

3. **Click Restart or just wait a few minutes until your Mac restarts automatically.**

4. **Hold down the C key while your Mac restarts.**

   You can release the C key when you see your Mac starting to boot up, such as displaying the Apple logo on the screen.

   This boots your Mac off the Mac OS X install disc. Your Mac starts up its Mac OS X installation program and displays a list of languages to choose.

   Booting and running off your install disc can be slow, so be patient.

5. **Select the language you want to use and click the arrow button in the bottom-right corner of the window.**

   An Install Mac OS X window appears.

6. **Choose Utilities⇨Disk Utility from the main menu.**

   The Disk Utility window appears.

7. **Click the startup drive in the left pane of the Disk Utility window.**

8. **Make sure the First Aid pane is visible. (If not, click the First Aid tab to call it up.)**

9. **Click the Repair Disk button.**

   The Repair feature of Disk Utility does what it can to fix any problems on your hard drive and informs you of its success — or failure.

10. **Choose Disk Utility⇨Quit Disk Utility.**

    The Install Mac OS X window appears again.

11. **Choose Installer⇨Quit Installer.**

    A dialog appears asking `Are you sure you want to quit the Installer?`”

12. **Click the Restart button in the dialog.**

Verifying disk permissions

Disk permissions apply to your startup disk and define what each program's files are allowed to access. If permissions aren't correct, your files could get scrambled, which can cause your Mac to act erratically or fail completely.

TECHNICAL STUFF

Disk permissions are similar to user permissions. With disk permissions, certain files are granted access to different parts of the computer. With user permissions, certain users are granted access to different files and folders stored on the hard drive.

REMEMBER

Unlike repairing a hard drive, you can verify and fix disk permissions without having to boot up from a separate hard drive or CD/DVD.

To verify disk permissions, follow these steps:

1. **Load the Disk Utility program (stored inside the Utilities folder in the Applications folder).**

   The Disk Utility window appears.

2. **Click on your startup hard drive in the left pane of the Disk Utility window.**
3. **Make sure the window is on the First Aid pane. (If not, click the First Aid tab to call it up.)**
4. **Click Verify Disk Permissions.**

   If Disk Utility finds any problems, it displays a message to let you know. Otherwise it displays a message to let you know all permissions are okay as shown in Figure 9-8.

5. **Click Repair Disk Permissions.**

   Disk Utility displays any messages concerning permission problems it found and repaired.

6. **Choose Disk Utility⇨Quit Disk Utility.**

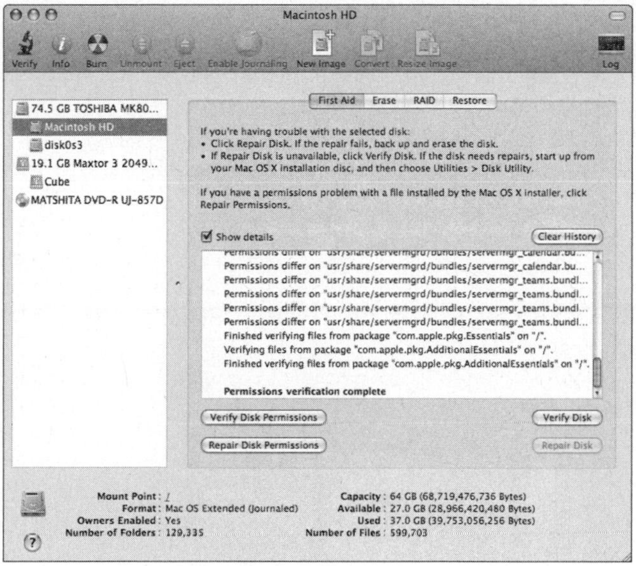

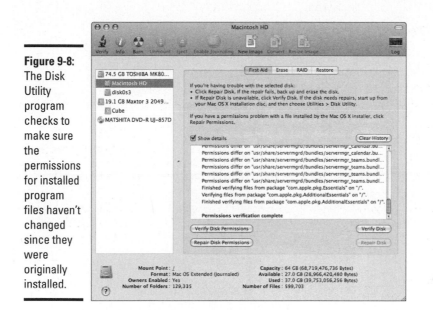

Figure 9-8: The Disk Utility program checks to make sure the permissions for installed program files haven't changed since they were originally installed.

Preventative Maintenance

Your Mac has daily, weekly, and monthly maintenance tasks that it runs periodically early in the morning (from 3:15 a.m. to 5:30 a.m.). If you leave your Mac on at night, it can perform these routine maintenance tasks all by itself. However, if your Mac is asleep during this time, it won't run these maintenance tasks.

You can wake yourself up between 3:15 a.m. and 5:30 a.m. every day and jiggle the mouse around to keep your Mac awake so it can run its maintenance tasks, or you can force your Mac to run its daily, weekly, and monthly maintenance tasks right now.

TIP

To automate running your Mac preventative maintenance programs, consider getting a free program called MacJanitor (`http://personalpages.tds.net/~brian_hill/macjanitor.html`).

To force your Mac to run its maintenance tasks, follow these steps:

1. **Load the Terminal program (located in the Utilities folder inside the Applications folder).**

   The Terminal window appears (refer to Figure 9-3).

2. **Type** sudo periodic daily **and press Return.**

   The Terminal window asks for your password.

   To make your Mac run weekly or monthly maintenance tasks, type **sudo periodic weekly** or **sudo periodic monthly,** respectively. Weekly and monthly tasks can take a long time to run. You'll know when a maintenance task is done when you see the cryptic-looking prompt (like *mycomputer$*) reappear.

3. **Type your password and press Return.**

   Wait until you see the Terminal prompt (like *mycomputer$*) reappear again, as shown in Figure 9-9.

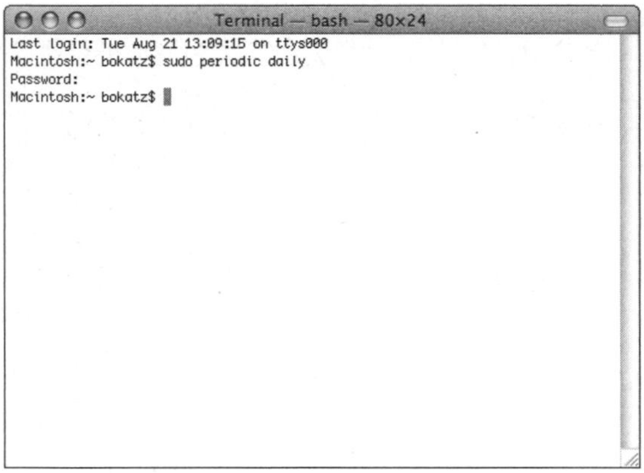
Terminal — bash — 80x24
Last login: Tue Aug 21 13:09:15 on ttys000
Macintosh:~ bokatz$ sudo periodic daily
Password:
Macintosh:~ bokatz$

Figure 9-9: When the Terminal prompt appears again, the Mac's maintenance tasks are finished running.

4. **Choose Terminal⇨Quit Terminal.**

Book II

Photos, Music, and Movies

"I tell you, it looks like Danny, it sounds like Danny, but it's NOT Danny!! I think the Mac has created an alias of Danny! You can see it in his eyes – little wrist watch icons!"

Contents at a Glance

Chapter 1: Playing with Audio 183
Chapter 2: Playing with Pictures 205
Chapter 3: Watching Videos on a Mac 223
Chapter 4: Using Front Row for Movies, Music, and Photos 239

Chapter 1: Playing with Audio

In This Chapter

- **Understanding audio file formats**
- **Playing audio files with iTunes**
- **Burning audio files to disc**

Since lugging around a case full of CDs (or even vinyl records or audio tapes) is cumbersome and bulky, more people are storing music as digital audio files. Not only are digital audio files much easier to store and copy, but storing individual songs as digital audio files means you need to carry only the songs you want to hear.

Besides storing music, audio files can also contain speeches, interviews, and radio shows. Many audio files that contain interviews or entire radio shows are called podcasts because they're commonly played on iPods.

Understanding Audio File Formats

Audio files offer tremendous advantages in storage and audio quality compared to previous forms of audio storage. However, there are literally dozens of different audio file formats out there, so to hear different audio files you may need to use different programs. This would be like having to buy two separate radios where one radio can receive only AM stations and the second radio can receive only FM stations.

Different types of audio file formats exist because each file format offers certain advantages. The three most popular types of audio file formats are

- Lossless
- Lossless compression
- Lossy compression

Any audio file format can be played on any computer with the right software.

Lossless audio files

The highest-quality audio files are called *lossless* because they never lose any audio data. As a result, lossless audio files offer the highest-quality sound, but they also create the largest file sizes.

The two most popular lossless audio file formats are WAV (Waveform audio format) and AIFF (Audio Interchange File Format). WAV files typically end with the `.wav` file extension, whereas AIFF files typically end with the `.aiff` or `.aif` file extension.

Both WAV and AIFF audio files are different ways to hold audio stored in the PCM (pulse code modulation) format. When you buy an audio CD of your favorite band, that CD stores music in the PCM format as well.

Compressed lossless audio files

Lossless audio files take up large amounts of space, so compressed lossless audio files are designed to squeeze audio data into a smaller file size. Three popular compressed lossless audio file formats are FLAC (which stands for Free Lossless Audio Codec), Shorten, and Apple Lossless.. FLAC files typically end with the `.flac` file extension, Shorten files typically end with the `.shn` file extension, and Apple Lossless files typically end with the `.m4a` file extension.

You can play Apple Lossless files in iTunes, but not FLAC or Shorten audio files. To play FLAC files, grab a free copy of SongBird (`www.songbirdnest.com`) or VLC Media Player (`www.videolan.org/vlc`). To play Shorten files, use Audion (`www.panic.com/audion`).

Compressed lossy audio files

A lossy audio file simply compresses a file by tossing out audio data to shrink the file size, much like pulling unnecessary clothing out of a suitcase to lighten the load. The greater the audio quality, the more audio data the file needs to retain and the bigger the file. The smaller the file, the less audio data the file can hold, and the lower the audio quality. As a result, most audio file formats strive for an optimal balance between audio quality and file size.

The amount of data an audio file format retains is measured in kilobits per second (Kbps). The higher the kilobits, the more data stored and the higher the audio quality. Table 1-1 shows approximate kilobit values and the audio quality they produce.

Streaming audio

Except for sound effects, most audio files are several megabytes in size. Before you can play such an audio file, you must first copy the entire file to your computer. Normally, this isn't a problem except if you want to listen to audio right away. To solve this problem, you have to use streaming audio.

Two features distinguish streaming audio from ordinary audio files. First, streaming audio plays as it's being downloaded to your computer. Second, streaming audio never gets saved to your hard drive.

The iTunes program (included with every Mac) can play streaming audio. Some other popular (and free) programs for listening to streaming audio include Audion (`www.panic.com/audion`), RealPlayer (`www.real.com`), and AOL Radio (`http://music.aol.com/radioguide/bb`).

Table 1-1 Audio Quality Comparisons

Bit Rate (Kilobits per Second)	*Audio Quality*
32 Kbps	AM radio quality
96 Kbps	FM radio quality
128–160 Kbps	Good quality, but differences from the original audio source can be noticeable
192 Kbps	Medium quality, slight differences from the original audio source can be heard
224–320 Kbps	High quality, little loss of audio quality from the original source

The most popular compressed lossy audio file formats are MP3 (MPEG-1 Audio Layer 3), AAC (Advanced Audio Coding), and WMA (Windows Media Audio). MP3 audio files are the most popular because the MP3 audio file standard was one of the first compression file formats that could smash audio files to a smaller size while still retaining much of their audio quality. You can recognize MP3 audio files by their `.mp3` file extension.

Because the MP3 audio file format is copyrighted, programmers have created a free equivalent audio file format called Ogg Vorbis, which uses the `.ogg` file extension. Ogg Vorbis offers slightly higher audio quality and slightly greater compression ratios.

Another alternative to MP3 files is the AAC audio file format. Like Ogg Vorbis, AAC audio files offer greater audio quality and smaller file compression than equivalent MP3 files. Unlike the Ogg Vorbis format, the AAC format offers a digital rights management (DRM) feature that allows copy protection. AAC files typically end with the `.aac` or `.m4a` file extension (if it does not have digital rights management) or the `.m4p` file extension (if it does have digital rights management).

To play Ogg Vorbis files, you need to convert them to MP3 or AAC files. One way to convert Ogg Vorbis (or other types of audio files) into MP3 files is to use the free audio-editing program, Audacity (`http://audacity.sourceforge.net`) or the VLC Media Player (`www.videolan.org/vlc`).

Playing Audio with iTunes

You can buy audio files of your favorite songs from services such as the iTunes Store. Perhaps the most popular way to get audio files is by importing (also known as "ripping") songs off an audio CD and storing them as audio files on your hard drive.

When you have an audio file, you need a special program that can play that audio file. To play the three most common audio files (MP3, AAC, and WAV) on your Mac, you can use iTunes. The iTunes program is a combination audio and video player, audio file converter, and disc-burning program so you can store your favorite audio files on a CD that you can play in your stereo.

You don't have to use iTunes to play audio CDs and digital audio files on your Mac. You can always use another audio player on your Macintosh (such as RealPlayer, which you can get for free at `www.real.com`, VLC Media Player at `www.videolan.org/vlc`, or Audion at `www.panic.com/audion`). Other audio players can be especially useful if you want to play oddball audio formats like Ogg Vorbis or FLAC, but in most cases, you'll probably find that iTunes works just fine.

Listening to CDs

You probably have audio CDs of your favorite albums, but rather than play them in a CD player, you can play them in your Mac by using iTunes. Much like a CD player, iTunes can play audio tracks on a CD in order or randomly. Even better, iTunes lets you selectively choose which audio tracks you want to hear. To play an audio CD in iTunes, follow these steps:

1. **Insert an audio CD into your Mac.**

   A dialog appears, asking whether you want to import all audio tracks on the CD into iTunes.

If you click Yes, iTunes makes copies of all the audio tracks on the CD, converts the copies into digital audio files, and then stores these new copies on your hard drive — a process known as *ripping.*

2. **Click No.**

   The dialog disappears. If you're connected to the Internet, iTunes displays the name of your album along with the names of every audio track, as shown in Figure 1-1.

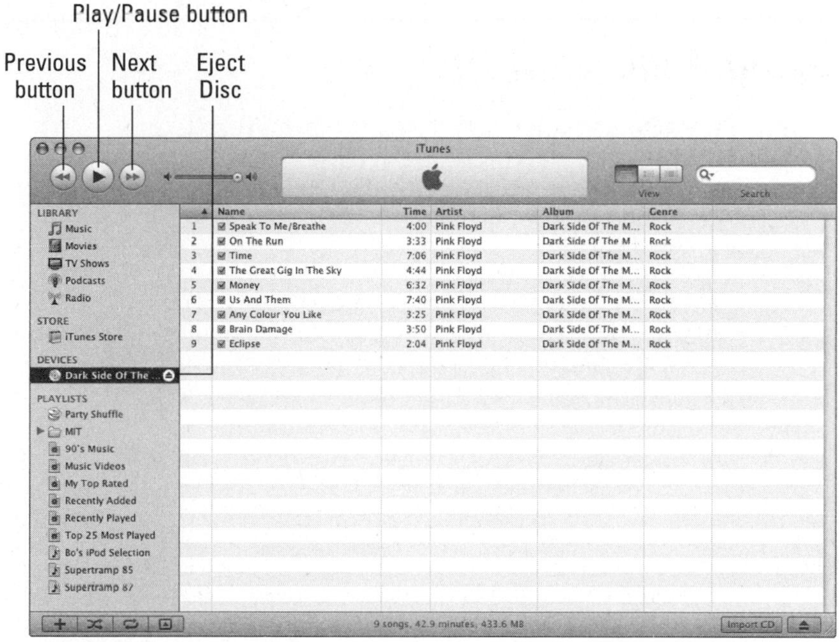

Figure 1-1: You can see all the audio tracks on your CD by name and track length.

3. **Click the Play button or press the space bar to start playing your selected audio tracks.**

   The Play button turns into a Pause button.

Here are some tricks you can use to enhance your CD-listening experience:

✦ **Volume slider:** Drag the volume slider to adjust the sound.

✦ **Selective play:** Deselect the check boxes of the audio tracks you don't want to hear.

✦ **Random play:** Choose Controls➪Shuffle to play your audio tracks in random order. Choosing the Shuffle command again turns off random play. You can keep turning this command off and on multiple times until you see a random order that you like.

- **Continuous play:** Choose Controls Repeat⇨All to continuously play all selected audio tracks on the CD. (Choose Controls⇨Repeat Off to turn off the repeat play feature.)

  If you select an audio track and then choose Controls⇨Repeat One, you can play a single audio track over and over again.

- **Adjust play:** Click one of the following buttons:
  - *Pause:* Temporarily stops playing audio.
  - *Previous:* Starts playing the currently selected audio track from the beginning. Clicking the Previous button a second time starts playing the previous audio track from the beginning.
  - *Next:* Skips the currently selected audio track and starts playing the next audio track.

When you're listening to an audio CD, you can eject it by choosing Controls⇨Eject Disc or clicking the Eject Disc icon.

Converting an audio disc into digital files

Having to insert a CD into your Mac every time you want to hear a few songs can be cumbersome, which is why you might find it easier to store your favorite songs as digital audio files instead.

The process of converting audio tracks on a CD into digital audio files is known as *ripping.*

To convert an audio disc into digital files, follow these steps:

1. **Insert an audio CD into your Mac.**

   A dialog appears, asking if you want to import all audio tracks on the CD into iTunes.

2. **Click Yes if you want to convert every audio track into a digital audio file.**

   The iTunes program plays your audio CD while it's copying all audio tracks to digital audio files. If you want to choose which files to select, click No and continue following the remaining steps.

3. **Choose iTunes⇨Preferences.**

   The iTunes Preferences window appears.

4. **Click the Advanced icon.**
5. **Click the Importing tab.**

   The Importing pane appears, as shown in Figure 1-2.

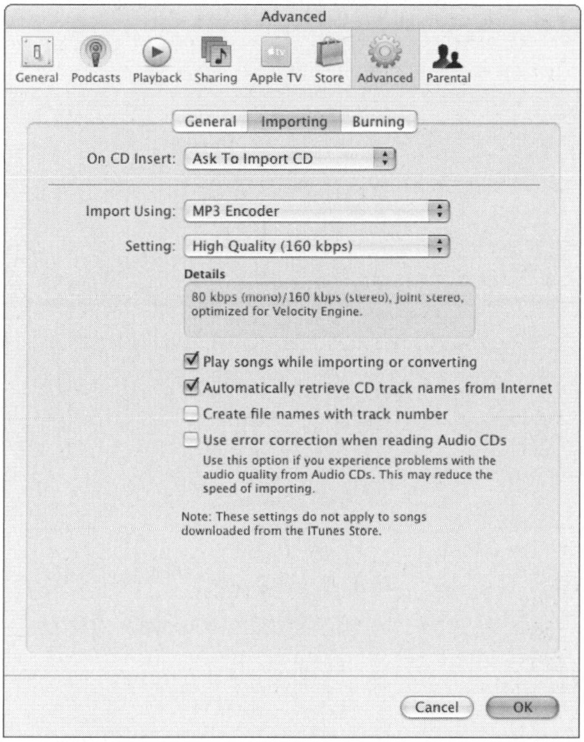

Figure 1-2: The Importing pane lets you define how iTunes converts CDs into digital audio files.

6. **(Optional) To specify what you want to happen whenever you insert an audio CD into your Mac, click the On CD Insert pop-up menu and choose one of the following:**
   - *Show CD:* Displays a list of audio tracks.
   - *Begin Playing:* Displays a list of audio tracks and starts playing the first track.
   - *Ask to Import CD:* Displays a dialog, asking whether you want to import all audio tracks from the CD.
   - *Import CD:* Automatically converts all audio tracks into digital files.
   - *Import CD and Eject:* Automatically converts all audio tracks into digital files and ejects the CD when it's done without playing any tracks.
7. **To specify which file format to use when importing, click the Import Using pop-up menu and choose one of the following:**
   - *AAC Encoder:* Stores audio tracks as AAC files.
   - *AIFF Encoder:* Stores audio tracks as AIFF files.

- *Apple Lossless Encoder:* Stores audio tracks as a losslessly compressed AAC file.
- *MP3 Encoder:* Stores audio tracks as MP3 files.
- *WAV Encoder:* Stores audio tracks as WAV files.

8. **Click the Setting pop-up menu and choose the audio quality for your files.**

   The higher the audio quality, the larger the file size.

9. **(Optional) Select or deselect one or more of the following check boxes:**

   - *Play songs while importing or converting:* Lets you hear your audio tracks as iTunes converts them to digital files.
   - *Automatically retrieve CD track names from Internet:* Identifies audio tracks by their song titles. If this option isn't selected, each audio track will have a generic name like Track 1.
   - *Create file names with track number:* Adds the track number to each digital file such as 01 – *TrackName.*
   - *Use error correction when reading Audio CDs:* Increases the chances that iTunes can retrieve and convert an audio track from a damaged or scratched CD.

10. **Click OK.**

    You're brought back to the main iTunes window.

11. **Deselect the check boxes of the songs you don't want to import.**

    Check marks should appear in the check boxes of the audio tracks you want o import.

12. **Click Import CD (the button appears in the lower-right corner of the iTunes window).**

    Your selected audio tracks get stored as digital audio files inside an iTunes folder, tucked inside the Music folder.

Importing digital audio files

Besides ripping audio tracks off a CD and storing them on your Mac, you might also get digital audio files from other people either through the Internet or handed to you on a flash drive. Before you can play any digital audio files in iTunes, you must first import those files, which essentially copies those digital audio files into the iTunes folder inside your Music folder. Until you import audio files into iTunes, you won't be able to play those audio files.

To import audio files into iTunes, follow these steps:

1. **Load iTunes.**

   Click the iTunes icon in the Dock or double-click the iTunes icon in the Applications folder.

2. **Choose File➪Import.**

   An Import dialog appears, as shown in Figure 1-3.

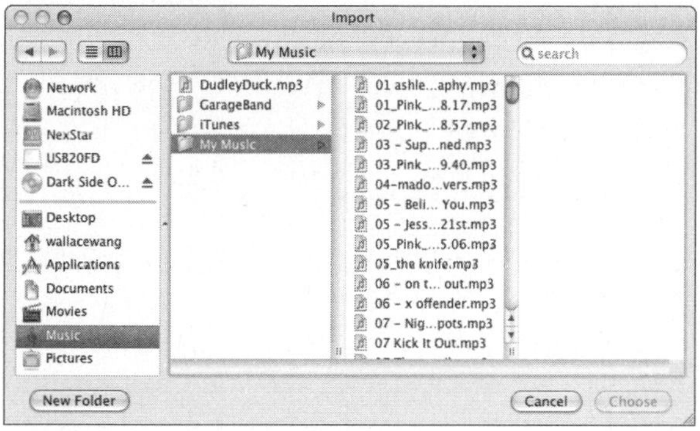

Figure 1-3: The Import dialog lets you copy an audio file from another part of your computer.

3. **Click the audio file you want to import into iTunes.**

   You might have to search for that file in different folders.

4. **Click the Choose button.**

Sorting your digital audio files

After you've stored some digital audio files in iTunes, you can sort through them to find the audio files you want. The iTunes program offers three different ways to display your audio files:

- ✦ **List view:** Displays audio files alphabetically by category, such as name, album, artist, or genre.
- ✦ **Album view:** Displays audio files grouped alphabetically by album name.
- ✦ **Cover Flow view:** Identical to the album view except that it displays album covers as 3-D images.

Displaying audio files in List view

The List view is best suited when you want to see as many names of your audio files as possible. In the List view, you can sort your audio files alphabetically so you can group audio files into different categories such as by Artist or Album. To see the List view, follow these steps:

1. **In iTunes, choose View➪List View (or click the List View icon).**

   The List view appears, as shown in Figure 1-4.

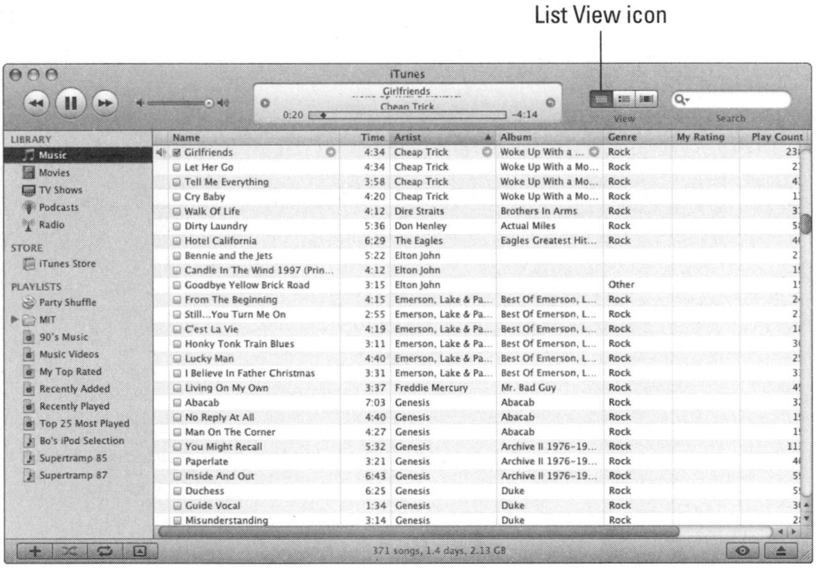

Figure 1-4: The List view lets you arrange your audio files alphabetically by categories such as Name or Artist.

2. **Click a category heading, such as Name or Artist.**

   When you click a category heading, iTunes sorts your entire audio file collection alphabetically in ascending order based on that category. If you click the same category again, iTunes sorts your audio files alphabetically in descending order.

REMEMBER

The List view makes it easy to find audio files from different artists.

Displaying audio files in Album view

The Album view visually groups songs next to specific album cover. If you find the List view too boring because it displays only text, try the Album view instead. To see the Album view, follow these steps:

1. **In iTunes, choose View➪Album View (or click the Album View icon).**

   The Album view appears, as shown in Figure 1-5.

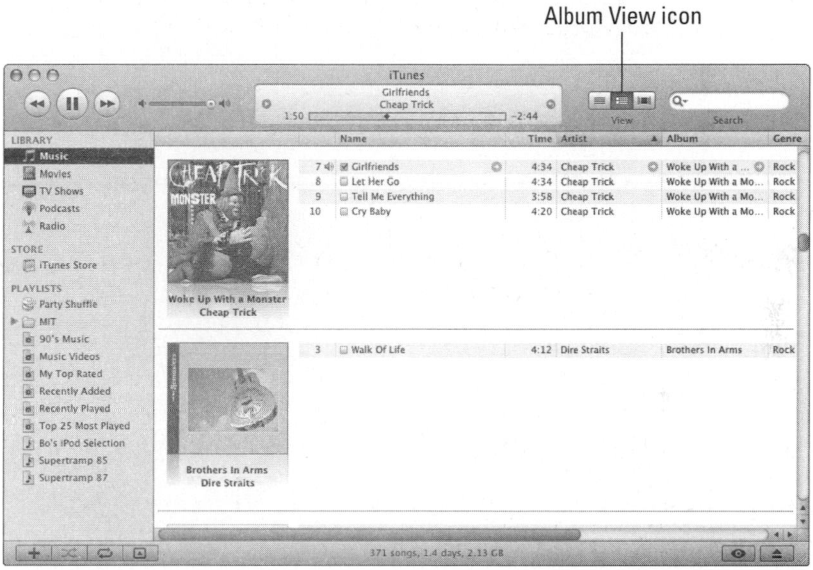

Figure 1-5: The Album view organizes songs alphabetically by album name.

2. **Use the scroll bars to view your favorite songs, organized according to album.**

Displaying audio files in Cover Flow view

Another way to sort through your audio file collection is with the Cover Flow view, which mimics the appearance of displaying album covers in a juke box, where you can flip through different album covers to find the songs you want to play. Like the Album view, the Cover Flow view lets you browse through your favorite songs sorted according to the album that they came from.

When displayed in the Album view, album covers may appear more than once. When displayed in the Cover Flow view, album covers appear only once.

REMEMBER

To download album cover artwork, you need an iTunes account. To create an iTunes account, choose Store➪Create Account. Creating an account won't cost you anything, but you will need to enter a credit card number in case you decide to buy anything from the iTunes online store.

To see the Cover Flow view, follow these steps:

1. **In iTunes, choose View⇨Cover Flow View (or click the Cover Flow View icon).**

   The Cover Flow view appears, as shown in Figure 1-6.

Figure 1-6: The Cover Flow view lets you flip through album covers to find the songs you want.

2. **Click an album cover to see the songs associated with that album.**

The Cover Flow view is basically a fancier version of the Album view.

Playing digital audio files

After you've imported one or more audio files into iTunes, you can view your list of audio files within the iTunes window, as outlined in the previous section. To play one or more digital files, follow these steps:

1. **Choose a view for displaying your audio file collection, such as List, Album, or Cover Flow view.**

   Check marks appear in the check boxes of all currently selected songs.

2. **Select the check boxes of the audio tracks you want to hear and deselect the check boxes of audio tracks you don't want to hear.**

   To deselect all audio tracks so you don't have to listen to them, hold down the ⌘ key and select a check box. To reselect all audio tracks, repeat the process.

3. **Click the Play button or press the space bar to start playing your selected audio tracks.**

   The Play button turns into a Pause button.

Searching for a song

To help you find a song, you can search by typing part of its name, album, artist, and so on. To search for a song, follow these steps:

1. **Click in the Spotlight search field that appears in the upper-right corner of the iTunes window and type part of the song, album, or other item that you want to find.**

   Each time you type a letter in the Spotlight search field, iTunes narrows down the total list of available songs in your music collection as shown in Figure 1-7.

2. **Click in the Close button of the Spotlight search field when you've found the song you want.**

Figure 1-7: Typing in the Spotlight search field helps you find a particular song in your music collection.

Using a playlist

One problem with playing digital audio files is that you must keep selecting the songs you want to hear. Rather than go through the hassle of selecting the same group of songs over and over again, you can select a group of songs once and store that list as a *playlist.* Now if you want to hear a group of songs, just select the playlist rather than each song individually.

You can create two types of playlists: an ordinary playlist and a Smart Playlist. An ordinary playlist is just a list of your favorite songs. A Smart Playlist lets you define rules for which songs to include, such as only songs that recorded by specific artists. As your audio file collection grows, a Smart Playlist can automatically include any new songs.

When you create an ordinary play list or a Smart Playlist, those playlists appear in the left pane of the iTunes window. By default, iTunes already includes several Smart Playlists labeled Recently Added or Top 25 Most Played.

REMEMBER

Playlists simply show you a group of related songs to make it easier to find the songs you want to hear.

Creating a playlist

The simplest playlist to create is one that contains specific songs, such as love songs or songs from your childhood. To create a playlist, follow these steps:

1. **In iTunes, hold down the ⌘ key and click each song you want to store in your playlist.**
2. **Choose File⇨New Playlist from Selection.**

   An untitled playlist appears in the left pane of iTunes under the Playlists category, and your chosen songs appear in the right pane.
3. **Type a name for your playlist.**

TIP

You can always edit a playlist name by double-clicking the name in the left pane.

Adding songs to a playlist

After you've created a playlist, you can always add or remove songs to that playlist at any time. To add a song to a playlist, follow these steps:

1. **In iTunes, move your cursor over a song you want to add to your playlist.**

2. **Click and drag the song onto the name of the playlist in the left pane of the iTunes window.**
3. **Release the mouse button when the pointer appears over your chosen playlist.**

Putting a song in a playlist doesn't physically move the song.

Deleting songs from a playlist

To delete a song from a playlist, follow these steps:

1. **In iTunes, click the playlist that contains the songs you want to delete from that playlist.**

   The right pane of iTunes shows all the songs in your chosen playlist.
2. **Click a song to delete.**
3. **Choose Edit➪Delete.**

   A dialog appears, asking whether you really want to remove the song from your playlist.
4. **Click Remove.**

Deleting a song from a playlist doesn't delete the song from your iTunes library.

To delete a song from your music collection, click Music under the Library category in the left pane of the iTunes window. Then right-click a song you want to delete and choose Delete. When a dialog appears, asking whether you want to delete the song from your library, click Remove. When a second dialog appears, click Move to Trash.

Creating a Smart Playlist

Manually adding and removing songs from a playlist can get tedious, especially if you keep adding new songs to your audio file collection. Instead of placing specific songs in a playlist, a Smart Playlist lets you define specific criteria for what types of songs to store in that playlist, such as songs recorded earlier than 1990 or songs under the Psychedelic Rock genre.

The three parts to using a Smart Playlist are

- ✦ Tagging songs
- ✦ Creating Smart Playlist rules to define which songs to include
- ✦ Editing existing Smart Playlists

Tagging songs

To accurately sort your song collection into Smart Playlists, you must first tag every song. Most songs, stored as digital audio files, already have some information stored in specific tags, such as the artist or album name. However, you might still want to edit or add new tags to help Smart Playlists sort your song collection.

To edit or add tags to a song, follow these steps:

1. **In iTunes, click a song that you want to tag.**
2. **Choose File⇨Get Info (or press ⌘+I).**

   An Info window appears.
3. **Click the Info tab.**

   The Info pane displays text boxes where you can type the song info, including album name, artist, and year recorded, as shown in Figure 1-8.

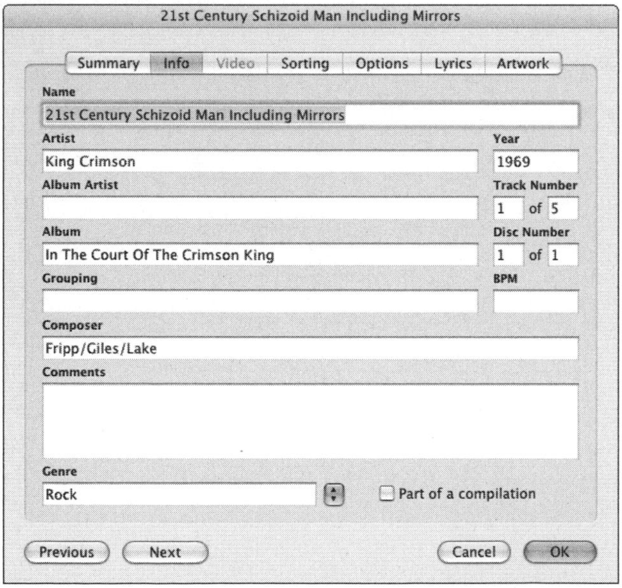

Figure 1-8: The Info pane lets you edit or type new labels to identify a song.

4. **Click in a text box and edit or type information.**

5. **In the same Info pane, choose a genre such as Rock or Classical from the Genre pop-up menu, as shown in Figure 1-9.**
6. **Click the Options tab.**

   The Options pane appears, as shown in Figure 1-10.
7. **Click in the My Rating box and choose one to five stars.**
8. **Click OK.**

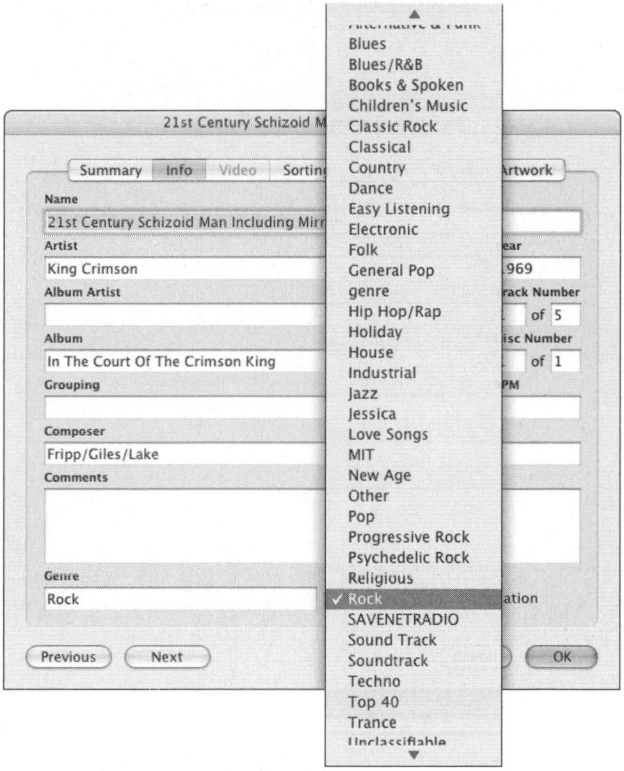

Figure 1-9: The Genre pop-up menu lets you group songs by category.

Defining a Smart Playlist rule

Smart Playlists use tags to automatically sort and organize your song collection. After you've added tags to your songs, you can create a Smart Playlist and define the type of songs you want that Smart Playlist to store. The specific criterion for choosing a song is called a *rule*.

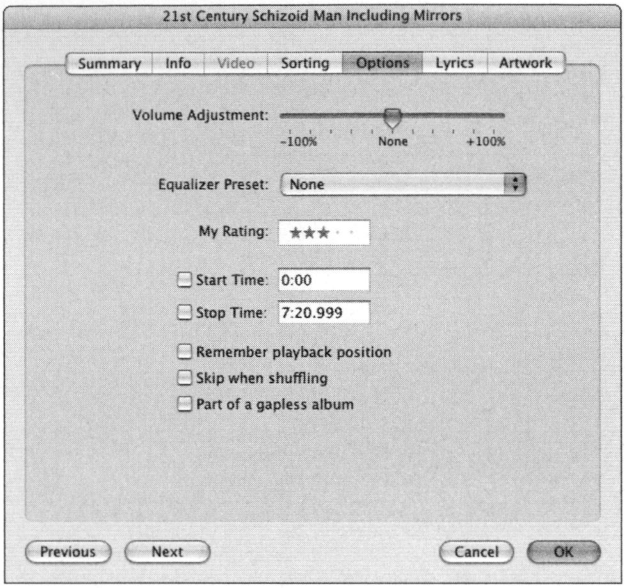

Figure 1-10: The Options pane lets you rate your songs with one to five stars.

To create a Smart Playlist, follow these steps:

1. **In iTunes, choose File➪New Smart Playlist.**

   A Smart Playlist dialog appears, asking that you define a rule for specifying which songs to store in the playlist, as shown in Figure 1-11.

Figure 1-11: The Smart Playlist dialog lets you define a rule for automatically storing certain songs.

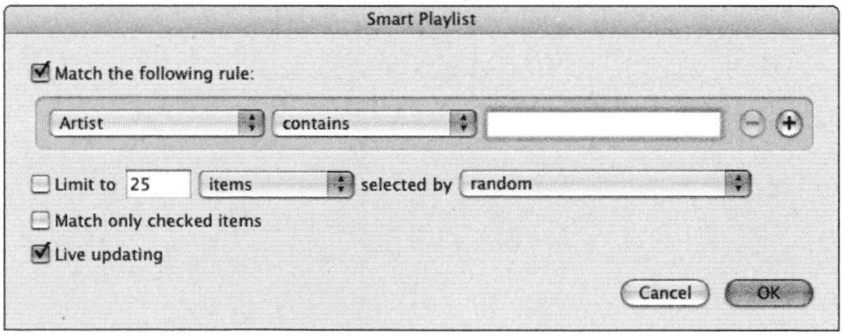

2. **Click in the first pop-up menu (the one on the left) and choose a label to use, such as Artist or Date Added, for deciding which songs to store, as shown in Figure 1-12.**

Figure 1-12: To define a rule, you must choose which criteria to use for your Smart Playlist.

3. **Click in the second pop-up menu (the one in the middle) and choose how to use your chosen label, as shown in Figure 1-13.**

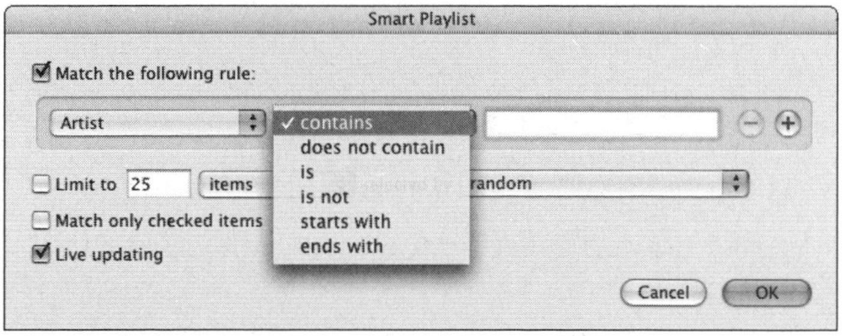

Figure 1-13: The second pop-up menu defines how to use your chosen label.

4. **Click in the text box and type a criteria, such as a specific date or an artist name.**
5. **(Optional) Select the Limit To check box and enter a number in the accompanying text box if you want to define the maximum number of songs/gigabytes/minutes/hours the Smart Playlist can hold.**

6. **(Optional) Select the Match Only Checked Items check box if you only want to store songs that both match your criteria and are also selected in the iTunes window.**
7. **(Optional) Deselect the Live Updating check box if you don't want Smart Playlist to automatically update its list of songs each time you add or remove a song from your iTunes song collection library.**
8. **Click OK.**

Editing a Smart Playlist

After you've created a Smart Playlist, you might want to go back and modify the way it works, such as adding more rules or editing any existing rules. To edit a Smart Playlist, follow these steps:

1. **In iTunes, select the Smart Playlist that you want to edit in the left pane of the iTunes window.**
2. **Choose File⇨Edit Smart Playlist.**

   The Smart Playlist dialog box appears (refer to Figure 1-10).
3. **Make any changes to your Smart Playlist rule and click OK when you're done.**

Deleting a playlist

If you create a playlist or a Smart Playlist, you might want to delete that list later. To delete a playlist, follow these steps:

1. **In iTunes, click a playlist that you want to delete in the left pane of the iTunes window.**
2. **Choose Edit⇨Delete.**

   A dialog appears, asking whether you really want to delete your playlist.

   Deleting a playlist doesn't physically delete the audio files from your iTunes library.
3. **Click Delete.**

Burning an Audio CD

After you've collected your favorite songs in digital audio files, you might want to save these files on a custom CD (often called a *mix CD* or just a *mix*) that you can play in your car or home stereo. To burn an audio CD, first create a playlist and then tell iTunes to copy all the songs in your playlist to an audio CD.

CDs can hold approximately 70–80 minutes worth of audio. More stereos can recognize and play CD-Rs although newer stereos can also recognize and play CD-RWs as well. (CD-Rs let you write to them exactly only once. CD-RWs let you erase and reuse them.)

To burn a disc using a playlist, follow these steps:

1. **In iTunes, choose iTunes➪Preferences.**

   A window appears.

2. **Click the Advanced icon.**
3. **Click the Burning tab.**

   The Advanced window displays different radio buttons for choosing the type of CD you want to burn such as Audio CD, MP3 CD, or Data CD, as shown in Figure 1-14.

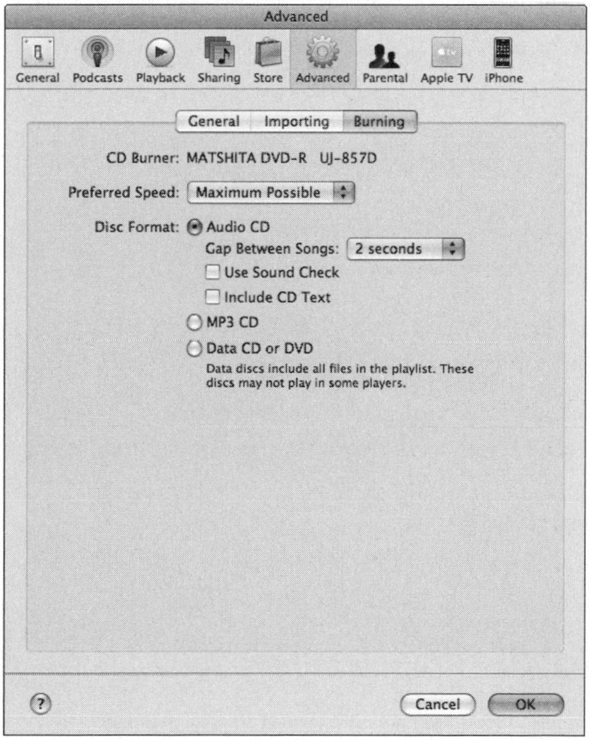

Figure 1-14: The Advanced window lets you choose the type of CD to burn.

4. **(Optional) Click the Preferred Speed pop-up menu and choose a disc burning speed such as Maximum Possible or 20x.**

   If the CDs you burn on your Mac don't play correctly on other CD players, choose a slower burning speed. Otherwise, use the Maximum Possible option.

5. **Select a radio button (Audio CD, MP3 CD, or Data CD) and click OK.**
6. **(Optional) Deselect the check boxes of any songs you don't want to burn to the CD.**
7. **(Optional) Arrange the songs in the order you want them to play on the CD.**

   To arrange songs in a playlist, click in the first column (that displays the number of each song) and then drag a song up or down to a new position.

8. **Choose File⇨Burn Playlist to Disc.**

   A dialog appears, asking you to insert a blank disc.

9. **Insert a blank CD-R or CD-RW into your Mac.**

   The top of the iTunes window displays the progress of your disc burning. You have enough time to go get a cup of coffee.

Chapter 2: Playing with Pictures

In This Chapter

- **Understanding digital photography**
- **Transferring pictures to your Mac**
- **Capturing pictures**
- **Editing pictures**

More people are taking pictures than ever before with digital cameras. Digital cameras let you capture a picture, see it right away, and then decide whether you want to keep it. Even better, after you've captured a picture, you can edit it to make it look better than it actually did in real life. With a little bit of creativity, you can even alter a digital image to create an image that never existed in the first place, such as pasting a horn on a horse to create a picture of a unicorn or adding a tentacle protruding from your mother-in-law's forehead.

Understanding Digital Photography

Instead of using film, digital photography captures images on memory storage devices. Not only does this make storing digital photographs easy on a computer, it also means you can make identical copies of your pictures at any time without losing the quality of your images. "Great," you say, but keep in mind that, when using a digital camera, you need to understand how digital cameras store images so you can transfer them to your Mac.

Understanding megapixels

Digital photographs capture images as a collection of tiny dots called *pixels*. A single picture consists of hundreds, thousands, or even millions of pixels. The greater the number of pixels used to create a picture, the sharper the overall image. To help you understand the capabilities of different digital cameras, manufacturers identify cameras by how many millions of pixels they can capture in each picture. This total number of pixels, called the *resolution,* ranges from 2 megapixels (MP) to 16 megapixels or more. Figure 2-1 shows how pixels create an image.

Figure 2-1: Every digital photograph is made up of pixels.

Generally speaking, the higher the megapixels of a digital camera, the sharper the image resolution. A picture captured with a 2-megapixel camera won't look as sharp as that same image captured with an 8-megapixel camera, especially if you enlarge it.

Understanding flash memory cards

Every time you take a picture with a digital camera, your camera needs to save that picture somewhere. Some digital cameras come with built-in memory, which can temporarily store any digital images that you capture. However, to store large numbers of pictures, most digital cameras can also store pictures on removable storage devices called *flash memory cards.*

Okay, in no particular order now, here are things to keep in mind about flash memory cards:

- **Reuse:** The biggest advantage of flash memory cards over film is that you can erase and reuse flash memory cards. Basically you can take as many pictures as the flash memory card can hold, copy your pictures to your Macintosh, and then erase the pictures off the flash memory card so you can use it again.
- **Resolution versus storage:** The number of pictures you can store on flash memory cards depends on the resolution of the pictures you take.

If you capture pictures at a high resolution, you can store far fewer pictures than if you captured those same pictures at a much lower resolution.

- **Storage and speed measurement:** Flash memory cards are often measured in terms of their storage size and speed. The amount of storage a flash memory card can hold is measured in megabytes (MB) and gigabytes (GB), such as 512MB or 2GB. The greater the storage capability of a flash memory card, the higher the cost.

  The speed of flash memory cards is often described as minimum read and write speeds, measured in megabytes per second (MB/sec) such as 10MB/sec. The higher the write speed of a flash memory card, the faster you can capture and store pictures. Sometimes the speed of a flash memory card may also be described as a number — 60x, for example — which basically tells you that the flash memory card is 60 times faster than the original flash memory cards.

TIP

- **Image recovery:** If you ever accidentally erase a picture off a flash memory card, don't panic (and don't store any more pictures on that flash memory card). If you buy a special file-recovery program such as MediaRECOVER (`www.mediarecover.com`) or Digital Picture Recovery (`www.dtidata.com`), you can often retrieve deleted pictures from any type of flash memory card. However, if you delete a picture and then store more pictures on the flash memory card, the new pictures will likely wipe out any traces of your deleted pictures, making it impossible to retrieve the deleted pictures ever again.

The following are the most popular flash memory cards:

- Compact Flash Type I (CFI) and Compact Flash Type II (CFII)
- Secure Digital (SD) and Plus Secure Digital (Plus SD)
- Memory Stick (MS), Memory Stick Pro (MS Pro), Memory Stick Duo (MS Duo), and Memory Stick Pro Duo (MS Pro Duo)
- xD Picture Cards (xD)

TECHNICAL STUFF

The reason why so many different types of flash memory cards exist is because each design is meant to set the "standard" for flash memory cards. Unfortunately, every flash memory card has its limitations, so companies keep coming up with newer designs to overcome these limitations. Because so many "standards" exist, the end result is that there is no standard.

The following sections discuss the popular flash memory cards in more detail.

Compact Flash Type I and Type II

First introduced in 1994, Compact Flash cards were one of the first flash memory cards available and also one of the largest. There are two types of Compact Flash cards: Type I (3.3 mm thick), or CFI; and Type II (5.0 mm thick), or CFII.

Because of the thickness differences, make sure you use the right Compact Flash cards for your digital camera and card reader. A digital camera and card reader that can use a CFII card can also use a CFI card, but the reverse isn't true. Because of their thickness and durability, professional photographers often use Compact Flash cards.

Secure Digital (Mini and Micro SD)

Secure Digital (SD) cards are much smaller than Compact Flash cards and offer built-in encryption to prevent storing copyright infringing materials such as illegal songs, although this encryption feature is rarely used.

Because of their small size, Secure Digital cards are slowly evolving into the standard for digital photography. Even smaller versions of Secure Digital cards include Mini and Micro SD cards.

Memory Stick, Memory Stick Pro, Memory Stick Duo, and Memory Stick Pro Duo

The Memory Stick format was developed by Sony, which means that only Sony devices (digital cameras, video camcorders, and PlayStations) use Memory Sticks for storing digital images. The original Memory Stick could store a maximum of only 128MB of data, so Sony created the Memory Stick Pro, which can hold up to 32GB worth of data. The Memory Stick Duo and Memory Stick Pro Duo look like an original Memory Stick cut in half.

Despite Sony's backing, the Memory Stick format has never gained popularity with other manufacturers. If you buy a Sony camera, you'll probably be stuck with using Memory Sticks, although some of the latest Sony cameras now use Secure Digital cards instead.

xD Picture Cards

Olympus and Fuji film invented the xD Picture Cards to provide yet another standard. Because the xD Picture Cards are fairly recent, far fewer cameras use xD Picture Cards — with the exception, of course, of Olympus cameras and some Fuji film cameras. An xD Picture Card is often more expensive than other flash memory cards, making them less attractive.

Understanding digital image file formats

When you take pictures, your digital camera stores those pictures in a specific graphics file format. The three most common file formats for storing digital photographs are

- ✦ **JPEG (Joint Photo Experts Group):** JPEG is the most common file format because it is recognized by most computers and offers the ability to compress images to shrink the overall file size. (*Compressing* a JPEG file means decreasing the number of colors used in an image, which shrinks the file size but lowers the visual quality.)
- ✦ **TIFF (Tagged Image File Format):** If picture quality is more important than file size, save your pictures as TIFF files. You can still compress TIFF files slightly, but TIFF files always retain all colors. As a result, a compressed TIFF file is almost always larger than an equivalent compressed JPEG file.
- ✦ **RAW (which doesn't stand for anything!):** A third type of file format is called RAW. RAW files offer greater visual quality; however, there is no single RAW file format standard. As a result, every digital camera manufacturer offers its own RAW file format.

  The biggest advantage is that RAW files allow for greater manipulation. As a result, professional photographers often use RAW files for greater control over manipulating their images. The biggest disadvantage is that RAW images take up a large amount of storage space and take longer for a digital camera to store them, which means you can't capture images in rapid succession like you can with JPEG files or ordinary film cameras.

Ultimately, there is no single "best" file format. If a digital camera lets you save images in different file formats, experiment to see which one you like best. You might prefer one type of file format, such as JPEG, for ordinary use but prefer RAW for capturing images in special situations such as taking pictures of a landscape that won't require capturing images quickly.

Transferring Digital Images to the Mac

To transfer pictures from a digital camera to your Mac, you have two choices. First, you can connect your digital camera to your Mac by using a USB cable. Second, pop the flash memory card out of your digital camera and plug it into a card reader (which you have to buy separately) that's plugged into your Mac.

No matter which method you use, your Mac then treats all the images stored on your digital camera's flash memory card as just another external drive that you can copy pictures from and paste them anywhere on your hard drive (such as in the Pictures folder).

When you connect digital camera to your Mac, it can automatically load a program to retrieve those images. Two programs commonly used to load digital images are iPhoto and the Image Capture program.

If you organize pictures in iPhoto, make iPhoto your default application to retrieve pictures from a digital camera. If you use a different program to organize your pictures, make Image Capture your default application.

Defining a default program for retrieving images

If you need to transfer digital images from a camera to your Mac on a regular basis, you can define a default program to use for retrieving these images by following these steps:

1. **Click the Finder icon in the Dock.**

   The Finder appears.

2. **Click Applications in the Finder's sidebar.**

   The contents of the Applications folder appear in the right pane of the Finder.

3. **Double-click the Image Capture icon.**

   The Image Capture window appears.

4. **Choose Image Capture⇨Preferences.**

   A Preferences window appears, as shown in Figure 2-2.

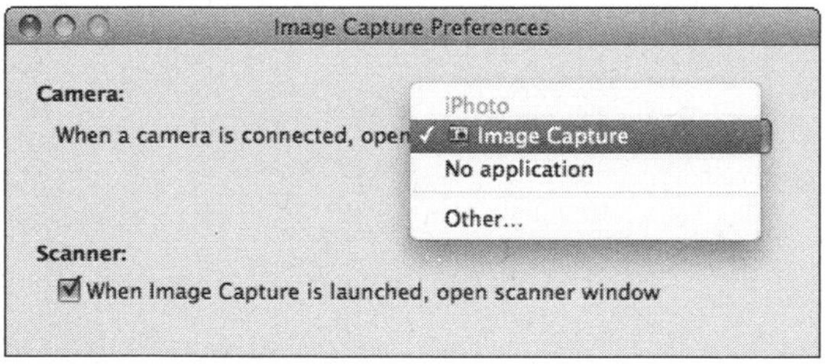

Figure 2-2: The Image Capture Preferences window lets you define a default application to work with a digital camera.

REMEMBER

You can also define a default application through iPhoto and the iPhoto Preferences window.

5. **Click the When a Camera Is Connected, Open pop-up menu and choose iPhoto or Image Capture.**

If you choose Other, you can pick a different program to run when you connect a digital camera to your Mac.

6. **Click the Close button of the Preference window.**
7. **Choose Image Capture⇨Quit Image Capture.**

Retrieving images using iPhoto

If you defined iPhoto as the default program to run when you connect a digital camera to your Mac, follow these steps:

1. **Connect your digital camera to your Mac by using a USB cable.**

   The iPhoto window appears, allowing you to view all the images available.

2. **Click an image that you want to transfer and click Import Selected.**

   If you click Import All, iPhoto retrieves all pictures stored on your digital camera.

   To select multiple images, hold down the ⌘ key and click each picture you want to import.

3. **Choose iPhoto⇨Quit iPhoto.**

Retrieving images using Image Capture

If you defined Image Capture as the default program to run when you connected a digital camera to your Mac, follow these steps:

1. **Connect your digital camera to your Mac by using a USB cable.**

   The Image Capture dialog appears, asking where you want to store your pictures as shown in Figure 2-3.

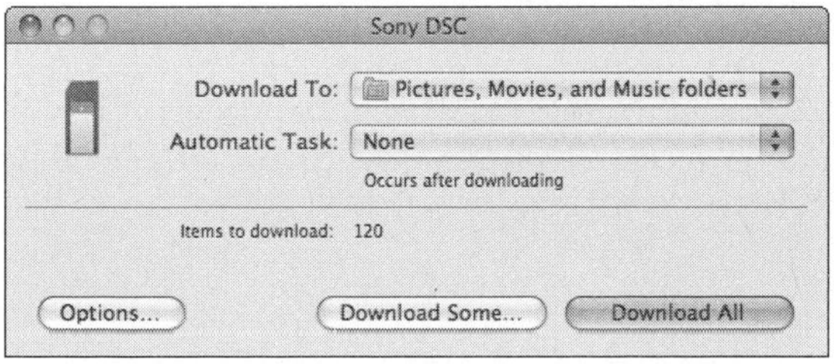

Figure 2-3: The Image Capture dialog lets you choose a folder to store your digital pictures.

TIP

You can also use the Image Capture program to capture and copy images from a scanner.

2. **Click the Download Some button.**

If you click the Download All button, you can copy all pictures stored on your digital camera.

The Image Capture window appears, allowing you to view all the images available, as shown in Figure 2-4.

Figure 2-4: The Image Capture window displays thumbnails of your images so you can see which ones to copy.

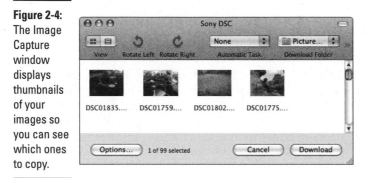

3. **Click an image that you want to transfer and click Download.**

   To select multiple images, hold down the Command key and click on each picture you want to import.

4. **Click Cancel.**
5. **Choose Image Capture➪Quit Image Capture.**

REMEMBER

After you've copied pictures off your digital camera to your Mac, you'll still have to erase the pictures off your flash memory card if you want to reuse it again.

A second way to transfer digital images is to use a separate device called a card reader, which plugs into your Macintosh through a USB port. (You have to buy a separate card reader if you want to use this method. Just yank the flash memory card out of your digital camera and plug it into the card reader. Your Mac now treats the flash memory card, through its card reader, as an external storage device.

WARNING!

Never yank a flash memory card out of a card reader because doing so might cause your Mac to scramble the data on that flash memory card. Before physically removing a flash memory card from a card reader, choose one of the following ways to safely remove a flash memory card from your Mac:

- Drag the flash memory card icon to the Trash icon in the Dock to eject it.
- Click the flash memory icon and choose File➪Eject.

- Click the flash memory icon and press ⌘+E.
- Right-click the flash memory icon and choose Eject from the menu that appears.
- Click the Eject button that appears to the right of the flash memory icon in the Sidebar of a Finder.

Capturing Pictures from Other Sources

If you don't have a separate digital camera, you might have a built-in digital camera in your Macintosh. This built-in camera, called iSight, appears in all newer Mac laptops and iMac models. To capture pictures using this built-in camera, the simplest method is to use a program called Photo Booth.

If you're the type who doesn't like taking pictures, you might prefer copying pictures off Web sites instead. By copying pictures off Web sites, you can find images that you wouldn't normally capture yourself, such as images of fighting in the Middle East or pictures of mountain climbers scaling Mount Everest.

Pictures stored on Web sites are usually copyrighted, so you cannot legally capture those pictures and reuse them for commercial purposes.

Capturing pictures with Photo Booth

If your Mac comes with an iSight camera built-in, you can capture pictures of yourself (or whoever's sitting in front of your Mac), using the Photo Booth program. When you take pictures using Photo Booth, your pictures get saved as JPEG files in a Photo Booth folder, tucked inside your Pictures folder.

To capture pictures with Photo Booth, follow these steps:

1. **Click the Finder icon in the Dock.**

   The Finder appears.

2. **Click Applications in the Finder's sidebar.**

   The contents of the Applications folder appear in the right pane of the Finder.

3. **Double-click the Photo Booth icon.**

   The Photo Booth window appears, displaying the current image seen through the iSight camera, as shown in Figure 2-5.

Figure 2-5: Photo Booth lets you capture pictures through your iSight camera.

TIP

If you click the Effects button, you can capture a picture using visual effects such as fish-eye or in front of a background such as the Eiffel Tower.

4. **Choose File➪Take Photo (or press ⌘+T).**

   Photo Booth counts down from 3, 2, and 1 before capturing your picture. Each captured picture appears at the bottom of the Photo Booth window.

TIP

   If you hold down the Option key while pressing ⌘+T, Photo Booth will take your picture right away without going through its usual 3, 2, 1 countdown.

5. **Choose Photo Booth➪Quit Photo Booth when you're done.**

   Photo Booth stores its pictures in a Photo Booth folder, inside the Pictures folder.

To erase all pictures captured by Photo Booth, follow these steps:

1. **Click the Finder icon in the Dock.**

   The Finder appears.

2. **Click Applications in the Finder's sidebar.**

   The contents of the Applications folder appear in the right pane of the Finder.

3. **Double-click the Photo Booth icon.**

   The Photo Booth window appears.

4. **Choose Edit⇨Delete All Photos.**

   A dialog appears, asking if you really want to delete all your pictures stored in the Photo Booth folder.

5. **Click OK to delete them or Cancel (if you changed your mind).**

REMEMBER

When you choose the Delete All Photos command, you'll remove all pictures stored in the Photo Booth folder inside the Pictures folder.

Capturing pictures off Web sites

By browsing through different Web sites, you can find a variety of different images that you might want to use for personal use, such as making greeting cards with the President's face on it.

To capture images off a Web page, follow these steps:

1. **Load your favorite Web browser, such as Safari.**
2. **Browse to a Web page and point the cursor at an image that you want to copy.**

   REMEMBER

   As a general rule, don't copy pictures off Web sites and reuse those pictures on a commercial Web site due to copyright rules.

3. **Right-click (Control-click) over your chosen image.**

   A pop-up menu appears, as shown in Figure 2-6.

4. **Choose one of the following:**
   - *Save Image to "Downloads":* Saves the picture in the Downloads folder, stored inside your Home folder.
   - *Save Image As:* Lets you choose a name for your picture and a folder to store that picture.
   - *Add Image to iPhoto Library:* Stores the image in iPhoto.
   - *Copy Image:* Copies the image so you can paste it into another program later.

Figure 2-6: Right-clicking a Web page image gives you a variety of choices for saving the picture.

TIP

The Save Image As option is the only one that lets you choose your own descriptive name for an image and specify the location where it is to be saved. All the other options save an image using that image's original filename, which might be something cryptic like `p009.jpg`, although you can always rename the file later if you want.

Editing Digital Images

One advantage that digital photographs have over traditional film is that you can easily edit and modify digital photographs just by using your computer. By controlling an image right down to the appearance of individual pixels, digital editing gives you the power to enhance pictures, remove unwanted portion of pictures, or create your own imaginary images from your fantasies and dreams.

Editing a picture is typically a two-step process. First, you must select which part of the picture you want to change. Second, you have to select a way to change it, such as deleting or coloring it.

To change a picture, you can modify a single pixel by changing its color. If you change the color of pixels, one by one, you'll eventually change the appearance of that picture.

Of course, modifying individual pixels can get tedious, so pixel editing is usually reserved for touching up small portions of an image. When faced with major reconstruction work, it's more common to modify an entire group of adjacent pixels. In order to do that, you first have to select the part of the picture you want to change.

To digitally edit a photograph, you need a digital editor such as one of the following:

- **Photoshop or Photoshop Elements (`www.adobe.com`):** Photoshop is the most popular (and expensive) program that graphics professionals use to manipulate images. A much cheaper and simpler version is Photoshop Elements, which offers the most commonly used features of Photoshop.
- **Photoline 32 (`www.pl32.com`):** A cross-platform (Windows and Mac) program that offers a low-cost alternative to Photoshop. Besides editing images, Photoline 32 can also create Flash and GIF animation.
- **PhotoStudio X (`www.arcsoft.com`):** Provides a wealth of features specifically designed for both modifying and organizing digital photographs.
- **Pixen (`http://opensword.org/Pixen`):** A free and simple image editor specifically designed to modify pixels in pictures.
- **Pixel (`www.kanzelsberger.com`):** A cross-platform image editor for editing digital images or creating digital artwork on its own.

The examples in the following sections use Photoshop Elements but all graphics editing programs work in similar ways.

Book IV, Chapter 1 provides more information about editing digital pictures using iPhoto.

Selecting all or part of a picture

When you're editing a digital photograph, you can select all or part of the picture. In most digital-editing programs, the shortcut key for selecting an entire image to change is ⌘+A.

Selecting all of a picture lets you use effects such as changing a color picture to black and white or brightening up the colors of an entire image, as shown in Figure 2-7.

Rather than change an entire picture, you might want to modify only part of a picture, such as highlighting a single object in a picture. You can also create a new picture that combines both pictures in a unique manner, as shown in Figure 2-8.

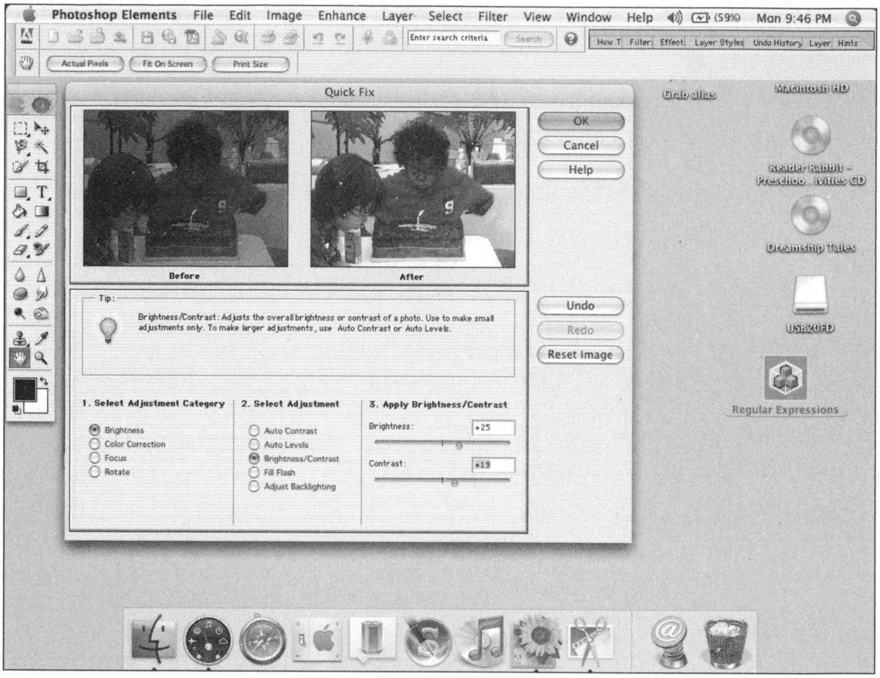

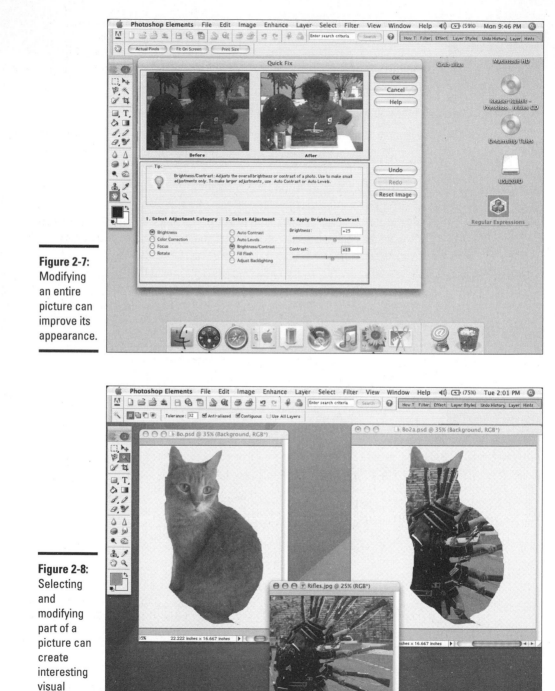

Figure 2-7: Modifying an entire picture can improve its appearance.

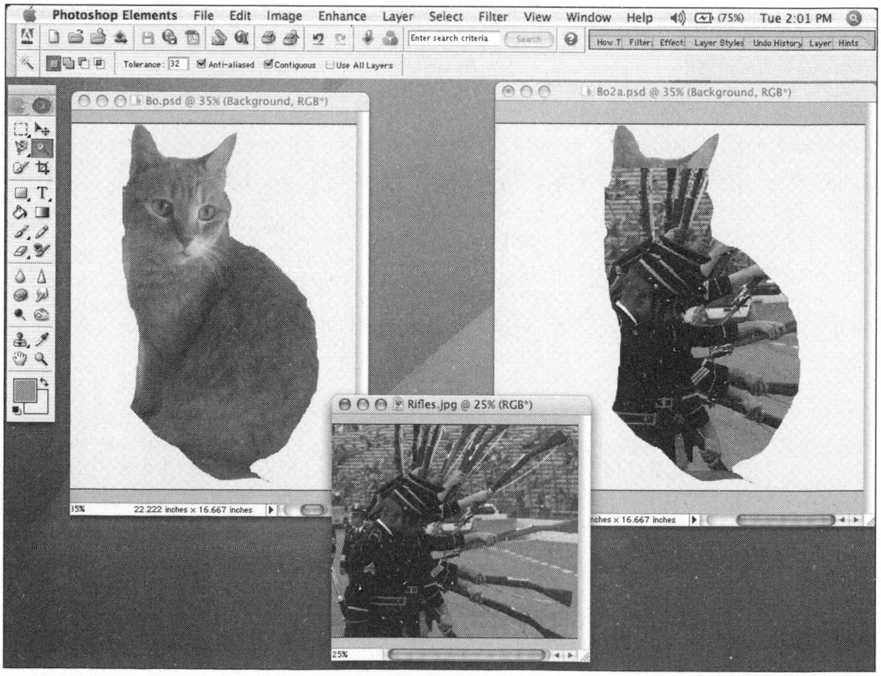

Figure 2-8: Selecting and modifying part of a picture can create interesting visual effects.

If you just want to select part of a picture, you have to use a selection tool. Most image-editing programs offer four types of selections tools:

- **Rectangular:** Selects a rectangular area of a picture.
- **Circular:** Selects a circular area of a picture.
- **Lasso:** Lets you drag the mouse around to define an area to select.
- **Magnetic Lasso:** Lets you drag the mouse around to select color boundaries in a picture. This tool lets you select irregularly shaped objects, such as a hand or a flower.

The basic steps to selecting part of a picture are

1. **Click a selection tool (Lasso, Rectangular, and so on) displayed in the toolbox, which is a collection of icons that typically appear on the left side of the window.**
2. **Drag the mouse over the part of the image you want to select.**

   As you drag the mouse, a dotted line appears that defines the area you selected as shown in Figure 2-9.

Figure 2-9: A dotted line, called a marquee, defines your selected area.

After you select part of a picture, you can choose a command to modify just that portion you selected, such as darkening or lightening or brightening the colors.

Changing colors

One common feature of digital editing programs is the ability to change colors in an image, either by touching up existing colors to make them brighter or by changing the colors altogether, such as turning a lady's pink scarf into a red one.

Such color replacement features are the basis for red-eye removal tools found in many digital editing programs. Red-eye often appears when the camera's flash makes a person's eyes appear with a reddish glow as if they're radioactive. Obviously, such red eyes can ruin an otherwise perfectly good picture, so red-eye removal tools basically replace the reddish tint in an image with another color such as black.

Of course, you can use the red-eye removal tool as a general color replacement tool as well. That way you can create unusual effects, such as changing someone's dark hair into blazing purple and pink, or changing the color of the sky from light blue to red.

The basic steps for using a red-eye removal tool are as follows:

1. **Click the Red-Eye Removal Tool in the toolbox, which generally appears on the left side of the window.**
2. **Click over the color that you want to replace (such as the red tint in a person's eye).**
3. **Click a color palette to choose a replacement color.**
4. **Drag the mouse over the part of your picture that you want to recolor.**

   If you drag the mouse over the color you selected in Step 2, your image-editing program replaces the color with the replacement color you chose in Step 3. If you drag the mouse over a different color than the one you chose in Step 2, dragging the mouse does nothing.

Adding and removing items in a picture

Part of the fun with digital photography is the ease with which you can add or delete items in a picture. By adding items to a picture, you can create unusual images that never existed, as shown in Figure 2-10.

The simplest way to add images is to copy all or part of a picture and paste it over a second picture. Of course, this can look as sloppy as clipping a picture out of a magazine and pasting it over another picture. Another way to add a picture is to follow these steps:

1. **Copy (or cut) an image from a picture, such as a person or an animal.**
2. **Select an area in a second picture where you want to paste an image.**

   By selecting an area, your copied image won't appear outside of the area of this selected boundary.

3. Paste the copied (or cut) image from Step 1 into the selected area from Step 2.

Figure 2-10: Adding items to a picture can create new images.

To paste into a selected area, choose Edit➪ Paste Into. Just be aware that other types of image-editing programs might not have a Paste Into command or might accomplish the same steps by using a different command altogether.

REMEMBER

The preceding steps represent just one way to copy and paste an image into a picture. There are dozens of ways to paste an image into a picture, depending on the features of your image-editing program.

Although adding images can create new pictures, removing items from a picture can clean up an image and make it more suitable for public viewing, as shown in Figure 2-11.

Normally, if you select part of an image and delete it, you'll leave a gaping hole in the picture. To delete an image while filling in the deleted area, you can use a special tool called a Clone Stamping Tool (which might go by different names in other image-editing programs).

The Clone Stamping Tool lets you copy and paste pixels from one part of a picture to another. This lets you copy background images, such as a wall, and paste it over someone's face, effectively erasing that person's face from the picture.

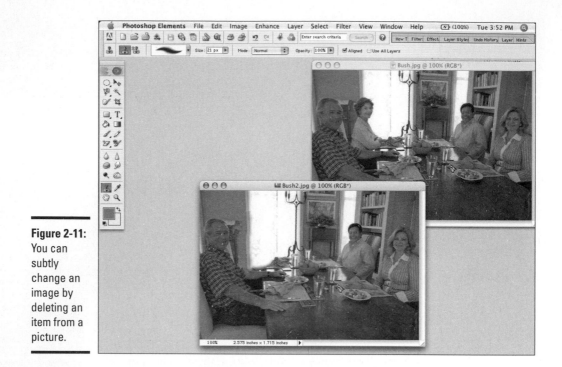

Figure 2-11: You can subtly change an image by deleting an item from a picture.

To use a Clone Stamping Tool, follow these steps:

1. **Click the Clone Stamping Tool in the toolbox, which is a collection of icons that typically appear on the left side of the window.**
2. **Click the part of the picture that you want to copy and paste to a new area of the picture.**

   The point where you click is called an *anchor point.* To define this anchor point, you might need to hold down a modifier key as you click, such as the Option or ⌘ key, depending on your program.
3. **Drag the mouse to "paint" over the picture with the image you clicked in Step 2.**

   If you clicked a brick wall in Step 2, dragging the mouse in Step 3 would paint that brick wall image over any part of your picture, effectively "erasing" that object. You might have to repeat this process several times to completely erase an image.

Chapter 3: Watching Videos on a Mac

In This Chapter

- Understanding movie formats
- Understanding digital movie formats
- Playing a digital video file
- Playing a VCD
- Playing a DVD

If you ever get bored, relax and watch a movie on your Mac. Not only can your Mac act like a DVD player, but your Mac can also bookmark and store your favorite scenes so you can always find your favorite parts of a movie.

Although many full-length movies appear on DVD, many shorter movies and videos are stored entirely as digital video files. Whether a movie is stored on DVD or as a digital video file, your Mac can play it at your convenience.

Understanding Video Disc Formats

The most common videodisc format is DVD (Digital Video Disc). However, this isn't the only videodisc format. An earlier video disc format is VCD (Video Compact Disc), which essentially stores video files on ordinary CDs. VCDs typically offer lower video quality than DVDs (comparable to videotape) and offer much less storage than DVDs.

Although DVDs are the current videodisc standard for most of the world, two competing standards have emerged as successors to DVDs: HD DVD (High-Definition Digital Versatile Disc) and Blu-ray discs.

HD DVD can store roughly three times as much data as ordinary DVDs (15GB for HD DVD versus 4.7GB for DVDs). Because HD DVDs are similar to ordinary DVDs, HD DVDs cost nearly the same to produce.

The main advantage of Blu-ray discs is that they can store much more data than even HD DVDs (25GB for a Blu-ray disc versus 15GB for an HD DVD). However, Blu-ray discs are also much more expensive to produce.

Currently, the Mac can play DVDs and VCDs out of the box, but if you want to watch video stored on HD DVDs or Blu-ray discs, you need to buy a special HD DVD or Blu-ray disc drive and a program to use it.

Understanding Digital Video Formats

Video discs are popular for storing and distributing videos, but with high-speed Internet connections and lower hard drive storage costs, storing full-length movies as a single digital video file has become both popular and practical. The biggest problem with digital video is the wide variety of digital video formats available. To play a digital video file, you need a video player program that accepts the type of video file you have. The following is a list of digital video file types and the programs that you can use to play them:

- **QuickTime (`.mov`):** Playable by the QuickTime Player that comes with every Mac.
- **Audio/Video Interleaved (`.avi`):** An older video file format introduced by Microsoft in 1992, although still commonly used today. To play AVI video files on a Mac, you'll need a separate video player such as the free VLC media player (`www.videolan.org`).
- **Windows Media Video (`.wmv`):** Playable on a Mac if you first install the Flip4Mac program (`www.flip4mac.com`), which allows the QuickTime Player to display Windows Media Video files.
- **DivX (`.divx`):** A high-quality video format known for storing DVD-quality video images in a digital video file format. DivX files can be played on a Mac with the free VLC media player (`www.videolan.org`) or the free DivX player (`www.divx.com`).

  Because DivX is a proprietary video file format, programmers have created a similar open source equivalent called Xvid (`www.xvid.org`).
- **Flash video (`.flv`):** A video file format commonly used on Web sites such as news sites that offer video (CNN and Reuters) along with YouTube, MySpace, and Yahoo! Video. You can play flash videos by using the free Adobe Flash player (`www.adobe.com`).
- **RealVideo (`.rm`):** A video file format often used for streaming video. RealVideo files can be played and viewed using the free Real Player program (`www.real.com`).
- **Moving Picture Expert Group (MPEG) (`.mpg`):** A video file format that consists of different versions, including
  - *MPEG-1:* Used for storing video on VCDs.
  - *MPEG-2:* Broadcast-quality video such as on SVCDs, DVDs, HD TV, HD DVDs, and Blu-ray discs.

* *MPEG-3:* Originally designed for HD TV but now rarely used.
* *MPEG-4:* For storing video on HD DVD and Blu-ray discs.

You can view MPEG videos with the QuickTime Player, the free VLC media player (`www.videolan.org`), or the commercial MacVCD player (`www.mireth.com`)

The QuickTime Player can't play MPEG videos if the audio is stored as AC3 (Dolby Digital) files.

Most video players are free because the companies developing and promoting a specific video file format want as many people as possible to use (and rely on) their particular video file format. Then these companies can make money by selling programs that create and store video in their specific file format.

Playing a Digital Video File

Playing a digital video file is as simple as double-clicking that file (or clicking the video file once and choosing File⇨Open), which opens the appropriate video player on your Mac and displays your video file on the screen. If you find a video file on a Web site, you can usually click the video file directly on the Web page to see it play within your browser.

Occasionally, you might find a video file format that you can't play on your Mac. In this case, you have two choices:

* Download and install a video player for that particular video file format.
* Convert the video file into a format that your Mac can play.

Sometimes it might be simpler just to download and install (yet another) free video player to watch video trapped in a different video file format. However, downloading and installing multiple video players can be annoying, so you might prefer to convert digital file formats instead. To convert digital video files, you need a special digital video file format conversion program.

To convert non-copy-protected DVD videos to a digital video file, such as an AVI or MPEG, you can use a free program called HandBrake (`http://handbrake.m0k.org`). In case you need to convert one digital video file format into another one (such as converting a DivX file into a QuickTime file), grab a copy of the oddly named ffmpegX (`www.ffmpegx.com`) or MPEG StreamClip (`www.squared5.com`).

By converting digital video files, you can store all your videos in a single file format, such as QuickTime, to avoid having to download and install half a dozen different video players just to watch one or two video files.

Playing a DVD

The most common video disc format is the DVD format. To play DVDs, just insert your DVD into your Mac. DVD Player loads and displays your DVD's main menu, as shown in Figure 3-1.

To choose from a DVD menu, just double-click an option, such as Play Movie or Special Features. Then sit back, pop some popcorn, and enjoy the show.

If you just want to watch a DVD from start to finish, you don't have to read the rest of this chapter. However, if you want to use some of the special features of DVD Player, keep reading.

Understanding full screen mode and window mode

One of the simplest ways to customize your video is to switch back and forth between full screen and window mode. In full screen mode, the video fills your entire computer screen. In window mode, the video fills only part of your computer screen while giving you access to the rest of your Mac Desktop such as the Dock and other program windows, as shown in Figure 3-2.

Figure 3-1: DVD Player displays the video's menus so you can choose what to watch.

Exiting and returning to full screen mode

The first time you insert a DVD into your Mac, DVD Player will likely display your video in full screen mode. To exit full screen mode, choose one of the following:

- ✦ Press Esc.
- ✦ Press ⌘+F.
- ✦ Click the Exit Full Screen button on the Controller, as shown in Figure 3-3.

REMEMBER

In full screen mode, you can view the DVD Player menu bar by moving the pointer to the top of the screen. You can also view the DVD Controller in full screen mode by moving the pointer to the bottom of the screen.

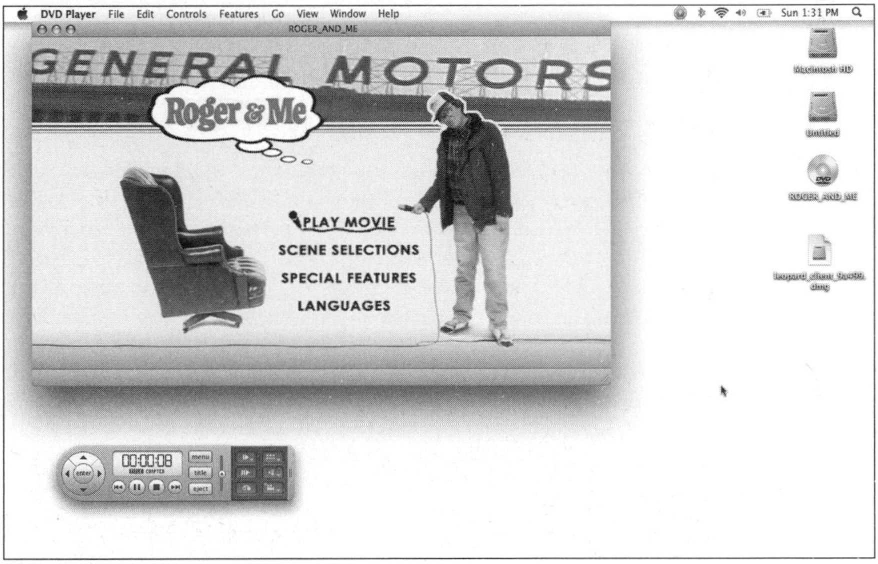

Figure 3-2: DVD Player can shrink a video inside a window on your Desktop.

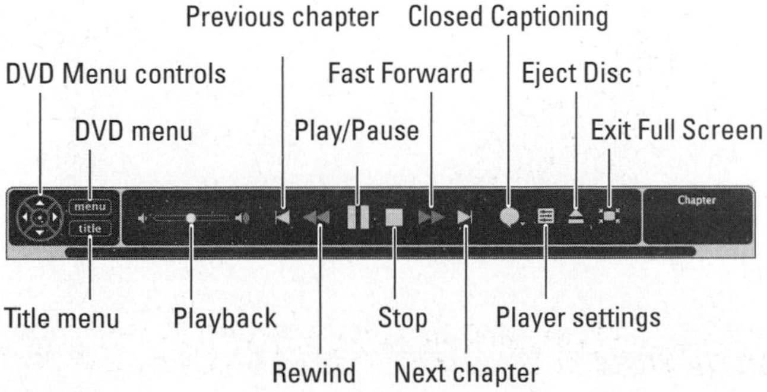

Figure 3-3: The Controller appears at the bottom of the screen.

To return to full screen mode, choose one of the following:

✦ Press ⌘+F.

✦ Choose View⇨Enter Full Screen.

Viewing a video in a window

When you exit full screen mode, your video appears in a window with the Controller displayed underneath the DVD window. (Refer to Figure 3-2.) By choosing the View menu, you can display a video in the following window sizes:

✦ Half Size

✦ Actual Size

✦ Double Size

✦ Fit to Screen

✦ Enter Full Screen

When viewing a video in a window, the Controller takes on a different *skin* (the display appearance), as shown in Figure 3-4.

Although the Controllers in both full screen and window mode allow you to control a DVD, each Controller offers slightly different features. You can access some features in both full screen and window mode, but many features are available only in one mode or the other.

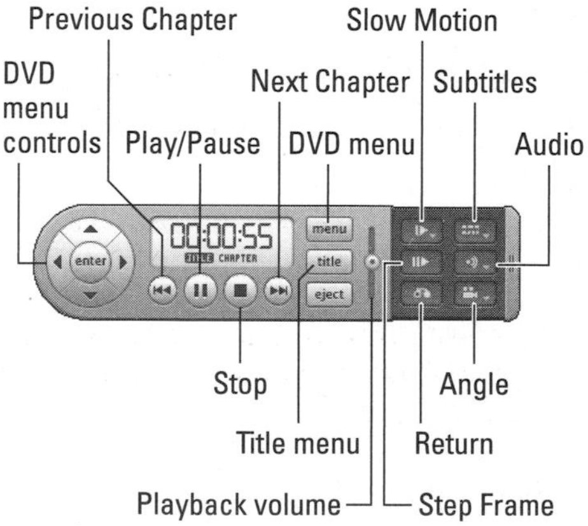

Figure 3-4: The Controller appears in new garb when underneath a video window.

To avoid letting any other window cover up part of your video window, choose View⇨Viewer Above Other Apps. To turn off this feature, choose the same command again.

Viewing the DVD and Title menus

Most DVDs include an initial menu that lets you choose what to watch, such as the feature presentation or trivia clips. Some DVDs also offer a Title menu that lets you pick different episodes, such as a DVD containing multiple episodes from a single TV show season. Some DVDs offer both an initial menu and a Title menu, and they might even start playing automatically.

To jump to the initial DVD or Title menu, try clicking the DVD Menu or the Title Menu button on the Controller.

Not all DVDs have a DVD or Title menu.

If you want to start the DVD from the very beginning just as if you inserted the DVD into your Mac for the very first time, follow these steps:

1. **If in full screen mode, move the pointer to the top of the screen to display the DVD Player menu bar.**
2. **Choose Go⇨Beginning of Disc.**

   Your DVD starts playing from the beginning.

Skipping through a video

Sometimes you might want to skip over or replay part of a video. To skip backward or forward through a video, follow these steps:

1. **Switch to full screen mode.**
2. **Click the Pause button.**
3. **Click one of the following buttons on the Controller:**
   - *Rewind:* Reverses the video a few frames and starts playing normally again
   - *Fast Forward:* Jumps the video ahead a few frames and starts playing normally again

When you click the Rewind or Fast Forward buttons, the video jumps ahead (or back) only a few frames. If you want to keep rewinding or fast-forwarding continuously, follow these steps:

1. **Switch to window mode.**
2. **Choose Controls⇨Scan Forward (or Scan Backwards).**

   Your video continuously rewinds or fast forwards.
3. **Click the Play button on the Controller or press the spacebar to play the video at its normal speed.**

You can also drag the slider at the bottom of the Controller (in full screen mode) to rewind or fast-forward a video.

Viewing frames in steps and slow motion

If you want to study a particular part of a video, the DVD Player lets you view individual frames one at a time, or view your video in slow motion. To view individual frames, follow these steps:

1. **Switch to window mode.**
2. **Click the Step Frame button on the Controller.**

   Each time you click the Step Frame button, the video advances one frame.
3. **Click the Play button on the Controller, or press the space bar to play the video at normal speed.**

Stepping through a video one frame at a time can get tedious, so a faster way to step through a video is in slow motion. To view your video in slow motion, follow these steps:

1. **Switch to window mode.**
2. **Click the Slow Motion button on the Controller or choose Controls➪Slow Motion.**
3. **Click the Play button on the Controller, or press the space bar to play the video at normal speed.**

Skipping by chapters

Most DVD videos are divided into segments called chapters, which are usually listed somewhere on or inside the DVD case. If you want to view a favorite scene, just jump to the chapter that contains your favorite scene.

To skip back to the previous chapter or forward to the next chapter, choose one of the following:

- Click the Previous Chapter or Next Chapter button on the Controller.
- Press the left- or right-arrow key while the video is playing.

To skip to a specific chapter, follow these steps:

1. **If in full screen mode, move the pointer to the top of the screen to display the DVD Player menu bar.**
2. **Choose Go➪Chapter.**

   A submenu appears listing all the available chapters.
3. **Click a chapter number.**

Placing bookmarks in a video

Sometimes your favorite parts of a movie don't correlate exactly to chapter sections on a DVD. In case you want to jump to a specific part of a video, you can create a bookmark.

REMEMBER

DVD Player saves your bookmarks on your hard drive, so if you pop the DVD out and back in again, your bookmarks are still preserved.

Creating a bookmark

To create a bookmark, follow these steps:

1. **If in full screen mode, move the pointer to the top of the screen to display the DVD Player menu bar.**
2. **Click the Pause button at the spot in the video where you want to place a bookmark.**
3. **Choose Controls⇨New Bookmark.**

   A Bookmark dialog appears, as shown in Figure 3-5.
4. **Enter a descriptive name for your bookmark in the text field and click Add.**

REMEMBER

If you select the Make Default Bookmark check box, you can jump to this bookmark in window mode by choosing Go⇨Default Bookmark.

Figure 3-5: The bookmark dialog lets you choose a descriptive name for your bookmark.

Jumping to a bookmark

After you've created at least one bookmark, you can jump to that bookmark by following these steps:

1. **If in full screen mode, move the pointer to the top of the screen to display the DVD Player menu bar.**
2. **Choose Go⇨Bookmarks.**

   A pop-up menu appears, listing all your saved bookmarks.
3. **Click the bookmark name you want to jump to.**

Deleting a bookmark

After you've created at least one bookmark, you can delete a bookmark by following these steps:

1. **If in full screen mode, move the pointer to the top of the screen to display the DVD Player menu bar.**
2. **Choose Window⇨Bookmarks.**

   A Bookmarks window appears, as shown in Figure 3-6.

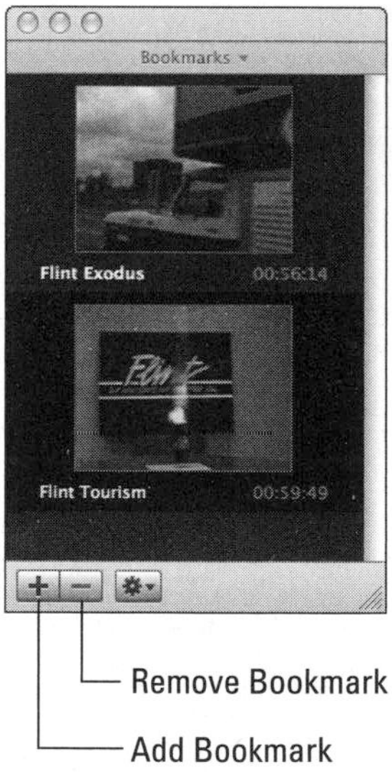

Figure 3-6: The Bookmarks window shows you all your bookmarks.

3. **Click to select the bookmark you want to delete and then click the Remove bookmark button (minus sign).**

   A dialog appears, asking whether you're sure you want to delete your chosen bookmark.

4. **Click OK (or Cancel).**
5. **Click the Close button of the Bookmarks window.**

TIP

If you click the Add bookmark button, you can add a bookmark at the video's currently paused position.

Creating video clips

A bookmark can mark the spot where you want to start viewing a video, but you can also create a video clip with a start and an end that you determine. That way, you can define a specific part of a video to watch again or show to others.

Creating a video clip

To create a video clip, follow these steps:

1. **If in full screen mode, move the pointer to the top of the screen to display the DVD Player menu bar.**
2. **Click the Pause button on the Controller when the video is at the point where you want to create the beginning of a video clip.**
3. **Choose Controls⇨New Video Clip.**

   A New Video Clip dialog appears, as shown in Figure 3-7.
4. **Click in the Clip Name text box and type a descriptive name for your video clip.**
5. **Drag the slider until you see the frame you want to use as the ending of your video clip.**
6. **Click the Set button to the left of the Start video box to define the starting point you chose in Step 2.**
7. **Click the Set button to the left of the End video box to define the ending point you chose in Step 5.**

   The Start box displays the frame that starts the beginning of your video clip, and the End box displays a frame that defines the end of your video clip.
8. Click Save.

REMEMBER

Your saved video clip isn't physically saved on your hard drive; just the start and ending positions are saved. To view a saved video clip, you have to insert your DVD back into your Mac.

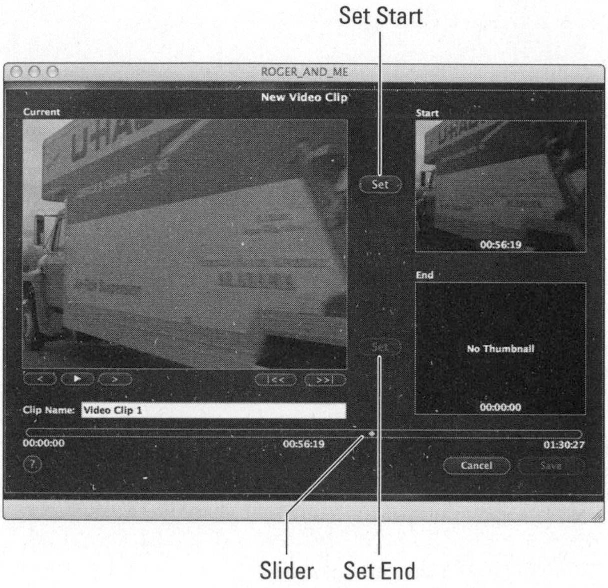

Figure 3-7: The New Video Clip dialog lets you choose a name for your video clip.

Viewing a video clip

To view a saved video clip, be sure your DVD is back in your Mac and then follow these steps:

1. **If in full screen mode, move the pointer to the top of the screen to display the DVD Player menu bar.**
2. **Choose Go⇨Video Clips.**

   A submenu appears, listing all the video clips you've created.
3. **Click the name of the video clip you want to watch.**

   Your video clip plays until it reaches the end frame you defined.

TIP

If you want to exit from your video clip, choose Go⇨Video Clips⇨Exit Clip Mode.

Deleting a video clip

To delete a video clip, follow these steps:

1. **If in full screen mode, move the pointer to the top of the screen to display the DVD Player menu bar.**

2. **Choose Window➪Video Clips.**

   A Video Clips window appears, as shown in Figure 3-8.

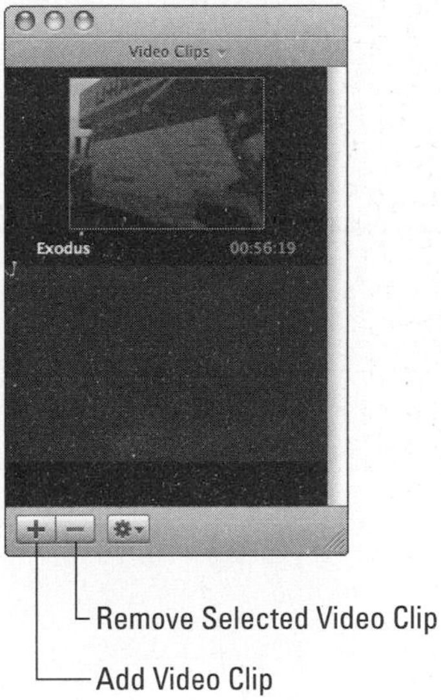

Figure 3-8: The Video Clip window lets you delete any saved video clips.

3. **Click to select the video clip you want to delete and then click the Remove Selected Video Clip button (minus sign).**

   A dialog appears, asking whether you're sure you want to delete your chosen video clip.

4. **Click OK (or Cancel).**

5. **Click the Close button of the Video Clip window.**

Viewing closed captioning

Many DVDs include closed captioning and subtitles. Closed captioning displays written dialogue on-screen in the same language that's being spoken — English, for example — whereas subtitles gives you a choice of reading dialogue on-screen in a language other than what's being spoken, such as French and Spanish.

To turn on closed captioning, choose one of the following:

- ✦ In window mode, choose Features➪Closed Captioning➪Turn On.
- ✦ In full screen mode, click the Closed Captioning button on the Controller and choose Turn On Closed Captioning.

To view subtitles in different languages, choose one of the following:

- ✦ In window mode, choose Features⇨Subtitles and then choose a language, such as French or Spanish.
- ✦ In full screen mode, click the Closed Captioning button on the Controller and choose a language under the Subtitles category.

REMEMBER

Not all DVDs offer closed captioning or subtitles.

Viewing different camera angles

Some DVDs, such as those containing video of concerts, offer a choice of multiple camera angles. This gives you a chance to view a DVD and, at a certain spot, switch from looking at the drummer to the lead guitarist.

To switch to different camera angle, also called just angles, choose one of the following methods:

- ✦ In window mode, click the Angle button on the Controller and choose an angle.
- ✦ In window mode, choose Features⇨Angle and choose an angle.
- ✦ In full screen mode, click the Streams/Closed Captioning button on the Controller and choose an angle under the Angle category.

REMEMBER

Not all DVDs offer different angles.

Choosing different audio tracks

Sometimes a DVD might offer multiple audio tracks, such as a default audio track and alternative audio tracks of foreign languages. To switch to different audio tracks, choose one of the following:

- ✦ In window mode, click the Audio button on the Controller and choose an audio track.
- ✦ In window mode, choose Features⇨Audio and choose an audio track.
- ✦ In full screen mode, click the Streams/Closed Captioning button on the Controller and choose an audio track under the Audio Streams category.

REMEMBER

Not all DVDs offer multiple audio tracks.

Customizing DVD Player

Normally, you can pop a DVD into your Mac and watch it play right away. However, you might want to take some time to customize DVD Player to change how it plays.

Parental controls

If you don't want your children watching certain DVDs, you can try turning on DVD Player's parental controls. These parental controls are designed either to block certain types of DVDs from playing or to prevent certain objectionable scenes from appearing while allowing the rest of the movie to be seen.

Because of the extra expense involved in adding parental control features to a DVD, many DVDs don't support parental controls. If you turn on parental controls, it's entirely possible to watch a totally inappropriate DVD on your Mac — just because the DVD itself hasn't been programmed to recognize any of the DVD Player's parental control features.

To turn on (or off) parental controls, follow these steps:

1. **If in Full Screen Mode, move the pointer to the top of the screen to display the DVD Player menu bar.**
2. **Choose Features➪Enable Parental Controls.**

   A dialog appears, asking for your password.
3. **Type your password and click OK.**

To disable parental controls, repeat the above steps, except in Step 2, and choose Features➪Disable Parental Controls.

Defining DVD Player preferences

DVD Player offers six categories for modifying how to play DVDs:

- **General:** Defines how DVD Player behaves when running, such as whether to start in full screen mode.
- **Disc Setup:** Defines the audio, subtitles, and DVD menus displayed.
- **Full Screen:** Defines how other program windows behave when a video appears in full screen mode.
- **Windows:** Defines how to display closed captioning in a window.
- **Previously Viewed:** Defines how to handle a DVD that has been ejected and inserted back into your Mac, such as whether to start playing the DVD at the beginning again or at the last scene viewed before you ejected the DVD.
- **High Definition:** Defines how to play high-definition DVDs if you have a HD DVD or Blu-ray drive attached to your Mac.

To change how your DVDs play, follow these steps:

1. **If in Full Screen Mode, move the pointer to the top of the screen to display the DVD Player menu bar.**
2. **Choose DVD Player — Preferences.**

   A Preferences dialog appears, as shown in Figure 3-9.

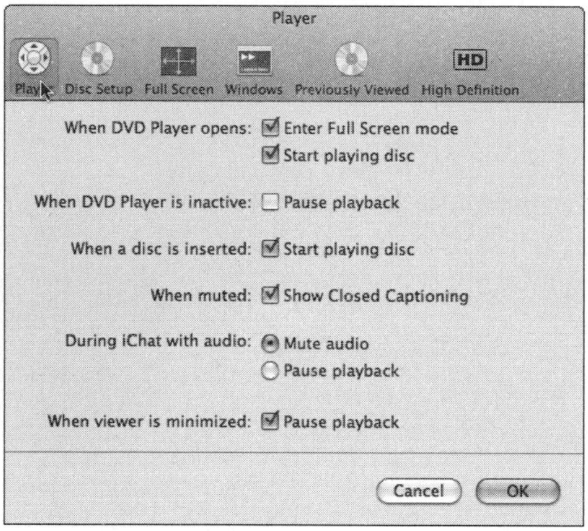

Figure 3-9: The Preferences dialog lets you customize different features of DVD Player.

3. **Click an icon, such as Player or Full Screen, and change any options.**

   Some of these options let you mute sound in case you receive an iChat invitation or defines colors for displaying closed captioning so you can see it easier on the screen. Feel free to experiment with different options to see which ones are most useful.
4. **Click the Close button of the Preferences dialog.**

Chapter 4: Using Front Row for Movies, Music, and Photos

In This Chapter

- Using the Apple Remote
- Accessing Front Row
- Playing movies and videos
- Playing music and podcasts
- Viewing pictures

If you want to watch videos, play music, or browse through digital photographs, you could load QuickTime Player, iTunes, and iPhoto and search for the videos, audio files, or pictures you want to hear or see. However, this can be clumsy, especially if you want to play music and browse through your photograph collection at the same time.

To give you another way to access your video, audio, and digital images, the latest Macs come with a program called Front Row. The whole purpose of Front Row is to integrate the features of the QuickTime Player, iTunes, the DVD Player, and iPhoto to make it easy for you to access your media without having to load a bunch of separate programs to do it.

Using the Apple Remote

The most common way to control Front Row is through the Apple Remote, although you can also control Front Row through the keyboard (in case you don't have an Apple Remote). The Apple Remote provides the following controls, as shown in Figure 4-1:

- **Up:** Moves the highlighting up one option.
- **Down:** Moves the highlighting down one option.
- **Next:** Fast forwards a file or selects the next item.
- **Previous:** Rewinds a file or selects the previous item.

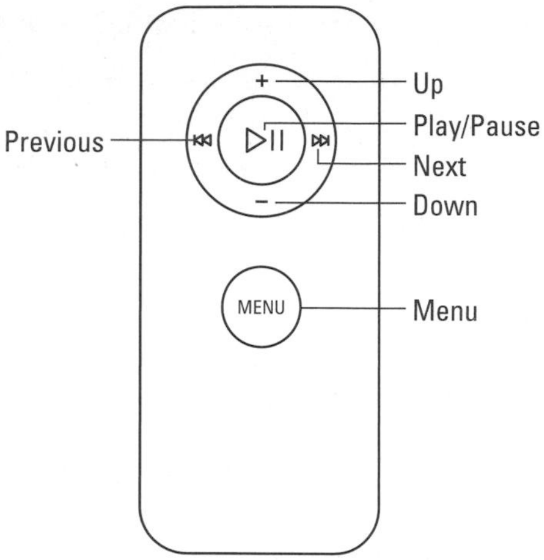

Figure 4-1: The Apple Remote provides standard remote control features.

- ✦ **Play/Pause:** Toggles between playing and pausing a file. Also used to select a highlighted option.
- ✦ **Menu:** Displays the initial Front Row menu. Also used to go back to a previous menu.

Although the Apple Remote can control the Front Row program, it can also control your Mac and other programs, such as Keynote, which can be handy if you want to control it from a distance, such as using a Mac to give presentations.

Making a Mac go to sleep

To make your Mac go to sleep using the Apple Remote, follow these steps:

1. **Hold down the Play/Pause button.**

   A sleeping Apple Remote icon appears on the screen.

2. **Release the Play/Pause button.**

   Your Mac obediently goes to sleep.

To wake up a sleeping Mac with the Apple Remote, just tap any button on the Apple Remote.

Booting up a Mac

If you've divided your hard drive into partitions and installed two different operating systems (such as using Boot Camp to install Windows), you can use the Apple Remote to help you choose which partition and operating system to use by following these steps:

1. **Hold down the Menu button and turn on (or restart) your Mac.**

   The hard drive icons that appear list all the bootable partitions you can choose.

2. **Press the Previous and Next buttons to select a hard drive.**
3. **Press the Play/Pause button to choose the selected hard drive.**

Controlling applications

You can use the Apple Remote to control several popular programs, including Keynote, iTunes, iPhoto, and DVD Player.

REMEMBER

The Apple Remote can control different programs, but it won't let you switch, open, or close programs. If you want to do this from a distance, use a wireless keyboard and mouse.

Controlling a Keynote presentation

By using the Apple Remote with Keynote, you can give and control a presentation without being near your Mac. To start a presentation, load Keynote and your presentation using your keyboard or mouse. At this point, you can view your presentation with the Apple Remote by pressing the Play/Pause button.

To view the next slide, press the Next button. To view the previous slide, press the Previous button. If you press the Menu button once, Keynote displays thumbnails of your slides, as shown in Figure 4-2.

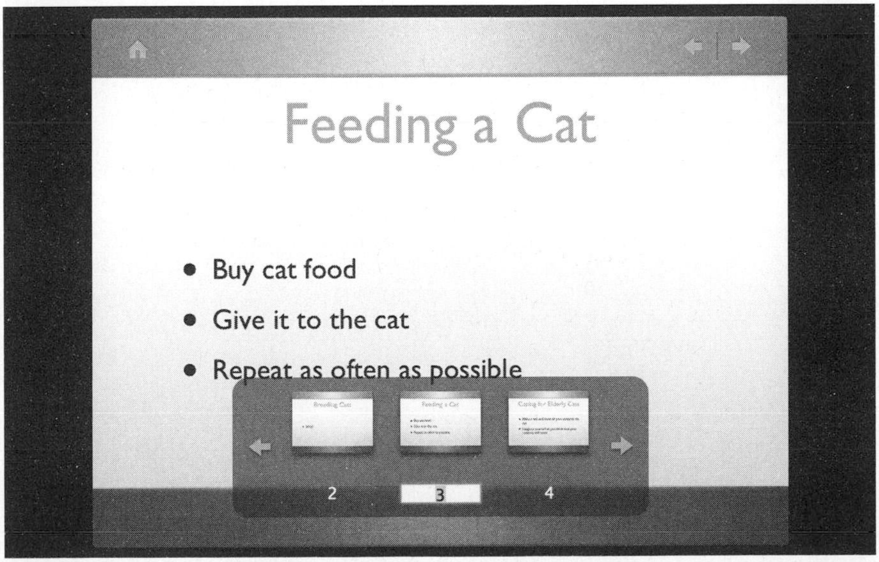
Feeding a Cat
Buy cat food
Give it to the cat
Repeat as often as possible
2
3
4

Figure 4-2: The Menu button displays thumbnails of your presentation.

If you hold down the Menu button, Keynote exits your presentation and returns you to the main Keynote screen.

Controlling iTunes

Using the Apple Remote with iTunes lets you control your music from across the room. To start playing a song, load iTunes using the keyboard or mouse and pick a playlist (or choose your entire music collection). At this point, you can press the Play/Pause button on the Apple Remote.

To start playing a song from the beginning, press the Previous button. If you press the Previous button twice in rapid succession, iTunes starts playing the previous audio track.

To jump to the next song, press the Next button. To raise the volume, press the Up button. To lower the volume, press the Down button.

Controlling iPhoto

Using the Apple Remote with iPhoto lets you control a photo presentation at a distance. To start showing a slideshow of all the images stored in iPhoto, load iPhoto using the keyboard or mouse, pick an album that contains the pictures you want to see, and then press the Play/Pause button on the Apple Remote.

To view the previous photograph, press the Previous button. To view the next photograph, press the Next button. To exit from your slideshow, hold down the Menu button.

Controlling DVD Player

With the Apple Remote and DVD Player, you can watch movies on your Mac while lounging on the sofa away from your desk. To start playing a DVD, load a DVD into your Mac and wait for the DVD Player program to load. (If DVD Player doesn't load automatically, you have to open it in the Applications folder using the keyboard or mouse.) After DVD Player starts running, you can control it by pressing the Play/Pause button on the Apple Remote.

To choose an option from the DVD menus, press the Previous/Next buttons and select an option by pressing the Play/Pause button. To raise the volume, press the Up button. To lower the volume, press the Down button.

Pairing an Apple Remote with a Mac

If you have two or more Mac computers, an iPod, or an Apple TV unit in the same room, your Apple Remote can accidentally control multiple items. In case you want to make sure an Apple Remote works with only one Mac, you can pair up that specific Apple Remote with one computer.

To pair an Apple Remote to a specific Mac, follow these steps:

1. **Hold the Apple Remote 4 to 6 inches away from the infrared (IR) port on the Mac you want it to control.**
2. **Press the Menu and Next buttons at the same time.**

   After a few seconds, a paired-remote icon appears on the screen.
3. **Release the Menu and Next buttons.**

   Your Apple Remote is now paired to work only with that specific Mac.

To unpair an Apple Remote from a specific Mac, follow these steps:

1. **Choose ⇨System Preferences on the Mac you want to unpair from an Apple Remote.**

   The System Preferences window appears.
2. **Click the Security icon under the Personal category.**

   The Security window appears.
3. **Click the General tab.**

   The General options appear, as shown in Figure 4-3.

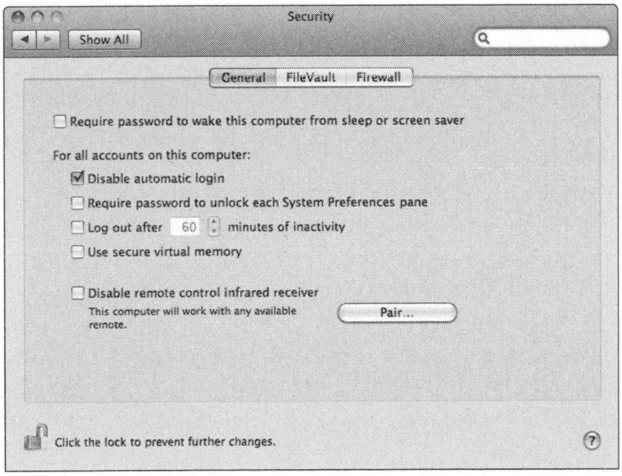

Figure 4-3: The General options of the Security window let you unpair an Apple Remote.

4. **Deselect the Disable Remote Control Infrared Receiver check box to let your Mac work with any Apple Remote.**

Accessing Front Row

You can easily control separate programs such as iTunes and DVD Player with the Apple Remote, but you must manually switch between different programs just to hear music, watch a movie, or look at your digital photographs. To overcome the hassle of working with multiple programs, Front Row provides a simple, consistent user interface for accessing all your media files whether they're stored in your Music, Movies, or Pictures folder.

REMEMBER

Before using Front Row, you need to store your favorite songs, podcasts, and music videos in iTunes; your favorite pictures in iPhoto; and your favorite movies in your Movies folder. Alternatively, you can have a CD or DVD in your Mac.

Starting Front Row

To start Front Row, choose one of the following:

- Press the Menu button on the Apple Remote.

  REMEMBER

  If you have a program running that can accept commands from the Apple Remote, such as Keynote, pressing the Menu button might control that program instead of starting Front Row.
- Double-click the Front Row icon in the Applications folder.
- Press ⌘+Esc.

Each time you start Front Row, the Front Row menu appears, as shown in Figure 4-4.

REMEMBER

The DVD option appears only if you have a DVD inserted in your Mac.

Highlighting an option in Front Row

To highlight an option on the Front Row menu, choose one of the following:

- Press the Up/Down buttons on the Apple Remote.
- Press the up- and down-arrow keys on the keyboard.

Selecting an option in Front Row

After you've highlighted an option on a Front Row menu, you can select that option by choosing one of the following:

- Press the Play/Pause button on the Apple Remote.
- Press Return on the keyboard.

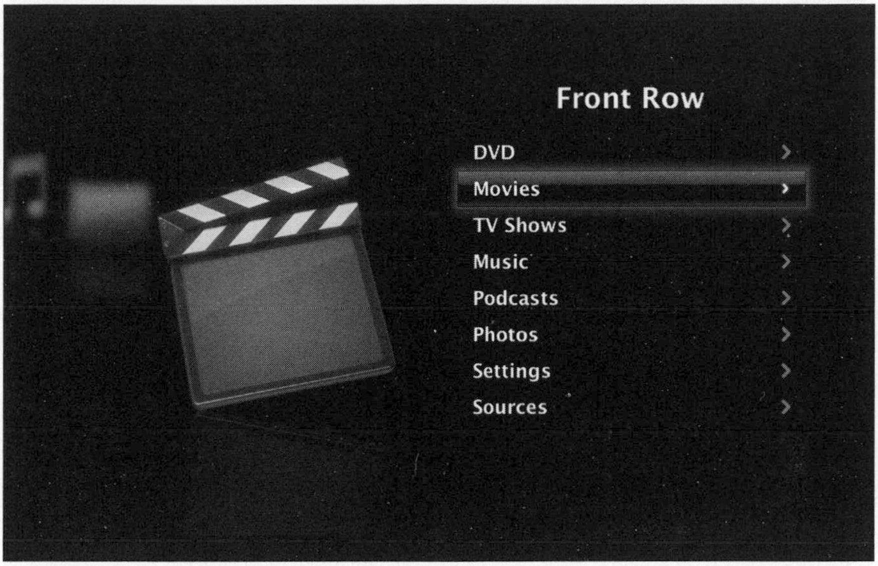

Figure 4-4: The Front Row menu gives you access to movies, music, and pictures on your Mac.

You find out more about different options in Front Row later in this chapter.

Exiting a Front Row submenu

To exit from a Front Row submenu and see the previous menu, choose one of the following:

- Press the Menu button on the Apple remote.
- Press Esc on the keyboard.

REMEMBER

If you keep pressing the Menu button on the Apple Remote or keep pressing Esc on the keyboard, you'll eventually exit from the main Front Row menu altogether, exiting Front Row in the process. This can be handy to get out of Front Row so you can run and control another program with the Apple Remote, like Keynote.

Playing Movies and Videos

Front Row can play DVDs or digital video files purchased from the iTunes Store — music videos, TV shows, full-length motion pictures, and the like. The four Front Row menu options that allow you to watch movies and videos are

- **DVD:** Plays a movie stored on a DVD.
- **Movies:** Plays digital video files such as movies you've either downloaded from the iTunes Store or off some other place on the Internet.

- ✦ **TV Shows:** Plays TV show segments and entire shows you've downloaded from the iTunes Store.
- ✦ **Music:** Plays music videos you've downloaded from the iTunes Store.

Playing a DVD

To play a DVD in Front Row, follow these steps:

1. **Start up Front Row by pressing the Menu button on the Apple Remote or by pressing ⌘+Esc.**

   The Front Row menu appears. (Refer to Figure 4-4.)
2. **Insert a DVD into your Mac.**
3. **Select the DVD menu option and press Play/Pause on the Apple Remote (or press Return on the keyboard).**

   The DVD starts playing and displays its DVD menu, which you can choose using the Apple Remote.

REMEMBER

If you had inserted the DVD into your Mac at some earlier point, you see a menu listing four options:

- ✦ **Resume Playing:** Starts playing at the last part of the DVD that you saw before ejecting the disc.
- ✦ **Start from Beginning:** Starts playing the DVD from the very beginning, including the usual FBI notice warning about copyright infringement.
- ✦ **Eject Disk:** Ejects the DVD.
- ✦ **DVD Menu:** Displays the DVD's menus.

Playing a digital video file

If you have digital video files stored on your Mac — movies you've created using iMovie and stored in your Movies folder, for example — you can play them through Front Row by following these steps:

1. **Start up Front Row by pressing the Menu button on the Apple Remote or by pressing ⌘+Esc.**

   The Front Row menu appears.
2. **Select the Movies option and press Play/Pause on the Apple Remote (or press Return on the keyboard).**

   A Movies menu appears, shown in Figure 4-5, listing three options to choose from:

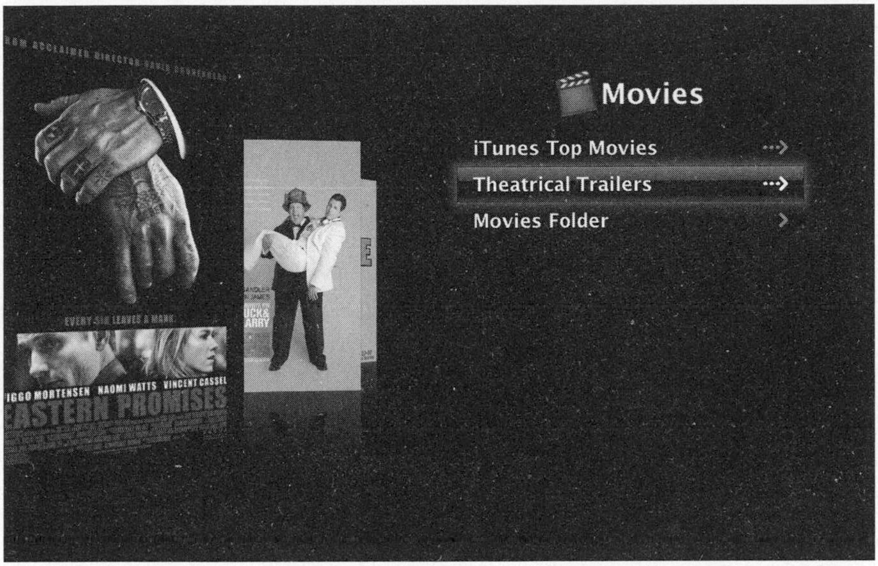

Figure 4-5: The Movies menu lets you view trailers or digital video files stored in your Movies folder.

- *iTunes Top Movies:* Displays trailers of the most popular movies purchased from the iTunes Store.
- *Theatrical Trailers:* Displays trailers of the latest movies currently in theaters.
- *Movies Folder:* Displays digital video files stored in your Movies folder.

3. **Select an option and press Play/Pause on the Apple Remote (or press Return on the keyboard).**

   If you select iTunes Top Movies or Theatrical Trailers, you see another menu listing your options, like the menu shown in Figure 4-6. If you select Movies Folder, you see a list of all digital video files stored in your Movies folder.

Playing a TV show

You can download TV shows from the iTunes Store and store them on your hard drive. To view your TV shows in Front Row, follow these steps:

1. **Start up Front Row by pressing the Menu button on the Apple Remote or by pressing ⌘+Esc.**

   The Front Row menu appears.

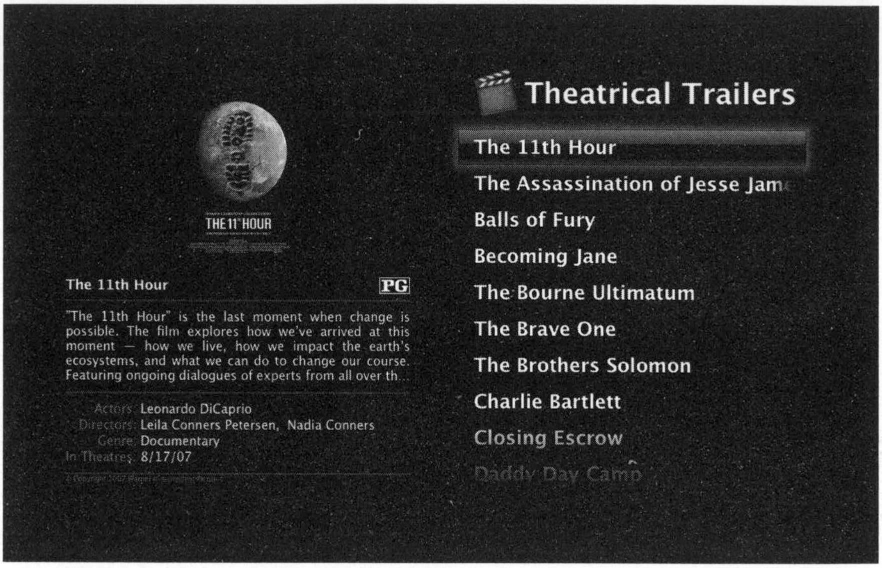

Figure 4-6: The Theatrical Trailers menu lets you choose a specific trailer to watch.

2. **Select the TV Shows option and press Play/Pause on the Apple Remote (or press Return on the keyboard).**

   The TV Shows menu appears, listing all TV shows currently stored on your hard drive, as shown in Figure 4-7. The iTunes Top TV Episodes option lets you view teasers of the latest shows. The Date and Show tabs let you rearrange how to view your list of shows, either by the date they were recorded or by their name.

3. **Select a TV show that you've downloaded on your hard drive or select the iTunes Top TV Episodes to view a menu of the latest TV episodes available on iTunes.**

4. **Press Play/Pause on the Apple Remote (or press Return on the keyboard).**

   If you selected iTunes Top TV Episodes, you have to select a specific episode to watch.

Playing a music video

If you've downloaded any music videos through iTunes, you can view them through the Music option on the Front Row menu. To view a music video, follow these steps:

1. **Start up Front Row by pressing the Menu button on the Apple Remote or by pressing ⌘+Esc.**

   The Front Row menu appears.

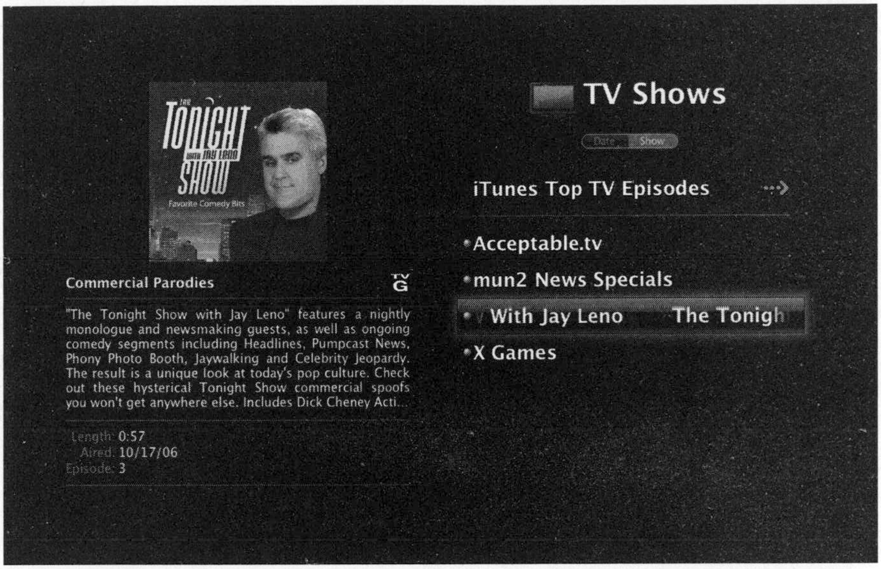

Figure 4-7: The TV Shows menu lets you view TV show episodes stored on your Mac.

2. **Select the Music option and press Play/Pause on the Apple Remote (or press Return on the keyboard).**

   A Music menu appears, as shown in Figure 4-8.

Figure 4-8: The Music menu lets you view music videos stored on your Mac or view teasers of music videos on iTunes.

3. **Select iTunes Top Music Videos (to see previews of music videos) or Music Videos (to see music videos already stored on your hard drive) and then press Play/Pause on the Apple Remote (or press Return on the keyboard).**

   An iTunes Top Music Videos or Music Videos menu appears.

4. **Select the music video you want to watch and press Play/Pause on the Apple Remote (or press Return on the keyboard).**

Playing Music and Other Sounds

Front Row can play CDs or audio files downloaded from the iTunes Store, such as songs, podcasts, and audiobooks. The following four Front Row menu options allow you to play audio files:

- **Audio CD:** Plays music stored on a CD.
- **Music:** Plays digital music files you've downloaded from iTunes.
- **Podcasts:** Plays digital audio files that contain interviews or recordings of radio shows.
- **Audiobooks:** Plays recordings of someone reading an entire book.

Playing an audio CD

To play an audio CD in Front Row, follow these steps:

1. **Start up Front Row by pressing the Menu button on the Apple Remote or by pressing ⌘+Esc).**

   The Front Row menu appears.

2. **Insert an audio CD into your Mac.**
3. **Select the Music option and press Play/Pause on the Apple Remote (or press Return on the keyboard).**

   A Music menu appears with the name of your audio CD displayed, as shown in Figure 4-9. If you aren't connected to the Internet, you see just Audio CD listed instead.

4. **Select the name of your audio CD and press Play/Pause on the Apple Remote (or press Return on the keyboard).**

   A list of songs from your audio CD appears.

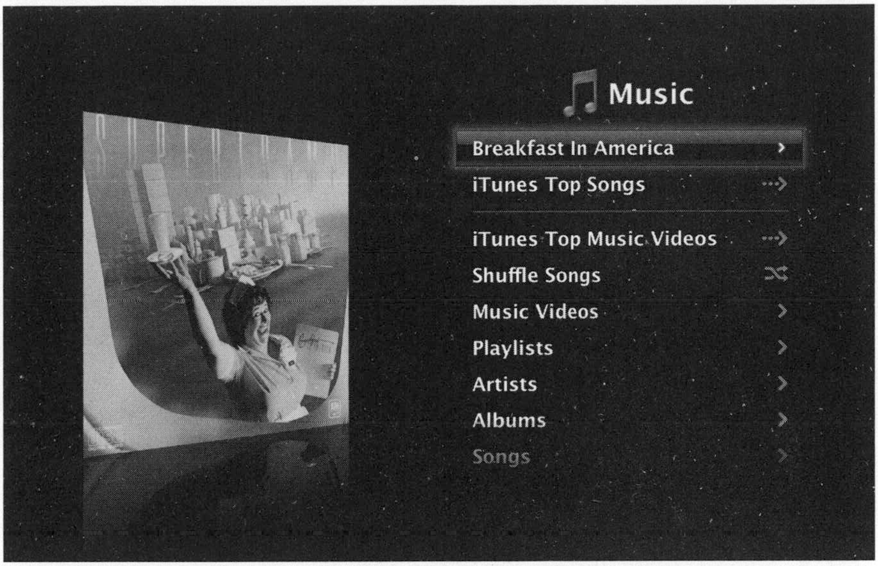

Figure 4-9: The Music menu displays the cover artwork and name of your audio CD.

5. **Select the first song you want to hear (or Shuffle Songs) and press Play/Pause on the Apple Remote (or press Return on the keyboard).**

   Front Row plays all the songs starting with the song you chose all the way down to the bottom of the list. If you chose Shuffle Songs, Front Row starts playing songs randomly.

Playing a digital audio file

If you're like most people, you'll eventually find yourself carrying fewer audio CDs around and just storing your favorite music as digital audio files instead. To hear digital audio files through Front Row, follow these steps:

1. **Start up Front Row by pressing the Menu button on the Apple Remote or by pressing ⌘+Esc.**

   The Front Row menu appears.

2. **Select the Music option and press Play/Pause on the Apple Remote (or press Return on the keyboard).**

   A Music menu appears, as shown in Figure 4-10. To keep you amused, album cover artwork flips by, showing you all the albums that your music collection has come from.

Figure 4-10: The Music menu displays a variety of ways to play your iTunes music.

3. **Select one of the following and press Play/Pause on the Apple Remote (or press Return on the keyboard):**
   - *Shuffle Songs:* Randomly mixes all the songs stored in iTunes.
   - *Playlists:* Lists all the playlists you've created in iTunes.
   - *Artists:* Lists all the recording artists' names.
   - *Albums:* Lists all albums that have at least one song you've stored in iTunes.
   - *Songs:* Lists all songs alphabetically that you've stored in iTunes.
   - *Genres:* Lists all song genres such as Country or Rock.
   - *Composers:* Lists all composers so you can pick the songs they've written.

Playing podcasts

Podcasts are recorded interviews or radio shows that you can download and hear at your convenience, which you can download through iTunes. After you've downloaded some podcasts, you can listen to them in Front Row by following these steps:

1. **Start up Front Row by pressing the Menu button on the Apple Remote or by pressing ⌘+Esc.**

   The Front Row menu appears.

2. **Select the Podcasts option and press Play/Pause on the Apple Remote (or press Return on the keyboard).**

   A Podcasts menu appears, listing all the podcasts you've downloaded and stored in iTunes.

3. **Select a podcast and press Play/Pause on the Apple Remote (or press Return on the keyboard).**

Playing audiobooks

Audiobooks are recordings of someone reading a book, which can be convenient to hear while you're exercising, eating, or commuting. After you've downloaded some audiobooks and stored them in iTunes, you can hear them through Front Row by following these steps:

1. **Start up Front Row by pressing the Menu button on the Apple Remote or by pressing ⌘+Esc.**

   The Front Row menu appears.

2. **Select the Music option and press Play/Pause on the Apple Remote (or press Return on the keyboard).**

   A Music menu appears.

3. **Select the Audiobooks option and press Play/Pause on the Apple Remote (or press Return on the keyboard).**

   An Audiobooks menu appears, listing all your audiobooks.

Understanding Apple TV

Front Row turns your Mac screen into an entertainment center, but what if you have a 52-inch high-definition TV in your living room? Rather than use Front Row to watch a DVD on your iMac's 20-inch screen, you might want to play that DVD on your 52-inch big-screen TV. In that case, you can ignore your Mac completely and buy a separate DVD player connected to your big-screen TV, or you can get Apple TV and control it using your Apple Remote.

Apple TV is nothing more than a box that physically connects to your TV through wires (which you'll have to buy separately from the Apple TV unit). After you've connected Apple TV to your TV screen, Apple TV wirelessly (or through cables if you prefer) connects to your Mac (or even a PC) to transfer movies from your computer to the Apple TV unit, which then broadcasts those movies on your big-screen TV. Essentially, Apple TV acts like a wired or wireless connection between your Mac and your big-screen TV for playing movies or TV show episodes that you've downloaded from iTunes.

4. **Select an audiobook title and press Play/Pause on the Apple Remote (or press Return on the keyboard).**

   Your chosen audiobook starts playing.

Viewing Pictures

If you have a bunch of photographs stored in iPhoto, you can view them in Front Row as an ongoing slideshow. This can be convenient to show different types of pictures during a party or family gathering. To view your iPhoto pictures in Front Row, follow these steps:

1. **Start up Front Row by pressing the Menu button on the Apple Remote or by pressing ⌘+Esc.**

   The Front Row menu appears.

2. **Select the Photos option and press Play/Pause on the Apple Remote (or press Return on the keyboard).**

   A Photos menu appears.

3. **Select a photo album such as Photos or Last 12 Months, and then press Play/Pause on the Apple Remote (or press Return on the keyboard).**

   Your slideshow appears on the screen.

Book III

Browsing the Internet

The 5th Wave By Rich Tennant

"I don't know what program you been usin' Frank, but it ain't the right one. Look – your menu bar should read, File, Edit, Reap, Gather..."

Contents at a Glance

Chapter 1: Browsing the Internet....................257
Chapter 2: Sending and Receiving E-Mail....................291
Chapter 3: Chatting in Real Time....................319
Chapter 4: Security for Your Mac....................335
Chapter 5: Setting up Your Own Web Site....................359

Chapter 1: Browsing the Internet

In This Chapter

- **Setting up an Internet connection**
- **Browsing Web sites**
- **Searching a Web page**
- **Saving Web pages**
- **Viewing and playing multimedia files**
- **Downloading files**

You can use a computer all by itself, but to get the most out of your Mac, you need an Internet connection. The Internet can also open up a whole new world for you by letting you browse and read news, watch movies, listen to radio stations, find and install new software, updated versions of your existing software, and shop online. For most people, an Internet connection is no longer an option but a necessity.

Setting Up an Internet Connection

From a technical point of view, your Mac can't connect directly to the Internet. Instead, your Mac must connect to another computer, run by a company called an Internet Service Provider (ISP); it's through the ISP that your Mac actually connects to the Internet.

To connect your Mac to an ISP, you have three options:

- Ethernet (also called high-speed or broadband)
- Wireless
- Dial-up access

Ethernet connection

An Ethernet connection, also known as a broadband connection, is the most popular way to connect to the Internet. The two most common broadband connections are through cable modems or DSL (Digital Subscriber Line) modems.

Ethernet cables have plugs that look like wider versions of a telephone plug. After you connect an Ethernet cable to your Mac and a cable or DSL modem, you can usually start using the Internet right away.

Macs can recognize an Ethernet Internet connection right away through something called the Dynamic Host Configuration Protocol (DHCP). Basically, DHCP means that your Mac is smart enough to connect to the Internet without you having to type a bunch of cryptic numbers and fiddle with confusing technical standards.

For more information about setting up a network and sharing a single Internet connection with multiple computers, see Book VII, Chapter 1.

Wireless access

Wireless access is popular because it allows you to connect to the Internet without stringing cables across the room to trip over. Most new Macs include built-in wireless capability, but if your Mac doesn't have this, you'll have to buy a special wireless receiver that plugs into your Mac.

If your Mac doesn't have a built-in wireless receiver, you can choose the Airport Extreme card (`www.apple.com/airportextreme`) that must be installed inside your Mac. You can also choose from a variety of other wireless receivers, such as the AfterTheMac wireless adapter (`http://afterthemac.com`) that plugs into a USB port.

After you have wireless access capability in your Mac, you need to connect to a wireless Internet network (often called Wi-Fi). Public libraries and many coffee houses offer free wireless Internet access, but you can set up your own wireless network at home or work by using a wireless router, which lets multiple computers share a single Internet connection.

A wireless router connects to your cable or DSL modem and broadcasts radio signals to connect your Mac wirelessly to the Internet.

Apple sells a wireless router called the Airport Extreme base station (`www.apple.com/airportextreme`), but you can actually buy any wireless router and hook it up to your high-speed Internet connection. The brand name of your wireless router is less important than the speed offered by the router, which is determined by the wireless standard the router uses. A *wireless standard* simply defines the wireless signal used to connect to the Internet. Table 1-1 lists the different wireless standards.

Table 1-1 Wireless Standards and Speeds of Different Routers

Wireless Standard	*Speed*	*Indoor Range*
802.11a	Up to 54 Mbps	30 meters (98 feet)
802.11b	Up to 11 Mbps	35 meters (114 feet)
802.11g	Up to 54 Mbps	35 meters (114 feet)
802.11n	Up to 248 Mbps	70 meters (229 feet)

The upload/download speed of wireless standards is measured in megabits per second (Mbps) although this maximum speed is rarely achieved in normal use. The speed and range of a wireless Internet connection will also degrade over distance or if obstacles appear between the Wi-Fi router and your Mac, such as walls or heavy furniture.

To connect to a wireless network, you need to make sure your router and the wireless receiver connected to your computer use the same wireless standard. If your router uses only the 802.11a standard but your computer can use only the 802.11b standard, you won't be able to connect.

Most routers and wireless receivers work with multiple standards. If you buy an Apple Airport Extreme base station (transmitter) and an Airport Extreme card (receiver), you won't have to worry about these wireless standards. If you buy a non-Apple wireless router, you might have to worry about which wireless standard the router uses.

The 802.11g wireless standard is currently the most popular wireless standard, but the newer 802.11n standard is becoming more popular because it offers greater range and higher speeds. Most routers are compatible with multiple standards, such as 802.11a, 802.11b, and 802.11g. The newer routers also include compatibility with the 802.11n standard.

If your Mac has wireless capability, you can connect to a wireless network (such as at a public library or coffeehouse) by following these steps:

1. **Load the Safari browser (or any other browser).**

   Safari displays a `You are not connected to the Internet.` Web page, as shown in Figure 1-1. You also see a Network Diagnostics button.

2. **Click the Network Diagnostics button.**

   A Network Diagnostics dialog appears, as shown in Figure 1-2.

3. **Select the Airport radio button and then click Continue.**

   The Network Diagnostics dialog displays a list of wireless networks that you can connect to, as shown in Figure 1-3.

Figure 1-1: A message and a Networks Diagnostics button appears when you aren't connected to the Internet.

4. **Select a wireless network name and click Continue.**

   A message appears, letting you know that you have changed your network settings, as shown in Figure 1-4.

   On private wireless networks, an additional dialog might appear, asking you to type a username and password.

5. **Click OK.**

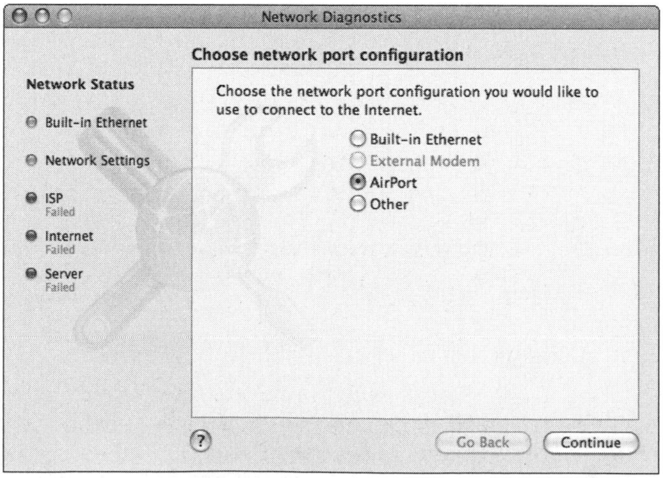

Figure 1-2: The Networks Diagnostics dialog lets you choose how to connect to the Internet.

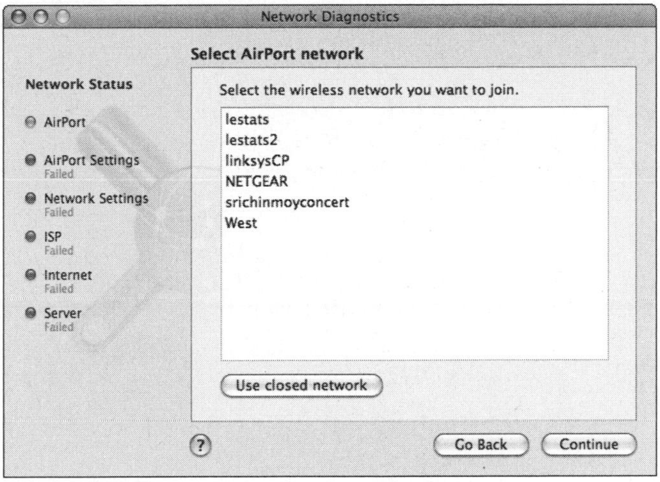

Figure 1-3: The Network Diagnostics dialog displays all available wireless networks nearby.

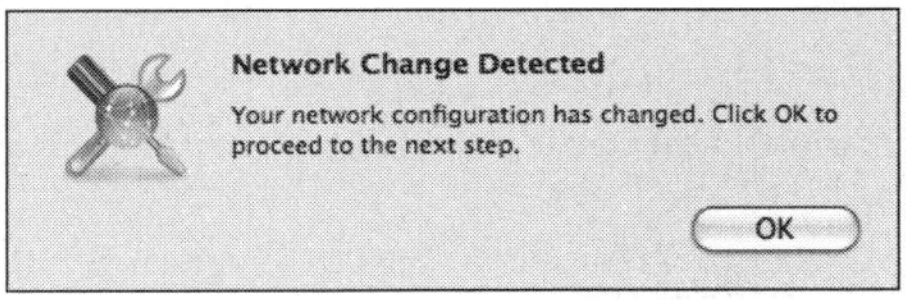

Figure 1-4: A message appears to let you know when you've changed your network settings.

The Network Diagnostics dialog tries to connect to your chosen wireless network. If it succeeds, it displays a message as shown in Figure 1-5, informing you that it has successfully connected.

6. **Click Quit.**

   Safari displays your home page on the Internet.

WARNING!

When connecting through a wireless Internet connection, your Mac essentially broadcasts any information you type (such as credit card numbers or passwords) through the airwaves. When connected through any wireless connection, assume that a stranger is peeking at your data. Then only type in data that you're comfortable giving away to others.

Dial-up access

Dial-up access involves using a telephone and a telephone modem, which lets you connect to an ISP and the Internet. Because telephone lines were designed for voice communication, they're terribly slow at transferring computer data. As a result, dial-up access is fast becoming obsolete.

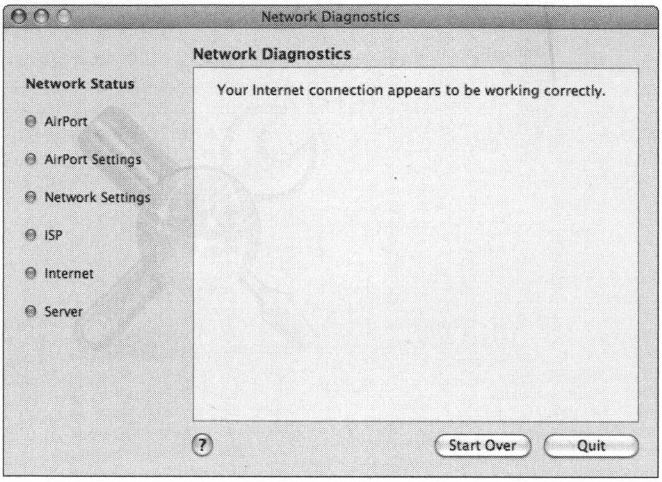

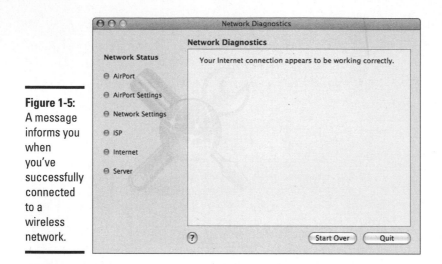

Figure 1-5: A message informs you when you've successfully connected to a wireless network.

A modem is a device that helps computers connect to the Internet. If your Internet connection uses cable, you need a cable modem. If your Internet connection uses DSL or a telephone line, you need a DSL modem or a telephone modem. Modems work only with specific types of Internet connections, so you can't substitute a telephone modem for a cable modem and expect it to work.

In many rural areas, dial-up access might be the only option for connecting to the Internet, because telephone and cable companies might not offer high-speed Internet service to isolated areas of the country.

To use dial-up access, you need a modem, which plugs into an ordinary telephone line. Newer Mac computers don't come with a modem, which means you'll have to buy an external modem from Apple (`www.apple.com`) or another company. If you have an older Mac, you might have a built-in modem. Just peek around your computer case and look for a plug for a telephone jack, which looks almost identical to an Ethernet port only slightly smaller.

Dial-up access is the slowest way to connect to the Internet. If you have a choice, use an Ethernet or wireless connection instead, because you'll be able to view Web sites much faster. Dial-up access will work, but it's like riding a tricycle down a freeway: You'll eventually get to your destination, but it will take a long time.

Configuring your dial-up modem

To connect to the Internet through a telephone line, you need to know the following:

✦ The telephone number of your ISP

- Your account name given to you by your ISP
- Your password to your account

The telephone number connects you to the ISP's computers, but you can't get access to the Internet unless you also have a valid account and password. After the ISP computer verifies that you A) have a valid account and B) know the right password, you can access the Internet.

To configure your Mac to use your telephone line to connect to the Internet, follow these steps:

1. **Choose ⇨System Preferences.**

   The System Preferences window appears.

2. **Click the Network icon under the Internet & Network category.**

   The Network window appears.

3. **Click the Modem icon in the left pane.**

   The Modem window appears and displays text boxes for entering your account name, password, and the telephone number to connect to your ISP's computer.

4. **Click Apply.**
5. **Click the Close button of the Network window.**

Using a modem

After you configure your dial-up access, you have to use the Internet Connect program to physically dial and connect to the Internet. To use the Internet Connect program, follow these steps:

1. **Click the Finder icon in the Dock.**

   The Finder appears.

2. **Click Applications in the Finder Sidebar.**

   The content of the Applications folder appears in the right pane of the Finder.

3. **Double-click the Internet Connect icon.**

   A dialog appears, displaying the account name and telephone number that you defined earlier. (If you didn't define an account name and telephone number, you can enter them now.)

4. **Click the Connect button.**

   After you've connected, you can load your browser and e-mail program to start using the Internet.

Browsing through Web Sites

After you connect to the Internet (through a dial-up, Ethernet, or wireless connection), you still need to run a Web browser. The most popular browser on the Mac is called Safari, and it comes free with every Mac. However, if you don't like Safari, you can always try another browser such as Firefox (`www.mozilla.com`) or Camino (`www.caminobrowser.org`).

Defining a home page

Every time you load your browser, it automatically loads a home page, which is the first Web page that you'll always see. (The default home page in Safari is the Apple Web site.)

REMEMBER

Throughout this chapter, all step-by-step instructions are given for Safari. Just keep in mind that other browsers (Firefox, Camino, and so on) work in similar ways.

To define a home page in Safari (if you don't like the default home page of `www.apple.com`), follow these steps:

1. **In Safari, choose Safari➪Preferences.**

   A Preferences window appears.

2. **Click the General icon.**

   The General pane appears, as shown in Figure 1-6.

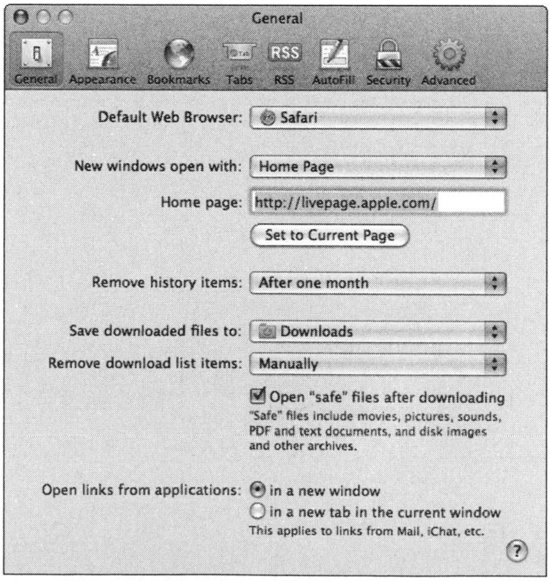

Figure 1-6: The General pane lets you type a new address for your home page.

3. **Click in the Home Page text box and type a Web site address, such as `www.yahoo.com`.**

   If you click the Set to Current Page button, you can make the currently displayed Web page your new home page without having to type the Web page's address. To use this feature, visit your favorite Web site immediately after Step 1. Then when you click the Set to Current Page button, you change your home page to the displayed Web page.

4. **Click the Close button of the Preferences window.**

Visiting a Web site

Although the first Web site you'll see will always be your home page, you probably don't want to stare at your home page all the time. To visit another Web site, you'll use the Web site's *address.*

Most Web site addresses consist of several parts, such as "`http://www.yahoo.com`":

- **`http://www`:** Identifies the address as part of the World Wide Web that uses the HyperText Transfer Protocol (http).

  Some Web sites omit the `www` portion of the name. Other Web sites use something unusual like `www2`. Just keep in mind that `www` is common, but not always necessary for a Web site address.

- **The domain name of the Web site (`yahoo`):** Most Web site names are abbreviations or smashed together names of the Web site, such as whitehouse for the White House's Web site.

- **A three-letter identifying extension such as `.com`:** The extension identifies the type of Web site, as shown in Table 1-2.

Table 1-2 Common Extensions Used in Web Site Addresses

Three-Letter Extension	*Type of Web Site*	*Examples*
`.com`	Often a commercial Web site, but can be any type of Web site	`www.apple.com`
`.gov`	Government Web site	`www.nasa.gov`
`.edu`	School Web site	`www.mit.edu`
`.net`	Network, sometimes used as an alternative to the `.com` extension	`www.earthlink.net`
`.org`	A nonprofit organization Web site	`www.redcross.org`
`.mil`	Military Web site	`www.army.mil`

Many Web sites in other countries end with a two-letter country address, such as `.uk` for the United Kingdom, `.ca` for Canada, and `.fr` for France.

When visiting different Web pages on a site, you might see additional text that identifies a specific Web page, such as `www.yahoo.com/sports` or `www.yahoo.com/movies`.

To visit a Web site by typing its Web site address, follow these steps:

1. **Load the Safari program.**

   The Safari window appears, displaying your current home page.

2. **Click in the address bar, as shown in Figure 1-7.**
3. **Type an address (such as `www.apple.com`) and press Return.**

   Safari displays the Web site corresponding to the address you typed.

If you type a Web site address and see an error message, it might mean one of a few things: You typed the Web site address wrong, your Internet connection isn't working, or the Web site is temporarily (or permanently) down.

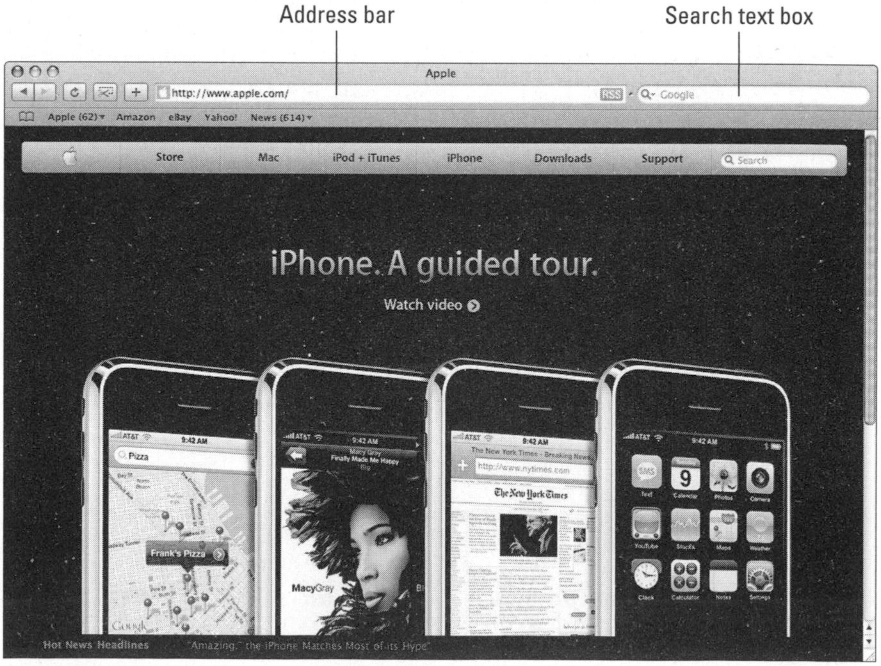

Figure 1-7: The address bar displays the current address and lets you type a new address.

Searching for Web sites

Typing a Web site address can get tedious. One way to find a Web site is to use a *search engine,* which is a special Web site that can look for other Web sites based on a word or phrase you type in. Because search engines are so convenient, Safari (and most other browsers) offers a built-in search engine text box in its upper-right corner. By typing a word or phrase that describes the kind of Web site you want, the search engine can find a list of related Web sites so you can click the one you want.

Safari uses the Google search engine. Other browsers, such as Firefox, might let you choose a different search engine to use.

To search for a Web site, follow these steps:

1. **Load the Safari program.**

   The Safari window appears, displaying your current home page.

2. **Click in the Search text box, type a word or phrase, and press Return.**

   The Safari window displays a Web page from Google, which lists Web sites related to the word or phrase you typed.

3. **Click the Web site you want to visit.**

If you mistype a word or phrase, the search engine might offer suggestions for the correct spelling at the same time it looks for Web sites that contain that misspelled word or phrase, which probably won't be the Web site you really want to see.

Every time you type a word or phrase in the Search text box, Safari (and most other browsers) saves the last ten words or phrases you searched. If you want to search for that same word or phrase later, just click the downward-pointing arrow that appears in the left side of the Search text box to display a menu. Then click the word or phrase you want to search for again.

Searching previously viewed Web sites

If you visit a Web site and find it interesting, you'll probably want to visit it again at a later time. Fortunately, Safari stores a list of your previously visited Web sites in its History menu for up to one year.

The default setting is to save visited Web sites for one month, but you can change this by choosing Safari⇨Preferences, clicking the General button, and then clicking the Remove history items pop-up menu to choose a time limit.

To view a list of the last Web sites you've visited, follow these steps:

1. **In Safari, choose History from the main menu.**

   A pull-down menu appears, displaying all the Web sites you've visited today. In addition, the History menu lists the past week's dates so you can view Web sites that you visited several days ago, as shown in Figure 1-8.

2. **Choose a Web site.**

   Safari displays your chosen site.

You can define how long Safari stores your previously visited Web sites by following these steps:

1. **In Safari, choose Safari⇨Preferences.**

   A Preferences window appears.

2. **Click the General icon.**

   The General pane appears, as shown in Figure 1-9.

3. Click in the Remove History Items pop-up menu and choose an option such as After One Month or After One Day.

   TIP: You might want to choose a shorter time period just in case you don't want other people to see which Web sites you've recently visited in the past, such as something really personal. Or choose History⇨Clear History.

4. **Click the Close button of the General window.**

TIP: Although the History menu only displays the past seven days, you can choose History⇨Show All History to view a list of all the Web sites you've visited in the time period specified by the Remove History Items pop-up menu in the General window.

Using bookmarks

Bookmarks let you store and organize your favorite Web sites into groups such as news sites, movie sites, or stock market sites. By organizing your favorite Web sites into groups, you can quickly find them again.

You can save and view bookmarks in two places as shown in Figure 1-10:

- The Bookmarks menu
- The Bookmarks bar

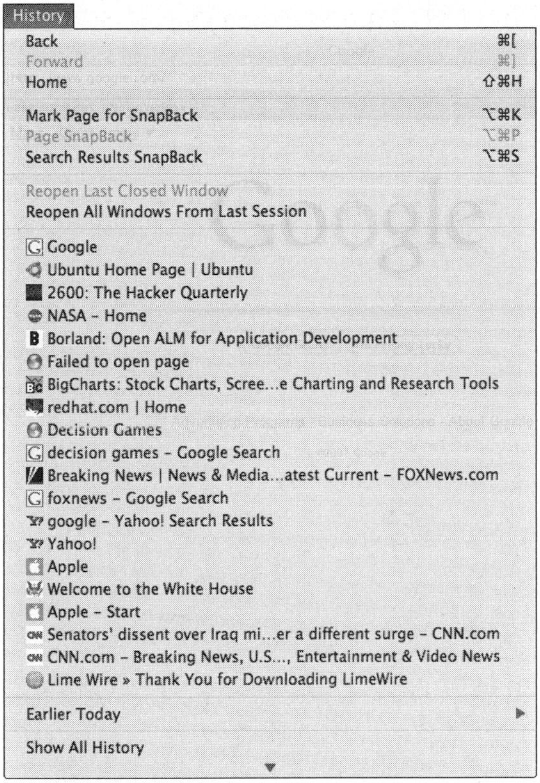

Figure 1-8: The History menu lets you revisit previously viewed Web sites.

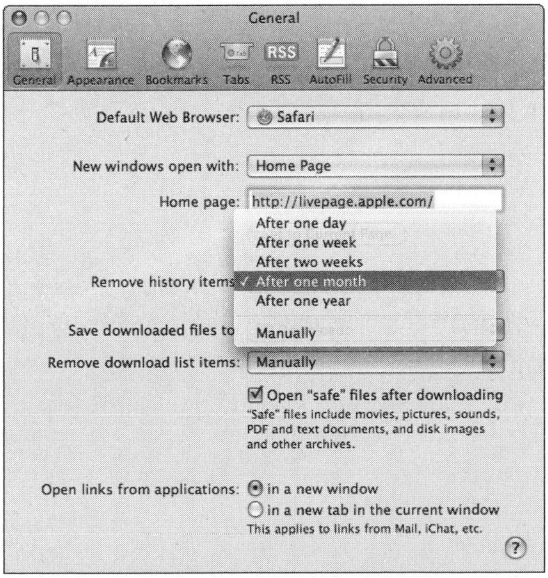

Figure 1-9: The Remove History Items pop-up menu lets you define how long Safari should save a list of your previously visited Web sites.

Figure 1-10: The Bookmarks menu is a pull-down menu. The Bookmarks bar displays the first few entries of the sites list directly on the browser.

Storing bookmarks on the Bookmarks menu tucks them out of sight. The drawback is that you must click the Bookmarks menu to find your bookmarks.

Storing bookmarks on the Bookmarks bar keeps the first few entries of your bookmarks visible and within easy access at all times. The drawback is that the Bookmarks bar at first can display only a limited number of bookmarks. (You have to click the arrow nest to Bookmarks Bar to see all entries.)

As a general rule, use the Bookmarks bar for one-click access to your favorite Web sites and use the Bookmarks menu to store Web sites that you don't access as often.

REMEMBER

Bookmarks behave the same whether they appear on the Bookmarks menu or the Bookmarks bar.

Adding bookmarks

To bookmark a Web site address in either the menu or the bar, follow these steps:

1. **In Safari, visit a Web site that you want to store as a bookmark.**
2. **Choose Bookmark⇨Add Bookmark (or click the plus sign button that appears to the left of the address box).**

   A dialog appears, as shown in Figure 1-11.
3. **Click in the Name text box and edit or type a descriptive name for your bookmark.**

   By default, the Name text box displays the current Web page's title, as defined by the Web page designer.

Figure 1-11: To create a bookmark, you need to type a descriptive name and define a location to store that bookmark.

4. **Click in the Location pop-up menu and choose a location for storing your bookmark.**

   You can choose the Bookmarks bar, Bookmarks menu, or a specific folder buried inside the Bookmarks bar or Bookmarks menu. (You discover how to create bookmark folders later, in the "Storing bookmarks in folder" section of this chapter.)

5. **Click Add.**

Deleting bookmarks

After you start saving bookmarks of your favorite Web sites, you might find that you have too many bookmarks that you don't use any more. To delete a bookmark, follow these steps:

1. **In Safari, choose Bookmarks⇨Show All Bookmarks.**

   Safari displays a window divided into two panes. The left pane displays a list of bookmark folders. (The Bookmarks bar and Bookmarks menu are considered folders.) The right pane displays the contents of the currently selected bookmark folder, as shown in Figure 1-12.

2. **Click on the folder, in the left pane, that contains the bookmark you want to delete.**

   The right pane displays the contents of your chosen bookmark folder, which might include bookmarks and additional folders that contain other bookmarks.

3. **(Optional) Click the triangle that appears to the left of any folder that appears in the right pane.**

   This displays the bookmarks stored in that particular folder. (You might need to repeat this step several times to find the bookmark you want.)

4. **Click to select the bookmark you want to delete.**

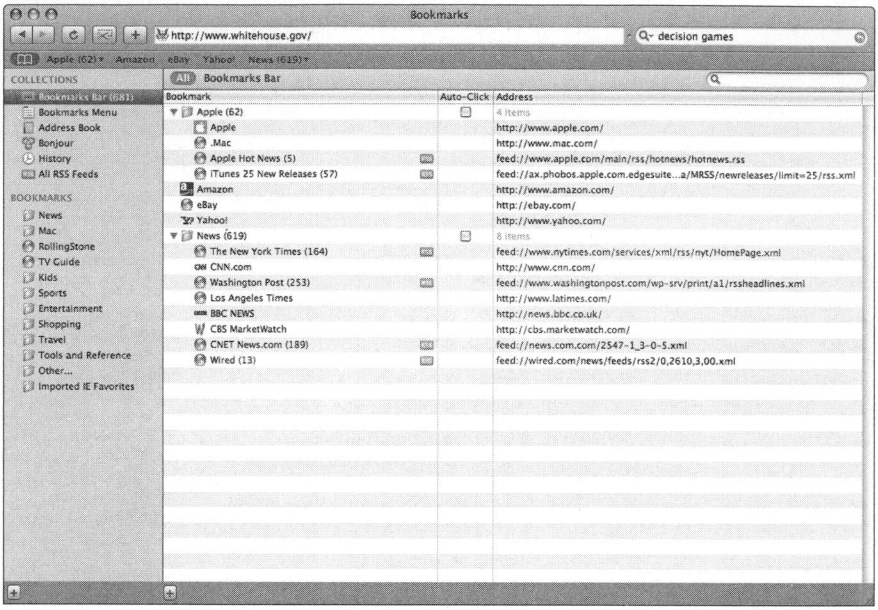

Figure 1-12: The Show All Bookmarks window displays your bookmarks and bookmark folders.

5. **Choose Edit➪Delete.**

   Your chosen bookmark disappears.

   TIP: You can also right-click a bookmark and, when a pop-up menu appears, choose Delete.

6. **Choose Bookmarks➪Hide All Bookmarks.**

Moving bookmarks

Your browser saves your bookmarks in the order you created them. However, this most likely isn't the order that you might want them in. To rearrange your bookmarks and put them in a more logical order, you can move a bookmark by following these steps:

1. **Choose Bookmarks➪Show All Bookmarks.**

   Safari displays a window divided into two panes. The left pane displays a list of bookmark folders. (The Bookmarks bar and Bookmarks menu are considered folders.) The right pane displays the contents of the currently selected bookmark folder.

2. **Click the folder, in the left pane, that contains the bookmark you want to move.**

   The right pane displays the contents of your chosen bookmark folder.

3. **(Optional) Click the triangle that appears to the left of any folder that appears in the right pane.**

   This step displays the bookmarks stored in that particular folder. (You might need to repeat this step several times to find the bookmark you want.)

4. **Click and drag the bookmark you want to move onto a folder in the left or right pane.**
5. **Release the mouse button.**

   Safari moves your chosen bookmark to its new location.

6. **Choose Bookmarks⇨Hide All Bookmarks.**

Storing bookmarks in folders

After you save a lot of bookmarks, you'll find that they might start cluttering up the Bookmarks menu or Bookmarks bar. To organize your bookmarks, you can store related bookmarks in folders. To create a bookmark folder, follow these steps:

1. **In Safari, choose Bookmarks⇨Show All Bookmarks.**

   Safari displays a window divided into two panes. The left pane displays a list of bookmark folders. (The Bookmarks bar and Bookmarks menu are considered folders.) The right pane displays the contents of the currently selected bookmark folder.

2. **Click Bookmarks bar or Bookmarks menu in the left pane to choose a location to store your folder.**
3. **(Optional) Click the triangle that appears to the left of a folder that appears in the right pane.**

   Clicking a triangle displays the contents of the folder.

4. **Click any bookmark or bookmark folder in the right pane.**

   When you create a bookmark folder, it appears inside the same folder that holds the bookmark or folder you clicked on in this step.

5. **Choose Bookmarks⇨Add Bookmark Folder.**

   An untitled bookmark folder appears.

6. **Type a descriptive name for your bookmark folder onto the newly created folder.**

   REMEMBER

   Your cursor is automatically put in place to label the new folder.

7. **Choose Bookmarks⇨Hide All Bookmarks.**

REMEMBER

After you've created a bookmark folder, you can copy or move existing bookmarks into that folder.

Using bookmarks

If you've saved bookmarks on both the Bookmarks menu and Bookmarks bar, you can choose bookmarks from either one. To choose a bookmark on the Bookmarks menu, follow these steps:

1. **In Safari, click the Bookmarks menu.**

   A list of bookmarks and folders appears.

2. **Do either of the following:**

   - Click a bookmark in the Bookmarks menu to view your chosen Web page.
   - Click a bookmark folder in the Bookmarks menu to view a submenu of additional bookmarks or folders. Then click the bookmark you want to view.

By default, Safari comes with several bookmarks already placed on the Bookmarks bar. To choose a bookmark on the Bookmarks bar, do either of the following:

- ✦ Click a bookmark in the Bookmarks bar to view your chosen Web page.
- ✦ Click a bookmark folder in the Bookmarks bar to view a pull-down menu of additional bookmarks or folders, as shown in Figure 1-13. Then click the bookmark you want to view.

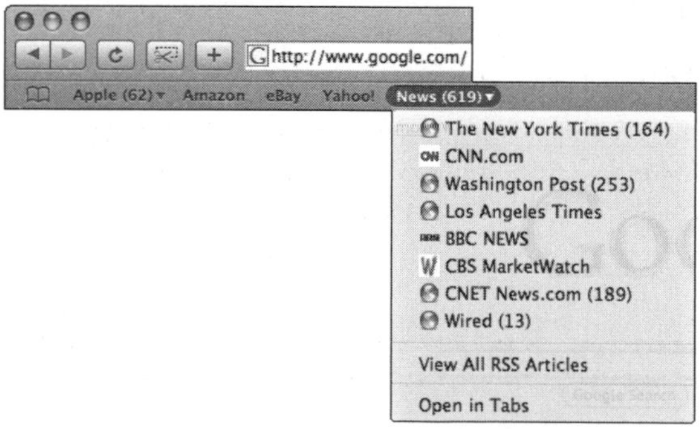

Figure 1-13: Bookmark folders appear on the Bookmarks bar as pull-down menus.

Importing and exporting bookmarks

After you've collected and organized bookmarks, you might become dependent on your bookmarks to help you navigate the Internet. Fortunately, if you ever want to switch browsers, you can export bookmarks from one browser and import them into another browser.

To export bookmarks from Safari, for example, follow these steps:

1. **In Safari, choose File➪Export Bookmarks.**

   A dialog appears, asking you to name your exported bookmarks and choose a folder to store them, as shown in Figure 1-14.

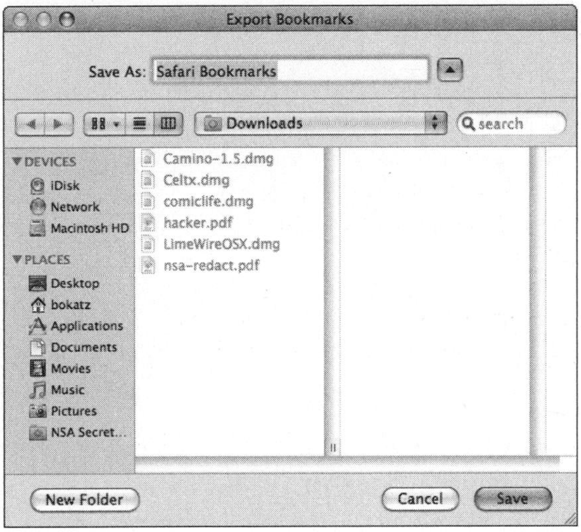

Figure 1-14: You can give your exported bookmarks a descriptive name and choose a location to store them.

2. **Click in the Save As text box and type a descriptive name for your bookmarks.**
3. **Choose a folder from the Where pop-up menu to store your bookmarks.**

   If you click the Arrow button that appears to the right of the Save As text box, a window appears displaying all the drives and folders you can choose to store your bookmarks.

4. **Click Save.**

After you've exported bookmarks from one browser, it's usually a snap to import them into a second browser. To import bookmarks into Safari, follow these steps:

1. **In Safari, choose File➪Import Bookmarks.**

   An Import Bookmarks dialog appears, giving you the chance to choose a volume and folder that contains the bookmarks exported by the other browser, as shown in Figure 1-15.

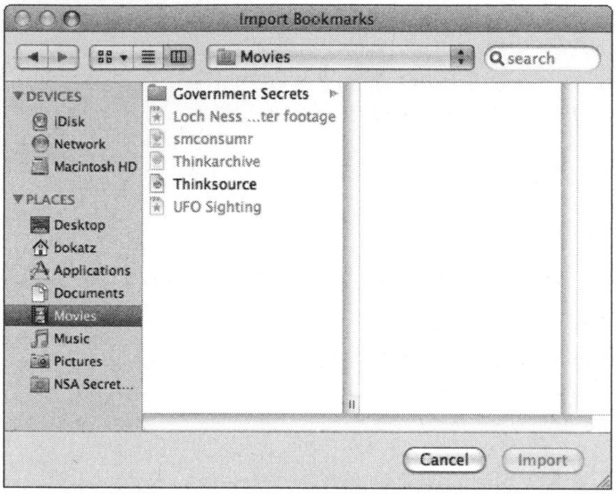

Figure 1-15: Safari can import bookmarks that another browser exported.

2. **Click the bookmark file you want to use and click the Import button.**

   Your imported bookmarks appear in an Imported folder that includes the date you imported the folder. At this point, you need to move this folder or its contents on the Bookmarks bar or menu to organize them.

Browsing with SnapBack

As you browse the Internet, you'll create a trail of Web pages that you once viewed. To help you navigate back and forth between the web pages you've viewed, browsers like Safari include a Back and Forward button.

After you've clicked the Back button at least once, you'll be able to use the Forward button. The Forward button simply reverses the action of the Back button and displays the Web page you viewed before clicking Back. If you click the Forward button enough times, you'll wind up at the last Web page you visited. The Back and Forward buttons typically appear as arrows pointing in opposite directions, as shown in Figure 1-16.

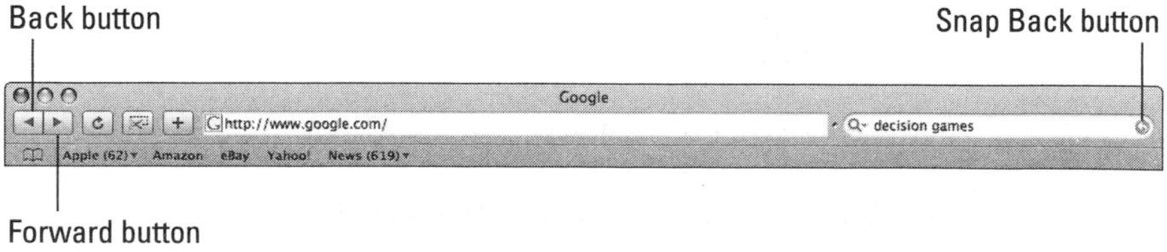

Figure 1-16: The Back and Forward buttons let you browse previously viewed Web pages.

As an alternative to clicking the Back button multiple times, Safari offers a special SnapBack feature. Unlike the Back button, which displays the previous Web page you viewed, SnapBack lets you jump back to any Web page designated as a SnapBack anchor point. There are four ways to create a SnapBack anchor point:

- ✦ Click a bookmark.
- ✦ Click a link in an e-mail message.
- ✦ Manually type a Web address (such as `www.google.com`) into the address bar.
- ✦ Choose History➪Mark Page for SnapBack.

So, if you type an address (such as `www.aol.com`) and then click different links, clicking the Back button would return you to each previous Web page in the order that you left them, but clicking the SnapBack icon would immediately jump you to the `www.aol.com` Web page.

REMEMBER

You can have only one Web page designated as a SnapBack anchor point at a time. The moment you create another SnapBack anchor point, Safari "forgets" the previous one.

After you've marked a page as a SnapBack anchor point, you can jump back to that Web page by doing one of the following:

- ✦ Click the SnapBack button that appears as an orange icon in the right of the address bar.
- ✦ Choose History➪Page SnapBack

Using tabbed browsing

One problem with browsing different Web sites is that you might want to keep a piece of one site visible while browsing a second site. Although you could open two separate browser windows, Safari and most other browsers offer a quick fix referred to as *tabbed browsing.* Essentially, tabbed browsing lets you easily jump back and forth between multiple Web pages in a single window — all you have to do is click the tab associated with the Web page. (See Figure 1-17.)

Creating additional tabs

When you load Safari, you see a single Web page (the home page) displayed. To create a tab, follow these steps:

1. **Choose File➪New Tab (or press ⌘+T).**

   An untitled tab appears.

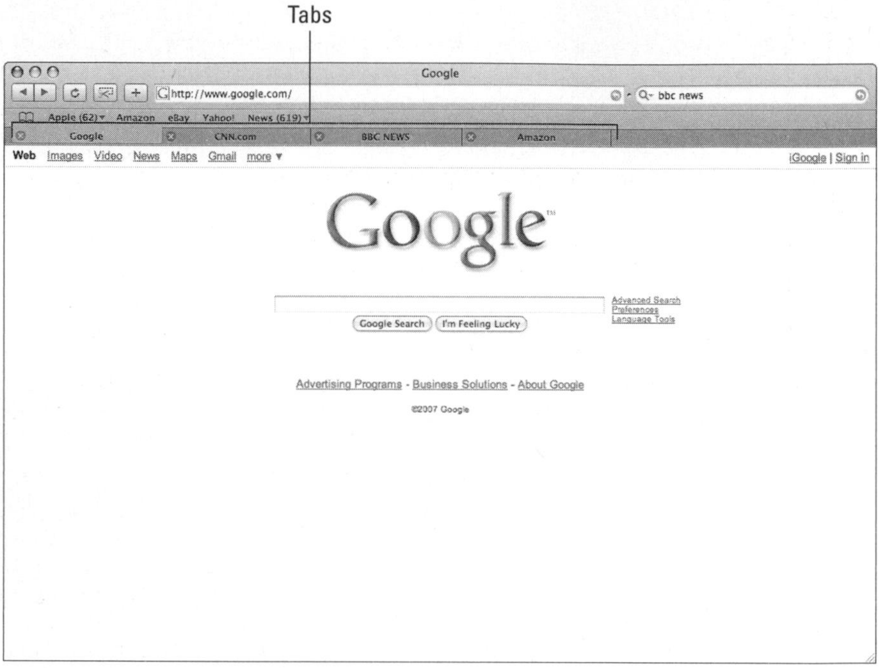

Figure 1-17: Tabbed browsing lets you cram multiple Web pages inside a single window.

2. **Type a Web site address or click a bookmark.**

   Safari displays your chosen Web page in your new tab.

Turning tabs into separate windows (and vice versa)

After you've created a tab and displayed a Web page inside that tab, you can "tear" that tab off to display it in a separate Safari window instead. To "tear" off a tab and turn it into a window, follow these steps:

1. **Move the cursor over the tab you want to convert into a separate window.**
2. **Click and drag the tab off the tab row.**

   The tab turns into a thumbnail image of the Web page displayed in that tab.
3. **Release the mouse button.**

   Safari turns your tab into a separate window.

Another way to turn a tab into a separate window is to follow these steps:

1. **Click the tab that you want to turn into a separate window.**
2. **Choose Window➪Move Tab to New Window or right-click a tab and choose Move Tab to New Window.**

To merge all Safari windows into separate tabs on a single window, choose Window➪Merge All Windows.

Deleting a tab

After you create a tab, you'll eventually want to get rid of that tab to avoid cluttering up your Safari window. To delete a tab, click the Close icon that appears in the left corner of each tab.

Using Web Clips

Rather than view an entire Web page, you might really care about only a certain part of a Web page that's frequently updated, such as sport scores, traffic congestion on local highways, or headline news. In case you want to view only part of a Web page, Safari lets you copy part of a Web page and store it as a Dashboard widget called a Web Clip.

Dashboard widgets are programs that perform a single task and pop up whenever you press F12. You find out more about Dashboard widgets in Book VI, Chapter 4.

When you store part of a Web page as a Web Clip, you can view that Web Clip in one of two ways:

✦ Click the Dashboard icon in the Dock.

✦ Press F12.

Creating a Web Clip

To create a Web Clip, follow these steps:

1. **In Safari, find the Web page you're interested in.**

   Usually that would mean a Web page that has a section that gets regularly updated — sports scores, traffic reports, election results, whatever.

2. **Click the Web Clip icon (which looks like scissors cutting around a dotted rectangle) or Choose File➪Open in Dashboard.**

   The Web page darkens and highlights a portion of the currently displayed Web page, as shown in Figure 1-18.

3. **Move the cursor over the part of the Web page that you want to view as a Dashboard widget.**
4. **Click the mouse button.**

   Handles appear around your chosen area.

5. **Move the cursor over a handle, then click and drag the mouse to change the size of the area you've selected on the Web page.**
6. **Click Add.**

   Your Web Clip gets added to Dashboard although you won't see anything until you choose the next step.

7. **Click the Dashboard icon on the Dock or press F12.**

   Dashboard displays your chosen part of the Web page in a widget, as shown in Figure 1-19.

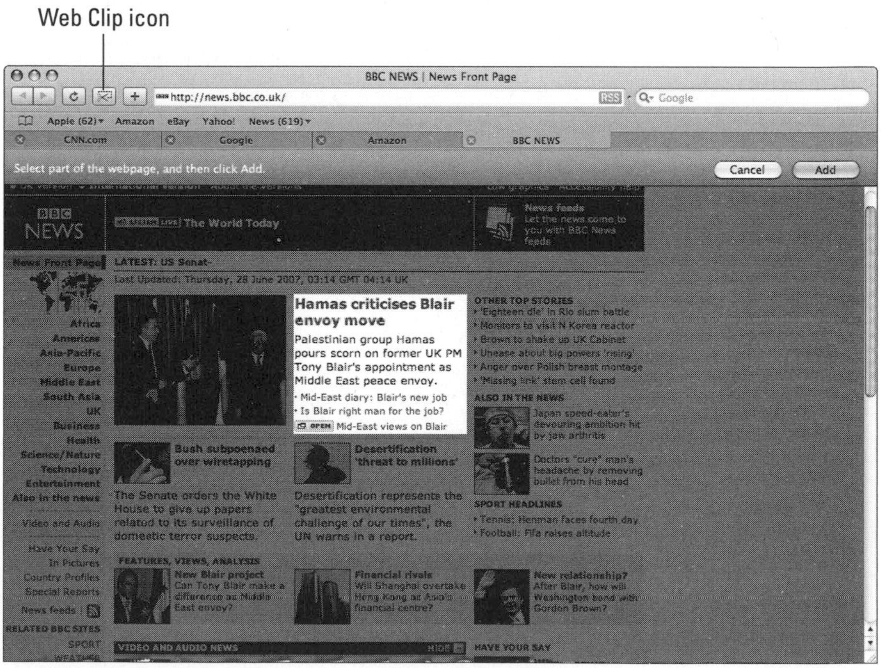

Figure 1-18: Web Clips let you display part of a Web page as a Dashboard widget.

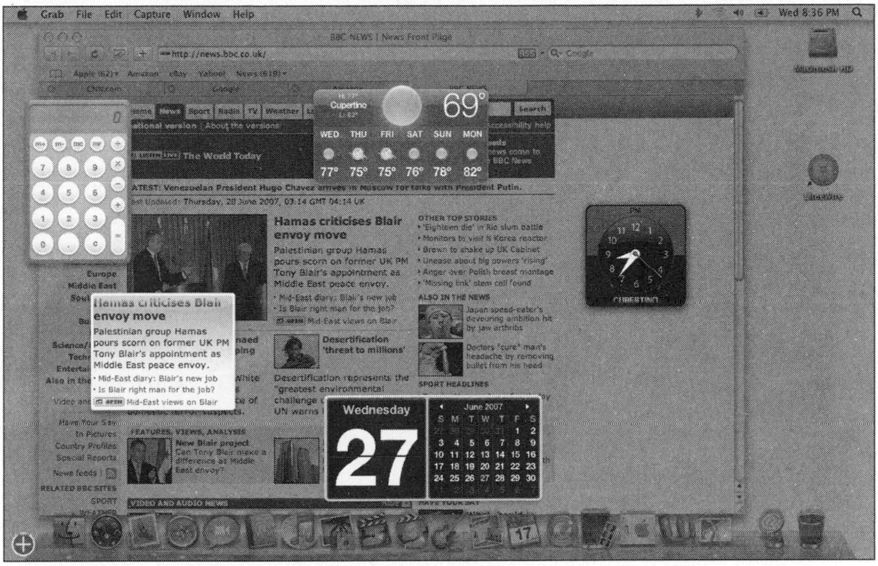

Figure 1-19: Web Clips appear as Dashboard widgets.

Deleting a Web Clip

After you've created a Web Clip, you might want to delete it later. To delete a Web Clip, follow these steps:

1. **Click the Dashboard icon in the Dock or press F12.**

   All your Dashboard widgets appear.

2. **Hold down the Option key and move the pointer over the widget you want to delete.**

   A close icon appears in the upper-left corner.

3. **Click in the Close button of the Web Clip widget.**

Search for Text on a Web Page

One quick way to skim a Web page is to search for specific words or phrases of what you want. So if you're visiting a Web site about investing, you might want to read about stocks and skip over anything related to real estate. To search for specific text, you can use Safari's Find feature.

The Find feature not only finds multiple instances of a word or phrase, but also highlights them on the Web page to make them easier to see and find. To search for text on a Web page, follow these steps:

1. **In Safari, find a Web page that you want to search.**
2. **Choose Edit⇨Find⇨Find (or press ⌘+F).**

   A Find banner (with text box) appears at the top of the Web page.
3. **Click in the Find text box and type a word.**

   The Find banner lists how many matches it found in the currently displayed Web page. Safari highlights the first match, as shown in Figure 1-20.
4. **Click the Next (or Previous) button to view the next (or previous) instance of the searched term.**

   If Safari can't find another match, it simply starts highlighting the previous words or phrases.
5. **Click the Done button in the Find banner when you're done searching through text.**

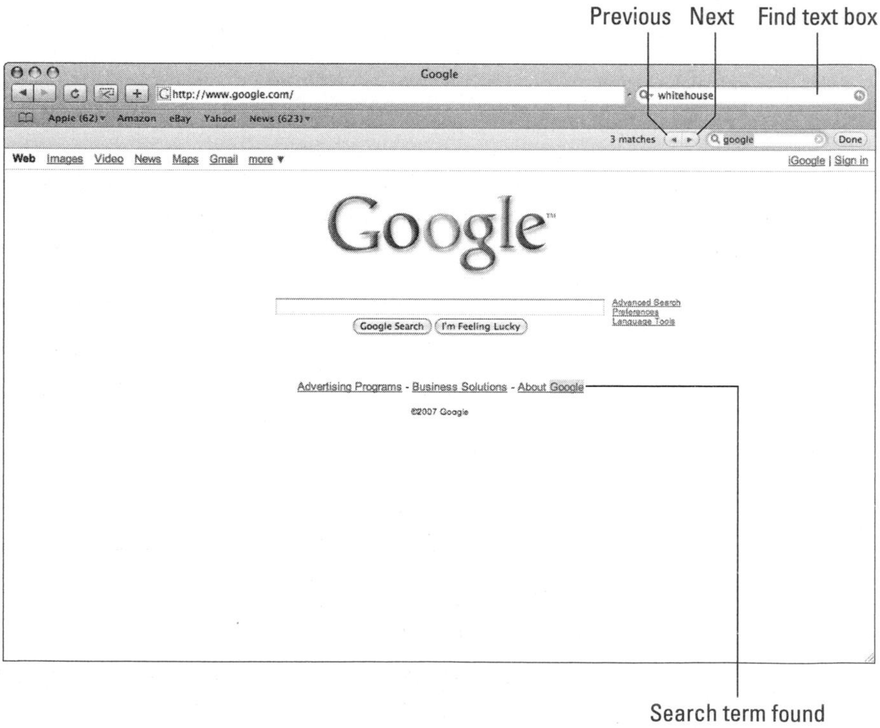

Figure 1-20: Safari highlights each match in a box.

Saving Web Pages

If you find an interesting Web page, you might want to save and share it with others. Some different ways to save and share a Web page include

- ✦ Saving a Web page as a file
- ✦ Printing a Web page
- ✦ Sending a Web page by e-mail
- ✦ Sending a Web page link by e-mail

The next few sections spell out each of these methods.

Saving a Web page as a file

When you save a Web page as a file, you physically store the complete text and graphics of that Web page on your Mac. Safari gives you two ways to save a Web page:

- ✦ As a Web archive
- ✦ As an HTML source file (called Page Source)

A Web archive is meant for viewing a Web page only in the Safari browser. Saving a Web page as an HTML source file lets you view and edit that file in any browser or Web page authoring program — which is neat if you want to figure out how someone designed that particular Web page.

If you view a Web page saved as Page Source, you might not see all the graphics properly without a live Internet connection.

TECHNICAL STUFF

HTML stands for HyperText Markup Language, which is a special language used to design the layout of all Web pages.

To save a Web page as a file, follow these steps:

1. **in Safari, find the Web page that you want to save.**
2. **Choose File⇨Save As.**

   An Export As dialog appears, as shown in Figure 1-21.
3. **Click in the Export As text box and type a descriptive name for your file.**

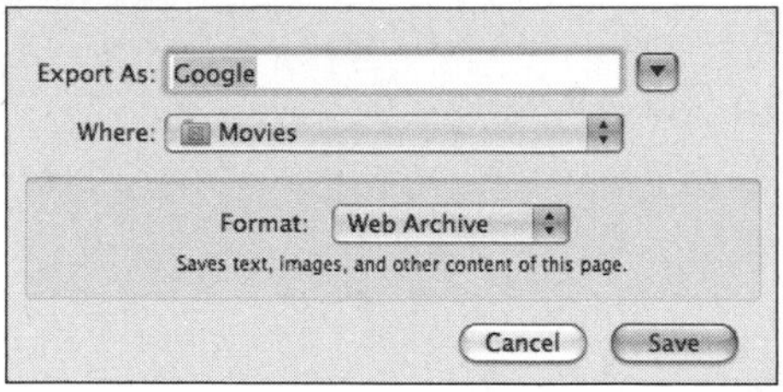

Figure 1-21: The Export As dialog lets you choose where and how to save a file.

4. **Click in the Where pop-up menu and choose a location to store your file.**

   If you click the Expand button, the Save As dialog expands to let you choose more folders to store your file.

5. **Click in the Format pop-up menu and choose Web Archive or Page Source**
6. **Click Save.**

After you save a file as a Web Archive or a Page Source, you can view that file again by following these steps:

1. **In Safari, choose File➪Open File.**

   An Open dialog appears.

2. **Click the Web Archive or Page Source file you want to view and click Open.**

   You might need to navigate through different drives and folders to find the file you want to open.

Only Safari can view a Web Archive file, but any browser can view a Page Source file.

Printing a Web page as a file

Rather than save a Web page as a file, you might just want to print it instead. To print a Web page, follow these steps:

1. **In Safari, find the Web page you want to print.**
2. **Choose File➪Print.**

   A Print dialog appears.

3. **Click in the Printer pop-up menu and choose the printer to use.**

   If you click the PDF button, you can save your Web page as a PDF file. If you click the Downward-pointing arrow to the right of the Printer pop-up menu, the Print dialog expands to let you select which pages to print.

4. **Click Print.**

Sending a Web page by e-mail

After saving a Web page as a separate file, you can then attach that file to an e-mail message to send it to a friend. This might be what you want to do if you want to send the same Web page to multiple people, but if you just want to send a Web page to just one person, you don't really have to save it as a file and then attach it to an e-mail message. You can just send a Web page as part of your e-mail message itself, as shown in Figure 1-22.

Figure 1-22: Sending a Web page as an e-mail message displays that Web page directly in the message text box.

If you use a different e-mail program with Safari, you may not be able to send a Web page as an e-mail message.

To send a Web page as an e-mail message, follow these steps:

1. **In Safari, find the Web page that you want to send.**

2. **Choose File➪Mail Contents of This Page.**

   The Mail program loads and displays your Web page in the message text box.

3. **Click in the To text box and type an e-mail address.**
4. **Click Send.**

Sending a Web page as a link

As an alternative to sending a Web page, you can just send a link to a Web page as part of your e-mail message. The main advantage of sending a link is that it doesn't take as much space as sending the actual Web page. To include a link in an e-mail message, follow these steps:

1. **In Safari, find the Web page that you want to share with others.**
2. **Choose File➪Mail Link to This Page.**

   Your e-mail program loads and displays the Web address of the currently displayed Web page in Safari.

3. **Click in the To text box and type an e-mail address.**

   Click Send.

REMEMBER

If you send a link to a Web page and that Web page or Web site gets changed or gets taken offline, anyone who clicks the link will see an error message and then might wonder why you sent a dead link.

Viewing and Playing Multimedia Files

The simplest Web pages consist of nothing but text and graphics. However, many Web sites offer content stored as video, audio, and PDF (Portable Document Format) files. Although your Mac includes many programs for viewing and listening to video, audio, and PDF files, you might still need additional software to view some Web sites.

Watching video

Many news sites offer videos that require Windows Media Player or RealPlayer. Figure 1-23 shows a typical message a Web site might display if you don't have the proper video player program installed on your Mac.

To download the Windows Media Player, visit Microsoft's Web site (`www.microsoft.com`). Microsoft actually gives you two choices. First, you can download the Windows Media Player for the Mac. However, Microsoft has stopped developing this program, so as a second choice, Microsoft offers a free program called Flip4Mac.

Some Web sites won't work unless you're using Microsoft Windows. In this case, you might need to run Windows on your Mac using one of the programs described in Book V, Chapter 4.

The Flip4Mac program basically allows the QuickTime player (which comes free with every Mac) to play video files designed to run only with the Windows Media Player. Given the choice between downloading the Windows Media Player for the Mac (which will no longer be updated and improved) or the Flip4Mac program (which will get updated and improved), you might as well download Flip4Mac.

Besides downloading and installing the Flip4Mac program, you should also download and install the RealPlayer program (`www.real.com`). After you have both Flip4Mac and RealPlayer installed, you should be able to watch most videos on every Web site you visit.

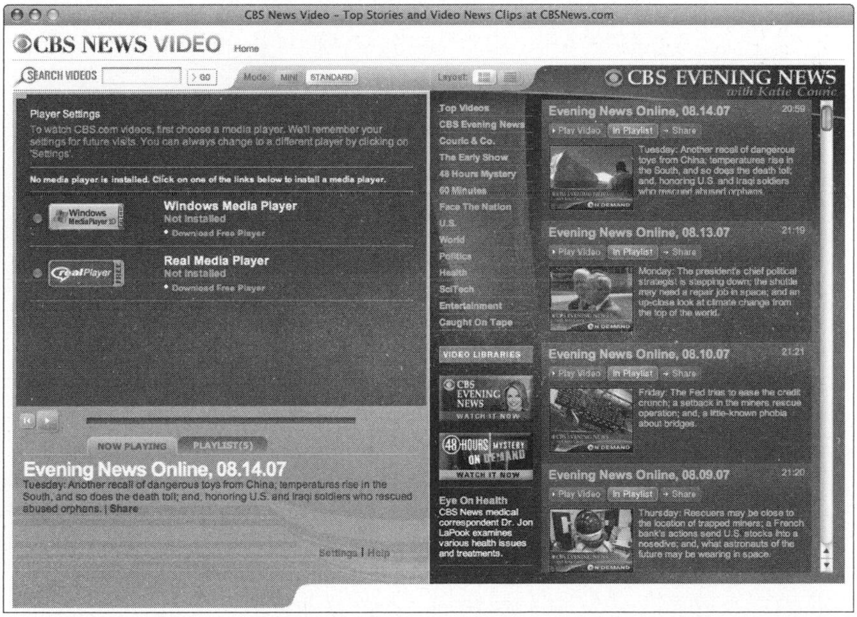

Figure 1-23: If you try to watch a video on some Web sites, you might see a message telling you which video player you need to install.

Listening to streaming audio

Many Web sites offer audio that you can hear, such as live interviews or radio shows. Such audio is often stored as *streaming audio,* which means as your computer downloads the audio file, it plays it right away without actually saving the file to your hard drive.

Sometimes you can listen to streaming audio through the iTunes program, sometimes you need a copy of Windows Media Player (or Flip4Mac), and sometimes you need a copy of RealPlayer.

Even worse, some Web sites won't let you listen to streaming audio unless you use a special program that runs only on the Windows operating system, such as SHOUTcast (`www.shoutcast.com`). In these cases, you simply can't listen to streaming audio from that particular Web site using your Mac.

The only way to run a Windows streaming audio program is to run that program on a copy of Windows on your Mac, using either the Boot Camp program or a virtualization program like Parallels (`www.parallels.com`) or Fusion (`www.vmware.com`). (See Book V, Chapter 4 for more information about running Windows on a Mac.)

Viewing PDF files

Some Web sites offer information stored in PDF (Portable Document Format) files, which is a special file format for storing the layout of text and graphics that appears identically on different computers. If a Web site offers a PDF file, you can view and scroll through it directly within Safari.

After you view a PDF file in Safari, you can save that file by choosing File➪Save As. If you double-click a PDF file icon, you can view the contents of that PDF file by using the Preview program included with every Mac.

You *can* view PDF files by using the Acrobat Reader program — a free download from Adobe (`www.adobe.com`) — but Acrobat Reader essentially duplicates the features of the Preview program that comes with every Mac. If you have problems printing certain PDF files in the Preview program, you might want to print them through the Acrobat Reader program instead.

Downloading Files

Part of the Internet's appeal is that you can find interesting files — music files or program files, for example — that you can download and/or install on your own computer. (When you copy a file off another computer and store it on your computer, that's called *downloading.* When you copy a file off your computer and store it on another computer, that's called *uploading.*)

Many software publishers offer free or trial versions of programs that you can download just by clicking on a button or link that says Download. After you download a file, you can copy or run it later.

Never download a file unless you trust the source. If you visit an unknown Web site, that unknown Web site might be trying to trick you into downloading a file that could delete files, mess up your computer, or even spy on your activities or bombard you with unwanted ads, so be careful.

Downloading a file

To start downloading a file, you must first find a link or button on a Web site that will start sending a file from another computer to your own Mac. With those preliminaries out of the way, do the following to actually download a file:

1. **In Safari, find a Web site that offers a file you can download.**
2. **Click this link or button to start downloading a file.**

   The Downloads window appears, showing the name of the file you're downloading and approximately how much time is remaining in the download, as shown in Figure 1-24.

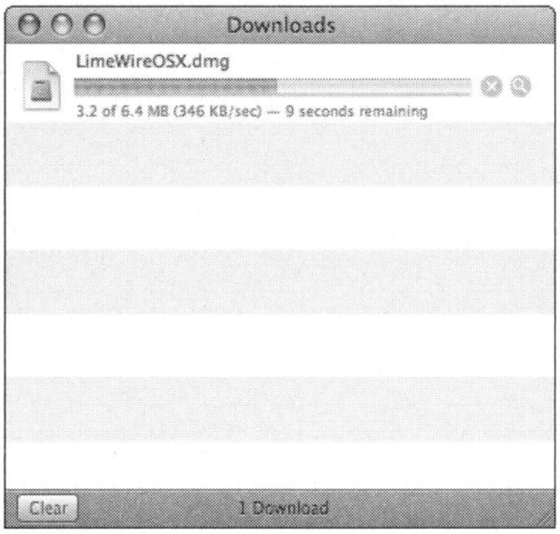

Figure 1-24: The Downloads window shows you how much longer you'll need to wait to finish downloading a file.

3. **Wait until your file is completely downloaded and then double-click that file to open it.**

   If you downloaded a program, that program might start running or installing itself on your Mac, so follow the on-screen instructions.

   If you click the Magnifying glass icon to the right of a file displayed in the Download window, you can view that file inside the Finder.

The Downloads window keeps track of every file you download. If you don't want others to see what you've been downloading, follow these steps to clear this Download window:

1. **In Safari, choose Window➪Downloads.**

   The Downloads window appears.

2. **Click Clear in the bottom left corner of the Downloads window.**

   The Downloads window clears itself.

3. **Click the Close button of the Downloads window.**

Chapter 2: Sending and Receiving E-Mail

In This Chapter

- Configuring an e-mail account
- Writing e-mail
- Receiving and reading e-mail
- Organizing e-mail

Sending and receiving e-mail is one of the most popular uses for the Internet. E-mail is fast, (almost always) free, and accessible to anyone with a computer and an Internet connection.

To send and receive e-mail, you first have to set up an e-mail account. The three types of e-mail accounts you can set up are called POP (Post Office Protocol), IMAP (Internet Message Access Protocol), and Exchange.

A POP e-mail account usually transfers (moves) e-mail from the POP server computer to your computer. An IMAP or Exchange e-mail account stores e-mail on its server, which allows multiple individuals to access the same e-mail account simultaneously. Most individuals have POP accounts, whereas many corporations have IMAP or Exchange accounts.

Setting Up an E-Mail Account

When you have an e-mail account, you'll often have two choices for reading and writing messages:

✦ Through a browser such as Safari

✦ Through an e-mail program such as the Mac's free program called Mail

REMEMBER

You don't have to choose between the methods — you can use both.

Accessing an e-mail account through a browser is simple because you don't need to know how to use another program, and you don't have to worry about knowing the technical details of your e-mail account. The drawback is that you need Internet access every time you want to read or respond to messages.

Accessing an e-mail account through an e-mail program lets you download messages so you can read or respond to them even if you aren't connected to the Internet. (Of course, you won't be able to send or receive any messages until you connect to the Internet again.) The drawback of using an e-mail program is that you must configure it to work with your e-mail account.

There are dozens of e-mail programs you can use, but the most popular one is the free Mail program that comes with every Mac. If you don't like Mail, you can download and install a free e-mail program such as Thunderbird (`www.mozilla.com`), or buy an e-mail program such as Microsoft Entourage (`www.microsoft.com`) or MailSmith (`www.barebones.com`).

If you plan to access your e-mail account only through a browser like Safari, you can skip this entire chapter because this chapter explains how to use the Mail program.

Gathering your e-mail account information

To make an e-mail program work with your e-mail account, you need to gather the following information:

- **Your username (also called an account name):** Typically a descriptive name (such as jerrysmith), a collection of numbers or symbols (such as 7300914 or 1m3990-4), or both (jerrysmith77). Your username plus the name of your Internet Service Provider (ISP) defines your complete e-mail address, such as jerrysmith77@aol.com.
- **Your password:** Any phrase that you choose to access your account. If someone sets up an e-mail account for you, he or she might have already assigned a password that you can always change later.
- **Your e-mail account's incoming server name:** The name of the computer that contains your e-mail messages. If you're using a POP account, the incoming server name is usually a combination of POP or the word "mail" and your e-mail account company, such as `pop.acme.com` or `mail.acme.com`.
- **Your e-mail account's outgoing server name:** The name of the computer that will send your messages to other people. The outgoing server name is usually a combination of SMTP (Simple Mail Transfer Protocol) and the name of the company that provides your e-mail account, such as `smtp.acme.com`.

If you don't know your account name, password, incoming server name, or outgoing server name, ask the company that runs your e-mail account. Without all this information, you won't be able to receive or send e-mail messages through a separate e-mail program.

Configuring your e-mail account

After you've collected the technical information needed to access your e-mail account, you need to configure the Mail program to work with your e-mail account by following these steps:

1. **Click the Mail icon in the Dock.**

   A New Account dialog appears, welcoming you to Mail.

2. **Click Continue.**

   Another New Account dialog appears, asking for your name and password, as shown in Figure 2-1.

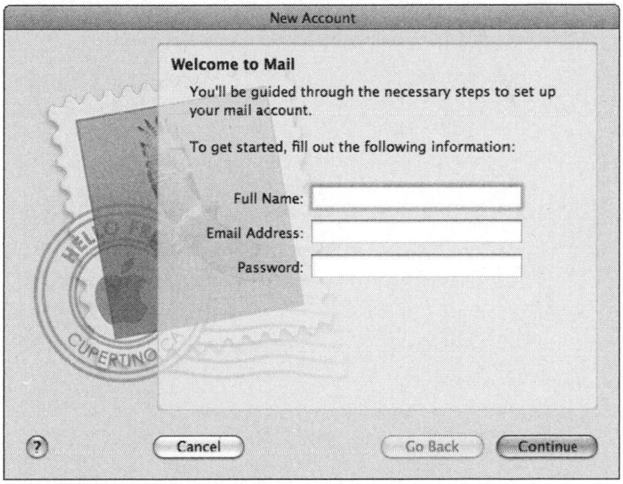

Figure 2-1: The New Account dialog asks for your name, e-mail address, and password.

3. **Enter your full name, e-mail address, and password in the text boxes.**

   Your full name is any name you want to associate with your messages. If you type "Zambar the Great" in the Full Name text box, all your messages will include "From: Zambar the Great." Your e-mail address includes your username plus ISP name such as billy394@earthlink.net. Your password might be case-sensitive, so type it exactly.

4. **(Optional) Select (or deselect) the Automatically Setup Account check box.**

   The Automatically Setup Account check box and the Create button appear after you've typed in your full name, e-mail address, and password. When the check box is selected, Mail will attempt to connect and configure itself automatically after you click the Create button. If this attempt fails, you'll have to manually configure the Mail program.

5. **Click Continue.**

   An Incoming Mail Server dialog appears, as shown in Figure 2-2.

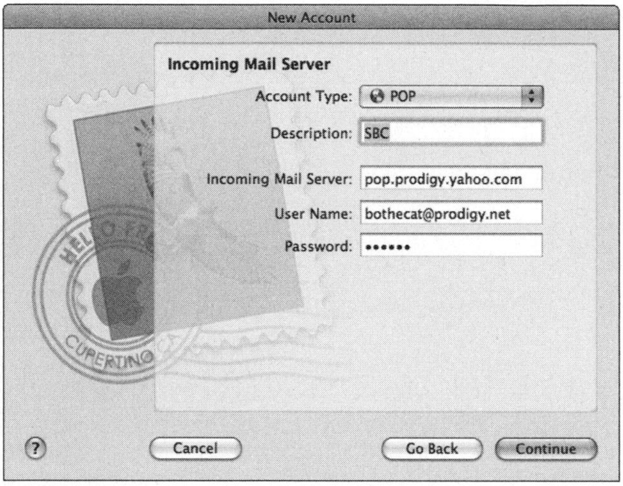

Figure 2-2: The Incoming Mail Server dialog lets you specify where to retrieve your e-mail.

6. **Choose your incoming mail server type from the Account Type pop-up menu.**

   Your choices here are .Mac, POP, IMAP, or Exchange.

   You would choose the .Mac account type only if you subscribe to the .Mac service.

7. **(Optional) Click in the Description text box and type a description of your account.**

   This description is for your benefit only, so feel free to type anything you want. Because you can configure Mail to access two or more e-mail accounts, you might want to identify an account as a Work account or a Yahoo! account.

8. **Click in the Incoming Mail Server text box and type the name of your server.**

   If you don't know this name, you'll have to ask your ISP or e-mail account provider.

9. **Click in the User Name text box and type your username.**

10. **Click in the Password text box and type your password.**

    Your password appears on-screen as a series of dots to keep people from peeking over your shoulder and seeing your password.

11. **Click Continue.**

The Outgoing Mail Server dialog appears, as shown in Figure 2-3.

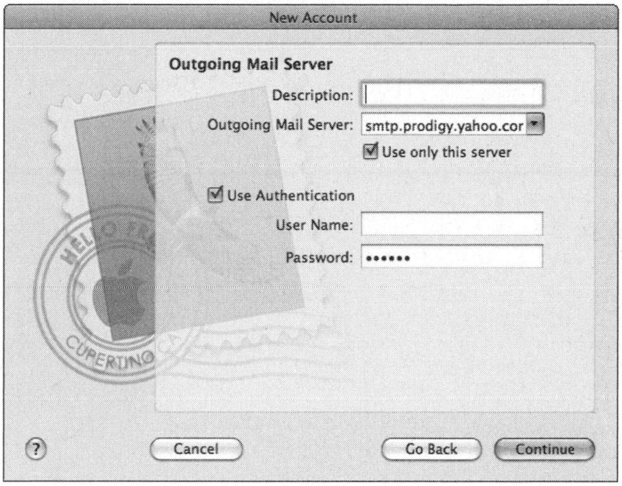

Figure 2-3: The Outgoing Mail Server asks for the name of the server to send your e-mail through to the rest of the Internet.

12. **(Optional) Click in the Description text box and type a description of your account.**

This description is for your benefit only, so feel free to type anything you want. If you type in the technical support number of your ISP as the outgoing mail server, you'll know who to call if you're having trouble.

13. **Click in the Outgoing Mail Server text box and type the name of your outgoing mail server.**

If you don't know this name, you'll have to contact your ISP or e-mail account provider.

14. **Click in the User Name text box and type your username.**

15. **Click in the Password text box and type your password.**

16. **Click Continue.**

The Account Summary dialog appears as shown in Figure 2-4.

17. **Click Create.**

The Mail window appears.

REMEMBER

You can configure the Mail program to retrieve e-mail from multiple e-mail accounts. To add more e-mail accounts, choose File⇨Add Account and repeat the preceding steps to define an incoming and outgoing mail server.

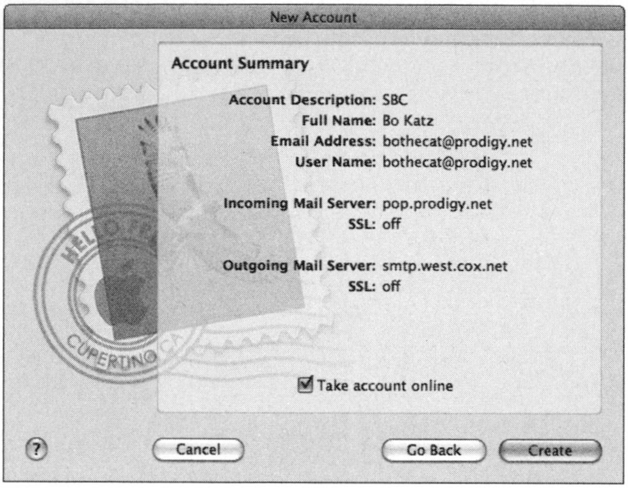

Figure 2-4: The Account Summary dialog shows your e-mail account settings.

Writing E-Mails

After you've configured Mail, you can start writing and sending e-mail to anyone all over the world (just as long as you have their e-mail address, that is). There are three ways to write and send an e-mail:

- Create a new message from scratch.
- Reply to a message you received from someone else.
- Forward a message you received from someone else.

Creating a new e-mail

When you're writing a message to someone for the first time, you have to create a new message by following these steps:

1. **In Mail, choose File⇨New Message (or click the New Message button).**

   A New Message window appears.

2. **Click in the To text box and type an e-mail address.**

   TIP: You can type multiple e-mail addresses in the To text box by separating each e-mail address with a comma, such as `john@yahoo.com, bill@microsoft.com`.

3. **Click in the Subject text box and type a brief description of your message for your recipient.**
4. **Click in the Message text box and type your message.**
5. **Click the Send button.**

Replying to a message

You'll often respond to a message that somebody else sent to you. When you reply to a message, your reply can contain the text that you originally received so the recipient can better understand the context of your reply.

REMEMBER

To reply to a message, you need to receive a message first. To receive messages, just click the Get Mail button. You find out more about receiving messages later in this chapter.

To reply to a message, follow these steps:

1. **In Mail, click the Inbox icon under the Mailboxes category in the left pane of the Mail window.**

   The right pane lists all the messages currently stored in your Inbox folder.

2. **Click to select a message in the right pane that you want to reply to.**
3. **Choose Message⇨Reply (or click the Reply button).**

   A Message window appears with the e-mail address of your recipient, the subject already typed in, and the text of the message so that the other person can understand the context of your reply.

   REMEMBER

   If you're replying to a message that was sent to you and several other people, you can reply to everyone who received the same message by choosing Message⇨Reply All or by clicking the Reply All button.

4. **Click in the Message text box and type a message.**
5. **Click Send.**

Forwarding a message

Sometimes you might receive a message and want to send that message to someone else. When you send a copy of a forwarded message, that message appears directly in the Message text box, as shown in Figure 2-5.

To forward a message, follow these steps:

1. **In Mail, click the Inbox icon under the Mailboxes category in the left pane of the Mail window.**

   The right pane lists all the messages stored in your Inbox folder.

2. **In the right pane, click to select a message that you want to forward.**
3. **Click the Forward button at the top of the Mail window.**
4. **Click in the To text box and type an e-mail address.**
5. **Click Send.**

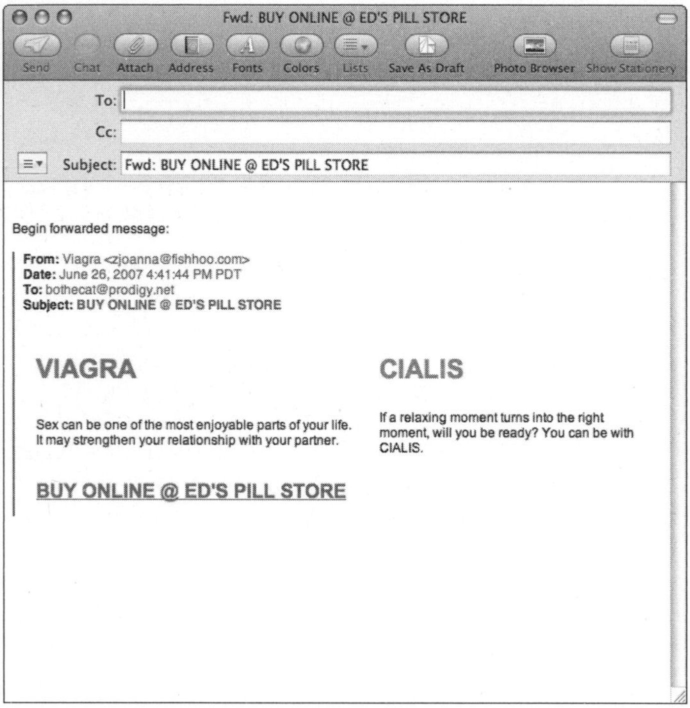

Figure 2-5: The text of a forwarded message appears directly in the Message text box.

Sending a file attachment

When you send an e-mail, you're basically sending text. However, sometimes you might want to send pictures or word processor documents. Anyone receiving your message and file attachment can then save the file attachment and open it later. Because so many people need to share Microsoft Word files or digital photographs, file attachments are a popular way to share files with others.

Your e-mail account may have a maximum file size limit you can send, such as 10MB. (If too many people send large file attachments, it could slow down e-mail access for other customers.) If you have a file larger than the maximum limit, you might have to send your files through a free, separate file-delivery service such as YouSendIt (`www.yousendit.com`), SendThisFile (`www.sendthisfile.com`), or BigUpload (`www.bigupload.com`).

To attach a file to a message, follow these steps:

1. **In Mail, open a Message window as described in one of the preceding sections.**

   You can open a Message window to create a new message, reply to an existing message, or forward an existing message.

2. **Choose File➪Attach File (or click the Attach button).**

   A dialog appears.

3. **Navigate through the folders to get to the file you want to send and then click it.**

   TIP: To select multiple files, hold down the ⌘ key and click each file you want to send. To select a range of files, hold down the Shift key and click on the first and last files you want to send.

4. **Click Choose File.**
5. **Click Send.**

Sending a message to multiple recipients

If you want to send the same message to several people, you can type multiple e-mail addresses, separated by a comma, in one or more of the following fields:

✦ To

✦ Carbon copy (Cc)

✦ Blind carbon copy (Bcc)

The To field is meant to hold e-mail addresses of people who you want to read your message. The Carbon copy (Cc) field is meant to hold e-mail addresses of people who you want to keep informed, but who don't necessarily need to write a reply.

TIP: When sending out a particularly important message, many people type the recipient's e-mail address in the To field and their own e-mail address in the Carbon copy field. This way they can verify that their message was sent out correctly.

When someone receives an e-mail message, he or she can read all the e-mail addresses stored in the To and Carbon copy fields. If you don't want anyone else to know who received your message, use Blind carbon copy. (It's possible to use both Carbon copy and Blind carbon copy in the same message.)

Whenever you write a message, the To field is always visible since you need to send your message to at least one e-mail address. However, Mail can hide and display both the Carbon copy and Blind carbon copy fields because you don't always want or need them to send every message your write.

To send multiple copies of the same message as Carbon copy or Blind carbon copy, follow these steps:

1. **In Mail, open a Message window as described in one of the preceding sections.**

   You can open a Message window to create a new message, reply to an existing message, or forward an existing message.

2. **(Optional) Choose View➪Cc Address Field if the Cc field isn't currently visible.**

   A check mark means the Cc text box appears in the Message window.

3. **(Optional) Choose View➪Bcc Address Field if the Bcc field isn't currently visible.**

   A check mark means the Bcc text box appears in the Message window.

4. **Click in the Cc and/or Bcc text box and type an e-mail address.**

   You can type multiple e-mail addresses in the To, Cc, and Bcc text boxes by separating each e-mail address with a comma, such as `john@yahoo.com, bill@microsoft.com`.

5. **Click Send.**

Using e-mail stationery

E-mail stationery consists of graphic designs and formatted text that you can edit. By using stationery, you can create e-mail messages that look more interesting than plain text.

Picking a stationery design

To use Mail's Stationery feature to create a new message, follow these steps:

1. **In Mail, choose File➪New Message (or click the New Message icon).**

   A New Message window appears.

2. **Click the Show Stationery button.**

   A list of stationery categories (Birthday, Photos, and so on) appears in the upper-left pane and a list of stationery designs appears in the upper-middle of the New Message window, as shown in Figure 2-6.

3. **Click a Stationery category, such as Sentiments or Birthday.**

   Each time you click a different category, the Mail window displays a list of stationery designs in that category.

4. **Click the stationery design that you want to use.**

   Your chosen stationery appears in the main section of the New Message window.

5. **Click any text and edit or type new text.**

Show/Hide Stationery button

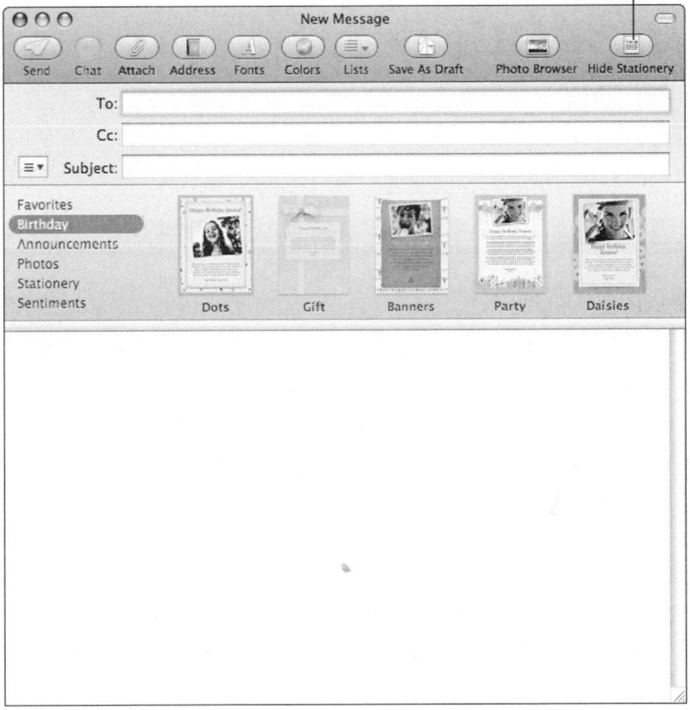

Figure 2-6: Stationery lets you choose from predesigned templates for different types of e-mail messages.

Modifying photographs in a stationery design

After you've chosen a stationery design, you can edit the text and replace it with your own personal message. If a stationery displays a photograph, you can replace the photograph with another picture, either one stored in iPhoto or one stored anywhere else on your hard drive.

To add your own pictures to a stationery design, follow these steps:

1. **Make sure the Mail program displays a stationery design that includes one or more pictures, as shown in top part of Figure 2-7.**
2. **Do one of the following actions:**
   - Call up the Finder by clicking the Finder icon in the Dock. (You might need to move the Finder and Mail windows so they appear side by side.)
   - Click the Photo Browser icon. The Photo Browser window appears, containing all the photographs you've stored in iPhoto.
3. **In either the Finder or the Photo Browser, navigate to the folder that contains a photograph that you want to use in your stationery.**

4. **Click and drag your chosen photograph onto the picture in your stationery design.**
5. **Release the mouse button.**

   Your chosen picture now appears in your stationery, as shown in the lower part of Figure 2-7.
6. **Click the Close button of the Finder or Photo Browser window.**

Figure 2-7: Click and drag to replace stationery pictures with your own images.

Spell and grammar checking

Although e-mail is considered less formal than other forms of communication, such as letters or subpoenas, you probably don't want your e-mail message riddled with spelling errors and typos that can make you look like an uneducated clod. That's why Mail provides a spell checker along with a grammar checker.

To use the built-in spell and grammar checker, you need to configure it first to define whether you want it to check as you type or wait until you're done typing.

Configuring the spell and grammar checker

By default, the Mail program has its spell checker turned on to check misspellings as you type. When Mail finds a misspelled word, it underlines the word in red. If you find this annoying or want to turn on the grammar checker too, you need to configure the spell and grammar checker. If you're happy with the way the spell checker works, you don't have to configure the spell or grammar checker at all.

To configure the spell and grammar checker, follow these steps:

1. **In Mail, choose Mail⇨Preferences.**

   A Preferences window appears.

2. **Click the Composing tab.**

   The Composing pane of the Preferences window appears.

3. **Choose one of the following options from the Check Spelling pop-up menu, as shown in Figure 2-8:**

   - *As I Type:* Underlines possible misspellings and grammar problems as you write.
   - *When I Click Send:* Spell and grammar checks your message before it's sent.
   - *Never:* Doesn't perform spell or grammar checking.

4. **Click the Close button of the Preferences window.**

Checking spelling and grammar

If you have spell checking turned on while you type, the spell checker will underline suspected misspelled words in red to help you find potential problems easily. If you want to spell and grammar check your entire message, follow these steps:

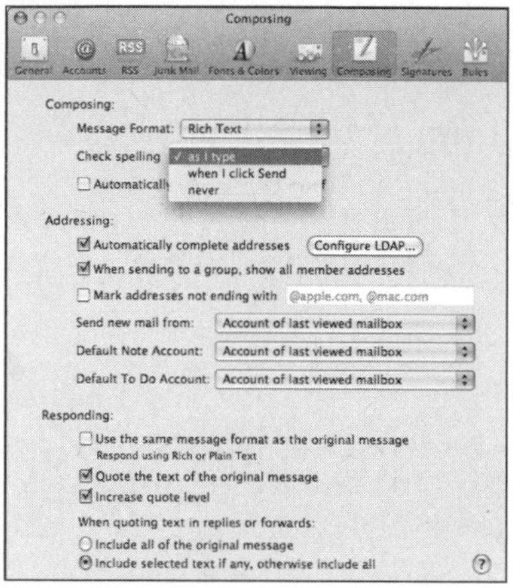

Figure 2-8: The Check Spelling pop-up menu provides spell and grammar checking options.

1. **Open a Message window as described earlier in this chapter.**

   You can open a Message window to create a new message, reply to an existing message, or forward an existing message.

2. **Choose Edit⇨Spelling and Grammar⇨Show Spelling and Grammar.**

   The spell and grammar check does its thing, with a Spelling and Grammar dialog appearing each time the Mail program finds a potentially misspelled word, as shown in Figure 2-9.

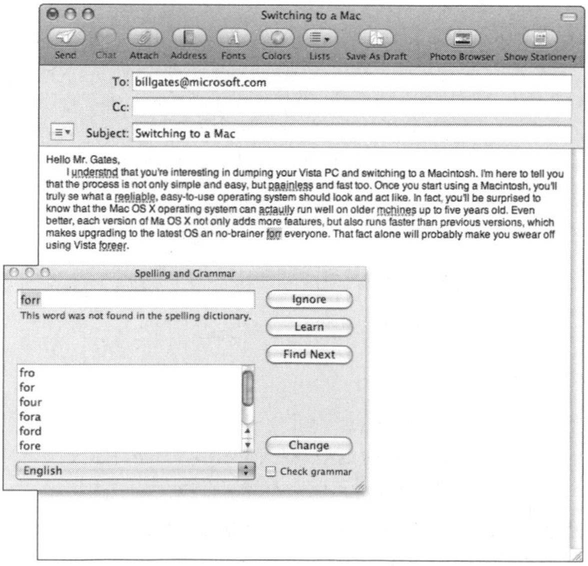

Figure 2-9: The Spelling and Grammar dialog suggests possible correct spellings.

3. **Click one of the following buttons:**
   - *Ignore:* Tells Mail that the word is correct.
   - *Learn:* Adds the word to the dictionary.
   - *Find Next:* Finds the next occurrence of the same misspelled word.
   - *Change:* Changes the misspelled word with the spelling that you choose from the list box on the left.
4. **Click Send.**

The spell and grammar checker can't catch all possible errors (words like *to* and *two* can slip past because the words are spelled correctly), so make sure you proofread your message after you finish spell and grammar checking your message.

Receiving and Reading E-Mail

After you start giving out your e-mail address to other people, you can start receiving e-mail. To receive e-mail, your e-mail program must contact your incoming mail server and download the messages to your Mac. Then you can either check for new mail manually or have the Mail program check for new mail automatically.

Retrieving e-mail

To check and retrieve e-mail manually in Mail, choose Mailbox⇨Get New Mail (or click the Get Mail icon). The number of new messages appears next to the Inbox icon.

Checking for new e-mail manually can get tedious, so you can configure Mail to check for new mail automatically at fixed intervals of time, such as every 5 or 15 minutes. To configure Mail to check for new messages automatically, follow these steps:

1. **In Mail, choose Mail⇨Preferences.**

   The Preferences window appears.
2. **Click the General icon.**

   The General pane appears, as shown in Figure 2-10.
3. **From the Check for New Mail pop-up menu, choose an option to determine how often to check for new messages.**

   You can check every minute, every 5 minutes, every 15 minutes, every 30 minutes, or every hour.

4. **(Optional) Choose a sound to play when you receive new messages from the New Mail Sound pop-up menu.**

   You can also choose None in case any sound bothers you.

5. **Click the Close button of the Preferences window.**

Mail can check for new messages only if you leave Mail running. If you quit Mail, it can't check for new messages periodically.

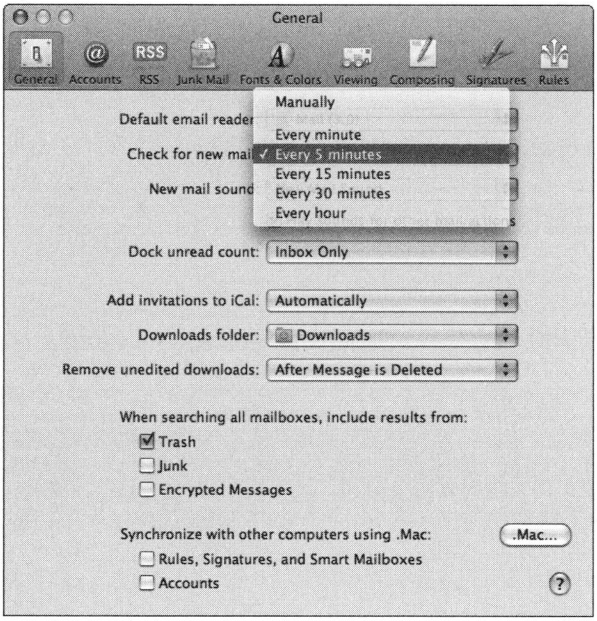

Figure 2-10: The General pane lets you define how often to check for new e-mail.

Reading e-mail

After you start receiving e-mail, you can start reading your messages. When you receive a new message, Mail flags it with a dot in the Message Status column, as shown in Figure 2-11.

To read a message, follow these steps:

1. **In Mail, click the Inbox icon in the left pane.**

   A list of messages stored in the Inbox appears.

2. **Do one of the following:**
   - Click a message and read the message in the Preview pane.
   - Double-click a message to display and read a message in a separate window.

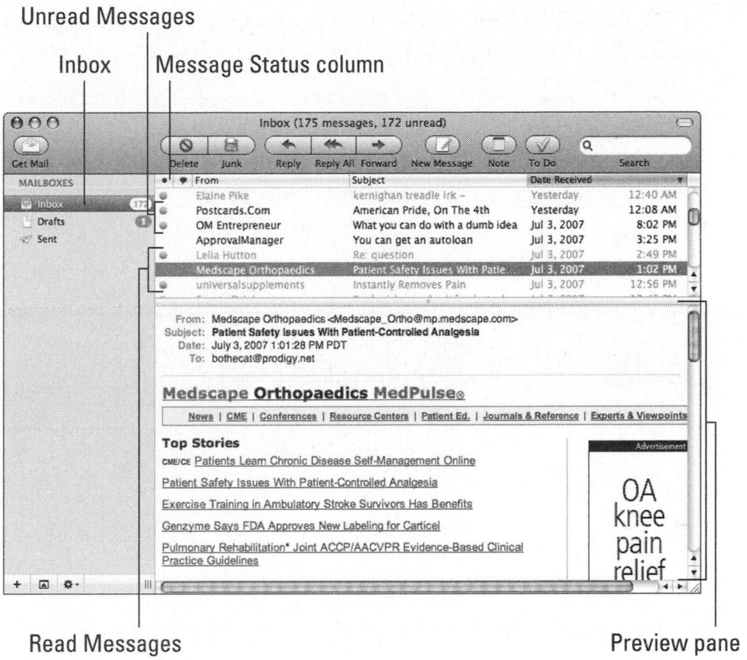

Figure 2-11: Mail shows you which messages you haven't read yet.

The advantage of the Preview pane is that you can scan your messages quickly by clicking each one without having to open a separate window. The advantage of reading a message in a separate window is that you can resize that window and see more of the message without having to scroll as often as you would if you were reading that same message in the Preview pane.

Viewing and saving file attachments

When you receive a message that has a file attachment, Mail identifies how many attachments there are and displays a Save button, as shown in Figure 2-12.

To save a file attachment, follow these steps:

1. **In Mail, click the Inbox icon in the left pane.**

   A list of messages stored in the Inbox appears.

2. **Click a message.**

   If the message has a file attachment, the number of attachments, the amount of space they take up, the Save button, and the Quick Look button all appear in the message headers that list who sent the message, the date sent, and the message subject.

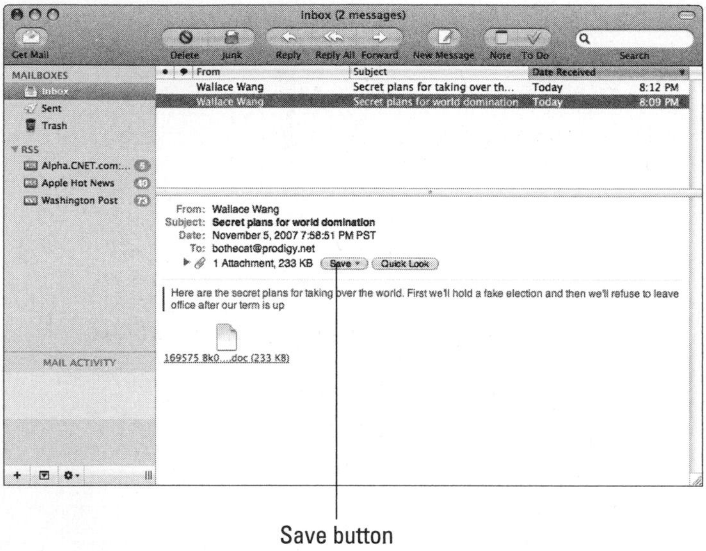

Figure 2-12: A Save button appears whenever a message includes a file attachment.

3. **(Optional) Click the Quick Look button.**

   A window appears, displaying the contents of your file attachment (or playing the file if it's a music or video file). Click the Close box of the Quick Look window when you're done looking at its contents.

4. **Click the Save button.**

   Mail saves your attachments into the Downloads folder stored inside your Home folder. (You may also access the Downloads folder on the Dock, to the left of the Trash icon.)

Storing e-mail addresses

Typing an e-mail address every time you want to send a message can get tedious — if you can even remember the address. Fortunately, Mail lets you store names and e-mail addresses in the Address Book program. Then you can just click that person's name to send a message without typing that person's entire e-mail address.

Adding an e-mail address to the Address Book

When you receive an e-mail from someone you like, you can store that person's e-mail address in the Address Book by following these steps:

1. **In Mail, click the Inbox icon in the left pane.**

   A list of messages appears in the right pane.

2. **Click to select a message sent by someone whose e-mail address you want to save.**
3. **Choose Message⇨Add Sender to Address Book.**

   Although nothing appears to happen, your chosen e-mail address is now stored in the Address Book.

REMEMBER

To view your list of stored names and e-mail addresses, you can open the Address Book by choosing Windows⇨Address Panel.

Retrieving an e-mail address from the Address Book

When you create a new message, you can retrieve an e-mail address from your Address Book. To retrieve an e-mail address, follow these steps:

1. **In Mail, choose File⇨New Message (or click the New Message icon).**

   A New Message window appears.
2. **Click the Address button (or choose Windows⇨Address Panel).**

   An Address Panel appears, as shown in Figure 2-13.

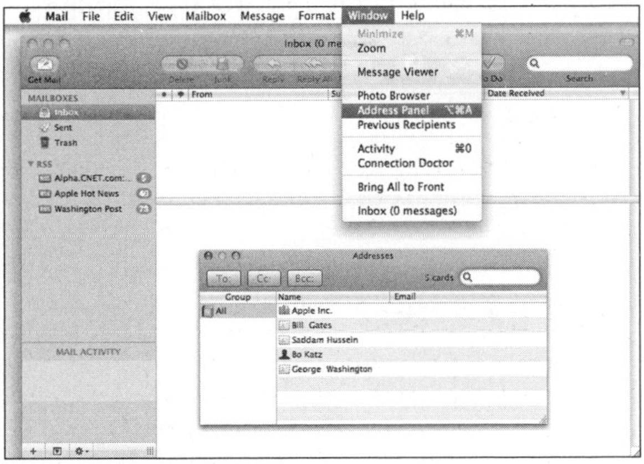

Figure 2-13: The Address Panel lets you pick an e-mail address.

3. **Click to select the name of the person you want to send a message to.**
4. **Click the To button.**

   Your chosen e-mail address appears in the To: text box. (If you click on the Cc or Bcc buttons, you can add an e-mail address to the Cc or Bcc text boxes, respectively.)
5. **Click the Close button of the Address Panel.**

Deleting a name and e-mail address from the Address Book

After you've stored names and e-mail addresses in your Address Book, you might want to delete some of them one day. To delete an e-mail address in the Address Book, follow these steps:

1. **Click the Address Book icon in the Dock (or double-click the Address Book icon in the Applications folder).**

   The Address Book window appears.

2. **Click the name you want to delete.**
3. **Choose Edit⇨Delete Card.**

   The Address Book deletes your chosen name.

   TIP: If you accidentally delete a name, you can retrieve it right away by choosing Edit⇨Undo Delete Record.

4. **Choose Address Book⇨Quit Address Book.**

Deleting messages

After you read a message, you can either leave it in your Inbox or delete it. Generally, it's a good idea to delete messages you won't need ever again, such as an invitation to somebody's birthday party back in July 2005. By deleting unnecessary messages, you can keep your Inbox organized and uncluttered.

To delete a message, follow these steps:

1. **In Mail, click the Inbox icon in the left pane.**

   A list of messages stored in the Inbox appears.

2. **Click the message you want to delete.**

   TIP: To select multiple messages, hold down the ⌘ key and click additional messages. To select a range of messages, hold down the Shift key, click the first message to delete, and then click the last message to delete, and release the Shift key.

3. **Choose Edit⇨Delete (or click the Delete button).**

REMEMBER: Deleting a message doesn't immediately erase it, but stores it in the Trash folder. If you don't go and "empty the trash," you still have the chance to retrieve deleted messages, as outlined in the next section.

Retrieving messages from the Trash folder

Each time you delete a message, Mail stores the deleted messages in the Trash folder. If you think you deleted a message by mistake, you can retrieve it by following these steps:

1. **In Mail, click the Trash folder.**

   A list of deleted messages appears.

2. **Click the message you want to retrieve.**
3. **Choose Message⇨Move To⇨Inbox.**

Emptying the Trash folder

Messages stored in the Trash folder continue to take up space, so you should periodically empty the Trash folder by following these steps:

1. **In Mail, choose Mailbox⇨Erase Deleted Messages.**

   A submenu appears, listing all the e-mail accounts in Mail.

2. **Choose either In All Accounts (to erase all deleted messages) or the name of a specific e-mail account (to erase messages only from that particular account).**

Organizing E-Mail

To help you manage and organize your e-mail messages, Mail lets you search and sort your messages. Searching lets you find specific text stored in a particular message. Sorting lets you arrange your messages in folders so one folder might contain personal messages and a second folder might contain business messages.

Searching through e-mail

To manage your e-mail effectively, you need to be able to search for the one (or more) message you want. To search through your e-mail for the names of senders or text in a message Subject line, follow these steps:

1. **In Mail, click in the Spotlight text box in the upper-right corner.**
2. **Type a word, phrase, or partial phrase that you want to find.**

   As you type, Mail displays a list of messages that match the text you're typing, as shown in Figure 2-14.

3. **Click a message to read it.**

Sorting e-mail

You can sort e-mail in ascending or descending order based on different categories, such as alphabetically by the sender, chronologically by date sent, or alphabetically by subject.

Figure 2-14: As you type in the Spotlight text box, Mail displays a list of messages that match your text.

> **TIP:** The easiest way to sort your e-mail is by clicking a column heading, such as From or Subject.

To sort your e-mail, you can also follow these steps:

1. **In Mail, choose View➪Sort By.**

   A submenu appears, as shown in Figure 2-15.

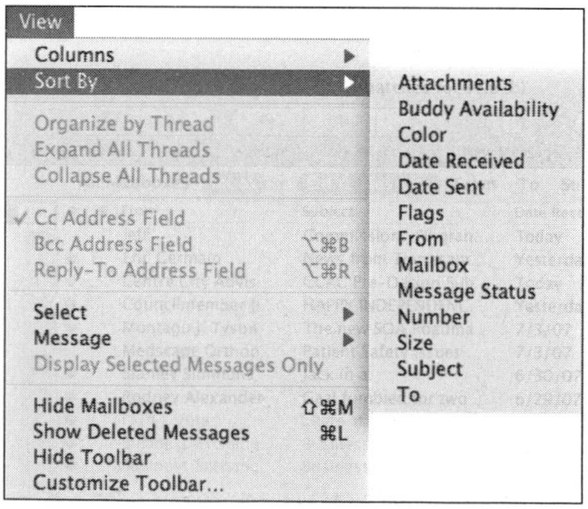

Figure 2-15: Mail lets you sort your e-mail messages in a variety of ways.

2. **Choose a criteria to sort, such as by Date Sent or Subject.**

   Mail then sorts the e-mail according to your whims.

Organizing e-mail with mailbox folders

When you receive e-mail, all of your messages get dumped in the Inbox. After a while, you might have so many messages stored there that trying to find related messages can be nearly impossible.

To fix this problem, you can create separate folders for organizing your different e-mails. After you've created a folder, you can group related messages together so you can quickly find them again later.

The most common type of e-mail to organize is junk e-mail, which you can route automatically into the Trash. Book III, Chapter 4 explains how to configure Mail to handle junk e-mail.

Creating a mailbox folder

To create a mailbox folder, follow these steps:

1. **In Mail, choose Mailbox⇨New Mailbox.**

   A New Mailbox dialog appears, as shown in Figure 2-16.

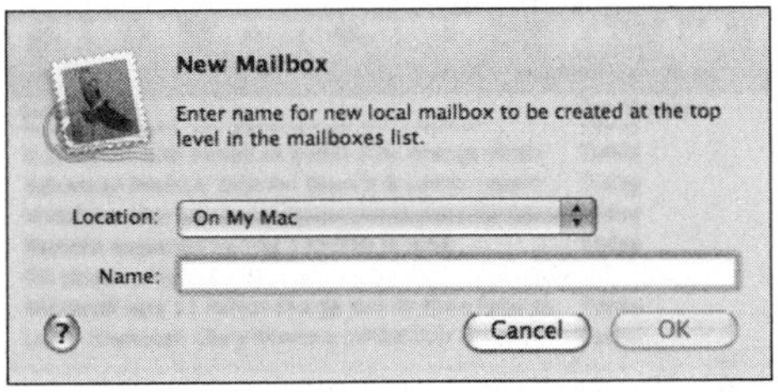

Figure 2-16: The New Mailbox dialog lets you choose a name for your mailbox folder.

2. **Click in the Name text box and type a descriptive name for your mailbox folder.**
3. **Click OK.**

   Your mailbox folder appears in the left pane of the Mail window.

Storing messages in a mailbox folder

When you create a mailbox folder, it's completely empty. To store messages in a mailbox folder, you must manually drag those messages into the mailbox folder. Dragging physically moves your message from the Inbox folder into your mailbox folder.

To move a message into a mailbox folder, follow these steps:

1. **In Mail, click the Inbox icon in the left pane to view all your messages.**
2. **Click to select a message that you want to move to your mailbox folder.**

   If you hold down the ⌘ key while clicking a message, you can select multiple messages. If you hold down the Shift key, you can click one message and then click another message to select those two messages and every message in between.
3. **Click and drag the selected message onto your mailbox folder.**
4. **Release the mouse button when the pointer highlights the mailbox folder.**

   Your selected messages now appear in the mailbox folder.

Deleting a mailbox folder

You can delete a mailbox folder by following these steps:

1. **In Mail, click on the mailbox folder you want to delete.**
2. **Choose Mailbox⇨Delete.**

   A dialog box appears, asking if you really want to delete your folder.

   When you delete a mailbox folder, you delete all messages stored inside.
3. **Click Delete.**

Automatically organizing e-mail with smart mailboxes

Mailbox folders can help organize your messages, but you must manually drag messages into those folders. To make this process automatic, you can use *smart mailboxes* instead.

A smart mailbox differs from an ordinary mailbox in two ways:

- A smart mailbox lets you define the type of messages you want to store automatically; that way, Mail sorts your messages without any additional work from you.
- A smart mailbox doesn't physically contain a message but only a link to the actual message, which is still stored in the Inbox folder (or any folder that you move it to). Because smart mailboxes don't physically move messages, it's possible for a single message to have links stored in multiple smart mailboxes.

Creating a smart mailbox

To create a smart mailbox, you need to define a name for your smart mailbox along with the criteria for the types of messages to store in your smart mailbox. To create a smart mailbox, follow these steps:

1. **In Mail, choose Mailbox➪New Smart Mailbox.**

   A Smart Mailbox dialog appears, as shown in Figure 2-17

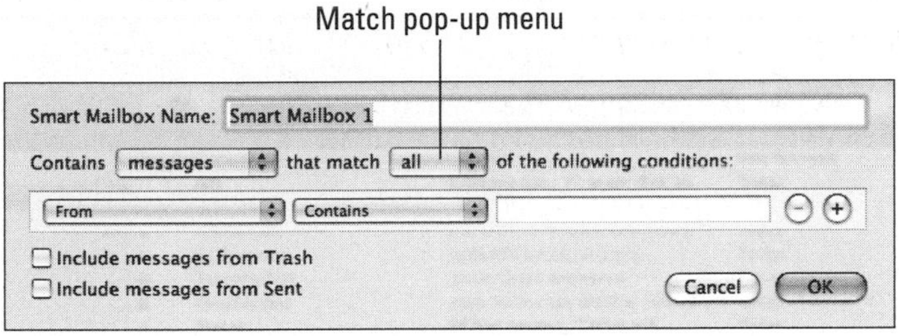

Figure 2-17: The New Smart Mailbox dialog lets you define the types of messages to store.

2. **Click in the Smart Mailbox Name text box and type a descriptive name for your smart mailbox.**
3. **Click in the Match pop-up menu and choose All (of the following conditions) or Any (of the following conditions).**
4. **Click the first criteria pop-up menu and choose an option, such as From or Date Received, as shown in Figure 2-18.**

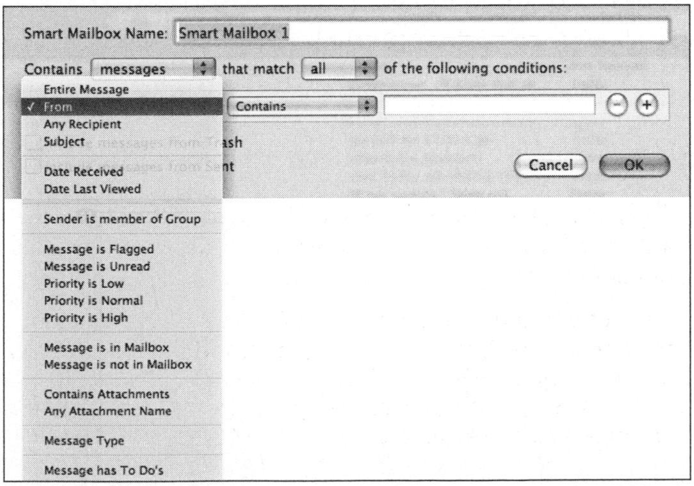

Figure 2-18: The first pop-up menu lets you choose criteria for the type of messages to include.

5. **Click in the second criteria pop-up menu and choose how to apply your first criteria, such as Contains or Ends with, as shown in Figure 2-19.**
6. **Click in the Criteria text box and type a word or phrase that you want to use for your criteria.**
7. **(Optional) Click the Add Rule icon (plus sign) and repeat Steps 5 through 7.**
8. **Click OK.**

   Your smart mailbox appears in the left pane of the Mail window. If any messages match your defined criteria, you can click your smart mailbox icon to see a list of messages.

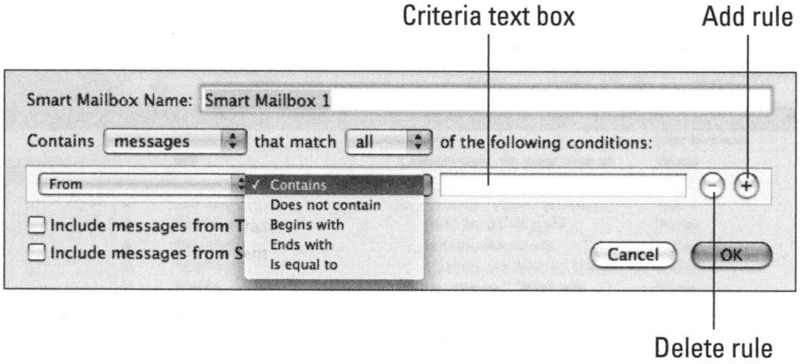

Figure 2-19: The second pop-up menu lets you choose how to apply your chosen criteria.

The messages stored in a smart mailbox are just links to the actual messages stored in your Inbox folder.

Deleting a smart mailbox

Deleting a smart mailbox doesn't physically delete any messages because a smart mailbox only contains links to existing messages. To delete a smart mailbox, follow these steps:

1. **In Mail, click the smart mailbox folder you want to delete.**
2. **Choose Mailbox➪Delete.**

   A dialog appears, asking whether you really want to delete your smart mailbox.
3. **Click Delete (or Cancel).**

Automatically organizing e-mail with rules

Smart mailboxes provide links to e-mail messages that physically remain in your Inbox folder. However, you might want to physically move a message out of the Inbox folder and into another folder automatically, which you can do by defining rules.

The basic idea behind rules is to pick criteria for selecting messages, such as all messages from specific e-mail addresses or subject lines that contain certain phrases, and route them automatically into a folder.

To create a rule, follow these steps:

1. **Choose Mail⇨Preferences.**

   A Preferences window appears.

2. **Click the Rules icon.**

   The Rules window appears, as shown in Figure 2-20.

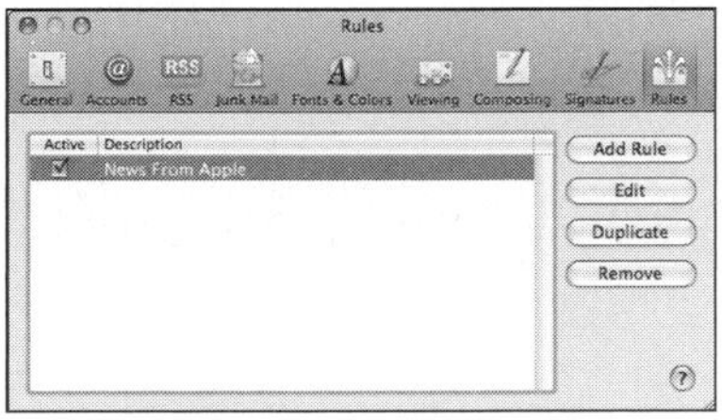

Figure 2-20: The Rules window shows you all the rules you've created and lets you create new ones.

3. **Click Add Rule.**

   The Rules window displays pop-up menus for defining a rule as shown in Figure 2-21.

   REMEMBER

   If you click an existing rule and click Edit, you can modify an exist-ing rule.

4. **Click in the Description text box and type a description of what your rule does.**

5. **Click in one or more pop-up menus to define how your rule works, such as what to look for or which folder to move the message into, as shown in Figure 2-22.**

6. **(Optional) Click the Plus Sign button to define another sorting criteria for your rule and repeat Steps 5 and 6 as often as necessary.**

7. **Click OK when you're done defining your rule.**

   A dialog appears, asking if you want to apply your new rule to your messages.

8. **Click Apply.**
9. **Click the Close button of the Rules window.**

   Mail now displays your messages sorted into folders according to your defined rules.

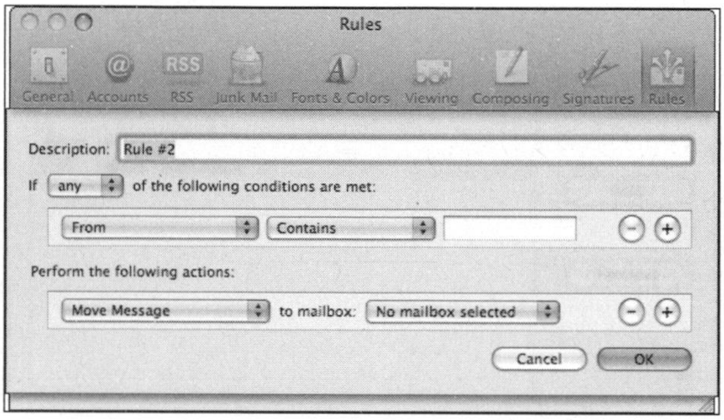

Figure 2-21: Clicking different pop-up menus lets you define a rule for routing your messages.

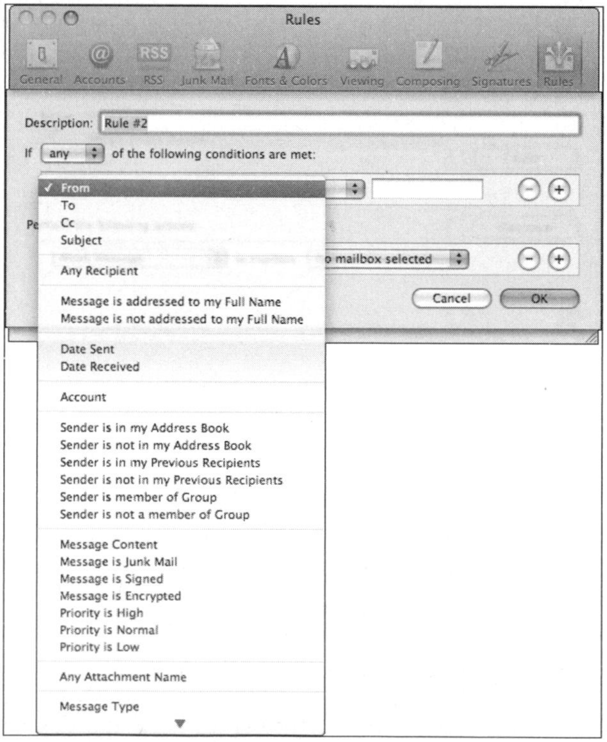

Figure 2-22: Pop-up menus provide different options for selecting messages to sort by your rule.

Chapter 3: Chatting in Real Time

In This Chapter

- **Setting up an account**
- **Creating a user profile**
- **Creating a chat**
- **Finding people to chat with**
- **Chatting via text, video, and audio**

The idea behind instant messaging is that you can communicate with someone over the Internet using text, audio, or even video — and it's all free.

Now you can swap messages with your friends, chat in real time across the planet, and even see each other through video images as you speak. Instant messaging offers another way for you to communicate with anyone in the world using an Internet connection and your Mac.

Although instant messaging can make communicating easy, instant messaging programs in the past have often been clumsy or difficult to use. That's why Apple designed iChat. Not only is iChat much easier to use than other instant messaging programs, but it also integrates video, audio, and text features so that anybody can start instant messaging their friends as easily as chatting over the telephone.

Setting Up an iChat Account

To chat with people on the Internet, you need to set up an account with one of the following services:

- **.Mac:** (Costs $99 a year.) If you create a free trial .Mac account and later cancel, you can still use your .Mac account name for free with iChat.
- **AOL Instant Messenger (AIM):** Available at `www.aim.com`. (Free.)

You can also set up accounts with Jabber (`www.jabber.org`) and Google Talk (`www.google.com/talk`), but these accounts aren't as easy to use with iChat as .Mac and AIM. If you want to make iChat as easy as possible to use, get a .Mac or AIM account.

After you have an account, you can set up an iChat account by following these steps:

1. **Load iChat by double-clicking on the iChat icon in the Applications folder.**

   A Welcome window appears.

2. **Click Continue.**

   A second iChat window appears, giving you a chance to enter your .Mac or AIM account, as shown in Figure 3-1.

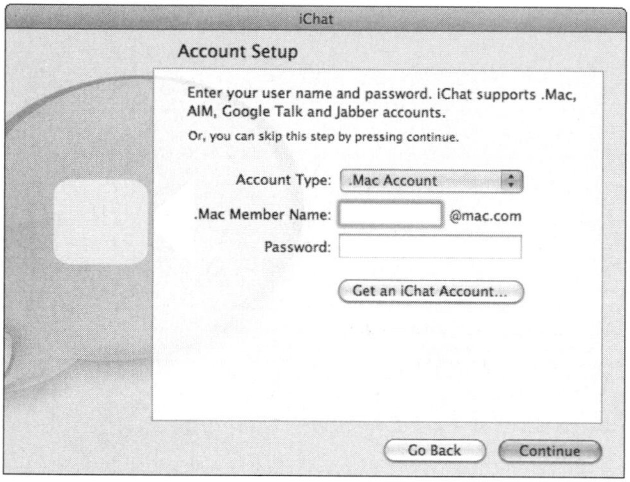

Figure 3-1: The iChat window asks for your account name.

3. **Choose your flavor of chat from the Account Type pop-up menu.**

   Your choices here include .Mac Account, AIM Account, Jabber Account, and Google Talk Account.

4. **Enter your account username in the Member Name text box.**

5. **Enter your password in the Password text box.**

   If you click the Get an iChat Account button, you see Apple's Web site, encouraging you to sign up for the .Mac service.

6. **Click Continue.**

   A third iChat window informs you that you've successfully set up an iChat account.

7. **Click Done.**

Setting up an account is only half the battle. Next you have to contact your friends to get their iChat account names and to give your iChat account name to others. (Think of account numbers as telephone numbers; you can't call a friend without first knowing her phone number, and similarly, you can't chat with someone if you don't know her account name.)

Storing names in a buddy list

A *buddy list* lets you store the account names of your friends. To contact a friend on your buddy list, just click his or her name in your buddy list.

To add a name to your buddy list, follow these steps:

1. **Load iChat.**

   If you don't see a Buddy List window, choose Window➪AIM Buddy List. (The AIM Buddy List lists all your buddy's addresses from various instant messaging services.)

2. **Choose Buddies➪Add Buddy.**

   A dialog appears, as shown in Figure 3-2.

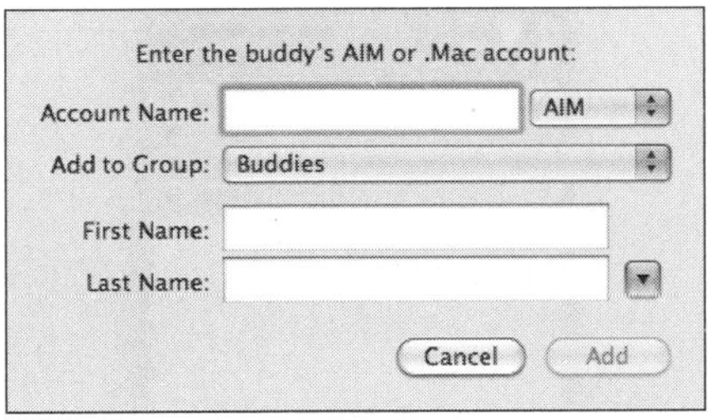

Figure 3-2: To add a new name, you must type an account name along with a real name.

3. **Click in the Account Name text box and type your friend's account name.**

4. **Click in the Account Name pop-up menu and chose AIM or .Mac, depending on which service your buddy uses.**

   iChat is designed to work seamlessly with AIM or .Mac accounts. Google and Jabber accounts are supported, but they require additional configuration, which is beyond the scope of this book.

5. **Click in the Add to Group pop-up menu and choose a group to store your friend's name under, such as Buddies or Family.**

   You can always change this group later.

6. **Enter the first and last name of your buddy in the appropriate text boxes.**

   Typing your buddy's first and last name is for your convenience only. If you don't know someone's first or last name, just leave it blank.

7. **Click Add.**

   Your new buddy appears in your buddy list.

Organizing a buddy list

When you add a name to your buddy list, you have to store it within an existing group, such as Buddies, Family, or Co-Workers. If you want, you can always move or copy a name to a different group or even create completely new groups, such as a group of people involved in a specific project — a community planning committee, say, or a Little League team, Boy Scout troop, or family reunion.

Moving a name to another group

The first time you add a name to your buddy list, you might have accidentally put a name in your Family group when you really want the name in the Friend group. To move a name to another group, follow these steps:

1. **Load iChat.**

   If you don't see a Buddy List window, choose Window⇨AIM Buddy List.

2. **Click a group name in the Buddy List window to reveal all the names stored within that group.**

   If you hold down the Option key and then perform Step 3, you can copy a name to another group.

3. **Click and drag a name onto a new group name.**

4. **Release the mouse button.**

   The name now appears in the new group.

Creating a new group

iChat includes a Buddies, Family, and Co-Workers group, but you might want to create new groups of your own. To create a group, follow these steps:

1. **In iChat, click the Add button (plus sign) that appears in the bottom-left corner of the Buddy List window.**

   A pop-up menu appears, as shown in Figure 3-3.

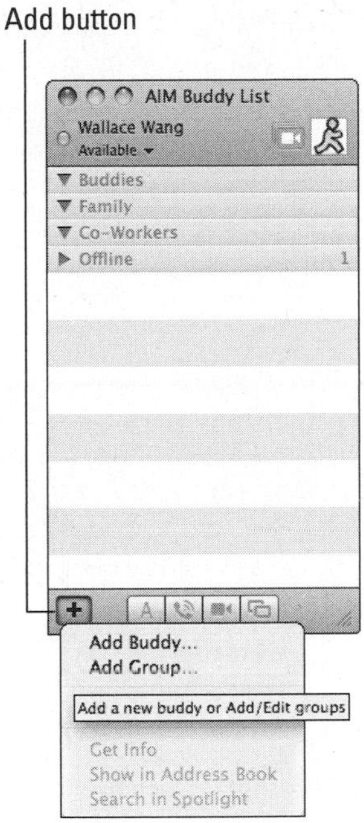

Figure 3-3: The Add button lets you create a new group.

2. **Choose Add Group.**

   A dialog appears, asking for a group name.

3. **Enter a descriptive name for your group in the Enter Group Name text box and then click Add.**

   Your new group appears in the buddy list. At this point, you have to copy or move names into your newly created group.

You can always rename a group by right-clicking the group and choosing Rename Group from the menu that appears.

Sorting names in a buddy list

To customize the appearance of your buddy list even more, you can sort names. Sorting lets you arrange names alphabetically by first or last name.

To sort names, follow these steps:

1. **In iChat, choose View⇨Sort Buddies.**

   A submenu appears, as shown in Figure 3-4.

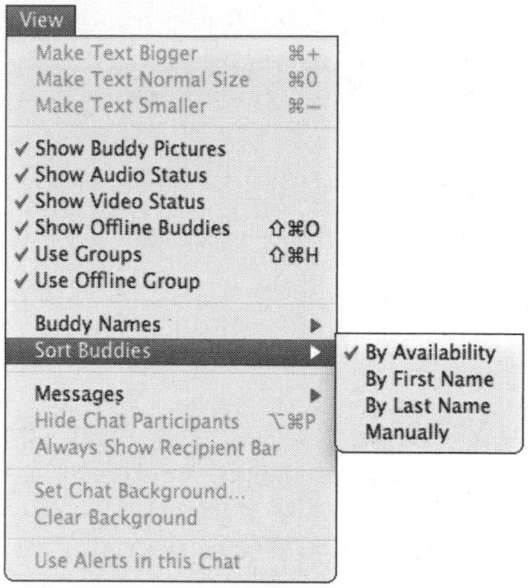

Figure 3-4: The Sort Buddies submenu lets you rearrange your buddy list.

2. **Choose one of the following:**
   - *By Availability:* Groups all buddies available for chatting.
   - *By First Name:* Sorts names alphabetically by first name.
   - *By Last Name:* Sorts names alphabetically by last name.
   - *Manually:* Lets you drag names to sort them any way you want.

Shortening names in a buddy list

iChat can display names as full names (John Doe), as shortened names (John), or by nicknames or handles (GeniusMan). For friends, it might be fun to display names based on handles, but for business use, it's probably best to stick with full or shortened names.

To define how to display names, follow these steps:

1. **In iChat, choose View⇨Buddy Names.**

   A submenu appears.

2. **Choose one of the following:**
   - Show Full Names
   - Show Short Names
   - Show Handles

Deleting names and groups in a buddy list

Eventually, you might want to prune names from your buddy list to make it easier to find the names of people you really do want to contact.

To delete a name from your buddy list, follow these steps:

1. **In iChat, click a group in your buddy list that contains the name you want to delete.**
2. **Click the name you want to delete.**
3. **Choose Buddies⇨Remove Buddy.**

   A dialog appears, asking whether you really want to delete the name.
4. **Click Delete (or Cancel).**

Rather than delete a name, you can also delete a group and all names stored in that group. To delete a group from your buddy list, follow these steps:

1. **In iChat, right-click a group that you want to delete.**

   A pop-up menu appears.
2. **Choose Delete Group from the pop-up menu.**

   A dialog appears, asking whether you really want to delete this group and all names in the group.
3. **Click Delete (or Cancel).**

Chatting with Someone

After you've stored a list of friends in your buddy list and given your account name to others to store in their buddy lists, you're ready to start chatting. Of course, before you can chat, you have to find someone who wants to chat.

You can chat with someone in three ways:

✦ **Text:** You type messages back and forth to each other.

✦ **Audio:** You can talk and hear the other person, much like a telephone.

✦ **Video:** You can talk, hear, and see the other person.

Anyone on your buddy list can use text chatting, because it requires only an Internet connection and a keyboard. (If someone doesn't have a keyboard or an Internet connection, he won't be on your buddy list in the first place.)

To participate in audio chatting, each person needs a microphone and speakers. Most Macs come with a built-in microphone, but you might want an external microphone, such as one on a headset, to capture your voice clearly.

REMEMBER

If your Internet connection is too slow, iChat might refuse to let you start an audio or video chat.

Initiating a text chat

To chat with anyone, you must first make sure that person is even available. The easiest way to find someone to chat with is to look at your buddy list. All names displayed in the Offline group are people unavailable at the moment. All names displayed in other groups, such as Family or Co-Workers, are currently connected to the Internet and might be available for chatting.

Just because someone is connected to the Internet doesn't necessary mean that he's in front of his computer and/or wants to chat at the moment.

Starting a text chat

To initiate a chat with someone listed in your buddy list, follow these steps:

1. **In iChat, browse through your buddy list until you see the name of someone who's available.**
2. **Click a name and click the Text Chat button at the bottom of the Buddy List window.**

   A chat window appears, as shown in Figure 3-5.

   The last button on the right is the Start Screen Sharing button, which lets you view the screen of another person's computer over the Internet.

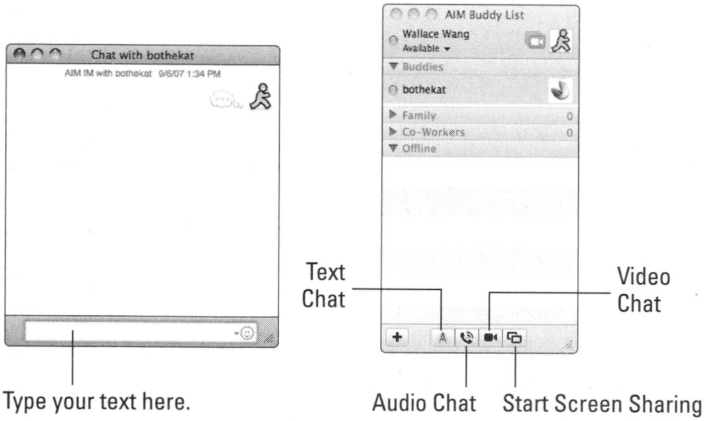

Figure 3-5: The chat window lets you type a message in the bottom text box.

3. **Click in the text box at the bottom of the chat window, type a message, and press Return on your keyboard.**

   The recipient of your message will see your message, as shown in Figure 3-6. The recipient can choose to Block, Decline, or Accept your invitation. If the recipient accepts your invitation to chat, you can start typing messages back and forth to each other. You type in the lower text box, and your dialog with the other person appears in the main text box.

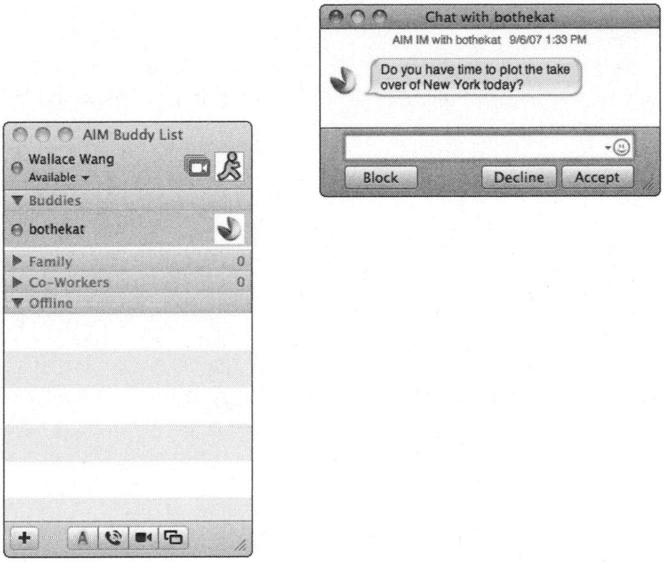

Figure 3-6: Your invitation to chat appears on the recipient's screen.

Starting a direct message text chat

When you create an ordinary text chat, your messages actually go through a central server, which means there's the slight possibility that someone could intercept your messages. In case you want more security when chatting with someone, you can initiate a *direct message* text chat instead. (Direct message chatting bypasses the central server and connects your computer directly to the other person's computer.)

Direct messaging can sometimes be blocked by a firewall. If this happens, you'll have to configure your firewall to allow direct messaging.

To initiate a direct message text chat, follow these steps:

1. **In iChat, browse through your buddy list until you see the name of someone who's available.**
2. **Right-click a name you want to contact and, when a pop-up menu appears, choose Send Direct Message.**

   A chat window appears (refer to Figure 3-5).
3. **Click in the text box at the bottom of the chat window, type a message, and press Return on your keyboard.**

   Your message shows on your buddy's computer screen. If the recipient accepts your invitation to chat, you can start typing messages (securely) back and forth to each other.

Starting a group text chat

Instead of chatting with a single person, you might want multiple people to chat at the same time. To create a group text chat, follow these steps:

1. **In iChat, browse through your buddy list until you see the name of someone who's available.**
2. **Hold down the ⌘ key and click each name that you want to invite to your group chat.**
3. **Click the Text Chat button at the bottom of the buddy list window.**

   A chat window appears (refer to Figure 3-5).
4. **Click in the text box at the bottom of the chat window, type a message that you want everyone to see, and press Return on your keyboard.**

Initiating an audio chat

To initiate an audio chat, everyone needs a microphone and speakers. You can initiate an audio chat by following these steps:

1. **In iChat, click a name on your buddy list and choose Buddies⇨Invite to Audio Chat (or click the Audio Chat button at the bottom of the Buddy List window).**

   A message appears, informing you that your audio chat invitation has been sent and that iChat is now waiting for a reply, as shown in Figure 3-7.

   REMEMBER: If this feature is dimmed, that means you don't have a microphone on your Mac or you don't have a fast enough Internet connection to support audio chatting.

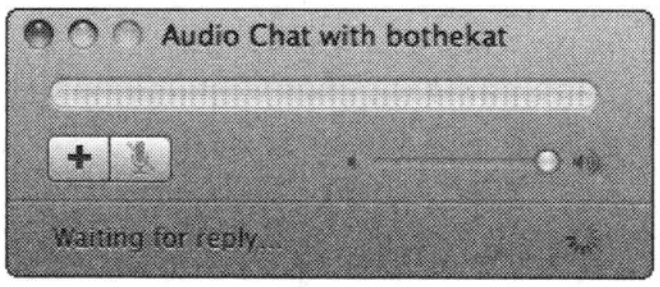

Figure 3-7: A message informs you when you're sending an audio chat invitation.

2. **Upon receiving your chat invitation on-screen, your potential chat partner can then click the message and choose Accept or Decline.**

   If your friend accepts, you can both start talking as if you were speaking over a telephone.

You might need to drag the volume slider to adjust the sound level. If you click the plus sign button, you can invite another person into your chat.

Initiating a video chat

To initiate a video chat, everyone's Mac needs a microphone, speakers, and a video camera. Most Macs have a built-in iSight video camera but for Macs without a built-in iSight camera, you have three options:

- ✦ Plug a digital video camcorder into your Mac's FireWire port.
- ✦ Buy the iMage USB webcam from Ecamm Network (`www.ecamm.com`).
- ✦ Plug an ordinary USB webcam into your Mac. You might need special software to make USB webcams work with your Mac, such as iChatUSBCam program from Ecamm Network (`www.ecamm.com`).

Although Apple no longer sells them any more, you can still find and use old iSight cameras that plug into a FireWire port.

After everyone (up to four people) has a video camera connected to their Macs along with a fast Internet connection (384 Kbps), you'll be able to participate in a video chat.

It's possible that your Mac has a camera and a fast Internet connection, but someone you want to contact does not. In that case, you might be stuck using an audio or text chat instead.

You can initiate a video chat by following these steps:

1. **In iChat, click a name on your buddy list and choose Buddies⇨Invite to Video Chat (or click the Video Chat button at the bottom of the Buddy List window).**

   Your invitation is sent, and a video chat window appears, showing you what the other person will see of you, as shown in Figure 3-8.

   If this feature is dimmed, that means you don't have the necessary equipment needed, such as not having a fast Internet connection or not having a camera hooked up to your Mac.

2. **(Optional) Choose Video⇨Show Video Effects.**

   A window appears, showing all the different visual effects you can choose, as shown in Figure 3-9.

3. **(Optional) Click a visual effect.**

   The video chat window now shows your chosen visual effect.

Figure 3-8: A preview window appears so you can see how you will look to others.

Figure 3-9: You can pick a unique visual effect to spice up your appearance.

4. **Your potential video chat partner either accepts or declines your invitation.**

   If someone accepts your video chat invitation, your picture appears in the bottom-right corner of the screen, and the other person's image fills up the rest of the screen, as shown in Figure 3-10.

Accepting (Or Blocking) a Chat Invitation

As soon as you connect to the Internet, your Mac broadcasts your availability on buddy lists with all of your friends. The moment someone wants to chat with you, you'll see a window.

Chat invitations can be fun to receive, but sometimes they can get annoying. As an alternative to taking time to click Decline on every chat invitation you receive, iChat offers several ways to decline invitations automatically.

Figure 3-10: A video chat lets you see and speak to another person.

Changing your status

You might love receiving and accepting chat invitations, but maybe you want to work without the distraction of chat invitations popping up on your screen. To let others know that you're busy at the moment, you can temporarily block chat invitations. This can be handy if you plan to start chatting soon, but not right away. (Otherwise, you might as well just exit iChat altogether.)

To keep people from contacting you, you can change the status that others see about you in their buddy list. Instead of seeing that you're Available, you can change your status to Away, Out to Lunch, On the Phone, or In a Meeting. To change your status, follow these steps:

1. **Choose iChat⇨My Status.**

   A submenu of different status choices appears, as shown in Figure 3-11.

   TIP: You can also click the pop-up menu (it displays the word Available) that appears directly underneath your name in the Buddy List window.

2. **Click a status line, such as Away or Out to lunch.**

   Your chosen status now appears in the buddy lists of other people.

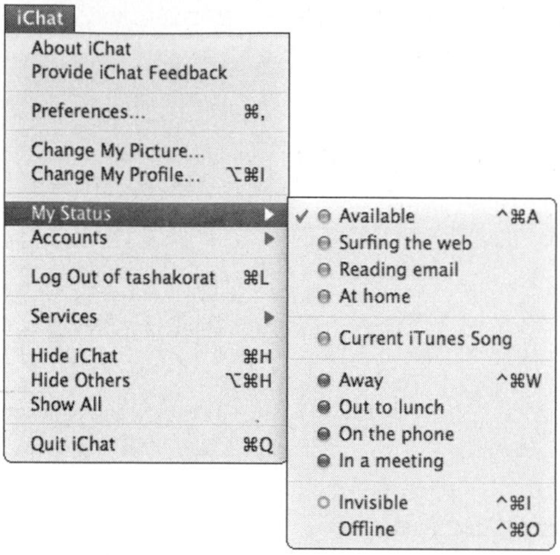

Figure 3-11: The My Status submenu provides a variety of status lines you can display.

You can also choose a different type of status line that allows chat invitations, such as Surfing the Web or Reading Email. If you choose Current iTunes Song, people can see the name of the song you're listening to at the moment. If you choose Custom, you can type your own message that others will see.

Becoming invisible

Another way to avoid receiving chat invitations is to make yourself invisible over the iChat network. This lets you see who on your buddy list might be available to chat, but when other people see your name on their buddy lists, your name appears as if you are offline and disconnected from the iChat.

To make yourself invisible over iChat, choose iChat➪My Status➪Invisible. By being invisible, you can monitor iChat messages without others knowing that you're there.

To make yourself visible again, choose iChat➪My Status and choose one of the status lines that accepts invitations, such as Available or At Home.

If you want others to think you're offline and unavailable, you can choose iChat➪My Status➪Offline.

Accepting (or blocking) chat invitations with privacy levels

Rather than block invitations from everyone, you might want to accept chat invitations from some people but block them from others. For example, someone might be annoying so you always want to block that person, but someone you like might need to reach you, so you always want that person to get through at any time.

When you receive an invitation, you could click the Block button every time, but you can automate the process to selectively decide who can reach you.

In iChat, you can define different privacy levels:

- **Allow Anyone:** Anyone can send you a chat invitation, even complete strangers.
- **Allow People in My Buddy List:** Allows only people you've stored in your buddy list to contact you.
- **Allow Specific People:** Allows you to define the names of allowed people to contact you.
- **Block Everyone:** Stops all chat invitations from friends, family, co-workers, and everyone else in the world.
- **Block Specific People:** Allows you to define the names of people you always want to keep from contacting you.

To set your privacy level, follow these steps:

1. **Choose iChat⇨Preferences.**

   A Preferences window appears.
2. **Click the Accounts icon.**

   The Accounts pane appears. You can store multiple instant messaging accounts, but you'll probably just have a single account to choose from.
3. **Click to select account listed in the Accounts pane whose privacy level you want to change**
4. **Click the Security tab.**

   The Security options appear, as shown in Figure 3-12.
5. **Click the radio button under the Privacy Level category that corresponds to your current desired privacy level.**

   For privacy, you might want to choose the Allow People in My Buddy List option.

   Note: If you select the Allow Specific People or Block Specific People radio buttons, you need to click the Edit List button to type the exact account names of the people you want to allow or block.
6. **Click the Close button of the Accounts window.**

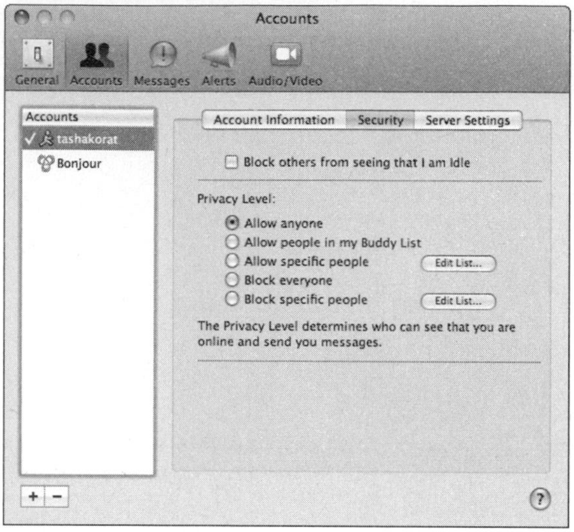

Figure 3-12: The Security pane lets you choose a privacy level.

Chapter 4: Security for Your Mac

In This Chapter

- Locking your Mac
- Setting up accounts and parental controls
- Dealing with junk e-mail

With the worldwide connectivity of the Internet, everyone is vulnerable to everything, including malicious software (known as *malware*) and malicious people with above average computer skills (known as *hackers*). Although threats over the Internet attract the most attention, your Mac is also vulnerable from more mundane threats, such as thieves who might want to steal your computer.

No matter how much you know about computers, you can always become a victim if you're not careful. So this chapter takes a look at the different ways to protect your Mac from both physical and cyber threats.

Locking Down Your Mac

Most people lock their car and house doors when they're away, so your Mac should be no exception. To physically protect your Mac, you can get a security cable that wraps around an immovable object (like that heavy rolltop desk you have in the den) and then attaches to your Mac. You can attach it by using glue, by threading it through a handle or hole in your Macintosh case, or by connecting it to a security slot built-in to your Mac. (The security slot is a tiny slot that a security cable plugs into. You might have to peek around the back or side of your Mac to find this security slot.)

Some companies that sell security cables are

- **Kensington** (`http://us.kensington.com`)
- **Targus** (`www.targus.com`)
- **Tryten** (`www.tryten.com`)

REMEMBER

Security cables can be cut. The main purpose of a security cable is to deter a thief who isn't carrying around a pair of bolt cutters.

After you've physically protected your Mac, you have two other ways to lock down your Mac and keep other people out. To stop intruders from sneaking into your computer if you step away from your desk, you need to use a password. To stop intruders from sneaking into your computer over the Internet, you need a program called a firewall.

All security features, like locks and passwords, can always be defeated by someone with enough time, determination, skill, and patience. Security can only discourage and delay an intruder, but nothing can ever guarantee to stop one.

Using passwords

Before you can ever use your Mac, you must configure it by creating an account name and password. If you're the only person using your Mac, you'll probably have just one account. If you disable automatic login, your password can keep others from using your Mac without your knowledge.

As a general rule, your password should be difficult for someone to guess but easy for you to remember. Unfortunately, that often means people use simple passwords. To make your password difficult to guess but easy to remember, you should create a password that uses a combination of letters and numbers, such as "checkm84u" (which sounds out the phrase "checkmate for you").

Two popular ways to create passwords include taking the first letter of a phrase that you'll never forget or using a name of a dead pet. By picking a memorable phrase, such as "I love my MacBook Pro" and turning it into a nonsensical combination of letters (ILMMP), you'll be able to remember your password easily, but others won't be able to guess it easily. Another alternative is the dead pet theory of passwords where you use the name of an animal you once owned. Presumably, nobody would ever know the name of a dog or cat you had when you were ten years old, so the name of a dead pet will be easy for you to remember but hard for someone to guess.

Changing your password

For additional security, you should change your password periodically. To change your password, follow these steps:

1. **Choose ⇨System Preferences.**

   The System Preferences window appears.

2. **Click the Accounts icon under the System category.**

   The Accounts window appears.

3. **Click the account name you want to modify under the My Account category in the left pane.**

   If you haven't created any additional accounts, you see only your own account listed.

4. **Click the Password tab.**

   The Password pane appears, as shown in Figure 4-1.

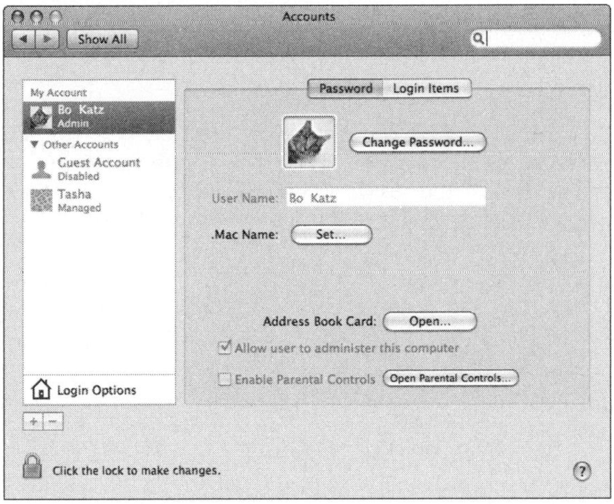

Figure 4-1: The Password pane lets you change your password.

5. **Click the Change Password button.**

   A dialog appears, displaying text boxes for typing your old password and then typing a new password twice to verify that you have typed your new password correctly, as shown in Figure 4-2.

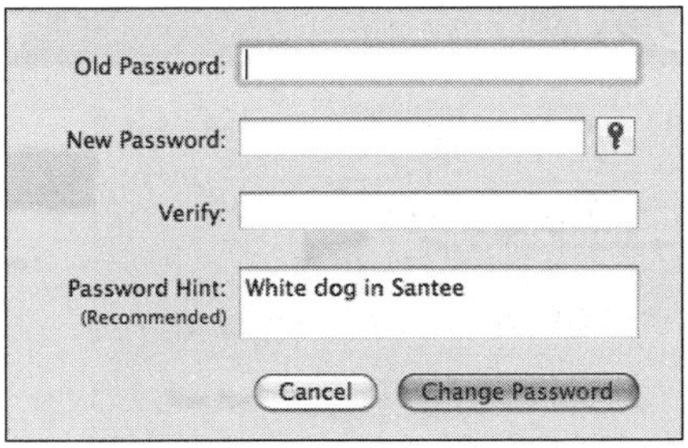

Figure 4-2: The Password dialog lets you change your password.

6. **Enter your current password in the Old Password text box.**
7. **Enter your new password in the New Password text box.**
8. **Enter your new password one more time in the Verify text box.**
9. **Enter a descriptive phrase into the Password Hint text box.**

   Adding a hint can help you remember your password, but it can also give an intruder a hint on what your password might be.
10. **Click Change Password.**

    The password dialog disappears.
11. **Click the Close button of the Accounts window.**

Applying your password

Normally, you need your password only to install new software on your Mac or when you log in to your account. That means, though, that after you log in to your account, anyone can use your Mac if you walk away and don't log out.

If you leave your Mac without logging out, your Mac will either go to sleep or display a screensaver. At this time, anyone could tap the keyboard and have full access to your Mac. To avoid this problem, you should password-protect your Mac when waking up from sleep or after displaying a screensaver.

For further protection, you can also password-protect your Mac from any changes. To keep someone from modifying the way your Mac works, you can even password-protect the System Preferences window. By applying password protection to different parts of your Mac, you can increase the chances that you'll be the only one who can control your computer.

If you're the only person who has physical access to your Mac, you won't have to worry about password protection, but if your Mac is in an area where others can access it easily, password protection can be one extra step in keeping your Mac private.

To password-protect different parts of your Mac, follow these steps:

1. **Choose ⇨System Preferences.**

   The System Preferences window appears.
2. **Click the Security icon under the Personal category.**

   The Security window appears.
3. **Click the System tab.**

   The System pane appears, as shown in Figure 4-3.

4. **(Optional) Select (or deselect) the Require Password to Wake This Computer from Sleep or Screen Saver check box.**

5. **(Optional) Select (or deselect) the Disable Automatic Login check box.**

   If this check mark is deselected, your Mac won't ask for a password before logging into your account.

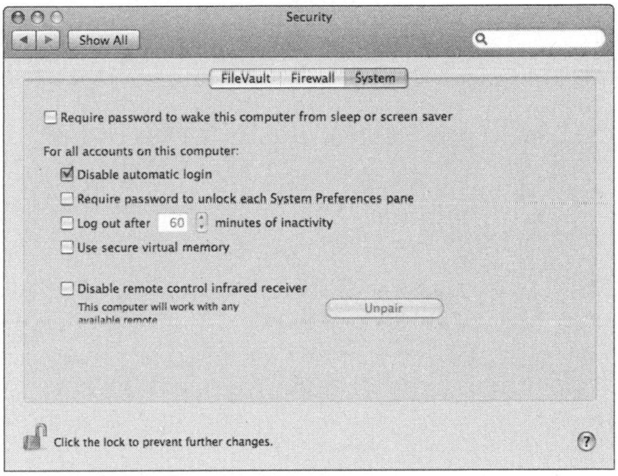

Figure 4-3: The System pane lets you choose different ways to password protect your computer.

6. **(Optional) Select (or deselect) the Require Password to Unlock Each System Preferences Pane check box.**

   If this check box is selected, nobody can modify the way your Mac works without the proper password.

7. **(Optional) Select (or deselect) the Log Out after ___ Minutes of Inactivity check box.**

   If selected, this option shuts down your account after a fixed period of time so anyone trying to access your computer will need your password to access your account.

   TECHNICAL STUFF

   Two additional check boxes appear, labeled Use Secure Virtual Memory and Disable Remote Control Infrared Receiver. The Secure Virtual Memory option means that your Mac will encrypt the temporary data that almost every program stores on your hard drive while the program is running. If you don't use secure virtual memory, other people might be able to read this temporary data that can remain on your hard drive even after you turn off your computer. Disabling the remote control infrared receiver simply keeps someone from controlling your Mac using an infrared remote control. (This option won't appear if your Mac doesn't have an infrared receiver, such as a Mac Pro.)

8. **Click the Close button of the Security window.**

Configuring a firewall

When you connect your Mac to the Internet, you essentially open a door to your Mac that allows anyone in the world to access your computer, copy or modify your files, or erase all your data. To keep out unwanted intruders, every computer needs a special program called a *firewall.*

A firewall simply blocks access to your computer while still allowing you access to the Internet so you can look at Web sites or send and receive e-mail. Every Mac comes with a built-in firewall that can protect you whenever your Mac connects to the Internet.

Many people use a special device, called a *router,* to connect to the Internet. A router lets multiple computers use a single Internet connection, such as a high-speed Internet connection. Many routers also include built-in firewalls, but it's still a good idea to use a firewall on your Mac for additional protection.

Although the default setting for this built-in firewall should be adequate for most people, you might want to configure your firewall to block additional Internet features for added security. For example, most people will likely need to access e-mail and Web pages, but if you never transfer files using FTP (File Transfer Protocol), you can safely block this service.

Don't configure your firewall unless you're sure you know what you're doing. Otherwise, you might weaken the firewall or lock programs from accessing the Internet and not know how to repair those problems.

To configure the built-in firewall, follow these steps:

1. **Choose ➪System Preferences.**

   The System Preferences window appears.

2. **Click on the Security icon under the Personal category.**

   The Security window appears.

3. **Click the Firewall tab.**

   The Firewall pane appears, as shown in Figure 4-4.

4. **Click the Advanced button.**

   The dialog that appears offers two check boxes.

5. **Select (or deselect) the following check boxes:**

   - *Enable Firewall Logging:* Maintains a record (log) of what the firewall has blocked. This can be useful to check whether the firewall is working.
   - *Enable Stealth Mode:* Makes the firewall refuse to respond to any outside attempts to contact it and gather information based on its responses.

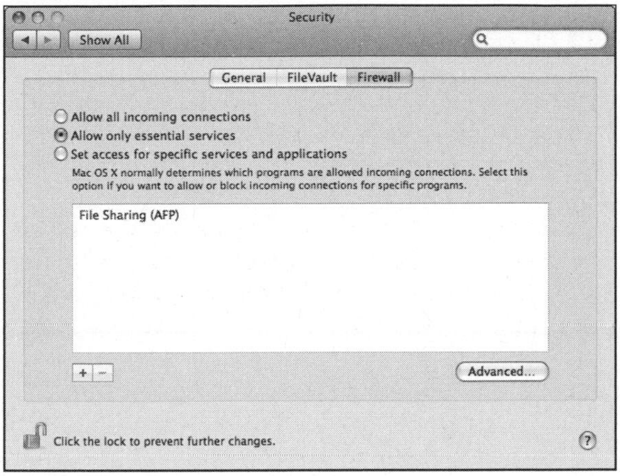

Figure 4-4: The Firewall pane displays your options for configuring the firewall.

6. **Click OK.**
7. **Select one of the following radio buttons:**
   - *Allow All Incoming Connections:* Allows other computers to send data to your Mac. (If you choose this, skip to Step 12.)
   - *Allow Only Essential Services:* Blocks other computers from trying to send your Mac data, although you can still connect out to the Internet and browse Web sites. (If you choose this, skip to Step 12.)
   - *Set access for Specific Services and Applications:* Allows you to choose which connections to allow and block.
8. **Click the plus sign button in the bottom-right corner.**

   A dialog appears, listing the contents of the Applications folder.
9. **Click a program that you want to allow access to the Internet.**
10. **Click Add.**

    Your chosen program appears under the Applications category.
11. **(Optional) To remove a program from the Applications list, click the program and click the minus sign button in the bottom-right corner.**
12. **Click the Close button of the Security window.**

Buying a firewall

Although the built-in Mac firewall works well, it only blocks incoming connections but allows all outgoing connections. Allowing all outgoing connections means a malicious program could communicate over the Internet without your knowledge. To prevent this problem, you need a firewall that can block both incoming and outgoing connections.

REMEMBER

You should use only one software firewall at a time, although it's possible to use one software firewall and a hardware firewall built into your router. If you use two or more software firewall programs, they may interfere with each other and crash your computer or keep each other from working.

If you want a more robust firewall than the one that comes with the Mac, consider one of the following:

- **NetBarrier** (`www.intego.com`)
- **Norton Personal Firewall** (`www.symantec.com`)

Dealing with spyware and RATs

On computers running Microsoft Windows, there are two big threats that exploit firewalls that don't block outgoing connections. The first of these threats, known as *spyware,* consists of programs that sneak on to your computer and then secretly connect to the Internet to retrieve ads that appear all over your screen.

A second type of program that requires an outgoing Internet connection is known as a RAT (Remote Access Trojan). Malicious hackers often trick people into downloading and installing a RAT on their computer. When it's installed, a RAT can connect to the Internet and allow the malicious hacker to completely control the computer remotely over the Internet, including deleting or copying files, conducting attacks through this other person's computer or sending junk e-mail (spam) through this other computer.

Although spyware and RATs are mostly restricted to Windows computers, there's a good chance that spyware and RATs will soon start infecting Mac computers as more people use the Mac. To guard against spyware and RATs, your Mac displays a dialog alerting you when you're running a program for the first time. This feature can alert you if spyware or a RAT tries to infect a Mac, but for further protection, consider a firewall that can block outgoing Internet connections.

One problem with a firewall is that, in the normal scheme of things, you never really know how well it's working. To help you measure the effectiveness of your current firewall, visit one of the following sites that will probe and test your computer, looking for the exact same vulnerabilities that hackers will look for.

- **Audit My PC** (`www.auditmypc.com`)
- **HackerWatch** (`www.hackerwatch.org/probe`)
- **Shields Up!** (`www.grc.com`)
- **Symantec Security Check** (`http://security.symantec.com`)

Because each firewall-testing Web site might test for different features, testing your Mac with two or more of the above sites can help ensure that your Mac is as secure as possible. Figure 4-5 shows the Shields Up! results from a test of the built-in Mac firewall.

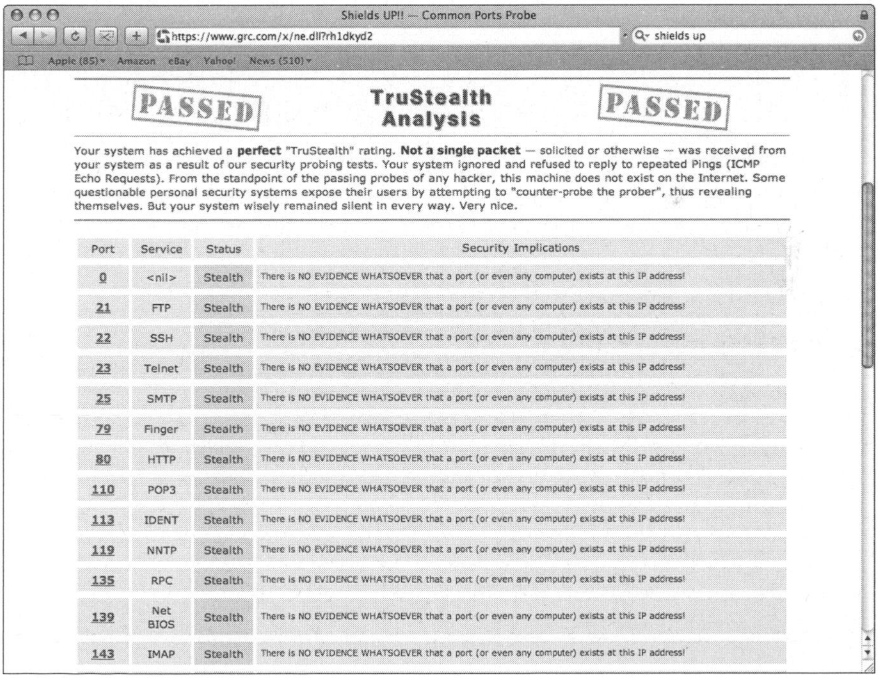

Figure 4-5: Despite its inability to block outgoing connections, the built-in Mac firewall does a decent job keeping intruders out of your Mac.

Creating Multiple Accounts

Every Mac needs at least one account that allows you to use your computer. However, if multiple people need to use your Mac, you probably don't want to share the same account, which can be like trying to share the same pair of pants.

One problem with sharing the same account is that one person might change the screensaver or delete a program that someone else might want. To avoid people interfering with each other, you can divide your Mac into multiple accounts.

Multiple accounts basically give your Mac a split personality. Each account lets each person customize the same Mac while shielding other users from these changes. So one account can display pink daffodils on the screen, and a second account can display pictures of sports cars in the background.

REMEMBER

To access any account, you need to log in to that account. To exit an account, you need to log out.

Not only do separate accounts keep multiple users from accessing each other's files, but creating multiple accounts also gives you the ability to restrict what other accounts can do. That means you can block Internet access from an account, limit Internet access to specific times, or limit Internet access to specific Web sites. (It's great for parents, of course, which is why such limits are referred to as *parental controls.*)

To protect your files and settings, you should create a separate account for each person who uses your Mac. You can create four types of accounts:

- **Administrator:** Gives the user access to create, modify, and delete accounts. You should have only one Administrator account.
- **Standard:** Gives the user access to the computer, but doesn't let the user create, modify, or delete accounts.
- **Managed with Parental Controls:** Gives the user restricted access to the computer based on the parental controls defined by an Administrator account.
- **Guest:** Gives the user access, but any files the user saves on the hard drive will get deleted when the guest account logs off.

The only difference between the Administrator and Standard accounts is that the Standard account cannot create, modify, or delete other accounts. Otherwise, a Standard account gives users unrestricted freedom to do anything they want on the Mac.

The Managed with Parental Controls and Guest accounts give users restricted access to what they can do on your Mac. The main difference is that a Guest account cannot save any files.

Creating a Managed with Parental Controls account

If you want users to be able to save files but you still want to restrict their access to the Internet or certain programs, you want to create a Managed with Parental Controls account. To do so, follow these steps:

1. **Choose ⌘⇨System Preferences.**

   The System Preferences window appears.

2. **Click the Accounts icon under the System category.**

   The Accounts window appears, as shown in Figure 4-6.

3. **Click the Lock icon in the bottom-left corner to give you the ability to add or create accounts.**

   A dialog appears, asking for your password.

4. **Enter your password in the Password text box and then click OK.**

   The dialog disappears, and you're back in the Accounts window.

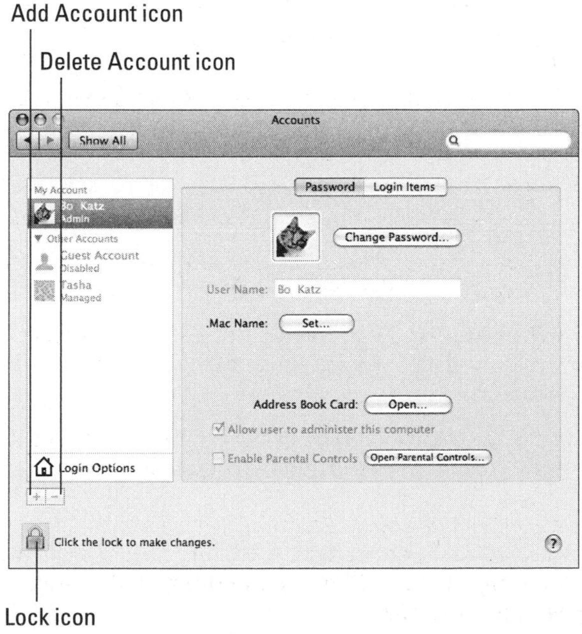

Figure 4-6: The Accounts window shows you all current accounts created on your Mac.

5. Click the Add Account (plus sign) icon.

An Accounts dialog appears, as shown in Figure 4-7.

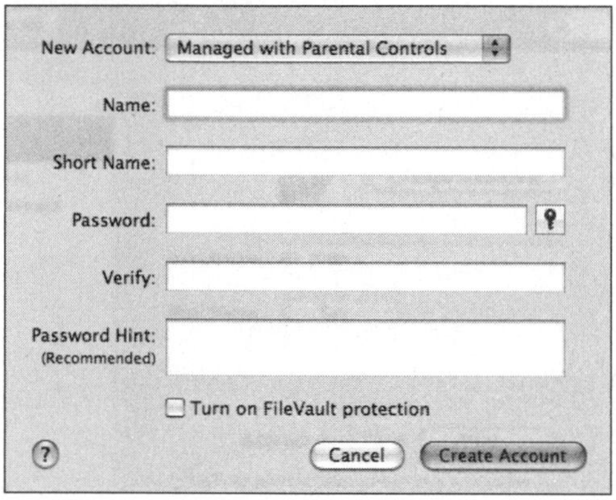

Figure 4-7: The Accounts dialog lets you define your new account.

6. Choose Managed with Parental Controls from the New Account pop-up menu.

Instead of choosing Managed with Parental Controls, you can instead choose Administrator or Standard to create an Administrator or Standard account.

7. Enter the name of the person who'll be using the account into the Name text box.

8. (Optional) Click in the Short Name text box and edit the short name that your Mac automatically creates.

9. Enter a password for this account in the Password text box.

10. Re-enter the password you chose in step 9 into the Verify text box.

11. (Optional) Enter a descriptive phrase to help remind you of your password into the Password Hint text box.

12. (Optional) Select the Turn on FileVault Protection check box, which allows the account user to encrypt files.

If you allow users to encrypt files, they will be able to hide the contents of their files from anyone — even folks with an Administrator account.

Keep in mind that turning on FileVault can make your Mac slower because it needs to take time to encrypt and decrypt your data.

If you turn on FileVault and forget your password, you'll never be able to access the FileVault encrypted data.

13. **Click the Create Account button.**

    The Accounts pane displays the name of your new account.

14. **Click the Close button of the Accounts window.**

Creating a Guest account

A Guest account is handy if you want multiple users to access your Mac. (If you have a Mac in a public lobby for anyone to use, for example, you want them to use only a Guest account.)

You can create only one Guest account because multiple users will access the same Guest account. To create a Guest account, follow these steps:

1. **Choose ➪System Preferences.**

   The System Preferences window appears.

2. **Click the Accounts icon under the System category.**

   The Accounts window appears (refer to Figure 4-7).

3. **Click the Lock icon.**

   A dialog appears, asking for your password.

4. **Enter your password in the Password text box and then click OK.**

   The dialog disappears and you're back in the Accounts pane.

5. **Click the Guest Account icon that appears in the left pane of the Accounts window, as shown in Figure 4-8.**

6. **Select the Allow Guests to Log into This Computer check box, which allows anyone to use your Mac's Guest account without needing a password.**

7. **(Optional) Select or deselect the Allow Guests to Connect to Shared Folders check box.**

   If this option is selected, a Guest account will be able to read files created by other accounts and stored in a special shared folder.

8. **Click the Close button of the Accounts window.**

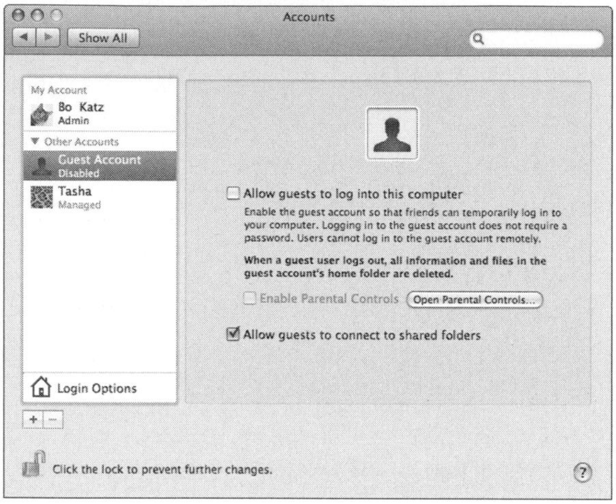

Figure 4-8: When you create a Guest account, you can define additional options for how the Guest account works.

Defining parental controls for a Guest account or a Managed with Parental Controls account

You can apply parental controls only to a Guest account or a Managed with Parental Controls account. After you've created a Guest account or at least one Managed with Parental Controls account, you can apply parental controls to those accounts.

There are several types of restrictions you can place on an account:

- **System:** Limits which programs the account can run.
- **Content:** Limits which Web sites the account can access.
- **Mail & iChat:** Limits the account to sending and receiving e-mail and instant messages from a fixed list of approved people.
- **Time Limits:** Prevents accessing the account at certain times or days.
- **Simple Finder:** Displays a simple Finder that's easier to use.
- **Administer Printers:** Prevents modifications to the printers connected to the Macintosh.
- **Burn CDs and DVDs:** Prevents saving data to a CD or DVD.
- **Password:** Prevents changing the account password.
- **Dock:** Prevents modifying the Dock.

To apply parental controls to an account, follow these steps:

1. **Choose ⇨System Preferences.**

   The System Preferences window appears.

2. **Click the Parental Controls icon under the System category.**

   A Parental Controls window appears, as shown in Figure 4-9.

3. **Click the Lock icon.**

   A dialog appears, asking for your password.

4. **Enter your password in the Password text box and then click OK.**

   The dialog disappears, and you're back in the Accounts pane

5. **Click the account icon, in the left list, to which you want to apply parental controls.**

6. **Click the System tab (if it isn't already selected).**

7. **(Optional) Select the Use Simple Finder check box.**

   This creates a Finder that's easier for novice Mac users to work with.

8. **Select the Only Allow Selected Applications check box.**

9. **Select or deselect the check boxes for the programs shown in the Check Applications to Allow list.**

10. **Click the gray triangle that appears to the left of the Other category.**

    A list of programs appears.

Figure 4-9: The Parental Controls window lets you define the restrictions for an account.

11. Select or deselect the check boxes of any additional programs you want to allow/disable.

12. (Optional) Select or clear the following four check boxes:

- Can Administer Printers
- Can Burn CDs and DVDs
- Can Change Password
- Can Modify the Dock

13. Click the Content tab.

The Content pane appears, as shown in Figure 4-10.

14. (Optional) Select the Hide Profanity in Dictionary check box.

15. Select one of the following radio buttons under the Website Restrictions category:

- Allow Unrestricted Access to Websites
- Try to Limit Access to Adult Websites Automatically
- Allow Access to Only these Websites

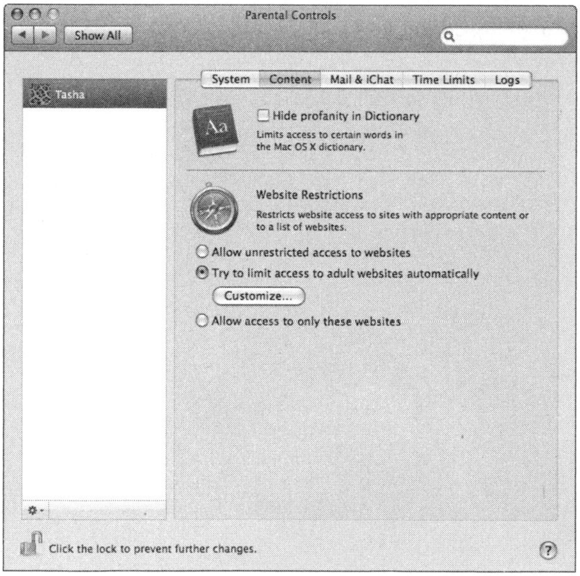

Figure 4-10: The Content pane lets you restrict what users can see.

REMEMBER

If you select the Allow Access to Only These Websites radio button, you can specify which Web sites the account can access. If you select the Try to Limit Access to Adult Websites Automatically, you can click a Customize button so you can type in the Web sites the account can always access and a second list of Web sites that the account can never access. In both cases, you must type in the address to allow or block, such as `www.nytimes.com` or `www.playboy.com`. Although the Try to Limit Access to Adult Websites Automatically option can automatically block most adult Web sites, you might need to enter additional addresses in case a particular Web site slips past the adult Web site filter.

16. **Click the Mail & iChat tab.**

    The Mail & iChat pane appears, as shown in Figure 4-11.

17. **Select the Limit Mail and/or Limit iChat check boxes.**

    These features let you define which e-mail or iChat addresses the account can access.

18. **Click the Add Name icon (plus sign).**

    A dialog appears, as shown in Figure 4-12.

19. **Enter the first and last name of a person that you approve of into the First Name and Last Name text boxes.**

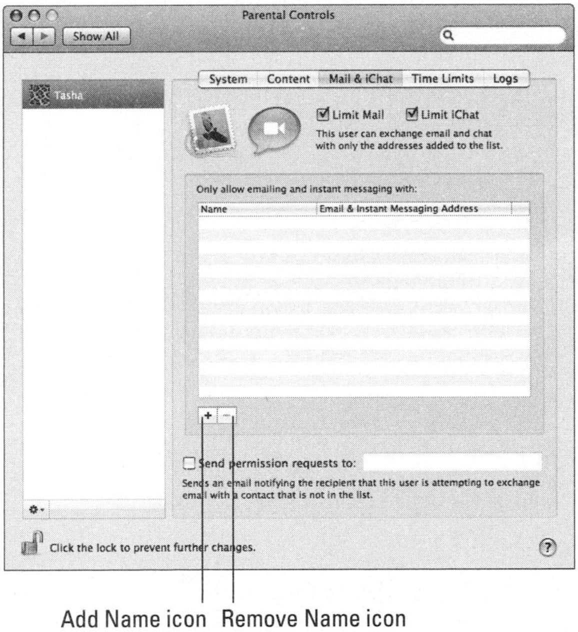

Figure 4-11: The Mail & iChat pane lets you restrict who the user can contact.

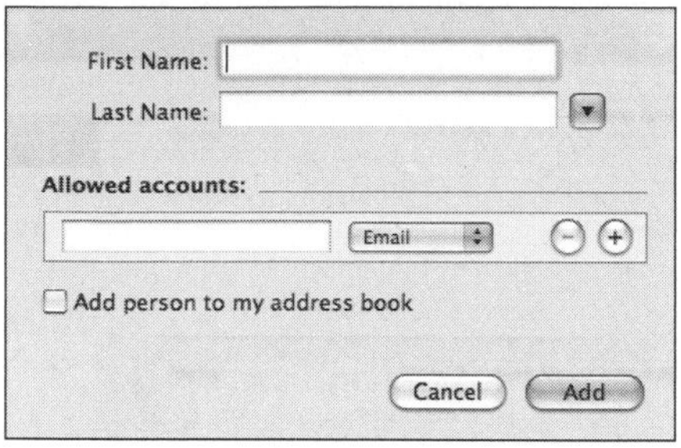

Figure 4-12: The dialog lets you specify the name and e-mail or instant messaging addresses of approved people.

20. **Enter an e-mail or instant messaging address of that approved person into the Allowed Accounts text box.**

    The iChat program can connect with anyone who uses the AIM (AOL Instant Messenger) or Jabber networks.

21. **Choose the account type (Email, AIM, or Jabber, for example) from the Allowed Accounts pop-up menu.**

22. **(Optional) Click the Add Name (plus sign) icon and repeat Steps 18 and 19 to specify another e-mail, AIM, or Jabber address of the person specified in Step 17.**

23. **Click Add.**

24. **Click the Time Limits tab.**

    The Time Limits pane appears, as shown in Figure 4-13.

25. **(Optional) Select the Limit Computer Use To check box under the Weekday Time Limits category and drag the slider to specify how much time the account can use your Mac.**

26. **(Optional) Select the Limit Computer Use To check box under the Weekend Time Limits category and drag the slider to specify how much time the account can use your Mac.**

27. **(Optional) Select the School Nights and Weekend check boxes under the Bedtime category and select the start and end times when you don't want the account to use your Mac, such as between 9:00 p.m. to 9:00 a.m.**

    The School Nights option defines Sunday – Thursday. The Weekend option defines Friday and Saturday.

28. **Click the Close button of the Parental Controls window.**

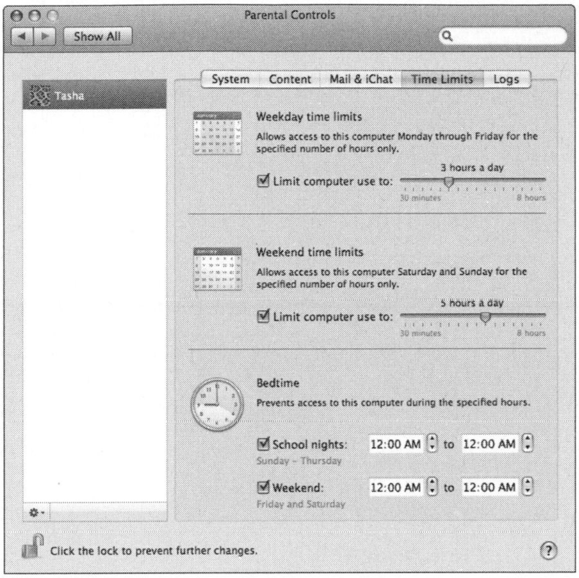

Figure 4-13: The Time Limits pane lets you specify certain days or times that the account can be used.

Monitoring a parental control managed account

After you create a Managed with Parental Controls account, you can view what that user has been doing on your Mac by reviewing the log files. The log files keep track of all the Web sites the user visited, tried to visit (and got blocked by the Mac parental controls), the programs run, and the people contacted through iChat. To view these log files, follow these steps:

1. **Choose ⌘⇨System Preferences.**

   The System Preferences window appears.

2. **Click the Parental Controls icon under the System category.**

   The Parental Controls window appears (refer to Figure 4-10).

3. **Click the account icon, in the left pane, whose log files you want to examine.**

4. **Click the Logs tab.**

   The Logs pane appears, as shown in Figure 4-14.

5. **Choose a time period for viewing from the Show Activity For pop-up menu, such as everything the user did in the past week or month.**

6. **Choose Website or Date from the Group By pop-up menu.**

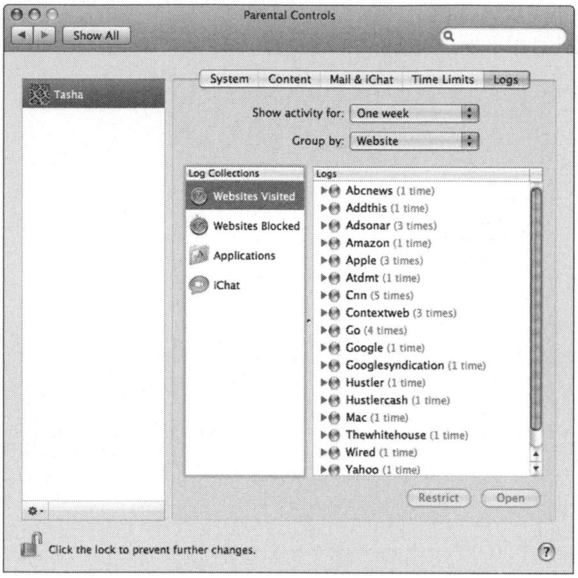

Figure 4-14: The Logs pane lets you investigate what the user does on your Mac.

7. **Click the Websites Visited, Websites Blocked, Applications, or iChat icon in the Log Collections list box to review the logs.**

   Figure 4-14 displays the Websites Visited list. In Figure 4-15, you can see the Websites Blocked list, which shows you all the sites the user tried (and failed) to access. If you peek at the Applications or iChat lists, you can see which programs ran on the account or which iChat addresses the account contacted.

   REMEMBER: Not all blocked Web sites are necessarily pornographic. Sometimes a blocked Web site could just be a blocked pop-up ad from an acceptable site.

8. **Click the Close button of the Parental Controls window.**

Dealing with Junk E-Mail

As soon as you get an e-mail address, you're going to start receiving junk e-mail, and there's nothing you can do to stop it. However, the Mail program gives you tools for handling the inevitable flow of junk e-mail so you can keep your e-mail account from getting overwhelmed. Two ways to manage your junk e-mail are by bouncing junk e-mail back to the sender or by filtering junk e-mail into a special junk folder.

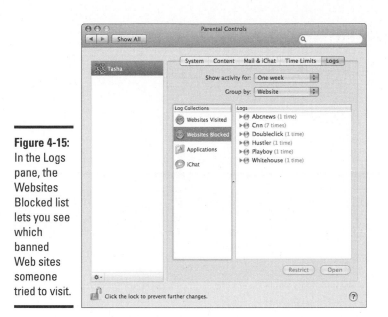

Figure 4-15: In the Logs pane, the Websites Blocked list lets you see which banned Web sites someone tried to visit.

WARNING!

Most junk e-mail messages are advertisements trying to sell you various products, but some junk e-mail are actually scams to trick you into visiting bogus Web sites that ask for your credit card number. Other times, junk e-mail might offer a malicious program, such as a computer virus, and try to trick you into downloading and installing it on your computer. By filtering out such malicious junk e-mail, you can keep your Mac safe.

Bouncing junk e-mail

When spammers send out e-mail, the majority of their messages get sent to nonexistent e-mail addresses. When this occurs, the mail server computer *bounces* the message back to the sender so the sender knows that the e-mail address is invalid. Then the spammer knows not to waste time sending that nonexistent e-mail address any more messages.

Fortunately, you can take advantage of this feature by bouncing unwanted messages back to the sender. When you bounce a message back to the sender, this bounced message makes it appear as if your e-mail address is invalid (although it's really not). Then the spammer will likely remove your e-mail address from the mailing list, so you'll receive less junk e-mail.

That's the theory, anyway. In real life, this can work if the spammer sent e-mail from a valid e-mail address. If the spammer sent junk e-mail through another computer (such as one hijacked without the owner's knowledge), bouncing e-mail will never reach the spammer, and your e-mail address will still continue receiving junk e-mail.

Although not perfect, bouncing junk e-mail back to its sender may help reduce your junk e-mail. To bounce a message, follow these steps:

1. **In Mail, click the Inbox icon in the left pane.**

   A list of messages appears in the right pane.

2. **Click a message that you consider to be junk.**
3. **Choose Message⇨Bounce.**

   A dialog appears, letting you know that bouncing messages works only if your unwanted message came from a valid e-mail address.

4. **Click the Bounce button (or click Cancel).**

Bouncing e-mail is more effective when you know the sender's e-mail address is valid, such as bouncing messages sent to you from an ex-boyfriend/girlfriend or spouse.

Filtering junk e-mail

More effective than bouncing is *filtering.* Filtering means that Mail examines the content of messages and tries to determine whether the message is junk. To improve accuracy, the Mail program will let you train it by letting you manually identify junk e-mail that its existing rules didn't catch.

After a few weeks of watching you identify junk e-mail, the Mail program's filters will eventually recognize common junk e-mail so it can route it automatically to a special junk folder. By doing this, the Mail program can keep your inbox free from most junk e-mail so you can focus on reading the messages that are actually important.

To train the Mail program to recognize junk e-mail, follow these steps:

1. **In Mail, click the Inbox icon in the left pane.**

   A list of messages appears in the right pane.

2. **Click a message that you consider to be junk.**
3. **Click the Junk icon.**

   This tells the Mail program's filters what you consider to be junk e-mail.

4. **Click the Delete icon at the top of the Mail window.**

   This deletes your chosen message and "trains" Mail to recognize similar messages as junk.

TIP

Although Mail's built-in junk e-mail filters can strip away most junk e-mail, consider getting a special junk e-mail filter as well. These e-mail filters strip out most junk e-mail better than Mail can do, but any junk e-mail that slips past these separate filters might later be caught by Mail's filters, which essentially doubles your defenses against junk e-mail. Some popular e-mail filters are SpamSieve (`http://c-command.com`), Spamfire (`www.matterform.com`), and Personal Antispam (`www.intego.com`). Spam filters cost money and take time to configure, but if your e-mail account is getting overrun by junk e-mail, a separate junk e-mail filter might be your only solution short of getting a new e-mail account altogether.

Chapter 5: Setting Up Your Own Web Site

In This Chapter

- Types of Web sites
- Creating a Web page
- Uploading your Web pages
- Using .Mac

After browsing the Internet and visiting different Web sites, you might get the urge to create your own Web site. If you own a business, a Web site can promote and advertise your services and products. If you can sell something that's easy to ship (such as books or posters as opposed to lead pipes or truck axles), you can set up on online store and sell products over the Internet.

Even if you don't have your own business, you can still take advantage of a Web site to promote yourself and your accomplishments. This can come in handy particularly if you're looking to promote yourself at your company or when looking for a new job. Think of a Web site as an online résumé that can highlight your services or skills.

All work and no play makes Jack a dull boy. Instead of creating a Web site for business, you might be more interested in creating a Web site for fun, such as promoting a hobby like raising tropical fish or collecting stamps. In this case, a Web site can be like having your own newsletter that anyone in the world can access and read.

Whatever your reasons for developing a Web site, your Mac can help you create your own online presence on the Internet with the least amount of hassle and the most amount of fun and enjoyment.

If you want a superfast and convenient way to set up your own Web site, skip ahead to the "Using .Mac" section at the end of this chapter.

Types of Web Sites

The basic idea behind any Web site is that you create your Web pages on your computer and then copy them to another computer that's connected to the Internet. This other computer, called a *server,* hosts your Web pages for the whole world to see.

The main reason you need to upload your Web pages on another computer (the server) is because the server is connected to a high-speed Internet connection (called a T1 or T3 line) that allows thousands of people to view your Web site simultaneously. A typical home Internet connection (dial-up or Ethernet) isn't fast enough to support hordes of people visiting your Web site at the same time.

At the simplest level, a Web page can consist of nothing but text. However, to make a Web page more visually appealing and inviting to read, most Web pages spice up their appearance with decorative graphics or colors. If static graphic images look too boring, you can add animated menus or short movies to make your Web site more interactive. To help design visually interesting Web pages, you often need to use a special Web page editing program.

After you've created your Web pages, you need to find a server computer that can display your Web pages (also known as *hosting* a Web site) on the Internet. Some popular Web site hosting options are:

- ✦ Free, advertiser supported Web site hosts
- ✦ Free, ISP (Internet Service Provider) Web site hosts
- ✦ Fee-based Web site hosts

Free, advertiser-sponsored Web site hosts

Because so many people like the idea of putting up their own Web sites, many companies offer free Web hosting to attract as many people as possible. In return for giving you storage space to host your Web pages, these free Web site hosts support themselves by displaying banner or pop-up ads all over your Web pages. If someone wants to visit your Web site, he or she might have to wade through some advertisements first.

Even worse, you can't control what type of advertisements might appear on your Web site. If you create a Web site praising American-built cars and encouraging people to support American autoworkers, the Web site host might stick advertisements for Honda or Toyota cars all over your Web pages, and there's nothing you can do about it.

Another drawback of free, advertiser-sponsored Web site hosts is that the specific Web site address will never be anything as simple as `www.apple.com`. Instead, free Web site hosts force you to use a convoluted Web site address that includes the Web site host name. So if you host your Web pages on a free site called Tripod or Geocities, your Web site's address might look like this:

```
http://mysite.tripod.com
```

or

```
http://www.geocities.com/mysite/2397
```

Such lengthy, nonintuitive Web site addresses work just like the simpler, more descriptive `www.mysite.com`, but they're harder to remember and even harder to type in correctly. Telling someone to visit `www.mysite.com` is easy to say and even easier to print on a business card. Telling someone to visit `http://www.geocities.com/mysite/2397` is much clumsier to say and even more confusing to write.

Despite the drawbacks of free, advertiser-supported Web site hosts, you can't overlook the fact that they're free to use, try, and play with for as long as you want. This gives you a chance to create and post your Web pages just to gain experience in designing aesthetically appealing Web pages and uploading them from your computer to a Web server computer.

TIP

By using a free Web hosting service, you can see whether you have the stamina to maintain and update a Web site regularly. Many people rush to create a Web site, furiously update and modify it for the first week, and then gradually lose interest and eventually abandon their site altogether. You can use a free Web hosting service as a trial before you shell out money for a fee-based Web hosting service.

Bottom Line: Because of their advertisements and non-intuitive Web site address, free Web site hosting services are fine for personal use or to gain experience designing and uploading Web pages, but you probably don't want to use them for business purposes. Some popular, free, advertiser-supported Web site hosting services are

- **Geocities** (`http://geocities.yahoo.com`)
- **Tripod** (`www.tripod.lycos.com`)
- **Google Pages** (`http://pages.google.com`)
- **FortuneCity** (`www.fortunecity.com`)

Although all of these Web hosting services are free, they offer different amounts of storage space and ads that appear on your Web pages, so compare these services until you find one that you like best.

Social networking Web sites

The latest trend among free Web site hosting is social networking sites such as MySpace (`www.myspace.com`) and Facebook (`www.facebook.com`). Social networking sites are free because they insert advertisements on everybody's Web pages. Unlike ordinary advertiser-supported Web site hosts, social networking sites won't always let you create your own Web pages on your computer. Instead, you have to create Web pages by customizing the social networking site's templates. The main advantage of social networking sites is that they make it easy for you to link your Web pages to other people's Web pages on the same social networking site.

The idea behind social networking sites is to give people a chance to express themselves and link up with friends and like-minded people. For instance, you could start a vegetarian cooking Web site and link your page with other vegetarians' Web pages.

If you want to meet hikers or sailing enthusiasts, social networking sites can help you find new friends. If you want to sell beef jerky online, social networking sites may not be the place to start a Web site any more than a cocktail party would be the place to hold a garage sale.

Social networking sites can be useful for business networking though. Connect with other computer programmers, graphic design artists, or construction workers and share tips for finding and looking for a job. A social networking site can be fun and useful for communicating with others in your line of work.

Free ISP Web site hosts

When you pay for Internet service from an Internet Service Provider (ISP), your ISP might throw in free Web site hosting as a bonus. Unlike advertiser-supported Web site hosting services that bury ads in your Web pages without your consent, free ISP Web site hosting services don't. The ISP figures that you're already paying it for its service, so Web site hosting is just a marketing tactic to entice people to sign up with that ISP anyway.

As a result, ISP Web site hosting gives you the benefits of experimenting with a free Web site without the drawbacks of unwanted advertisements. However, your Web site address will still likely contain something convoluted and non-intuitive like `http://www.ispname.net/myname/4872`.

Of course, not every ISP offers free Web site hosting as part of your ordinary Internet subscription. Some ISPs charge extra, and others don't offer free Web site hosting at all. If your ISP doesn't offer free Web site hosting, you'll be forced to use a different Web site host or switch to a different ISP altogether.

Because of the lack of obtrusive ads, Web sites hosted on free ISP Web sites are more often used for personal use rather than setting up on-line stores. (Some ISPs might even restrict businesses from setting up business sites due to the bandwidth problems that might occur if too many people visit the Web site every day.)

Fee-based Web site hosting service

Free Web site hosting services can be great for having fun or teaching yourself how to design Web pages and upload them on a Web server. However, free Web site hosting services often limit the amount of storage space you can use. The less storage space available, the fewer Web pages, graphic images, and additional files (such as sound or video) you can put on your Web site. If you want a Web site with no ads, more storage space, and a descriptive Web site address (called a *domain name*), you'll need to pay a fee-based Web site hosting service.

TIP

Many advertiser-supported Web hosts offer both a free and a subscription-based plan. The free plan lets you create Web sites that include ads and a bizarre Web site address. The fee-based plan removes ads and gives you a descriptive Web site address such as `www.apple.com`. By offering a free and fee-based plan, these Web site hosting services give you the option of experimenting with designing a Web site and then transferring it to its own domain name (like `www.symantec.com`) without having to change Web site hosting companies.

The first step to using a fee-based Web site hosting service is to compare prices and features offered. Prices vary from as low as $1.99 a month to as high as $19.99 a month or more, depending on what additional options you might want. (What one Web site hosting service might consider an option, another might throw in free as part of its basic package.) Some basic features to look for are

- **Storage space:** The more storage space, the more Web pages, pictures, videos, animation, and so on you can post on your Web site. Typical storage space ranges from 10GB up to 250GB or more. If your Web site needs to store files, especially audio or video files, you need more space than someone who just wants to display a picture of a pet lizard.
- **File transfer limitation:** Defines how much data others can copy off your Web site. A high transfer rate might be necessary if you offer files for people to download, such as pictures or music files.
- **Number of e-mail accounts:** The more e-mail accounts offered, the better. If you're running a company Web site, you don't want to bump into a limitation of only 12 e-mail accounts if your company suddenly starts growing.

- **E-mail storage space:** The more storage space, the more messages all of your e-mail accounts can hold. If you don't have enough e-mail storage space, it's possible to fill your e-mail accounts to the brim with too many messages, which you'll then have to erase to make room for new messages.
- **Domain name registration:** If you want your Web site to have a descriptive address like `www.logitech.com`, you need to register that particular name so no one else can use it. For convenience, many Web hosting services will register a domain name at a low price. Otherwise, you'll have to register the domain name yourself.
- **Number of domain names:** Some Web site hosting services let you use only one domain name. If you want to create two or more Web sites, you'll have to pay more. Other Web site hosting services let you host multiple domain names for one low price.

After you pick a Web hosting service, you need to pick a domain name for your Web site. Many domain names are already taken (such as `www.whitehouse.gov` or `www.foxnews.com`).

To check whether a domain name is already taken, do a search on a site like Whois.net (`www.whois.net`).

After you decide on a descriptive domain name, you need to register it either through your Web site hosting service or through a separate domain name registration service.

Registration means picking a name that no one else is using, paying a one-time fee, and then paying periodic fees to maintain that domain name. If you don't continue paying to maintain your domain name, you'll lose it. Registration fees typically cost $5 to $25 a year, although some Web site hosting services will pay this fee for you as long as you keep using their services.

After you pick a Web site hosting service and register a domain name, you can always transfer your domain name (and all your Web page files) to a different Web site hosting service that offers lower rates or better service.

Multiple domain names can point to the same Web site. This can be handy to ensure that people reach your Web site no matter what Web site address they use. For example, the official Trend Micro Web site domain name is `http://us.trendmicro.com`, but you can also visit Trend Micro's Web site by using the `www.antivirus.com` domain name. In case you want to redirect a domain name that you own (such as `www.microsoft.com`) to a cryptic Web site address (such as `www.freeweb.com/3940/4937`), you can use DyNS (`www.dyns.cx`).

After you've picked and registered a domain name and paid to use a specific Web hosting service, you'll be ready to create and upload your Web pages.

Creating Web Pages

Creating a Web page can be as simple or as difficult as you want to make it. If you want to slap together a simple Web page, you can do that in about five minutes. If you have a specific design for a Web page that involves custom graphics and fancy animation, that might take you a few days, a few weeks, or more.

To create a Web page, you have four options:

- Write HTML (HyperText Markup Language) code using a text editor.
- Use a general-purpose program, such as a word processor or desktop publishing program, to save a document as an HTML file.
- Use a built-in Web page creation program offered by your Web site hosting service, such as Yahoo! Site Builder or Google Page Creator. These programs simplify the process of creating and editing Web pages, but you can use them to create Web pages only for that particular site.
- Use a dedicated Web page creation program, such as iWeb.

REMEMBER

You actually have a fifth option, and that's to pay someone else to create a Web site for you. For business owners who don't want the hassle of creating and maintaining a Web site, this option is probably the best, but if you want to create a Web site honoring your cat or goldfish, it's much cheaper to create Web pages yourself.

Creating a Web page with HTML code

The most primitive, but most powerful way to create a Web page is by writing HTML code. Every Web page, no matter how simple or how complicated, consists of nothing but HTML code that defines exactly what to display. (To create fancy visual effects such as pull-down menus, Web pages might also use programs or languages such as Flash or JavaScript.)

REMEMBER

If you want to peek at the HTML code that defines your favorite Web page, visit that Web page in Safari and then choose View➪View Source to get a listing of the page's code, as shown in Figure 5-1.

Although HTML code might look confusing, it's actually fairly simple to learn. Then again, learning how to change your car's oil or how to replace a leaky toilet is also fairly simple, but most people don't want to do it.

Figure 5-1: Every Web page ultimately consists of cryptic HTML code.

To design Web pages in HTML code, start off by learning about how HTML codes work. (Pick up a copy of *HTML, XHTML & CSS For Dummies,* 6th Edition, by Ed Tittel and Jeff Noble). Next, you need to use a text editor, which is a special program often used to write programs or HTML commands. Unlike a word processor, a text editor won't wrap your words to the next line or change fonts. The most popular text editor for the Mac is BBEdit (`www.barebones.com`). If you don't want to pay for a text editor like BBEdit, get the free, less-featured version of BBEdit called TextWrangler. For another free text editor for writing HTML code, get Taco HTML Edit (`http://tacosw.com`).

Creating Web pages with other programs

Almost every program (word processor, spreadsheet, presentation, and desktop publishing) can save documents as HTML files, with the extension `.html`. To check whether your favorite program can do so, follow these steps:

1. **Choose File➪Save As.**

   A Save As dialog appears.

   REMEMBER

   With some programs, you might be able to choose File➪Export.

2. **Look for a file format option such as Web Page or HTML File, as shown in Figure 5-2.**

   If you find this option, the program can save documents as HTML files.

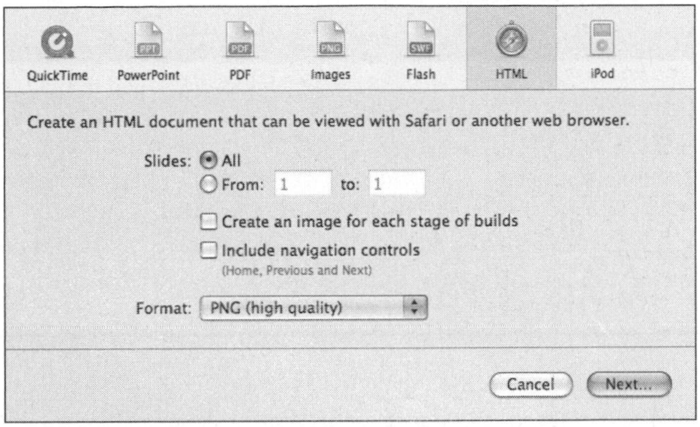

Figure 5-2: Web pages must always be saved in the HTML file format.

The advantage of using your favorite word processor or presentation program to create a Web page is that you don't have to learn anything new (other than how to save your documents as an HTML file). The disadvantage of creating Web pages from your favorite program is that you might still need to customize the Web page to include other features. For example, to add navigation buttons on your Web page, you have to edit that Web page in an HTML editor or dedicated Web page designing program instead.

Creating Web pages with dedicated Web page designers

If you're serious about designing Web pages, you should get a dedicated Web page designing program. Such programs often give you a choice of designing a Web page graphically (by plopping graphic images on a page around boxes filled with text) or by editing or writing HTML code.

Often times you can start designing a Web page visually and then switch to tweaking the HTML code to make your Web page look exactly the way you want. By giving you this dual capability for creating a Web page, dedicated Web page designing programs give you the most control over the appearance of your Web pages.

There are two types of dedicated Web page designing programs: consumer and professional versions. Web page designing programs designed for consumers are much easier to use because they offer fewer features for modifying a Web page.

For a free, consumer version Web page designing program, grab a copy of Nvu (`www.nvu.com`). If you're willing to pay for a Web page designing program, try RapidWeaver (`www.realmacsoftware.com`), Freeway (`www.softpress.com`), or Coda (`www.panic.com`).

Every Mac includes a free Web page designing program, iWeb, which can create Web pages quickly and easily. See Book IV, Chapter 4 for more information about using iWeb.

If you want to use a Web page designing program that the professionals use, be prepared to spend a few hundred dollars to get a copy of Dreamweaver (`www.adobe.com`). Besides using Dreamweaver, professional Web designers might also use Photoshop (to create or edit digital photographs) along with Illustrator and Flash (to create animation).

No matter how you create a Web page, the end result will always be an HTML file along with other files such as graphic images. So it's entirely possible to create a Web page in Dreamweaver, edit it in Nvu or RapidWeaver, and then tweak it further using BBEdit. The type of program you use to create a Web page is less important than your skill in designing and creating a Web page.

Uploading Web Pages

After you've created one or more Web pages, they're trapped on your computer. To share your Web pages over the Internet, you need to transfer the files to a Web site hosting service. (Web site folks refer to this as *uploading* your files.) The most common way to transfer Web page files from your computer to a Web site server computer is to use something called FTP (File Transfer Protocol).

To use FTP, you need a special program called an FTP client. The FTP client lets you choose one or more files to transfer off your hard drive and then copy those files to a specific location on the Web site hosting computer.

When you transfer files through FTP, you must make sure you transfer all files. Typically, a Web page consists of the Web page itself (an HTML file) and one or more graphic images that appear on that Web page (often stored as GIF or JPG files). If you forget to transfer a graphic image with your Web page, your Web page will appear without that graphic image, which can leave a noticeable gap in your Web page.

Also when transferring files through FTP, you must know the exact location to store your Web page files on the Web site server computer, which you can get from your Web site hosting service. If you store your Web page and graphic files in the wrong folder, your Web page won't appear correctly when viewed over the Internet.

Some popular free FTP client programs include Cyberduck (`http://cyberduck.ch`), RBroser (`www.rbrowser.com`), and NcFTP Client (`www.ncftp.com`). If you feel better about buying a commercial FTP client, buy a copy of Transmit (`www.panic.com`) or Fetch (`www.fetchsoftworks.com`).

Using .Mac

To create your own Web site, you need to take care of finding a Web site hosting service, designing your own Web pages, transferring your Web page files and graphic images using an FTP client, and knowing the exact location to store all your files. You might also need to worry about registering a domain name if you want a descriptive address like `www.cbsnews.com`. If all this sounds clumsy and complicated, you're right.

To make designing Web pages easy, you can use iWeb, but to make creating and posting a Web site easy, you can use the optional .Mac Web hosting service. (.Mac costs $99 a year, but Apple offers a free 60-day trial and places like Amazon.com might sell a .Mac subscription at a discount.)

The main idea behind .Mac is to eliminate the minor details necessary to create a Web site. You don't have to worry about finding a Web site hosting service (you just use .Mac), and you don't have to worry about finding an FTP client and learning how to use it. Instead, you just have to choose File⇨Publish to .Mac from within iWeb to transfer your files and store them in the right place automatically.

More about .Mac

The .Mac service is actually more than just a Web site hosting service. First, .Mac offers a traditional Web site hosting service along with the ability to just post your digital photographs and movies directly from iPhoto and iMovie. If all you want to do with a Web site is post pictures for others to see, you can skip the whole process of creating Web pages altogether and go straight to posting pictures and videos using .Mac.

Second, .Mac offers the ability to copy and store all your important files on Apple's own computers. That way if a fire torches your house or a Russian spy satellite plummets out of orbit and smashes into your apartment (crushing your Mac and your external hard drive at the same time), your files will still be safely stored on .Mac.

Third, .Mac subscribers often receive offers for free or discounted software along with tutorials for using different types of programs. If you take advantage of enough of these software offers, you might save enough money to justify the cost of your .Mac subscription.

Finally, .Mac gives you yet another e-mail account as part of its price. Unlike other types of e-mail accounts, .Mac won't automatically attach an advertisement to your e-mail messages. Although you can get a free e-mail account from many sites such as Yahoo! or Google, having yet another e-mail account is a nice option, especially if your current e-mail accounts are getting overrun with junk e-mail and you want to start fresh with a new e-mail account.

As wonderful as .Mac sounds, here's why you might want to think twice about subscribing to .Mac:

✦ **The cost is steep.** At $99 a year, .Mac isn't the least expensive Web site hosting option available. For the same amount of money, you might find a Web site hosting service that offers more storage and features than .Mac.

✦ **You might not be using iWeb and iPhoto.** Both iWeb and iPhoto are great programs, but if you use another Web page designing program (such as Dreamweaver) or another digital photo organizing and editing program (such as Adobe Photoshop Lightroom), all the slick integration of .Mac with iPhoto and iWeb will be useless.

✦ **You might not need the extra features of .Mac.** Offline storage might be nice, but you can find many free or less expensive offsite storage sites such as ElephantDrive (`www.elephantdrive.com`), XDrive (`http://xdrive.com`), or MediaMax (`www.mediamax.com`). Having another e-mail account might also be convenient, but you can create virtually an unlimited number of free e-mail accounts on dozens of different Web sites.

When you first turned on your Mac, Apple probably tried to convince you to sign up for .Mac. If you resisted this low-key sales pitch, you can still join .Mac by visiting `www.apple.com/dotmac` and signing up for your free trial or (if you're already convinced) an annual .Mac subscription plan.

The .Mac service offers the easiest way to create your own Web sites with a minimum of hassle, so if the traditional way of setting up a Web site sounds too confusing or time-consuming, sign up for .Mac and start posting your Web sites right away. You might find the convenience of .Mac is worth the cost.

Book IV

Working with iLife and iWork

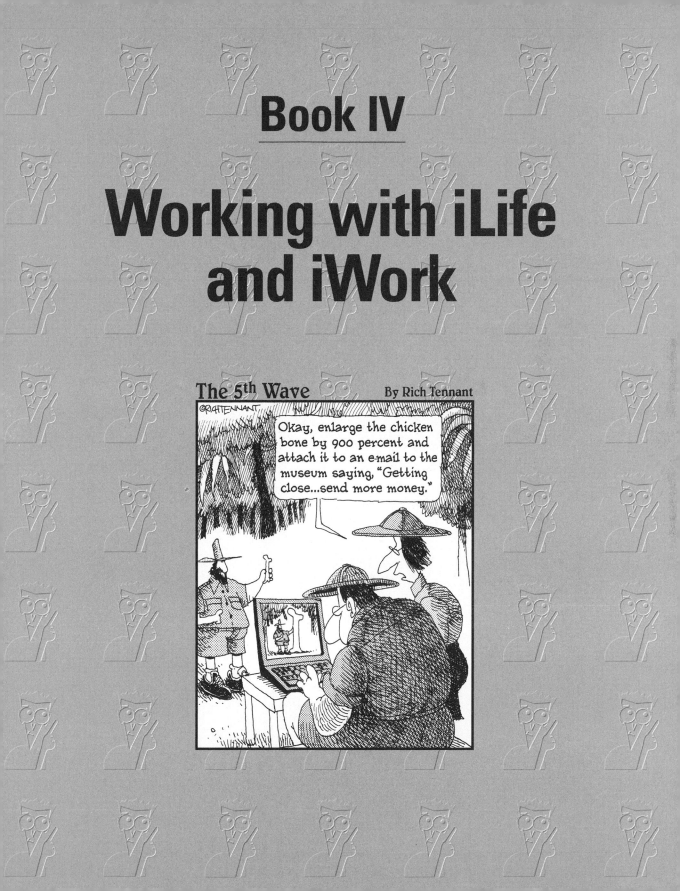

The 5th Wave
By Rich Tennant
©RICHTENNANT
Okay, enlarge the chicken bone by 900 percent and attach it to an e-mail to the museum saying, "Getting close...send more money."

Contents at a Glance

Chapter 1: Storing Memories with iPhoto 373
Chapter 2: Using iMovie 401
Chapter 3: Using iDVD 425
Chapter 4: Creating Web Sites with iWeb 443
Chapter 5: Using GarageBand 459
Chapter 6: Writing and Publishing with Pages 481
Chapter 7: Making Presentations with Keynote 509
Chapter 8: Doing Calculations with Numbers 535

Chapter 1: Storing Memories with iPhoto

In This Chapter

- **Importing pictures into iPhoto**
- **Organizing Events**
- **Organizing pictures**
- **Editing pictures**
- **Sharing pictures with others**

Think of iPhoto as a place where you can dump your digital photographs so you can find them again later. In iPhoto, all your pictures get stored in a Library. The Library provides three ways to organize your pictures:

- Events
- Albums
- Folders

Events typically contain pictures captured on the same day. Albums typically contain pictures grouped by a common theme, such as pictures of animals or cars. Folders can hold and organize multiple albums.

REMEMBER

You find out more about creating folders and albums later in this chapter, in the "Storing pictures in albums and folders" section.

After organizing your pictures, iPhoto also lets you edit your pictures to modify colors or clip out unwanted portions. When your pictures look perfect, you can print them on either your own printer or (for an added cost) through a printing service. From start to finish, iPhoto can take care of organizing your pictures so you can focus on taking even more pictures.

Importing Pictures

Before you can organize your pictures, you need to store them in iPhoto. If you have pictures stored in other folders on your hard drive, on other storage devices (such as CDs or DVDs), or trapped inside a digital camera, the first step is to copy those pictures into iPhoto.

To copy pictures into iPhoto — or, to use the accepted lingo, to *import* pictures into iPhoto — follow these steps:

1. **Insert or connect the storage device — thumb drive, digital camera, CD, whatever — that contains the pictures you want to import into iPhoto.**

   If your pictures are already stored in a folder on your hard drive, skip this step.

2. **Load iPhoto.**

   Double-click the iPhoto icon in the Applications folder, or click the iPhoto icon in the Dock. The iPhoto window appears.

3. **Choose File⇨Import to Library.**

   An Import Photos dialog appears, as shown in Figure 1-1.

Figure 1-1: The Import Photos dialog lets you choose the device and folder that contains pictures.

4. **Click the drive, in the far left column, that contains the pictures you want to import.**

5. **Choose one of the following:**

   - Click the folder, in the middle column, that contains the pictures you want to import. (This selects all pictures in that folder.)
   - Double-click the folder, in the middle column, that contains the pictures you want to import and then click on the picture, in the right column, that you want to import. (To select multiple pictures, hold down the ⌘ key and click each picture. To select a range of pictures, click the first picture you want to import, hold down the Shift key, and then click the last picture to import to highlight all the pictures in between.)

6. **Click Import.**

   iPhoto imports your pictures and organizes them into an Event.

TIP

A fast way to import pictures into iPhoto is to drag and drop those pictures over the iPhoto icon in the Dock.

Organizing Events in the Library

The iPhoto Library can store literally thousands of pictures, which can soon get as disorganized as dumping a decade's worth of photographs in a closet and then wondering why you can never find a specific picture easily.

Just as most people organize pictures in albums, boxes, or bags, so can iPhoto organize groups of pictures in one place. In iPhoto, a group of related pictures is called an *Event.*

The main purpose of Events is to group related pictures together. One Event might contain pictures you captured of a UFO, and a second Event might hold pictures of your kid's Little League game. After you've grouped related pictures in an Event, you'll be able to find what you need quickly and easily.

Creating an Event

When you import pictures, iPhoto automatically organizes them as Events, based on the day the picture was captured. Organizing Events by day can automatically sort pictures into one Event (the first day of your vacation when you visited London) and a second Event (the second day of your vacation when you visited Paris).

You can also create an Event manually by choosing Events➪Create Events.

Browsing through an Event

An Event can represent a single picture, but it more likely represents several pictures. To view all the pictures stored in a single Event, iPhoto lets you browse through all the pictures just by moving the pointer from left to right across the Event.

If you'd rather see all the pictures stored in a single Event at once, double-click the Event to display them, as shown in Figure 1-2.

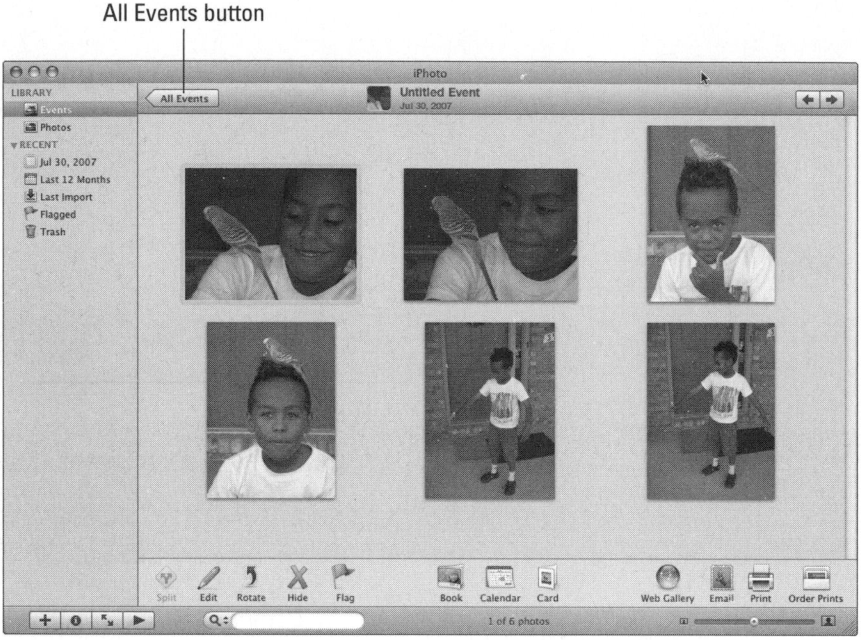

Figure 1-2: Double-clicking an Event expands all the pictures in the iPhoto window.

Naming an Event

To make finding pictures easier, you can give all Events a descriptive name so you'll have a rough idea what type of pictures are stored in that Event without having to browse through them first. To give your Events a descriptive name, follow these steps:

1. **Click the Events category under Library in the left pane of the iPhoto window.**

   The iPhoto window displays all your Events in the right pane. If you haven't named your Events, each Event may display the date when you captured those pictures as its name.

2. **Click the Event name, which appears directly under the Event picture.**

   A yellow box highlights the Event. A text box appears along with the number of pictures stored in that Event, as shown in Figure 1-3.

3. **Type a new, descriptive name for your Event and press Return.**

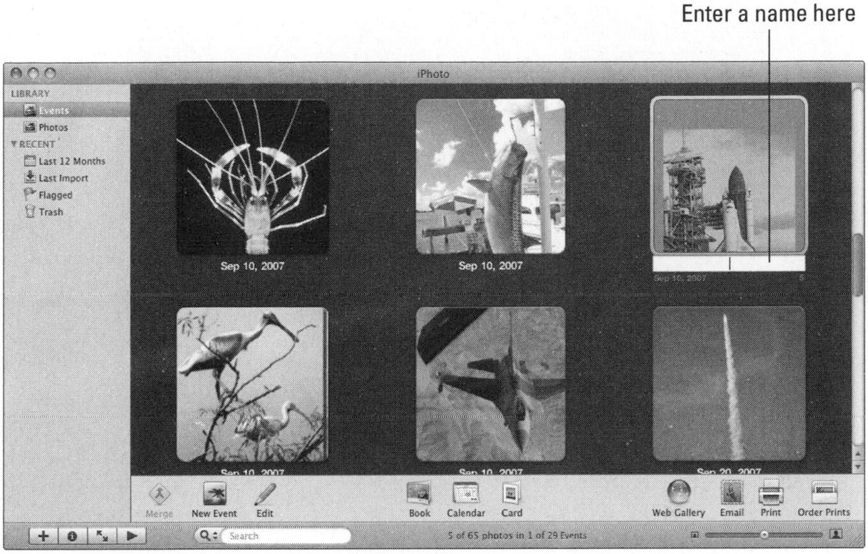

Figure 1-3: An Event's title and number of pictures appear when you move the pointer over an Event.

Merging Events

You might have pictures stored as separate Events, but you might later decide that the pictures in both Events really should be grouped together in a single Event. In this case, you can merge two Events into a single Event by following these steps:

1. **Click the Events category under Library in the iPhoto sidebar.**

   The iPhoto window displays all your Events in the right pane.

2. **Move the pointer over an Event you want to move or merge into another Event.**

3. **Click and drag the Event over the Event you want to merge it with.**

   The pointer turns into an arrow with a green plus sign, as shown in Figure 1-4.

4. **Release the left mouse button when the pointer appears over an Event.**

   A dialog appears, asking whether you want to merge the two Events.

5. **Click Merge.**

   Your two Events now appear as a single Event.

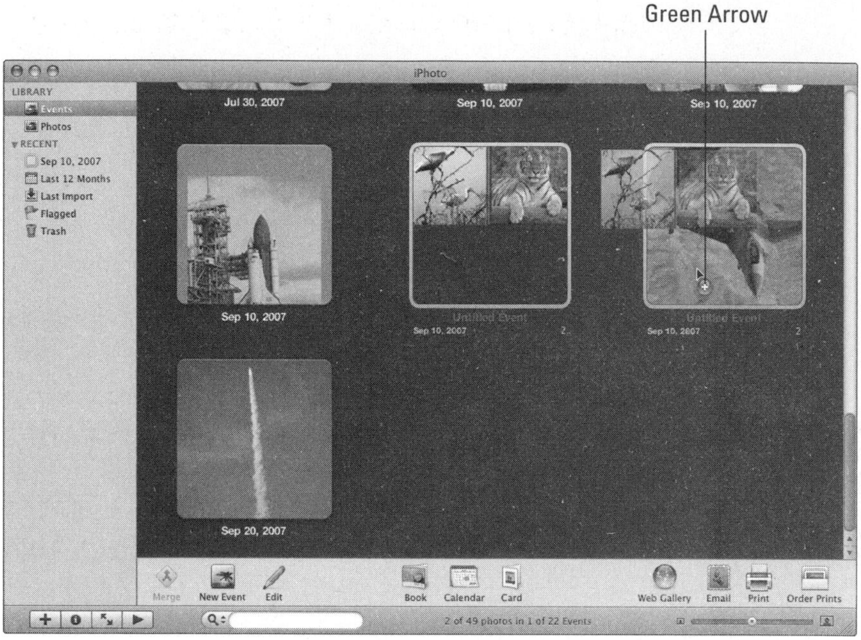

Figure 1-4: A green plus sign appears under the pointer to identify when two Events merge.

Splitting an Event

Sometimes an Event might contain too many pictures. In this case, you might want to store pictures in separate Events. To split an Event, follow these steps:

1. **Click the Events category under Library in the iPhoto sidebar.**

   The iPhoto window displays all your Events in the right pane.

2. **Double-click an Event you want to split.**

   The pictures in your Event appear in the iPhoto window (refer to Figure 1-2).

3. **Hold down the ⌘ key and click each picture you want to split into a separate Event.**

   A yellow border highlights each chosen picture.

4. **Choose Events⇨Split Event.**

   Your chosen pictures now appear in a separate Event.

5. **Click the All Events button.**

   Your original and newly split Events appear highlighted with a yellow border.

Moving pictures from one Event to another

If a picture appears in one Event but you think it should appear in a different Event, you can always move that picture. To move a picture from one Event to another, follow these steps:

1. **Click the Events category under Library in the iPhoto sidebar.**

   The iPhoto window displays all your Events in the right pane.

2. **Click the Event that contains the picture you want to move.**

3. **Hold down the ⌘ key and click the second Event to which you want to move a picture.**

   Yellow borders appear around both Events.

4. **Double-click one of the highlighted Events.**

   The iPhoto window splits in half, with pictures of the two Events stacked on top of each other in the two halves, as shown in Figure 1-5.

5. **Click and drag the picture you want to move over the area containing the pictures of the second Event.**

6. **Release the mouse button.**

   Your chosen picture now appears in the other Event.

7. **Click the All Events button to see all your Events again.**

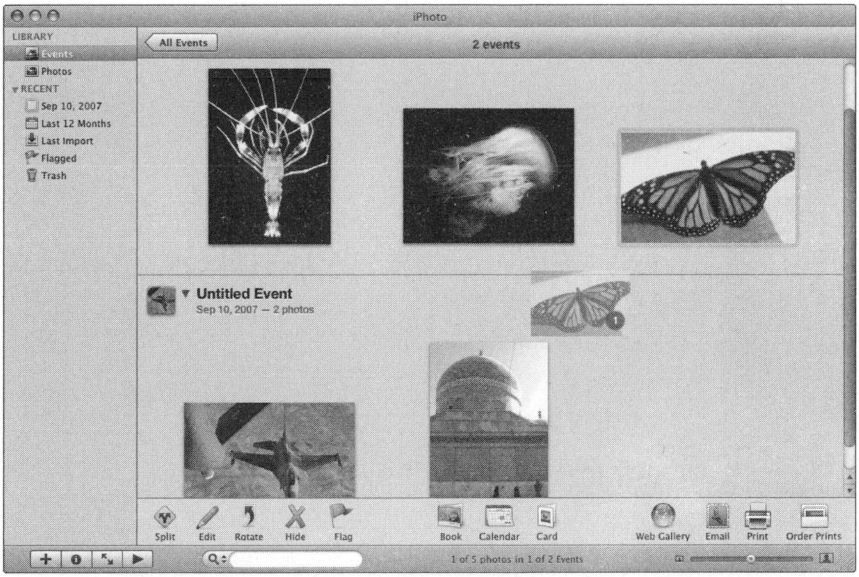

Figure 1-5: Dragging lets you move a picture from one Event to another.

Sorting Events

The more Events you create to store your pictures, the harder it can get to find what you need. To help keep you organized, iPhoto lets you sort your Events by different criteria:

- **Date:** Lets you sort Events by time.
- **Title:** Lets you sort Events by title.
- **Manually:** Lets you sort Events by clicking and dragging them.

You can also sort pictures by rating and keywords, but you must first give a picture a rating or keyword, which you find out about later in this chapter.

Sorting by date or title

Sorting by date makes it easy to find pictures based on the time you remember capturing those pictures. Sorting by title is helpful after you've given all Events a descriptive title and want to find a picture stored under a specific Event title.

To sort Events by date or title within the iPhoto window, follow these steps:

1. **Click the Events category under Library in the iPhoto sidebar.**

   The iPhoto window displays all your Events in the right pane.

2. **Choose View⇨Sort Events.**

   A submenu appears with a check mark next to the current way you have your Events sorted, as shown in Figure 1-6.

3. **Choose By Date, By Title, Ascending, or Descending.**

   Your Events now appear resorted by the criteria you chose.

If you choose Ascending or Descending, iPhoto resorts your Events based on the sorting method that appears with a check mark in the Sort Events submenu.

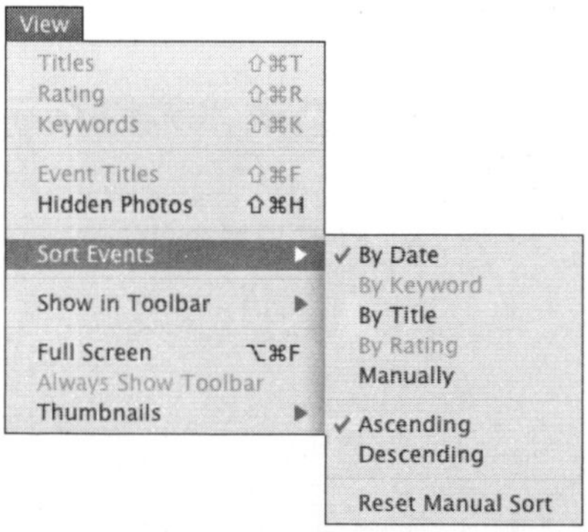

Figure 1-6: The Sort Events submenu lists the different ways to sort Events.

Sorting manually

Another way to sort Events is by clicking and dragging them around within the iPhoto window. This gives you the freedom to arrange pictures in Events based on your own preferences, regardless of date or titles. For example, you might put all your family Events near the top of the iPhoto window to make it easy to find pictures of different family members if you're putting together a newsletter for a family reunion.

To sort Events manually within the iPhoto window, follow these steps:

1. **Click the Events category under Library in the iPhoto sidebar.**

   The iPhoto window displays all your Events in the right pane.

2. **Click and drag an Event you want to move to its new location.**

   When you move an Event between two other Events, the other Events slide out of the way to make room.

3. **Release the mouse button when you're happy with the new position of the Event.**

Organizing Pictures

After you've stored pictures in separate Events, you might want to view and organize individual pictures stored in an Event.

Viewing pictures stored in a single Event

If you want to view pictures in only one Event, follow these steps:

1. **Click the Events category under Library in the iPhoto sidebar.**

   The iPhoto window displays all your Events in the right pane.

2. **Double-click an Event.**

   All your pictures in that Event appear in the iPhoto window, as shown in Figure 1-7.

3. **Click the All Events button in the upper-left corner of the iPhoto window to view all your Events again.**

Figure 1-7: Double-clicking an Event displays all the pictures in that Event.

Viewing pictures stored in all Events

Rather than view pictures stored in a single Event, you might want to view all your pictures in separate Events at the same time. To view pictures in all Events, follow these steps:

1. **Click the Photos category under Library in the iPhoto sidebar.**

   The iPhoto window displays all your pictures. If you have hidden any photos temporarily from view (by choosing Photos⇨Hide Photos), you can view those hidden photos by choosing View⇨Hidden Photos and making sure a check mark appears to the left of Hidden Photos.

2. **Choose View⇨Event Titles so a check mark appears to the left of Event Titles.**

   Note: If a check mark already appears to the left of Event Titles, skip this step.

   Displaying Event Titles lets you see how your pictures are organized into different Events, as shown in Figure 1-8.

3. **Click the triangle to the left of the Event title to display or hide pictures in an Event.**

   This step works only if a check mark appears to the left of Event Titles on the View menu.

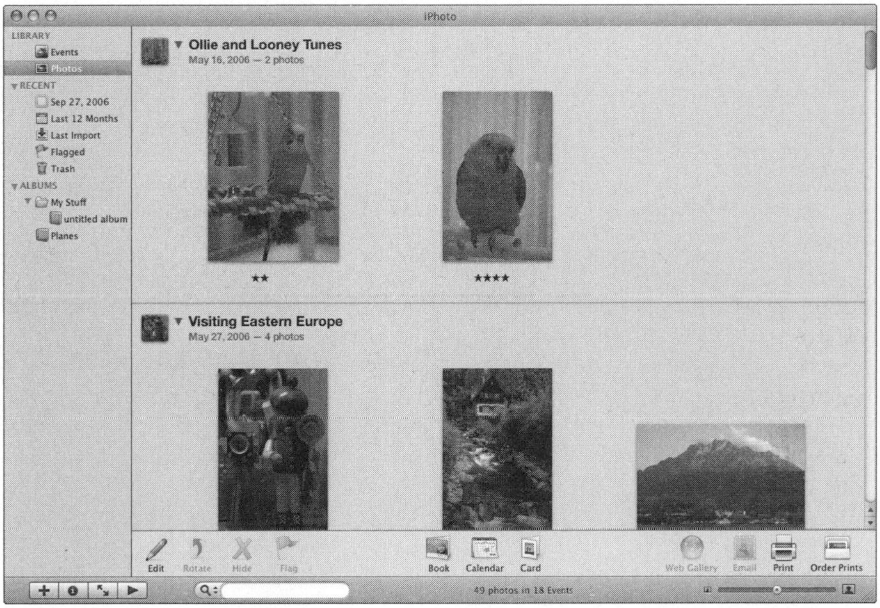

Figure 1-8: The Photos category lets you view all your pictures.

Naming pictures

Every digital camera stores pictures with generic filenames like `DSC_846`. Fortunately, you can replace these generic titles with more descriptive names.

In iPhoto, you can give descriptive names to your Events and descriptive names to individual pictures as well. So an Event might be named "Spring Break," and pictures stored in that Event might be named "Day 1: Partying," "Day 2: Drinking," and "Day 3: Hangover."

To name individual pictures stored in an Event, follow these steps:

1. **Choose one of the methods mentioned earlier (in the section "Viewing pictures in a single Event" or "Viewing pictures stored in all Events") to view individual pictures.**
2. **Choose View⇨Titles.**

   Note: If a check mark already appears to the left of Titles, skip this step.

   Titles appear underneath every picture.
3. **Click the title that you want to change.**

   A text box appears, as shown in Figure 1-9.

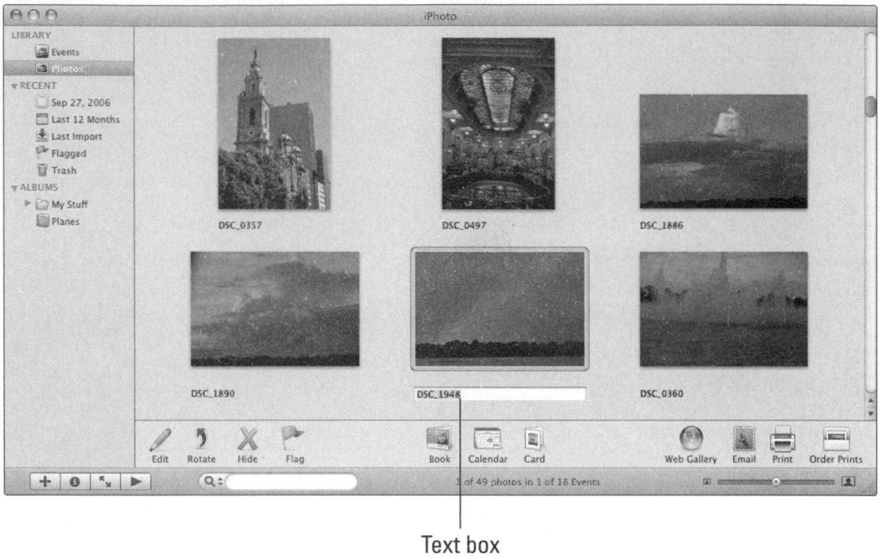

Figure 1-9: Descriptive titles can help you find pictures easier.

4. **Type a new name for your picture or use the arrow and Delete keys to edit the existing name.**
5. **Press Return when you're done.**

After you've named all pictures in an Event, you can sort them by choosing View➪Sort Photos➪By Title. Then you can choose View➪Sort Photos➪Ascending (or Descending) to sort by titles in ascending or descending order.

Rating pictures

Some pictures are better than others, so another way to sort and organize pictures is by rating them from zero to five stars. To rate pictures, follow these steps:

1. **Choose one of the methods mentioned earlier (in the section "Viewing pictures in a single Event" or "Viewing pictures stored in all Events") to view individual pictures.**
2. **Choose View➪Rating.**

   Note: If a check mark already appears to the left of Rating, skip this step.

   Titles appear underneath every picture.
3. **Click a picture to rate and choose Photos➪My Rating.**

   A submenu of stars appears, as shown in Figure 1-10.

TIP One fast way to rate pictures is to right-click a picture and choose the My Rating submenu to pick a star rating. A second way is to click on a picture and press ⌘-0 through ⌘-5 to rate a picture from zero to five stars.

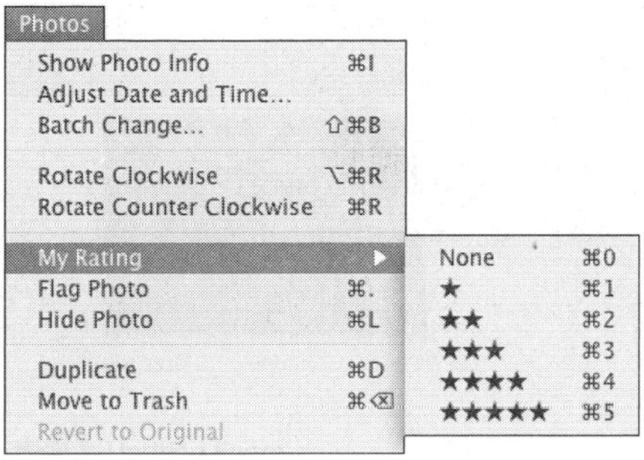

Figure 1-10: You can rate each picture with zero to five stars.

TIP After you've rated all pictures in an Event, you can sort them by choosing View➪Sort Photos➪By Rating. To change whether to sort by ascending or descending rating, choose View➪Sort Photos➪Ascending (or Descending).

Adding keywords to a picture

A *keyword* helps you organize pictures based on categories such as Favorite, Birthday, or Kids. By placing keywords on pictures, you can quickly find all Birthday or Kids pictures.

To add a keyword to a picture, follow these steps:

1. **Choose one of the methods mentioned earlier (in the section "Viewing pictures in a single Event" or "Viewing pictures stored in all Events") to view individual pictures.**
2. **Click a picture that you want to label with a keyword.**

   TIP If you hold down the ⌘ key, you can click two or more pictures to assign the same keyword to all of them.
3. **Choose Window➪Show Keywords.**

   A Keywords window appears, which displays several common keywords that iPhoto has already provided for you, as shown in Figure 1-11.

   TIP To add your own keywords to the Keywords window, click Edit Keywords. When an Edit Keywords dialog appears, click the plus sign button to type your own keywords into the Keywords window. (You can also click a keyword and then click the minus sign button to remove a keyword from the Keyword window.) If you click the Shortcut button, you can assign a key to represent a keyword. That way you can choose View➪Keywords to display a keywords text box underneath each picture, click in that text box, and press your shortcut key to add a keyword to that picture quickly.

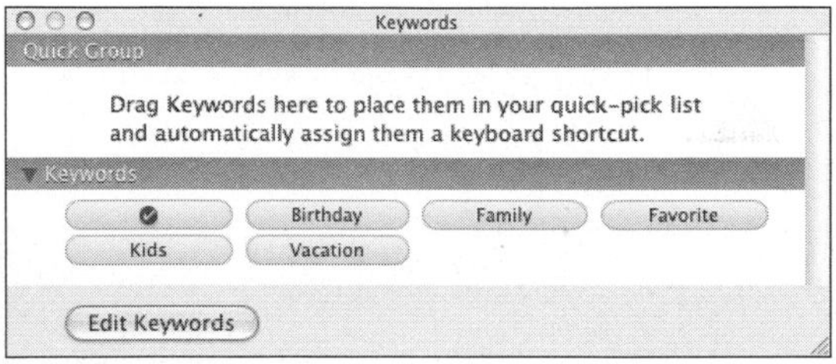

Figure 1-11: The Keywords window displays a list of keywords you can use.

4. **Click a keyword.**

   Your chosen keyword appears underneath the picture you selected.

   If you click the same keyword in the keyword window, iPhoto removes the keyword from your chosen picture.

After you've added keywords to pictures in an Event, you can sort them by choosing View➪Sort Photos➪By Keyword. Then you can sort alphabetically by keyword by choosing View➪Sort Photos➪Ascending (or Descending).

Storing pictures in albums and folders

Sorting and organizing pictures into Events can get cumbersome. For example, you might have dozens of birthday pictures stored in separate Events. Although you can store all these birthday pictures in the same Event, you might also want to keep them grouped with other pictures in separate Events that represent different years.

To keep pictures stored in separate Events while also grouping them together at the same time, you can create an *album.* An album groups related pictures together without removing them from the Events they're currently stored in.

Creating albums and organizing pictures manually

To create an album and store pictures in it, follow these steps:

1. **Choose File➪New Album.**

   A dialog appears, as shown in Figure 1-12.

For another way to create an album, click the plus sign button in the bottom-left corner of the iPhoto window. When a dialog pops up, click the Album button, type a name for your album, and click Create.

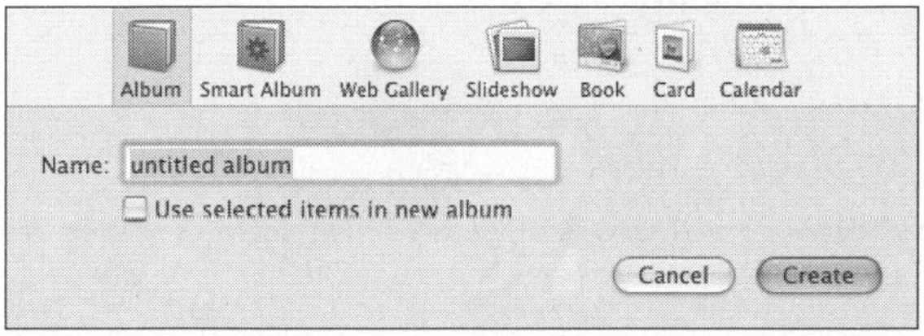

Figure 1-12: A dialog appears so that you can name your album.

2. **Type a descriptive name for your album and click Create.**

   Your album name appears under the Albums category in the iPhoto sidebar.

3. **Choose one of the methods mentioned earlier (in the section "Viewing pictures in a single Event" or "Viewing pictures stored in all Events") to view individual pictures.**

4. **Click and drag a picture you want to add to your album onto the album folder in the iPhoto sidebar.**

   You can select multiple pictures by holding down the ⌘ key and clicking each picture you want to add to an album.

5. **Release the mouse button to copy your picture to the album.**

6. **Repeat Steps 4 and 5 for each additional picture you want to copy into the album.**

   Now, if you click the album name in the iPhoto sidebar, you can see all the pictures in that album.

Any changes you make to a picture stored in an album automatically appears in the same picture stored in an Event (and vice versa).

The preceding steps create an empty album which you can then fill up with pictures. If you want to select pictures to store in an album first, follow these steps:

1. **Select one or more pictures that you want to store in an album.**

2. **Choose File⇨New Album From Selection.**

   A dialog appears, asking for a name for your Album.

3. **Type a descriptive name for your album and click Create.**

Creating albums and organizing pictures automatically

In case manually dragging pictures in and out of albums is too troublesome, you can set up a Smart Album from within iPhoto that will store pictures automatically.

To create a Smart Album that can store pictures automatically, follow these steps:

1. **Choose File⇨New Smart Album.**

   A dialog appears, asking for a name for your Smart Album.

2. **Type a descriptive name for your album in the Smart Album Name text box.**
3. **Click in the first pop-up menu and choose a criterion, such as Keyword or Rating, as shown in Figure 1-13.**
4. **Click in the second and third pop-up menus to define the criterion you chose in Step 3, such as choosing only pictures with a rating of four stars or with the Birthday keyword.**
5. **(Optional) Click the plus sign button to define another criterion and repeat Steps 3 and 4.**
6. **Click OK.**

   Your Smart Album now stores pictures based on your chosen criteria.

TIP

If you create too many albums, you can organize them into folders by choosing File⇨New Folder and dragging each album into that folder.

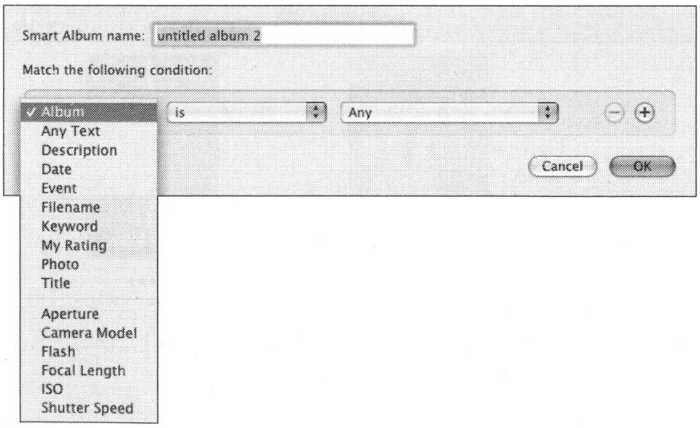

Figure 1-13: You must define the type of pictures you want the Smart Album to store automatically.

Deleting pictures, albums, and folders

Many times you'll import pictures into iPhoto and decide that the picture isn't worth saving after all. To keep your iPhoto Library from getting too cluttered, you should delete the pictures you don't need.

Besides deleting individual pictures, you can also delete albums and folders that contain pictures you don't want. When you delete an album or folder (which contains albums), you don't physically delete any pictures; you just delete the folder or album that contains the pictures. The original pictures are still stored in the iPhoto Library.

To delete a picture, album, or folder, follow these steps:

1. **Click and drag the picture, album, or folder you want to delete onto the Trash icon in the iPhoto sidebar.**

   A dialog appears, asking whether you really want to delete your selected items.

2. **Click Delete.**

TIP

Press ⌘+Z or choose Edit➪Undo Delete if you want to recover your deleted items right away.

Editing Pictures

Besides organizing your pictures, iPhoto lets you edit them as well. Such editing can be as simple as rotating or cropping a picture, or it can be as complicated as removing red-eye from a photograph or modifying colors.

REMEMBER

If you need more detailed or sophisticated editing, get a program like Adobe Photoshop Elements (`www.adobe.com`).

Rotating a picture

Sometimes pictures appear sideways when you first import them into iPhoto. To rotate a picture so you can see it right-side up, follow these steps:

1. **Choose one of the methods mentioned earlier (in the section "Viewing pictures in a single Event" or "Viewing pictures stored in all Events") to view individual pictures.**

2. **Click a picture.**

   Editing buttons (including the Rotate button) appear at the bottom of the iPhoto window, as shown in Figure 1-14.

3. **Click the Rotate button until you're happy with the new position of your picture.**

   If you hold down the Option key and click the Rotate button, you can rotate a picture in the opposite direction.

Figure 1-14: The editing tools appear at the bottom of the iPhoto window.

Cropping a picture

Cropping a picture lets you select only the part of the picture you want to keep. To crop a picture, follow these steps:

1. **Choose one of the methods mentioned earlier (in the section "Viewing pictures in a single Event" or "Viewing pictures stored in all Events") to view individual pictures.**
2. **Click a picture.**

   Editing buttons appear at the bottom of the iPhoto window (refer to Figure 1-14).
3. **Click the Edit button.**

   A new series of editing buttons appears at the bottom of the iPhoto window, as shown in Figure 1-15.
4. **Click the Crop button.**

   A white box appears on your picture, as shown in Figure 1-16.

5. Click and drag an edge or corner of the white box to reshape the box.

If you select the Constrain check box, you can pick a specific size option for your picture, such as square or 4 x 3.

6. Click the Apply button.

Your cropped picture appears.

7. Click the Done button.

Figure 1-15: Clicking the Edit button displays a new series of editing buttons.

Figure 1-16: Cropping a picture involves positioning a white box around the part of the image to keep.

Straightening a picture

Sometimes a picture may appear slightly cockeyed, so iPhoto lets you straighten an image out by following these steps:

1. **Choose one of the methods mentioned earlier (in the section "Viewing pictures in a single Event" or "Viewing pictures stored in all Events") to view individual pictures.**
2. **Double-click a picture.**

   Editing buttons appear at the bottom of the iPhoto window (refer to Figure 1-14).
3. **Click the Edit button.**

   A new series of editing buttons appears at the bottom of the iPhoto window (refer to Figure 1-15).
4. **Click the Straighten button.**

   A yellow grid appears over your image along with a slider, as shown in Figure 1-17.
5. **Move the pointer over the slider, hold down the mouse button, and drag the mouse left or right to straighten the image.**

   If you click the Decrease/Increase angle of photo icons that appear on opposite ends of the slider, you can adjust the angle of your picture by 0.1 of a degree.
6. **Click the Done button.**

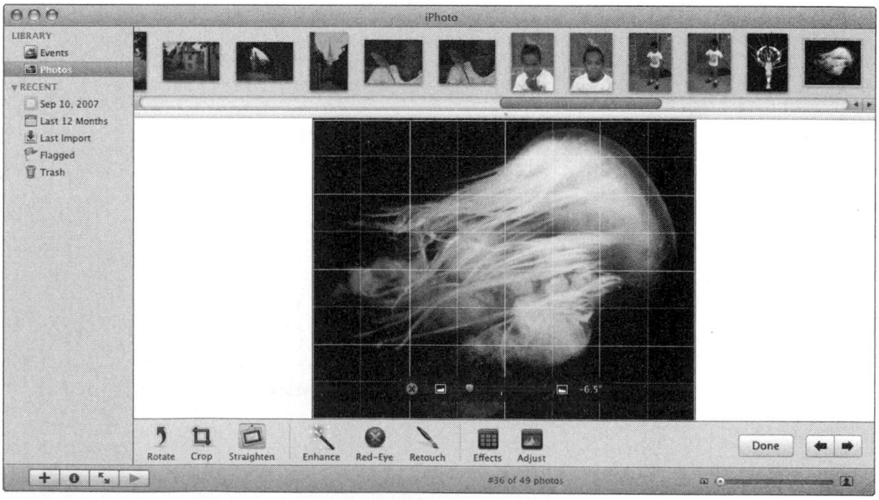

Figure 1-17: Dragging the slider lets you tilt an image.

Fixing a picture

Not every picture looks perfect, so iPhoto gives you three tools to try and fix an image:

- **Enhance:** Fixes brightness and contrast problems.
- **Red-eye:** Removes red-eye caused by flash photography.
- **Retouch:** Lets you drag the mouse to remove wrinkles, pimples, and other minor blemishes.

To fix a picture, follow these steps:

1. **Choose one of the methods mentioned earlier (in the section "Viewing pictures in a single Event" or "Viewing pictures stored in all Events") to view individual pictures.**
2. **Double-click a picture.**

   Editing buttons appear at the bottom of the iPhoto window (refer to Figure 1-14).
3. **Click the Edit button.**

   A new series of editing buttons appears at the bottom of the iPhoto window (refer to Figure 1-15).
4. **Click the Enhance button.**

   Your picture changes appearance by appearing brighter and easier to see details.
5. **If necessary, click the Red-Eye button and then click the red-eye in the picture.**

   The red color in a person's eye is replaced with a darker, more natural color.
6. **If necessary, click the Retouch button, move the pointer over the part of the picture you want to modify, and then click and drag to erase an area and replace it with colors from the surrounding area.**
7. **Click Done.**

Adding visual effects to a picture

Just for fun, you can add visual effects to your pictures, such as making them look like faded pictures taken decades ago or placing them inside a circle with blurred edges. To add effects to a picture, follow these steps:

1. **Choose one of the methods mentioned earlier (in the section "Viewing pictures in a single Event" or "Viewing pictures stored in all Events") to view individual pictures.**

2. **Double-click a picture.**

   Editing buttons appear at the bottom of the iPhoto window (refer to Figure 1-14).

3. **Click the Edit button.**

   A new series of editing buttons appears at the bottom of the iPhoto window (refer to Figure 1-15).

4. **Click the Effects button.**

   An Effects window appears, as shown in Figure 1-18.

5. **Click an effect.**

   Note: You can click multiple effects.

6. **Click the Done button.**

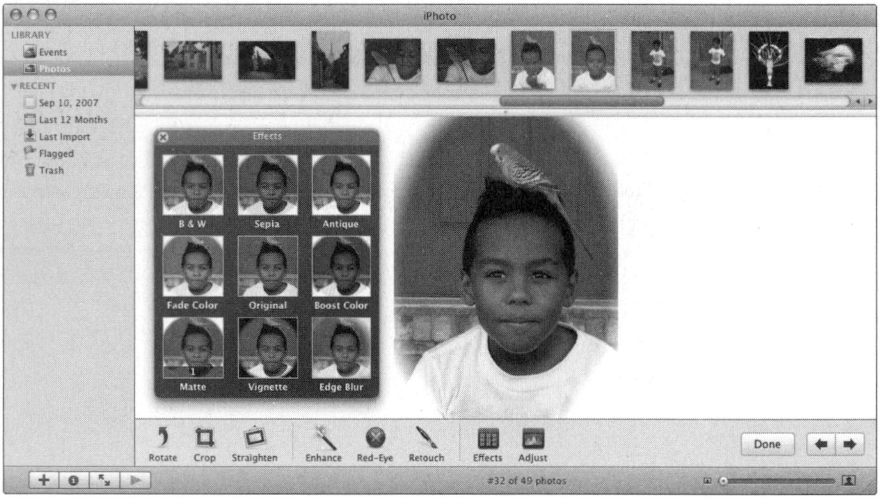

Figure 1-18: The Effects window lets you choose a way to modify your picture.

Controlling colors in a picture

In case you need more advanced editing features, iPhoto lets you adjust contrast, saturation, tint, exposure, and other parts of a picture by following these steps:

1. **Choose one of the methods mentioned earlier (in the section "Viewing pictures in a single Event" or "Viewing pictures stored in all Events") to view individual pictures.**

2. **Double-click a picture.**

   Editing buttons appear at the bottom of the iPhoto window (refer to Figure 1-14).

3. **Click the Edit button.**

   A new series of editing buttons appears at the bottom of the iPhoto window (refer to Figure 1-15).

4. **Click the Adjust button.**

   An Adjust window appears as shown in Figure 1-19.

Figure 1-19: The Adjust window provides multiple ways to modify the colors in a picture.

5. **Adjust any of the following settings:**

   - *Exposure:* Lightens or darkens a picture.
   - *Contrast:* Alters the differences between light and dark areas.
   - *Highlights:* Increases detail in a picture by lightening or darkening areas.
   - *Shadows:* Lightens or darkens shadow areas of a picture
   - *Saturation:* Alters the intensity of colors in a picture
   - *Temperature:* Alters colors by making them dimmer (colder) or brighter (hotter).
   - *Tint:* Adjusts the red/green colors in a picture.
   - *Sharpness:* Adjusts the focus of a picture.
   - *Reduce Noise:* Alters the graininess of a picture.

   TIP: If you decide that your original picture looked better without any adjusted settings, click the Reset button.

6. **Click Done.**

Sharing Pictures

There's no point in taking pictures if you don't share them with others. To help you publicize your pictures to the world, you can print them out, store them on a Web page, e-mail them to others, or burn them to a CD/DVD. For an added fee, you can print out your pictures as books, calendars, or greeting cards.

Printing pictures

You can print individual pictures or groups of pictures on your home printer by following these steps:

1. **Choose one of the methods mentioned earlier (in the section "Viewing pictures in a single Event" or "Viewing pictures stored in all Events") to view individual pictures.**
2. **Hold down the ⌘ key and click all the pictures you want to print.**
3. **Click the Print button or choose File➪Print.**

   A Print dialog appears, as shown in Figure 1-20.

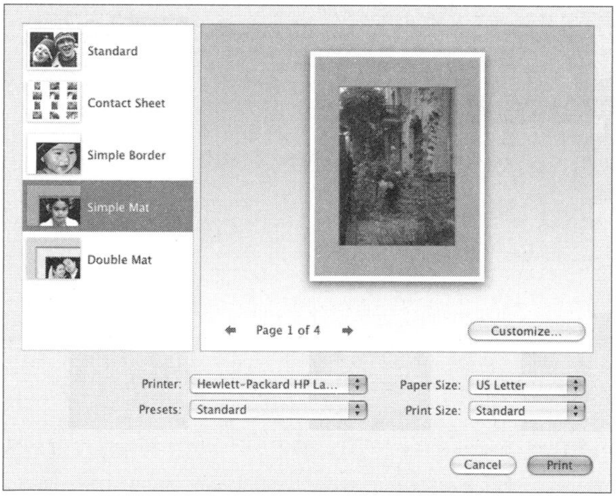

Figure 1-20: The Print dialog lets you choose different ways to print your pictures.

4. **Click one of the following print styles:**
   - *Standard:* Prints pictures to fill the entire page.
   - *Contact Sheet:* Prints thumbnail images of multiple pictures on a single page.
   - *Simple Border:* Prints one picture per page with a plain border around the edge.

- *Simple Mat:* Prints one picture per page with a tinted border around the edge.
- *Double Mat:* Prints one picture per page with two borders around the edges.

5. **Choose the following pop-up menu options:**
   - *Printer:* Defines which printer to use (if you have more than one printer).
   - *Paper Size:* Defines what size paper to use.
   - *Presets:* Provides pre-defined printing settings.
   - *Print Size:* Defines the size to print each picture, such as 3 x 5 or 8 x 10.
6. **Click the Print button.**

REMEMBER

You can click the Order Prints button in the bottom-right corner of the iPhoto window to have your pictures sent to Kodak for printing (for a fee, of course). You can also click the Book, Calendar, or Card button to create photo books, calendars, or greeting cards from your pictures.

E-mailing pictures

If you store some interesting pictures, you can e-mail them to your friends through Mail. If you use a different e-mail program, such as America Online or Entourage, you can configure iPhoto to work with your e-mail program by following these steps:

1. **Choose iPhoto⇨Preferences.**

   A Preferences window appears.
2. **Click the General button.**
3. **Click the Email Photos Using pop-up menu and choose your e-mail program, such as America Online, Eudora, Mail, or Entourage.**
4. **Click the Close button of the Preferences window.**

After you've configured your e-mail program to work with iPhoto, you can send a picture by following these steps:

1. **Choose one of the methods mentioned earlier (in the section "Viewing pictures in a single Event" or "Viewing pictures stored in all Events") to view individual pictures.**
2. **Hold down the ⌘ key and click on all the pictures you want to send.**
3. **Click the Email button or choose Share⇨Email.**

   A Mail Photo dialog appears, letting you choose a size for your picture, as shown in Figure 1-21.

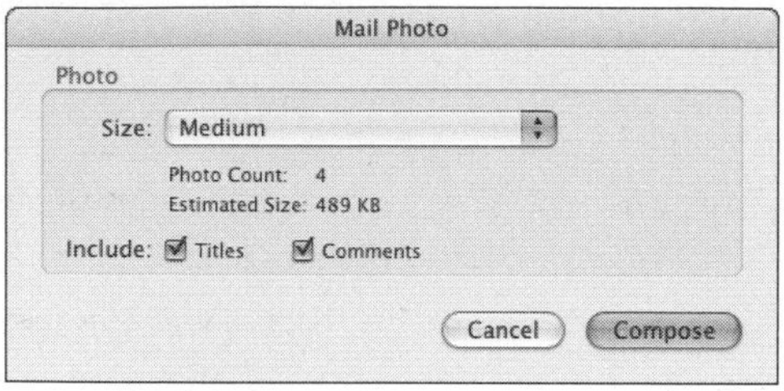

Figure 1-21: The Mail Photo dialog lets you choose how to e-mail pictures.

4. **Choose any options in the Mail Photo dialog.**
   - *Size:* Lets you define how big (or small) you want your picture to be. Use smaller pictures if you or the recipient has a slow Internet connection.
   - *Titles:* Includes the pictures title.
   - *Comments:* Includes any comments you may have added to the picture.
5. **Click Compose.**

   A Mail window appears.
6. **Type any additional message, enter an e-mail address, and click Send.**

Saving pictures to a CD/DVD

If you want to give someone a copy of your pictures, you can store them on CD/DVD so they can shove the CD/DVD into their own computer. To save pictures on CD/DVD, follow these steps:

1. **Choose one of the methods mentioned earlier (in the section "Viewing pictures in a single Event" or "Viewing pictures stored in all Events") to view individual pictures.**
2. **Hold down the ⌘ key and click all the pictures you want to save.**
3. **Choose Share⇨Burn.**

   A dialog appears, telling you to insert a blank CD/DVD into your Mac.
4. **Insert a blank CD/DVD and click OK.**

   Your photos are burned to your CD/DVD.

REMEMBER

Not all Mac computers can write to a DVD, so make sure your Mac can use the type of disc you want to save your pictures on.

Using pictures in iWeb and iDVD

After you've stored pictures in iPhoto, you can import them directly into iDVD (to burn them on to a DVD, complete with fancy menus and music) or into iWeb (to place on Web pages). To transfer pictures from iPhoto into iDVD or iWeb, follow these steps:

1. **Choose one of the methods mentioned earlier (in the section "Viewing pictures in a single Event" or "Viewing pictures stored in all Events") to view individual pictures.**
2. **Hold down the ⌘ key and click all the pictures you want to use.**
3. **Choose one of the following:**
   - Share➪Send to iWeb➪Photo Page (or Blog). This loads iWeb and creates a photo album page displaying all your chosen pictures.
   - Share➪Send to iDVD. This loads the iDVD program and your chosen photographs so you can arrange them in the order you want.

REMEMBER

If you have a .Mac account, you can post your pictures as a Web Gallery or slide show by clicking the Web Gallery button at the bottom of the iPhoto window, choosing Share➪Web Gallery, or Share➪.Mac Slides.

Ordering books, calendars, and cards

For a fee, you can take your favorite iPhoto pictures and have them printed in books, as calendars, or as greeting cards. To choose to print your pictures on a book, calendar, or greeting card, follow these steps:

1. **Choose one of the methods mentioned earlier (in the section "Viewing pictures in a single Event" or "Viewing pictures stored in all Events") to view individual pictures.**
2. **Hold down the ⌘ key and click all the pictures you want to use.**
3. **Click the Book, Calendar, or Card button at the bottom of the iPhoto window.**

   A dialog appears, asking that you choose a particular style — a Picture Book or Picture Calendar, for example — as shown in Figure 1-22.

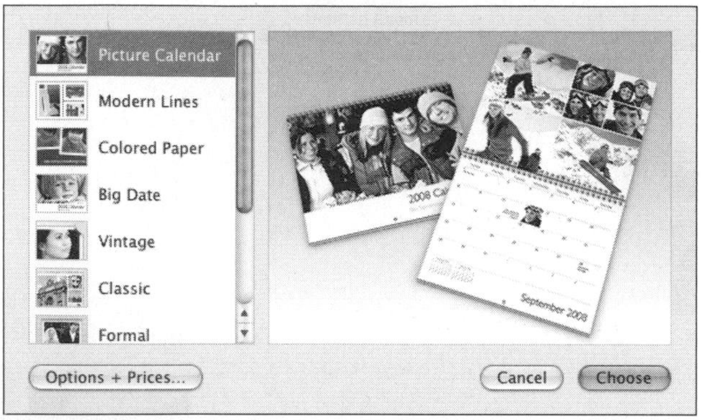

Figure 1-22: The dialog lets you choose a specific type of book, calendar, or card to create.

4. **Click a type and click Choose.**

   Depending on the type of project you want to create (a book, calendar, or card), you might need to pick additional options. Eventually, the iPhoto window displays a blank book, calendar, or card for you to drag your pictures on to design them, as shown in Figure 1-23.

5. **Click the Buy button when you're done designing your project.**

   Prices for books and calendars typically cost $10 to $30, and greeting cards cost $2 each. Your order goes directly to Apple, although Kodak does the actual printing.

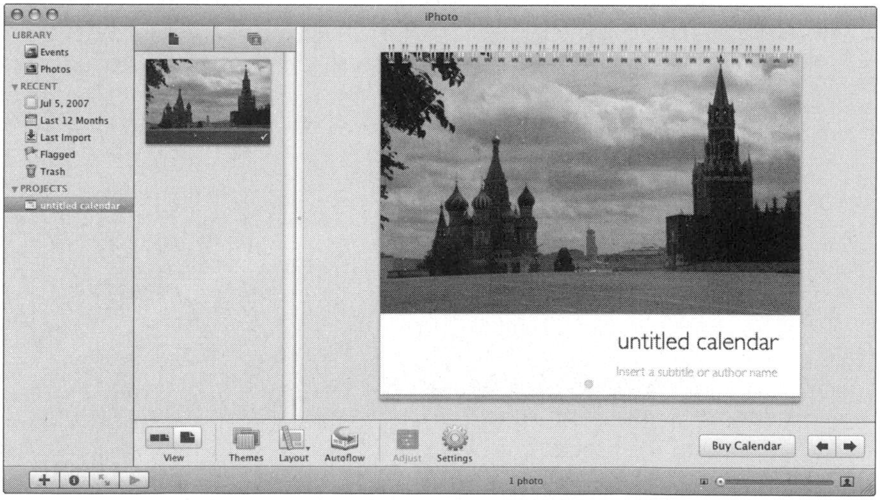

Figure 1-23: To design a project, drag the pictures you've selected.

Chapter 2: Using iMovie

In This Chapter

- **Discovering how iMovie works**
- **Storing video**
- **Browsing and organizing video**
- **Adding transitions and effects**
- **Saving videos**

If you have a digital video camcorder, you can create home movies. To make your home movies fancier and more professional-looking, though, use iMovie. That way, you can turn your home movies into a polished product that you can upload to video-sharing sites such as YouTube, play on video iPods, or just view on your Mac. Any digital home movie you might have, iMovie can improve it with the help of your skill and creativity.

How iMovie Works

The iMovie program consists of an Event Library and a Project Library. The Event Library appears in the bottom-left corner of the iMovie window and is where you store videos. When you want to work your magic and come up with a film project, you'll pick and choose parts of any video you have stored in the Event Library, and you'll copy these parts (know as *clips*) into the Project Library, which appears in the upper-left corner of the iMovie window.

REMEMBER

The Event Library contains your raw, unedited video, whereas the Project Library contains the copies of your video that you can modify. If you accidentally erase or mess up a video in the Project Library, you can just retrieve the original footage from the Event Library and start all over again.

Organizing the Event Library

The more videos you store, the more crowded the Event Library will get, and the harder it will be to find what you want. When you store a new video in the Event Library, iMovie gives you the option of creating an event folder, which identifies the date you imported the video file into iMovie.

Organizing videos in the Event Library by date can be helpful, but you might prefer identifying Events by descriptive name instead. To rename an Event, follow these steps:

1. **Click the Finder icon in the Dock.**

   The Finder appears.

2. **Double-click the iMovie icon in the Applications folder.**

   The iMovie window appears.

3. **(Optional) Choose Window⇨Event Library if the Event Library is not visible.**

4. **Double-click an Event in the Event Library in the bottom-left corner of the iMovie window.**

   Your chosen Event name appears highlighted.

5. **Type a descriptive name or press the arrow and Delete keys to edit the existing Event name.**

Storing video in different Event folders can help you find the video you want. If you want to edit video of your family vacation, just click the Event folder for that day or span of days to display your video.

The Event Library displays each video file as a series of thumbnail images. To define how to divide a video into multiple thumbnail images, drag the slider in the bottom-right corner of the iMovie window. Dragging this slider to the left divides your video into more thumbnail images, whereas dragging this slider to the right divides your video into fewer thumbnail images.

Instead of forcing you to browse through your entire video to find the one part you need, iMovie lets you jump straight to a scene that contains the footage you want to use. After you've found the video footage that you want to edit, just copy that video footage into the Project Library by dragging it with the mouse.

Organizing the Project Library

The Project Library appears in the upper-left corner of the iMovie window. You can divide the Project Library into different folders where one folder might contain your family vacation video, and a second folder might contain the footage you captured of a UFO you spotted hovering outside of New Mexico. To view (or hide) the Project Library, choose Window⇨Project Library.

REMEMBER

You can copy and store the same video footage in two or more projects.

In the Project Library, you can rearrange, trim, and delete video clips to create your movie. This is where you can also add titles or sound effects to your edited video.

The basic steps for using iMovie are

- Store and organize video in the Event Library.
- Copy video footage out of the Event Library and store it in a folder (project) inside the Project Library.
- Edit your video clips in the Project Library.
- Save your video as a digital video file for viewing on other computers, on DVD, or over the Internet.

Importing a Video into the Event Library

The Event Library holds all your videos, acting as your personal stock film vault. By storing videos in the Event Library, you can selectively pick and choose footage from old videos to use in any new projects.

To store video in the Event Library, you must import a video from one of three sources:

- A digital video camera
- A project created and saved using an earlier version of iMovie
- A digital video file stored on your hard drive

Importing from a digital video camera

To *import* (that is, to copy) a movie that you've captured with a digital video camera, follow these steps:

1. **Connect your digital video camera to your Mac through a USB or FireWire cable, as appropriate for your camcorder.**
2. **Double-click the iMovie icon inside the Applications folder to load iMovie.**

   The iMovie window appears.
3. **Choose File⇨Import from Camera.**

   An Import window appears.
4. **Click Import.**

   An Import dialog appears, as shown in Figure 2-1.

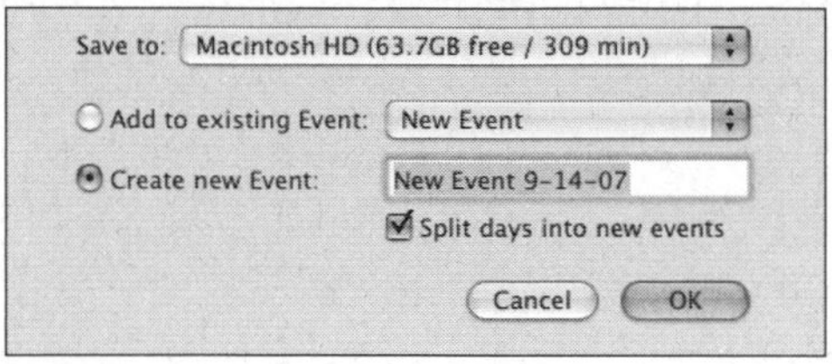

Figure 2-1: The Import dialog lets you define how to classify a movie.

5. **Select one of the following radio buttons:**

   - *Add to Existing Event:* Stores the video as part of an existing event in the Event library.
   - *Create New Event:* Stores the video as a new event in the Event library. The default name for the Event will be the current date, but you can always type a more descriptive name.

6. **Select or deselect the Split Days into New Events check box.**

   Many video camcorders time-stamp any video footage you capture, so this option divides a video into parts where each part represents all video footage shot on the same day.

7. **Click OK.**

   The Import dialog displays your video in real time.

8. **Click Stop when you want to stop importing video.**

   Your imported video appears as thumbnail images in the lower pane (the Event pane) of the iMovie window, as shown in Figure 2-2. After you import a video, your original video footage remains on your video camcorder, so you might want to go back and erase it.

REMEMBER

You can define how many thumbnails to divide a video by dragging the slider in the bottom-right corner of the iMovie window.

REMEMBER

iMovie divides a video into separate scenes where each scene displays the first frame of a video clip. By browsing through these thumbnail images of scenes, you can see which scene is likely to contain the video footage you want to use.

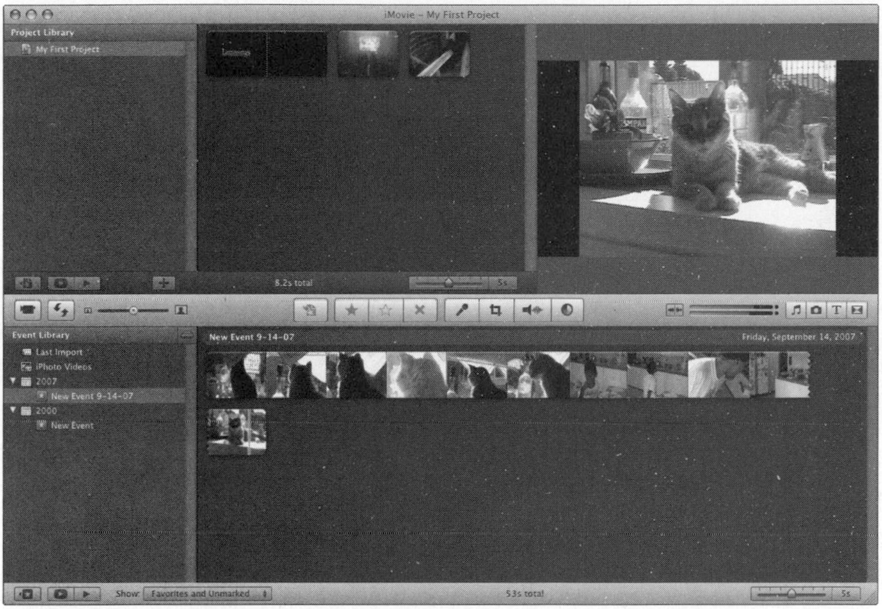

Figure 2-2: iMovie automatically separates a video into separate scenes.

Importing a digital video file

If you have any digital video files stored in QuickTime, MPEG-4, or digital video (DV) files lying around on your hard drive, you can import them into iMovie. To import a digital video file, follow these steps:

1. **Choose File⇨Import Movies.**

   An Open dialog appears, as shown in Figure 2-3. You might need to navigate through different drives and folders to find the file you want to import.

2. **Select the digital video file you want to import.**
3. **Click the Save To pop-up menu and choose a drive to store your video.**
4. **Select one of the following radio buttons:**
   - *Add to Existing Event:* Stores the video as part of an existing event in the Even Library
   - *Create New Event:* Stores the video as a new event in the iMovie Event Library.
5. **Choose how you want to handle importing 1080i video from the Import 1080i Video As pop-up menu.**

   The Large option reduces the frame size of the video to 960 x 540 pixels, whereas the Full option displays the frame size at the complete 1,920 x 1,080 pixels.

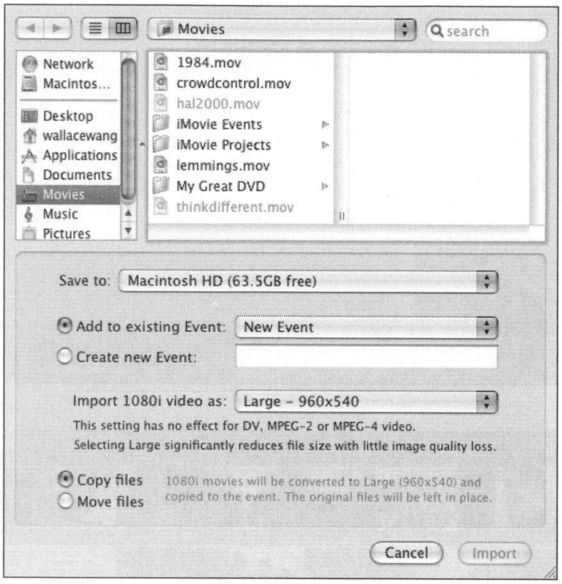

Figure 2-3: The Open dialog lets you import digital video files.

6. **Select the Copy Files or Move Files radio button.**

   The Copy Files option leaves your original file and creates a duplicate file to store in iMovie. The Move Files option physically transfers your chosen video file and moves it into iMovie.

7. **Click Import.**

   Your imported movie appears as thumbnail images in the iMovie window.

Working with Projects

The Project Library contains folders for storing your separate video projects. One project might contain your family vacation movies, and a second project might contain movies of your daughter's soccer games. Projects contain one or more video clips from movies stored in the Event Library.

Creating an iMovie project

To create a project, follow these steps:

1. **Choose File⇨New Project.**

   A dialog appears, as shown in Figure 2-4.

2. **Enter a descriptive name for your project in the Project Name text box.**

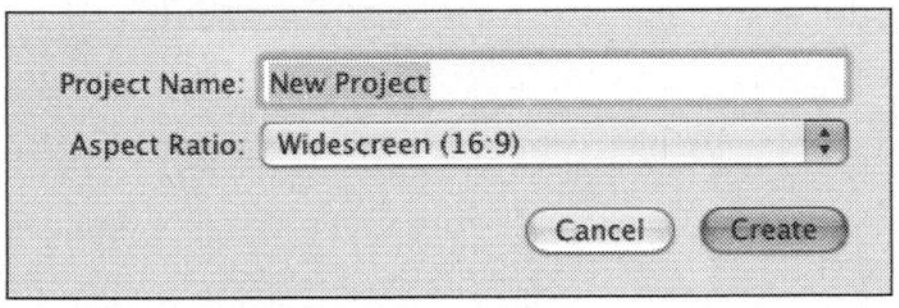

Figure 2-4: The New Project dialog lets you choose a name and aspect ratio for your video project.

3. **Choose Standard, iPhone, or Widescreen from the Aspect Ratio pop-up menu.**

   The aspect ratio optimizes your video project for displaying on different devices. If you want to view your video on a TV set, choose Standard or Widescreen. If you want to view your video on a mobile phone, choose the smaller iPhone aspect ratio.

4. **Click the Create button.**

   A Drag Media Here to Create a New Project pane appears in the Project Library section of the iMovie window, as shown in Figure 2-5.

   The stage is set for your cinematic masterpiece.

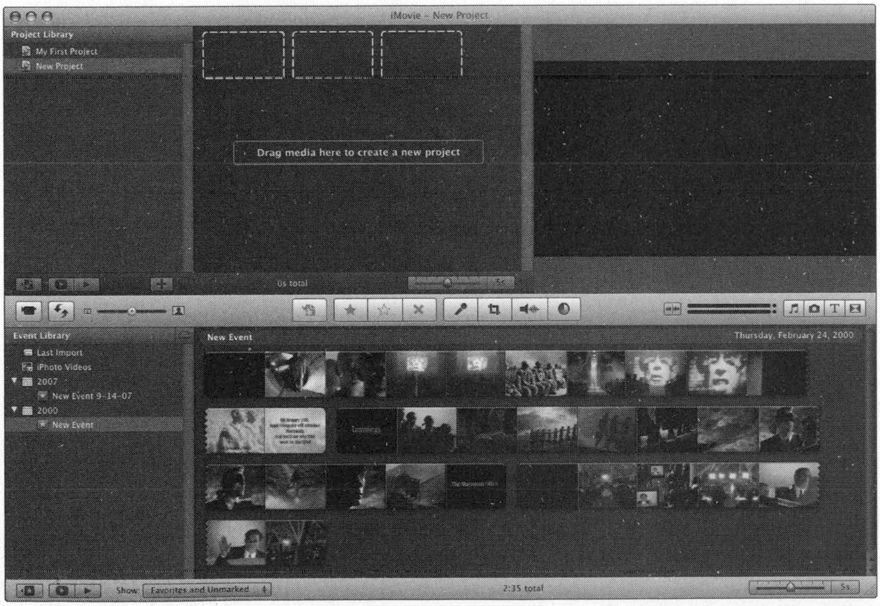

Figure 2-5: The Drag Media Here to Create a New Project pane is where you can arrange video clips.

Selecting video clips

Whether you want to create a new project or edit an existing one, you need to add video clips from the Event Library and place them in a folder stored in the Project Library.

Before you can select a video clip to store in a project, you need to see exactly what part of a video you want to clip. To help you find any part of a video, iMovie displays an entire video as a series of images that appear like individual frames of a filmstrip. To find a specific part of a video, you can skim through a video. When you find the part of a video you want to use, just copy it and paste it into a project folder.

Skimming a video

Skimming a video lets you see the contents of a video file just by moving the mouse over the video images. To view a video by skimming, follow these steps:

1. **Move the pointer over any one of the thumbnail images of a video file when displayed in the Event Library section of the iMovie window.**

   A red vertical line appears over the thumbnail image, as shown in Figure 2-6.

Red vertical line

Figure 2-6: A red vertical line shows you the position of the current image in a video file.

2. **Move the mouse left and right to watch your video in the upper-right corner of the iMovie window.**

   The faster you move the mouse, the faster the video plays. Moving the mouse to the left plays the video backwards. Moving the mouse to the right plays the video forwards.

Selecting a video clip

After you see the part of a video you want to use, you need to select that video clip by following these steps:

1. **In the Event Library section of the iMovie window, move the pointer to the beginning of the part of the video that you want to use.**
2. **Click and drag to the right.**

   A yellow rectangle appears to define the size of your clip, as shown in Figure 2-7. You can drag the handles to define the exact frame to start and end your video clip.
3. **Release the mouse button when you're happy with the portion of the video that your clip contains.**

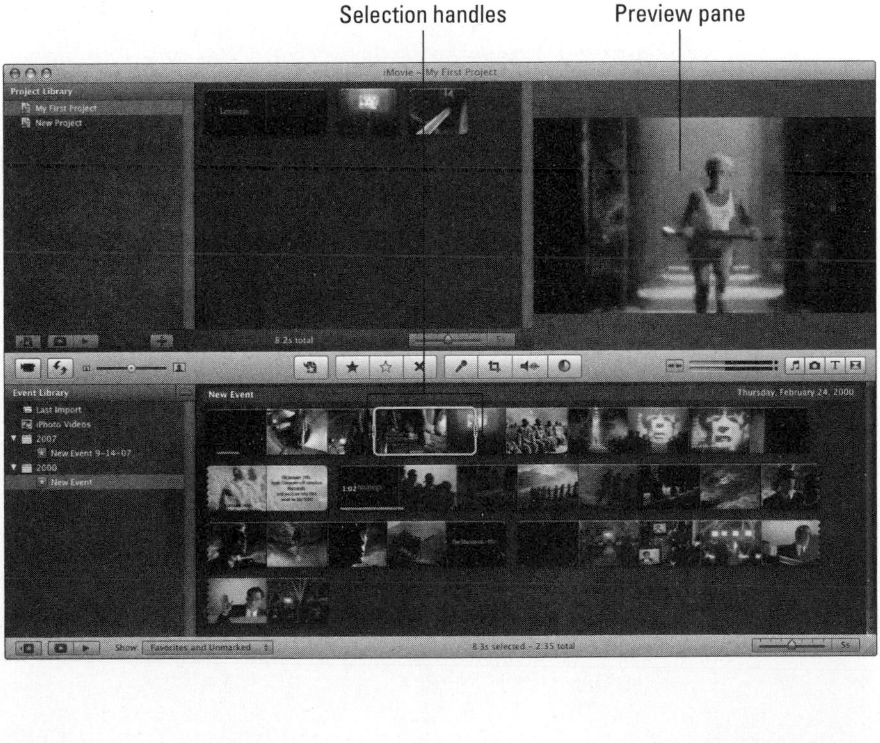

Figure 2-7: A yellow rectangle defines the size of a video clip.

After you've selected a video clip, you can view it by choosing one of the following:

- ✦ Move the mouse over the left selection handle until the pointer turns into a two-way pointing arrow. Then double-click to view your video clip in the Preview pane in the upper-right corner of the iMovie window.
- ✦ Right-click the video clip and choose Play Selection from the menu that appears.

Placing a video clip in a project

After selecting a video clip, you can place it in a project folder. Video clips in a project folder appear as thumbnail images so you can browse through your collection of video clips. To place a video clip in a project folder, follow these steps:

1. **Make sure you have defined a video clip within a yellow rectangle, as described in the preceding section.**
2. **Click a project folder displayed in the Project Library listing in the upper-left corner of the iMovie window.**

   Thumbnail images of any video clips already stored in the project appear.

   Note: If you haven't added any video clips to a project, you see a Drag Media Here to Create a New Project message, along with three dotted rectangles (refer to Figure 2-5).
3. **Move the pointer inside the yellow rectangle of the video clip you selected.**

   The pointer turns into a hand icon.
4. **Click and drag the selected video clip onto the project folder; then release the mouse button (see Figure 2-8).**

   Your selected video clip appears as a thumbnail image in the Project Library section of the iMovie window.

Deleting video clips

In case you store a video clip in a project folder and then decide you don't need that video clip any more, you can delete it from that project.

Deleting a video clip from a project does not delete the video clip from the Event Library.

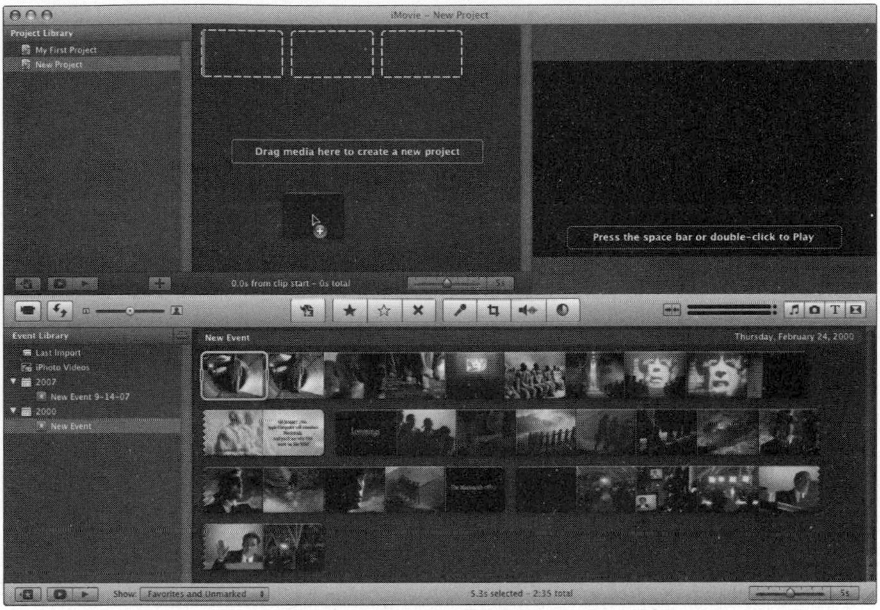

Figure 2-8: Dragging a video clip lets you store it in a project folder.

To delete a video clip from a project, follow these steps:

1. **Click a project folder in the Project Library window.**

   The project window, in the center, displays all the video clips stored in the selected project folder.

2. **In the project window, click the video clip that you want to delete.**

   A yellow rectangle border surrounds your chosen video clip.

3. **Choose Edit⇨Delete Selection (or press Delete).**

Deleting a project

In case you're done with a project or decide you no don't want it anymore, you can delete an entire project folder.

WARNING!

When you delete a project folder, you also delete any video clips stored inside that project. However, the original videos (from which you copied clips to store in the Project Library) remain in the Event Library.

To delete a project, follow these steps:

1. **Click the project folder you want to delete in the Project Library listing on left-hand side of the iMovie window.**
2. **Choose File⇨Move Project to Trash.**

TIP

If you accidentally delete a project, you can retrieve it again by pressing ⌘+Z or choosing Edit➪Undo Delete Project.

Printing a project

Each project folder displays thumbnail images of one or more video clips. If you want to review the order and images of the video clips stored in a project, you can print these images on paper. Obviously, this printout of your project thumbnails can't show you the moving images of your video, but they can show you the organization of your video clips.

To print the thumbnail images of video clips stored in a project folder, follow these steps:

1. **Click a project folder in the Project Library listing.**
2. **Choose File➪Print Project.**

   A Print dialog appears.
3. **(Optional) Drag the slider, in the bottom-right corner of the iMovie window, to define how many thumbnail images to display.**

   If you drag the slider to the right, you'll display fewer thumbnail images. Drag the slider to the left, and you'll display more thumbnail images.
4. **Click the Preview button to see how your project will appear on paper, as shown in Figure 2-9.**
5. **Click Print.**

Editing Video Clips in a Project

After you've placed one or more video clips in a project folder, you'll usually want to edit those video clips to put them in the best order, trim unnecessary footage, and add titles and audio to spice up your entire video.

Rearranging the order of video clips

A project plays video clips in sequence, but you might want to change the order that your video clips play. To rearrange the order of your video clips in a project, follow these steps:

1. **Click a project folder in the Project Library listing.**

   Thumbnail images of all your video clips appear in the center pane (the project window) of the iMovie window.
2. **Click a video clip you want to move.**

   A yellow rectangle appears around your chosen video clip.

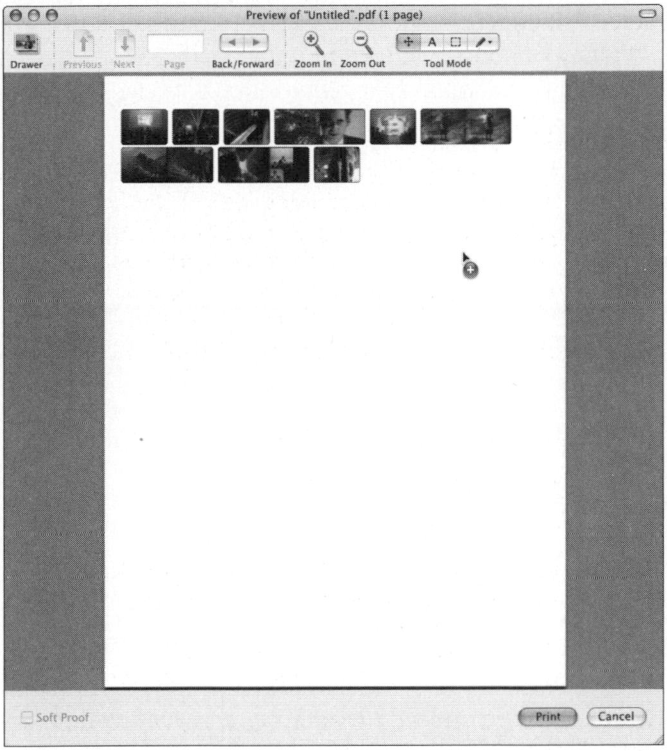

Figure 2-9: The preview shows you how your printed video clip images will appear on paper.

3. **Move the pointer inside the yellow rectangle of your selected video clip.**

   The pointer turns into a hand icon.

4. **Click and drag the selected video clip behind another video clip.**

   Vertical lines appear to show you where your video clip will appear.

5. **Release the mouse button.**

   Your video clip now appears in its new location.

Adjusting the size of a video clip

Sometimes a video clip contains a little too much extra footage that you'll need to trim. Other times, you might have trimmed a video clip a little too much and need to add more footage. In either case, you can fix this problem and change the size of your video clip by following these steps:

1. **Click a project folder in the Project Library listing.**

   Thumbnail images of all your video clips appear in the center pane (the project window) of the iMovie window.

2. **Move the pointer over a video clip.**

   A yellow rectangle highlights the video clip, and you see a Clock icon in the bottom-left corner of the video clip, as shown in Figure 2-10.

3. **Click the Clock icon.**

   A Trim Clip pane appears. It displays a yellow rectangle that contains the current size of your video clip, along with dimmed thumbnail images of the original video that you used to copy a video clip, as shown in Figure 2-11.

4. **Move the pointer over a handle on the left or right side of the yellow rectangle that defines the size of your video clip.**

   The pointer turns into a two-way pointing arrow.

5. **Click and drag a handle to increase or decrease the size of your video clip.**

6. **Click the Play button to view your edited video clip.**

7. **Click Done when you're happy with the images stored in your video clip.**

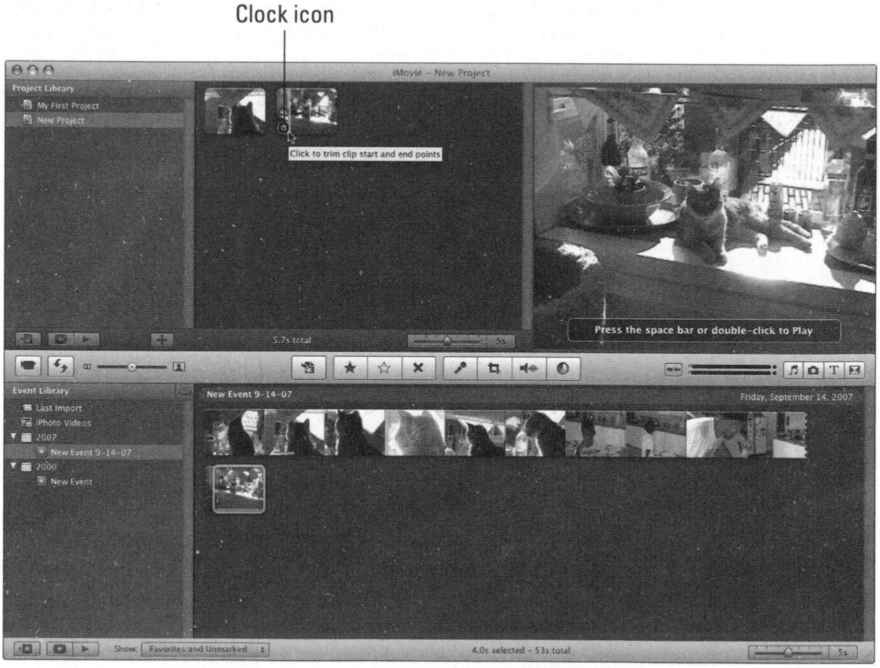

Figure 2-10: Moving the pointer over a video clip displays a Clock icon.

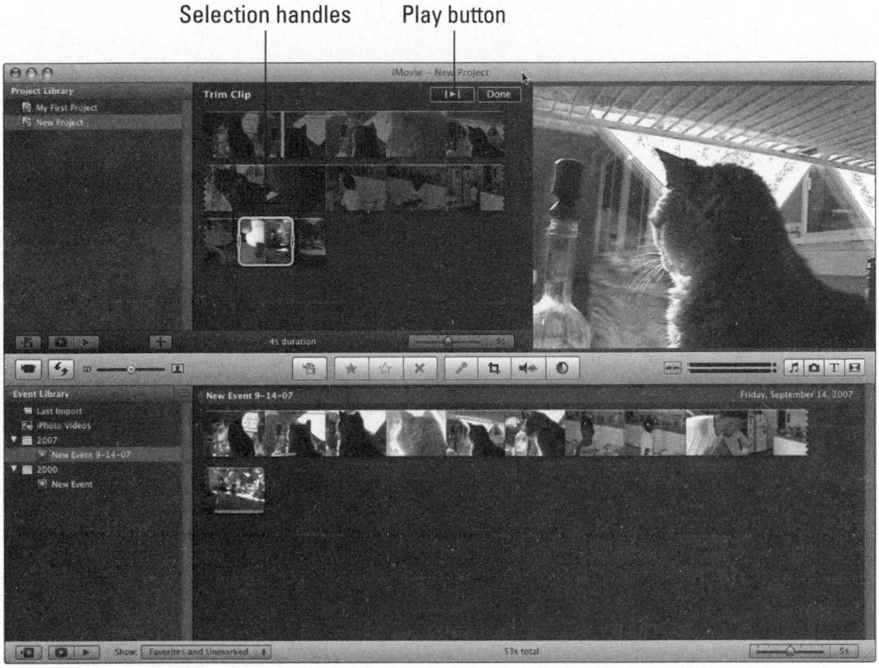

Figure 2-11: The Trim Clip pane lets you adjust the size of your video clip.

Adding titles

Many times, you might want to add titles to your video, such as at the beginning or end. (Beginning titles can display the video's name and purpose, and the ending titles can list the credits of the people who put the video together.)

Titles can appear by themselves or be superimposed over part of your video. To create titles for a project, follow these steps:

1. **Click a project folder in the Project Library listing.**

   Thumbnail images of all your video clips appear in the center pane (the project window) of the iMovie window.

2. **Click the Titles button on the iMovie toolbar.**

   A list of different title styles appears in the Titles browser, as shown in Figure 2-12.

3. **Click and drag a title from the Titles browser onto a video clip or in between two clips.**

4. **Release the mouse button.**

Figure 2-12: The Titles button shows (or hides) different title styles you can use.

If you release the mouse button over a video clip, your title appears superimposed over the video image, as shown in Figure 2-13. If you release the mouse button in between video clips, your title appears as a separate video clip.

5. **Click the blue title balloon that appears over a video clip.**

   Your chosen title format appears in the Preview pane.

6. **Double-click the text you want to edit and type new text, or use the arrow and Delete keys to edit the existing title.**
7. **Click the Show Fonts button to display a Fonts window that lets you choose a different font, font size, and typeface for your text.**
8. **Click the Play button to preview how your titles appear.**
9. **Click Done.**
10. **Click the Titles button to hide the list of available title styles from view.**

    All titles appear as blue title balloons in the project window.

REMEMBER

To delete a title, click the title balloon and press Delete, or choose Edit ➪ Delete Selection.

Figure 2-13: Titles can appear as separate clips or superimposed over existing video clips.

Adding transitions

Normally, when you place video clips in a project folder, those video clips play one after another. Rather than abruptly cutting from one video clip to another, you can add transitions that appear in between video clips. To add a transition, follow these steps:

1. **Click a project folder in the Project Library listing.**

   Thumbnail images of all your video clips appear in the center pane (the project window) of the iMovie window.

2. **Click the Transitions button on the iMovie toolbar.**

   A list of different transitions appears in the Transitions browser, as shown in Figure 2-14.

3. **Click and drag a transition in the Transitions browser between two video clips in the project window.**

   Some different types of transitions include Cube (which spins a cube on the screen where a different video clips appears on each side of the cube) and Page Curl (which peels away one video clip like a piece of paper).

4. **Release the mouse button when a vertical line appears between two video clips.**

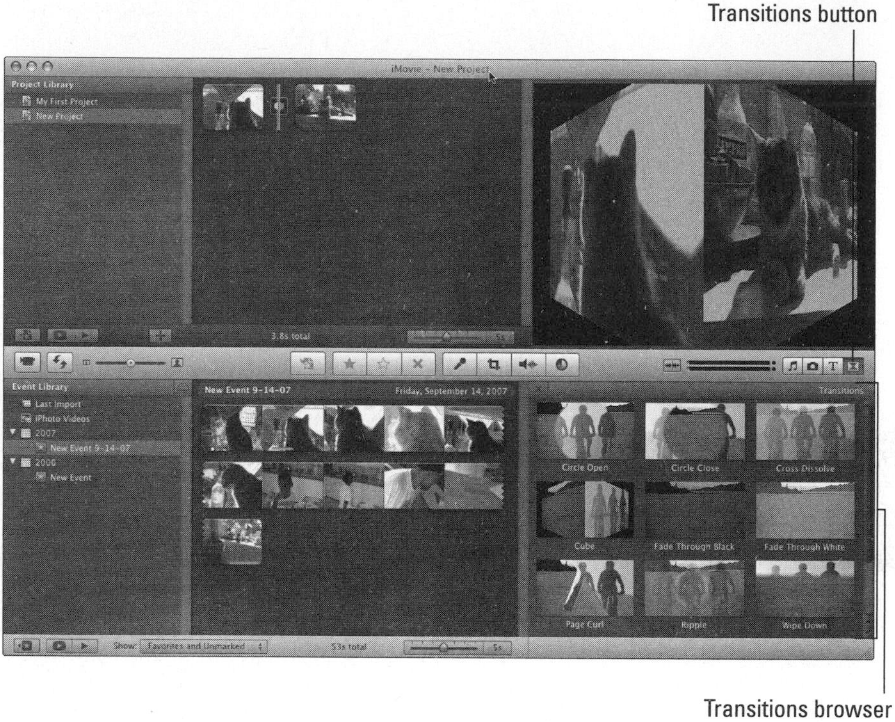

Figure 2-14: Transitions let you create unique visual effects in between video clips.

5. **Move the pointer over the transition.**

   Move the pointer to the right, and the transition plays forward. Move the pointer to the left, and the transition plays backwards.

6. **Click the Transitions button again to hide the list of available transitions.**

Adding audio files

To spice up your video, you can add audio files that play background music or sound effects to match what appears on your video — a car honking, say, or maybe a telephone bell ringing. To add an audio file to a project, follow these steps:

1. **Click a project folder in the Project Library listing.**

   Thumbnail images of all your video clips appear in the center pane (the project window) of the iMovie window.

2. **Click the Music and Sound Effects button on the iMovie toolbar.**

   A list of audio files appears in the Music and Sound Effects browser, as shown in Figure 2-15.

Figure 2-15: Audio files can add music or sound effects to your videos.

3. **In the Music and Sound Effects browser, click an audio file library to use, such as iTunes, GarageBand, or iLife Sound Effects.**

   A list of audio files appears.

4. **Click and drag an audio file onto a video clip displayed in the center pane (the project window) of the iMovie window.**

   A red vertical line appears over the video clip to show you where the audio file will start playing.

5. **Release the mouse button.**

6. **Click the Music and Sound Effects button to hide the list of available audio files.**

Saving a Video

The whole point of organizing video clips in a project is to create a polished video. With iMovie, you can save your project to view on a computer, in iTunes, on an iPod or iPhone, or even on YouTube. You can even save the same video project to different formats in case you need to view your video on your Mac but also want to post a copy on YouTube for other people to enjoy.

If you've created an interesting video that you might want to add to other programs, such as a presentation program, you can save a video in the Media Browser to use in other programs.

Saving a project as a digital video file

You might want to save your iMovie project as a digital video file so you can burn it to DVD later (using iDVD) or give a copy to someone who wants to view it on their own computer. When you save a project as a digital video file, you can save it as an MPEG-4 or a QuickTime file.

Creating an MPEG-4 file

To save a project as an MPEG-4 digital video file, follow these steps:

1. **Click a project folder in the Project Library listing.**

   Thumbnail images of all your video clips appear in the center pane (the project window) of the iMovie window.

2. **Choose Share⇨Export Movie.**

   The Export Movie dialog appears, as shown in Figure 2-16.

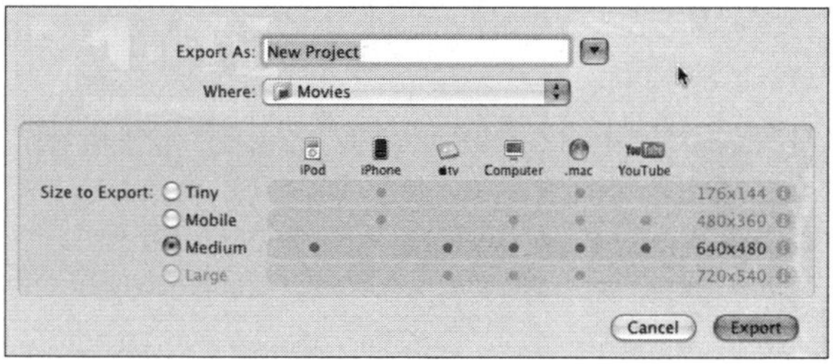

Figure 2-16: The Export Movie dialog lets you choose the resolution for playing on different devices.

3. **Select a Size to Export radio button (such as Medium or Tiny) and click Export.**

   The different sizes available define the frame size. Smaller frame sizes are designed for viewing on smaller screens, such as an iPhone screen, whereas larger frame sizes are designed for viewing on bigger screens, such as a computer or TV set.

Saving (and removing) a video for iTunes

If you create a particularly interesting video and store it on your hard drive, you might later have trouble finding it again. To fix this problem, save your videos in your iTunes library. This way you can quickly find and play videos later.

To save a project that you can play in iTunes, follow these steps:

1. **Click a project folder in the Project Library listing.**

   Thumbnail images of all your video clips appear in the center pane (the project window) of the iMovie window.

2. **Choose Share⇨iTunes.**

   A dialog appears, as shown in Figure 2-17.

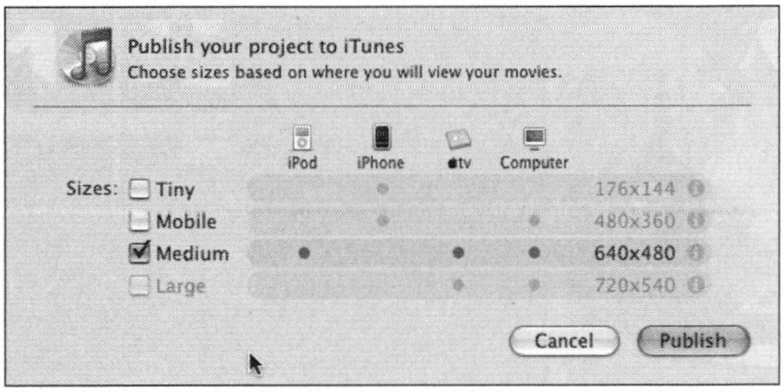

Figure 2-17: The Publish to iTunes dialog lets you choose the resolution for playing on different devices.

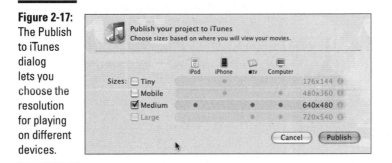

3. **Select or deselect one or more check boxes (such as Medium or Tiny) and click Publish.**

   The different sizes define the frame size of your video. Smaller sizes make your video look best on small screens, such as on mobile phones. Larger sizes make your video look best on larger screens, such as on a TV set. Your movie now appears in your iTunes library on your hard drive.

REMEMBER

After you've saved a movie to iTunes, you can remove it by choosing Share⇨Remove from iTunes.

Saving (and removing) a project for YouTube

One of the latest Internet trends is *video-sharing,* where people post movies on the Internet for everyone to download and enjoy. The most popular video-sharing site (at least at the time of this writing) is YouTube.

In case you've captured an interesting video that you want to post on YouTube, you can save your project to YouTube after setting up a YouTube account (`www.youtube.com`). Then you can upload a video from iMovie to YouTube by following these steps:

1. **Click a project folder in the Project Library listing.**

   Thumbnail images of all your video clips appear in the center pane (the project window) of the iMovie window.

2. **Choose Share➪YouTube.**

   A dialog appears, as shown in Figure 2-18.

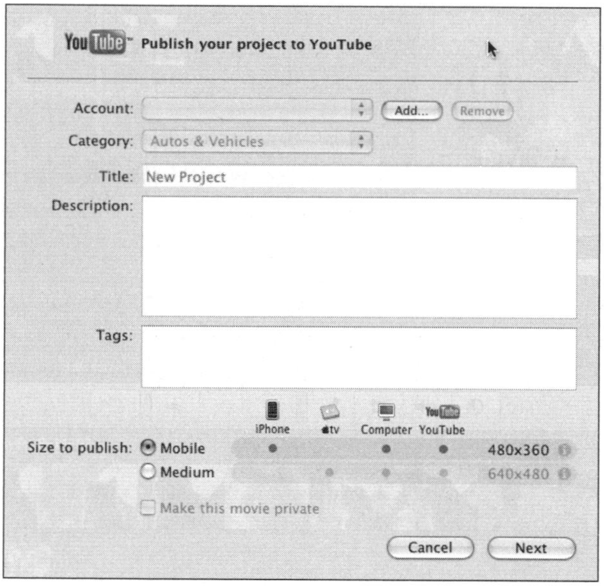

Figure 2-18: The YouTube dialog lets you choose an account, category, and resolution size to store your video.

3. **Click the Account and Category pop-up menus and choose an option.**

4. **Enter information to identify your video in the Title, Description, and Tags text boxes.**

   The information you type to identify your video can help others find it on YouTube when they want to see videos that offer comedy, dogs, or other categories.

5. **Select one of the Size to Publish radio buttons (Mobile or Medium) and click Next.**

   Choose Mobile if you want to create a video frame size of 480 x 272 pixels, which is designed for viewing on small screens, such as on an iPhone. Choose Medium if you want to create a video frame size of 640 x 360 for viewing on an ordinary TV screen. After you click Next, a dialog appears, warning about copyright infringement.

6. **Click the Publish button.**

REMEMBER

After you've saved a movie to YouTube, you can remove it by choosing Share⇨Remove from YouTube.

Saving (and removing) a project in the Media Browser

If you store your movie in the Media Browser, you can access and insert that movie into any program that uses the Media Browser, such as the iWork suite along with many iLife programs (such as iDVD and iWeb) and non-Apple software such as Toast (`www.roxio.com`).

To save a movie in the Media Browser, follow these steps:

1. **Click a project folder in the Project Library listing.**

   Thumbnail images of all your video clips appear in the center pane (the project window) of the iMovie window.

2. **Choose Share⇨Media Browser.**

   The Media Browser dialog appears, as shown in Figure 2-19.

3. **Select or clear one or more Sizes check boxes, such as Tiny or Medium.**

   The different sizes define the frame size, and the dots identify the type of devices that your video can play on.

4. **Click the Publish button.**

REMEMBER

After you've saved a movie to the Media Browser, you can remove it by choosing Share⇨Remove from Media Browser.

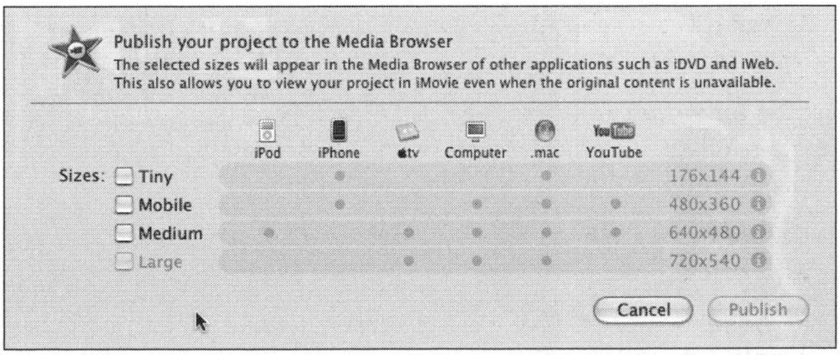
Publish your project to the Media Browser
The selected sizes will appear in the Media Browser of other applications such as iDVD and iWeb.
This also allows you to view your project in iMovie even when the original content is unavailable.
iPod
iPhone
tv
Computer
.mac
YouTube
Sizes:
Tiny
Mobile
Medium
Large
176x144
480x360
640x480
720x540
Cancel
Publish

Figure 2-19: The Media Browser dialog lets you choose different resolutions.

Chapter 3: Using iDVD

In This Chapter

- **Burning a DVD from a video camcorder**
- **Creating a DVD with the Magic iDVD option**
- **Working with iDVD projects**

If you simply wanted to share digital photographs and movies with others, you could burn your pictures and movies as separate files onto a DVD. Friends and family could see your pictures or movies, but they'd have to search through the DVD's directory structure to find each individual file. Although this method works, it makes looking at pictures and movies about as tedious as browsing a hard drive, looking for word processor or spreadsheet documents.

To make DVDs useful for both storing and presenting digital pictures and movies, use the iDVD program. iDVD lets you create photo slideshows or movies complete with menus and graphics that can play on any DVD player. If you ever dreamed of creating your own Hollywood-style DVDs to present your home movies or digital photographs, iDVD will help you achieve your dreams.

To create a DVD, iDVD gives you three choices:

- **OneStep DVD:** Transfers a video directly from a digital video camcorder to a DVD.
- **Magic iDVD:** Provides a variety of DVD templates that you can modify for creating menus to organize the content of digital photographs and movies stored on the DVD.
- **A DVD project:** Lets you create custom DVD menus and graphics for storing and presenting digital photographs and movies.

REMEMBER

To burn DVDs using iDVD, you need a Mac that can write to DVDs. If your Mac can't write to DVDs, you can still create an iDVD project, but you'll have to transfer it to another Mac to create your DVD.

Burning a Video Straight to DVD

The OneStep DVD option lets you burn a video from your video camcorder and store it to a recordable DVD in your Mac. When you insert your finished

DVD into a DVD player, your video simply starts playing immediately, with no fancy DVD menus or graphics.

Although the OneStep DVD option creates the illusion of burning video from a camcorder direct to a DVD, it's actually encoding your video to an MPEG-2 video file format and creating various files on your hard disk before it burns these files to a DVD.

To burn a video to a DVD with the OneStep DVD option, follow these steps:

1. **Load iDVD. (Click on the iDVD icon on the Dock or double-click on the iDVD icon in the Applications folder to load iDVD.)**

   The iDVD opening window appears, as shown in Figure 3-1.

2. **Click the OneStep DVD button.**

   A dialog appears, telling you to connect your video camcorder to your Mac and insert a recordable DVD.

3. **Connect your video camcorder to your Mac using a FireWire cable.**
4. **Insert a recordable DVD in your Mac.**
5. **Click OK.**

   A dialog appears to let you know when the DVD has finished burning.

6. **Click Done.**

   The DVD remains in your Mac so you can either view it using the DVD Player or eject it yourself.

Figure 3-1: The iDVD opening window displays your options for creating a DVD.

Creating a DVD with the Magic iDVD Option

The Magic iDVD option provides predesigned templates that you can customize to create DVD menus. To choose the Magic iDVD option, follow these steps:

1. **Load iDVD.**

   The iDVD opening window appears (refer to Figure 3-1).

2. **Click the Magic iDVD button.**

   The Magic iDVD window appears, as shown in Figure 3-2.

3. **Type a descriptive name for your DVD in the DVD Title text box.**

4. **(Optional) Click on the Themes pop-up menu and choose a category of themes, such as 7.0 Themes or 6.0 Themes.**

   The Themes pop-up menu provides themes used by different versions of iDVD. So, if you wanted to use themes used by version 6.0 of iDVD, choose 6.0 Themes. (The current version of iDVD is 7.0.)

5. **Choose a theme, such as Vintage Vinyl or Sunflower, from the Themes browser.**

   Each theme offers a different appearance for your DVD menus. Each theme name describes its appearance, so Sunflower displays a big sunflower while Vintage Vinyl displays an old turntable and vinyl record.

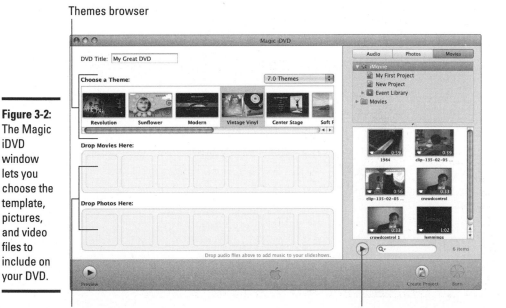

Figure 3-2: The Magic iDVD window lets you choose the template, pictures, and video files to include on your DVD.

6. **In the right pane of the Magic iDVD window, click the Movies tab.**

   A list of movies stored in your Movies folder appears.

7. **Click and drag a movie that you want to add to your DVD onto the Drop Movies Here drop well.**

   To select multiple movies, hold down the ⌘ key and click each movie you want to add to your DVD.

   If you click a movie and click the Play button, you can see a thumbnail image of your movie.

8. **In the right pane of the Magic iDVD window, click the Photos tab.**

   A list of photos stored in iPhoto appears (refer to Figure 3-2).

9. **Click and drag a picture that you want to add to your DVD onto the Drop Photos Here drop well.**

   To select multiple pictures, hold down the ⌘ key and click each picture you want to add to your DVD.

   Each drop well represents a separate slideshow. Generally, you'll want to put several pictures in the same drop well to create a slideshow of multiple pictures. Underneath each drop well, iDVD lists the number of slides currently stored, such as "2 slides."

10. **In the right pane of the Magic iDVD window, click the Audio tab.**

    A list of audio files stored in iTunes and GarageBand appears.

11. **Click and drag an audio file that you want to play during a photo slideshow onto the Drop Photos Here drop well.**

    Pictures that include audio appear with an audio icon over them, as shown in Figure 3-3.

    Keep in mind that, if you add a 3-minute audio file over a slideshow (drop well) that contains 3 slides, each slide will appear for 1 minute until the entire audio file finishes playing. If you add a 3-minute audio file to a slideshow of 30 slides, each slide will appear for 0.1 minutes. So the more slides (pictures) you add, the faster the images pop up and disappear while an audio file plays.

12. **Click the Preview button in the lower-left corner.**

    An iDVD Preview window appears with a controller (which mimics a typical handheld remote control) so you can take your DVD through its paces to make sure it works the way you want, as shown in Figure 3-4.

13. **Click Exit on the controller on the screen.**

    The Magic iDVD window appears again.

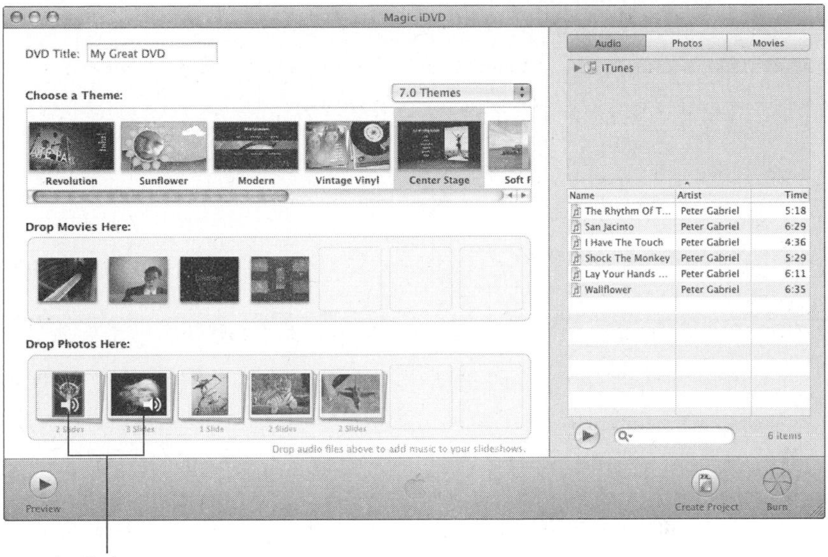

Audio icons

Figure 3-3: An audio icon identifies pictures that include an audio file.

14. **Select one of the following:**

- *Create Project:* Lets you save your DVD design to modify it later.
- *Burn:* Burns your music, pictures, and movies using your chosen DVD theme. If you choose this option, you'll need to insert a recordable DVD in your Mac.

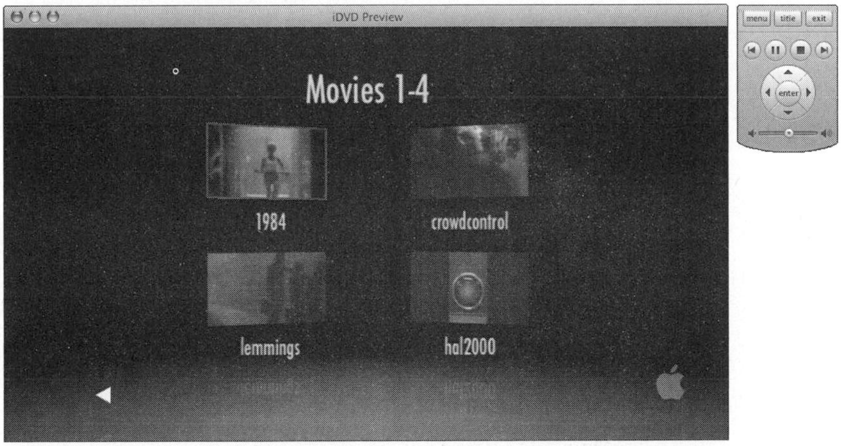

Figure 3-4: The iDVD Preview window shows you how your DVD will look when played.

Working with iDVD Projects

For maximum flexibility, you can design your own DVD menus and add graphics to give your DVD a polished, professional look. When you create your own DVD project, you can save it and edit it later.

The different parts of an iDVD project are

- ✦ **Title menu:** Displays a list of the different contents of the DVD, such as movies or slideshows.
- ✦ **Slideshows:** Displays a slideshow of multiple digital photographs.
- ✦ **Movies:** Displays a movie.
- ✦ **Text:** Displays text on-screen — useful for providing instructions or descriptions about the DVD.
- ✦ **Submenus:** Displays another screen where you can offer additional slideshows or movies.
- ✦ **Opening content:** Displays a photo or movie that appears as soon as someone inserts the DVD into their DVD player. In many commercial DVDs, the opening content is usually an FBI warning about copyright infringement.

REMEMBER

Not every iDVD project uses all of the preceding parts. At the very least, an iDVD project needs a title menu and at least one slideshow or movie.

To create a DVD project, follow these steps:

1. **Load iDVD.**

   The iDVD opening window appears (refer to Figure 3-1).

2. **Click the Create a New Project button.**

   A Create Project dialog appears, as shown in Figure 3-5. (If you already created a project and want to edit it, all you need to do is click the Open an Existing Project button.)

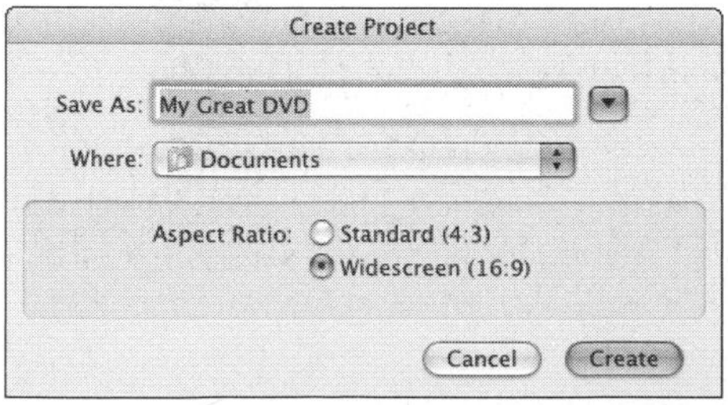

Figure 3-5: The Create Project dialog lets you define a name and aspect ratio for your DVD.

3. **Enter a descriptive name for your project into the Save As text box.**
4. **Click in the Standard (for ordinary TV screens) or Widescreen (for widescreen TVs) radio button under the Aspect Ratio group.**

   Choosing Standard optimizes your DVD project for an ordinary TV set, although it will still play on a widescreen TV — it just won't look as nice. Likewise, choosing Widescreen lets a DVD project play on an ordinary TV set, but it won't look as nice as on a widescreen TV.
5. **Click the Create button.**

   An iDVD project window appears, as shown in Figure 3-6. You can now proceed with sprucing up your project.
6. **Click the Themes button in the bottom-right corner of the iDVD Project window.**

   The Themes browser appears in the right pane of the window.
7. **(Optional) Click on the Themes pop-up menu and choose a category of themes such as 7.0 Themes or 6.0 Themes.**

   The Themes pop-up menu provides themes used by different versions of iDVD. So if you wanted to use themes used by version 6.0 of iDVD, choose 6.0 Themes. (The current version of iDVD is 7.0.)
8. **Choose a theme, such as Vintage Vinyl or Sunflower, from the Themes browser.**

   Each theme offers a different appearance for your DVD menus. Each theme name describes its appearance, so Sunflower displays a big sunflower while Vintage Vinyl displays an old turntable and vinyl record.

Figure 3-6: The iDVD project window lets you design your menus.

9. **Choose a theme from the Themes browser.**

   Your chosen theme appears in the iDVD window, as shown in Figure 3-7. Depending on the theme you choose, you might see Drop Zones where you can place pictures or video.

10. **Choose File➪Save.**

    After saving your iDVD project, you can quit the iDVD program or continue with the next section to add pictures to your title menus.

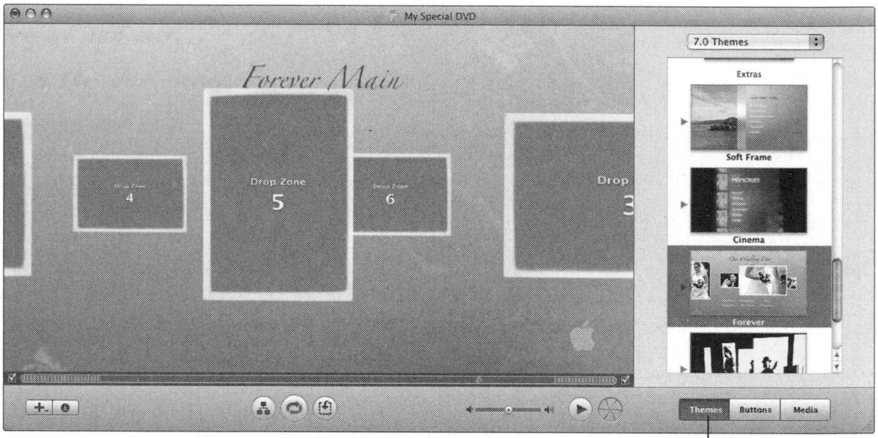

Figure 3-7: Your chosen theme appears in the iDVD project window.

Adding photos to a title menu theme

Some themes just display a colorful graphic background but others provide placeholders for adding your own pictures to further customize the theme. To add your own pictures

1. **Open the iDVD project you want to add pictures to.**

   You can open a previously saved project by choosing File➪Open or the Open an Existing Project button when iDVD first loads.

2. **Click the Media button in the bottom-right corner of the iDVD project window.**

   The Audio, Photos, and Movies tab appear in the upper right corner of the iDVD window.

3. **Click the Photos button.**

   A list of photos stored in iPhoto appears, which you can add to your title menu.

4. **Click the Edit Drop Zones button.**

   A list of Drop Zones appears, as shown in Figure 3-8.

5. **Click and drag a photo onto a Drop Zone and release the mouse button.**

   Your chosen picture now appears as part of the DVD theme.

6. **Repeat Step 7 for any additional photographs you need to add to another Drop Zone.**

7. **Choose File⇨Save.**

   After saving your iDVD project, you can quit the iDVD program or continue with the next section to add options to your title menus.

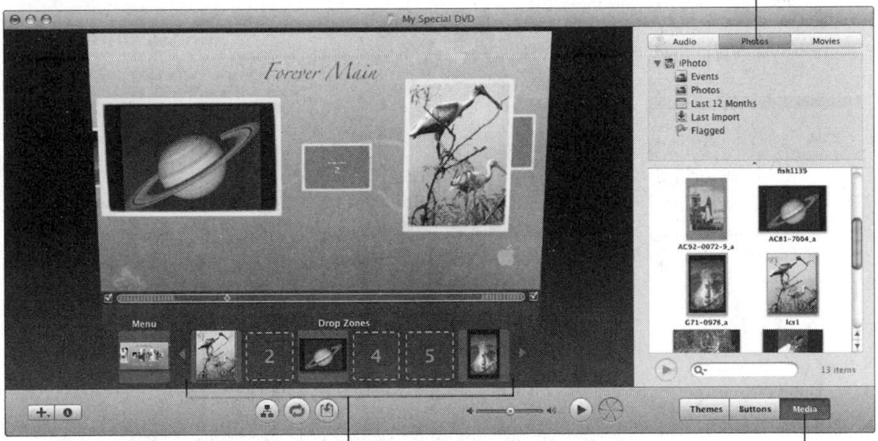

Figure 3-8: You can drag and drop photos to customize a DVD menu.

Adding options to the title menu

After you've defined a theme and possibly added some photos for your title menu, you can add options that the viewer can choose. The four types of options you can display on the title menu are

- ✦ Slideshow menus
- ✦ Movie menus
- ✦ Text
- ✦ Submenus

Creating a Slideshow

When a viewer selects a Slideshow menu option, the DVD displays one or more digital photographs. To add a slideshow option to the title menu, you need to create a menu that allows viewers to choose your slideshow. Then you need to create the slideshow itself by following these steps:

1. **Choose Project⇨Add Slideshow (or press ⌘+L).**

   A My Slideshow button appears on your title menu, as shown in Figure 3-9.

2. **Click the My Slideshow button.**

   The My Slideshow text appears highlighted and displays Font, Style, and Font Size pop-up menus, as shown in Figure 3-10.

3. **Type descriptive text for your slideshow button.**

4. **(Optional) Click in the Font, Style, or Font Size pop-up menus to choose how to format your text.**

5. **Double-click your slideshow button.**

   The iDVD project window displays a Drag Images Here box. Now you can start building the slideshow itself.

6. **Click and drag a photograph displayed in the right pane onto the Drag Images Here box and then release the mouse button.**

   To select multiple pictures, hold down the Command key and click on each picture you want to select.

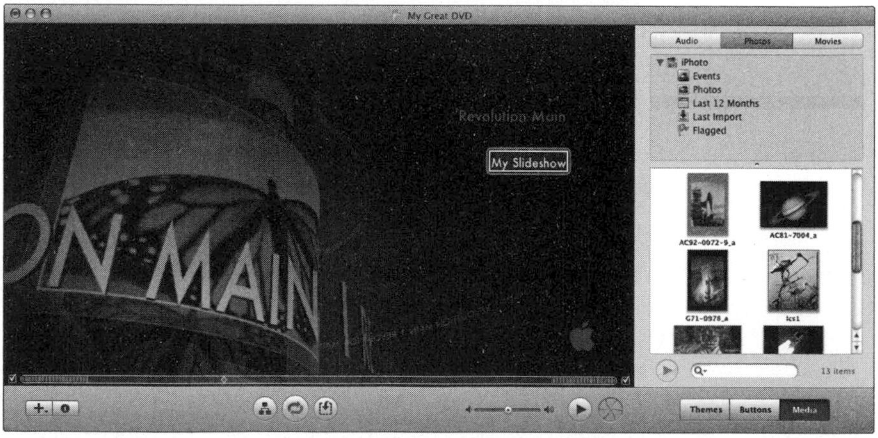

Figure 3-9: A slideshow menu button appears as a generic My Slideshow option.

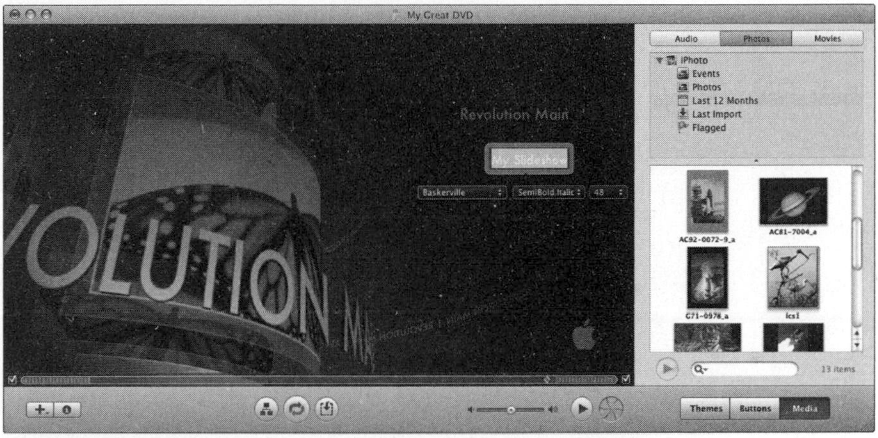

Figure 3-10: A slideshow menu button's pop-up menus let you customize the appearance of the slideshow button.

7. Your chosen pictures appear in the Slideshow window, numbered to show you the order in which your pictures will appear, as shown in Figure 3-11.

   A slideshow can hold up to 99 pictures.

8. **(Optional) Click in the Slide Duration pop-up menu and choose a new time period for how long a slide stays onscreen, such as 1 or 10 seconds.**

9. **(Optional) Click in the Transition pop-up menu and choose a transition to display between slides, such as Dissolve or Twirl.**

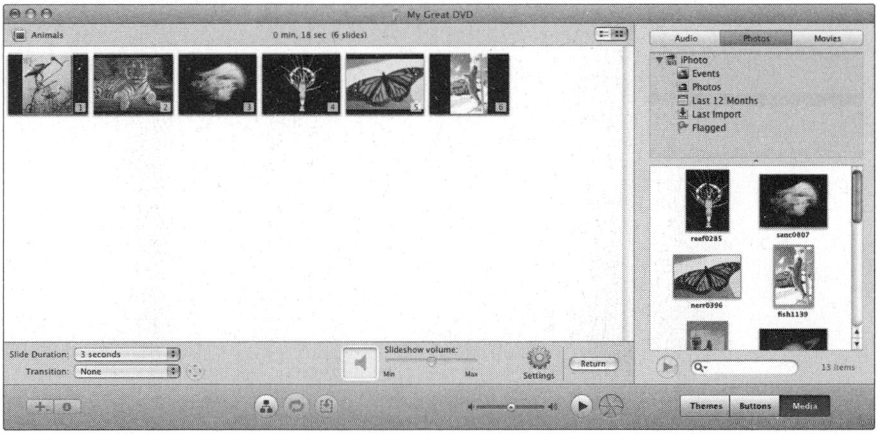

Figure 3-11: A slideshow consists of multiple pictures.

10. **(Optional) Click the Audio button, click and drag an audio file from the listing in the right pane onto the Audio drop well (it looks like a speaker icon to the left of the Slideshow volume slider), and then release the mouse button.**

11. **(Optional) If you added an audio file to a slideshow, click the Slide Duration pop-up menu and choose how long you want the audio file to play, such as 10 seconds.**

    If you add an audio file to a slideshow, the Slide Duration pop-up menu defaults to the Fit To Audio option, which means your pictures appear until the audio file is done playing.

12. **Click Return.**

    Your DVD title menu appears again.

13. **Choose File⇨Save.**

You need to create a different slideshow menu option for each slideshow you want to include on your DVD.

Creating a Movie menu option

When a viewer selects a Movie menu option, the DVD plays a movie. To create a Movie menu option on the title menu, follow these steps:

1. **Choose Project⇨Add Movie.**

   An Add Movie Here button appears, as shown in Figure 3-12.

2. **Click and drag a movie displayed in the right pane onto the Add Movie Here button and then release the mouse button.**

   The name of your movie appears on the button.

3. **Choose File⇨Save.**

For a faster way to create Movie menu buttons, just click and drag a movie shown in the right pane anywhere onto your title menu and then release the mouse button to create a button that will play your chosen movie.

Creating text

Sometimes you might want to add text on a title menu to provide additional descriptions or instructions. To add text on the title menu screen, follow these steps:

1. **Choose Project⇨Add Text (or choose ⌘+K).**

   A Click to Edit text box appears.

Figure 3-12: An Add Movie Here button provides a link to a movie.

2. **Click the Click to Edit text box.**

   Font, Style, and Font Size pop-up menus appear, as shown in Figure 3-13.

3. **Type descriptive text for your slideshow button.**
4. **(Optional) Click in the Font, Style, or Font Size pop-up menus to choose how to format your text.**
5. **Choose File⇨Save.**

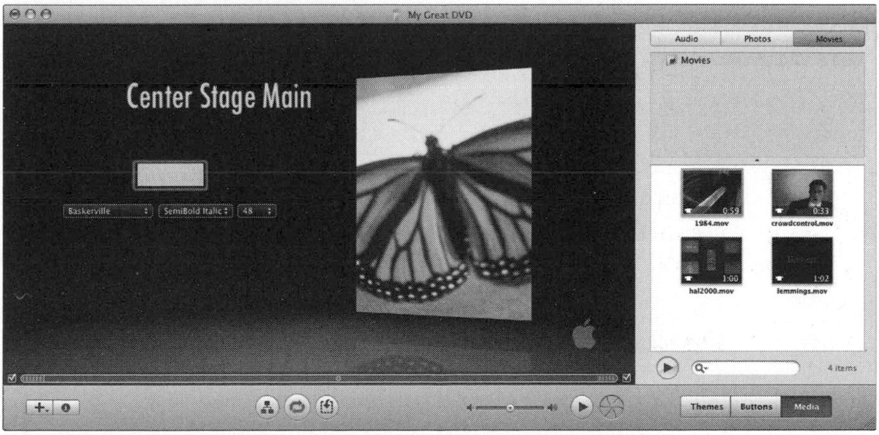

Figure 3-13: A Click to Edit text box lets you type text that appears on the title menu screen.

Creating a submenu

If you have too many options on the title menu, the title menu can look cluttered. To fix this, you might need to create a submenu on your title menu and then place additional Slideshow or Movie options on this submenu. To create a submenu, follow these steps:

1. **Choose Project➪Add Submenu.**

   A My Submenu button appears.
2. **Click the My Submenu button.**

   Font, Style, and Font Size pop-up menus appear.
3. **Type descriptive text for your submenu button.**
4. **(Optional) Click in the Font, Style, or Font Size pop-up menus to choose how to format your text.**
5. **Double-click the submenu button.**

   The iDVD window displays a new screen where you can add slideshows, movies, text, or even additional submenus.
6. **Choose Project➪Add Title Menu Button.**

   The Title Menu button lets viewers jump back to the title menu from your submenu. At this point, you need to add a Slideshow or Movie menu option on your submenu.

Moving and deleting buttons

After you create a Slideshow, Movie, Submenu, or Text button on a screen, you can move or delete it. To move a button, follow these steps:

1. **Click the button you want to move.**

   The text inside your button appears highlighted.
2. **Click and drag your selected button to its new location and then release the mouse button.**

Rather than move a button, you might want to delete it altogether. To delete a button, follow these steps:

1. **Click the button you want to delete.**

   The text inside your button appears highlighted.
2. **Choose Edit➪Delete.**

   Your button disappears in an animated puff of smoke.

Defining opening content for your DVD

You can display a picture or a movie as soon as someone inserts your DVD into a DVD player, which is called the opening content. This opening content appears before the title menu appears. To define a picture or movie to display as the opening content, follow these steps:

1. **Choose View⇨Show Map (or click the Show the DVD Map icon, which looks like a miniature organization chart with a box connected to two other boxes).**

   The iDVD window displays a blank content box that displays the message `Drag content here to automatically play when the disc is inserted`, as shown in Figure 3-14.

2. **Click the Photos or Movies button at the top of the right pane to display either your iPhoto pictures or the movies stored in your Movies folder.**
3. **Click and drag a picture or movie onto the blank content box.**
4. **Release the mouse button.**

REMEMBER

The Show Map command can be particularly useful so you can see the layout of your entire iDVD project.

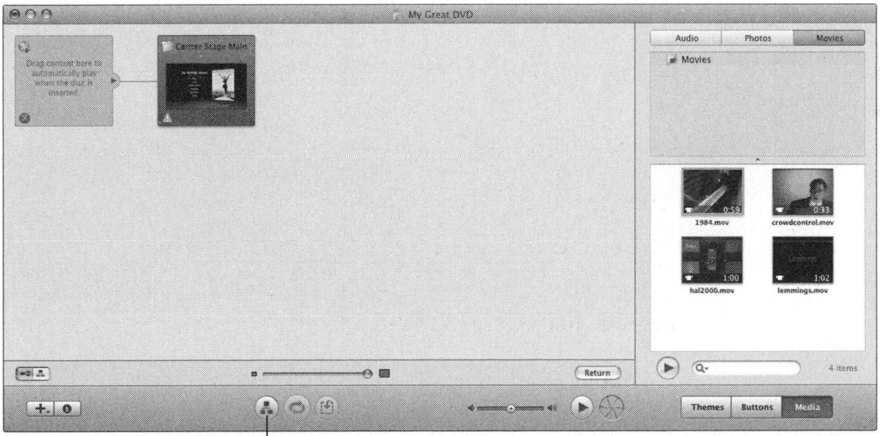

Figure 3-14: The map view of your iDVD project displays the blank content box.

Saving your iDVD project

After you're finished designing your DVD project, you can save your entire project in one of three ways:

- As a DVD
- As a disc image (`.img`) file
- As files stored in a VIDEO_TS folder

Burning to a DVD

When you save your iDVD project to a DVD, you create a DVD that you can give to anyone to play on any DVD player. To burn an iDVD project to a DVD, follow these steps:

1. **Insert a blank DVD into your Mac.**
2. **Choose File⇨Burn DVD.**

Saving to a disc image

As an alternative to saving an iDVD project to a DVD, you can also save an iDVD project to a disc image. A *disc image* is a single file that contains the entire contents of a drive or folder. By storing an iDVD project as a disc image, you can transfer a single (large) file to someone over the Internet. Then that person can open that disc image to retrieve the entire contents of your iDVD project and burn the disc image contents to a DVD.

To save your iDVD project to a disc image, follow these steps:

1. **Choose File⇨Save as Disc Image.**

   A Save Disc Image As dialog appears.
2. **Type a descriptive name for your disc image in the Save As text box.**
3. **Choose a location to store your disc image from the Where pop-up menu.**
4. **Click Save.**

Saving to a VIDEO_TS folder

You can also save your entire iDVD project inside a VIDEO_TS folder, which essentially lets you store the contents of your iDVD project as separate files stored in a folder. By storing a DVD in a folder, you can play your DVD directly off the hard drive.

To save your iDVD project to a folder, follow these steps:

1. **Choose File⇨Save as VIDEO_TS Folder.**

   A Save VIDEO_TS Folder As dialog appears.

2. **Type a descriptive name for your folder in the Save As text box.**
3. **Choose a location to store your folder from the Where pop-up menu.**
4. **Click Save.**

When you save an iDVD project as a VIDEO_TS folder, you can open and play the contents of that VIDEO_TS folder by using the DVD Player program in the Applications folder of any Mac. If you later decide to burn the contents of a VIDEO_TS folder to a DVD, make sure you burn the DVD in UDF format to create a DVD that can play in other DVD players.

Chapter 4: Creating Web Sites with iWeb

In This Chapter

- Understanding the parts of a Web page
- Creating Web sites
- Designing Web pages
- Publishing Web pages

Almost everyone has a Web site these days. Some people use Web sites to publicize their businesses, and others use Web sites as their sole means of reaching customers, such as online sellers of books, food, or pet products. Some people run Web sites focusing on their favorite hobbies, such as gardening or Star Trek trivia. No matter what your interests and needs, setting up a Web site can be fun, rewarding, and perhaps profitable as well.

Although creating Web pages isn't difficult, it's not as straightforward as you might hope. That's why Apple created iWeb, a special program designed to make creating Web pages easy, fun, and fast. With iWeb, you can create professional-looking Web pages in minutes instead of days.

When creating Web pages, make sure the information you put on those Web pages is something that won't embarrass you later.

The Parts of a Web Page

Think of a Web page as an endless sheet of paper that you can stretch in all directions to make it as large or as small as you want. On this sheet, you can paste text, pictures, graphics, movies, songs, and even programs for others to access. To help guide people around your Web pages, you also need to add navigational aids called *hyperlinks,* also commonly called *links.* By clicking a link, people can jump from one Web page to another or from one location on a page to another location on that same Web page. Figure 4-1 shows the typical parts of a Web page.

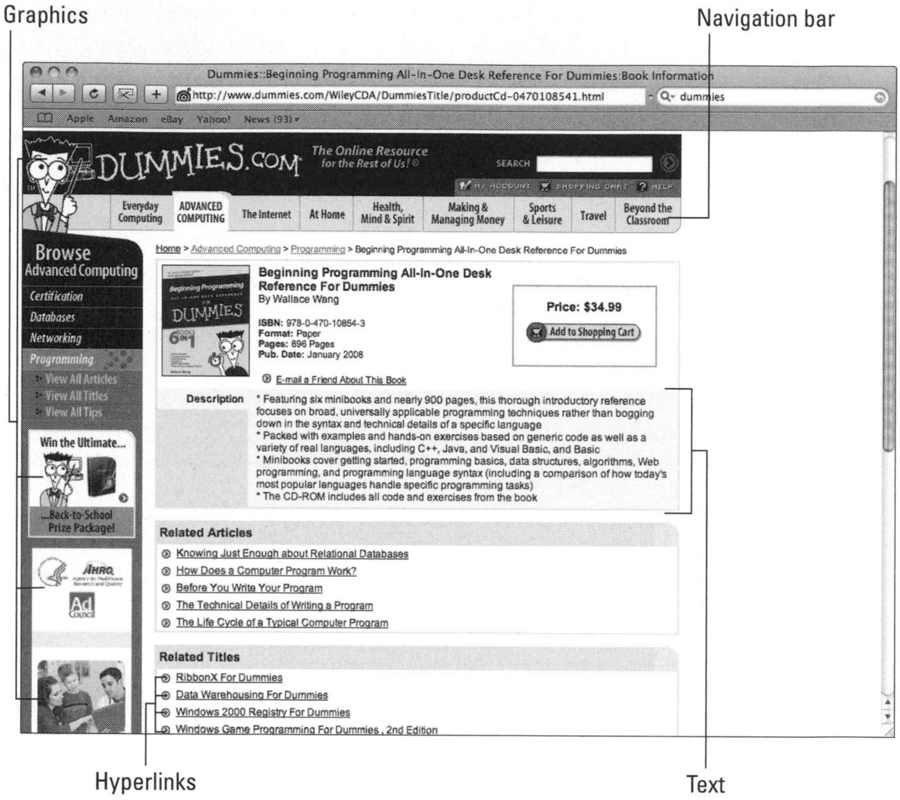

Figure 4-1: A Web page consists of text and graphics.

The purpose of text

Text generally serves two purposes. First, text provides content on a Web page, such as a news story or a step-by-step description for how to bake a cake. Second, text is often used to create hyperlinks to other Web pages or to entirely different Web sites altogether.

To make text easy to find and read, you can add color, change the fonts and font size, or display text in different styles such as bold and italics. Some Web pages might contain lots of text (such as a news site like CNN (`www.cnn.com`), whereas others might contain a minimal amount of text, such as a Web site displaying photographs with text simply listing the photograph's name or topic.

The purpose of graphics

Graphics can serve a purely decorative function, such as a company logo displayed in the corner of the Web page. Besides decorative purposes, graphics can also be used as content and as hyperlinks.

As content, graphics provide information, such as photographs on a news site or pictures of your family on a personal site. Instead of showing pictures, some graphics can display decorative text in ways that ordinary text cannot produce. For example, a Web site for a plant nursery might have its name displayed in text or graphics. When displayed as text, the nursery's name might appear in a different font or bold. When displayed as a graphic image, that same nursery's name could appear in different fonts as well as having a picture of a vine intertwined between the characters of the nursery's name.

It's impossible to search for text stored as a graphic image. That's why many Web sites list an e-mail address as a graphic image; if they list that e-mail address as text, another computer can scan the Web site for text that contains an e-mail address to send junk e-mail.

Finally, graphics, like text, are often used to create hyperlinks, such as menus that offer options for displaying different Web pages. Such graphic hyperlinks often provide you with a more colorful way to present hyperlinks than plain text, such as appearing as buttons or pull-down menus.

Putting together a Web page

To create a Web page with other programs, you have to learn the cryptic language that creates Web pages, known as HTML (*H*yper*T*ext *M*arkup *L*anguage). Since learning the HTML language just to create a Web page might be intimidating, iWeb simplifies this task by creating HTML code for you "behind the scenes." All *you* have to do is arrange objects (text and graphics) on a Web page.

Although you could create a Web page starting with a blank page, it's far easier to create a Web page by modifying a one that's already been designed for you. With iWeb, you can choose from a variety of predesigned Web page templates, which already contain background graphics, text, and pictures that you can customize. Such templates act like a library of term papers that you can modify and pass off as your own.

Creating a Web Site in iWeb

Every Web site contains one or more Web pages. To design a Web site, you need to decide how many Web pages you need, the purpose for each Web page, and the overall appearance you want to use for each Web page.

The number of Web pages you need can vary depending on the Web site's purpose If you're putting together an online store to sell food, books, or pet supplies, you might need dozens (or even hundreds) of separate Web pages to list all your products. You can always add and delete Web pages as you need them.

After you know (approximately) how many Web pages you'll need and what you want each Web page to offer, the next step is to pick a theme, which defines the overall appearance of each Web page, such as a background color or decorative graphic along the borders.

Picking a theme

A theme provides a consistent appearance for every Web page that makes up your Web site. One part of your Web site might list products for sale, so you might use one theme for product listings. Another part of your Web site might list company news so those Web pages might use a different theme. Themes simply help visually organize similar information.

To pick a theme for your Web pages, follow these steps:

1. **Load iWeb. (Click the iWeb icon on the Dock or double-click the iWeb icon in the Applications folder.)**
2. **Choose File➪New Site.**

   A dialog appears, listing different themes in the Theme list on the left and displaying the appearance of specific types of Web pages on the right, as shown in Figure 4-2.
3. **Click a theme in the Theme list.**

   Each time you click a different theme, the Web pages in the right pane show you how that new theme displays each type of Web page — Welcome page, About Me page, Photos page, whatever.

If you click in the pop-up menu in the upper left corner of the iWeb dialog, you can choose themes used with older versions of iWeb such as version 2.0, 1.1, or 1.0.

4. **Click one of the following types of Web pages in the right pane:**
   - *Welcome:* Introduces your Web site. The Welcome page is typically the first Web page visitors see when they visit a specific site such as `www.dummies.com`.
   - *About Me:* Describes yourself or your company.
   - *Photos:* Displays digital pictures, such as those stored in iPhoto, for everyone to see.
   - *My Albums:* Displays groups of different photo categories for people to browse.
   - *Movie:* Displays a digital video that people can watch directly in your Web page.

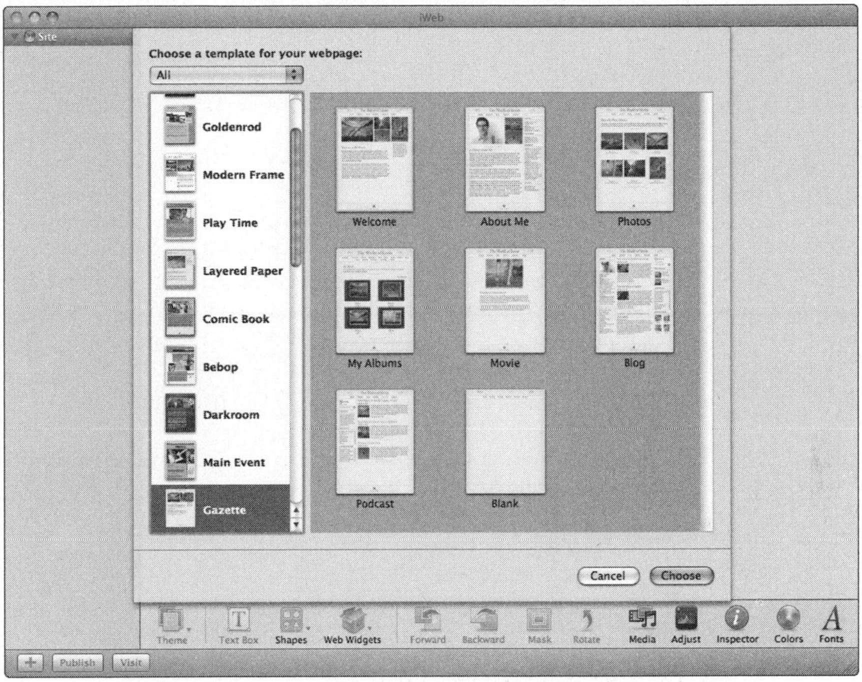

Figure 4-2: Every theme displays Web pages in a slightly different appearance.

- *Blog:* Provides space for typing your thoughts about different topics.
- *Podcast:* Displays lists of audio recordings (podcasts) that others can hear directly off your Web page.
- *Blank:* Provides a Web page that incorporates a specific theme so you can add anything you want to it.

5. **Click Choose.**

   The Web page that appears in the iWeb window is all decked out in your chosen theme, as shown in Figure 4-3. You may see pictures of strange people and gibberish text. This is known as placeholder text and graphics, which you'll have to replace, as explained later in this chapter in the "Designing a Web Page" section.

Adding new pages

Because Web sites typically contain more than one Web page, you often need to add more Web pages to your Web site. To add a Web page, follow these steps:

1. **Choose File⇨New Page (or press ⌘+N).**

   The list of available Web page templates appears again with your current theme already highlighted (refer to Figure 4-2).

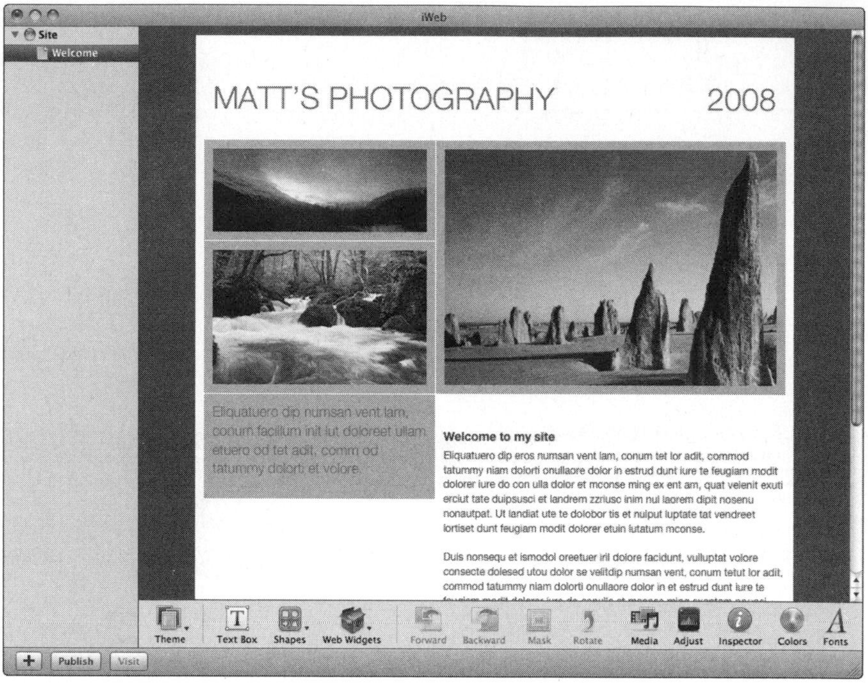

Figure 4-3: A Welcome page shows up in the iWeb window.

2. **Select a new page you want to add, such as Podcast or My Albums, and then click Choose.**

   Your new Web page appears in the iWeb window.

Deleting Web pages

If you've added too many Web pages or suddenly find you don't need a Web page after all, you can delete that Web page. To delete a Web page, follow these steps:

1. **Click the Web page that you want to delete in the sidebar of the iWeb window.**
2. **Choose Edit➪Delete Page.**

   Your chosen Web page disappears, along with any text or graphics you stored on that Web page.

REMEMBER

If you accidentally delete a Web page, press ⌘+Z or choose Edit➪Undo to retrieve the deleted Web page.

Designing a Web Page

With the exception of the Blank Web page template, every iWeb template displays a Web page filled with placeholder text and graphic images that you can then replace with your own text and pictures.

Replacing placeholder text

Placeholder text is meant to give you a rough idea of what the text might look like on the Web page. To change placeholder text, follow these steps:

1. **In the sidebar of the iWeb window, click the Web page that you want to modify.**

   Your chosen Web page appears in the right pane of the iWeb window.

2. **Double-click the text you want to edit or replace.**

   Your chosen text appears highlighted.

3. **Type new text or press the arrow and Delete keys to edit the existing text.**

TIP

Instead of typing new text, you can always copy text from another program and paste it over the placeholder text instead.

Replacing placeholder graphics

Placeholder graphics are meant to give you some idea how a picture would work in a particular area of your page. To replace placeholder graphics with some graphics of your own, follow these steps:

1. **In the sidebar of the iWeb window, click the Web page you want to modify.**

   Your chosen Web page appears in the right pane of the iWeb window.

2. **Click the Media button that appears at the bottom of the iWeb window.**

   A Media window appears.

3. **Click the Photos button.**

   Your iPhoto library appears in the Media Browser, as shown in Figure 4-4.

4. **Click and drag a picture you want to use onto the placeholder graphic image you want to replace.**

5. **Release the mouse button.**

   Your iPhoto picture now appears on your Web page.

6. **Click the Close button of the Media window.**

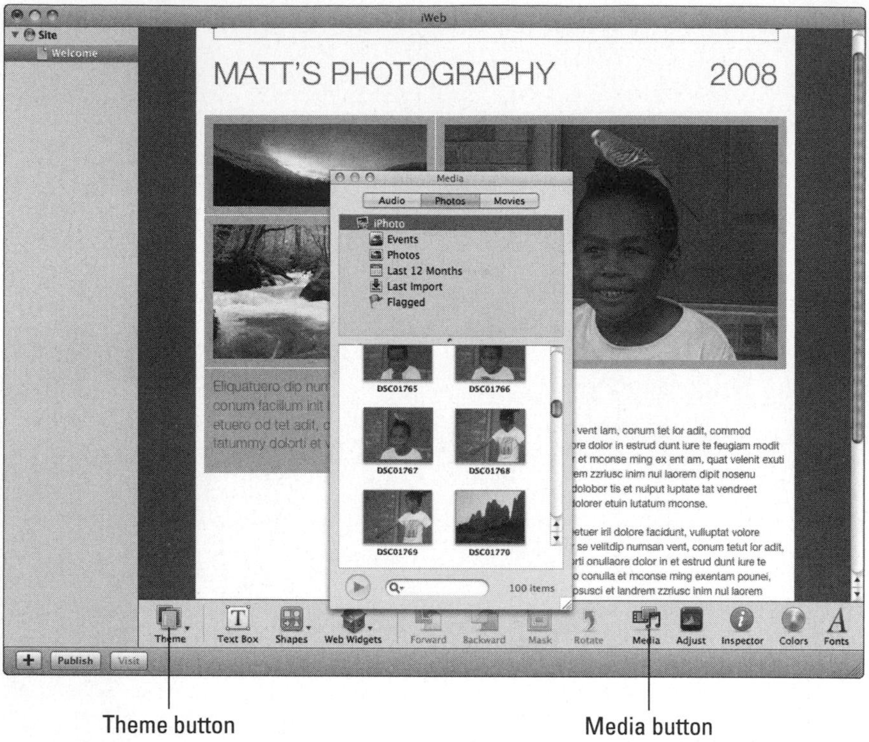

Figure 4-4: The Media browser displays all your iPhoto pictures.

Changing the Web page theme

You might end up modifying a Web page with text and graphics and suddenly realize that you don't like the theme you chose after all. To change a Web page's theme while leaving your content (text and graphics you've added) unchanged, follow these steps:

1. **In the sidebar of the iWeb window, click the Web page you want to modify.**

   Your chosen Web page appears in the right pane of the iWeb window.

2. **Click the Theme button that appears at the bottom-left corner of the iWeb window.**

   A pop-up menu of different themes appears, as shown in Figure 4-5.

3. **Click a new theme.**

   Your Web page changes to match your chosen theme.

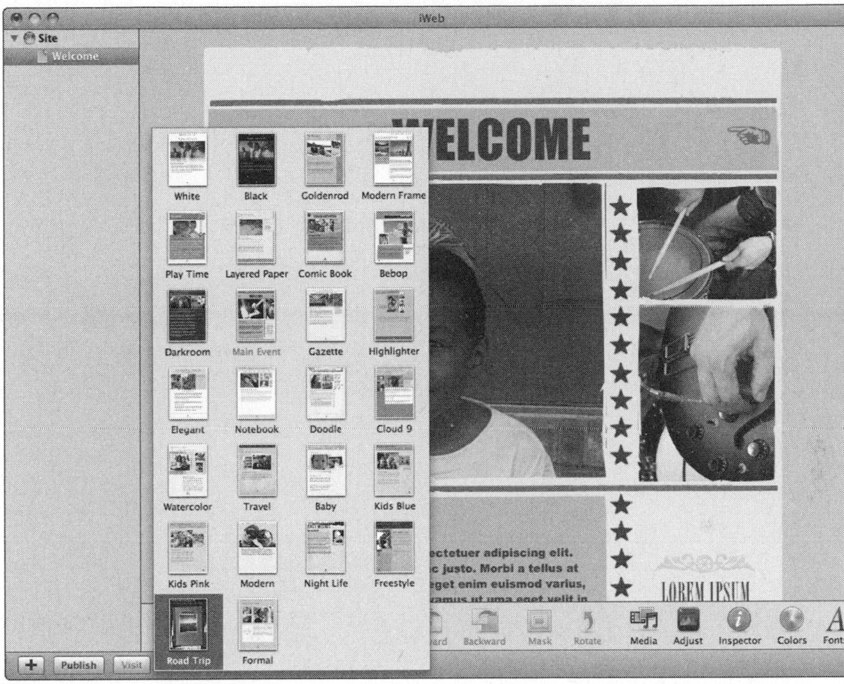

Figure 4-5: The Theme button lets you pick a new theme for a specific Web page.

Customizing the Parts of a Web Page

Making an iWeb template your own by replacing placeholder text and graphics certainly makes creating Web pages easy, but sooner or later, you'll come across a template that doesn't have the text and graphics positioned exactly where you want them. To further customize a Web page, you need to know how to add, move, resize, delete, and arrange text and graphics on a Web page. You can modify existing objects or create new objects for storing text and graphics.

Moving an object

To move text or graphics to another part of your Web page, follow these steps:

1. **Move the pointer over the text or graphics you want to move.**
2. **Click and drag the text or graphics to a new location.**
3. **Release the mouse button.**

   The text or graphics stays put in its new location.

Resizing an object

To resize text or graphics to make it bigger or smaller, follow these steps:

1. **Click to select the text or graphics you want to resize.**

   Handles appear around your chosen object, as shown in Figure 4-6.

2. **Move the pointer over a handle until the pointer turns into a two-way pointing arrow; then click and drag the handle to change the size of your object.**

3. **Release the mouse button when you're happy with the new size of the text or graphic object.**

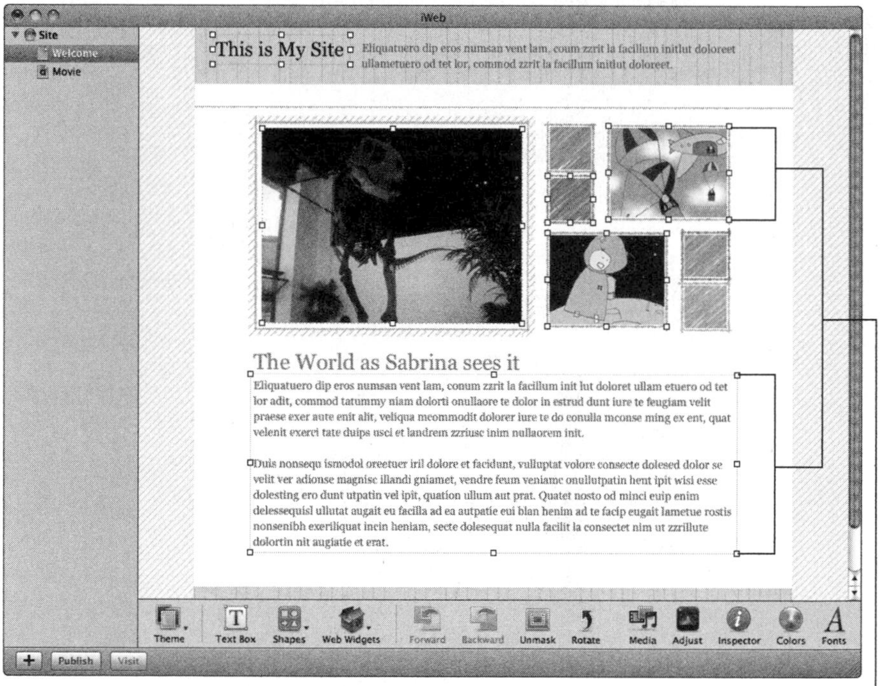

Selection handles

Figure 4-6: Handles appear when you select an object.

Rearranging an object

If you move or resize an object, it might cover up another object as shown in Figure 4-7. To fix this problem, you might need to rearrange which object appears over another one.

Think of each object (text or graphic) as a sheet of paper that can lie over or slide under another object.

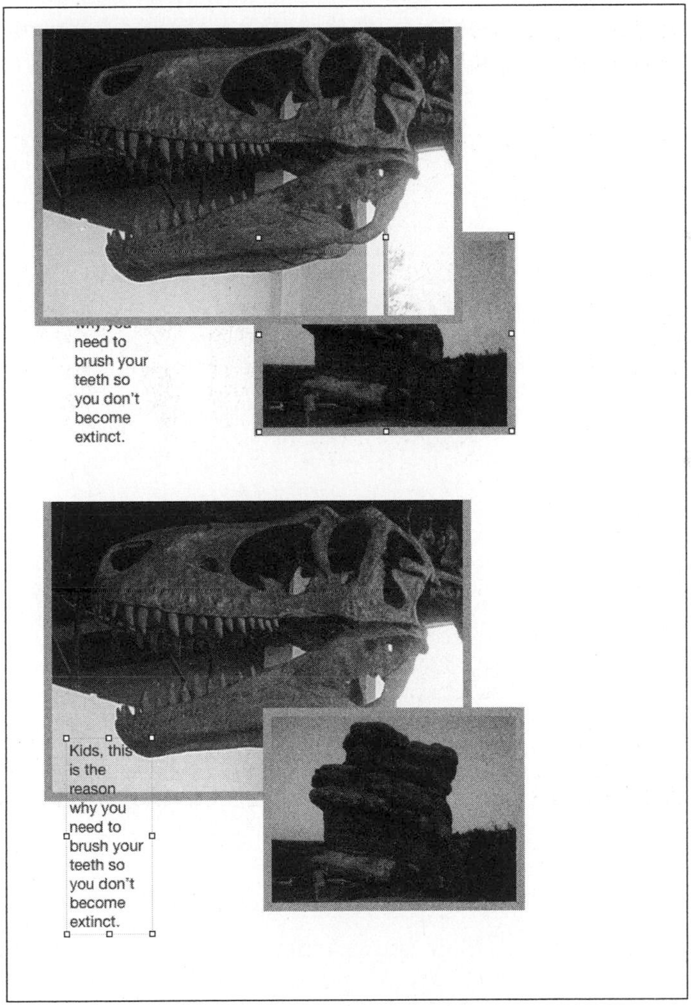

Figure 4-7: Objects can cover part of another object.

To rearrange which object appears on top of another one, follow these steps:

1. **Click to select the text or graphics that you want to place over (or under) another object.**

   Handles appear around your selected object.

2. **Choose one of the following:**

   - *Arrange➪Bring Forward:* Moves the selected object over one object that might be overlapping it. If multiple objects cover your selected object, you might not see any difference.
   - *Arrange➪Bring to Front:* Moves the selected object on top of all overlapping objects.
   - *Arrange➪Send Backward:* Moves the selected object underneath one object that it may be covering.
   - *Arrange➪Send to Back:* Moves the selected object underneath all other overlapping objects.

Deleting objects

To delete one or more objects, follow these steps:

1. **Click to select the text or graphics that you want to delete.**

   To select multiple objects, hold down the Shift key and click each object you want to delete.

2. **Press Delete or choose Edit➪Delete.**

If you delete an object by mistake, press ⌘+Z or choose Edit➪Undo.

Working with text

Text always appears on a Web page inside a text box, which you can move and resize on a Web page. If you create a Web page from a template, it will likely have a text box on the page that you can fill with your own text. If you create a blank Web page, or need more room to display text, you may need to create a text box.

Creating a text box

To create a text box, follow these steps:

1. **Click the Text Box icon at the bottom of the iWeb window or choose Insert➪Text Box.**

   A blinking cursor appears in the middle of your Web page.

2. **Type your text.**

If you have any existing objects on the Web page, the text box might appear over an existing object. When you type, you might have a hard time seeing your text, so press ⌘+A to see your text.

3. **Click anywhere on the Web page away from your newly created text box.**
4. **Click your newly created text box to display handles around your newly created text box.**
5. **Click and drag to move and/or resize the text box.**

Formatting text

After you type text inside a text box, you can format it by following these steps:

1. **Double-click the text box that contains the text you want to modify.**
2. **Select the text you want to modify; alternatively, press ⌘+A (or choose Edit⇨Select All) to select all the text in the text box.**
3. **Choose Format⇨Font.**

   A submenu of options appears, as shown in Figure 4-8.
4. **Choose an option from the Font submenu, such as Bold or Show Fonts.**

   If you click the Fonts button in the bottom-right corner of the iWeb window, a Fonts dialog appears, letting you pick a font to use.

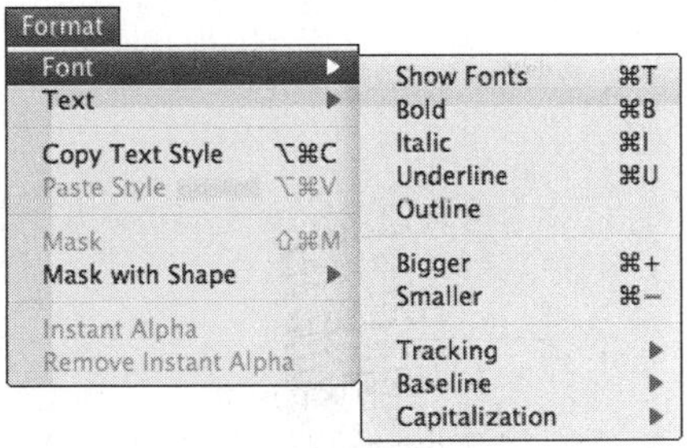

Figure 4-8: The Font submenu displays different ways to format text.

Creating a text hyperlink

Besides making text look pretty inside a text box, you might also want to turn text into a *hyperlink* — the highlighted or underlined link that can jump a reader to another Web page or Web site. To create a hyperlink, follow these steps:

1. **Double-click the text box that contains the text you want to turn into a hyperlink.**
2. **Select the text you want to turn into a hyperlink.**

3. **Choose Insert⇨Hyperlink.**

   A submenu appears, as shown in Figure 4-9.

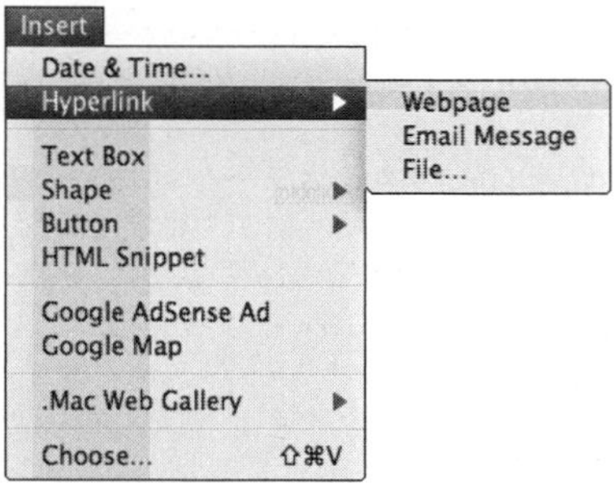

Figure 4-9: The Hyperlink submenu gives you three different options.

4. **Choose one of the following to display a Link pane, as shown in Figure 4-10:**

   - *Webpage:* Links to a specific Web site such as `www.dummies.com`.
   - *Email Message:* Links to an e-mail address such as `billgates@microsoft.com`.
   - *File:* Links to a file, such as a PDF or text file, which others can download off your Web page.

5. **Choose the options in the Link pane.**

   The options displayed in the Link pane will look different depending on the option you chose in step 4. For example, if you chose to create a Webpage link, you need to type the Web site address to link to, such as `www.dummies.com`. If you create an Email Message link, you'll need to specify the email address such as `sjobs@apple.com`.

6. **Click the Close button of the Link pane.**

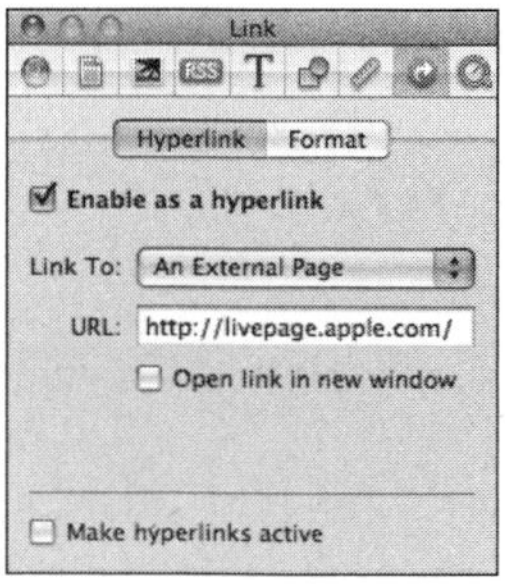

Figure 4-10: The Link pane lets you customize your hyperlink.

Working with graphics

You can add and place digital photographs, simple graphic shapes like arrows, or even videos anywhere on a Web page. If you create a Web page from a template, the template will likely provide placeholder graphics for you to add your own pictures. However, if you want to add more pictures, or if you started with a blank Web page, you can add more graphics to any Web page.

REMEMBER

Graphics can take time to transfer over the Internet, so the more graphics you place on a Web page — and the larger the graphic images you use — the longer the Web page will take to load and display in someone's Web browser. Don't be afraid to use graphics, but don't go overboard either.

Adding a picture to a Web page

To add a picture to a Web page, follow these steps:

1. **Click the Media button at the bottom of the iWeb window.**

   The Media Browser appears.

2. **Click the Photos tab.**

   A list of pictures stored in iPhoto appears.

3. **Click and drag a picture from the Media Browser onto your Web page.**
4. **Release the mouse button.**

   Your chosen picture appears on your Web page. (You might need to move or resize the picture.)

5. **Click the Close button of the Media Browser.**

REMEMBER

The preceding steps let you add an iPhoto image to a Web page. However, if you have a picture that isn't stored in iPhoto, you can add that picture to a Web page by choosing Insert⇨Choose. When a dialog appears, navigate to the graphic file you want, click to select it, and then click Insert.

Adding a movie to a Web page

Besides adding pictures, you can also add movies to a Web page, which people can view when they visit your site. To add a movie to a Web page, follow these steps:

1. **Click the Media button at the bottom of the iWeb window.**

   The Media Browser appears.

2. **Click the Movies tab.**

   A list of movies stored in your Movies folder appears in the Media Browser.

3. **Click and drag a movie from the Media Browser onto your Web page.**
4. **Release the mouse button.**

   Your chosen movie appears on your Web page. (You may need to move or resize the picture.)
5. **Click the Play button to preview your movie.**
6. **Click the Close button of the Media Browser.**

Publishing Your Web Pages

After you create all the Web pages that make up your Web site, you need to publish your Web pages. If you have a .Mac account, you can choose one of the following two options:

- **File⇨Publish to .Mac:** Sends the current Web page to your .Mac account. Your Web page is now available for viewing.
- **File⇨Publish All to .Mac:** Sends all the Web pages of your Web site to your .Mac account. Your entire Web site is now updated.

The Publish to .Mac option is best if you're updating a single Web page. The Publish All to .Mac option is best when you've made massive changes to your Web pages or if you're posting your Web site for the first time.

If you don't have a .Mac account, you can choose the File⇨Publish to a Folder. This stores all your Web pages, plus any additional files such as pictures and movies, in a folder that you define. After you've stored all your Web pages to a folder, you need to use a File Transfer Protocol (FTP) program to transfer all the files from this folder to your Web hosting service. (See Book III, Chapter 5 for more information about setting up a Web site.)

TIP

A popular (and free) FTP program is Cyberduck (`http://cyberduck.ch`).

Chapter 5: Using GarageBand

In This Chapter

- Playing instruments with Magic GarageBand
- Recording your music
- Recording your podcasts
- Saving your music

GarageBand lets you record, play, alter, and arrange any types of sounds to create your own music. If you already know how to play an instrument, GarageBand provides accompanying instruments such as drums, keyboards, and guitars that you can include in recordings of your own music. If you don't know how to play an instrument at all, GarageBand turns your Macintosh into a full-fledged band where you can control the sound of each instrument, arrange the separate audio tracks, and smash them together to create your own hit songs.

Although designed for recording, modifying, and playing music, GarageBand can record, modify, and save any type of audio files. If you're not interested in making music, you can use GarageBand to clean up recorded speech and save them as podcasts that you can distribute to the rest of the world.

Whether you want to record and arrange music or recorded speech, the three main tasks for using GarageBand are:

- Recording audio
- Arranging and modifying audio
- Saving the finished audio file

Whatever your needs, GarageBand can satisfy your artistic side or serious side, or just give you another way to amuse yourself with your Macintosh.

Recording Audio

Since GarageBand works with audio, the first task is to record audio into GarageBand using your computer's built-in microphone, an external microphone, or audio input (such as a keyboard or guitar plugged directly into your Macintosh).

If you don't have a real instrument, GarageBand provides a variety of software instruments, which are basically different musical instruments such as pianos, guitars, and drums that you can play and control through your Macintosh. All you have to do is specify the notes and tempo to play and software instruments let you hear your music played by different instruments.

Apple sells additional Jam Packs, which provide additional software instruments such as ethnic instruments, vocalists, or symphony orchestras.

Recording audio through Magic GarageBand

Magic GarageBand is great for creating a certain type of background music quickly and easily. For example, if you're creating a Keynote presentation to present to cowboys, you might want country music playing in the background. Rather than hunt up a country song, just fire up Magic GarageBand, pick the Country musical genre, modify the song by choosing different instruments, and you have yourself an instant country song without even knowing how to play an instrument.

Each musical genre in Magic GarageBand only plays one stock song that you can modify. If you want a country song, Magic GarageBand creates the same country song. It's up to you to customize this song to make it different if you want. If you want to create your own country song, you'll have to create a new music project rather than use Magic GarageBand.

To create a Magic GarageBand, follow these steps:

1. **Load GarageBand.**

   A dialog appears as shown in Figure 5-1.

Figure 5-1: The Garage Band dialog lets you choose the type of project to create.

2. **Click Magic GarageBand.**

   A Magic GarageBand window appears, listing different musical genres such as Rock, Jazz, or Funk, as shown in Figure 5-2.

3. **Click on a musical genre, such as Blues or Country.**

4. **Click on the Snippet or Entire Song radio button and then click the Play button to hear a snippet or entire song played in your chosen genre.**

5. **Click Audition.**

   The Magic GarageBand window displays a stage and instruments, as shown in Figure 5-3.

6. **Click on an instrument on the stage.**

   The bottom of the Magic GarageBand window displays all available variations of that instrument for your perusal.

7. **Click on the instrument variant you want in the bottom of the GarageBand window.**

   Your chosen instrument variant appears on the stage.

8. **Click the Play button to hear how the song or snippet sounds with your new instruments.**

   Essentially, Magic GarageBand plays one stock song that you can modify by choosing the types of instruments to play.

9. **Repeat steps 6 – 8 for any additional instruments you want to change.**

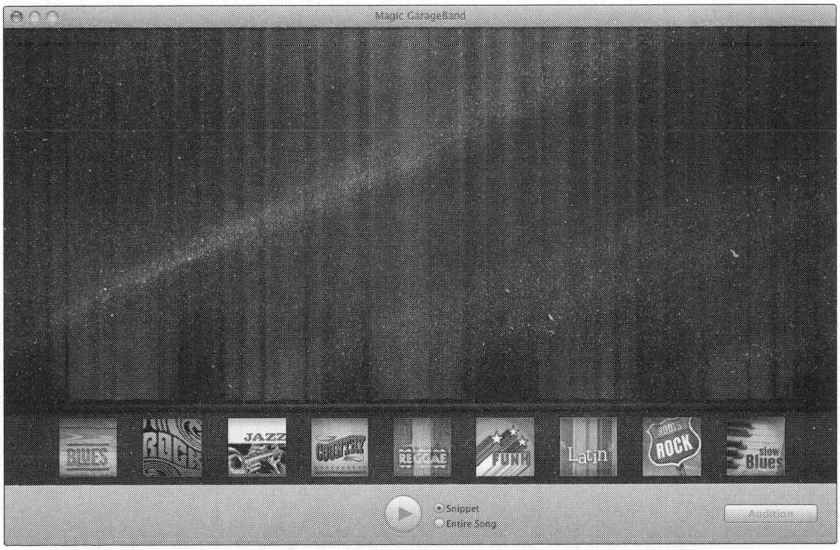

Figure 5-2: The Garage Band icons provide different musical genres to pick.

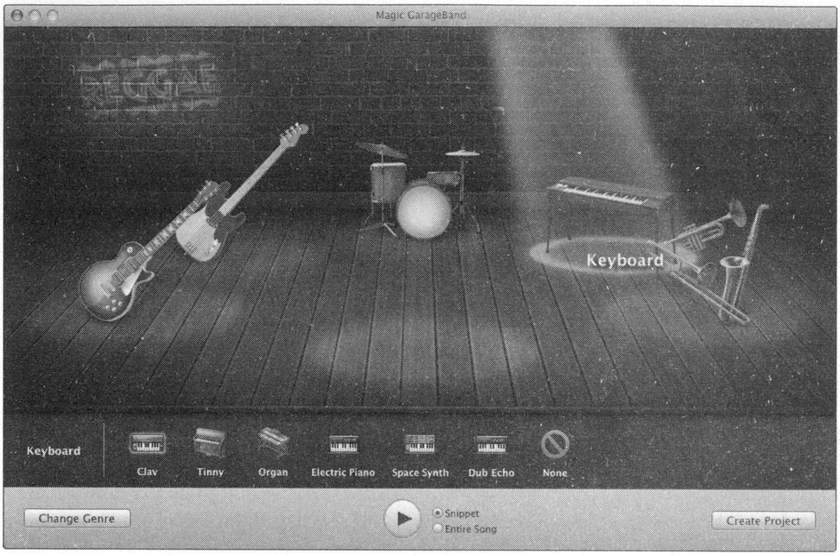

Figure 5-3: The Magic Garage Band displays all the instruments of the band.

10. **Click Create Project when you're happy with the instruments in your band.**

    GarageBand displays a window that contains all your instruments arranged in separate tracks as shown in Figure 5-4. At this point, you can modify the song.

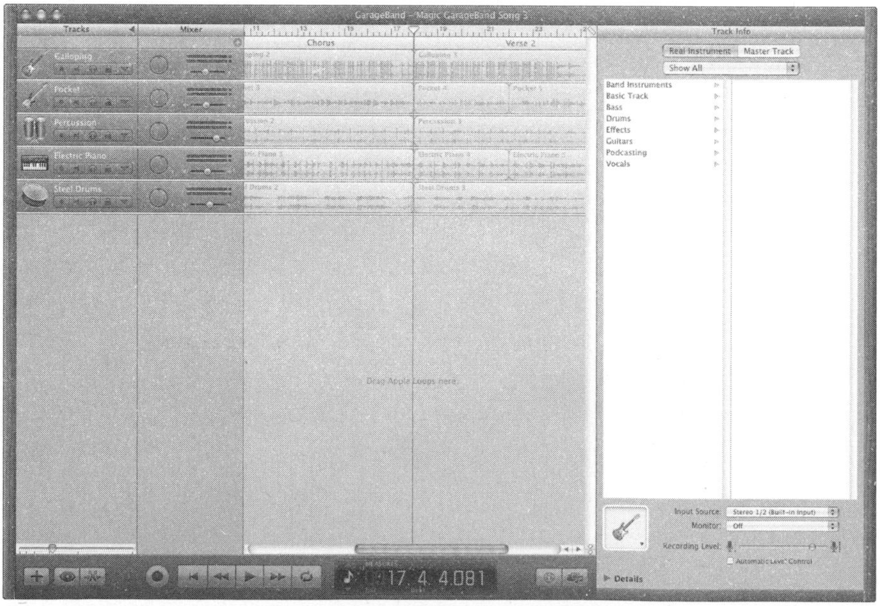

Figure 5-4: The Project window displays all the audio parts of each instrument.

Creating music with software instruments

Magic GarageBand can be handy for creating an instant song from a specific musical genre, but GarageBand also lets you specify the notes to play so GarageBand's software instruments can play your music instead.

Software instruments give you a chance to create music starting with one instrumental track and gradually layering other tracks until you've defined the parts for an entire band. To use software instruments, you need to specify the instrument you want to use, such as a baby grand piano or a steel string acoustic guitar. Then define the notes you want that instrument to play using a virtual keyboard where you can click or press the notes you want to play.

To create a software instrument, follow these steps:

1. **Load GarageBand.**

   A dialog appears (refer to Figure 5-1).

2. **Click New Music Project.**

   A New Project dialog appears, as shown in Figure 5-5.

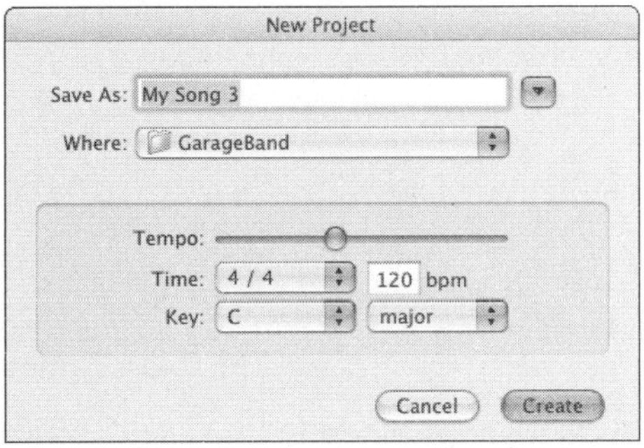

Figure 5-5: The New Project dialog lets you define your project.

3. **Enter a descriptive name for your project in the Save As text box.**
4. **Choose a location for storing your project from the Where pop-up menu.**
5. **(Optional) Change the Tempo, Time, bpm (beats per minute), and key options.**

   You can always change these options later.

6. **Click Create.**

   A window appears, displaying a virtual keyboard and a single audio track for a Grand Piano, as shown in Figure 5-6.

7. **To change the instrument for your single track, choose Track⇨Show Track Info (or click the View/Hide Track Info button in the bottom right corner of the GarageBand window).**

   A Track Info pane appears, as shown in Figure 5-7.

8. **Click on an instrument category (such as Strings or Bass) and then click on the specific type of instrument to use (such as Trance Bass or Electric Piano).**

9. **Click on the virtual keyboard to hear how your chosen instrument sounds.**

10. **(Optional) Click the Musical Typing button on the virtual keyboard, or choose Windows ‡ Musical Typing.**

    A Musical Typing keyboard appears as shown in Figure 5-8. The Musical Typing keyboard allows you to press keys on your Mac keyboard to play certain notes, which you may find more convenient than using your mouse to click keys on the virtual keyboard.

11. **Click the Record button and click on the virtual keyboard or type on the Musical Typing keyboard to record the notes as you play.**

12. **Click the Record button again to stop recording and click the Play/Stop button.**

13. **Click the Go to Beginning button and click Play to hear the notes you've recorded.**

In case you want to add another software instrument, follow these steps:

1. **Choose Track⇨New Track.**

   A dialog appears, asking if you want to create a real or software instrument track.

2. **Click the Software Instrument Track radio button and click Create.**

   The new instrument track appears in the GarageBand window.

3. **Choose Track⇨Show Track Info to display the Track Info window. (If this window already appears, skip this step.)**

4. **Click the Software Instrument button.**

   A list of instrument types appears such as Organs, Guitars, and Drum Kits.

5. **Click on an instrument type.**

   The right column displays specific types of instruments.

6. **Click on a specific instrument in the right column, such as Electric Piano.**

   Your newly added instrument track will now play using your chosen instrument.

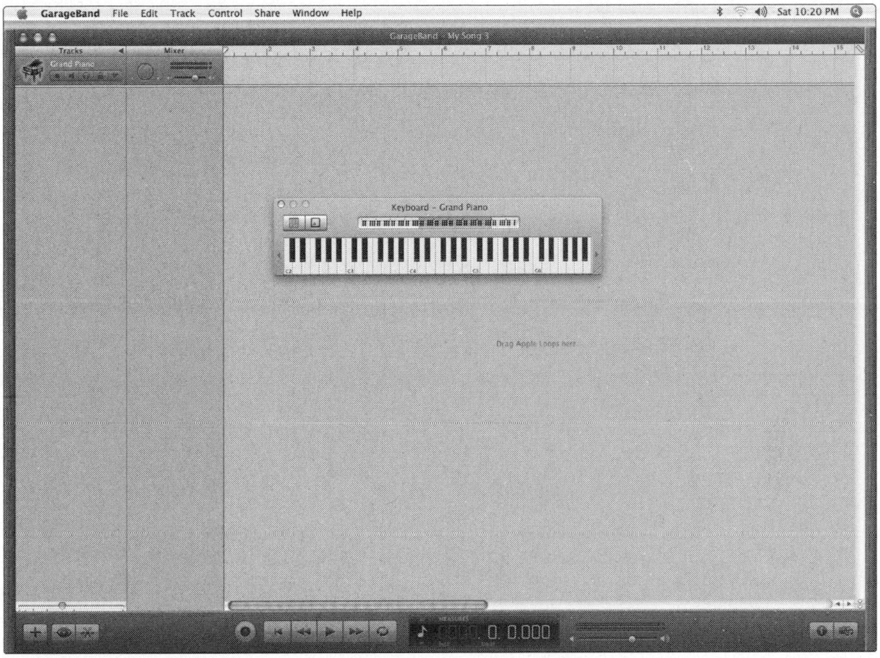

Figurc 5-6: Time to tickle the ivories.

Figure 5-7: The Show Track window displays a list of different instruments you can choose.

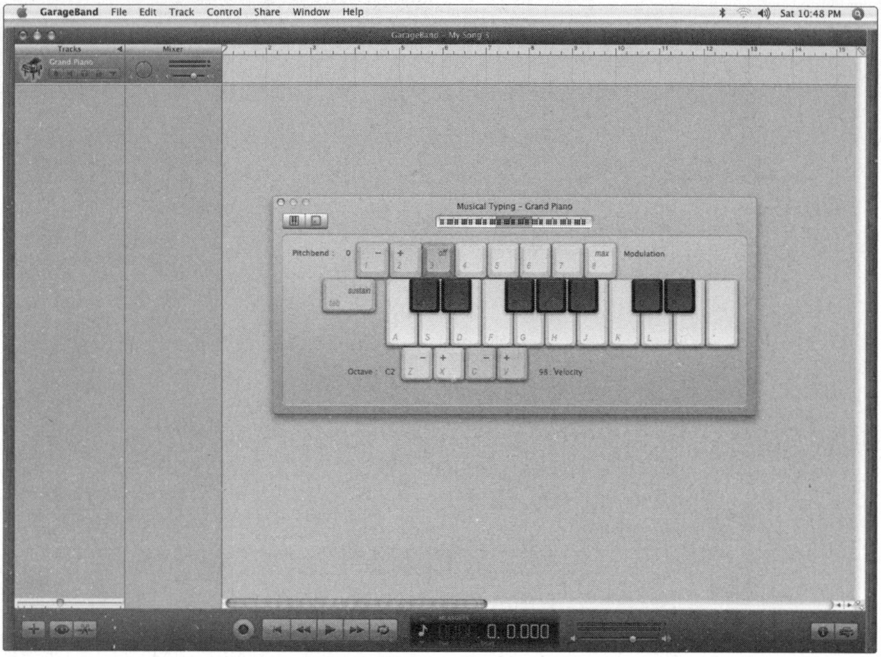

Figure 5-8: The Musical Typing keyboard lets you use the keyboard as a musical instrument.

Playing with a real instrument

The easiest way to play music is with a real instrument connected to your Macintosh, such as through a USB port. By playing with a real instrument, you can record yourself, alter the sound, and even save your recording so you can play along with your own recording. To record a real instrument connected to your Macintosh, follow these steps:

1. **Load GarageBand.**

   A dialog appears (refer to Figure 5-1).

2. **Click New Music Project.**

   A New Project dialog appears (refer to Figure 5-5).

3. **Enter a descriptive name for your project in the Save As text box.**
4. **Choose a location for storing your project from the Where pop-up menu.**
5. **(Optional) Change the Tempo, Time, bpm (beats per minute), and key options.**
6. **Click Create.**

   A window appears, displaying a virtual keyboard and a single audio track for a Grand Piano (refer to Figure 5-6).

7. **Click to select the Grand Piano track and choose Track➪Delete Track.**
8. **Choose Track➪New Track.**

   A dialog appears, asking if you want to use a software instrument or a real instrument, as shown in Figure 5-9.

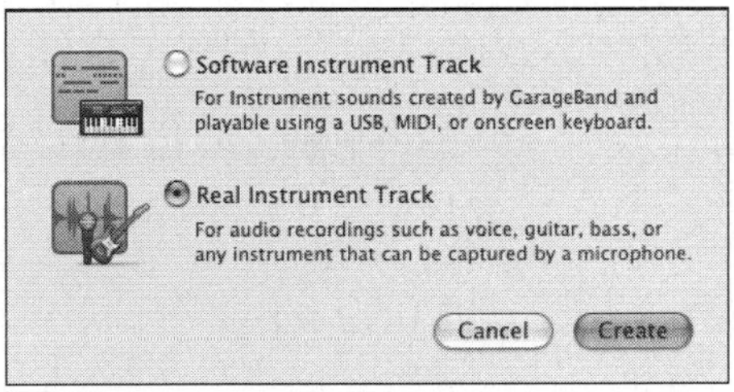
Software Instrument Track
For instrument sounds created by GarageBand and playable using a USB, MIDI, or onscreen keyboard.
Real Instrument Track
For audio recordings such as voice, guitar, bass, or any instrument that can be captured by a microphone.
Cancel
Create

Figure 5-9: A dialog lets you choose between a real or software instrument.

9. **Click the Real Instrument radio button and click Create.**

   A No Effects track appears along with a Track Info pane, as shown in Figure 5-10.
10. **Click an instrument category in the Track Info pane, such as Guitars or Bass.**
11. **Click on a specific instrument type in the right list of the Track Info pane, such as Classic Rock or Metal.**

    The instrument you choose in this step defines how GarageBand plays your real instrument. So if you have a keyboard hooked up to your Mac, you can use this step to make your keyboard sound like horns, drums, or guitars.
12. **Click on the Input Source pop-up menu and choose the option for how your instrument is connected to your Macintosh (such as through a USB port or other type of connection).**
13. **Click the Monitor pop-up menu and choose On or Off to define if you want to hear audio through the speakers or not.**

    To prevent feedback, choose On with Feedback Protection. If you still experience feedback, you might want to choose the Off option instead.
14. **Drag the Recording Level slider or click the Automatic Level Control check box to let GarageBand set the level.**

    Lowering the recording level can reduce feedback. If you select the Automatic Level Control check box, the Monitor option (from step 13) turns off.

Figure 5-10: The Track Info window lets you define the type of instrument you're using.

15. **(Optional) Click the Details category at the bottom of the Track Info pane to display additional options for modifying the sound of your instrument as shown in Figure 5-11.**

16. **Click the Record button on your track and start playing away.**

    When you're done playing, click the Record button again.

Editing Audio

To record audio, click the Record button and start playing. GarageBand includes a metronome (Control ‡ Metronome) that you can toggle on and off. If you want to play along with previously recorded tracks, you can choose Control ‡ Count In so you'll know when to start playing.

Splitting a track

When you first record an instrument, GarageBand saves it as a single long track. To make it easier to edit this track, you can split a track into parts that you can later modify individually, save and reuse, delete, or rearrange in a new position.

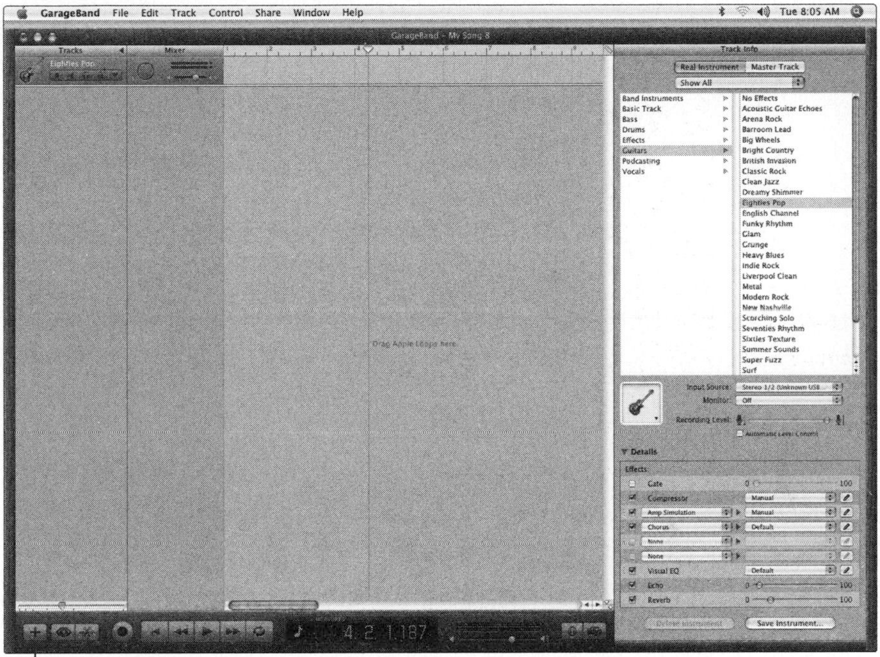

Add Track button

Figure 5-11: The Details category of the Track Info pane lets you further refine your instrument's sound.

To split a track, follow these steps:

1. **Click to select a track that you want to split.**

   GarageBand highlights your chosen instrument.

2. **Drag the slider (which displays a vertical red line) where you want to split the track.**

   TIP

   If you can't find the slider, click the Go to Beginning button to move the slider to the beginning of your track.

3. **Choose Edit⇨Split or press Command+T.**

   GarageBand splits your track, as shown in Figure 5-12.

Joining a track

If you split a track, you can always join the back together again later. To join two adjacent parts of a track, follow these steps:

1. **Click on the first part of the track that you want to join.**

Figure 5-12: Splitting a track can make it easier to edit.

2. **Hold down the Shift key and click on the second part of the track you want to join.**
3. **Choose Edit⇨Join or press Command+J.**

   GarageBand connects the two parts together.

Moving tracks

After you've recorded two or more tracks, you may want to adjust how each track plays relative to one another. For example, you can make one track play before or after a second track to create interesting audio effects. To move tracks, follow these steps:

1. **Click on the track that you want to move.**

   GarageBand highlights your selected instrument track.

   For more flexibility, split a track into multiple parts so that way you can move each part separately.
2. **Click and drag the track to the left or right to adjust the relative positions of the two tracks.**
3. **Release the left mouse button when you're happy with the new arrangement of the track.**

Figure 5-13 shows a before and after appearance of different tracks rearranged to start and end at different times.

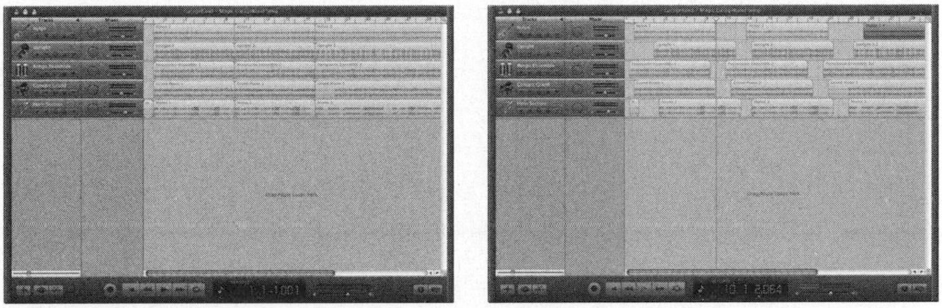

Figure 5-13: Moving tracks can adjust how they play in relation to one another.

Arranging tracks by regions

Moving individual parts of a track can help you change the way multiple instruments sound together. However, after you've moved multiple tracks to play at different times, you may want to move and arrange entire chunks of a song (called regions) to move related parts of a song played by different instruments.

To arrange tracks, follow these steps:

1. **Choose Track⇨Show Arrange Track.**

   A blank track appears at the top of the GarageBand window.

2. **Click the Add Arrange Region button (the plus sign) that appears on the blank track at the top of the window as shown in Figure 5-14.**

   An untitled region appears as shown in Figure 5-14.

3. **Double-click on the region name and type a descriptive name.**
4. **Move the mouse to the left and right margins of the highlighted region to select part of your song.**
5. **Repeat steps 2 – 4 to create, name, and define multiple regions, as shown in Figure 5-15.**
6. **Click and drag a region name to the left or right to move an entire region to rearrange your song.**

   Regions separate to show you where your dragged region will appear in a song, as shown in Figure 5-16.

TIP

If you hold down the Option key while dragging a region to a new location, you'll copy that region rather than move it.

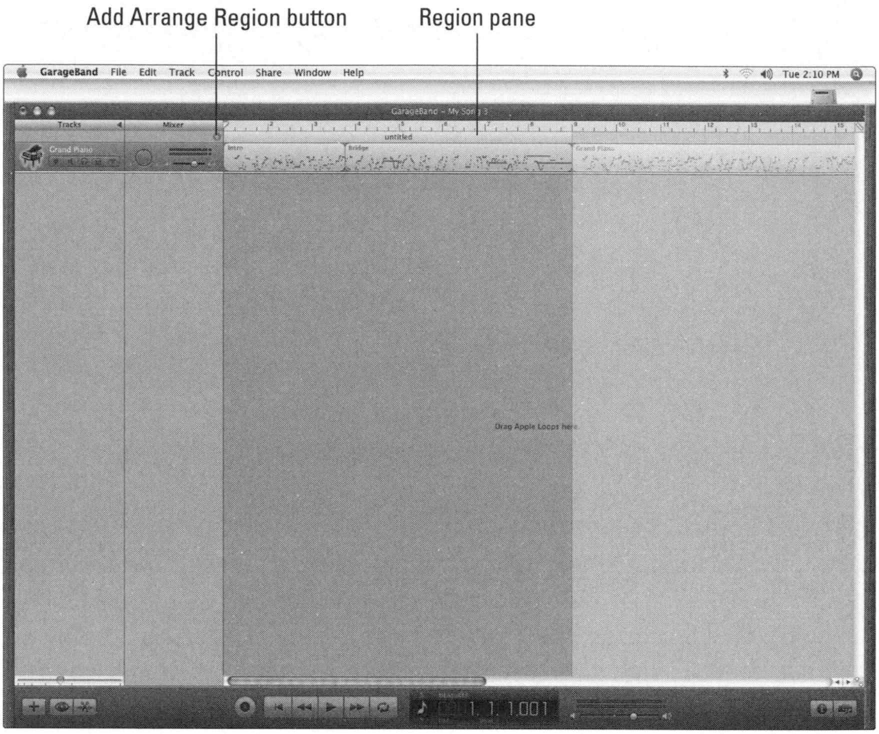

Figure 5-14: Clicking the Add Arrange Region button displays an untitled region.

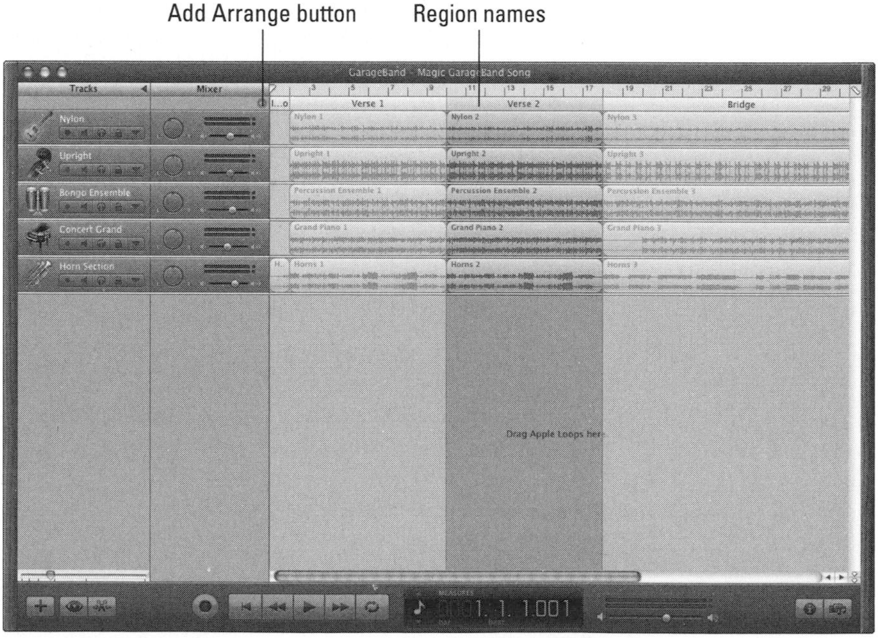

Figure 5-15: Multiple regions can help you identify the parts of your song.

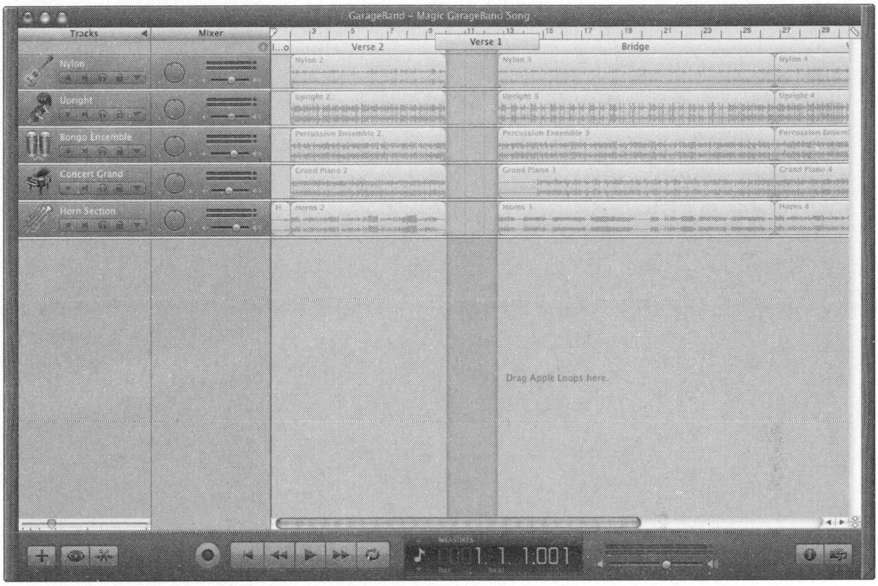

Figure 5-16: By moving a region, you can rearrange entire chunks of a song.

Modifying the key and tempo

You can move tracks and/or regions around in a GarageBand song to radically change the way a song sounds, but you can also just change the key or tempo to introduce a slight (or maybe even a major) change. Changing the key can modify the way a song sounds while changing the tempo speeds up or slows down a song without making the song sound high-pitched or like it's running down.

To change the time, key, tempo, you use the LCD Mode, which mimics an LCD (liquid crystal display) at the bottom of the GarageBand window. By changing what the LCD Mode displays, you can modify items like the key and tempo of your tracks.

To change both the key and tempo, follow these steps:

1. **Choose Project from the LCD Mode pop-up menu near the bottom of the GarageBand window, as shown in Figure 5-17.**

   By choosing Project, the LCD Mode displays the current key and tempo of your track.

2. **Click on the Go to Beginning button and then click Play to hear your song.**

   By playing your song, you can adjust the key and tempo and hear your changes in real-time as they occur.

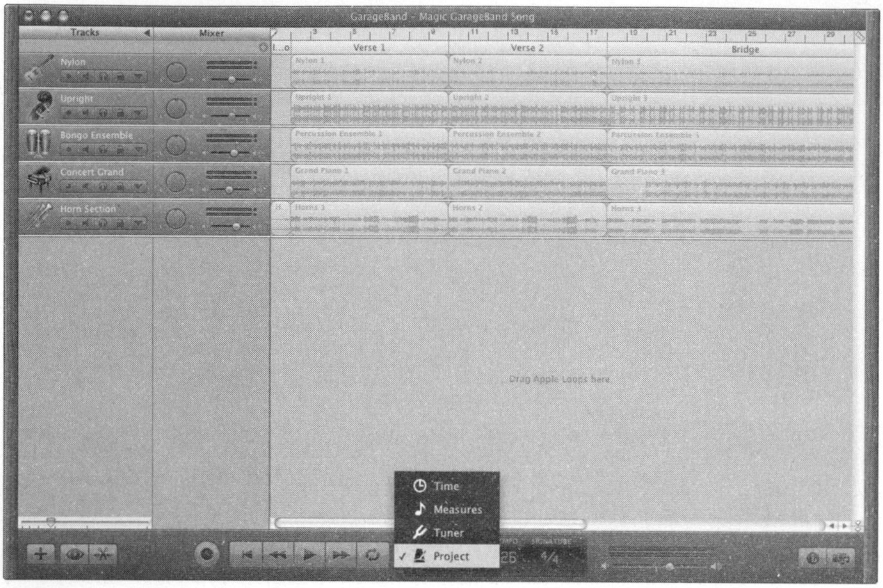

Figure 5-17: The LCD Mode pop-up menu changes the information displayed about your song.

3. **Click the Key pop-up menu and choose a key, such as F or G, as shown in Figure 5-18.**
4. **Click Tempo pop-up menu.**

   A vertical slider appears.
5. **Drag the vertical slider up or down to speed up or slow down the tempo of your song.**

Saving Music

After you're done arranging and modifying your song, you can choose File➪Save to save your GarageBand project (so you can edit it later). However, if you want to share your creation with others, you can save your audio file in the following locations:

- As a song in the iTunes library
- As a song stored anywhere on your hard disk
- On a CD

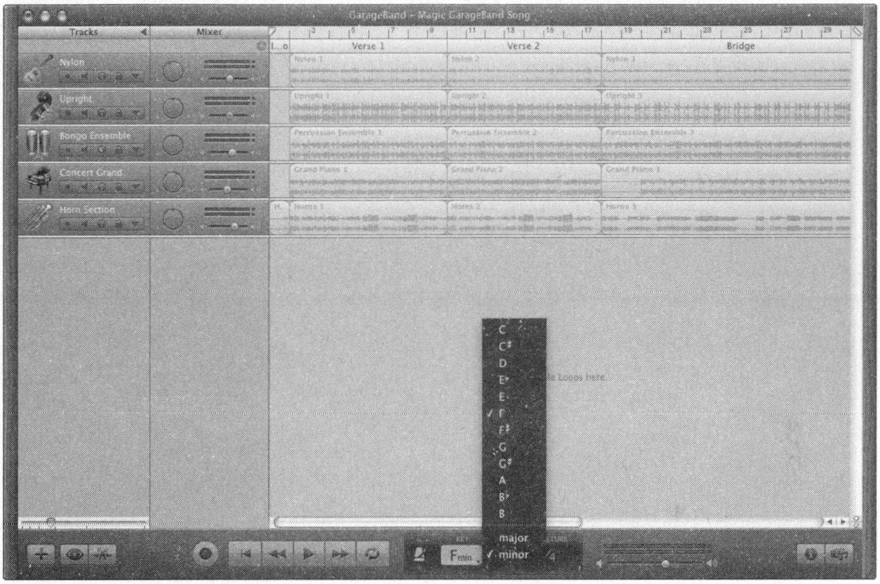

Figure 5-18: The Key pop-up menu lets you change the key that your song plays in.

Saving a song in iTunes

If you've created a song that you'd like to save and play later, you can store that song in iTunes by following these steps:

1. **Choose Share⇨Send Song to iTunes.**

   A dialog appears, as shown in Figure 5-19.

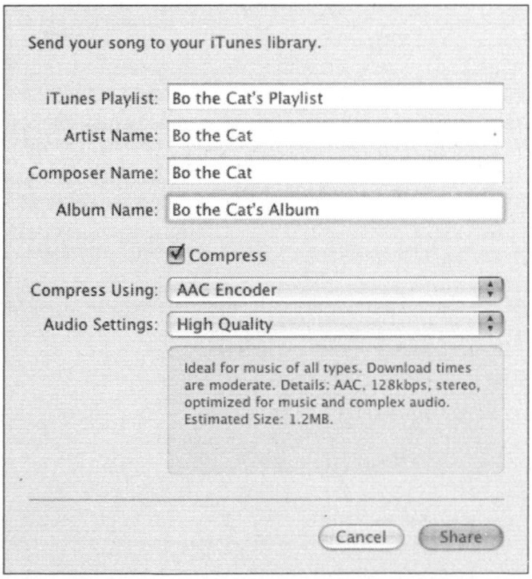

Figure 5-19: Garage Band lets you choose a playlist, artist name, and audio setting for your song.

2. **Click in the iTunes Playlist, Artist Name, Composer Name, and Album Name text boxes and enter in any information you want to store.**

   By default, GarageBand uses your name in each text box.

3. **Make sure the Compress check box is selected and then choose either AAC or MP3 Encoder from the Compress Using pop-up menu.**

   The Compress option smashes your audio file as small as possible while still retaining audio quality. If you don't compress your audio file, it may be too large for transferring over the Internet.

4. **Choose either Good, High, or Higher Quality from the Audio Settings pop-up menu.**
5. **Click Share.**

   Your song appears in your iTunes library.

Saving a song to disk

If you don't want to store your song in iTunes, you can save your song as a separate audio file that you can store anywhere, such as on an external hard disk or a USB flash drive. To save your song as an audio file, follow these steps:

1. **Choose Share⇨Export Song to Disk.**

   A dialog appears.

2. **Make sure the Compress check box is selected and then choose either AAC or MP3 Encoder from the Compress Using pop-up menu.**
3. **Click in the Audio Settings pop-up menu and choose Good, High, or Higher Quality.**
4. **Click Export.**

   An Export to Disk dialog appears.

5. **Enter a name for your audio file in the Save As text box.**
6. **Choose a location for storing your project from the Where pop-up menu.**
7. **Click Save.**

Burning a song to CD

If you created a song that you want to share with others, you can burn it to a CD and then give the CD away. To burn a song to a CD, follow these steps:

1. **Choose Share⇨Burn Song to CD.**

   A dialog appears, telling you that it's waiting for a blank CD.

2. **Insert a blank CD into your Macintosh and click Burn.**

Recording Podcasts

Podcasts are recorded audio files that contain speech, such as interviews, radio talk show broadcasts, or just monologues of a single person talking about anything they want. If you store your podcast on a Web site, anyone in the world can download and listen to your podcast.

To customize your podcasts, GarageBand lets you add other audio, picture, or video files using the Media Browser, which appears in the upper right corner of the GarageBand window.

Recording speech

The most important part about a podcast is recording spoken words, either through the internal microphone in your Macintosh, an external microphone plugged into your Macintosh, or even a recording of an iChat audio conversation using a program such as Conference Recorder (`www.ecamm.com`), Audio Hijack (`www.rogueamoeba.com`), or WireTap Studio (`http://www.AmbrosiaSW.com`).

To record a podcast, follow these steps:

1. **Load GarageBand.**

   A dialog appears (refer to Figure 5-1).
2. **Click Create New Podcast Episode.**

   A New Project from Template dialog appears.
3. **Enter a descriptive name for your podcast in the Save As text box.**
4. **Choose a location for storing your project from the Where pop-up menu.**
5. **Click Create.**

   The GarageBand window appears as shown Figure 5-20.
6. **Click the Male or Female Voice track, click the Record button, and start speaking.**

   Choosing a Male or Female Voice track makes GarageBand optimize recording for males or females. If you've already captured audio and stored it in iTunes or GarageBand, click on the Audio button in the Media Browser window, click on GarageBand or iTunes, and drag an audio file on to the Male or Female Voice track.
7. **Click the Record button and start talking.**
8. **Click the Stop button when you're done talking.**

Refer to the earlier section, "Editing Audio," for instructions on editing your podcast audio file.

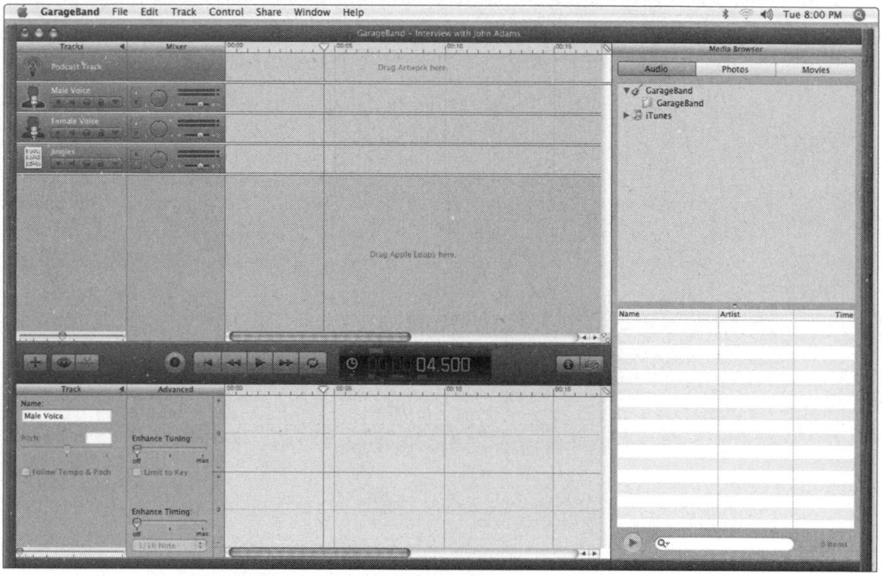

Figure 5-20: The Garage Band window displays a Male and Female Voice track along with a Jingles track.

Adding jingles and audio effects

After you've recorded you or someone else speaking, you may want to add music or sound effects to enhance your podcast. For example, you could have introductory music that fades away as soon as you start speaking.

To prevent any background jingles or audio effects from drowning out the spoken portion of your audio, GarageBand offers a feature called Ducking, which mutes background music when the Male or Female Voice track starts playing. To turn the Ducking feature on or off, choose Control⇨Ducking.

To add audio effects, follow these steps:

1. **Choose Control⇨Show Loop Browser, or click the View/Hide the Loop Browser button.**

   The Loop Browser appears, as shown in Figure 5-21.

2. **Click on an Effects category, such as Jingles or Sound Effects.**
3. **Click and drag an audio effect onto the Jingles Track.**
4. **Release the left mouse button.**

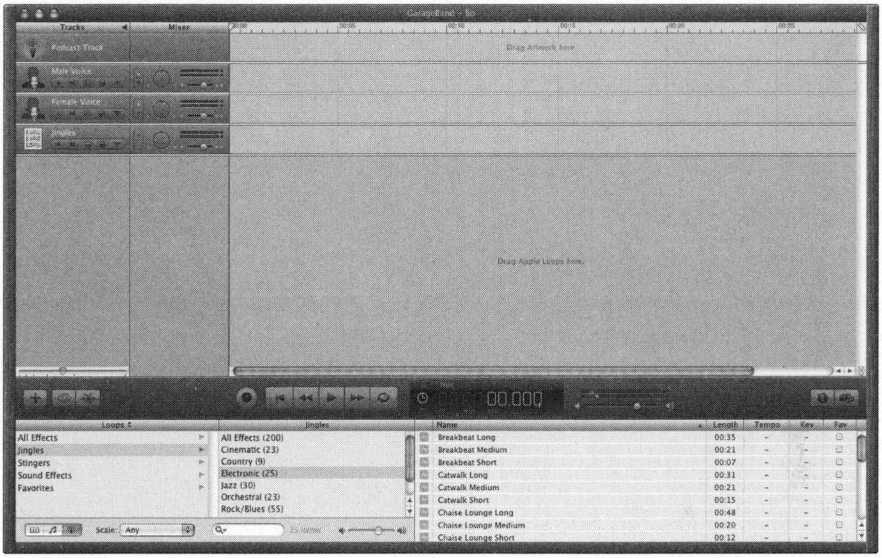

Figure 5-21: The Loop Browser provides categories of music, jingles, and sound effects.

Adding pictures

Although podcasts are meant to be heard, you can add pictures to your podcast to represent your entire recording or just individual parts of your podcast.

REMEMBER

Adding pictures to a podcast is only useful when listening to your podcast on a device that can also display pictures, such as an iPod Photo.

To add pictures to a podcast, follow these steps:

1. **Choose Control⇨Show Editor, or click the View/Hide the Track Editor button — the one sporting a pair of scissors — near the bottom left corner of the GarageBand window.**

   The Track Editor pane appears at the bottom of the GarageBand window.

2. **Choose Control⇨Show Media Browser.**

   The Media Browser pane appears, as shown in Figure 5-22.

3. **Click on the Photos button in the Media Browser.**

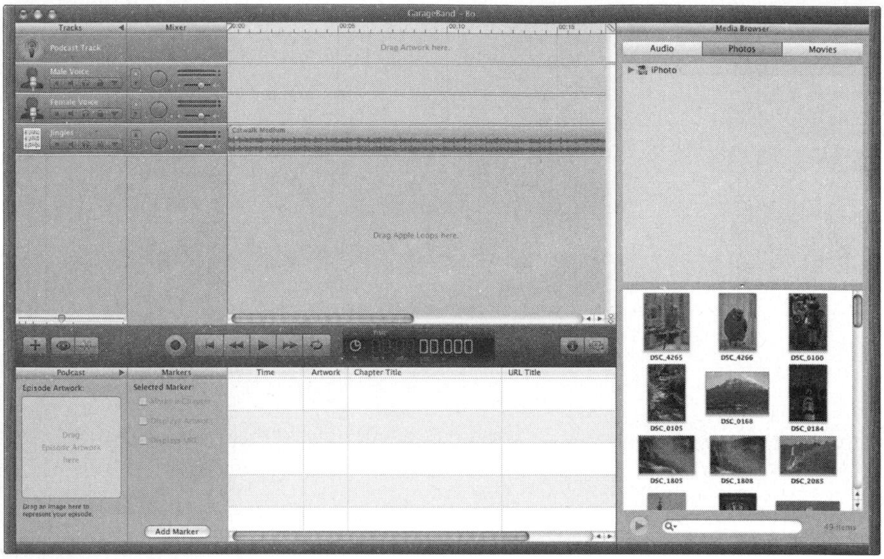

Figure 5-22: The Media Browser pane lists all pictures stored in iPhoto while the Track Editor pane displays blank areas for adding pictures.

4. **Click and drag a picture from the Media Browser onto either the Episode Artwork box or the Artwork column in the Track Editor pane and then release the left mouse button.**

   The Episode Artwork box is where you can place a picture to represent your entire podcast. The Artwork column is where you can place a picture to represent separate chapters (parts) of your podcast. You can have only one picture in the Episode Artwork box, but you can have multiple pictures in the Artwork column.

5. **(Optional) For each picture you placed in the Artwork column, click in the Time column and define the time when you want each picture to appear as your podcast plays.**

REMEMBER

When you're done editing your spoken audio and adding sound effects and pictures, you're ready to share your podcast with the world. Sharing a podcast is identical to sharing an audio file in iTunes, as an audio file on your hard disk, or directly on a CD. For information about saving a podcast in different ways, refer to the previous section, "Saving Music."

Chapter 6: Writing and Publishing with Pages

In This Chapter

- Using document templates
- Creating text
- Formatting text
- Using text boxes
- Working with graphics
- Polishing a document

Pages is a combination word processor and desktop publishing program. As a word processor, Pages lets you type, edit, and format text quickly and easily. As a desktop publisher, Pages lets you arrange graphics and text boxes on a page to create business cards, menus, newsletters, or brochures.

Because Pages offers a dual personality as a word processor and a desktop publishing program, you can switch between the features you need in a single program. You can start writing and then decide to design your pages. Halfway through designing your pages, you might feel the urge to write again.

Pages is part of the iWork suite — and it ain't free. Your Mac may have a trial version of Pages that lets you play with the program to see if it meets your needs.

Working with Document Templates

To help you get started writing, Pages supplies a variety of document templates. By choosing a document template, you can just enter new text or customize the appearance of the template so you don't have to create everything from scratch.

Pages offers two types of templates: Word Processing and Page Layout. Word Processing templates are designed mostly for writing (relatively) plain and simple, while Page Layout templates are designed mostly for when you're mixing text and graphics. (You can always add pictures to a Word Processing template or write in a text box on a Page Layout template.)

The main difference between Word Processing templates and Page Layout templates is that you can type directly on a page in a document created from a Word Processing template. If you want to type text on a document created from a Page Layout template, you have to create a text box and place that text box somewhere on your page.

A second difference is that you must manually add (or delete) pages in a Page Layout template (by choosing the Insert➪Pages or Edit➪Delete Page commands). With a Word Processing template, Pages automatically adds pages as you type and deletes pages as you delete text.

In general, if you need a document that contains mostly text, such as letters or reports, start with a Word Processing template. If you need a document that consists mostly of pictures, or if you need to create newsletters, magazine pages, or Web pages, start with a Page Layout template.

After you create a document using a Word Processing (or Page Layout) template, you can't switch to a new template. If you want to use a different template, you have to create another document.

To choose a document template, follow these steps:

1. **Load Pages by double-clicking the Pages icon in the Applications folder (or choose File➪New if Pages is already running).**

   A dialog appears, displaying different templates you can choose, as shown in Figure 6-1.

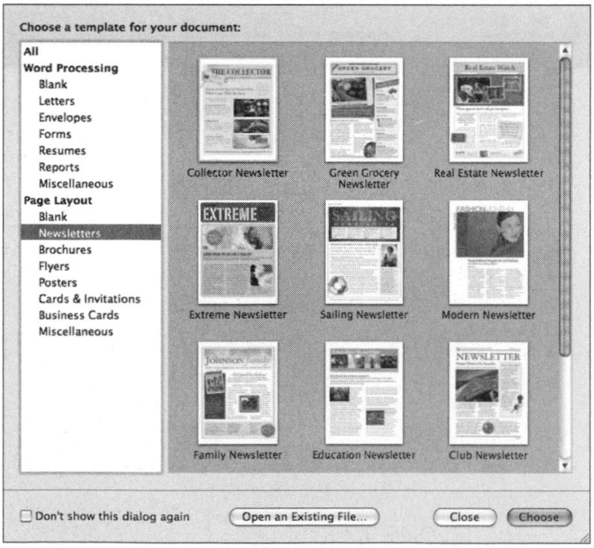

Figure 6-1: Pages provides a variety of templates to help you create a document quickly.

2. **Select a template category under the Word Processing or Page Layout headings in the listing on the left.**

   The templates for your selected category appear in the main pane of the dialog.

3. **Click in the right pane to select a template and then click the Choose button.**

   Pages displays your chosen template.

REMEMBER

If you want to start out with a blank document, click on the Blank template under the Word Processing category.

Replacing placeholder text

Nearly every template contains placeholder text that shows you gibberish that you'll have to replace with your own text. To change text in a template, follow these steps:

1. **Double-click the placeholder text you want to change.**

   Pages selects the entire placeholder text, which can be as short as a single sentence or as large as several paragraphs, as shown in Figure 6-2.

2. **Type any new text you want to replace the placeholder text.**

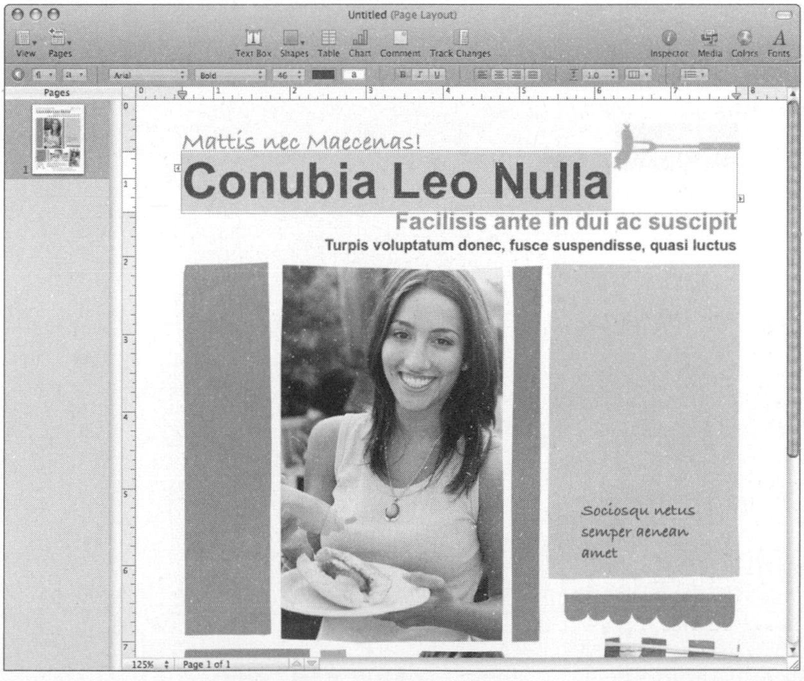

Figure 6-2: To replace placeholder text, just double-click it and type new text.

Replacing placeholder pictures

Many templates display placeholder pictures. Unless you happen to like the picture included with a template, you'll probably want to replace it with one of your own by following these steps:

1. **Click the Media icon (the one displaying a musical note) on the toolbar, or choose View⇨Show Media Browser.**

   The Media Browser window appears.

2. **Click the Photos tab in the Media Browser window to view all the pictures stored in iPhoto.**
3. **Click and drag a picture from the Media Browser window onto any placeholder picture in your document.**
4. **Release the mouse button.**

   Pages replaces the placeholder picture with the picture you chose from the Media Browser window, as shown in Figure 6-3.

5. **Click the Close button on the Media Browser window.**

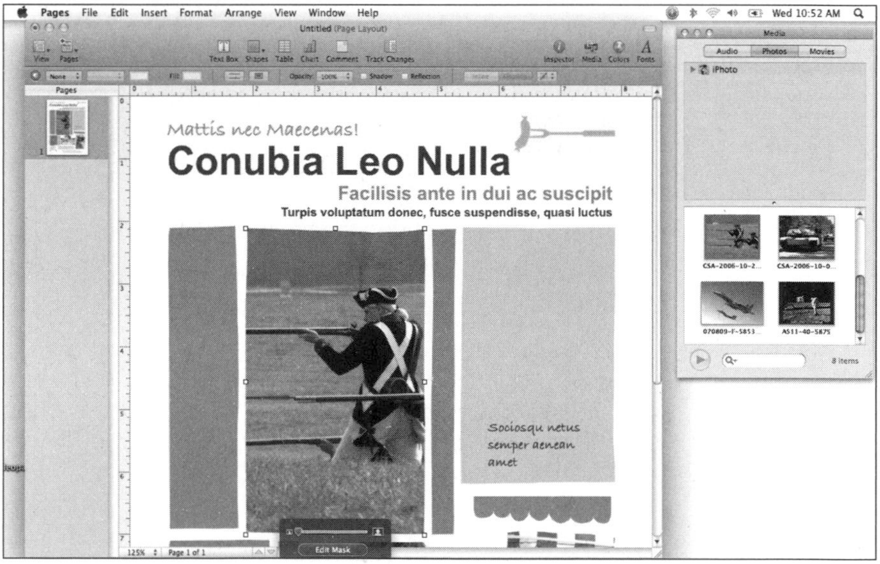

Figure 6-3: The Media Browser window lets you drag and drop pictures directly on your document.

Working with Text

Text can appear directly on a page or inside a text box. Word Processing templates let you type text directly on a page, but you can always add text boxes and type text inside those text boxes later. Page Layout templates allow you to type text only inside text boxes.

You can always tell what type of template your document is based on by peeking at the title bar of the document window, which identifies your document by name followed by either (Word Processing) or (Page Layout).

The advantage of typing text directly on a page is that you can keep typing and Pages automatically creates new pages as you type. The disadvantage of typing text directly on a page is that it's harder to define exactly where the text will appear on a page.

The advantage of using text boxes is that you can move them anywhere on a page. The disadvantage of typing text in a text box is that text boxes can display only a limited amount of text. (If you need to type a large amount of text, you may need to link text boxes together so when text overflows one text box, it automatically flows into another one.)

Editing text

Whether you're typing text directly on a page or inside a text box, you can edit text by adding, deleting, or rearranging it.

Adding text

Any new text you type appears wherever the cursor is located. To add text, just place the cursor where you want the new text to appear, click, and then type away.

If a cursor immediately appears when you click, that means you've moved the cursor inside text that appears directly on a page. If a box surrounds the text that you clicked, that means you clicked inside a text box. In that case, you have to move the pointer over the text inside the text box and click a second time.

Deleting text

You can delete text in two ways:

- Move the cursor next to characters you want to erase. To delete characters that appear to the *left* of the cursor, press the big Delete key (the one that appears to the right of the +/= key). To delete characters that appear to the *right* of the cursor, press the little Delete key (also called the Forward-Delete key, which appears to the left of the End key).

Not all keyboards have this Forward-Delete key.

- Select text and then press Delete.

You can select text by holding down the Shift key and moving the cursor using the arrow keys, or you can drag the mouse over text to select it.

Rearranging text

After you've written some text, you may need to rearrange it by copying or moving chunks of text from one location to another. You can copy and move text between two text boxes or from one part of a text page to another part of the same page — or to another page all together.

To copy and move text, you can use the Cut, Copy, and Paste commands on the Edit menu, but you might find it quicker to select and drag text using the mouse. Here's how it's done:

1. **Select the text you want to copy or move.**

   If you want to copy text, hold down the Option key while doing Step 2. If you want to move text, you don't need to hold down any keys.
2. **Click and drag the selected text, to a new location.**
3. **Release the mouse button to finish copying or moving your text.**

Formatting text

To make text look more appealing, you can format text to use different fonts, display text in italics, change the size of text, or add color to text. To give you fast access to different formatting options, Pages displays a Format Bar near the top of the Pages window. To view (or hide) the Format Bar, choose View⇨Show (or Hide) Format Bar.

To format text, select the text you want to format and then do any of the following:

- Click the **Font pop-up menu** on the Format Bar as shown in Figure 6-4, and then choose a font from the menu that appears.
- Click the **Style pop-up menu** on the Format bar and choose a style such as Regular or Heading 1. (Choosing Bold or Italic from the Style pop-up menu is identical to clicking on the Bold or Italic icon on the Format Bar.)
- Click the **Font Size pop-up menu** on the Format Bar and choose a size, such as 12 or 24.

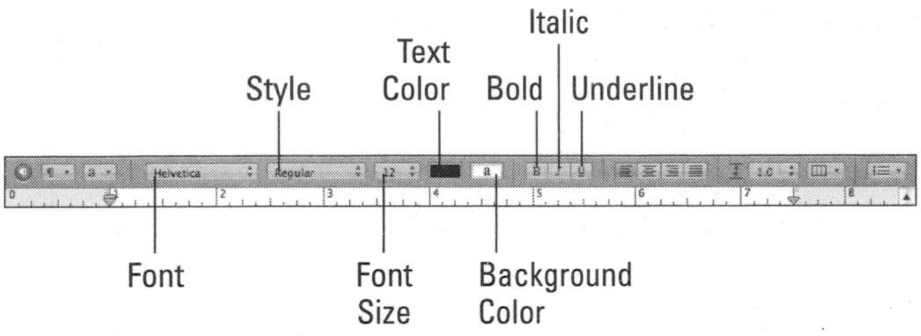

Figure 6-4: The Format bar lets you choose different fonts, sizes, and typefaces.

- Click the **Text Color button** on the Format Bar. A color menu appears, as shown in Figure 6-5. Click a color to change the color of your selected text.
- Click the **Background Color button** on the Format bar. A color menu appears, much like the one for the text color. Click a color to appear in the background of your selected text.
- Click the **Bold, Italic, or Underline icons** on the Format bar.

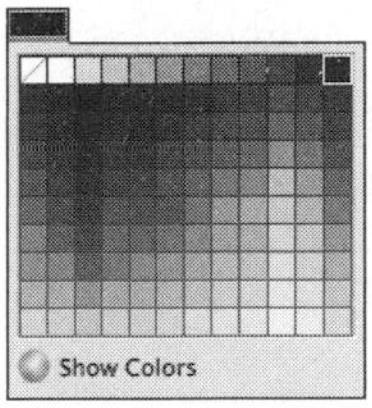

Figure 6-5: Clicking the Text Color icon displays a color menu.

If you suddenly change your mind about any of the formatting changes you made, choose Edit⇨Undo or press ⌘+Z to reverse the last changes you made.

Adjusting text spacing and margins

You can change how letters look by messing with the font, but you can also change the way a block of text looks by changing how it's spaced on the page. In concrete terms, this means changing:

- **Line spacing:** Defines how close lines in a paragraph appear.
- **Text justification:** Defines how text aligns within the left and right margins.
- **Margins:** Defines the left and right boundaries that text can't go past.

Changing line spacing

Line spacing can vary from 0.5 to 2.0. (A value of 1.0 is single spacing, and a value of 2.0 is double spacing.) To change line spacing, follow these steps:

1. **Select at least two lines of text you want to modify.**
2. **Click the Line Spacing pop-up menu on the Format Bar and choose a number such as 1.5 or 2.0, as shown in Figure 6-6.**

REMEMBER

Line spacing values less than 1.0, such as 0.5, can cause lines to overlap, which makes the text hard to read.

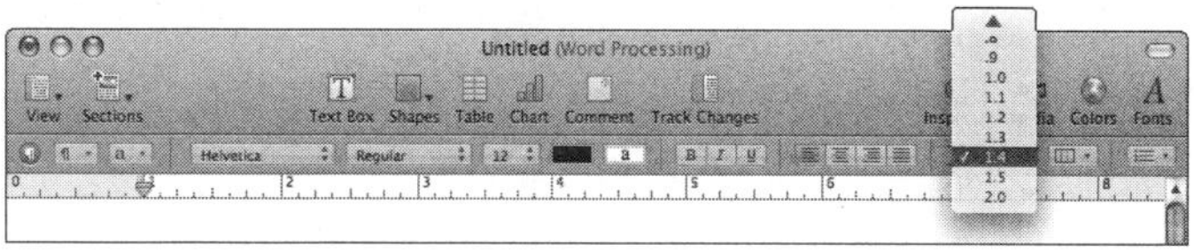

Figure 6-6: Line spacing can make text appear squashed or far apart.

Changing justification

The four types of justification are

- ✦ **Align left:** Text appears flush against the left margin but ragged along the right margin
- ✦ **Center:** Each line of text is centered within the left and right margins, so text appears ragged on both left and right margins
- ✦ **Align right:** Text appears flush against the right margin but ragged along the left margin
- ✦ **Justify:** Text appears flush against both the left and right margins, but extra spaces appear between words and characters

Figure 6-7 shows four paragraphs. The first is aligned left, the second is centered, the third is aligned right, and the final paragraph is justified.

To set your text justification, follow these steps:

1. **Select the text you want to modify.**
2. **Click the Align left, Center, Align Right, or Justify icons on the Format bar.**

Defining margins

The left and right margins only define text that appears on the page (Word Processing layout). The left and right margins of text boxes are defined by the text box size.

To define the left and right margins of text, you can use the ruler, which appears at the top of the Pages window. The ruler lets you define an exact location for your margins, such as placing the left margin exactly 1.5 inches from the left side of the page.

To define the left and right margins of text, follow these steps:

1. **Select the text you want to modify.**
2. **Click and drag the Left Margin marker to a new position on the ruler and then release the mouse button, as shown in Figure 6-8.**

   The Left Margin marker looks like an upside-down blue triangle that appears on the left side of the ruler.

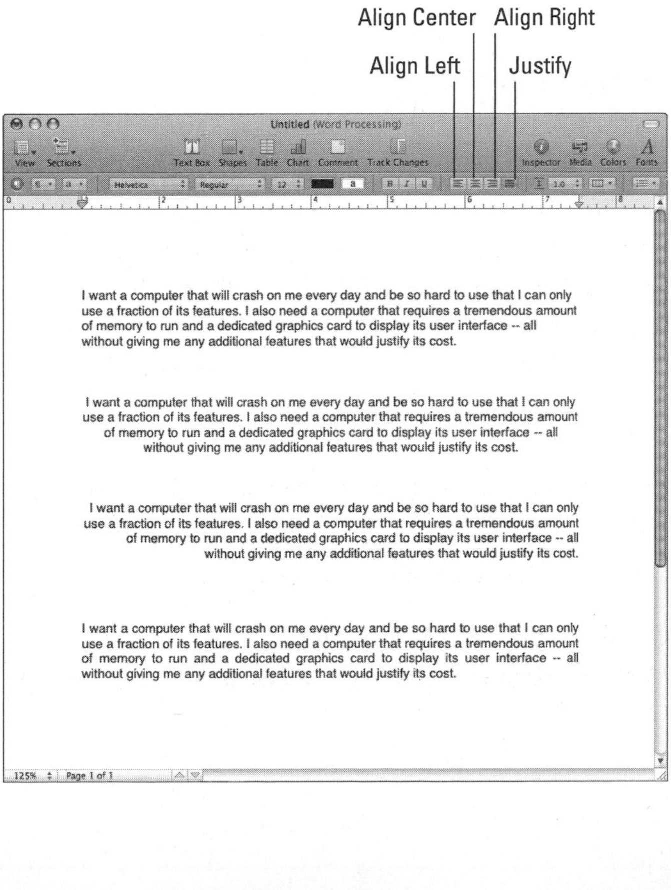

Figure 6-7: Justifying text can make paragraphs appear in different ways.

If the ruler isn't visible, choose View⇨Show Rulers.

3. **Click and drag the Indent marker to a new position on the ruler and then release the mouse button (refer to Figure 6-8).**

   The Indent marker looks like a thin blue rectangle that appears over the Left margin marker.

4. **Click and drag the Right Margin marker to a new position on the ruler and then release the mouse button (refer to Figure 6-8).**

   The Right Margin marker looks like an upside-down blue marker that appears on the right side of the ruler.

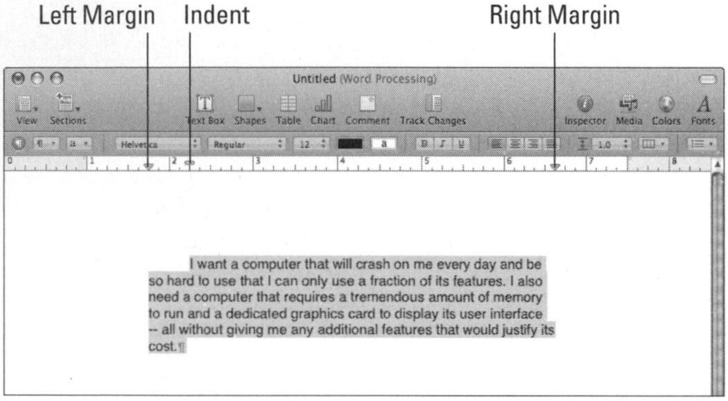

Figure 6-8: The ruler provides markers that you can drag to adjust paragraph margins.

Dragging the Left and Right margin markers on the ruler is a fast way to adjust the margins, but for a more precise way, follow these steps:

1. **Select the text you want to modify.**
2. **Click the Inspector icon (the one that looks like a little "i" in a blue circle) in the upper-right corner of the Pages window, or choose View⇨Show Inspector.**

   An Inspector window appears.

3. **Click the Text Inspector icon (the big T).**
4. **Click the Tabs tab, as shown in Figure 6-9.**
5. **Enter a value in the First Line, Left, or Right text box or click the up and down arrows to chose a value.**
6. **Click the Close button of the Text Inspector window.**

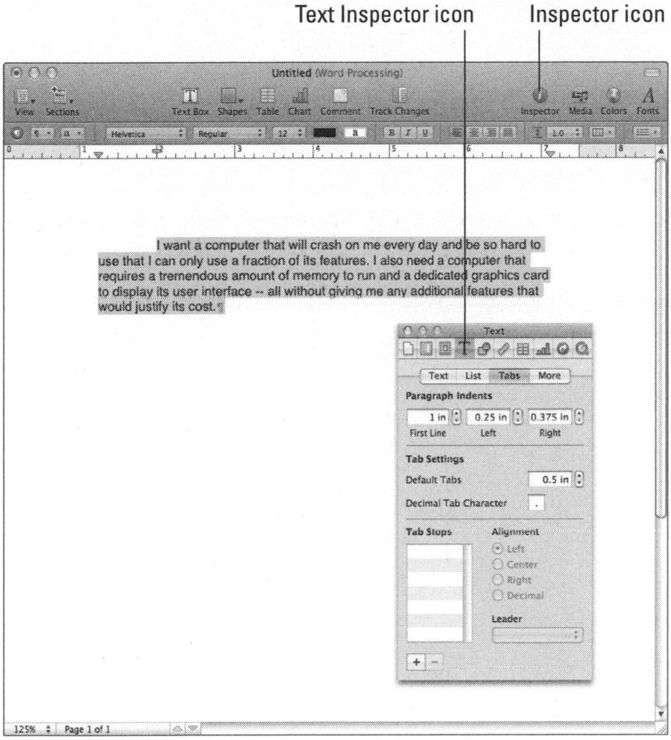

Figure 6-9: The Text Inspector window lets you choose precise values for adjusting the margins of text.

Using Formatting Styles

You might have a favorite way to format text. Although you could manually change each formatting feature, you might find it faster and easier to use styles instead. *Formatting styles* store different types of formatting that you can apply to text. By using and creating formatting styles, you can format text quickly and easily.

Applying styles

The following are the three types of styles you can apply to text:

- **Paragraph styles** affect an entire paragraph where the end of a paragraph is defined by a line that ends where you pressed Return.
- **Character styles** can affect characters or words.
- **List styles** affect multiple lines of text where each line of text ends when your press Return. (Think To Do lists or bullet points.)

Using a paragraph style

To apply a paragraph style, follow these steps:

1. **Click on the text (or move the cursor inside the text box) you want to modify.**
2. **Click the Paragraph Styles button, which appears as a gray button with a paragraph symbol and a downward pointing arrow on the far left of the Format Bar.**

   A menu of available paragraph styles appears, as shown in Figure 6-10.

   If you can't see the Format bar, choose View⇨Show Format Bar.
3. **Click a style.**

   Pages formats your entire paragraph.

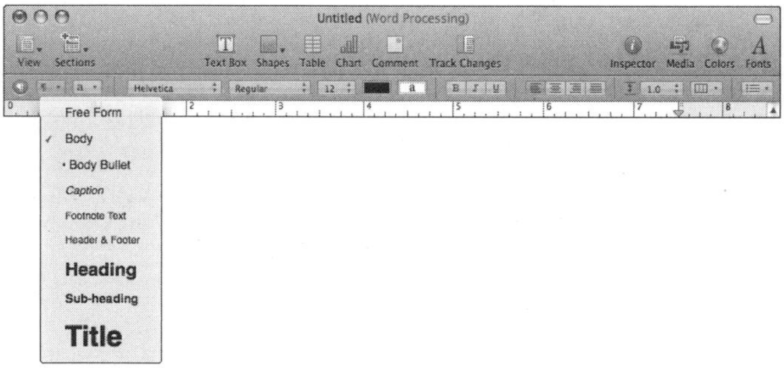

Figure 6-10: The Paragraph Styles button and menu.

Using a character style

To apply a character style, follow these steps:

1. **Select the text you want to modify.**
2. **Click the Character Styles button, which appears as a gray button with a small letter "a" and a downward pointing arrow on the far left of the Format Bar.**

   A menu of available character styles appears, as shown in Figure 6-11.
3. **Click a style.**

   Pages formats your selected text.

Some character styles, such as Emphasis and Italics, work identically as the Bold and Italics buttons on the far right of the Format Bar.

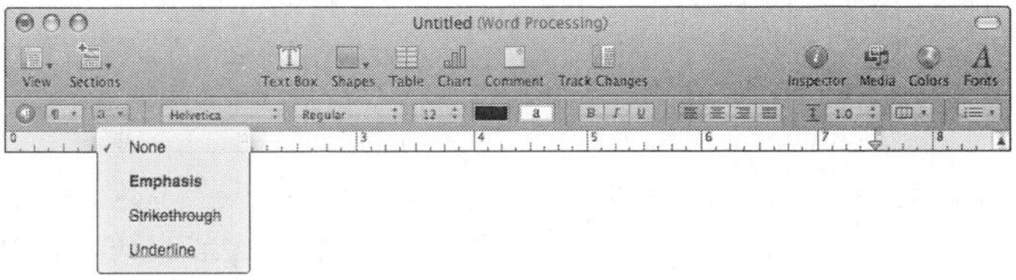

Figure 6-11: The Character Styles button and menu.

Using a list style

To apply a list style, follow these steps:

1. **Move the cursor where you want to start typing a list.**
2. **Click the List Styles button, which is the last gray button on the far right of the Format bar.**

   A menu appears, as shown in Figure 6-12.
3. **Click a list style, such as Harvard or Bullet.**
4. **Type some text and press Return.**

   Pages displays your list in your chosen list style, such as numbered or bullet list.
5. **Repeat Step 4 for each additional line of your list.**

REMEMBER

To turn off List mode, click the List Styles button and choose None.

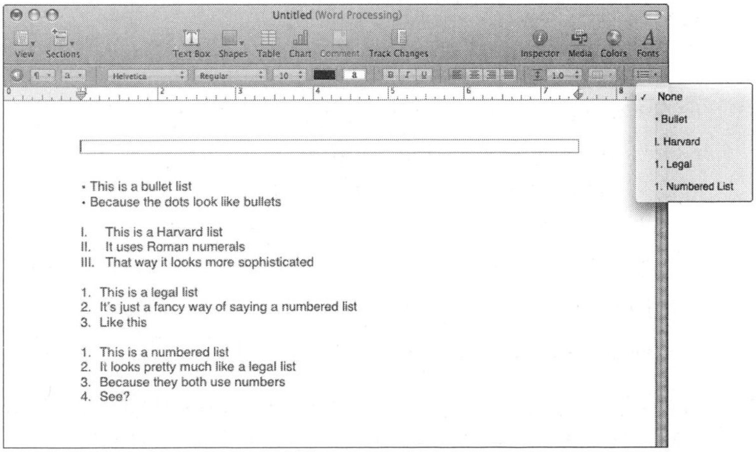

Figure 6-12: The List Styles menu displays the different types of lists you can create.

Using the Styles Drawer

For a fast way to select Paragraph, Character, or List styles, use the Styles Drawer. The Styles Drawer pops out from the right side of a Pages document and displays different styles to use while showing how text appears in each style. By using the Styles Drawer, you can quickly pick a style to format text.

To use the Styles Drawer, follow these steps:

1. **Select the text you want to modify.**
2. **Click the Styles Drawer button.**

   A drawer appears, listing all the available styles, as shown in Figure 6-13.
3. **Click a style in the Styles Drawer.**

   Your text takes on the characteristics of your selected style
4. **Click the Styles Drawer button to hide the Styles Drawer.**

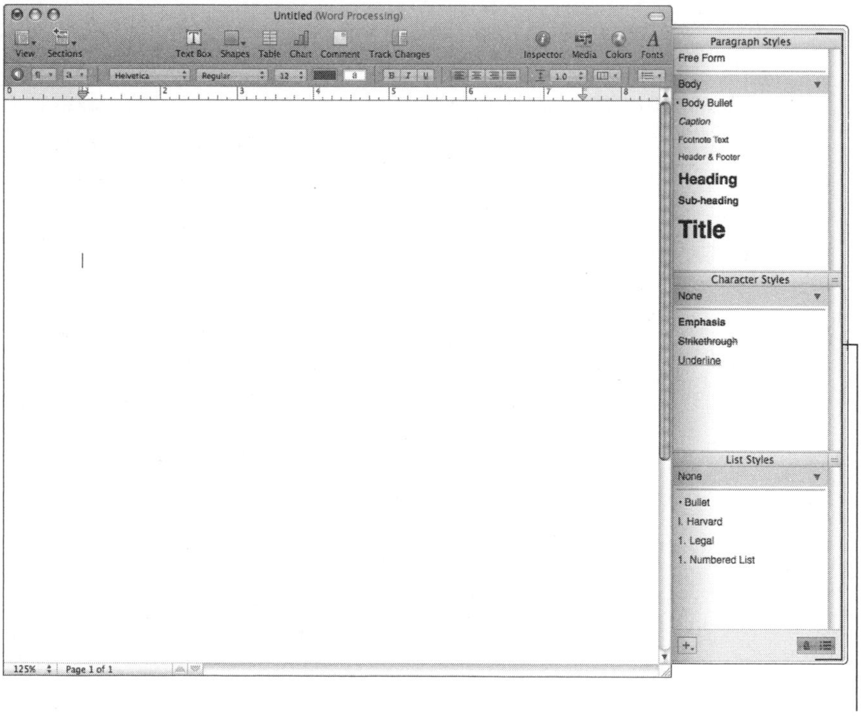

Styles Drawer

Figure 6-13: The Styles drawer lists all available styles at once.

Creating temporary styles

Pages provides paragraph, character, and list styles, but you might need to format text in a certain way that Pages doesn't offer. In that case, you can copy the style from existing text and paste that style to format other text automatically.

Copying and pasting formatting

To copy and paste formatting from existing text, follow these steps:

1. **Format text in a certain way, such as changing the fonts and font size.**
2. **Click (or move the cursor) inside the formatted text.**
3. **Choose Format⇨Copy Character Style (or Copy Paragraph Style).**
4. **Select text that you want to format the same way as the text you chose in Step 1.**
5. **Choose Format⇨Paste Character Style (or Paste Paragraph Style).**

   Pages copies your style over the text you selected in Step 4.

Saving a formatting style

If you format text a certain way repeatedly, you might want to save your formatting as a style that appears in the Styles Drawer. That way you can choose that style later just by clicking on the name of your saved style.

To save your own style in the Styles Drawer, follow these steps:

1. **Format text in a certain way, such as changing the fonts and font size.**
2. **Click (or move the cursor) inside the formatted text.**
3. **Click the Styles Drawer button to open the Styles Drawer.**
4. **Click the Plus sign button in the bottom left corner of the Styles Drawer.**

   A New Paragraph Style dialog appears.

5. **Type a descriptive name for your style and click OK.**

   Your style name now appears in the Styles Drawer. The next time you need to use this style, select text and click on this style name in the Styles Drawer.

REMEMBER

To delete a style from the Styles Drawer, right-click on the style and choose Delete Style. When a dialog appears, click in the pop-up menu to choose a style to format text currently formatted by the style you want to delete. Then click Replace.

Creating and Placing Text Boxes

Text boxes hold text that you can place anywhere on a page (even in the middle of other text). You can create and place text boxes on both word processing and page layout documents.

Creating a text box

To create a text box, follow these steps:

1. **Choose Insert➪Text Box or click the Text Box icon.**

   Pages displays a text box, as shown in Figure 6-14.

2. **Type new text inside the text box.**

   Pages keeps your text within the boundaries of the text box.

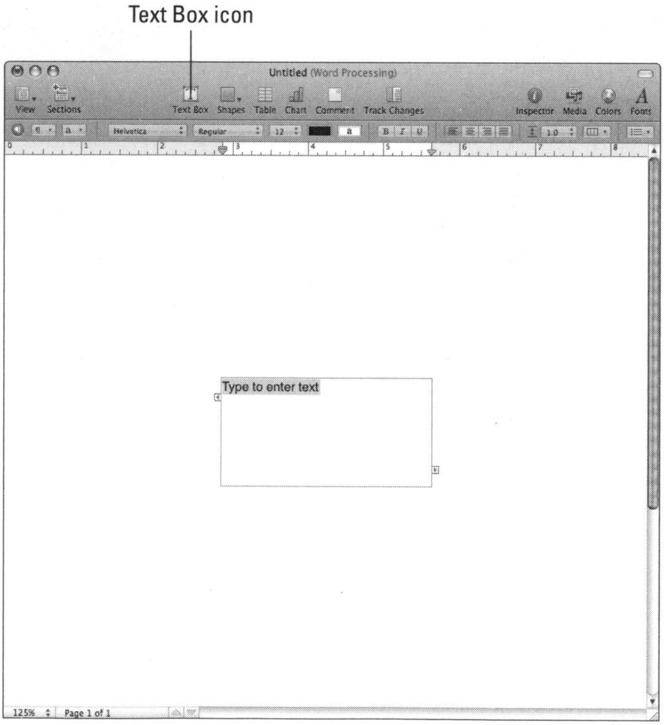

Figure 6-14: A text box appears in the middle of a page.

Moving a text box

After you've created a text box, you'll probably want to move it. To move a text box, follow these steps:

1. **Move the cursor inside the text box.**
2. **Click and drag the text box to its new location.**
3. **Release the mouse button when you've arrived at your destination.**

Resizing a text box

Sometimes a text box will be too large or small for the amount of text you typed inside of it. To fix this problem, you can resize a text box by following these steps:

1. **Click anywhere inside the text box.**

   Handles appear around the text box border, as shown in Figure 6-15.

2. **Move the pointer over a handle until the pointer turns into a two-way pointing arrow.**

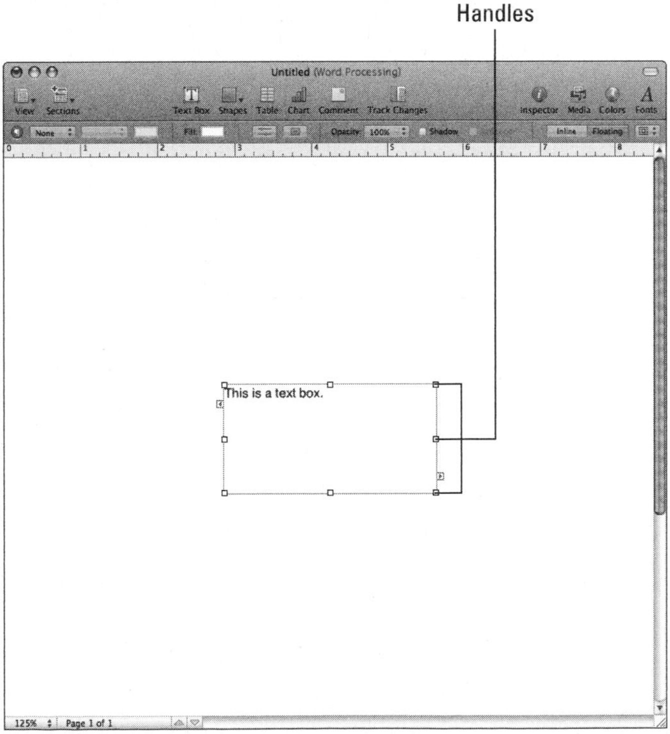

Figure 6-15: Handles appear when you click a text box.

3. **Click and drag a handle to resize the text box.**
4. **Release the mouse button when you're happy with the size of the text box.**

Creating linked text boxes

If you type more text than a text box can display, you see a *Clipping Indicator* icon — it appears as a plus sign inside a square at the bottom of the text box, as shown in Figure 6-16.

When you see the Clipping Indicator at the bottom of a text box, you have two choices. First, you can resize the text box so it can display more text, as described in the preceding section. This might not always be practical because you might not want to expand a text box any larger.

As a second alternative to dealing with too much text, you can link text boxes. Linked text boxes allow text from one text box to flow into another text box.

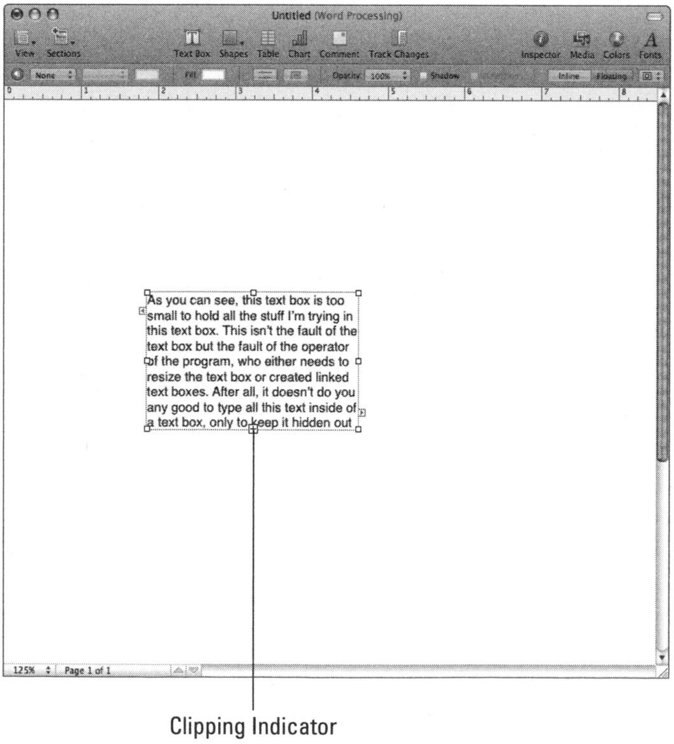

Figure 6-16: The Clipping Indicator appears when a text box is too small to display all the text stored inside of it.

Linking text boxes

To link text boxes, follow these steps:

1. **Click a text box that displays a Clipping Indicator at the bottom.**

   Blue tabs appear on the sides of the text box.

2. **Click the blue tab on the right side of the text box.**

   A message appears, telling you to click an existing text box or anywhere on the page to create a new text box, as shown in Figure 6-17.

3. **Click an existing text box or click anywhere on the page to create a new text box.**

   Pages displays a blue line linking your two text boxes and moves overflowing text from the first text box to the linked second text box, as shown in Figure 6-18.

Depending on how much text you have, you can link multiple text boxes together in a daisy chain.

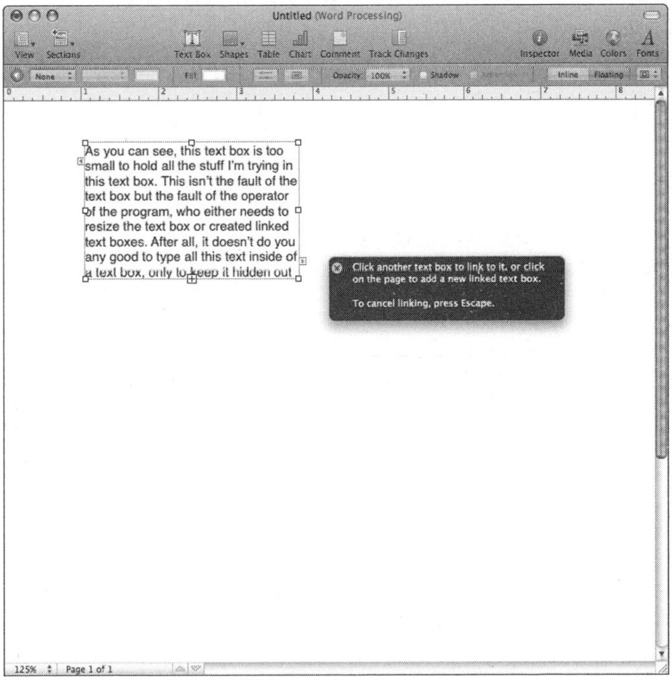

Figure 6-17: To link a text box, you can click an existing text box or have Pages create a new text box for you automatically.

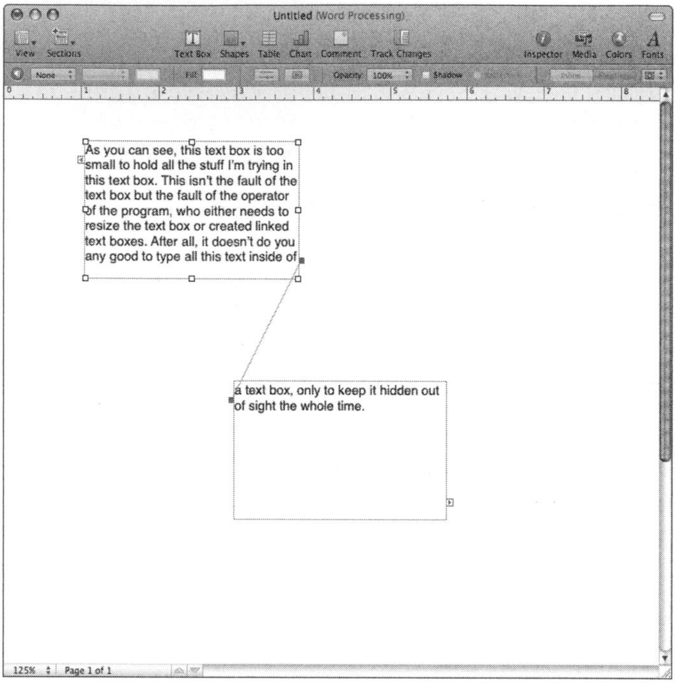

Figure 6-18: Pages identifies linked text boxes with a blue connecting line.

Unlinking text boxes

After you've linked two or more text boxes, you might decide you don't want linked text boxes after all. To unlink text boxes, follow these steps:

1. **Click the text box that you want to unlink from another text box.**
2. **Choose one of the following:**
   - Choose Format➪Text Box➪Break Connection into Text Box
   - Move the pointer over the end of the connection line, hold down the mouse button, drag the mouse away from the text box, and release the mouse button.

When you unlink text boxes, the text fills up (and overflows) the first text box, leaving the unlinked text box empty.

Wrapping text around a text box

A new text box often appears near other text. To prevent a text box you've added from covering up other text, you need to wrap the (already present) text around the new text box. To define how to wrap text around a text box, follow these steps:

1. **Click on a text box.**
2. **Click the Inspector icon (which looks like a little "i" in a blue circle) in the upper right corner of the Pages window, or choose View⇨Show Inspector.**

   The Inspector window appears.
3. **Click the Wrap Inspector button (which appears to the left of the big "T" button).**

   The Wrap Inspector options appear as shown in Figure 6-19.

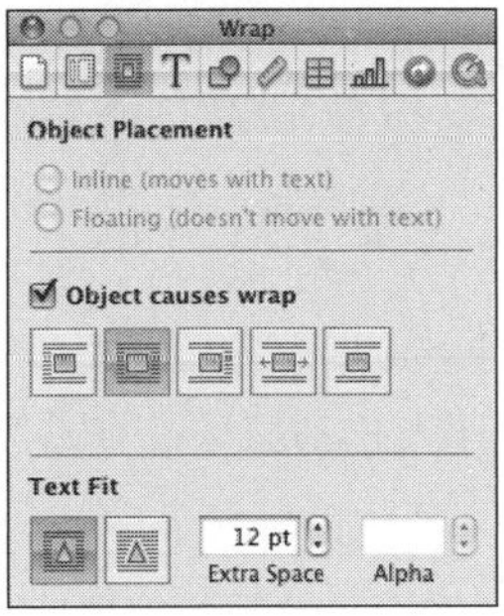

Figure 6-19: The Wrap Inspector offers different ways text can appear around a text box.

4. **Select the Object Causes Wrap check box.**
5. **Click on a text wrap button.**

   The five different text wrap buttons are:
   - *Wrap Text on the Left*
   - *Wrap Text Around*
   - *Wrap Text on the Left or Right* (whichever has more space)
   - *Wrap Text Above and Below*

Working with Digital Photographs

If you have digital photographs stored in iPhoto, you can paste those pictures directly into a Pages document and manipulate those pictures as well.

Adding a picture

To add a picture from iPhoto into a document, follow these steps:

1. **Click the Media icon on the toolbar.**

   The Media Browser appears.

2. **Click the Photos tab, as shown in Figure 6-20.**
3. **Click and drag a picture from the Media Browser onto your document.**
4. **Release the mouse button.**

   Pages displays your chosen image in the document.

Moving and resizing a picture

After you've placed a picture in a document, you might need to resize or move it. To move a picture, follow these steps:

1. **Click and drag the picture to a new position.**
2. **Release the mouse button when you're happy with the new location of the picture.**

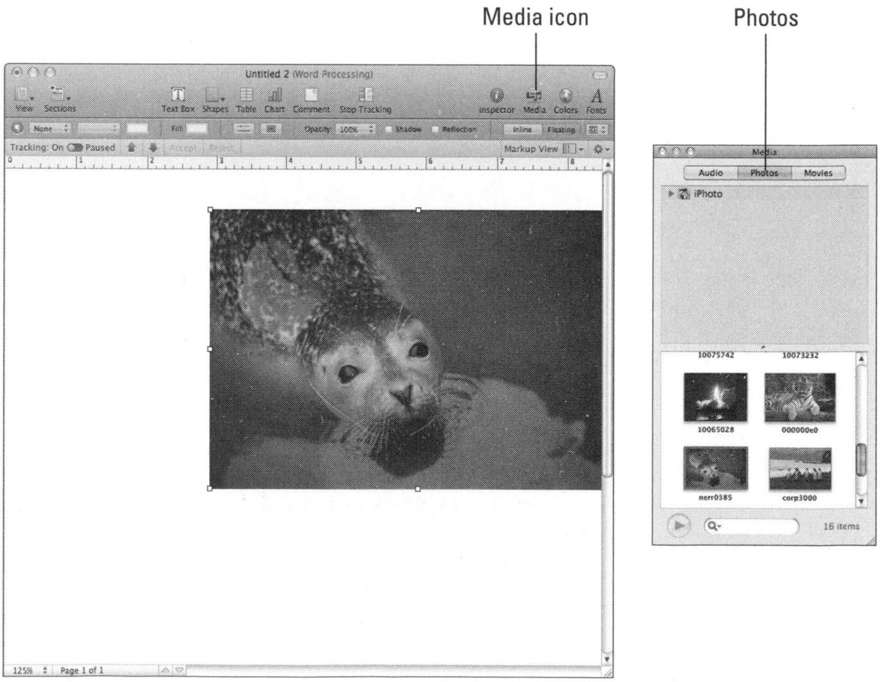

Figure 6-20: The Photos tab in the Media Browser lets you browse your iPhoto library.

To resize a picture, follow these steps:

1. **Click the picture you want to resize.**

   Handles appear around your chosen picture.

2. **Move the pointer over a handle until the pointer turns into a two-way pointing arrow.**

3. **Click and drag the handle to resize your picture.**

4. **Release the mouse button when you're happy with the new size of the picture.**

Modifying a picture

Pages provides two ways to modify the appearance of a picture: Masking and Instant Alpha. *Masking* acts like a cookie cutter that displays only part of an image within a shape. *Instant Alpha* makes part of an image transparent so that you can remove parts of the image, such as the sky in the background.

Masking a picture

To apply a mask over a picture, follow these steps:

1. **Click the picture you want to mask.**

   Handles appear around your chosen picture.

2. **Choose Format⇨Mask (or Format⇨Mask with Shape and choose a shape, such as Right Triangle or Diamond.**

   Your chosen mask appears over your picture, as shown in Figure 6-21.

3. **Move the pointer over the mask handles, then click and drag the handles to resize the mask.**

4. **Move the pointer over the dimmed portion of the picture outside the mask and then click and drag the dimmed part to adjust which part of the picture appears within the mask.**

5. **Click Edit Mask.**

   Pages displays your completed masked picture, as shown in Figure 6-22.

TIP

If you drag the slider above the Edit Mask button, you can resize the picture to make it larger or smaller.

REMEMBER

You can apply only one mask on a picture at a time. If you want to apply a different mask to a picture, you must remove the first mask by clicking the masked picture and then choosing Format⇨Unmask.

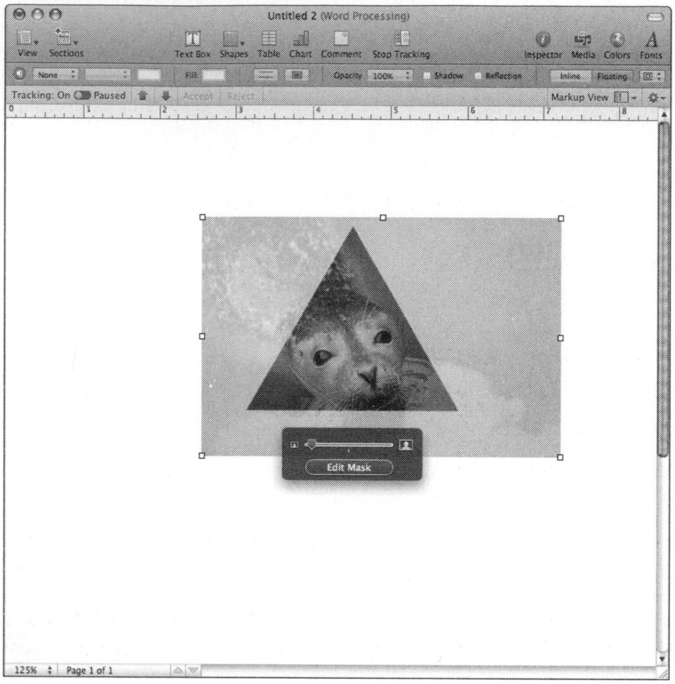

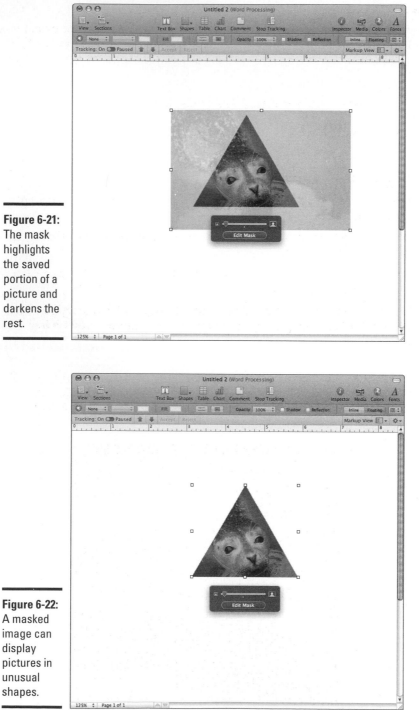

Figure 6-21: The mask highlights the saved portion of a picture and darkens the rest.

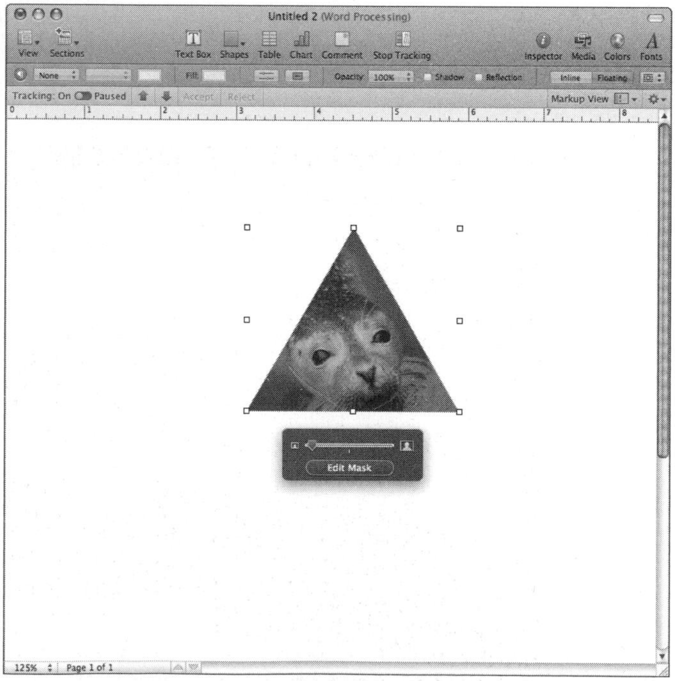

Figure 6-22: A masked image can display pictures in unusual shapes.

Turning a picture transparent with Instant Alpha

The Instant Alpha feature lets you cut away parts of a picture. For example, if you have a picture of a person's face, you might want to trim away the background image of the wall so you see only the person's face and not the wall behind.

To use the Instant Alpha feature, follow these steps:

1. **Click the picture you want to modify.**

   Handles appear around your chosen picture.

2. **Choose Format⇨Instant Alpha.**

   A dialog appears over your picture, telling you how to use the Instant Alpha feature.

3. **Click and drag your mouse over the portion of your picture that you want to make transparent (such as the sky).**

   Pages highlights all parts of your picture that are similar in color to the area that you originally pointed, at as shown in Figure 6-23.

4. **Release the mouse button when you're happy with the portion of the picture that the Instant Alpha feature has highlighted and turned transparent.**

Figure 6-23: Dragging the mouse can highlight similar colors to remove from a picture.

You can use the Instant Alpha feature multiple times to remove different colors from the same picture.

Polishing Your Document

When you're done designing your document, you're ready to show it to the world. Of course, before you show your document to others, you should spell check your document. Fortunately, Pages is happy to help you check a document's spelling. Then you can choose to save your document in a variety of formats to ensure that others can read it.

Spell checking a document

Pages can spell check your entire document, including text trapped inside text boxes and shapes. To spell check an entire document, follow these steps:

1. **Choose Edit⇨Spelling⇨Spelling.**

   (If you choose Edit⇨Spelling⇨Check Spelling, Pages highlights misspelled words but won't offer any suggestions.)

   A dialog appears, highlighting misspelled words and offering possible corrections, as shown in Figure 6-24.

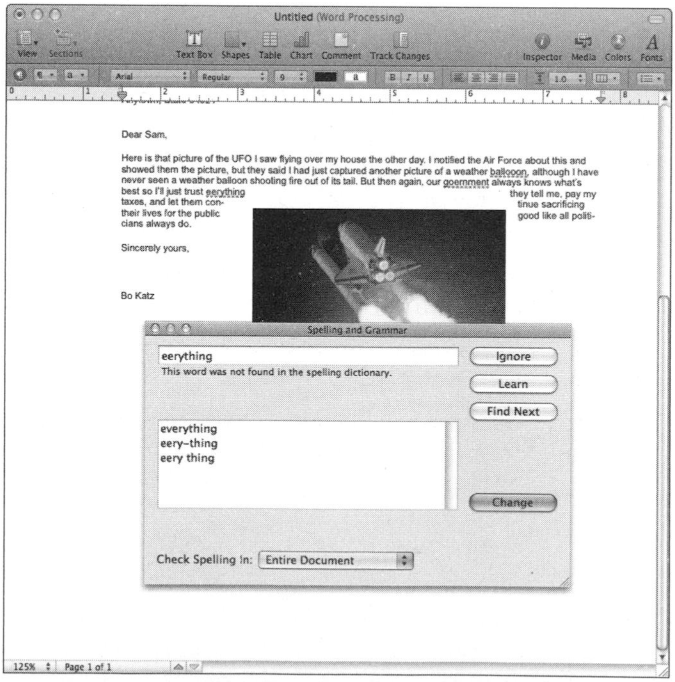

Figure 6-24: The Spelling and Grammar dialog lets you pick from a list of correctly spelled words.

2. **Choose one of the following:**
   - *Ignore:* Skips over the misspelled word.
   - *Learn:* Stores the selected word in Pages' dictionary
   - *Find Next:* Looks for the next misspelled word.
   - *Change:* Changes the misspelled word with the word selected in the list box.
3. **Click the Close button of the Spelling dialog at any time to make it go away.**

TIP

Pages can check your spelling as you type. The moment Pages identifies a misspelled word, it underlines it with a red dotted line. If you right-click (Control-click) over any word underlined with a red dotted line, Pages displays a pop-up menu of correctly spelled words that you can choose. If you want to turn off spell checking as you type, choose Edit➪Spelling➪Check Spelling As You Type to clear the check mark in front of this command.

REMEMBER

It's a good idea to proof-read your document even after spell-checking, since the spell checker only makes sure the word is correctly spelled. If you've typed "I have to cats" when you really meant to type "I have two cats," no spell checker on earth is going to flag that.

Exporting a document

When you choose the File➪Save command, Pages saves documents in its own proprietary file format. However, if you want to share your Pages documents with others who don't have the Pages program, you'll need to export your document into another file format, such as

- ✦ **PDF:** Saves your document as a series of static pages stored in the PDF Adobe Acrobat file format that can be viewed (but not necessarily edited) by any computer with a PDF viewing program.
- ✦ **Word:** Saves your document as a Microsoft Word file, which can be opened by any word processor that can read and edit Microsoft Word files.
- ✦ **RTF:** Saves your document as a Rich Text Format (RTF) file, which many programs can open and edit.
- ✦ **Plain Text:** Saves your document as text without any formatting or graphic effects.

The PDF file format preserves formatting 100 percent, but doesn't let anyone edit that file unless they use a separate PDF editing program such as Acrobat Pro. If someone needs to edit your document, both the Word and RTF options preserve Pages documents well. The Plain Text option is useful only if you can't transfer your Pages document to another program as a Word or RTF file.

To export a Pages document, follow these steps:

1. **Choose File➪Export.**

   A dialog appears, as shown in Figure 6-25.

2. **Select an option such as Word or RTF.**
3. **Click Next.**

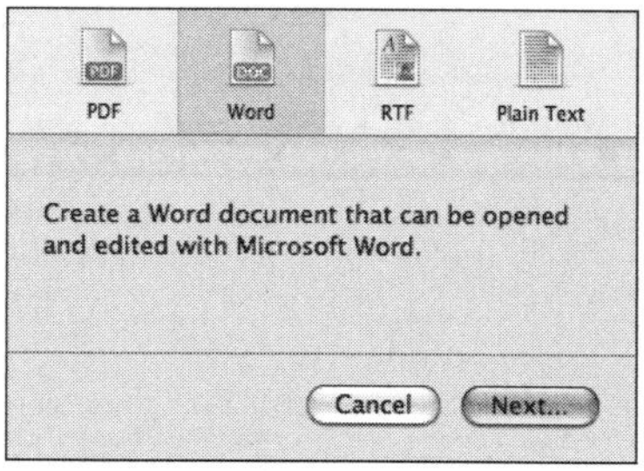

Figure 6-25: The Export dialog lets you choose a format to save your Pages document.

4. **In the new dialog that appears, enter a name for your exported document in the Save As text box.**
5. **Continuing down the dialog box, click to select the folder where you want to store your presentation.**

   You might need to switch drives or folders until you find where you want to save your file.

6. **Click Export.**

When you export a document, your original Pages document remains untouched in its original location where you last saved it.

Chapter 7: Making Presentations with Keynote

In This Chapter

- Creating a presentation
- Adding and deleting slides
- Manipulating text
- Working with graphics
- Modifying pictures and movies
- Using transitions
- Showing off a presentation

If you need to inform or convince a group of people about a subject, you often need to make a presentation. Although you could give a presentation just by talking, it's harder to emphasize certain points and ideas through words alone. That's why you need a presentation program like Keynote.

Keynote can take the hassle out of creating, organizing, and giving a presentation so you can concentrate more of your time on talking to an audience and less of your time fumbling around with transparencies, whiteboards, and felt markers that stain your fingertips and emit an unpleasant odor.

Best of all, Keynote can spice up your presentation by including audio and visual effects, from playing music and movies to showing visually interesting effects — stuff like text sliding across the screen or dissolving away into nothingness. Such effects can enhance your presentation and help hold an audience's attention.

REMEMBER

Keynote comes as part of the $79 iWork suite. Your Mac may come with a trial version of iWork, which lets you try Keynote to see if you might find it useful.

Creating a Presentation

An entire Keynote presentation consists of one or more slides, where a slide displays information to make a single point. Each slide typically contains text, as shown in Figure 7-1, although graphics, video, and audio can make an appearance as well.

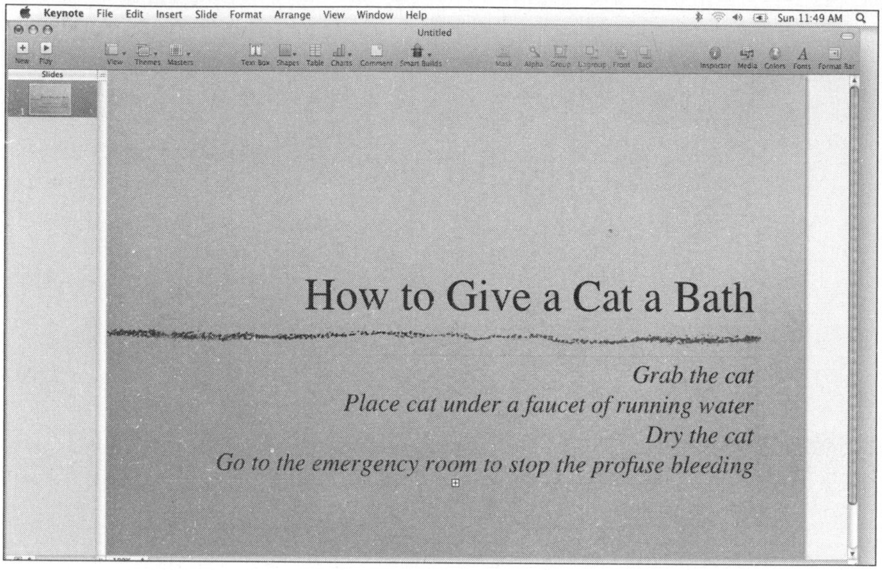

Figure 7-1: The appearance of a typical slide.

To make your slides more interesting to watch, you can also add *transition* effects that appear when you switch from one slide to another. To further emphasize the information on a particular slide, you can add individual visual effects to specific items, such as making text rotate or making a graphic image glide across the screen and halt in place.

The basic steps to creating a presentation in Keynote involve

1. Pick a theme to use for your presentation.
2. Creating one or more slides.
3. Typing text or placing graphics on each slide.
4. (Optional) Adding an audio or video file to each slide.
5. (Optional) Adding visual effects to animate an entire slide or just the text or graphics that appear on that slide.

The rest of this chapter goes into detail about each of these steps.

Working with Themes

A presentation consists of multiple slides. While you could create a generic presentation where plain black text appears against a white background, this can be boring. To spice up your presentation, Keynote provides pre-designed background graphics called themes, which provide a consistent appearance for your slides such as the font, size, style, and background color.

Choosing a theme for a new presentation

A *theme* defines the appearance of text and graphics on a slide, although you can always modify this later. To pick a theme, follow these steps:

1. **Load Keynote by double-clicking on the Keynote icon in the Applications folder (or choose File⇨New if Keynote is already running).**

   A dialog appears, displaying different themes you can choose, as shown in Figure 7-2.

2. **Click a theme and then click the Choose button.**

   Keynote creates the first slide of your presentation using your chosen theme. At this point, you can add text, graphics, audio, or video to the slide, or you can add new slides.

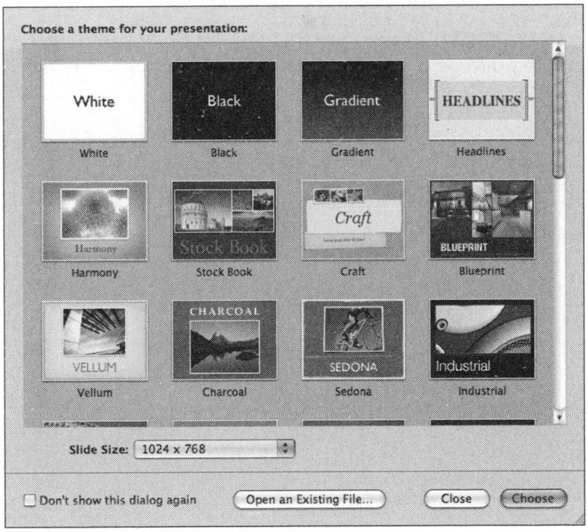

Figure 7-2: Keynote provides a variety of themes for your presentations.

Defining a default theme

If you have a favorite theme, you can make it the default theme that Keynote uses every time you create a new presentation. To define a default theme, follow these steps:

1. **Load Keynote.**
2. **Choose Keynote⇨Preferences.**

   The Preferences window appears.

3. **Click the General Icon.**

   The General Preferences pane appears, as shown in Figure 7-3.

4. **Under the For New Documents category, select the Use Theme radio button.**

   The first time you select the Use Theme radio button, a Theme dialog appears right away. After this first time, you'll have to choose a theme by selecting the Use Theme radio button and then clicking Choose.

5. **Click to select the theme you want to use as the default theme and then click Choose.**

6. **Click the Close button of the Preferences window.**

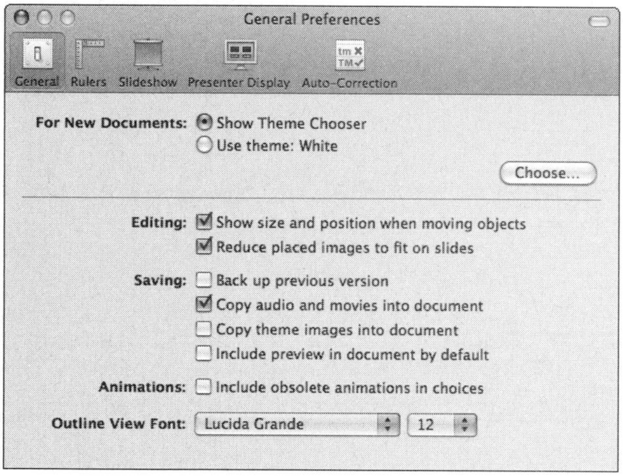

Figure 7-3: The General Preferences pane lets you pick a default theme.

Changing Presentation Views

After you've created a presentation, Keynote offers four different ways to view a presentation:

- **Navigator:** Useful for both editing individual slides and manipulating all the slides in an entire presentation.
- **Outline:** Useful for viewing and editing just the text that appears on slides, as shown in Figure 7-4.
- **Slide Only:** Useful for editing the text and graphics of a single slide, as shown in Figure 7-5.
- **Light Table:** Useful for manipulating a large number of slides in a presentation, as shown in Figure 7-6.

To switch to a different view, choose View from the Keynote menu and then choose Navigator, Outline, Slide Only, or Light Table.

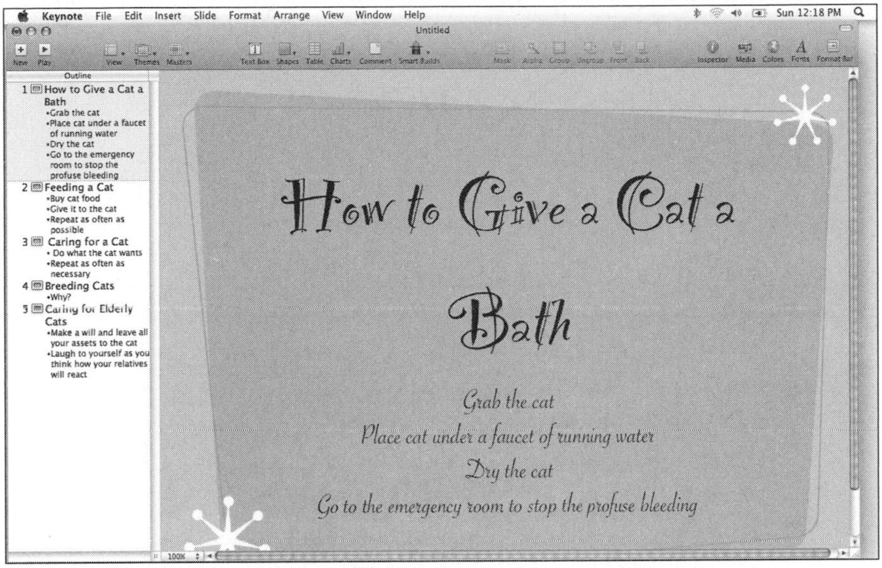

Figure 7-4: Outline view helps you edit text without the distraction of graphics.

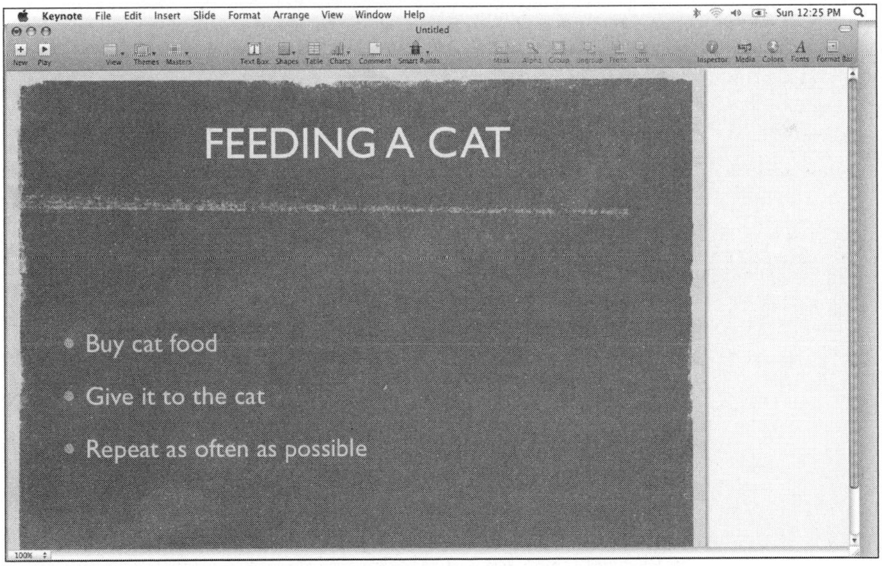

Figure 7-5: Slide Only view helps you focus on editing one slide at a time.

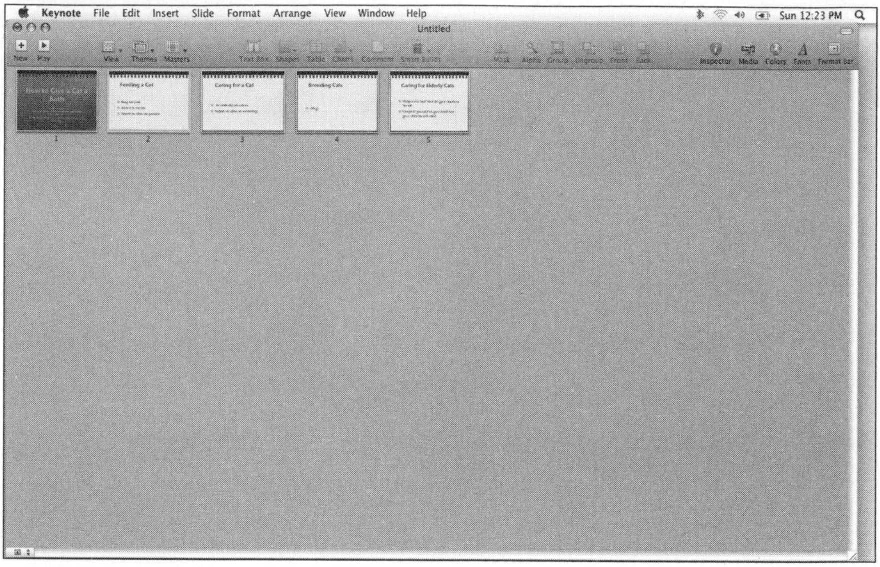

Figure 7-6: Light Table view displays slides in rows and columns for easy rearranging.

Working with Slides

When you create a new presentation, that presentation contains just one slide. Because you'll usually need more than one slide to create a presentation, you'll probably want to add more slides. And if you go overboard and add too many slides, you can always winnow out a few.

When working with slides, you often need to select multiple slides in the Slide Organizer pane or the Light Table view. If you hold down the ⌘ key, you can click and select multiple slides. If you hold down the Shift key and click two different slides, you select a range of slides.

Adding a slide

To add a slide to a presentation, follow these steps:

1. **Click a slide in either the Slide Organizer pane or in the Light Table view.**

   Your new slide will appear directly after the slide that you click on.

2. **Choose one of the following to add a new slide:**

   ✦ Click the New (plus sign) icon

   ✦ Choose Slide➪New Slide

   ✦ Click a slide in the Slide Organizer pane or Light Table view and press Return

   ✦ Right-click a slide and choose New Slide

Your newly created slide adapts the theme of the previous slide (the slide you selected in Step 1).

Rearranging slides

After you've created two or more slides in a presentation, you might want to rearrange their positions.

Keynote displays slides in the order they appear in the Slide Organizer. The top slide appears first, followed by the slide directly underneath, and so on.

To rearrange slides in a presentation, follow these steps:

1. **Choose one of the following:**
   - View➪Navigator (Displays slides vertically in the Slide Organizer pane.)
   - View➪Light Table (Displays slides in rows and columns.)
2. **Click and drag a slide in the Slide Organizer pane (or Light Table view) to its new position.**

   In Navigator view, Keynote displays a horizontal line with a downward-pointing arrow to show you where your slide will appear if you release the mouse button, as shown in Figure 7-7. In Light Table view, Keynote moves slide icons out of the way to show you where your new slide will appear.

Arrow

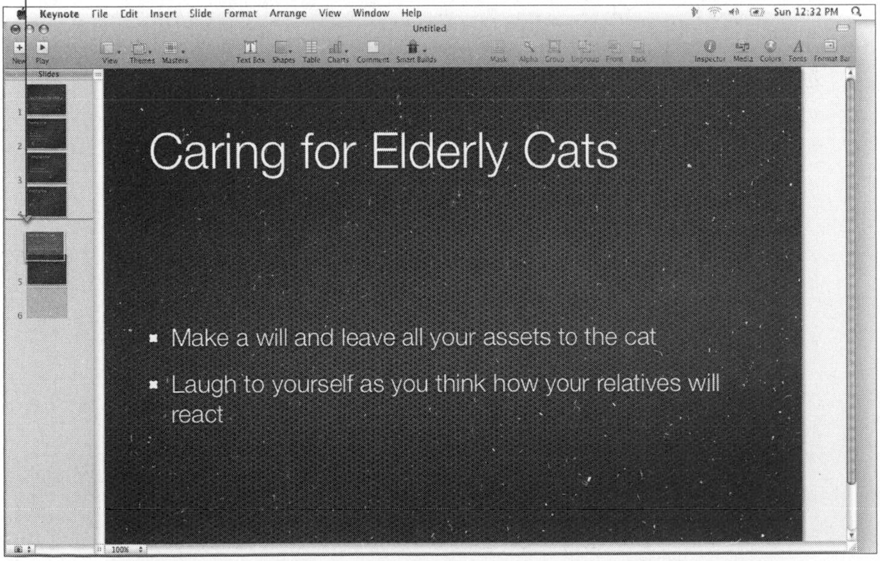
Keynote File Edit Insert Slide Format Arrange View Window Help
Sun 12:32 PM
Untitled
Caring for Elderly Cats
Make a will and leave all your assets to the cat
Laugh to yourself as you think how your relatives will react

Figure 7-7: A horizontal line and downward-pointing arrow shows you where your new slide will appear in the Navigator or Outline view.

3. Release the mouse button when you're happy with the new position of the slide in your presentation.

Deleting a slide

Eventually, you might find that you don't need a slide any more. To delete a slide, follow these steps:

1. **In either the Slide Organizer pane or Light Table view, select the slide(s) that you want to delete.**
2. **Choose one of the following:**
   - ✦ Press Delete.
   - ✦ Choose Edit⇨Delete.
   - ✦ Right-click and choose Delete.

TIP

If you delete a slide by mistake, choose Edit⇨Undo Delete (or press ⌘+Z).

Grouping slides

Many times, two or more slides are so closely related that you'd never use one slide without the other. To make sure adjacent slides stay together, Keynote lets you organize them into a group. After you've organized two or more slides as a group, you can move and delete the entire group of slides as easily as moving or deleting a single slide.

Putting slides in a group

To create a group, follow these steps:

1. **Choose View⇨Navigator.**
2. **Move all the slides that you want to place in a group so they all appear stacked over one another in the Slide Organizer pane.**
3. **Click the second slide of the group.**
4. **Hold down the Shift key and click the last slide of the group.**
5. **Press Tab.**

   Keynote indents your selected slides. Your group consists of all the indented slides plus the nonindented, first slide of the group, as shown in Figure 7-8.

REMEMBER

You can create groups of slides within other groups of slides.

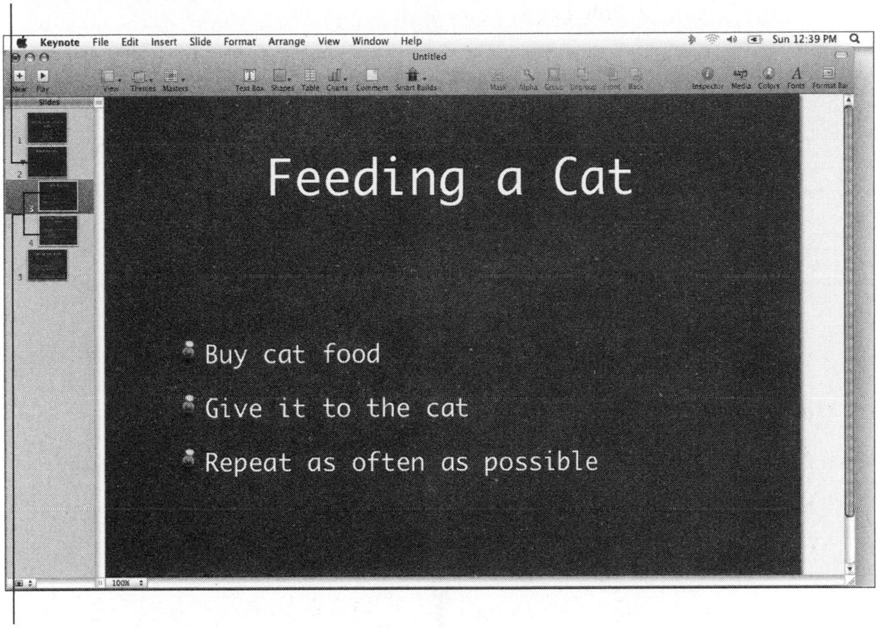

Figure 7-8: Grouped slides appear indented underneath the first slide of the group.

Moving a group

After you've created a group of two or more slides, you can treat that group as a single item and move it. To move a group, follow these steps:

1. **Choose View⇨Navigator.**
2. **Move the pointer over the first slide of the group you want to move.**

   The first slide of a group displays a triangle to its left.
3. **Click and drag the slide group to a new location in the Slide Organizer pane.**

   As you drag a group, Keynote displays all the slides of that group.
4. **Release the mouse button.**

   Your entire group of slides appears in its new location.

Deleting a group

You can easily delete an entire group of slides at the touch of a button, so be careful. To delete a group of slides, follow these steps:

1. **Choose View⇨Navigator.**

2. **Move the pointer over the first slide of the group you want to delete.**
3. **Press Delete.**

   Keynote deletes your entire group.

If you delete a group of slides by mistake, press ⌘+Z or chose Edit➪Undo Delete.

Manipulating Text

Text appears on a slide in a text box. Most slides contain two text boxes, where the top text box defines the title of a slide and the bottom text box displays the bullet points of a slide (refer to Figure 7-1).

The title of a slide typically defines the purpose of the slide, and the bullet points underneath provide supporting ideas. A slide can have only one Title text box and one Bullet Point text box, but each Bullet Point text box can contain multiple bullet points.

Editing text on a slide

Initially, every slide contains an empty Title text box and an empty Bullet Point text box. To place text on a slide, follow these steps:

1. **Choose View➪Navigator.**
2. **In the Slide Organizer pane, click the slide that you want to edit.**

   Your chosen slide appears.
3. **Double-click the placeholder text that appears in the Title or Bullet Point text boxes.**
4. **Type text or use the arrow keys and Delete key to edit existing text.**

To ensure you don't give a presentation filled with typos and misspelled words, check the spelling in your presentation by choosing Edit➪Spelling➪Spelling.

Formatting text

After you've created text, you can format it by changing fonts, font size, or color. Formatting can emphasize text or make it prettier.

Use fonts and colors sparingly. Using too many fonts or colors can make text harder to read. When choosing colors, make sure you use colors that contrast with the slide's background color. For instance, light-yellow text against a white background will be nearly impossible to read.

Changing fonts

To change the font of text, follow these steps:

1. **In the Slide Organizer pane, select the slide that contains the text you want to modify.**
2. **Double-click the text box that contains the text you want to modify.**
3. **Select the text you want to format by clicking and dragging with the mouse or holding down the Shift key while pressing the arrow keys.**
4. **Click the Fonts icon on the Keynote toolbar.**

   The OS X Fonts window appears, as shown in Figure 7-9.

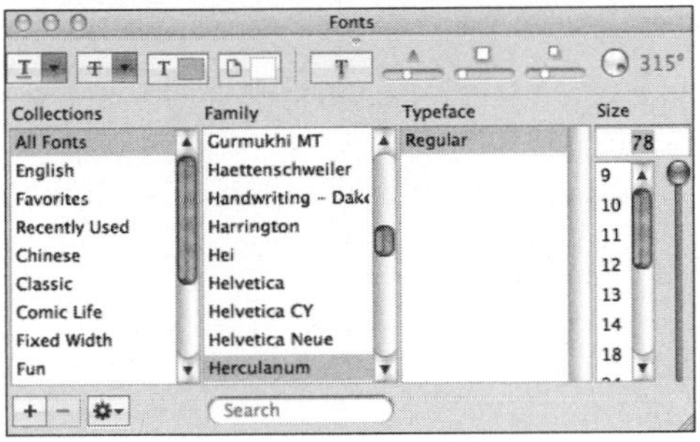

Figure 7-9: The Fonts window lets you choose a font to modify text.

Changing colors

To change the color of text, follow these steps:

1. **In the Slide Organizer pane, click the slide that contains the text you want to modify.**
2. **Double-click the text box that contains the text you want to color.**
3. **Select the text whose color you want to change by clicking and dragging the mouse or holding down the Shift key while pressing the arrow keys.**
4. **Click the Colors icon in the Keynote toolbar.**

   The OS X Color Picker window appears, as shown in Figure 7-10.
5. **Click on the desired color in the color wheel that appears in the Colors window**

   Keynote immediately uses your selected color to color the text you selected in Step 3.

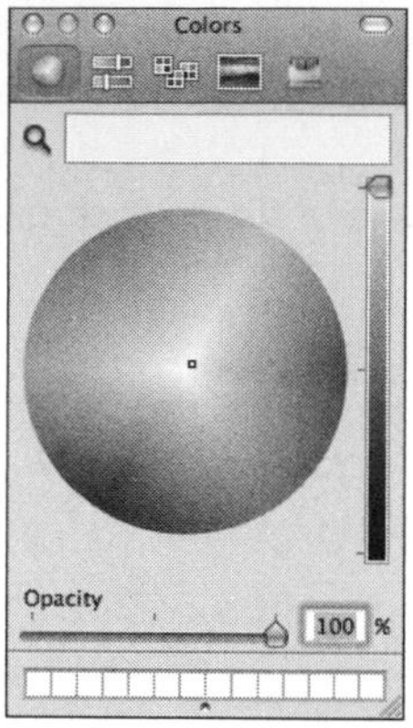

Figure 7-10: The Color Picker lets you choose a text color.

TIP

The top of the Colors window provides a variety of different color pickers that display colors as sliders, color spectrums, or even as crayons. So if you don't like the color wheel, click on a different color picker and use that one instead.

Adding Media Files

Text by itself can be as monotonous to read as the flight arrival and departure screens at an airport. To make your presentation more appealing, add sound, pictures, and movies. Sound can be an audio recording of a song stored in iTunes or edited in GarageBand, pictures can be digital photographs stored in iPhoto, and movies can be short video clips you've edited and stored in iMovie.

Adding sound

You can add any audio file stored in iTunes or GarageBand. To add sound to a slide, follow these steps:

1. **In the Slide Organizer pane, click the slide where you want to play an audio file.**
2. **Click the Media icon on the Keynote window toolbar.**

   The Media browser appears.
3. **Click the Audio tab.**

   The Media browser displays the iTunes and GarageBand folders, as shown in Figure 7-11.
4. **Click the iTunes or GarageBand folder.**

   The bottom section of the Media browser displays all the available files you can choose.

5. **Click and drag an audio file from the Media browser onto your slide and then release the mouse button.**

   Keynote displays an audio icon directly on your slide to let you know that when this slide appears in your presentation, it will automatically play your chosen audio file.

6. **Click the Close button of the Media browser.**

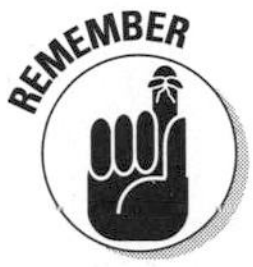

Although the audio icon appears when you're editing a Keynote presentation, it won't appear when you show your presentation.

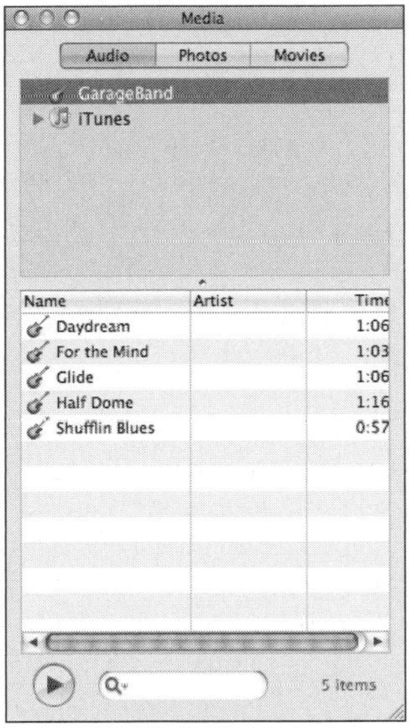

Figure 7-11: The Audio pane in the Media browser lets you choose an audio file from iTunes or Garage Band.

Adding iPhoto pictures

If you've stored digital pictures in iPhoto, you can paste those pictures on any slide in a Keynote presentation by following these steps:

1. **In the Slide Organizer pane, click the slide where you want to add a picture.**
2. **Click the Media icon on the Keynote window toolbar.**

   The Media browser appears.

3. **Click the Photos tab.**

   The Media browser displays all the pictures stored in iPhoto, as shown in Figure 7-12.

4. **Click and drag a picture from the Media browser onto your slide and then release the mouse.**

   Your chosen picture appears on your slide.

5. **Click the Close button of the Media browser.**

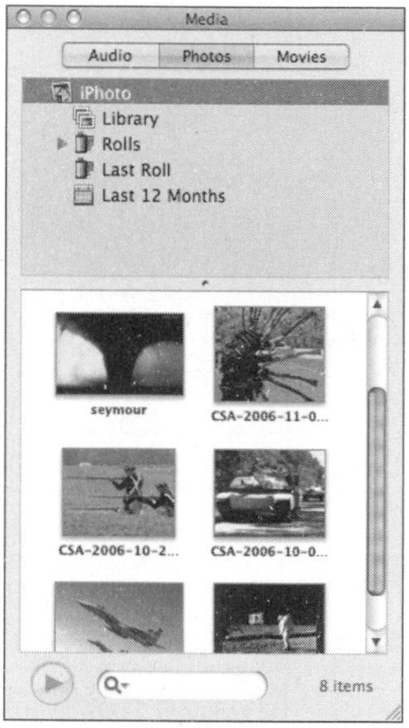

Figure 7-12: The Photo pane in the Media browser lets you choose a picture from iPhoto.

Adding iMovie videos

If you've downloaded, edited, and saved any digital videos, you can paste those movies on any slide. When you give your presentation, the movie will start playing automatically. To add a movie to a slide, follow these steps:

1. **In the Slide Organizer pane, click the slide where you want to play a video.**
2. **Click the Media icon on the Keynote window toolbar.**

   The Media browser appears.

3. **Click the Movies tab.**

   The Media browser displays all the movies stored in your Movies folder, as shown in Figure 7-13.

4. **Click and drag a movie file from the Media browser onto your slide and then release the mouse.**

   Your chosen movie appears on your slide.

5. **Click the Close button of the Media browser.**

Figure 7-13: The Movies pane in the Media browser lets you add a movie to a slide.

Editing Pictures and Movies

After you've pasted a picture or movie on to a slide, you can always move, resize, or even modify that picture. Moving and resizing a picture or movie lets you place a picture or movie in the exact spot you want it to appear on a slide. Modifying the picture lets you either correct an image or create unusual visual effects.

Moving and resizing a picture or movie

To move or resize a movie, follow these steps:

1. **In the Slide Organizer pane, click the slide where you want to move or resize a picture or movie.**
2. **Click the picture or movie.**

   Handles appear around your chosen picture or movie.
3. **To move a picture or movie, place the cursor over the middle of the image, click and drag the picture or movie to a new location on the slide, and then release the mouse button.**
4. **To resize a picture or movie, click and drag a handle to resize the picture or movie and then release the mouse button.**

TIP

If you hold down the Shift key while resizing a picture or movie, you'll retain the height and width proportions.

Modifying a picture

Keynote provides two ways to modify the appearance of a picture: Masking and Instant Alpha. Masking lets you display just a portion of an image, such as an oval or star-shaped area. Instant Alpha lets you make part of an image transparent so that the background of a slide can be seen through an image.

Masking a picture

A mask acts like a cookie cutter that you plop over a picture to save anything *inside* the cookie cutter shape, but hide any part of a picture that appears *outside* this cookie cutter shape. Keynote provides a rectangular mask and a variety of other shaped masks such as ovals, stars, arrows, and triangles.

To apply a mask on a picture, follow these steps:

1. **In the Slide Organizer pane, click the slide that contains the picture you want to mask.**
2. **Click the picture you want to mask.**

   Handles appear around your chosen picture.
3. **Choose Format⇨Mask (or Format⇨Mask with Shape and choose a shape such as Polygon or Diamond).**

   Your chosen mask appears over your picture, as shown in Figure 7-14.

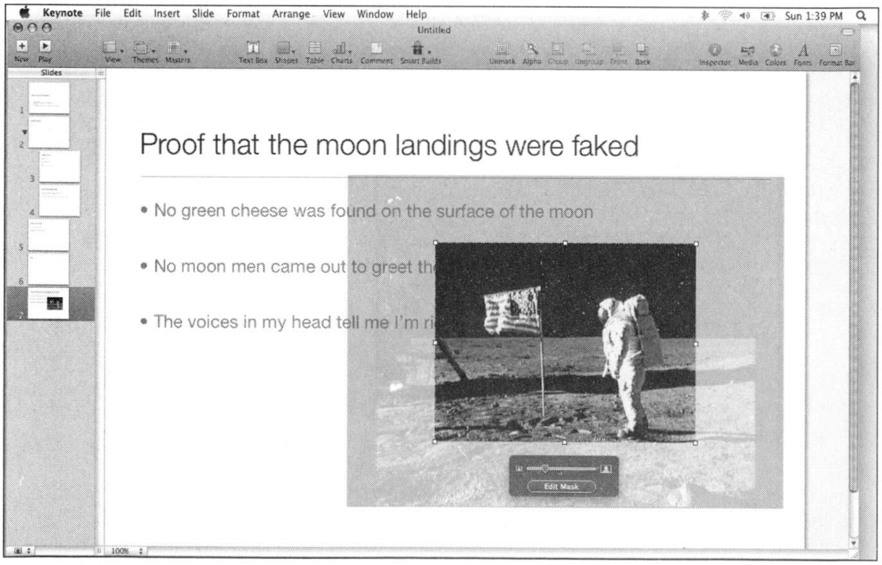

Figure 7-14: The mask highlights the saved portion of a picture and dims the rest.

4. **Click and drag a mask handle to resize the mask.**

   If you hold down the Shift key while dragging a mask handle, you'll retain the height and width aspect ratio.

5. **Move the pointer over the dimmed portion of the picture outside the mask, then drag over the dimmed portion to adjust which part of the picture appears within the mask.**

6. **Click the Edit Mask button.**

   Keynote masks your picture, as shown in Figure 7-15.

You can apply only one mask on a picture at a time. If you want to apply a different mask over a picture, you must remove the first mask by choosing Format➪Unmask.

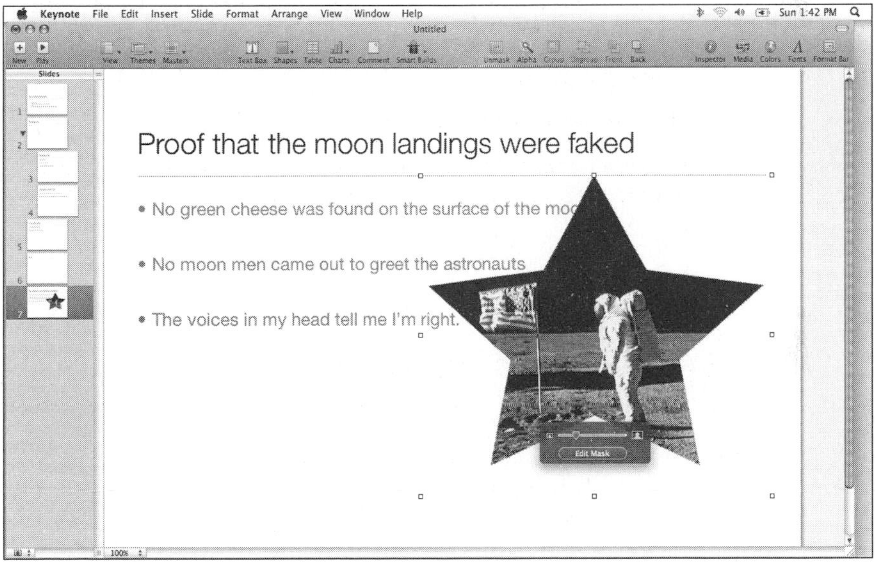

Figure 7-15: A masked image can create an unusual visual effect on a slide.

Turning a picture transparent with Instant Alpha

Keynote's Instant Alpha feature lets you remove a portion of a picture. This can create unusual visual effects by stripping unwanted portions of a picture, such as the sky, and just keeping the parts you like, as shown in Figure 7-16.

To use the Instant Alpha feature, follow these steps:

1. **In the Slide Organizer pane, click the slide that contains the picture you want to modify.**
2. **Click the picture you want to modify.**

   Handles appear around your chosen picture.
3. **Choose Format⇨Instant Alpha (or click the Alpha icon on the Toolbar at the top of the Keynote window).**

   A dialog appears over your picture, telling you how to use the Instant Alpha feature.
4. **Place the pointer over the portion of your picture that you want to make transparent (such as the sky) and then drag the mouse.**

   Keynote highlights all parts of your picture that are similar in color to the area that you originally pointed at, as shown in Figure 7-17.
5. **Release the mouse button when you're happy with the portion of the picture that the Instant Alpha feature has highlighted and turned transparent.**

REMEMBER

You can use the Instant Alpha feature multiple times to remove different colors from the same picture. If you make a mistake, choose Edit⇨Undo Instant Alpha or press ⌘+Z.

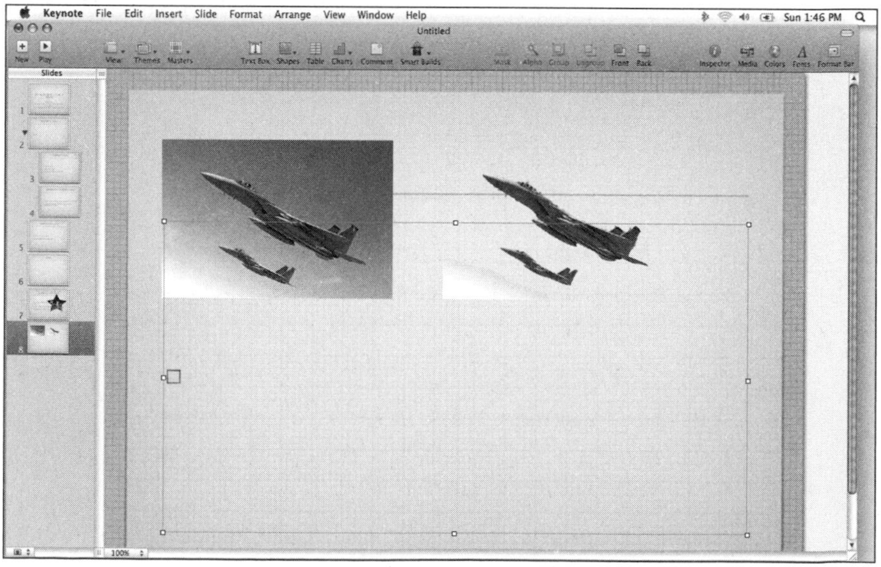

Figure 7-16: The Instant Alpha feature can strip away the unwanted parts of a picture.

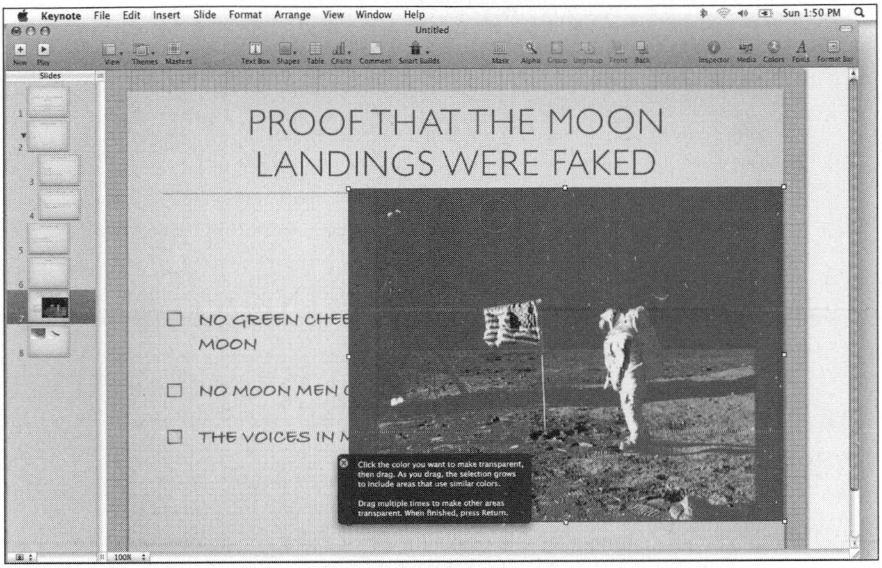

Figure 7-17: Dragging the mouse highlights similar colors to eliminate.

Creating Transitions and Effects

To make your presentations visually interesting to watch, you can add transitions that define how slides, text, and graphics appear and disappear. Slide transitions define how a slide disappears from the screen. Text and graphic effects define how the text or graphic initially appears on the slide, how it disappears off a slide, and how it can move around a slide.

Creating a slide transition

To create a slide transition, follow these steps:

1. **Choose View⇨Navigator.**
2. **In the Slide Organizer pane, click the slide that you want to display with a transition.**
3. **Choose View⇨Show Inspector (or click the Inspector icon).**

   An Inspector window appears.
4. **Click the Slide Inspector icon in the Inspector window and click the Transition tab, as shown in Figure 7-18.**
5. **Click in the Effect pop-up menu and choose an effect such as None (to remove any transitions), Fall, or Flip.**

   The Slide Inspector gives you a preview of what your transition will look like.

6. **(Optional) Depending on the transition effect you chose, you might need to define other options such as the Direction or Duration of your transition.**
7. **Click the Close button of the Inspector window.**

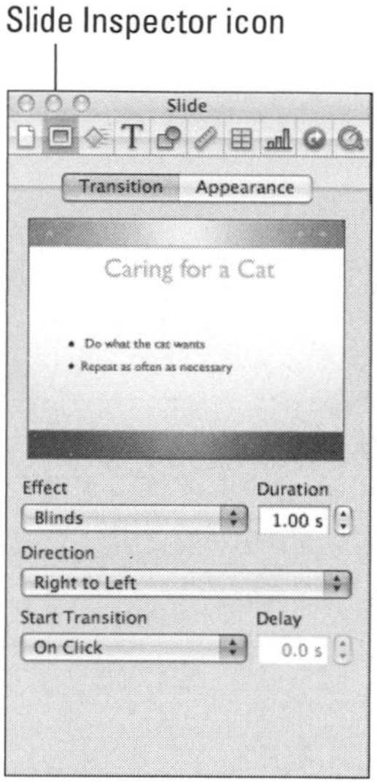

Figure 7-18: The Transitions tab in the Slide Inspector pane lets you define a transition.

Creating text and graphic effects

Keynote offers three ways to create text and graphic effects:

- **Build In:** Defines how text and graphics enter on a slide. (If you choose a Build In transition, the text and graphics won't appear initially on the slide.)
- **Build Out:** Defines how text and graphics exit off a slide.
- **Action:** Defines how text and graphics move on a slide.

To define an effect for text or graphics, follow these steps:

1. **Choose View➪Navigator.**
2. **In the Slide Organizer pane, click the slide that contains the text or graphic you want to display with a visual effect.**
3. **Click the text or graphic you want to modify.**

   Handles appear around your chosen text or graphic.

4. **Choose View➪Show Inspector or click the Inspector icon.**

   An Inspector window appears.

5. **Click the Build Inspector tab in the Inspector window.**

   The Build Inspector pane appears, as shown in Figure 7-19.

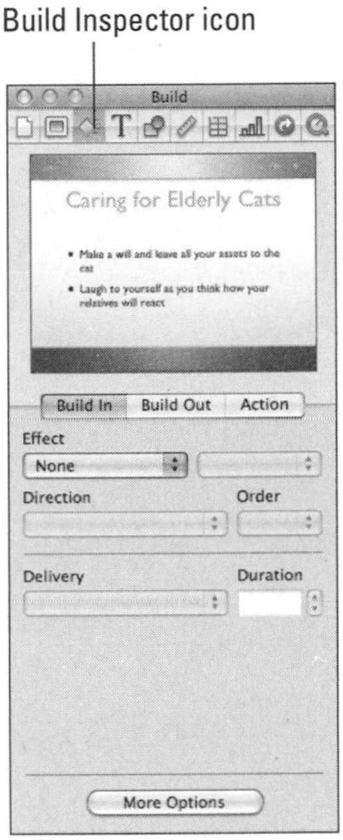

Figure 7-19: The Build Inspector pane lets you choose an effect for text or graphics on a slide.

6. **Click the Build In, Build Out, or Action button.**
7. **Choose an option from the Effect pop-up menu.**

   Rotate and Opacity are nice choices.

8. **(Optional) Depending on the effect you chose, you might be able to choose additional ways to modify that effect.**
9. **Click the Close button of the Inspector window.**

Making text and graphics move on a slide

If you choose the Action button for text or graphics, you can choose the Move Effect, which lets you define a line that the text or graphic follows as it moves across a slide. To define a line to move text or graphics on a slide, follow these steps:

1. **Choose View➪Navigator.**

2. **In the Organizer pane, click the slide that contains the text or graphic you want to display with a visual effect.**
3. **Click the text or graphic you want to modify.**

   Handles appear around your chosen text or graphic.
4. **Choose View⇨Show Inspector, or click the Inspector icon.**

   An Inspector window appears.
5. **Click the Build Inspector tab.**

   The Build Inspector pane appears (refer to Figure 7-19).
6. **Click the Action button.**
7. **Choose Move from the Effect pop-up menu.**

   Keynote displays a red line that shows how your chosen text or graphic will move, as shown in Figure 7-20.
8. **(Optional) Click and drag the handle at the beginning or end of the red line to move the line or change the line length.**

   Moving the red line changes the direction your chosen text or graphics moves. Changing the line length determines how far your chosen text or graphics moves.
9. **(Optional) Click the Straight Line or Curved Line button under the Path heading in the Inspector window to change how your object moves.**
10. **Click the Close button on the Inspector window.**

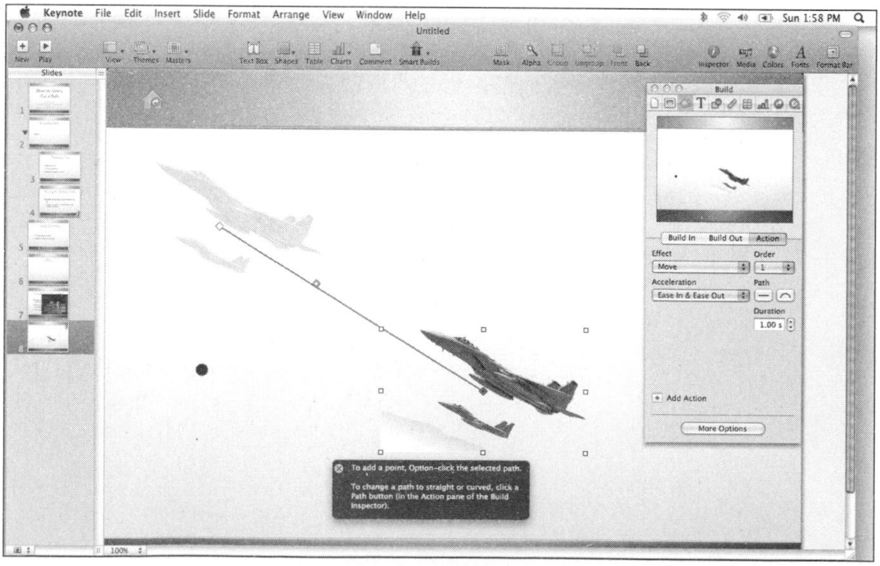

Figure 7-20: Keynote displays the path of text or graphic on a slide.

Polishing Your Presentation

When you're done modifying the slides in your presentation, you'll need to show your presentation to others. You might give a presentation in person or just pass out your presentation to others so they can view it at their leisure without you around.

Viewing a presentation

After you've finished creating a presentation, you need to view it to see how it actually looks. The slide order or visual effects might have looked good when you put your presentation together, but when viewed in its entirety, you might suddenly notice gaps in your presentation. To view a presentation, follow these steps:

1. **Choose View➪Navigator.**
2. **In the Organizer pane, click the first slide you want to view.**

   If you click the first slide of your presentation, you can view your entire presentation. If you click a slide in the middle of your presentation, you can view only that part of your presentation from that slide to the end.
3. **Choose View➪Play Slideshow.**

   The slide you chose in Step 2 appears.
4. **Click the mouse button or press the space bar to view each effect and slide.**

   If you're at the last slide of your presentation, clicking the mouse button or pressing the space bar exits out of your presentation.
5. **(Optional) Press Esc if you want to stop viewing your presentation before reaching the last slide.**

Rehearsing a presentation

Viewing a presentation lets you make sure that all the slides are in the right order and that all effects and transitions work as you expect. Before giving your presentation, you might want to rehearse it and let Keynote show you approximately how much time you spend on each slide.

REMEMBER

Rehearsing can give you only a guess of the time needed to give your presentation. In real life, the audience and conditions around you might interfere with your timing, such as an impatient audience sitting in a stuffy conference room where the air conditioning suddenly breaks down.

To rehearse a presentation, follow these steps:

1. **Choose View⇨Navigator.**
2. **In the Slide Organizer pane, click the first slide you want to view.**
3. **Choose View⇨ Rehearse Slideshow.**

   Keynote displays your slides with a timer underneath, as shown in Figure 7-21.
4. **Practice what you're going to say when presenting each slide and then press the space bar or click the mouse button to advance to the next slide.**

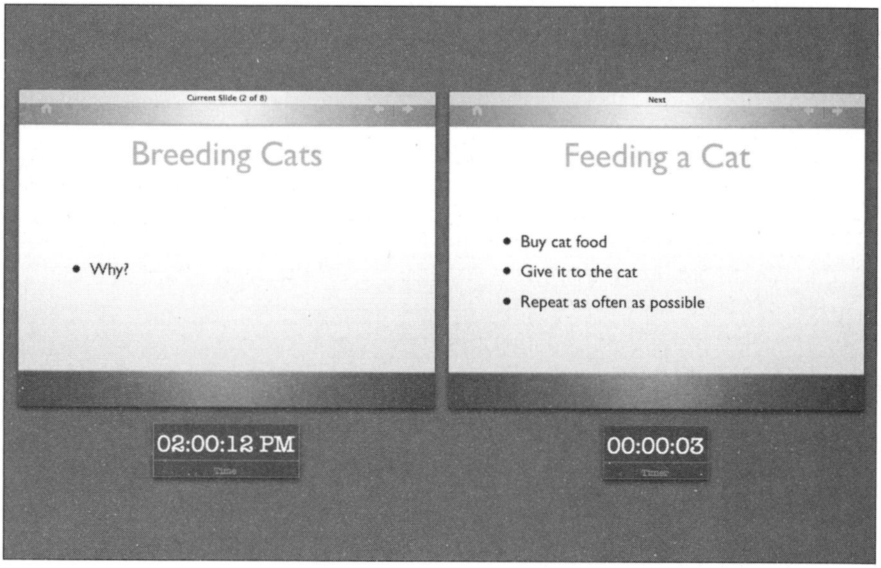

Figure 7-21: Keynote tracks how much time you spend on each slide.

Exporting a presentation

When you give a presentation, you'll probably do it directly from your Mac. However, there may come a time when you'll need to save your presentation to run on a different type of computer. Fortunately, Keynote lets you save (or *export*) a Keynote presentation in one of the following file formats:

- ✦ **QuickTime:** Saves your presentation as a movie that can be played on a Windows or Mac computer that has the free QuickTime player. This movie preserves all transitions and visual effects.

+ **PowerPoint:** Saves your presentation as a PowerPoint file that you can edit and run on any computer that runs PowerPoint. (Certain visual effects and transitions might not work in PowerPoint.)
+ **PDF:** Saves your presentation as a series of static images stored in the PDF Adobe Acrobat file format that can be viewed by any computer with a PDF viewing program. Any interesting visual or transition effects between slides will be lost.
+ **Images:** Saves each slide as a separate graphic file.
+ **Flash:** Saves your presentation as a movie that can be played on any computer that has the free Flash player. This movie preserves all transitions and visual effects.
+ **HTML:** Saves each slide as a separate Web page. Any interesting visual or transition effects between slides will be lost.
+ **iPod:** Saves your presentation as a movie specially designed to play on an iPod.

If you want to preserve your visual effects and transitions, save your presentation as a QuickTime, iPod, or Flash movie. If you want to preserve and edit your presentation, save it as a PowerPoint file.

To export a Keynote presentation, follow these steps:

1. **Choose File⇨Export.**

   A dialog appears, as shown in Figure 7-22.

2. **Click an option such as the QuickTime or PowerPoint icon.**

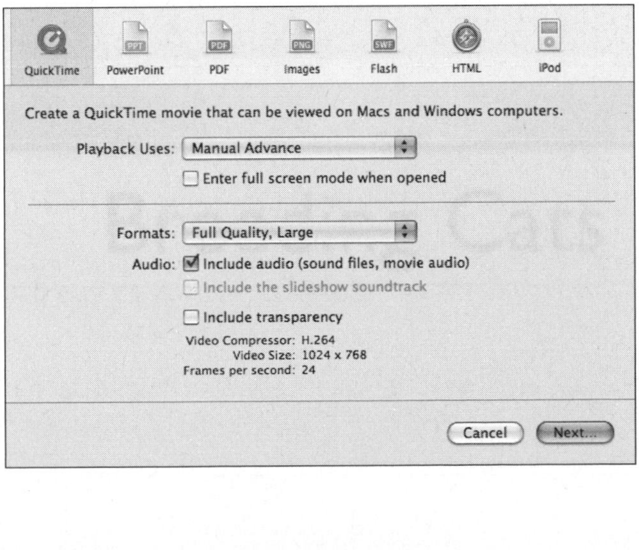

Figure 7-22: The Export dialog lets you choose a format to save your Keynote presentation.

3. **(Optional) Depending on the option you choose in Step 2, you might see additional ways to customize your presentation.**
4. **Click Next.**

   Another dialog appears, showing all the drives and folders on your hard drive.
5. **Click the folder where you want to store your presentation.**

   You might need to switch drives or folders until you find where you want to save your file.
6. **Click the Export button.**

When you export a presentation, your original Keynote presentation remains untouched in its original location where you last saved it.

Chapter 8: Doing Calculations with Numbers

In This Chapter

- Getting to know the parts of a Numbers spreadsheet
- Creating a spreadsheet
- Using sheets
- Working with tables
- Adding data to a table
- Working with charts
- Polishing a spreadsheet
- Sharing your spreadsheet efforts

Numbers is a spreadsheet program designed to help you manipulate and calculate numbers for a wide variety of tasks, such as balancing a budget, calculating a loan, and creating an invoice. The Numbers program not only lets you organize numbers and perform calculations on them, but the program also lets you create line, bar, and pie charts that graphically help you analyze and understand what your data means. By making calculations easy and creating charts from your numbers even easier, Numbers can help you make sense out of any numeric data.

Understanding the Parts of a Numbers Spreadsheet

Basically, a Numbers spreadsheet consists of one or more *sheets,* which are completely blank like an empty sheet of paper. On each sheet, you can place the following items, as shown in Figure 8-1:

- Tables
- Charts
- Text boxes
- Pictures

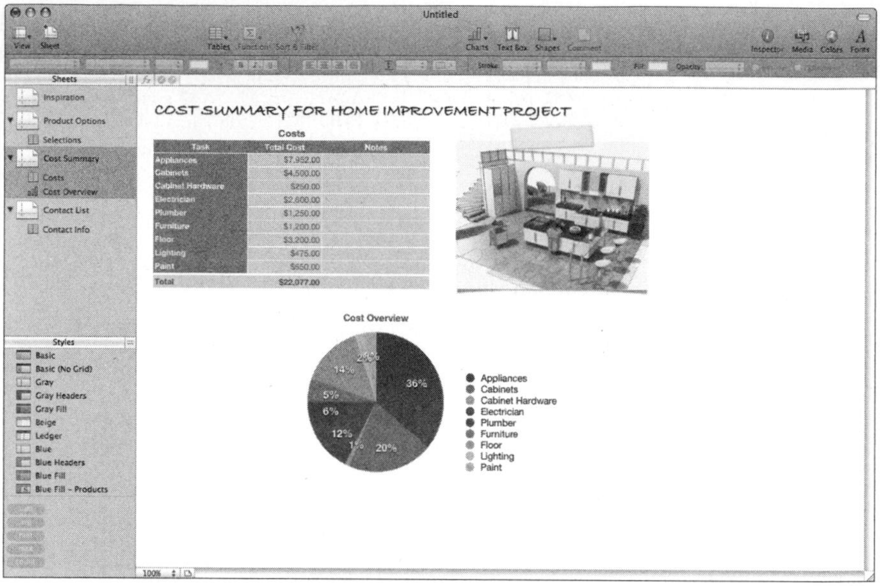

Figure 8-1: The parts of a Numbers spreadsheet.

A *table* consists of rows and columns. The intersection of a row and column is called a *cell,* which is where you can type and store numbers, text, and formulas, as shown in Figure 8-2.

A *chart* displays data stored in a table. Common types of charts are line, bar, pie, and column charts, as shown in Figure 8-3.

Both *text boxes* and *pictures* serve mostly decorative functions. A text box lets you type and store text independent of the rows and columns in a table. Pictures let you add decorative images on a sheet, such as a company logo. By letting you arrange tables, charts, text boxes, and pictures on a sheet, Numbers helps you manipulate numbers and present your information in a visually appealing way that ordinary spreadsheets can't match.

Putting together a spreadsheet is a pretty simple process. The following list points out the highlights:

✦ **Start with a sheet.** When you create a new Numbers file, either from scratch or using a template, Numbers automatically creates one sheet with one table on it. From there, it's your job to start filling that table with data. Add more tables if you want — yes, a sheet can hold multiple tables — or start spicing up your data presentation with charts or pictures. (More on that later.)

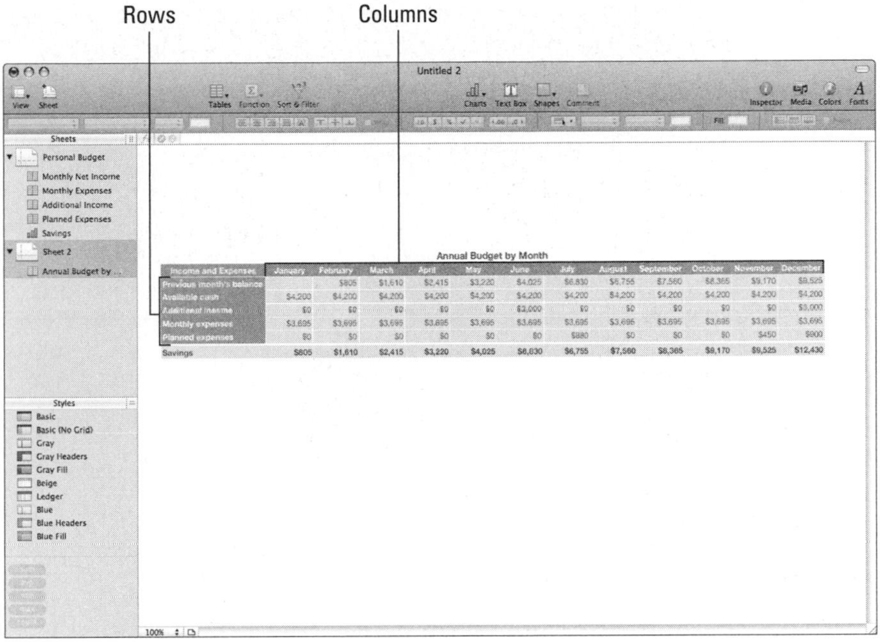

Figure 8-2: The parts of a table.

- ✦ **Fill a table with numbers and text.** After setting up at least one table on a sheet, you can move the table around on the sheet and/or resize it, as spelled out later in this chapter. When you're happy with the table's position on the sheet and the table's size, you can start typing numbers into the table's rows and columns. Of course, a long list of numbers is relatively meaningless, so you also need to type text in a table that identifies what those numbers mean, such as "August Sales" or "Number of Screwdrivers Sold."
- ✦ **Create formulas.** After you've typed numbers in a table along with descriptive text, you also need to enter formulas that manipulate one or more numbers in certain ways, such as adding a column of numbers. Formulas take your numbers and calculate a result, such as identifying how much your company made in sales last month or how a single sales person's sales results have changed each month since the beginning of the year.

Formulas not only calculate useful results, but they also let you enter hypothetical numbers to see possible results. For example, if every sales person improved his or her sales results by 5 percent every month, how much of an increase in cash would that bring in to the company? Now, what happens if every sales person lowered his or her sales results by 3 percent every month? By typing in different values, you can ask "What if?" questions with your data and formulas.

- **Visualizing data with charts.** Just glancing at a dozen numbers in a row or column might not show you much of anything. That's why Numbers lets you create charts based on your data. By turning numeric data into line, bar, or pie charts, Numbers can help you spot trends in your data.
- **Polish your sheets.** Most spreadsheets consist of rows and columns of numbers with a bit of descriptive text thrown in for good measure. Although functional, such spreadsheets are boring to look at. That's why Numbers gives you the chance to place text boxes and pictures on your sheets to make your information (tables and charts) look pretty for printing.

Creating a Numbers Spreadsheet

To help you create a spreadsheet, Numbers provides a handful of templates that you can use or modify. If you prefer, you can use the blank template to create a spreadsheet (one sheet with one table on it) from scratch. If you design a particularly useful spreadsheet, you can even save it (by choosing File⇨ Save as Template) as a template to use in the future.

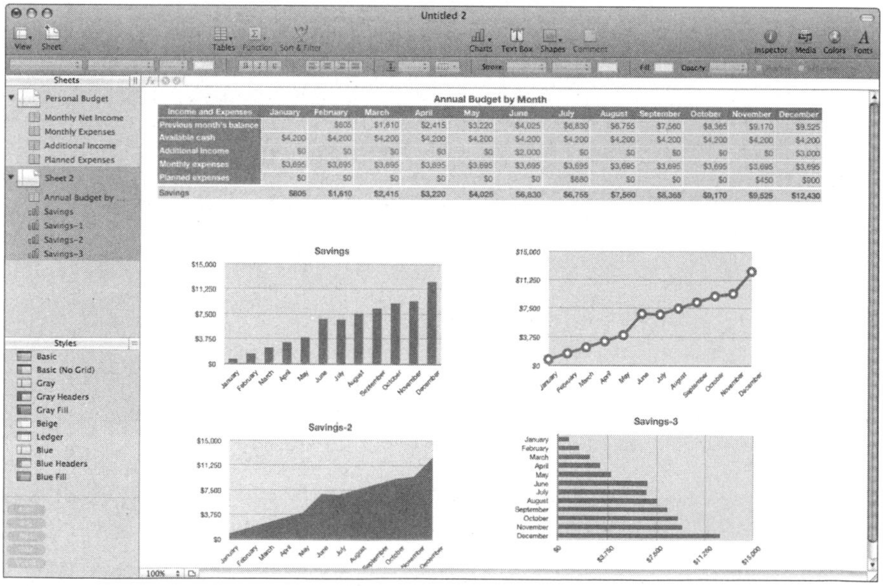

Figure 8-3: Numbers can create different types of charts to help you visualize the meaning of your data.

To create a spreadsheet based on a template, follow these steps:

1. **Load Numbers by double-clicking on the Numbers icon in the Applications folder (or choose File➪New if Numbers is already running).**

   A dialog appears, displaying the different templates you can choose from, as shown in Figure 8-4.

2. **Click a template category in the listing on the left, click a particular template displayed in the main pane, and then click Choose.**

   Numbers displays your chosen template.

   If you want to start out with a blank spreadsheet, click the Blank template in the listing on the left.

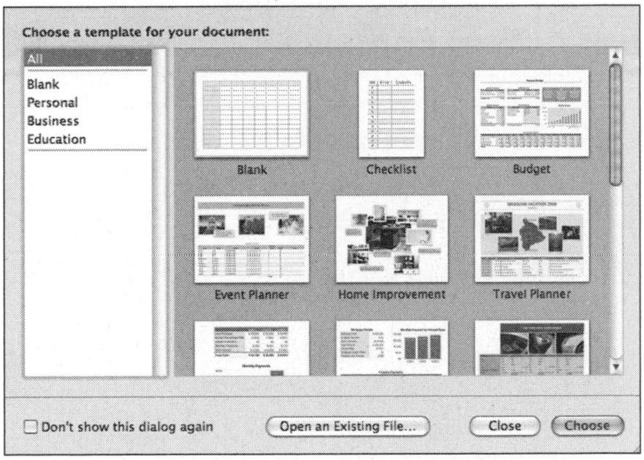

Figure 8-4: Numbers provides a variety of spreadsheet templates organized into categories such as Personal or Business.

Working with Sheets

Every Numbers spreadsheet needs at least one sheet. A sheet acts like a limitless page that can hold any number of tables and charts. Ideally, you should use sheets to organize the information in your spreadsheet, such as using one sheet to hold January sales results, a second sheet to hold February sales results, and a third sheet to hold a line chart that shows each sales person's results for the first two months.

When you create a new spreadsheet, it initially starts out with one sheet, but you can always add more if you want.

To help organize your sheets, Numbers stores the names of all your sheets in the Sheets pane on the left. Indented underneath each sheet is a list of all tables and charts stored on that particular sheet.

To view the contents of a specific sheet, just click that sheet name in the Sheet pane. To view a particular table or chart, first find the sheet that contains that table or chart. Then click that specific table or chart.

Adding a sheet

You can always add another sheet if you need one. When you add a sheet, Numbers creates one table on that sheet automatically. To add a sheet, choose one of the following:

- ✦ Choose Insert⇨Sheet.
- ✦ Right-click anywhere inside the Sheet pane and choose New Sheet.
- ✦ Click the Sheet icon that appears above the Sheet pane.

Deleting a sheet

If you need a sheet to go away, clear out, disappear, whatever, you can delete it. When you delete a sheet, you'll also delete any tables or charts stored on that sheet. To delete a sheet, follow these steps:

1. **Click the sheet you want to delete in the Sheet pane.**
2. **Choose one of the following:**
   - Press the Delete key.
   - Right-click on a sheet name and choose Delete Sheet.
   - Choose Edit⇨Delete.

   A dialog appears, asking whether you really want to delete the sheet.
3. **Click Delete (or Cancel).**

Adding a table or chart

A sheet can hold one or more tables and charts. When you add a table or chart, the table or chart is blank. To add a table or chart, follow these steps:

1. **In the Sheet pane, click the sheet where you want to add a table or chart.**
2. **Choose one of the following and select an option, as shown in Figure 8-5 or 8-6:**
   - Click the Tables icon (or choose Insert⇨Table).
   - Click the Charts icon (or choose Insert⇨Chart).

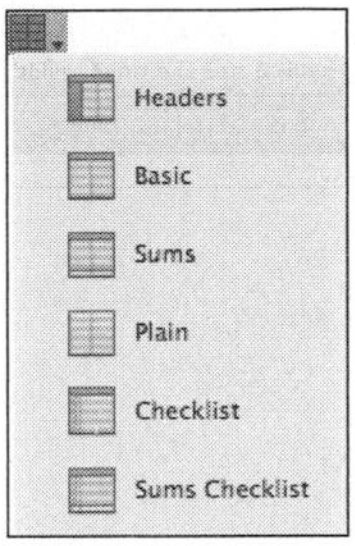

Figure 8-5: The Tables menu lists different types of tables you can add.

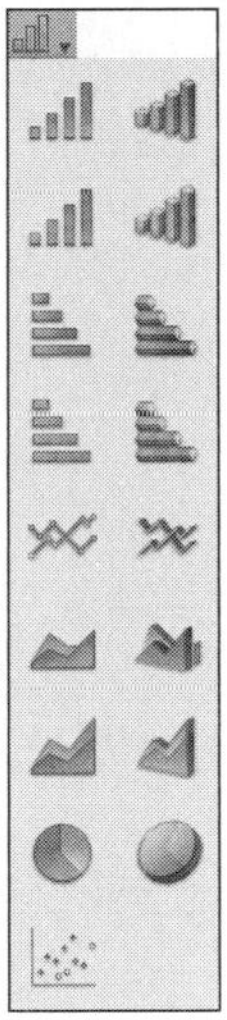

Figure 8-6: The Charts menu lists different types of charts you can add.

Deleting a table or chart

When you create a table or chart, you don't have to keep it forever. You can quietly make it go away and then pretend it was never there. Keep in mind, though, that when you delete a table, Numbers deletes all data (numbers, text, and formulas) stored on that table. To delete a table or chart, follow these steps:

1. **In the Sheet pane, click the table or chart you want to delete.**
2. **Choose one of the following:**
   - Press the Delete key.
   - Right-click on a table or chart and choose Delete.
   - Choose Edit➪Delete.

Naming sheets, tables, and charts

Numbers gives each sheet, table, and chart a generic name, such as Sheet 2, Table 1, or Chart 3. To help you better understand the type of information stored on each sheet, table, and chart, you should use more descriptive names, especially once you start adding multiple tables and charts (which you'll find out about later in this chapter).

To name a sheet, table, or chart in the Sheet pane follow these steps:

1. **Choose one of the following:**
   - Double-click a sheet, table, or chart name.
   - Right-click a sheet, table, or chart name and choose Rename.
2. **Type a new name or use the arrow keys and the Delete key to edit an existing name.**

REMEMBER

Choose a descriptive name for your sheets, tables, and charts. The names you choose are purely for your benefit.

Designing Tables

A table consists of row and columns, with columns labeled using capital letters (Column C or Column H) and rows labeled using numbers (Row 4 or Row 28). The intersection of a row and column is a *cell,* which is where you can type numbers, text, or formulas.

Them's the basics. If you have that down, you have enough info to make a simple table. But there's oh so much more you can do.

Moving a table

After creating a table on a sheet, you might want to move it to a better position. To move a table, follow these steps:

1. **In the Sheets pane, click the table that you want to move.**

   Numbers displays your selected table.
2. **Click anywhere inside the table.**

   The table displays column and row headings, a Move corner (in the upper left corner of the table), and a Resize corner (in the bottom-right corner of the table), as shown in Figure 8-7.
3. **Move the pointer over the Move corner until the pointer turns into an arrow with a four-way pointing arrow underneath.**

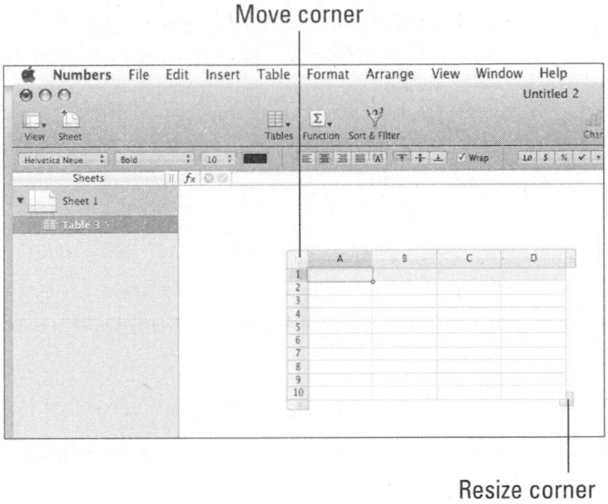

Figure 8-7: The Move and Resize corners appear at opposite corners of a table.

4. **Click and drag the table to a new location on the sheet.**
5. **Release the mouse button when you're happy with the table's new location.**

Resizing a table

You might need to resize a table for various reasons: to fit it in a small space, to make it larger and easier to read, and so on. Numbers offers two ways to resize a table. First, you can make a table larger (or smaller) while retaining the same number of rows and columns, which increases the height and width of rows and columns. The second way to resize a table automatically adds (or removes) rows and columns so all rows and columns inside the table retain the same physical dimensions.

To stretch or shrink a table (without adding or subtracting rows or columns), follow these steps:

1. **In the Sheets pane, click the table that you want to resize.**

   Numbers displays your selected table with handles around it.
2. **Move the pointer over a handle until the pointer turns into a two-way pointing arrow.**
3. **Click and drag a handle to enlarge or shrink the table.**

   Notice that any data inside the table grows or shrinks as well.
4. **Release the mouse button when you're happy with the size of your table.**

To resize a table by adding or subtracting rows and columns, you use the Resize corner. Just follow these steps:

1. **In the Sheets pane, click the table that you want to resize.**

   Numbers displays your selected table with handles around it.

2. **Click anywhere inside the table.**

   The table displays column and row headings, a Move corner, and a Resize corner (refer to Figure 8-7.)

3. **Move the pointer over the Resize corner in the bottom right corner of the table.**

4. **Click and drag the Resize corner to resize the table on the sheet.**

   As you drag the Resize corner, you add (or delete) rows and columns.

5. **Release the mouse button when you're happy with the table's number of rows and columns.**

Adding a row or column

You can add a row or column in the middle of a table or at the end. If you add a row or column in the middle of a table, the newly added row or column will move existing data. If you add a row or column at the end of a table, you just make the table a little bit larger.

TIP

To add multiple columns or rows, highlight two or more column or row headings, click on the Table menu, and then choose Add Columns Before/After or Add Rows Above/Below.

To add a row or column in the middle of a table, click in a row or column, choose Table and then choose one of the following from the Table menu:

- **Add Row Above:** Inserts a new row directly above the currently selected cell.
- **Add Row Below:** Inserts a new row directly below the currently selected cell.
- **Add Column Before:** Inserts a new column to the left of the currently selected cell.
- **Add Column After:** Inserts a new column to the right of the currently selected cell.

TIP

If you move the pointer over a row or column heading (such as column D or row 5), a downward-pointing arrow appears, and you can click it to display a menu. From this menu, you can choose any of the options in the preceding list.

Deleting a row or column

To delete a row or column, choose one of the following:

- ✦ Click a cell inside the row or column you want to delete and then choose Table➪Delete Row (or Delete Column).
- ✦ Right-click a cell inside the row or column you want to delete, and then choose Delete Row (or Delete Column) from the shortcut menu.
- ✦ Move the pointer over the row or column heading (such as column A or row 3), click the downward-pointing arrow that appears, and choose Delete Row (or Delete column).

TIP

You can delete multiple columns or rows by highlighting two or more column or row headings, clicking the Table menu and then choosing Delete Columns or Delete Rows.

Resizing rows and columns

Rows and columns define the size of cells. However, a cell that's too small may not show all the information stored in that cell. To fix this problem, you can resize rows and columns.

Resizing the fast way

To resize a row or column using the mouse, follow these steps:

1. **Move the pointer over the border between two row or column headings, such as between columns A and B.**

   The pointer turns into a two-way pointing arrow around a vertical or horizontal line.

2. **Click and drag the mouse up/down or right/left to resize the row or column.**

3. **Release the mouse button when you're happy with the size of your row or column.**

TIP

If you have data stored inside a row or column, Numbers can automatically resize the row or column to fit the largest item stored in that row or column. To automatically resize a row or column, click a cell inside the row or column you want to resize and choose Table➪Resize Columns to Fit Content (or Resize Rows to Fit Content).

Resizing the precise way

If you want to resize a row or column to a specific height or width, follow these steps:

1. **Click a cell inside the row or column you want to resize.**
2. **Choose View➪Inspector.**

   An Inspector window appears.
3. **Click the Table Inspector icon in the Inspector window toolbar, as shown in Figure 8-8.**
4. **Click in the Row Height or Column Width text box and type a value, or click the up/down arrows in that text box to define a value.**
5. **Click the Close button of the Inspector window.**

Table Inspector icon

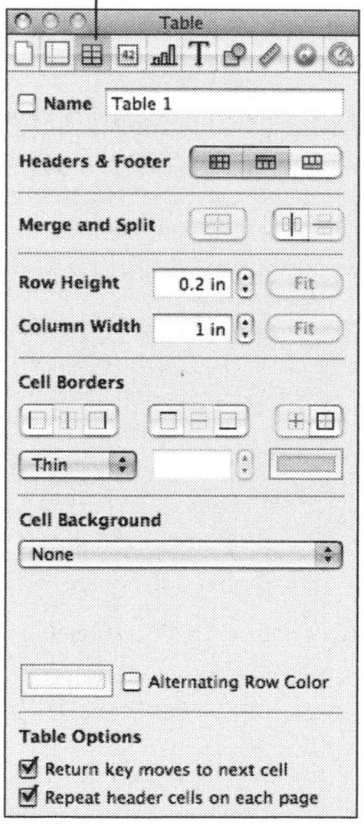

Figure 8-8: The Table Inspector pane displays text boxes to precisely define a Row Height or Column Width.

Formatting a table

To make your table easier to read, you can format it with a style, which basically provides different ways to color row and column headings of an entire table with one click of the mouse. To format a table, follow these steps:

1. **In the Sheet pane, click the table that you want to format.**

   Numbers displays your chosen table.

2. **Click a formatting style, such as Ledger or Blue Headers, in the Styles pane in the bottom-left corner of the Numbers window.**

   Numbers formats your table. If you don't like the way your table looks, choose another of the ten styles available.

Typing Data into Tables

The three types of data you can store inside a table are

- Numbers
- Text
- Formulas

To type anything into a table, follow these steps:

1. **Select a cell by clicking it or by pressing the arrow keys.**
2. **Type a number, text, or formula.**
3. **Press Return to select the cell below, press Tab to select the cell to the right, or click in any cell where you want to type new data.**

   Numbers formats your table. If you don't like the way your table looks, choose another of the ten styles available.
4. **Repeat Steps 2 and 3 for each additional item you want to type into the table.**

Formatting numbers and text

When you type a number in a cell, the number will look plain like 45 or 60.3. To make your numbers more meaningful, you should format them. For example, the number 39 might mean nothing, but if you format it to appear as $39.00, your number now clearly represents a dollar amount.

To format numbers, follow these steps:

1. **Click to select one cell or click and drag to select multiple cells.**

   Numbers draws a border around your selected cell(s).

   REMEMBER

   If you select empty cells, Numbers will automatically format any numbers you type later into those cells.

2. Click one of the following icons on the Format bar, as shown in Figure 8-9:

- *Decimal:* Displays numbers with two decimal places, such as 3.19.
- *Currency:* Displays numbers with a currency symbol, such as $3.19.
- *Percentage:* Displays numbers as a percentage, such as 3.19%.
- *Increase decimal places:* Displays numbers with an additional decimal place, such as 3.190.
- *Decrease decimal places:* Displays numbers with one less decimal place, such as 3.2.

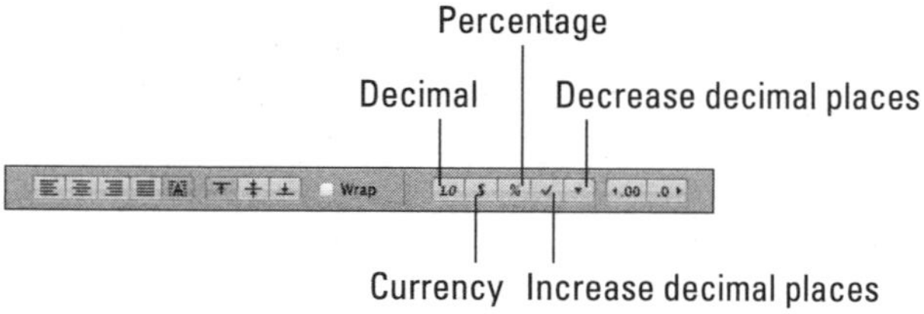

Figure 8-9: The Format bar displays icons for quickly formatting numbers.

TIP

To customize the way formatting works, such as changing the currency format from displaying dollar symbols to Euros or Swiss francs, follow these steps:

1. **Select the cells that contain one or more numbers.**
2. **Click the Inspector icon or choose View⇨Show Inspector.**

   An inspector window appears.
3. **Click the Cells Inspector icon in the Inspector window toolbar, as shown in Figure 8-10.**

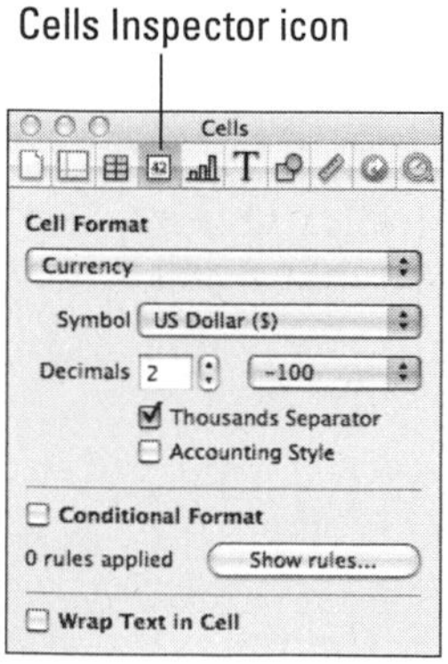

Figure 8-10: The Cells Inspector pane lets you customize different number formats.

4. **Choose a format from the Cell Format pop-up menu.**

   The Currency format is always nice.

5. **Choose any options to customize your chosen format.**

   For example, if you chose the Currency format in Step 4, you can click a Symbol pop-up menu to define the type of symbol (dollar sign, Euro, and so on) that appears with each number.

6. **Click the Close button of the Inspector window.**

To make your text prettier, you can choose different fonts and styles by following these steps:

1. **Select the cells that contain text.**
2. **Click on one of the following on the Format bar, as shown in Figure 8-11:**
   - *Font:* Displays a variety of fonts.
   - *Style:* Displays different options such as bold or italic.
   - *Font size:* Displays a range of sizes such as 9 or 24.
   - *Text color:* Displays a color window for coloring numbers or text.

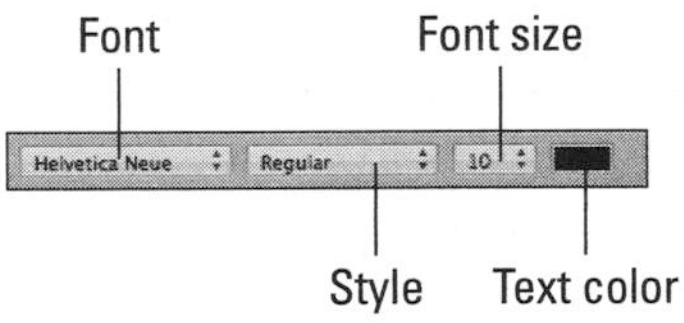

Figure 8-11: The Format bar displays pop-up menus for changing the font of selected cells.

Typing formulas

The main purpose of a table is to use the numbers you've stored in cells to calculate a new result, such as adding a row or column of numbers. To calculate and display a result, you need to store a formula in a cell.

Numbers provides three ways to create formulas in a cell:

- ✦ Quick formulas
- ✦ Typed in formulas
- ✦ Functions

Using Quick Formulas

To help you calculate numbers in a hurry, Numbers offers a variety of Quick Formulas that can calculate common results, such as

- ✦ **Sum:** Adds numbers.
- ✦ **Average:** Calculates the arithmetic mean.
- ✦ **Minimum:** Displays the smallest number.
- ✦ **Maximum:** Displays the largest number.
- ✦ **Count:** Displays how many numbers you selected.
- ✦ **Product:** Multiples numbers.

To use a Quick Formula, follow these steps:

1. **Select two or more cells that contain numbers.**
2. **Click the Function icon or choose Insert⇨Function and choose a Quick Formula (Sum, Average, Minimum, Maximum, Count, or Product).**

   Numbers displays your calculates results.

REMEMBER

If you highlight a row of numbers, the Quick Formula displays the result to the right. If you highlight a column of numbers, the Quick Formula displays the result at the bottom of the column. If you highlight both rows and columns of numbers, the Quick Formula displays the result at the bottom of each column.

Typing in a formula

Quick Formulas are handy when they offer the formula you need, such as adding rows or columns of numbers with the Sum formula. However, most of the time you'll need to create your own formulas.

Basically, every formula consists of two parts:

- ✦ **Operators:** Perform calculations such as addition (+), subtraction (-), multiplication (*), and division (/).
- ✦ **Cell references:** Define where to find the data to use for calculations.

A typical formula looks like this:

```
= A3 + A4
```

This formula tells Numbers to take the number stored in column A, row 3 and add it to the number stored in column A, row 4.

To type a formula, follow these steps:

1. **Click in (or use the arrow keys to highlight) the cell where you want the formula results to appear.**
2. **Type =.**

   The Formula Editor appears, as shown in Figure 8-12.

   TIP

   You can move the Formula Editor if you move the pointer over the left end of the Formula Editor where the pointer turns into a hand. Then click and drag the Formula Editor to a new location.

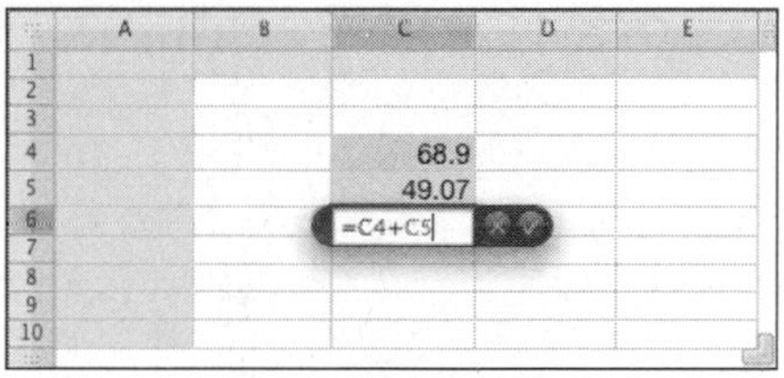

Figure 8-12: The Formula Editor lets you create and edit a formula stored in a cell.

3. **Click a cell that contains the number you want to include in your calculation.**
4. **Type an operator, such as * for multiplication or / for division.**
5. **Click another cell that contains the number you want to include in your calculation.**
6. **Repeat Steps 4 and 5 as often as necessary.**
7. **Click the Accept (or Cancel) button on the Formula Editor when you're done.**

   Numbers displays the results of your formula. If you change the numbers in the cells you defined in Steps 3 and 5, you can see Numbers calculate a new result instantly.

TIP

For a fast way to calculate values without having to type a formula in a cell, you can use Instant Calculations. Just select two or more cells that contain numbers, and you can see the Instant Calculations in the bottom-left corner of the Numbers window, as shown in Figure 8-13.

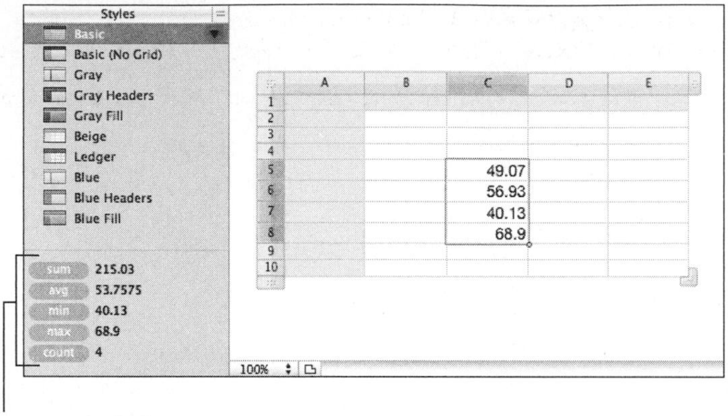

Figure 8-13: Instant calculations can show you results without you typing a formula first.

Instant calculations

Using functions

Typing simple formulas that add or multiply is fairly easy. However, many calculations can get more complicated, such as trying to calculate the amount of interest paid on a loan with a specific interest rate over a defined period of time.

To help you calculate commonly used formulas, Numbers provides a library of *functions* — prebuilt formulas that you can plug into your table and define what data to use without having to create the formula yourself.

To use a function, follow these steps:

1. **Click in (or use the arrow keys to highlight) the cell where you want the function results to appear.**
2. **Click the Function icon.**

   A pull-down menu appears.
3. **Choose More Functions.**

   An Insert Function dialog appears, as shown in Figure 8-14. It displays all the available functions.
4. **Click a Function category in the left pane, such as Financial or Statistical.**

   The right pane displays only those functions stored in that category.
5. **Click a function in the right pane and click the Insert button.**

   The Formula Editor appears, containing your chosen function.

6. **Edit the formula by typing the cell names (such as C4) or clicking the cells that contain the data the function needs to calculate a result.**

7. **Click the Accept (or Cancel) button on the Formula Editor.**

   Numbers shows your result.

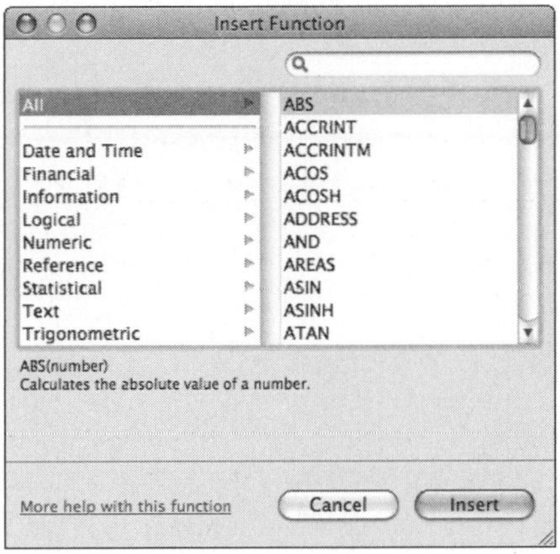

Figure 8-14: The Insert Function dialog displays all available functions that Numbers provides.

Formatting data entry cells

After you create formulas (or functions) in cells, you can type new numbers in the cells defined by a formula or function and watch Numbers calculate a new result instantly. Typing a new number in a cell is easy to do, but sometimes a formula or function requires a specific range of values. For example, if you have a formula that calculates the sales tax, you might not want someone to enter a sales tax over 10% or less than 5%.

To limit the types of values someone can enter in a cell, you can use one of the following methods, as shown in Figure 8-15:

✦ **Sliders:** Lets the user drag a slider to choose a value within a fixed range.

✦ **Steppers:** Lets the user click up and down arrows to choose a value that increases or decreases in fixed increments.

✦ **Pop-up menus:** Lets the user choose from a limited range of choices.

Formatting a cell with a slider or stepper

A *slider* or *stepper* is useful when you want to restrict a cell to a range of values, such as 1 to 45. The main difference between the two is that a slider appears next to a cell, whereas a stepper appears inside a cell.

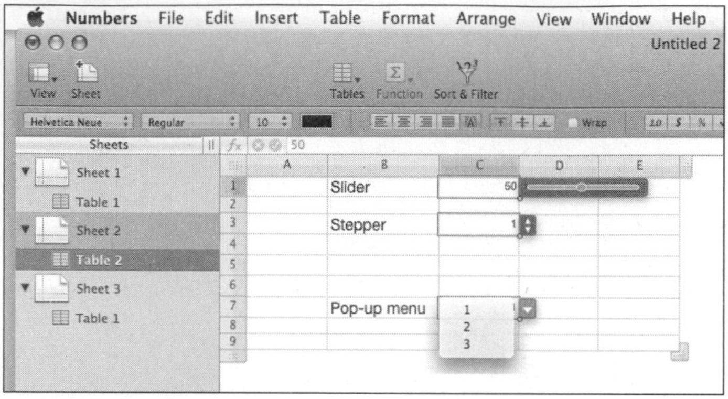

Figure 8-15: Sliders, steppers, and pop-up menus restrict the types of values a cell can hold.

To format a cell with a slider or stepper, follow these steps:

1. **Click in a cell that you want to restrict to a range of values.**
2. **Click the Format button (it looks like a downward-pointing arrow) on the Format bar and choose Slider or Stepper from the pull-down menu that appears, as shown in Figure 8-16.**

   A Cells Inspector window appears, as shown in Figure 8-17.

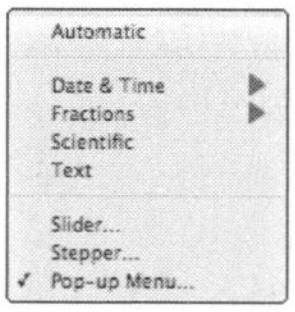

Figure 8-16: Choosing your restraint.

3. **Click in the Minimum text box and type the minimum acceptable value.**
4. **Click in the Maximum text box and type the maximum acceptable value.**
5. **Click in the Increment text box and type a value to increase or decrease when the user drags the slider or clicks the up and down arrows of the stepper.**
6. **Click the Close button of the Inspector window.**

   Numbers displays a slider next to the cell. Users have a choice of typing a value or using the slider to define a value. If you type a value outside the minimum and maximum range defined in Steps 4 and 5, the cell won't accept the invalid data.

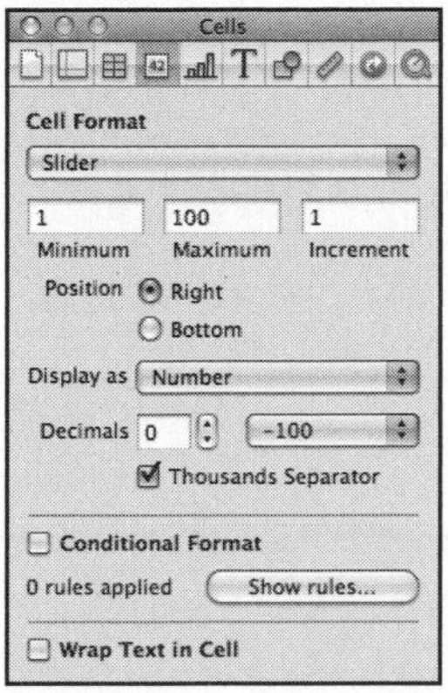

Figure 8-17: The Cells Inspector pane lets you define the range of values for a slider or stepper.

Formatting a cell with a pop-up menu

A pop-up menu restricts a cell to a limited number of choices. To format a cell with a pop-up menu, follow these steps:

1. **Click in a cell that you want to restrict to a limited choice of values.**
2. **Click the Format button (it looks like a downward-pointing arrow) that appears on the Format bar.**

   A pull-down menu appears (refer to Figure 8-16).
3. **Select Pop-up Menu from the pull-down menu.**

   A Cells Inspector window appears, as shown in Figure 8-18.

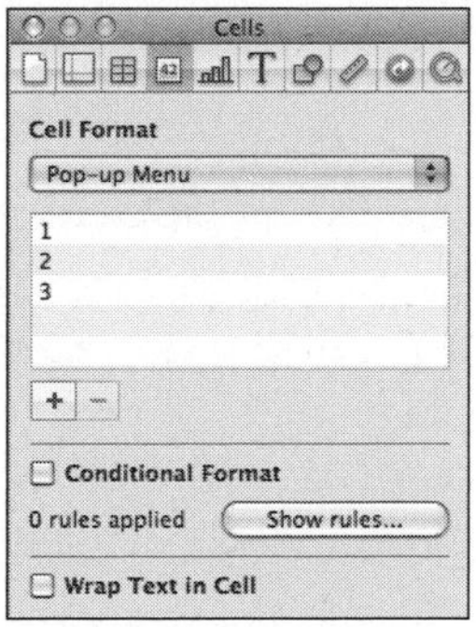

Figure 8-18: The Cells Inspector window lets you define a list of values.

4. **In the Cells Inspector window, click in the list box under the Cell Format pop-up menu and then click the plus (+) or minus (-) sign buttons to add or remove an item from the pop-up menu list.**
5. **Click the Close button of the Cells Inspector window.**

   Numbers displays a pop-up menu that lists choices when users click in that cell.

Deleting data in cells

After you type data into a cell, you might later want to delete that data. Numbers provides two ways to delete data in cells:

- Delete data but retain any formatting.
- Delete data and formatting.

To delete data but retain any formatting, follow these steps:

1. **Select one or more cells that contain data you want to delete.**
2. **Press Delete or choose Edit⇨Delete.**

To delete both data and formatting in cells, follow these steps:

1. **Select one or more cells that contain data and formatting you want to delete.**
2. **Choose Edit⇨Clear All.**

Making Charts

Charts help make sense out of your numeric data by turning numbers into pictures that can show trends or help you spot patterns such as identifying which sales person is most consistent (and which ones are consistently the best and worse).

Creating a chart

Creating a chart is a three-step process. First, you have to decide what numeric data you want to turn into a chart. Second, you need to choose a specific type of chart to create, such as a line chart or pie chart. Finally, you have to decide whether you want to create a 2-dimensional or 3-dimensional chart.

REMEMBER: A 3-D chart might look cool, but it can often make understanding your data harder. You might need to experiment with different charts until you find the one that displays your data the best.

To create a chart, follow these steps:

1. **Highlight the data you want to convert into a chart.**

   You can highlight data by dragging the mouse or by holding down the Shift key and pressing the arrow keys.

2. **Click the Charts icon.**

   A pull-down menu of different chart types appears.

3. **Click on a chart type.**

   Numbers creates your chart, along with a Chart Inspector window, as shown in Figure 8-19.

   REMEMBER: If you don't like the chart type you chose, click in the Chart Type icon in the Chart Inspector pane and choose a different chart type.

4. **Click the Close button of the Inspector window.**

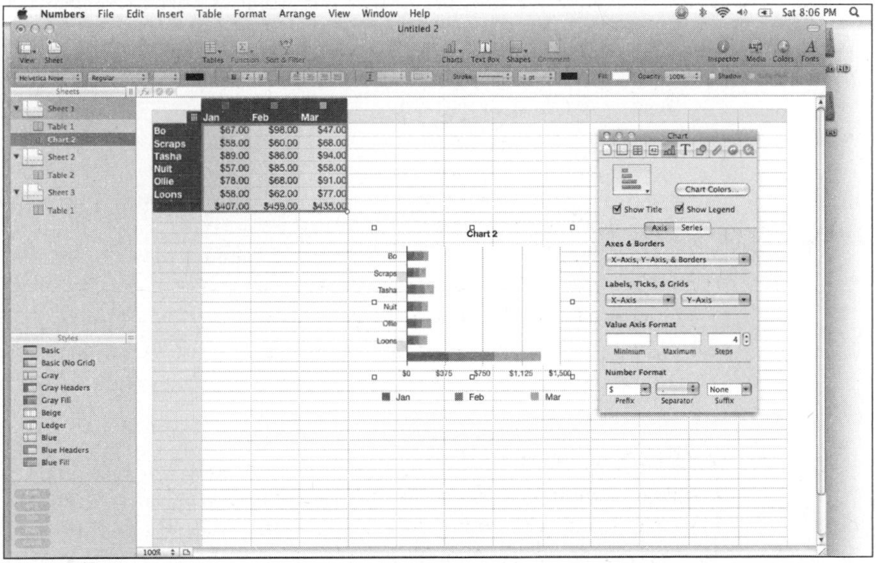

Figure 8-19: A chart appears directly on a sheet.

Editing a chart

After you've created a chart, you might need to edit it later. To edit your chart, follow these steps:

1. **Click the chart name in the Sheet pane that you want to edit.**

   Numbers displays your chart with handles around its edges.

2. **Choose View⇨Show Inspector.**

   The Chart Inspector pane appears, giving you options you can modify.

3. **Choose any options in the Chart Inspector pane.**

   You might want to change the title of your chart or hide the legend that explains what each color represents.

4. **Click the Close button of the Inspector window.**

Manipulating a chart

A chart is just another object that you can move, resize, or delete.

Any time you resize, move, or delete a chart, you can always reverse your action by pressing ⌘+Z or choosing Edit⇨Undo.

Moving a chart on a sheet

To move a chart, follow these steps:

1. **Click a chart name in the Sheets pane.**

   Numbers displays your chart with handles around it.

2. **Click over the middle of the chart, hold down the mouse button, and drag the chart to a new location.**

3. **Release the mouse button when you're happy with your chart's new home.**

Moving a chart from one sheet to another sheet

To move a chart to a different sheet, follow these steps:

1. **Click and drag the chart name underneath a Sheet icon of a different sheet in the Sheet pane.**

2. **Release the mouse button when you're happy with the location of your chart.**

   Numbers displays your chart on the other sheet. You may need to move the chart to a specific location on the sheet, just to make your chart look nicer.

Resizing a chart

To resize a chart, follow these steps:

1. **Click a chart name in the Sheets pane.**

   Numbers displays your chart with handles around it.

2. **Move the pointer over a handle until the pointer turns into a two-way pointing arrow.**
3. **Click and drag the handle to resize the chart.**

   Release the mouse button when you're happy with the size of your chart.

Deleting a chart

To delete a chart, choose one of the following:

- Click a chart name in the Sheets pane and then choose Edit➪Delete.
- Right-click a chart name in the Sheets pane and choose Delete.

Making Your Spreadsheets Pretty

Tables and charts are the two most crucial objects you can place and arrange on a sheet. However, Numbers also lets you place text boxes, shapes, and pictures on a sheet. Text boxes can contain titles or short descriptions of the information displayed on the sheet, shapes can add color, and pictures can make your entire sheet look more interesting.

Adding a text box

To add a text box to a sheet, follow these steps:

1. **In the Sheet pane, click the name of a sheet you want to add the text box to.**

   Numbers displays your chosen sheet and any additional objects that might already be on that sheet, such as tables or charts.

2. **Click the Text Box icon (or choose Insert➪Text Box).**

   A text box appears on the sheet.

3. **Type any text you want to appear in the text box. (Press Return to type text on a new line.)**
4. **(Optional) Select any text that you've typed and choose any formatting options from the Format bar, such as different fonts or font sizes.**

To edit a text box, double-click that text box.

Adding a picture

To add a picture from iPhoto into a document, follow these steps:

1. **In the Sheet pane, click the name of a sheet you want to add a picture to.**

   Numbers displays your chosen sheet and any additional objects that are already on that sheet, such as tables or charts.

2. **Click the Media icon.**

   The Media browser appears.

3. **Click the Photos tab, as shown in Figure 8-20.**

4. **Click and drag a picture from the Media browser onto a blank area of your sheet.**

   If you drag a picture over a table, Numbers displays your picture as a tiny image inside a single cell, which probably isn't what you want.

5. **Release the mouse button.**

   Numbers displays your chosen image on the sheet.

6. **Click the Close button of the Media browser.**

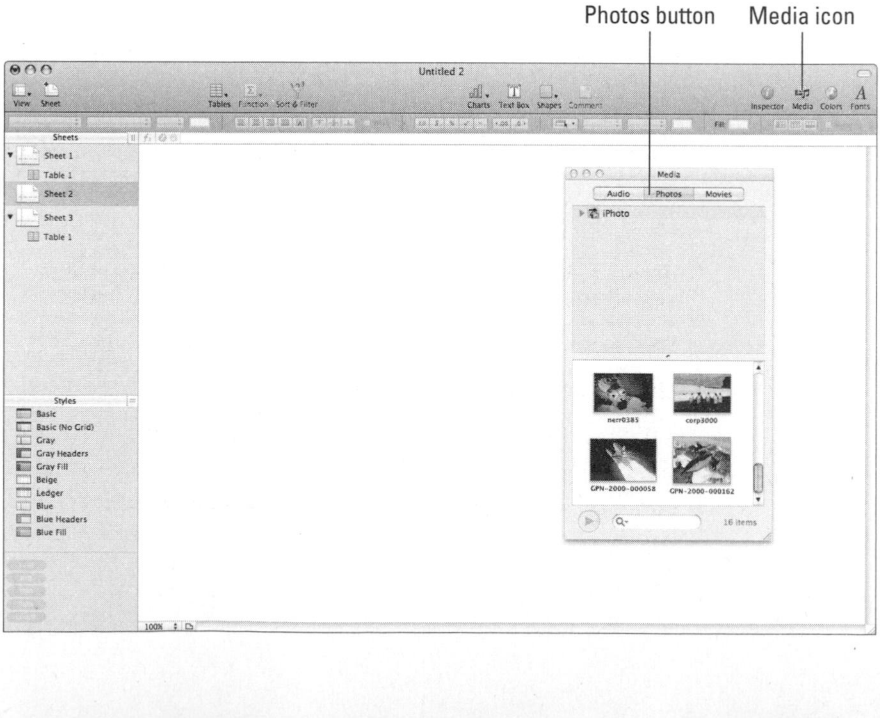

Figure 8-20: The Photos pane in the Media window lets you browse your iPhoto library.

Deleting text boxes, shapes and pictures

In case you want to get rid of an object, you can delete it by following these steps:

1. **In the Sheet pane, click the name of the sheet containing the object you want to delete.**
2. **Click the object (text box, shape, or picture) you want to delete.**

   Handles appear around your object.
3. **Press the Delete key.**

Sharing Your Spreadsheet

You've put a lot of effort into making your spreadsheet presentable. Now's the time to actually *present* it, which usually means sharing your spreadsheet with others by printing it out or saving it as a file.

Printing a spreadsheet

In other spreadsheet programs, you can print your spreadsheet and chart — only to find that part of your chart or spreadsheet gets cut off by the edge of the paper. To avoid this problem, Numbers displays a Content Slider, which lets you magnify or shrink an entire sheet so that it fits and prints perfectly on a page.

To shrink or magnify a sheet to print, follow these steps:

1. **In the Sheet pane, click the name of a sheet you want to print.**
2. **Choose File⇨Show Print View (or View⇨Show Print View).**

   Numbers displays a page and shows how the charts and tables on your sheet will print, as shown in Figure 8-21.
3. **Drag the Content Slider to magnify or shrink your data until it fits exactly the way you want on the page.**

   The Content Slider is located at the bottom center of the Print View window.
4. **Choose File⇨Print (or press ⌘+P).**

   A dialog appears asking how many copies to print, which pages to print, and which printer to use.
5. **Choose the print options you want and click Print.**

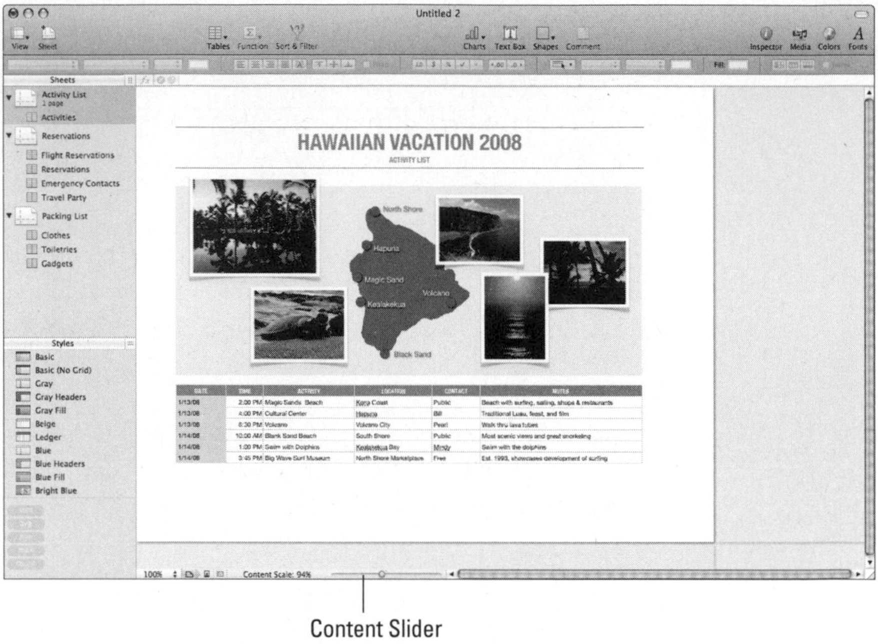

Figure 8-21: The Print View shows you exactly how your sheet will print on paper.

Exporting a spreadsheet

When you choose the File➪Save command, Numbers saves your spreadsheet in its own proprietary file format. If you want to share your spreadsheets with others, you need to export your spreadsheet into another file format, such as:

✦ **PDF:** Saves your spreadsheet as a series of static pages stored in the PDF Adobe Acrobat file format that can be viewed by any computer with a PDF viewing program.

✦ **Excel:** Saves your spreadsheet as a Microsoft Excel file, which can be opened and edited by any spreadsheet that can read and edit Microsoft Excel files.

✦ **CSV:** Saves your spreadsheet in Comma-Separated Values format, a universal format that preserves only data, not any charts or pictures you have stored on your spreadsheet.

The PDF file format preserves formatting 100 percent, but you'll need extra software to edit it. Generally, if someone needs to edit your spreadsheet, save it as an Excel file. The CSV option is useful only for transferring your data to another program that can't read Excel files.

To export a spreadsheet, follow these steps:

1. **Choose File⇨Export.**

   A dialog appears as shown in Figure 8-22.

2. **Click an icon such as PDF or Excel.**
3. **Click Next.**

   A dialog appears, letting you choose a name and location to save your exported spreadsheet.

4. **Enter a name for your exported spreadsheet in the Save As text box.**

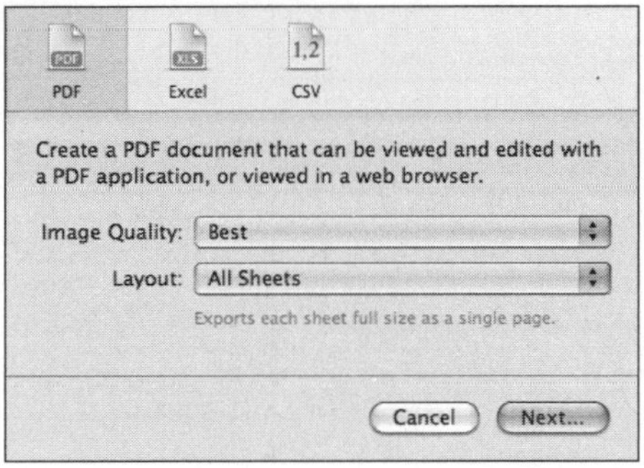

Figure 8-22: The Export dialog lets you choose a format to save your spreadsheets.

5. **Click the folder where you want to store your spreadsheet.**

   You might need to switch drives or folders until you find where you want to save your file.

6. **Click Export.**

   REMEMBER: When you export a spreadsheet, your original Numbers spreadsheet remains untouched in its original location where you last saved it.

Book V

Other Mac Programs

"Guess who found a Kiss merchandise site on the Web while you were gone?"

Contents at a Glance

Chapter 1: Word Processing on the Mac 567

Chapter 2: Office Suites on the Mac 581

Chapter 3: Painting and Drawing on a Mac 597

Chapter 4: Running Windows on a Mac 613

Chapter 5: Having Fun with a Mac 627

Chapter 1: Word Processing on the Mac

In This Chapter

- ✔ **Understanding basic word-processor features**
- ✔ **Choosing a word processor**
- ✔ **Working with various word-processor file formats**

A *word processor* lets you create, save, change, and rearrange text. After you've written text, a word processor can spell and grammar check your words and format your text to make it look pretty.

Besides arranging text, word processors can also do simple page layout that lets you include graphics and wrap text around these graphic images. If you need to write long documents, word processors can keep track of page numbering, displaying headers and footers at the top and bottom of each page, and they even create an index automatically. If you need to work with words, you need a word processor.

The Basic Features of Word Processing

The three basic aspects of word processing are creating a document, editing it, and formatting it. Editing involves adding, deleting, and moving or copying text from one part of your document to another. Formatting changes the appearance of text without changing the text itself. You can make text bigger or smaller, underline or italicize it, and change the line spacing or paragraph margins, to name a few formatting actions.

Creating a document and adding text

Word processor files are called *documents.* You can create a document from a blank page or from a template that provides formatting, such as a newsletter template that divides text into columns using a specific font and font size.

Whether you create a document from a blank page or a template, you need to add new text wherever the cursor appears. In most programs, the cursor appears as a vertical, blinking line that acts like a pointer. You can move the cursor using either the keyboard or the mouse. To move the cursor, press the up-, down-, left-, or right-arrow keys or move the mouse and click the screen wherever you want to enter text. Then just type away!

Almost every word processor offers shortcut keys that can move the cursor to specific places in the document, such as to the beginning or end of a line or to the next or previous word. Some common word processor shortcuts appear in Table 1-1.

Table 1-1 Common Word Processor Keystrokes

Keystroke	*Purpose*
⌘+N	Create a new document
⌘+O	Open an existing document
⌘+S	Save the current document
⌘+F	Find text
⌘+B	Bold text
⌘+I	Italicize text
⌘+U	Underline text
⌘+P	Print the current document

Copying or cutting text

After typing text, you can always move or copy that chunk of text to another location. *Copying* text lets you place a duplicate of your selected text somewhere else; *cutting* text deletes the selected text and lets you move it to a new location. You can copy or cut text by following these steps:

1. **Select (highlight) the text to copy or move.**

   Select the text by clicking at the beginning of the text you want to select, holding down your mouse button, dragging the pointer over the text, and releasing the mouse button. If you prefer using the keyboard, place the cursor at the start of the text and then hold down the Shift key while pressing the appropriate arrow key until the text is highlighted.

2. **Copy or cut the text:**

   - *Copy:* Choose Edit➪Copy or press ⌘+C.
   - *Cut:* If you want to eliminate the text where it is and move it somewhere else, choose Edit➪Cut instead, or press ⌘+X.

3. **Move the cursor to the location where you want the text to appear.**

4. **Choose Edit➪Paste or press ⌘+V to place the text in its new location.**

TIP: Many word processors let you quickly cut and paste text by selecting text and then dragging it to a new location with the mouse. Similarly, you can copy text by selecting it, holding down the Option key, and then dragging the selected text to a new location with the mouse.

Deleting text

You need to be able to erase those pesky typos or whole chunks of text. Thankfully, a word processor lets you zap your errors out of existence. The Mac keyboard might have two Delete keys for eliminating individual characters, as follows:

- ✦ Pressing the big Delete key (the one that appears to the right of the + and = key) deletes characters to the *left* of the cursor.
- ✦ Pressing the small Delete key (the one that appears to the left of the End key) deletes characters to the *right* of the cursor.

REMEMBER

Not all Mac keyboards have both types of Delete keys.

If you hold down either Delete key, you delete multiple characters.

To delete a large chunk of text, such as an entire sentence, paragraph, or group of paragraphs, the fastest way is to select the text and then press either Delete key.

TIP

If you delete text by mistake, choose Edit⇨Undo or press ⌘+Z to put it right back. If you choose the Undo command multiple times, you can undo each previous action one at a time.

Formatting text

Formatting text changes its appearance. For instance, you can display text in different colors, fonts, or sizes. To format text, you must first select the text you want to change and then choose a way to format it. Figure 1-1 shows different ways to format text.

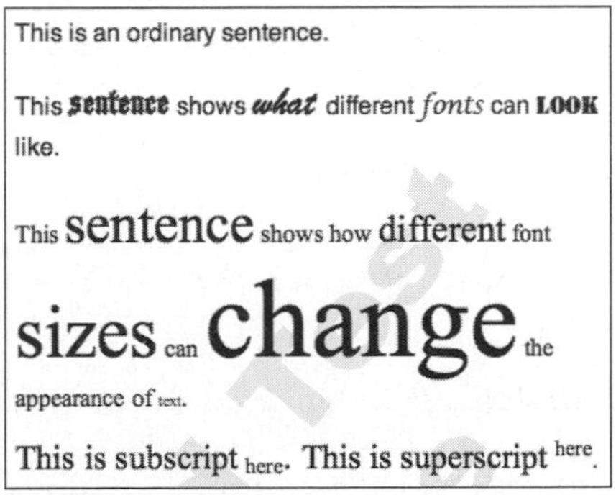
This is an ordinary sentence.
This sentence shows what different fonts can LOOK like.
This sentence shows how different font sizes can change the appearance of text.
This is subscript here. This is superscript here.

Figure 1-1: Formatting text simply changes its appearance.

To format text, you typically have two choices after you select the text you want to modify:

- ✦ Click the Format menu and then choose the type of formatting such as changing the Font.
- ✦ Click the Format toolbar, which displays buttons for changing paragraph justification or font size.

TIP

If you format text a certain way and suddenly decide that it looks ugly, choose Edit⇨Undo or press ⌘+Z to remove the formatting and return your text to its previous appearance.

Formatting pages

Another way to change the appearance of text is to format all or part of a page. Formatting a page simply changes the physical location of text on the page, as shown in Figure 1-2.

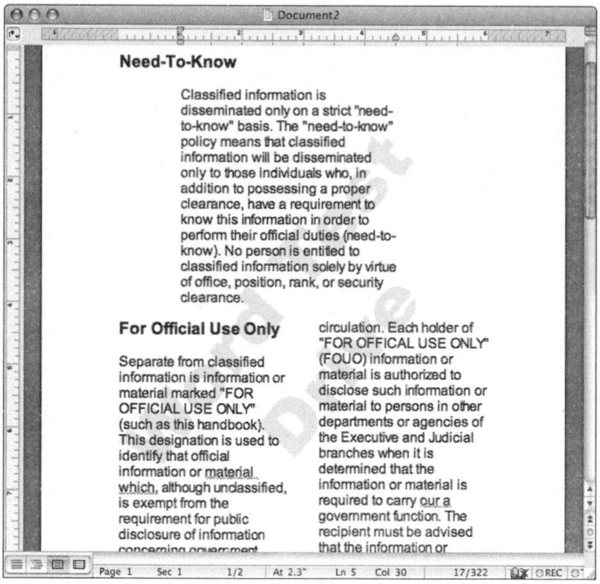

Figure 1-2: Formatting a page defines the physical location of text.

Some common page formatting options are:

- ✦ **Line spacing:** Defines the space that appears between lines in a paragraph.
- ✦ **Paragraph margins:** Defines the left and right edges that the text appears in between.
- ✦ **Columns:** Divides a page into vertical areas. When text fills one column, it can flow into the next column.

Choosing a Word Processor

Two important aspects of any word processor are its features and its compatibility with other programs. Features are important because one word processor might lack a feature that a different word processor offers, such as the ability to add footnotes to a page or generate a table of contents automatically.

Compatibility is important because users often share word processor documents with other people without printing out the documents at all. Multiple users can add comments or mark up text and then pass the revised document to others who can see the original text and the newly added text (often displayed in colors).

TextEdit

If your word processing needs are simple, such as writing letters or reports occasionally, use the free TextEdit program that comes with every Mac. Like most commercial word processors, TextEdit provides a spelling and grammar checker and can read and write to Microsoft Word documents, which makes sharing documents much easier with others.

Although TextEdit lacks features such as templates for reusing different page layouts, TextEdit does offer the unusual feature of letting you type right to left (unlike the traditional left to right). By allowing right to left typing, TextEdit can work with foreign languages such as Hebrew.

Microsoft Word

The TextEdit word processor that comes free with every Mac might be sufficient for many people, but if you need to share word-processor documents with someone who uses Microsoft Word, you might prefer using Microsoft Word as well. Microsoft Word isn't necessarily the best word processor, but it offers three features that make it a popular and often the most practical choice for business and academic users:

- ✦ Nearly guaranteed file compatibility with Microsoft Word users running Windows
- ✦ Collaboration tools that allow multiple users to add and review comments written by others
- ✦ Advanced features for creating indexes, tables, footnotes, and graphics

REMEMBER

The biggest advantage of Microsoft Word is that so many other people use Word on both Windows and the Mac, so sharing and collaborating with Word files are nearly flawless. If you need to share files with others regularly, especially those using Windows or different types of programs such as desktop publishing programs, the path of least resistance is to use Microsoft Word.

In an effort to get everyone to buy and use Microsoft Word, Microsoft sells a low-cost, student edition of Microsoft Office (which includes Microsoft Word). This student edition is identical to the retail version, although the retail version might include additional programs such as Microsoft Entourage. If you're a student, or the parent of one, and just want Microsoft Word, buying the student edition can save you several hundred dollars.

Microsoft Word alternatives

Perhaps the most intriguing alternative to Microsoft Word is the free, open source AbiWord (`www.abisource.com`) word processor. AbiWord offers many advanced features such as the ability to create tables, footnotes, and bullet lists.

The main difference between Microsoft Word and AbiWord is that Microsoft Word offers a huge library of templates and clip art to help you create new documents, whereas AbiWord offers only a handful of templates. In addition, AbiWord's features might be similar to Microsoft Word's, but they might not be as polished. For example, Microsoft Word's spelling and grammar checker tends to catch more errors than AbiWord's spelling and grammar checker.

One major feature missing in AbiWord is the ability to collaborate on documents and display revision marks. Although a newer version of AbiWord will likely offer this feature eventually, the lack or limit of collaboration tools in AbiWord might make you stay with Microsoft Word.

Open source is a term used to describe any program that not only is free to use and copy but also makes its source code (the actual written instructions used to create the program) freely available for anyone to copy, modify, and use.

Besides being free to use and copy, AbiWord also runs on multiple operating systems, including Windows, Mac OS X, and Linux. (Microsoft Word runs only on Windows and Mac OS X, and the Windows version of Microsoft Word looks and behaves slightly differently than the Mac OS X version.) If you need a word processor that looks and acts the same on multiple operating systems and don't require all the features of Microsoft Word, AbiWord might be a better choice than Word.

If you need to write in a foreign language, AbiWord even supports left-to-right typing (useful for Hebrew or Arabic) along with spell-checking dictionaries in 30 languages.

To maximize compatibility when sharing documents, AbiWord can also open and save files in several popular file formats, including Microsoft Word, Rich

Text Format, OpenOffice, and WordPerfect documents. With its ability to open and save files in different formats, AbiWord lets you share documents with others no matter which word processor they use. (As noted previously, all document sharing among varying programs runs the risk of some incompatibilities.)

Because AbiWord is free, you have nothing to lose by trying it. If it works for you, then keep using it. If it doesn't do what you want, then use another word processor. If you know anything about programming, you can even peek at the source code and rewrite the program to make it work exactly the way you want.

Three other popular word processors that have a small but loyal following are Nisus (`www.nisus.com`), Mariner Write (`www.marinersoftware.com`), and Mellel (`www.redlers.com`). As does AbiWord, Nisus, Mariner Write, and Mellel offer most of the features of Microsoft Word, including the ability to open and save files in Microsoft Word format and save different types of formatting as reusable styles. If you don't need all the features of Microsoft Word, you might like Nisus, Mariner Write, or Mellel better.

The latter three word processors focus on creating a smaller, slimmer, and easier word processor than Microsoft Word. The main drawback is that these three programs aren't free, but the cost is still a fraction of the price of Microsoft Word.

For another Microsoft Word alternative, consider Apple's iWork, which includes the Pages word processor, which you discover more about in Book IV, Chapter 6.

Specialized word processors

The specialized word processors in this section can help you with particular tasks. If you have a special need, there might be a special program to fill that need.

Ordinary word processors might be fine for writing reports and letters, but if you need to write only certain types of documents, you might prefer a more specialized word processor. For example, you might like Letter Star (`www.objectpark.net`), which makes writing letters easy, especially if you need to write form letters. Just type your letter and specify where to insert someone's name, address, or other custom information, and Letter Star can print form letters. Although other word processors offer the ability to create form letters and insert data such as names and addresses (known as mail-merge), Letter Star simplifies the process.

For aspiring authors, Z-Write (`www.stonetablesoftware.com`) offers a combination outliner and word processor. By helping you organize your writing into parts, such as chapters for novelists or scenes for a screenwriter, Z-Write helps keep your ideas organized and divides a larger idea into small pieces to make tackling a large project much easier.

Screenplays, teleplays, or stage plays require proper formatting, and if you'd rather not worry about all those details, you can use a specialized scriptwriting word processor such as Final Draft (`www.finaldraft.com`), Movie Magic Screenwriter (`www.screenplay.com`), or Montage (`www.marinersoftware.com`). These programs can automatically format your script as you type.

Final Draft, Movie Magic Screenwriter, and Montage cost money, but you can grab a copy of the free, open source scriptwriting program called Celtx (`www.celtx.com`), shown in Figure 1-3. As do most open source programs, Celtx runs on Windows, Mac OS X, and Linux, so if you use other operating systems regularly, Celtx might be your only choice. (Final Draft and Movie Magic Screenwriter run on both Windows and Mac OS X; Montage runs only on Mac OS X.)

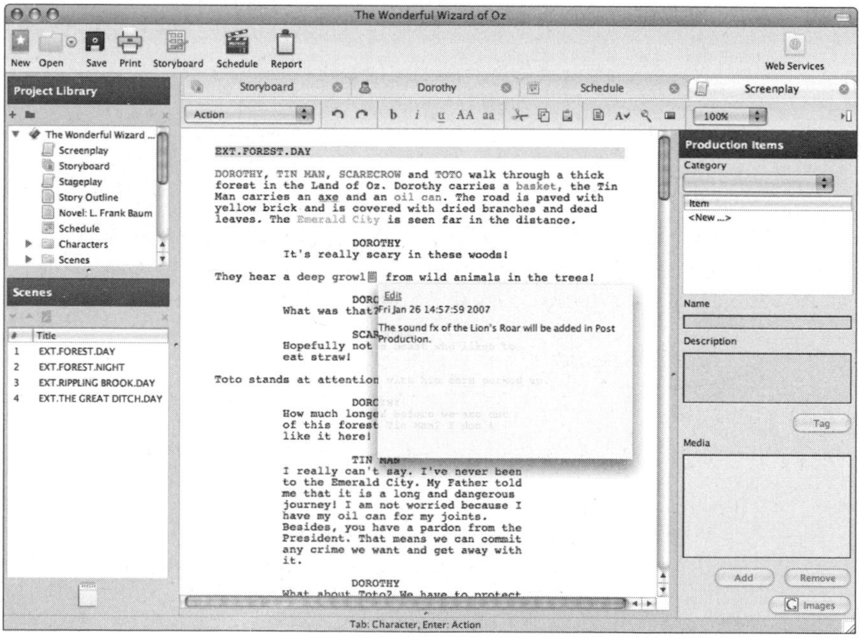

Figure 1-3: Script formatting word processors help you write a script while automatically formatting your text as you write.

Word Processor File Formats

Although most word processors work the same, they all tend to store documents in different file formats. Most word processors can open and save files that other word processors can use as well, but any time you share documents between two different word processors (even two different versions of the same word processor), you risk the chance that one word processor won't be able to use the files created by another word processor.

Also, just to let you know, there isn't a TextEdit format. TextEdit uses other common file formats.

The Microsoft Word .doc and .docx format

Originally, every word processor created its own file format to lock customers into using that particular word processor. That's the reason why so many people use Microsoft Word. It's not that people love Microsoft Word (they don't) or that Microsoft Word is the best word processor available (it isn't). It's just that so many people use Microsoft Word that if you need to share word processor documents with others, it's much easier just to use Microsoft Word, too.

The newest version of Microsoft Word, Word 2008 on the Mac, uses a file format with the extension `.docx`, which is based on XML (eXtensible Markup Language). Although this file format is fairly new, many word processors (such as Microsoft Word, Pages '08, and TextEdit) can now open and edit a `.docx` file format.

Earlier versions of Microsoft Word used a different file format, with the extension `.doc` — the unofficial "standard" for sharing word processor documents. Other word processors can also open, edit, and save `.doc` files, but they sometimes mess up the formatting in tables, headers, or footnotes.

REMEMBER

Older versions of Microsoft Word cannot open the Word 2008 `.docx` files. However, Microsoft (`www.microsoft.com`) offers a free Microsoft Office Open XML File Format Converter, which can take files stored in the `.docx` format and convert them into the older `.doc` format.

RTF (Rich Text Format) files

Not all word processors can open and display Microsoft Word files, so Microsoft created a word processor file format "standard" called Rich Text Format (RTF) files. The main purpose of the RTF file format is to allow word processors to share documents while retaining all formatting.

Because Microsoft has published the RTF file format for anyone to read and study, nearly every word processor can reliably read, write, and edit any documents stored in RTF files. For nearly guaranteed compatibility between different word processors, use RTF files to share documents.

REMEMBER

For maximum file compatibility, the free TextEdit program that comes with every Mac can read and write RTF and Microsoft Word `.doc` files.

Text (ASCII) files

An even older standard for sharing documents between word processors is called *text* or *ASCII files.* The main difference between text and RTF files is that RTF files can retain formatting of text whereas text files contain only text, with no formatting whatsoever. Every word processor can use text files, but if you need to share documents that contain formatting, stick with RTF files.

One reason to share documents as text files is if you need to share a document with a really old computer and word processor that can't recognize RTF files. Another reason to use text files is when you need to take a word processor document and pour it into a desktop publishing program or other program.

Open Document (.odf) files

One of the newest standards for word processor documents is called the Open Document format (`.odf`). The idea behind Open Document is to provide a format that retains complex formatting (such as tables, indexes, charts, and bullet lists) but whose technical specifications are kept publicly available. This way, anyone can create a word processor that can read, edit, and save documents in the Open Document format. (The Open Document format is the standard file format used by the free OpenOffice suite, which you can find out about in Book V, Chapter 2.)

Although the Open Document standard isn't in widespread use, it's likely to grow in popularity. To maintain compatibility with Open Document files, it's a good idea to check if your word processor can save, edit, and create Open Document files as well.

TECHNICAL STUFF

Several countries (France, Belgium, Norway, Japan, Finland, and Germany) are now pushing to store official publications in a universal file format, such as Open Document, for guaranteed accessibility in the future. For more information about the Open Document standard, visit OASIS (Organization for the Advancement of Structured Information Standards) at `www.oasis-open.org`.

Web page (HTML) files

You can use many word processors as simple Web page editors by saving documents in the HyperText Markup Language (HTML) format, which is used by Web sites to display text and graphics in a Web browser. The HTML file format is best for turning word processor documents into Web pages but can also be used for sharing documents between different word processors.

Although HTML is a file format standard publicly available to anyone who cares to read the technical specifications for creating and storing data in an HTML file, every word processor tends to save, open, and edit HTML files in different ways. So it's possible to create an HTML file that looks perfect in one word processor, but when opened in a different word processor (or Web page editor), that same HTML file might look skewed.

Portable Document Format (PDF) files

In the old days, *sharing* meant storing a document in a file format that another word processor could open. If two people used different word processors, there was a chance that they couldn't share documents, even if they only wanted to look at the document but not edit it.

To address this problem, Adobe created a universal file format for displaying documents called PDF or Adobe Acrobat files. A PDF file acts like a printed version of your document, except that it's stored in an electronic file (which you can, of course, print).

The Mac can view the contents of an PDF file using its Preview program. Users of other computers must view the contents of a PDF file using a special PDF reader, such as the free Adobe Acrobat Reader program (`www.adobe.com`). Because the Adobe Acrobat Reader program runs on several different operating systems (including Mac OS X, Windows, and Linux), some word processors, such as Pages '08, let you save documents in the PDF file format so that you can share your document with anyone.

PDF files preserve the exact appearance of your document. For that reason, PDF files are great for sharing files that you want others to read but don't want others to modify (although they still can with the right program, such as Acrobat Pro). That's why the government distributes tax forms as PDF files and many companies publish press releases in this format.

REMEMBER

If you're more concerned about letting others view your document but not necessary edit it, share it as a PDF file. If you want others to edit your document, store it in another file format, such as RTF, instead.

Converting File Formats

Every word processor chooses a default file format to save your documents, although you can always change this file format at any time, as shown in Figure 1-4.

If you need to share files between different word processors, you have two choices. First, you can change the default file format used by your word processor. If you need to share documents, both of you could agree to use a specific file format (such as RTF) and save your files in that format.

A second solution is to save your documents in the default file format of your word processor and then save a second copy of your document in a different file format. To save an existing document in a different file format, the general steps are as follows:

1. **Choose File⇨Save As.**

   A Save As dialog appears.

2. **Click the pop-up menu that defines a file format for saving documents.**

   A list of different formats appears, as shown in Figure 1-4.

3. **Choose the file format you want to use.**
4. **Click Save.**

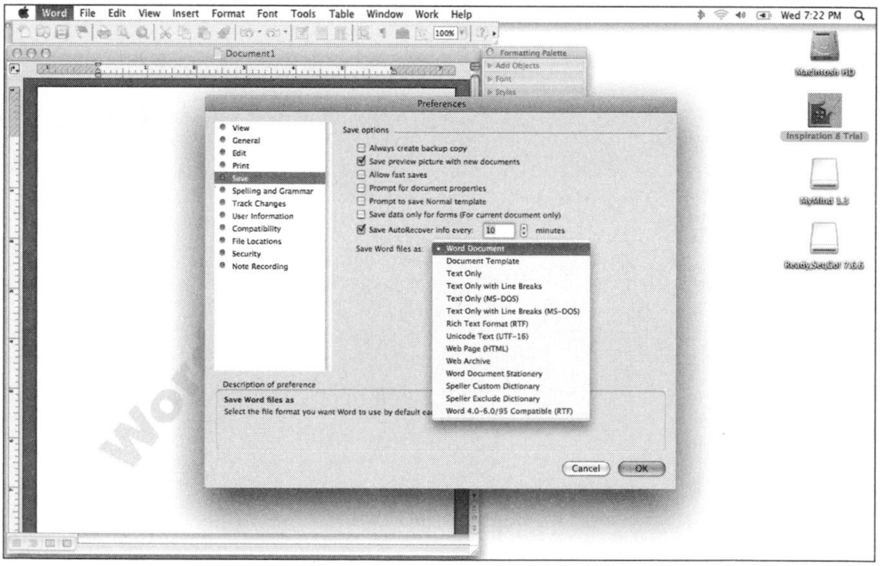

Figure 1-4: Every word processor lets you choose a default file format to use.

If you need to use documents stored in different file formats, you might want a dedicated file-conversion program such as MacLink Plus (`www.dataviz.com`). In contrast to a word processor that can typically open and save documents in only a handful of different file formats, MacLink Plus can convert and save documents stored in dozens of different file formats, including obscure file formats such as WordStar, MultiMate, OfficeWriter, WriteNow, and ClarisWorks/AppleWorks.

With so many different word processors available, take your time to find the one you like best. As long as you're happy with your word processor, it doesn't really matter what anyone else uses.

Chapter 2: Office Suites on the Mac

In This Chapter

- **Understanding spreadsheets**
- **Understanding presentation programs**
- **Comparing office suites**
- **Understanding office suite file formats**

Most businesses rely on word processors, spreadsheet applications, and presentation programs to do most of the heavy lifting for essential office functions. Instead of buying these programs separately, most people buy them in sets known as *office suites.* Besides costing less than buying the programs individually, office suite programs are designed to work together. Not only can you share data among all programs in an office suite, but each office suite program uses similar menus and commands.

Although many people are familiar with word processors (if not, refer to Book V, Chapter 1), fewer people understand the purpose and advantages of spreadsheets and presentation programs. The first part of this chapter briefly describes what these two programs do and why you might want to use them.

Understanding Spreadsheets

Word processors are great for manipulating text, but when you need to manipulate (or *crunch*) numbers to balance your budget, you need a spreadsheet. Think of a spreadsheet like a super calculator. Just feed a spreadsheet 4 or 4,000 numbers, and it happily crunches (adds, subtracts, multiplies, and divides) them quickly and accurately.

To make a spreadsheet calculate numbers, you need to create and store formulas in the spreadsheet. Formulas can be as simple as adding several numbers or as complicated as solving a third-order differential equation; the choice is yours.

Even better, spreadsheets let you examine your formulas so you can spot errors in the formulas or in the numbers you're feeding into the formula.

Such error-checking lets you create and calculate spreadsheets with a speed and accuracy not possible with a calculator or adding machine.

The parts of a spreadsheet

Every spreadsheet consists of a grid that consists of rows and columns. The intersection of a row and column forms a block called a *cell*, as shown in Figure 2-1.

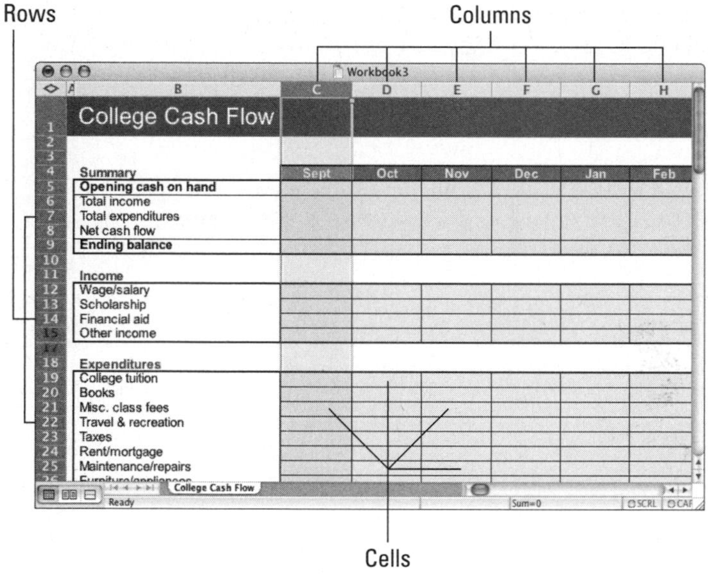

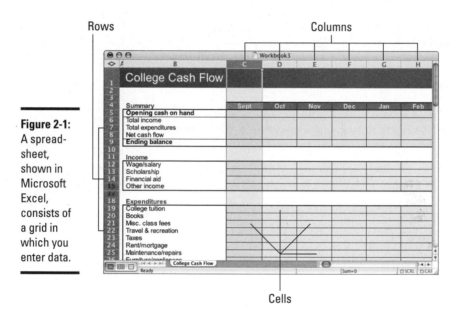

Figure 2-1: A spreadsheet, shown in Microsoft Excel, consists of a grid in which you enter data.

When you type numbers into a spreadsheet, you always type them into a cell, which are aligned in rows and columns (refer to Figure 2-1).

Two types of data you can type in a spreadsheet are numbers and text. Numbers can represent anything, such as quantities or measurements. Text typically identifies what your data represents, as in the following:

Sales Person	Weekly Sales
Sally May	$648.20
Bob Jones	$710.54
Derek Kale	$609.86
Mary Sands	$448.25

At the simplest level, a spreadsheet lets you organize numbers and text labels in rows and columns. However, the heart of any spreadsheet is its formulas, which can calculate results based on the numbers stored in different cells. Any cell can contain a formula. A formula can be as simple as adding two numbers or as complicated as multiplying 4,000 numbers. You can type a formula in a cell and then edit it later using the Formula Bar (refer to Figure 2-1).

Calculating results with formulas

A *formula* is a special type of text that tells the computer how to use numbers, stored in different cells, to calculate a new result. Although a formula can define specific numbers to calculate (such as 23 + 76.09), the real power of a spreadsheet comes from defining which cells to calculate. Because you can type different numbers into a cell, changing a number in a cell feeds different data into a formula.

A *cell reference* identifies a specific cell by its column heading (a letter) and row heading (a number), as shown in Figure 2-2.

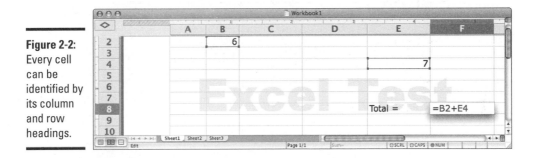

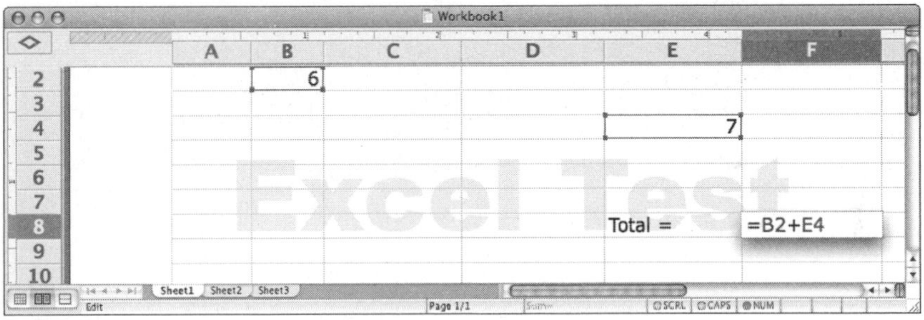

Figure 2-2: Every cell can be identified by its column and row headings.

If you want a formula to use a number stored in a specific cell, you have to use cell references in your formula, such as

= B2 + E4

This formula tells the spreadsheet, "Take the number stored in cell B2 and add it to the number stored in cell E4. Then display the results in the cell where you typed this formula."

By using cell references rather than actual numbers, formulas can always calculate the same type of results (addition, subtraction) no matter what numbers you store in different cells.

By combining addition, subtraction, division, and multiplication in various ways, you can create even the most complicated formulas, such as determining the monthly payments on a loan that charges a fixed interest rate every year over a ten-year period. To spare you the trouble of creating commonly used formulas, such as calculating logarithms or interest rates, most spreadsheet programs include prebuilt formulas called functions. By using functions, you can make a spreadsheet calculate the most complicated formulas to solve any mathematical problem.

Formatting text and numbers

After you've entered some numbers and created formulas to manipulate those numbers, you can format your spreadsheet to make it look nicer or present your data more effectively. By shading column I, this spreadsheet makes numbers displayed in that column easier to find and read. By shading rows 9 and 13, the spreadsheet helps separate data, as shown in Figure 2-3.

Besides formatting text, you can also format numbers. Formatting numbers can include defining how many decimal places appear; whether to use commas to separate the digits of a large number; whether to display numbers with currency signs; and whether to display negative numbers in red or in parentheses.

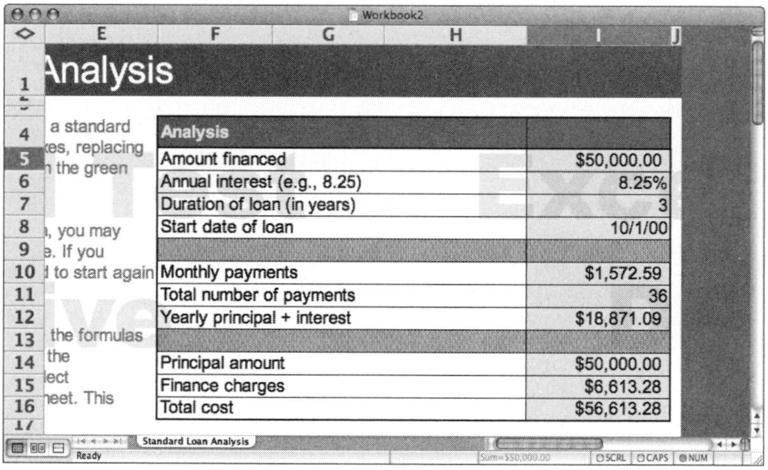

Figure 2-3: Formatting text, rows, and columns can make different elements stand out.

To change the formatting of one or more cells, you need to open a dialog. In Excel, you can right-click one or more cells and choose Format Cells to display the dialog as shown in Figure 2-4. In Numbers, you need to select one or more cells and choose View➪Show Inspector to see a similar dialog.

In the dialog in Figure 2-4, you first need to select a category that defines the type of data that you want to format, such as numbers or currency. Then you need to select specific options for each type of formatting. For example, selecting the Numbers category lets you choose how many decimal places to display, but selecting the Currency category offers a different option that lets you choose the type of currency symbol to display.

REMEMBER

Formatting is never necessary, but it can make your spreadsheet easier to read and understand.

Making numbers meaningful with charts

Staring with a spreadsheet loaded with rows and columns of numbers can seem like driving in a heavy fog. What are you supposed to be seeing in those numbers? Are those sales figures going up or down, and by how much? But translate your numbers into pie, bar, or line charts, and presto! It all seems so much clearer now. Figure 2-5 shows some types of charts that you can create in standard spreadsheet programs.

To create a chart, you must select the cells containing the data you want to show in your chart, which includes the actual numbers along with labels that identify what those numbers represent such as sales per month. Then you can choose the type of chart you want to create. To display the dialog in Figure 2-5 using Excel, you can just click a Chart Wizard button. In Numbers, you can choose a chart by clicking a Chart button.

Charts help you spot trends that would be impossible to identify just by looking at lists of numbers. For example, a pie chart can show you which sales people account for the largest amount of income, and a line chart can show you which sales person has been gradually increasing (or decreasing) sales over time.

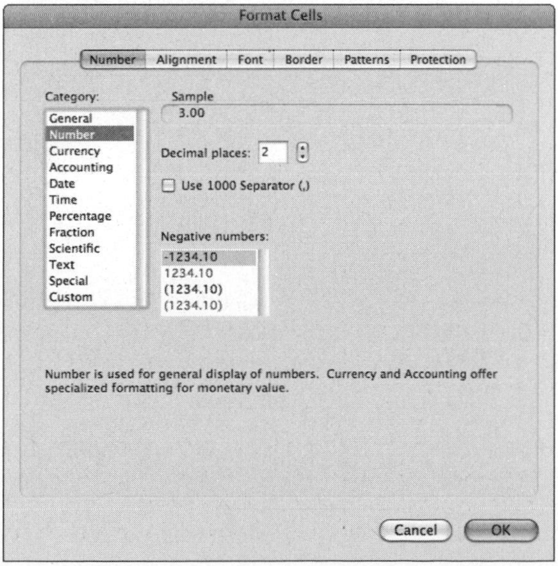

Figure 2-4: Formatting numbers can make your numbers easier to read and understand.

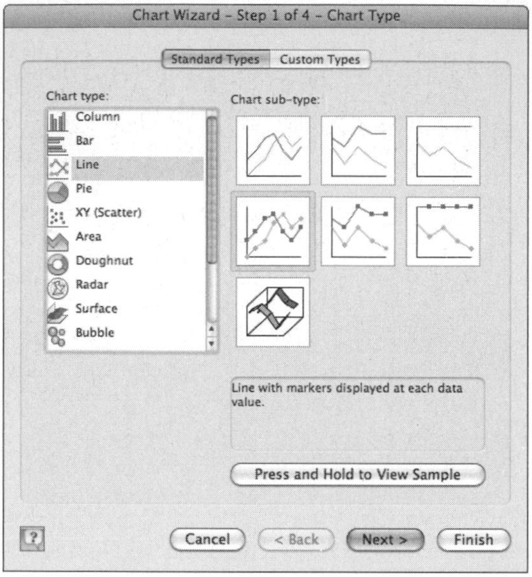

Figure 2-5: Charts can make long lists of numbers meaningful.

Understanding Presentation Programs

In the old days, giving a presentation often meant printing text and graphics on a transparent sheet of plastic and slapping it on an overhead projector. Obviously, this method of presenting information was clumsy and tedious. Not only did you have to print everything on transparent plastic sheets, but you had to keep them in the right order. If you needed to make any changes, you'd have to print a new transparent sheet all over again.

Presentation programs solve this problem by making it easy to create and edit a presentation, even at the last minute. Plus you can include animation, sound, or movies, which is impossible to do with static transparencies on an overhead projector.

Every presentation consists of one or more slides, with a slide typically displaying a single chunk of information. So the first slide of a presentation might display a brief introduction identifying the speaker or the topic of the presentation. The second slide might explain how sales results are going down, and a third slide might display a list of ideas for increasing sales.

Displaying text

Text can appear by itself on a slide or combined with a graphic image, such as a pie chart. Text generally consists of a heading and brief supporting items such as bullet points, as shown in the PowerPoint screen in Figure 2-6.

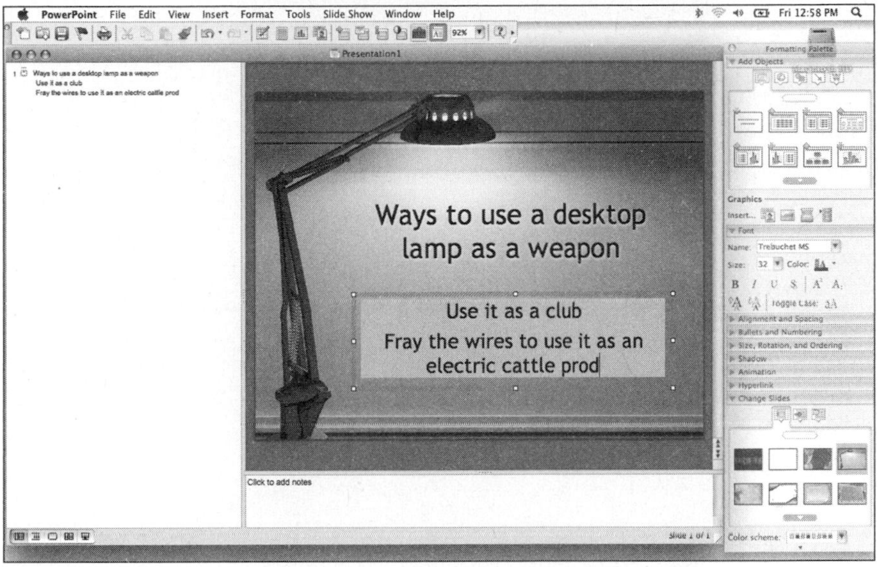

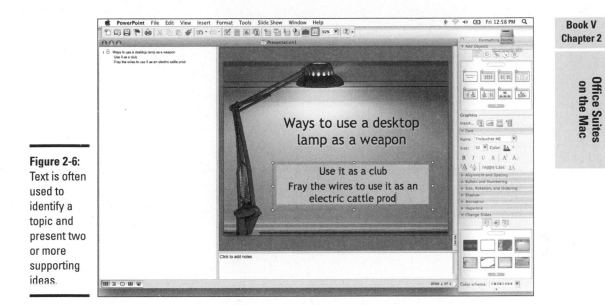

Figure 2-6: Text is often used to identify a topic and present two or more supporting ideas.

As do word processor programs, presentation programs let you format text to use different fonts, change the font size, or display text in color.

TIP

Format your text in ways that make it easier to read, especially for people sitting in the back of the room watching your presentation. For instance, make sure the text is large enough, and if you color your text, make sure it contrasts with the background (using light-colored text on a dark background, and vice versa).

Displaying graphics

A presentation that consists entirely of text can often get monotonous. To keep people from falling asleep, spruce up your presentation with graphics. You might, for example, sprinkle informative images, such as pie or bar charts, throughout your slide show. You can also use purely decorative graphics, such as a company logo. (See Figure 2-7 for a graphic displayed in PowerPoint.)

Things can really get interesting when you animate your graphics. A simple, static line chart can show how sales are rising or falling, but it's much more dramatic to watch an animated line chart change before your eyes.

Besides cartoon images, graphics can also include actual still photographs or video. If you were giving a presentation in front of advertising executives, you could play a short video of a competitor's TV commercial, concluding with a demo video of your own commercial. By adding animation and video, presentation programs can become more compelling and convincing.

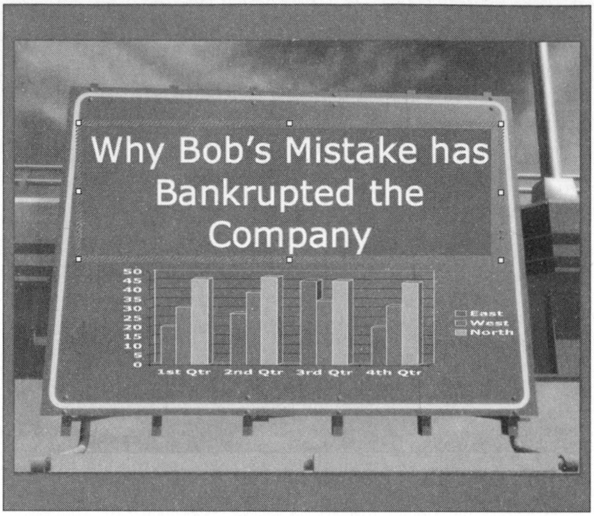

Figure 2-7: Enliven your presentation with graphics.

Spicing up presentations with transitions

If your presentation doesn't use or need video or animated graphics, you can still spice up your presentation by using transitions. A transition can animate the way text appears on a slide or how each slide appears.

Adding a transition to text can make your text drop in place, one letter at a time, or swirl around the screen before settling into place. Like formatting text, adding transitions to text is meant to highlight your message and make it more interesting for people to read.

Transitions can make individual slides more interesting to watch as well. Instead of having one slide disappear and another one appear in its place, a transition can make one slide dissolve and reveal the next slide underneath. Such slide transitions are meant to capture the audience's attention and make your entire presentation visually interesting. (Now all you have to worry about is making it informative and useful.)

WARNING!

When using transitions, don't get carried away. Too many transitions can get more distracting than entertaining, so use transitions sparingly.

Rearranging slides

Perhaps most important, presentation programs let you rearrange your slides easily, making it possible to create a presentation and customize it for different audiences. For example, if you're presenting to a group of engineers and scientists, you might add more slides displaying technically oriented information. If you had to give that same presentation to a group of investors and business executives, you could simply skip over the technically oriented slides without having to delete them.

Comparing Office Suites

Office suites typically bundle several programs that offer the most common features you'll need for personal or business use. The most common office suite is Microsoft Office. Because Microsoft Office is so popular on Windows, using Microsoft Office for the Mac allows you to share files easily with little risk of file incompatibilities.

Choosing an office suite often boils down to these factors:

- **Compatibility:** If you need to share files with others, you need maximum file compatibility. Identify the office suite being used by people who you need to share files with. Then use the same office suite that these people are using. If you don't want to use that office suite, look for a similar office suite that can work with files created by other office suites.
- **Cost:** The cost of an office suite can also influence your decision because some office suites cost nearly as much as a new computer (Microsoft Office).
- **Features:** Look at the features offered by each program in the office suite. Although office suites tend to offer similar features, they always offer something different, either a feature that a competing office suite doesn't offer or a slicker way of doing something that another office suite does.

One of the newest office suites available is iWork, which you can read about in Book IV, Chapters 6, 7, and 8.

If you already have a word processor but just need a spreadsheet, consider getting Mesa (`www.plsys.com`), which is a low-cost ($34) spreadsheet that's designed to be simpler to use than other spreadsheets.

Microsoft Office

The most popular office suite is Microsoft Office, which includes Microsoft Word (word processor), Microsoft Excel (spreadsheet), Microsoft PowerPoint (presentation program), and Microsoft Entourage (e-mail and personal organizer program).

If you're switching over from a Windows computer, you might already be familiar with Microsoft Office, so getting the Mac version will make the transition from Windows to the Mac that much easier.

One drawback of Microsoft Office is that it offers so many features that the programs can be hard to learn and use. If you just need an office suite for personal use, Microsoft Office can do the job in much the same way that a baseball bat can do the job of a fly swatter. For many people, Microsoft Office offers way more features than they'll ever need, so if you fit into this category, you might want to consider some alternatives.

ThinkFree Office

One of the more interesting alternatives to Microsoft Office is a competing office suite dubbed ThinkFree Office (`www.thinkfree.com`), which is offered in two versions: a desktop version and an online version.

The desktop version of the ThinkFree office suite includes a word processor, spreadsheet, and presentation program that can open, edit, and save documents in Microsoft Word, Excel, and PowerPoint formats.

The drawback of ThinkFree Office is that it doesn't work 100 percent exactly like Microsoft Office, and there's always the possibility that ThinkFree Office won't be able to open and display complex Microsoft Office documents correctly. However, if you don't need all the features of Microsoft Office and don't create complicated documents, ThinkFree Office is the perfect low-cost alternative.

For an even better alternative, try the free online version of ThinkFree Office, shown in Figure 2-8. Unlike the desktop version, which requires you to install the programs on your Mac, the online version of ThinkFree Office works entirely through your Web browser. As long as you have a fast and reliable Internet connection, you can create, edit, and save files using ThinkFree Office anywhere in the world.

Of course, if you don't have access to an Internet connection, you won't be able to edit documents using the online ThinkFree, so you might still want to buy the desktop version of ThinkFree when you need to work without an Internet connection.

ThinkFree even offers a special portable edition of its ThinkFree Show presentation program. This portable edition lets you create, edit, and save presentations on your iPod so that you can carry and give your presentations through your iPod rather than lug your laptop Mac around.

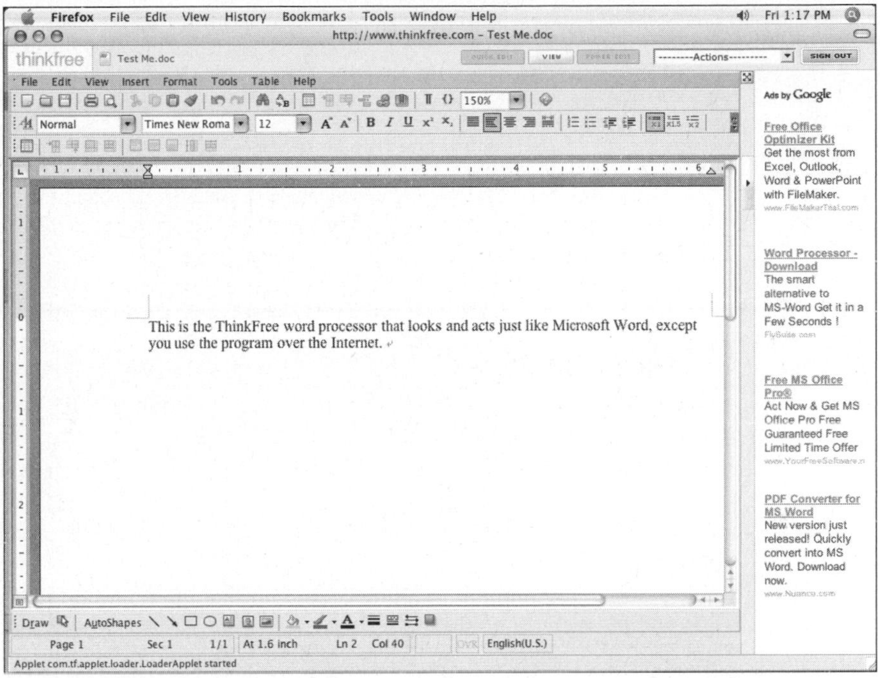

Figure 2-8: To use the online version of ThinkFree Office, you need an Internet connection and a Web browser.

Google Docs & Spreadsheets

For another free, online office suite, try Google Docs & Spreadsheets (`www.google.com`), which lets you use a Microsoft Word– and Excel-compatible program to write documents and create spreadsheets using any computer that has an Internet connection and a browser. Figure 2-9 shows a Google spreadsheet in action.

If you need to collaborate on word processor documents or spreadsheets with others, ordinary office suites force you to e-mail files back and forth. With Google Docs & Spreadsheets, you and another person can collaborate on a word processor document or spreadsheet file online in real time.

As with the online version of ThinkFree Office, Google Docs & Spreadsheets is useless if you don't have an Internet connection, but if you do most of your creating and editing at a computer hooked up to the Internet, Google Docs & Spreadsheets is another free alternative to Microsoft Office.

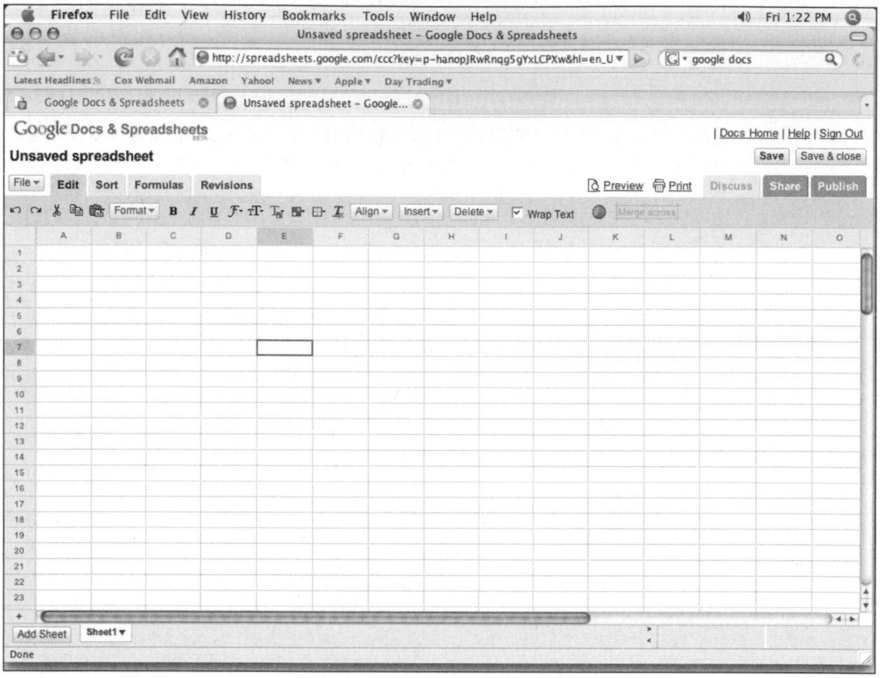

Figure 2-9: A Google online spreadsheet.

NeoOffice and OpenOffice

If the free, online version of ThinkFree Office appeals to you but you don't want to rely on the Internet to create and edit your documents, consider the free, open source NeoOffice (`www.neooffice.org`) and OpenOffice (`www.openoffice.org`). OpenOffice is an open source project to create a free office suite that runs under the Mac OS, Windows, and Linux. Best of all, OpenOffice includes a wealth of programs specifically designed for business use including:

- ✦ OpenOffice Writer (word processor)
- ✦ OpenOffice Calc (spreadsheet)
- ✦ OpenOffice Impress (presentation program)
- ✦ OpenOffice Base (database program)
- ✦ OpenOffice Draw (drawing program)

Although OpenOffice Writer, Calc, and Impress mimic Microsoft Word, Excel, and PowerPoint, respectively, OpenOffice Base is a relational database similar to Microsoft Access, which is available only on Windows computers. Relational databases let you store large amounts of data and are used by many businesses to track inventory or manage customer lists. OpenOffice

Draw is a vector drawing program, similar to CorelDRAW or Adobe Illustrator, which lets you draw organizational charts or flowcharts.

OpenOffice is a free version of a commercial office suite called StarOffice, developed and marketed by Sun Microsystems (`www.sun.com`). If you need technical support, you can buy the commercial version of StarOffice, which is identical to OpenOffice.

One glaring flaw of OpenOffice is that its current version runs on X11, which is a windowing system designed for the Unix operating system, which is what Mac OS X is based on. As a result, installing and running OpenOffice on a Mac requires technical expertise, which might scare novices away from OpenOffice.

The OpenOffice programmers are working to create a native Mac version of OpenOffice, which might be available by the time you read this.

Since OpenOffice originally did not run on the Mac, a separate team of programmers took it upon themselves to develop their own Mac version of OpenOffice, which they dubbed NeoOffice.

NeoOffice is identical to OpenOffice except that NeoOffice runs only on the Mac. If you want to run OpenOffice and don't want to wait for an official Mac version of OpenOffice to be developed someday, grab a free copy of NeoOffice instead. Figure 2-10 shows the presentation program that's part of the NeoOffice suite. Just think of NeoOffice as OpenOffice but with the friendly Mac user interface.

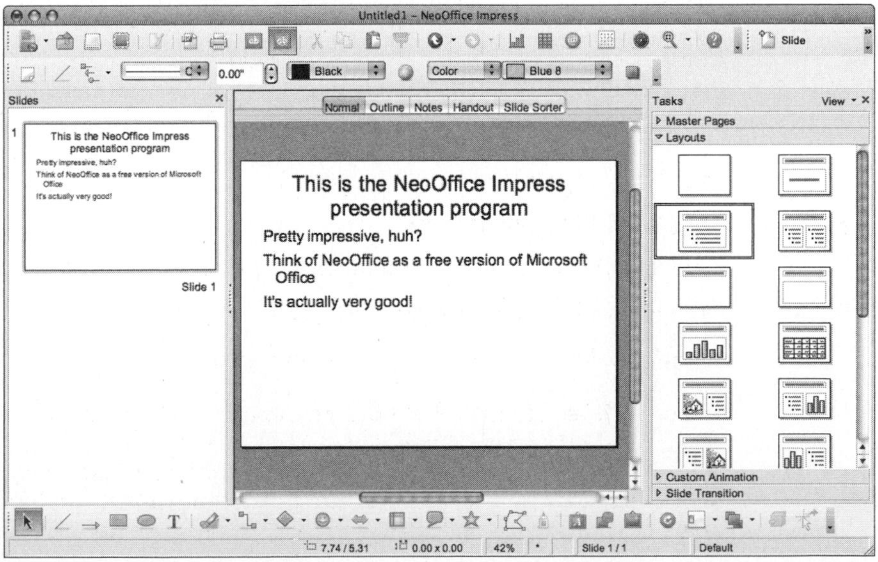

Figure 2-10: NeoOffice brings the power of OpenOffice to your Mac.

Databases

Although most office suites don't include a database, most businesses need the ability to store, sort, and retrieve data. Currently, the most popular database for the Mac is FileMaker (`www.filemaker.com`), which has long been acknowledged as one of the easiest database programs to use on any personal computer. A simpler version of FileMaker, sold by the same company, is called Bento.

Another popular database program available for the Mac is 4th Dimension (`www.4d.com`). Although not as easy to use as FileMaker, 4th Dimension is a hit with programmers who want to create their own custom databases.

RagTime

One unusual business suite is called RagTime (`www.ragtime-online.com`). In contrast to most office suites, which offer a word processor, spreadsheet, and presentation program, RagTime provides a word processor, spreadsheet, and desktop publishing program. The reason for this is that RagTime focuses on helping you create printed business reports.

By using RagTime's word processor to create text and its spreadsheet to calculate numeric results, you can easily transfer this information into RagTime's desktop publishing program to create reports that would be difficult to create in a word processor.

Best of all, if you make any changes in your word processor or spreadsheet, RagTime immediately updates those changes as they appear in your desktop publishing document. In this way, RagTime ensures that your desktop publishing document will always contain the latest information automatically. Although RagTime is relatively expensive ($495), the price might be worth it if you need to create business reports on a regular basis.

MarinerPak

For a low-cost, simple office suite, consider MarinerPak (`www.marinersoftware.com`), which combines Mariner Write (a word processor) with Mariner Calc (a spreadsheet). Mariner Write can open, edit, and save Microsoft Word documents, and Mariner Calc can open, edit, and save Microsoft Excel files.

Although not as full featured as Microsoft Word or Excel, both Mariner Write and Mariner Calc are far easier to use and less expensive as well ($89.95). If you're looking for a word processor and spreadsheet that won't leave your scratching your head or pulling out hair, you might find MarinerPak to be just what you're looking for.

Office Suite File Formats

Because Microsoft Office is the most popular office suite, nearly every office suite can open, edit, and save to Microsoft Office file formats. The Microsoft Word file format uses the `.doc` extension, Excel uses `.xls`, and PowerPoint uses `.ppt`.

The 2007 version of Microsoft Office uses a new file format with the extension `.docx` (Word), `.xlsx` (Excel), and `.pptx` (PowerPoint), respectively. Not all office suites can open, edit, and save to these new file formats yet, so if you need to be able to open documents with these new file formats, make sure to obtain an office suite that 's compatible.

Although the Microsoft Office file formats are the most popular for storing data, office suites actually use many other file formats. Most of these other file formats are designed to retain compatibility with older programs, but if you need to use data trapped in these file formats, make sure your office suite knows how to use them.

See Book V, Chapter 1 for more information about word processor file formats.

Spreadsheet file formats

Because so many people use Microsoft Excel, its `.xls` file format has become the *de facto* standard spreadsheet file format for transferring information. As is the Microsoft Word `.doc` format, the Excel `.xls` format is proprietary, which means that a complicated spreadsheet file might not appear correctly in another spreadsheet.

A last-resort file format is known as comma-separated value format (`.csv`). Basically, a `.csv` file just stores the data without retaining any of its formatting. To separate data, `.csv` files use commas. This is a universal spreadsheet file format, which means that every spreadsheet can open and create `.csv` files.

To prevent spreadsheet data from ultimately getting trapped in file formats that fall out of use, an open source standard for spreadsheets has been developed called Open Document Spreadsheets (`.ods`). Although not in widespread use, expect more spreadsheets to start offering the ability to open, edit, and save spreadsheets in the OpenDocument format.

Presentation file formats

The dominant presentation file format is Microsoft PowerPoint (which uses the .ppt extension). In contrast to word processor documents or spreadsheet files, presentations rarely contain data that you might need to save and reuse in the future. As a result, most presentation programs can import and export PowerPoint files, but they might use their own proprietary file format to store the presentations.

To define a universal presentation file format standard, there's an OpenDocument standard for presentations (.odp). Although not in widespread use yet, expect more presentation programs to offer the ability to open and save presentations in the OpenDocument format.

Generally, the simplest way to avoid dealing with different file formats is to use the exact same programs that everyone else is using, which usually means using Microsoft Office. However, if absolute compatibility with others isn't important or you're willing to deal with the occasional hassle of incompatible files, you can find plenty of alternative office suites that can turn your Mac into a business productivity tool.

Chapter 3: Painting and Drawing on a Mac

In This Chapter

- Understanding painting versus drawing
- Working with common raster-editing features
- Using vector-editing features
- Choosing a painting and drawing program
- Understanding graphic file formats

The Mac is best known for its graphics capabilities. Although many companies, such as Adobe, sell virtually identical graphics programs for both Mac and Windows computers, the vast majority of professional artists and graphics designers prefer the Mac.

One common way to play with graphics is to modify an existing image. Many people capture pictures using a digital camera and then touch up those pictures using a graphics editing program.

Another way to use graphics is to create an image from scratch. Creating graphics from scratch isn't necessarily difficult — it's just time-consuming. As a result, creating graphics is the realm of most professionals, whereas editing graphics is commonly used by both amateurs and professionals.

Understanding Painting versus Drawing

The two types of graphics programs are painting and drawing programs. The main difference between these two forms of graphics lies with the way they create, edit, and display pictures.

A painting program draws pictures using individual dots called *pixels.* A single picture can consist of thousands of individual pixels. By changing the color of these pixels, you can change the appearance of an image.

Pictures made up of pixels are also called *raster images.* When you take a picture with a digital camera, your camera stores that picture as a raster image. If you capture a picture using a scanner, your scanner saves that image as a raster picture too. The most popular raster-editing program is Adobe Photoshop.

The biggest disadvantage of raster images is that you can't resize them. The more you enlarge a raster image, the grainier and chunkier it gets, as shown in Figure 3-1.

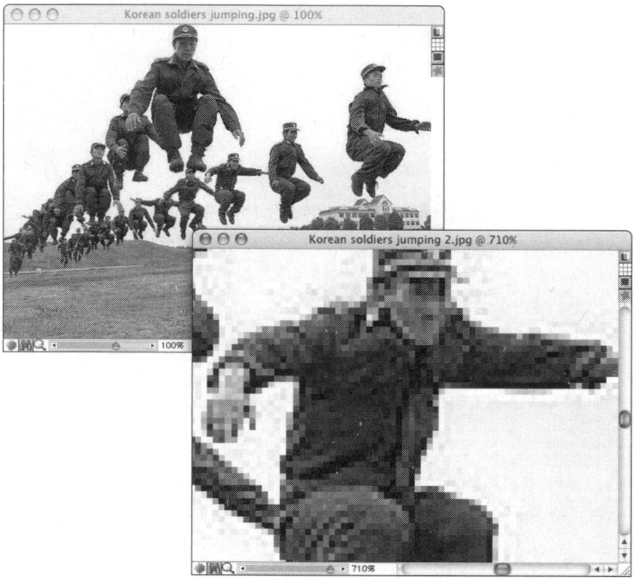

Figure 3-1: Enlarged raster images appear chunky and grainy.

The alternative to a painting program is a drawing program. Drawing programs store pictures as *vector graphics.* Whereas a raster image physically draws an image on the screen, vector graphics store images as mathematical equations that define how to display an image on the screen.

A vector graphics picture consists of multiple items called primitives, such as points, lines, curves, and shapes. A mathematical equation tells the computer where to place items and how wide, tall, or long or what color to display each item. As a result, vector graphics generally don't display the subtle details that a raster image does, but vector graphics can be resized without ever losing their resolution, as shown in Figure 3-2.

Vector graphics typically consist of separate items that you can modify and manipulate individually. This gives vector graphics more of a cartoon look than a realistic image. Because the resolution of vector graphics remains sharp no matter how large you make the picture or what resolution you use to display the image on a screen, vector graphics are used in many Web page advertisements and animated movies. One popular vector graphics program is Adobe Flash.

Figure 3-2: Vector graphics display sharp resolution no matter how much you enlarge them.

Many companies sell libraries of clip art images that you can use to spice up a document or desktop publishing file. Sometimes these clip art images are vector images, which let you resize them without degrading their appearance, but sometimes these clip art images are raster images, which means resizing them can make them look grainy.

Common Raster-Editing Features

Editing involves a two-step process. First, you must select the item you want to modify. Second, you have to choose a command to modify your selected item.

In most programs, such as a word processor or a spreadsheet, you can easily select text by dragging the mouse. In a graphics program, selecting parts of a picture can be much harder because, in contrast to text, there isn't always a clear boundary of what to choose. When looking at a digital photograph of a man, how can you tell the computer to select just the man's face but not his mustache or hat? Computers see every raster image as just as series of colored pixels, so selecting which pixels you want to manipulate can be tricky.

To help you select all or part of an image, raster-editing programs offer different types of tools that usually appear as icons in a group known as a *toolbox,* as shown in Figure 3-3. By selecting the right tool, you can use the mouse to select and manipulate a picture in different ways.

The toolbox shown in Figure 3-3 comes from Photoshop Elements, but other graphics programs will likely display different tool icons in different positions.

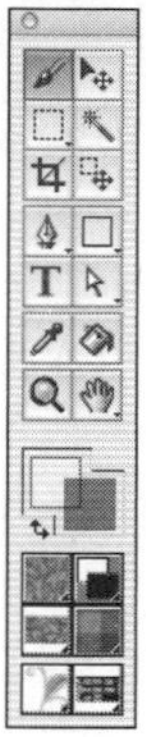

Figure 3-3: Raster-editing programs offer a toolbox of icons that represent different ways to manipulate a picture.

Selecting an entire picture

The simplest way to select a raster image is to select an entire image by pressing ⌘+A. (In some programs, you can also choose this command by choosing Edit➪Select All or just Select➪All.)

After you select an entire picture, you can modify that entire picture by rotating, making it lighter or darker, increasing/decreasing its contrast, and converting a color picture black and white.

Many raster-editing programs also offer a Select Invert command. So if you want to select a large area of a picture except for a small region in the middle, it's actually easier to select the small region in the middle first. Then you can choose the Select Invert command, and you'll actually select the large region that you want.

Selecting an area

Instead of selecting a whole picture, you can also select just part of a picture. You can't select part of a picture until you first choose a selection tool, which typically appears in a toolbox (refer to Figure 3-3).

One of the simplest ways to select part of a picture is to select a rectangular or elliptical area. To select a rectangular or circular part of a picture, follow these steps:

1. **Click the rectangular or elliptical selection tool in the Toolbox and move the pointer over the part of the picture you want to select.**

2. **Hold down the mouse button and drag the mouse.**

   The selection tool draws a dotted line, called a *marquee,* around your selected item, as shown in Figure 3-4.

Figure 3-4: Dragging the mouse draws a marquee around your selection.

Selecting an irregular shape

The problem with the rectangular and elliptical selection tools is that the part that you want to edit will almost never be perfectly rectangular or elliptical. Because images in a picture are often irregularly shaped (think of the shape of a man's face in a digital photograph), most raster-editing programs offer a special tool called a Lasso tool.

The Lasso tool lets you drag the mouse and draw the boundaries of the area you want to select by dragging the mouse, as shown in Figure 3-5.

Variations of the Lasso Tool

Although the Lasso tool can select irregular shapes, it can also be clumsy to use because it requires a steady hand to drag the mouse exactly where you want to select part of a picture. To compensate for this, some programs offer two varieties of the Lasso Tool called the Polygonal Lasso tool and the Magnetic Lasso tool.

The Polygonal Lasso tool lets you point and click to draw straight lines. By letting you click the mouse around an area, the Polygonal Lasso tool makes it easy to select an irregularly shaped part of a picture.

The Magnetic Lasso tool lets you drag the mouse around an area, but it's smart enough to detect contrast differences between different parts of a picture. So rather than force you to drag the mouse exactly around a selected area in a picture, the Magnetic Lasso tool lets you drag the mouse approximately near an area you want to select, and the Magnetic Lasso tool automatically selects the boundary of an area.

Figure 3-5: The Lasso tool can select an irregular shape.

Selecting with the Magic Wand

Dragging the mouse to select an area might still be difficult, especially if the item you want to select consists of multiple irregular shapes like a tree branch. In cases like this, it might be easier to select the color of a picture by using the Magic Wand tool.

The Magic Wand tool selects adjacent pixels based on color. So if you want to select the blue sky behind a tree, you can click the Magic Wand tool and then click the blue sky. The Magic Wand tool would automatically select the blue pixels that you clicked, along with any adjacent blue pixels. By adjusting the sensitivity of the Magic Wand tool, you can make it select more or fewer pixels. If you select the Magic Wand tool and click the black portion of a picture, you select all adjacent black areas as shown in Figure 3-6.

Erasing pixels

One common way to modify a picture is to erase part of it, which you can do by using the Eraser tool. When you choose the Eraser tool, you can drag the mouse over a picture and wipe out all pixels underneath, as shown in Figure 3-7.

By changing the shape and size of the eraser tool, you can trim away parts of a picture without erasing the parts that you want to keep. For added flexibility, many raster-editing programs offer a Magic Eraser tool. Like the Magic Wand tool, which selects an area based on similar colors, the Magic Eraser tool erases adjacent pixels that contain similar colors.

Figure 3-6: The Magic Wand can select areas that contain similar colors.

Figure 3-7: The Eraser tool wipes out anything that you drag the mouse over.

Using the paint brush and paint bucket

Rather than erase part of your picture, you might want to color pixels. By changing the color of pixels, you can change the appearance of an image, such as creating a third eye on someone's forehead or coloring in a tear in a scanned photograph to make the tear disappear.

To color pixels, raster-editing programs offer a Paint Brush and Paint Bucket tool. The Paint Brush tool lets you use the pointer as a brush by clicking and dragging the mouse.

If you need to paint a large area, dragging the mouse with the Paint Brush tool can get tedious, so raster-editing programs offer a Paint Bucket tool, which colors in any enclosed area. To use the Paint Bucket tool, just click it in the Toolbox and then click the color that you want to use. Next, click the part of your picture that you want to color and your chosen color floods that part of your picture as if you spilled a bucket of paint over it.

As an alternative to clicking a color, many raster-editing programs off a special Eyedropper tool. The purpose of the Eyedropper tool is to let you choose an existing color in your picture. After you click a color in your picture, the Paint Brush or Paint Bucket tool can use that to color another area.

Common Vector-Editing Features

Unlike raster-editing programs that modify individual pixels, vector graphics–editing programs modify objects. To create a picture, a vector graphic program gives you various tools for drawing different types of objects, called *primitives.* Some common primitive objects are lines, curves, and points.

After you create a picture using primitive objects, you can modify those primitives using a variety of tools that scale (enlarge or shrink) or reshape those primitives.

Moving and resizing objects with the Selection tool

Vector graphics consist of multiple objects. When you use the Selection tool, you can move or resize one or more objects by selecting them with a Selection tool and then dragging them with the mouse. To use the Selection tool, follow these steps:

1. **Click the Selection tool, which usually appears as a dark arrow pointer, in the toolbox.**
2. **Click an object you want to modify, such as a line.**

   Handles appear around your object, as shown in Figure 3-8, which displays the EazyDraw program.
3. **(Optional) To move your selected object, move the pointer over your selected object, hold the mouse button, and drag the mouse.**

   Release the mouse button when you're happy with the new location of your object.
4. **(Optional) To resize your selected object, move the pointer over a handle, hold down the mouse button, and drag the mouse.**

   Release the mouse button when you're happy with the new size of your object.

TIP

After selecting an object with the Selection tool, you can press Delete if you want to remove that selected object.

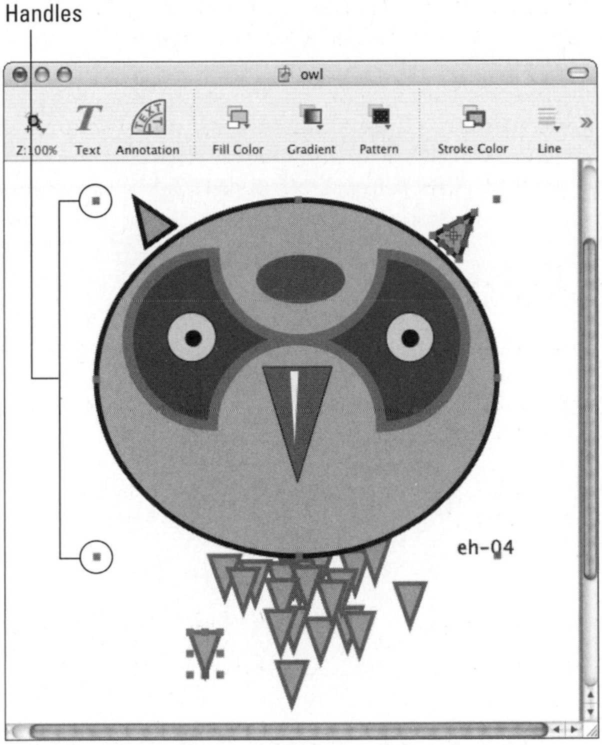

Figure 3-8: The Selection tool lets you choose an object to modify.

Reshaping an object with the Direct Selection tool

Rather than move or change the size of an object, you might want to modify the shape of an object, which you can change using the Direct Selection tool. This tool often appears as a white arrow pointer directly underneath the Selection tool icon in the toolbox.

When you click an object with the Direct Selection tool, that object displays anchor points and direction points. *Anchor points* appear as squares directly on an object. By dragging an anchor point, you can reshape an object. *Direction points* appear as lines with a circle or point on each end. By dragging a direction point, you can reshape the curve of an object. Figure 3-9 shows an image displayed in the Intaglio drawing program.

Vector graphics programs sometimes use different terms to describe identical items. For example, Adobe Illustrator uses the term Direct Selection tool; another program might call it a Point Selection tool. Just remember that the names might be different, but the functions remain the same.

To use the Direct Selection tool, follow these steps:

1. **Click the Direct Selection tool, which usually appears as a white arrow pointer, in the toolbox.**
2. **Click an object you want to modify, such as a line.**

   Anchor and direction points appear on your chosen object.

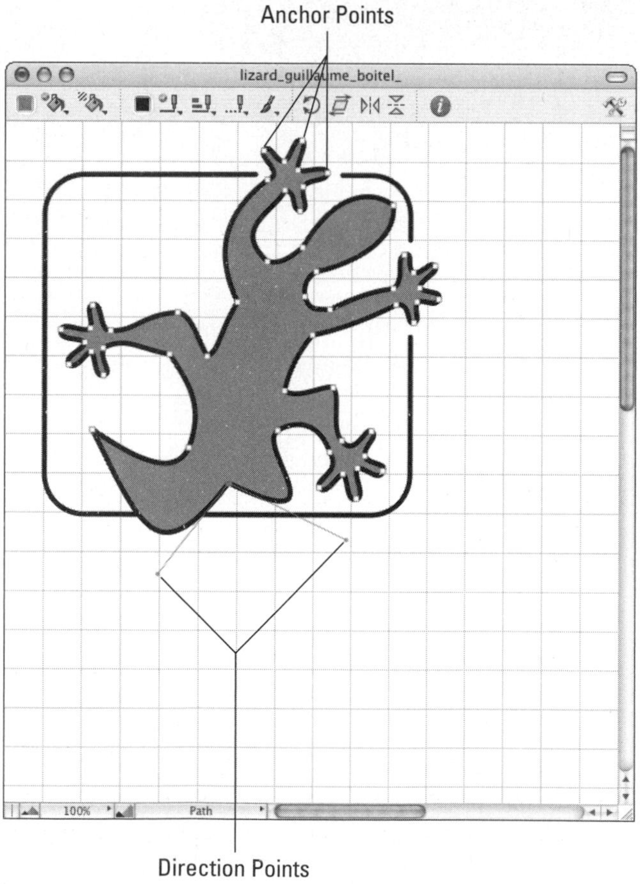

Figure 3-9: The Direct Selection tool lets you reshape an object.

3. **(Optional) To reshape your chosen object, move the pointer over an anchor point, hold down the mouse button, and drag the mouse.**

   Release the mouse button when you're done.

4. **(Optional) To change the curve of an object, move the pointer over a direction point, hold down the mouse button, and drag the mouse.**

   Release the mouse button when you're done.

Drawing lines

To create lines, vector graphics programs typically offer a Pencil tool, a Line tool, a Pen tool, and different Shape tools, as shown in Figure 3-10.

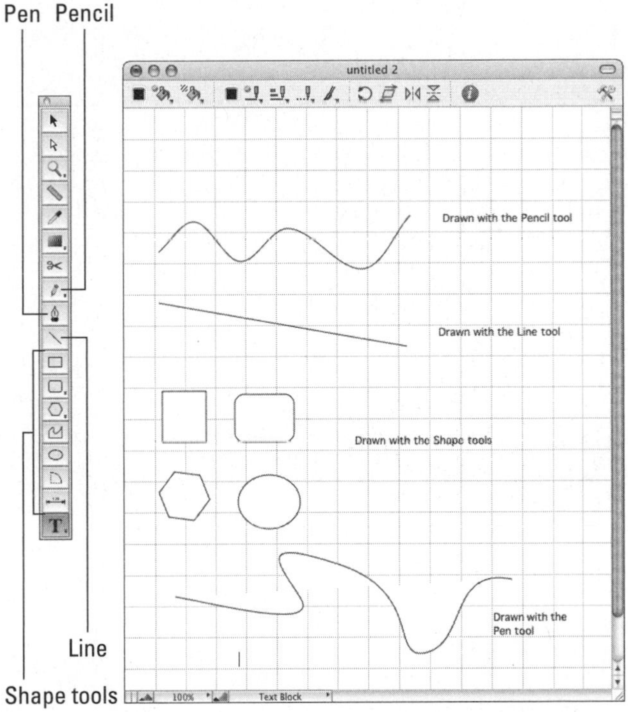

Figure 3-10: The Pencil, Pen, Line, and Shape tools let you create new objects.

The Pencil tool lets you draw a line by dragging the mouse. This lets you create lines of any shape created by the path along which you move the mouse.

The Line tool lets you draw straight lines by dragging the mouse. After you draw a straight line, you can always reshape it later, but if you need a perfectly straight line, the Line tool will meet your needs.

The Shape tools (Rectangle, Rounded Rectangle, Polygon, and Oval) let you draw specific shapes, which you can always reshape later.

The Pen tool lets you draw a line by clicking define points. Each time you click another point, the drawing program automatically draws a connecting straight line. To curve a line, you can drag direction points that appear. Some drawing programs may also let you drag the Pen tool to create curved lines.

Choosing a Painting and Drawing Program

If you're a professional or aspiring graphics designer, your only real choices are Adobe Photoshop, Adobe Illustrator, and Adobe Flash (`www.adobe.com`). All three programs are heavily used in the graphics design industry.

Although these programs are mandatory for graphics design professionals, most other people will likely find Photoshop, Illustrator, and Flash too expensive and complicated to use. As an alternative to these three professional-quality programs, you can find plenty of low-cost (or even free) programs that offer most of the features of these programs.

Photoshop alternatives

Perhaps the best alternative to Photoshop is a similar, less expensive program dubbed Photoshop Elements, which is also sold by Adobe. Adobe markets Photoshop to professionals and Photoshop Elements to digital photography hobbyists who want to touch up their digital photographs quickly and easily.

If you like the idea of an easy-to-use digital photography editor, consider these other programs that are also geared for beginners: PhotoStudio (`www.arcsoft.com`), Color It! (`www.microfrontier.com`), GraphicsConverter (`www.lemkesoft.com`), and PhotoLine 32 (`www.pl32.com`).

Although it's not much cheaper or easier to use than Photoshop, another alternative raster editor is Corel Painter X (`www.corel.com`). Whereas Photoshop specializes in editing digital photographs, Corel Painter specializes in mimicking the use of ordinary artist tools, such as drawing with charcoal or creating oil paintings on different types of paper and canvases where your ink or oil paints can drip and soak into the surface just like the real thing. If you're an aspiring artist and want a program specifically designed to mimic the handheld tools you're already familiar with, Corel Painter might actually be a better choice than Photoshop.

Specialized digital photography editors and organizers

Programs such as Photoshop can help you edit and modify digital photographs, but they do nothing to help you organize your digital photographs. If you work exclusively with digital photographs, you might want to skip Photoshop and consider two different programs, Adobe Photoshop Lightroom (`www.adobe.com`) and Apple Aperture (`www.apple.com`), which are especially designed for professional photographers.

Both Lightroom and Aperture are designed to organize, sort, edit, and store your digital photographs. Both programs also offer nondestructive editing, which means your original digital image is never changed. This means that you can always return to your original image without having to make a separate copy of that image.

After you've made any changes to a digital photograph, you can organize and sort it in a library so that you can find it again. You can also create a slideshow of your favorite images or print your pictures in different ways (such as one big picture on a page or several smaller pictures on a page).

Think of Lightroom and Aperture as advanced versions of the iPhoto program. If you need only to organize your digital images occasionally, iPhoto should be sufficient. But if you're constantly storing, editing, and organizing digital images, consider Lightroom or Aperture.

Before you buy any raster editor, grab a free copy of Paintbrush (`http://paintbrush.sourceforge.net`). If you have children, grab a free copy of TuxPaint (`www.tuxpaint.org`), a simple painting program designed to help kids learn the basics of painting with a computer.

Illustrator alternatives

Although designed mostly for editing raster images, Adobe Photoshop also includes some vector drawing capabilities. If you need to create vector drawings every now and then, you can use Photoshop and never bother with a separate vector graphics program at all. However, you may prefer using a simpler vector drawing program instead.

For a free vector graphics program, just use the Draw program included in both OpenOffice (`www.openoffice.org`) and NeoOffice (`www.neooffice.org`), which are office suites described in Chapter 2 of this minibook. If you need to draw diagrams, organizational charts, or flow charts, consider OmniGraffle (`www.omnigroup.com`).

In case you need a drawing program for creating technical illustrations, you could use any drawing program, but you might be better off using Canvas X (`www.deneba.com`). Besides letting you create technical drawings, Canvas X also offers options for scientific imaging and geographical information systems (GIS), which can be handy if you need to draw molecular structures or create maps.

If you just want a simpler, less expensive version of Illustrator, consider Intaglio (`www.purgatorydesign.com`). Instead of attempting to offer as many features as possible, as Illustrator does, Intaglio offers the basic features that most people need 90 percent of the time. As a result, Intaglio lets you focus more on your work and less on trying to find the features you need.

Another low-cost drawing program for novices is Lineform (`www.freeverse.com`). One unique feature of Lineform is that of artistic strokes, which combines the visual appearance of brush strokes found in painting programs with the ability to edit and manipulate them as separate objects, as in a drawing program.

A third low-cost drawing program is EazyDraw (`www.eazydraw.com`). Although geared for beginners, EazyDraw actually offers some advanced features for mechanical drawings, printed circuit layouts, and electronic schematics.

If you want to create simple animated drawings, get iDraw (`www.macpoweruser.com`), which can save your drawings as animated GIF, Flash, or QuickTime movies. Despite its animation capabilities, iDraw offers a simplified user interface that won't overwhelm you with options.

Flash alternatives

Flash actually consists of two separate programs. First, there's the Flash development program, which lets you design and create Flash animation. Second, there's the free Flash player, which lets your browser display Flash movies and animation. If you need to create Flash animation for different purposes, you can buy the Flash development program (`www.adobe.com`).

If you want to create cartoons in Flash but don't want to buy the Flash development program, you can pick two alternatives called Toon Boom Studio (`www.toonboom.com`) and Anime Studio (`www.e-frontier.com`). Although both programs use the Flash file format, they provide tools to help you create and animate cartoons much faster than the Flash development program.

Both programs specialize in helping you draw characters, animate them, and even synchronize audio with the movements of their mouths so that the characters appear to be speaking correctly. If you're just getting started with

Flash animation, you can buy an entry-level version of either program. When you get familiar with creating Flash animation, move up to the professional versions of these programs.

Graphic File Formats

Because Adobe Photoshop, Illustrator, and Flash lead the market in raster editing, vector graphics, and vector graphics animation, the three most important file formats are Photoshop's PSD format, Illustrator's AI format, and Flash's SWF format. Although these file formats are the most popular, most painting and drawing programs can use other file formats as well.

REMEMBER

You can easily save a vector graphics file as a raster file, but then you lose the ability to manipulate the objects of that picture. If you save a raster picture as a vector graphics picture, you won't be able to modify its parts as though it were a true vector graphics picture. (Adobe Illustrator offers a raster-to-vector graphics conversion feature, but most drawing programs don't.) If you need to manipulate individual parts of a picture, create and save your picture as a vector graphics file. If you need to manipulate individual pixels, create and save your picture as a raster file.

Raster (painting) formats

Besides Photoshop PSD files, another popular raster file format is known as TIFF (Tagged Image File Format). TIFF was designed as a universal graphics file format, so most graphics programs can save and open TIFF files.

TIFF files are, like Photoshop PSD files, often large, which makes them impractical for use on Web pages. To display graphics on a Web page, Web designers use three different file formats that compress images while retaining much of the visual quality. The most popular of these raster compressed file formats is JPEG (Joint Photographic Experts Group), which is also used by many digital cameras.

JPEG files are great for storing photographic quality images, but if you just need simple graphics, such as company logos or cartoons, then you'll find that the GIF (Graphics Interchange Format) file format is more popular. Because the GIF format was once patented, a free alternative soon appeared known as PNG (Portable Network Graphics).

PNG files offer better compression than GIF files and unlike JEPG files, PNG files can shrink files down in size without tossing out data, thus preserving image quality.

One file format used exclusively with digital cameras is RAW, which stores images in a format that must be converted before you can edit or print it. The advantage of the RAW format is its ability to store more data about an image, which can give you higher-quality digital photographs. Two big drawbacks with the RAW format is that these files tend to be much larger than equivalent JPEG files, and every digital camera manufacturer creates its own RAW format that are incompatible with RAW formats created by other digital cameras. If you can't convert your RAW formats into a universal file format such as JPEG, your images could get trapped in a particular RAW format forever.

Vector graphics (drawing) formats

Adobe Illustrator AI files are the most popular vector graphics formats, so many drawing programs can open and save AI files and save files in an open standard called SVG (Scalable Vector Graphics).

Another popular open standard format for vector graphics is EPS (Encapsulated PostScript). Much like SVG files, EPS files are often used as an intermediary file format to transfer files from one drawing program to another.

Although not an open standard, many vector graphics programs can also store pictures as PDF (Portable Document Format) files. PDF files are used to display the exact formatting and appearance of a picture so that others can view and print it on their own computers. To read PDF files, you can use the Preview program that comes with every Mac, or you can download a free copy of the Adobe Acrobat Reader.

If you run across a graphics file format that you can't open, try to convert it using GraphicConverter (`www.lemkesoft.com`) or DeBabelizer (`www.equilibrium.com`).

Chapter 4: Running Windows on a Mac

In This Chapter

- **Understanding why you might need Windows**
- **Giving your Mac a split personality with Boot Camp**
- **Running virtual machines**
- **Using CrossOver Mac**

Whether you like it or not (probably not), Microsoft Windows is the most used operating system in the world. (Note that "most used" doesn't necessarily mean "most popular" or "most respected.") If you're using a Mac, chances are good you don't want to use a Windows PC.

As much as you might enjoy using your Mac, sometimes you might need to run Windows because you need to use a program that can run only on Windows. When faced with this dilemma, you have a choice:

- You can buy a Windows PC and use that computer just to run the Windows program you need. However, this is not only inconvenient but also expensive.
- As a more practical alternative, you can run Windows on your Mac. Ever since Apple started using the same parts as ordinary Windows PCs (that is, Intel processors), you've been able to actually turn your Mac into a Windows PC.

Of course, turning your Mac into an ordinary Windows PC is a lot like buying a Ferrari and turning it into a garbage truck. You can do it, but why would you want to?

Instead of wiping out your hard drive and running Windows on it, you have other ways to run Windows on your Mac that still let you use all the features that made you want to use a Mac in the first place.

REMEMBER

Purist Mac enthusiasts might shudder at the thought of Windows tainting their hard drive, but many programs run only on Windows, such as astrology or stock picking programs, and custom applications developed by a company for in-house use.

Giving Your Mac a Dual Personality with Boot Camp

To install Windows on a Mac, you can split your hard drive in half (the split portions are called *partitions*) and use one partition to store Windows and a second to store Mac OS X. By storing two different operating systems on your hard drive, you can choose which operating system to use every time you turn on your computer. To divide your hard drive into partitions and install Windows, Apple provides a program called Boot Camp.

To use Boot Camp, you need the following:

✦ A Mac that uses an Intel processor

✦ Version 10.5 or higher of the Mac OS X operating system

✦ A printer for printing out instructions for installing Boot Camp

✦ At least 10GB free on your hard drive

✦ The latest firmware updates

Firmware is software stored on your Mac's circuit board. Firmware basically tells your Mac how to turn itself on and work with all of its hardware components. If Apple has released new firmware for your Mac, you can find and retrieve it by clicking on the Apple menu and choosing Software Update.

✦ A legitimate copy of Windows XP SP2 or any version of Vista (Basic, Home, Business, or Ultimate editions)

You must use a full, 32-bit version of Windows XP or Vista that comes on a single CD or DVD. If you use an upgrade version, a 64-bit version, or a version that comes on multiple discs (CDs), you cannot install Windows using Boot Camp.

Follow these basic steps to use Boot Camp:

1. Make sure your Mac can run Boot Camp.
2. Create a partition on your hard drive and install Windows.

The following sections give the details you need to complete these steps.

Making sure you can run Boot Camp

If you have a new Mac, chances are very good that you'll be able to run Boot Camp. However, the older your Mac is, the lower your chances are of being able to use this program.

Identifying the hardware capabilities of your Mac

To identify the processor, firmware version, and version number of the Mac OS X operating system running on your computer, follow these steps:

1. **Click the Apple menu and choose About This Mac.**

   An About This Mac window, shown in Figure 4-1, appears.

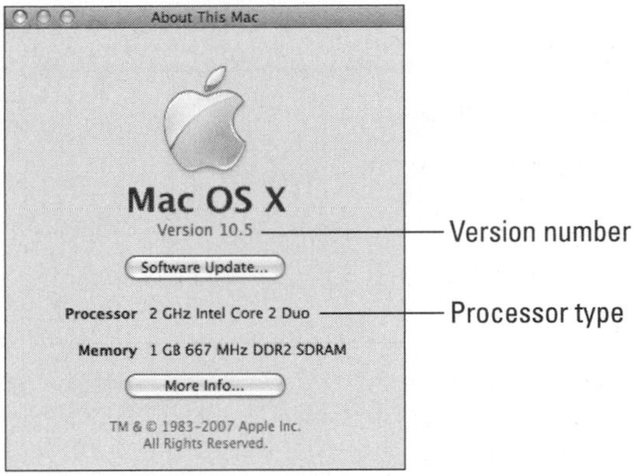

Figure 4-1: The About This Mac window identifies the processor type and version of Mac OS X.

2. **Make sure the processor type contains the word *Intel,* such as Intel Core 2 Duo.**

   If the processor type contains the term *PowerPC,* you can't use Boot Camp.

3. **Make sure the version number is 10.5 or higher.**

   If the version number is lower, such as 10.3, you can't use Boot Camp until you get a newer version of Mac OS X.

4. **Click the Close button of the About This Mac window.**

Identifying the amount of free space on your hard drive

You need at least 10GB of free space on your hard drive to install both Boot Camp and Windows. To find out how much free space you have left on your hard drive, click the Finder icon in the Dock and, in the Finder window that opens, click the Macintosh HD icon in the left pane. If you look at the status bar at the bottom of the Finder window, you can see how much space is available on your hard drive.

Installing Windows

When you're certain your Mac can run Boot Camp, you need to go through two more steps before you can install Windows. First, you need to partition your hard drive. This reserves a chunk of your hard drive for Windows. Some good news here: Creating a partition and installing Windows on your computer are tasks you have to do only once (unless your hard drive crashes and you have to reinstall everything all over again).

Second, you need to install Windows on your newly created hard drive partition. Installing Windows can be time-consuming but isn't necessarily difficult. The two most technical parts of installing Windows on a Mac involves partitioning your hard drive and choosing that partition to install Windows on.

Partitioning divides your hard drive in two parts: one part for Mac OS X and the second part for Windows. After you partition your hard drive, you must tell Windows which partition to install on, and you must specify the partition designated for Windows.

If you install Windows on the wrong partition, you'll wipe out everything on your Mac. If you don't feel comfortable partitioning a hard drive and choosing the right partition to install Windows on, get a more knowledgeable friend to help you.

To install Windows, follow these steps:

1. **Open the Finder window by clicking the Finder icon on the Dock.**
2. **Choose Go⇨Utilities.**

   The contents of the Utilities folder appear in the right pane.
3. **Double-click the Boot Camp Assistant icon.**

   A Boot Camp Assistant window appears, informing you of the process of using Boot Camp, as shown in Figure 4-2.
4. **(Optional) Click the Print Installation & Setup Guide button.**

   A Print dialog appears.
5. **Change the default settings, such as changing the paper size, and click OK.**

   A second Print dialog appears, letting you choose a specific printer and number of copies to print.
6. **Choose a printer and click the Print button.**

   The Installation & Setup Guide prints out, and the Boot Camp Assistant window appears again (refer to Figure 4-2).

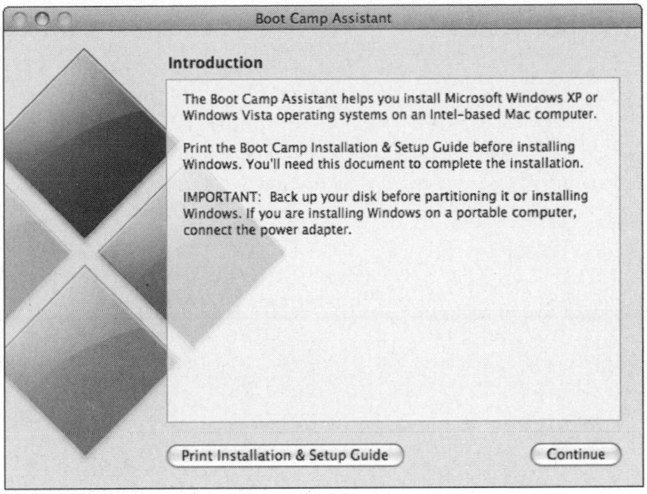

Figure 4-2: The introductory Boot Camp Assistant window tells you what you need to run Boot Camp.

7. **Read the Installation & Setup Guide for the most current instructions for installing Boot Camp and then click the Continue button.**

   The Boot Camp Assistant window displays a Create a Partition for Windows box, as shown in Figure 4-3.

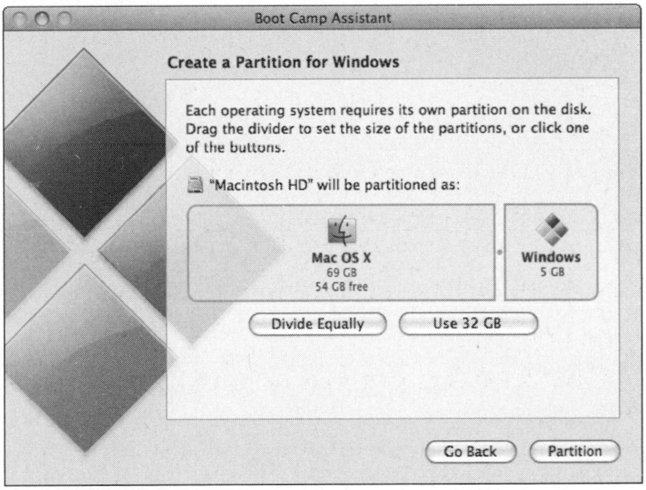

Figure 4-3: The Create a Partition Windows box lets you define how much hard drive space to allocate for Windows.

8. **Click the Partition button.**

9. **Move the pointer over the divider between the Macintosh partition and the Windows partition, hold down the mouse button, and drag the mouse left or right to choose a partition size.**

   TIP

   If you're installing Windows XP, the minimum partition size should be 5GB. If you're installing Vista, the minimum partition size should be 8GB. You might want to choose an even larger partition size if you plan to install many Windows programs.

10. **Click the Partition button.**

    Boot Camp partitions your hard drive. (This process might take a little while.) When partitioning is completed, another Boot Camp Assistant window appears, asking you to insert your valid Windows installation disc in your Mac, as shown in Figure 4-4.

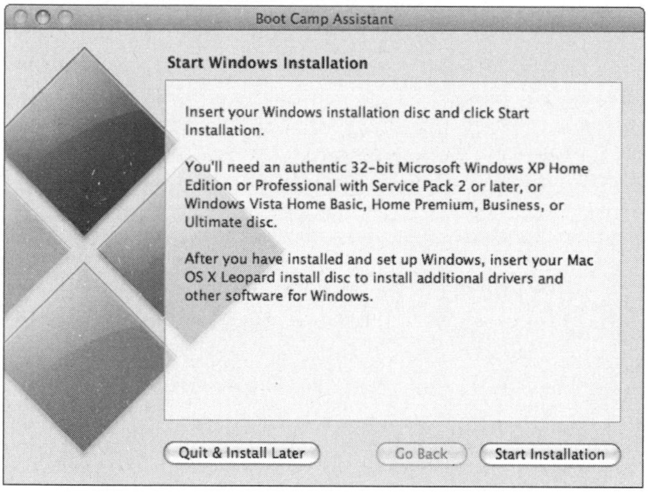

Figure 4-4: The Boot Camp Assistant window lets you know when to insert your Windows installation disc.

11. **Insert your Windows installation disc in your Macintosh and then click Start Installation button.**

    WARNING!

    When the Windows installation program asks you which partition to install on, look for the partition that's the same size you specified in Step 8 and has the words BOOT CAMP displayed. If you choose the wrong partition, Windows might install on the partition used by your Mac, which could wreck your files and bring your entire Mac crashing to its knees.

12. **Follow the Windows installation instructions on the screen, and when the installation is finished, eject the disc.**

    Be patient. Installing Windows can take time and Windows will reboot several times during installation, so don't panic if the screen suddenly goes blank.

Choosing an operating system with Boot Camp

After you've used Boot Camp to install Windows on your Mac, you can use Boot Camp to choose which operating system to run by following these steps:

1. **Restart your computer and hold down the Option key until two disk icons appear.**

   The two disk icons are labeled Windows and the second labeled Macintosh HD. (If you changed the name of your Mac's hard disk, you'll see this name displayed instead.)

2. **Double-click the Windows or Macintosh Startup Disk icon.**

   Your chosen operating system starts up.

REMEMBER

To switch to a different operating system, you have to shut down the current operating system and repeat the preceding steps to choose the other operating system.

If you start up your Mac without holding down the Option key, your Mac starts up the default operating system. You can define the default operating system in Mac OS X by following these steps:

1. **Within Mac OS X, click the Apple menu and choose System Preferences to make the System Preferences window appear.**

2. **In the System Preferences window, click the Startup Disk icon under the System category.**

   Windows shows you the Startup Disk window (see Figure 4-5), which asks for the CD or DVD driver disc you burned earlier.

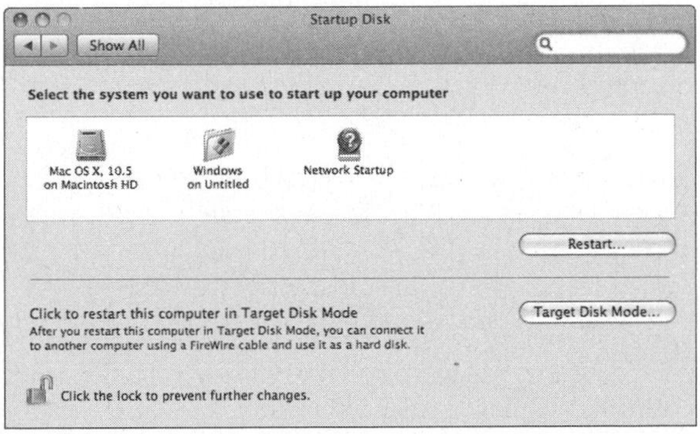

Figure 4-5: The Startup Disk window lets you choose which partition to make the default startup disk.

3. Click the Mac OS X or Windows icon and click the Restart button.

If you click the Target Disk Mode button, you can make your Mac appear like an external hard drive when connected to another computer through a FireWire cable.

If you want to wipe out the partition on your hard drive that contains Windows, you can do so by following these steps:

1. **Double-click the Boot Camp Assistant icon in the Utilities folder.**

   An Introduction dialog appears.

2. **Click the Continue button.**

   A Select Task dialog appears.

3. **Click the Create or remove a Windows partition button and click the Continue button.**

   A Restore Disk to a Single Volume dialog appears.

   Wiping out your Windows partition deletes all data stored on that partition that you created using Windows.

4. **Click the Restore button.**

Using Virtual Machines

One problem with Boot Camp is that it forces you to run either Windows or Mac OS X. If you want to run Windows and Mac OS X at the same time and switch between one or the other, you need to use a virtualization program such as Parallels (`www.parallels.com`) or Fusion (`www.vmware.com`).

Virtualization is a technology that lets you run multiple operating systems at the same time where each operating system time-shares the computer's hardware. Because the operating system isn't really controlling the computer's hardware completely, the operating system is called a *virtual machine* (as opposed to a real machine).

Parallels and Fusion work in similar ways by creating a single file on your Mac hard drive that represents a virtual PC hard drive that contains the actual Windows operating system plus any additional Windows programs you might install, such as Microsoft Office.

When you run Parallels or Fusion, the program boots up from this virtual hard drive while your original Mac OS X operating system continues to run. This lets you run another operating system, such as Windows, inside a separate Mac OS X window, as shown in Figure 4-6.

Because the operating system stored on the virtual hard drive has to share the computer's processor and memory with Mac OS X, operating systems running on virtual machines tend to run slightly slower than the same operating system running on a computer all by itself.

Besides letting you run multiple operating systems simultaneously, virtualization programs also let you run different types of operating systems. As mentioned previously, Boot Camp works only with Windows XP SP2 or Vista, but virtualization programs let you run any operating system that can run on Intel processors, including older versions of Windows (such as Windows 98 or Windows 2000), Linux (such as Ubuntu or Red Hat), obscure operating systems (such as Solaris or OpenBSD), or long-abandoned operating systems (such as MS-DOS or OS/2).

More people are likely to run Windows than OS/2 or Solaris, so both Parallels and Fusion offer additional features to make using Windows as seamless as an ordinary Mac program.

Instead of forcing you to load Windows and then load a specific program within Windows, virtualization programs let you store a Windows program icon directly on the Desktop or on the Dock so that it behaves exactly like a Mac program icon.

Clicking a Windows program icon loads Windows and the Windows program at the same time without showing the Windows desktop or the Windows Start menu. By integrating Windows programs as if they were Mac programs, virtualization programs shield you from the clunky Windows interface.

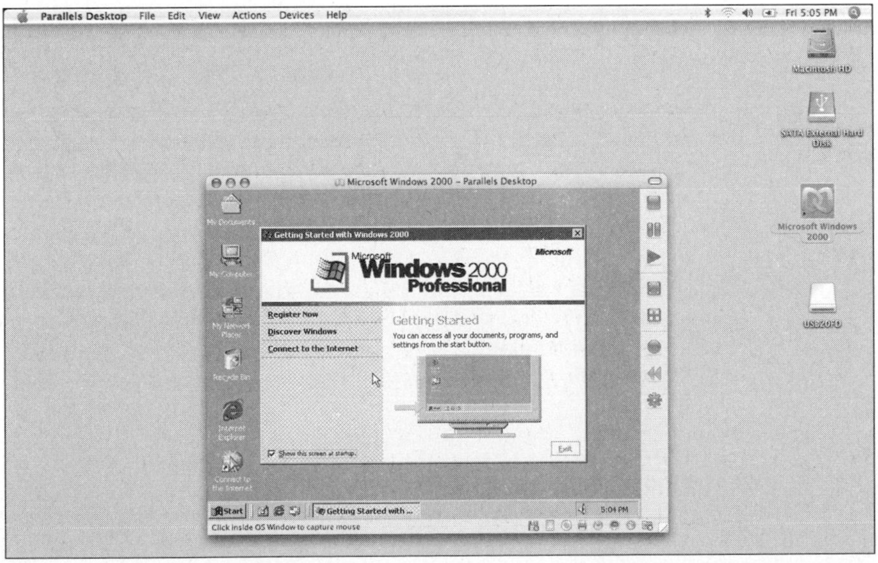

Figure 4-6: A virtualization program lets you run Windows inside a separate Mac window.

The background of Figure 4-7 shows the Mac desktop and the VMware Fusion menu bar (VMware Fusion is the virtualization program running). Running inside a Mac window is the Windows Internet Explorer browser. Notice that this window displays Internet Explorer's menus and the ugly appearance of a Windows screen trapped inside the simple yet elegant design of the Mac user interface.

Another feature related specifically to Windows is data sharing. If you open a program such as WordPerfect in Windows and type some text, you can copy that text out of Windows and paste it directly into any Mac program (and vice versa). This further integrates Windows programs into the Mac and gives you a chance to transfer data between Mac and Windows programs.

Besides letting you cut, copy, and paste text and graphics between Windows and Mac programs, virtualization programs also let you create shared folders where you can store files that you can access from either Windows or Mac OS X. This lets you run a Windows-specific program, save the file in the shared folder, and then retrieve the file from the Mac.

To ease the migration from Windows to the Mac, virtualization programs can clone your existing Windows PC and duplicate it, with all your data and programs, on to the Mac. You can essentially use your old Windows PC as a virtual computer on your Mac.

Because everyone knows that Windows isn't the most reliable operating system around, virtualization programs let you save snapshots of your virtual machine's current state. That way, if Windows crashes and wipes itself out, the virtualization program can load a previously saved snapshot to restore your virtual machine to an earlier time when it was working.

If you need to run Windows and Mac programs, virtualization programs offer the best combination of convenience and simplicity. However, virtualization programs have slight drawbacks that you should know about:

- **Program delay:** When you run Windows and Windows programs within Boot Camp, that program has total access to your computer's hardware, which means the program will run as fast as it would on a normal PC. However, when you run Windows within a virtualization program, the virtualization program demands attention from the Intel processor, which means that both Windows and Mac programs can run slightly (or dramatically) slower than normal.

  For programs like word processors or browsers, this slight delay might not be noticeable, but for programs that demand speed, such as high-end graphics program like Adobe Photoshop, this speed difference can become noticeable and annoying.

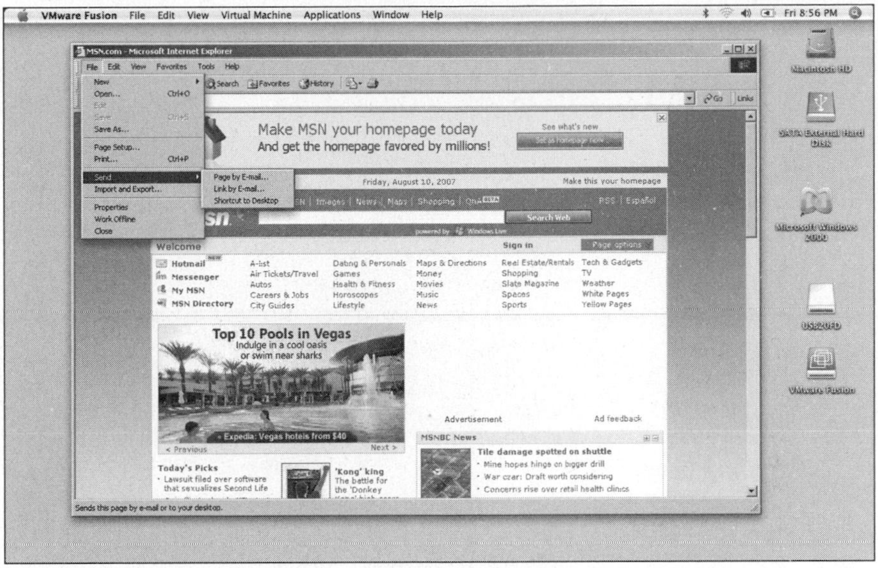

Figure 4-7: A virtualization program can disguise any Windows program in a Mac window.

✦ **Memory hogging:** A second problem with virtualization programs is that loading and running additional operating systems (besides Mac OS X) gobbles up memory. If your Mac has 1GB of RAM, you'll have the bare minimum needed to run Windows XP on your Mac. If you want to run Vista on your Mac, you need at least 2GB of RAM for acceptable performance. To ensure that your Mac doesn't slow to a crawl when running another operating system, you should have at least 2GB of RAM.

Buying extra memory ($100), a virtualization program ($80), and a legitimate copy of Windows ($200–$400) drives up the cost of running Windows on your Mac. Even worse, all this money still leaves you stuck using an ugly Windows program.

✦ **Slower performance for advanced video games:** Although most Windows programs work flawlessly when run within a virtualization program, the most notable exceptions are high-performance video games, such as flight simulators. Such high-performance video games require a separate graphics card with plenty of memory to create realistic visual effects. Running such programs in a virtualization program typically means slow, choppy performance that can be annoying at best or render the game completely unplayable at worst.

If you're switching from a Windows PC to a Mac, virtualization programs can help ease your migration to the Mac. If you're already a Mac user, virtualization programs ensure that you'll always be able to run both Windows and Mac programs for maximum compatibility with everyone.

Using CrossOver Mac

With Boot Camp, Parallels, and Fusion, you need to buy a separate copy of Windows. If the idea of wasting your money on Windows just to run a handful of programs makes you nauseous, consider a unique program called CrossOver Mac (`www.codeweavers.com`). CrossOver Mac lets you run Windows programs without a copy of Windows. The program works by fooling Windows programs into thinking they're really running on a Windows PC.

CrossOver Mac lets you pop a Windows CD into your Mac and install the Windows program on a simulated PC that CrossOver Mac creates automatically on your Mac. After you've installed a Windows program, CrossOver Mac displays the normal Windows icons inside a Finder window. Double-clicking the Windows program icon runs that Windows program on your Mac, as shown in Figure 4-8.

Unfortunately, CrossOver Mac isn't perfect. Like Parallels and Fusion, CrossOver Mac runs only on Intel Macintosh computers. A more crucial limitation is that CrossOver Mac works with only a handful of Windows programs, so you can't run any Windows program on a Mac with CrossOver Mac and expect it to run flawlessly.

To help you determine whether your favorite Windows program will work with CrossOver Mac, the product's Web site (`www.codeweavers.com/compatibility/browse/name`) lists all known programs that have been tested and verified to work correctly. Each program is given a ranking, as follows:

- **Gold:** The program works flawlessly on the Mac.
- **Silver:** The program works with occasional problems.
- **Bronze:** The program runs, but you might run into minor problems.
- **Honorable Mention:** The program has been tested to run correctly, but it isn't officially supported, so you might run into minor (or major) problems.
- **Untested:** Nobody has tried the program yet, so you might be the first.
- **Known not to work:** The program won't work no matter how hard you cry, beg, or pray.

Because testing each program for compatibility with CrossOver Mac can take time, most Gold-ranked programs are older versions of popular Windows programs, such as Microsoft Office 2000.

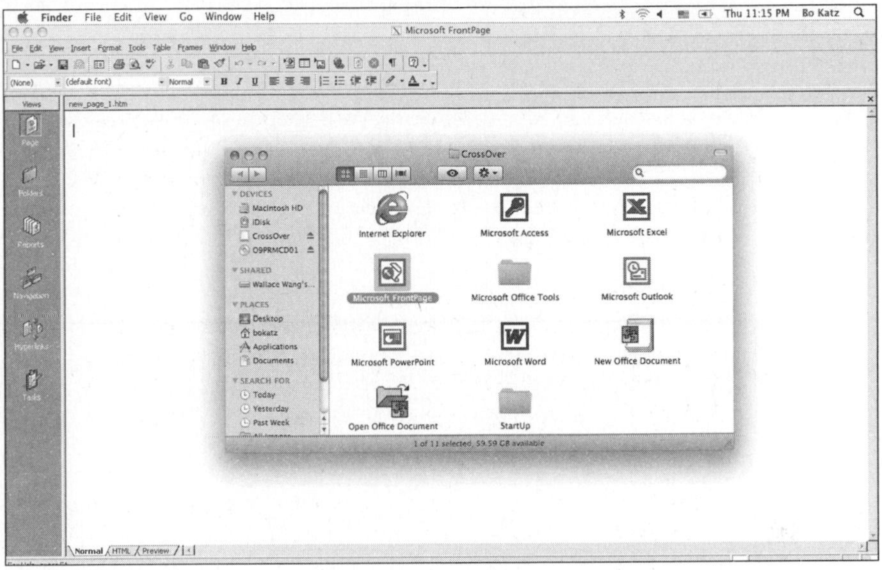

Figure 4-8: CrossOver Mac lets you run a handful of Windows programs without running Windows.

If you need to run the latest Windows programs, a little-known Windows program, or a custom Windows program, CrossOver Mac probably won't let you run it. However, if you need to run only a handful of older, popular programs, CrossOver Mac might be the ideal solution. Just try the trial version with your favorite Windows program, and if it works, buy the commercial version of CrossOver Mac. Then you can happily use your favorite Windows program while secretly pretending you're really being productive with a Mac.

Chapter 5: Having Fun with a Mac

In This Chapter

- Learning a foreign language
- Learning to play music
- Teaching yourself to type
- Expanding your mind
- Managing your hobby
- Playing video games

Work, work, work. We all work too much, so kick back, fire up your Mac, and blow off steam with your favorite video game. Your Mac is be great for helping you get stuff done, but your Mac is even better for helping you have some fun without breaking any laws to do it. There are loads of ways you can have fun with your Mac. You can start with several free games that can turn your computer into a chess, checkers, or tic-tac-toe opponent. If you get tired of these games, you can always buy more, and you have a vast array of video games to choose from.

Games can double as effective learning tools, too. With the right programs, you can turn your Mac into an inspiring math, grammar, or science tutor for children, or a motivating foreign language or music teacher for yourself. Or, rather than pick up a new skill, you can use your Mac to help with your current hobbies. Although Macs might not help you hang-glide or belly dance, your Mac can run unique programs covering everything from needlepoint to gardening to collecting and trading baseball cards. Read on to explore some ideas for enjoying your free time (or ways to goof off during your so-called work time).

¿No Hablas Español? Then Get Crackin'!

Perhaps you've always wanted to learn another language but never found the time to go to a class. Well, these days, you can learn almost anything — on your own schedule, and without having to step foot outside your own front door. So, what are you waiting for?

The best way to learn any foreign language is to immerse yourself in it through listening, speaking, and reading it. Your Mac can't literally put you on the streets of, say, Barcelona, but it can act as a friendly guide and tutor while exposing you to the voices of native speakers. You can even speak into a microphone and have your pronunciation analyzed (a great way to hone your accent before anyone hears you and questions which language you're trying to speak). Whether you're learning a foreign language in school, for fun, or for business, you can use programs on your Mac to practice speaking, reading, and even writing a foreign language.

For free language lessons, visit the BBC site at `www.bbc.co.uk/languages`, where you can find introductory vocabulary lessons, pronunciation audio files, and videos in a variety of languages. (See Figure 5-1.) These introductory lessons won't make you fluent in a new language, but they can teach you the basics.

Another useful (and free) language Web site is UniLang (`http://home.unilang.org`), which is a community-run site that provides free resources to anyone interested in learning practically any language, including Lithuanian, Afrikaans, and Gaelic. Some of its many language resources include children's stories, phrasebooks, and vocabulary lists so that you can make your own flash cards.

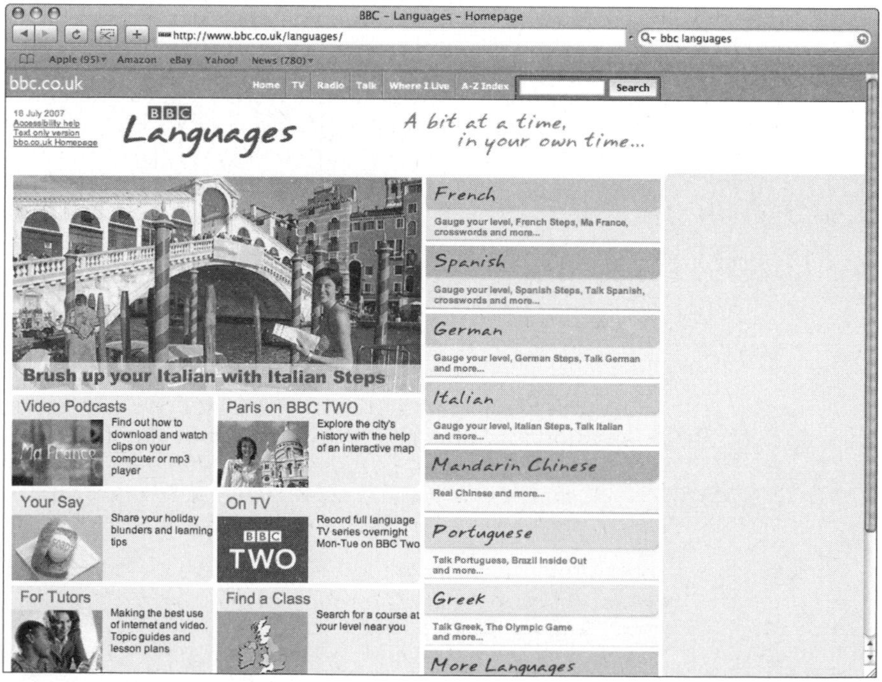

Figure 5-1: The BBC Web site offers a variety of free video and audio files to teach different languages.

Free language lessons can get you started, but for more advanced language lessons, you'll probably have to buy a language course. Here are some good ones to consider:

✦ **Berlitz** (`www.berlitzbooks.com`): Provides audio courses that focus on helping travelers master useful phrases that they'll likely need when they travel overseas, such as "I have gotten sick five times since drinking the local water" or "What do you mean I have to pay for toilet paper in a public restroom?"

✦ **Pimsleur** (`www.pimsleurapproach.com`): Named after its creator, Dr. Paul Pimsleur, the Pimsleur method focuses on teaching foreign languages primarily by listening to the most commonly used words in each language. Besides emphasizing listening, the Pimsleur method also encourages responding by gradually piecing together the grammar of a language through constant repetition and practice. Pimsleur's principle is that anyone can learn a new language in the same way that babies learn to speak, which is by listening and then attempting to speak back to their parents (until they're old enough to start arguing with their parents).

✦ **Transparent Language** (`www.transparent.com`): Offers free language articles (so that you can practice reading), free language games, and free introductory language lessons to teach you how to recognize and speak basic vocabulary so you can communicate with people in other countries without resorting to hand signals.

✦ **Rosetta Stone** (`www.rosettastone.com`): One of the most acclaimed language courses, Rosetta Stone emphasizes listening, reading, writing, and speaking another language. By focusing on four different elements of learning any language, Rosetta Stone is the closest you can get to immersing yourself in another country. Figure 5-2 shows different phrases on the screen that you can choose in response to hearing a question in a foreign language. By turning learning into a game, you can pick up a new language while having fun in the process.

✦ **Unforgettable Languages** (`www.unforgettablelanguages.com`): If you have trouble remembering foreign words, you might try this course, which teaches foreign words by relating them to another word. For example, to help you remember that the Mandarin word for tree (*shu,* pronounced like "shoe"), you're told to think of a shoe in a tree. By using such vivid word associations, this course can make memorizing vocabulary words fun (especially if you can find naughty words that sound similar to foreign language phrases).

✦ **Power-Glide** (`www.power-glide.com`): These courses make learning a new language interactive through videos, stories, and games. By reinforcing language concepts in multiple ways, Power-Glide helps make learning and remembering a foreign language as effortless as possible.

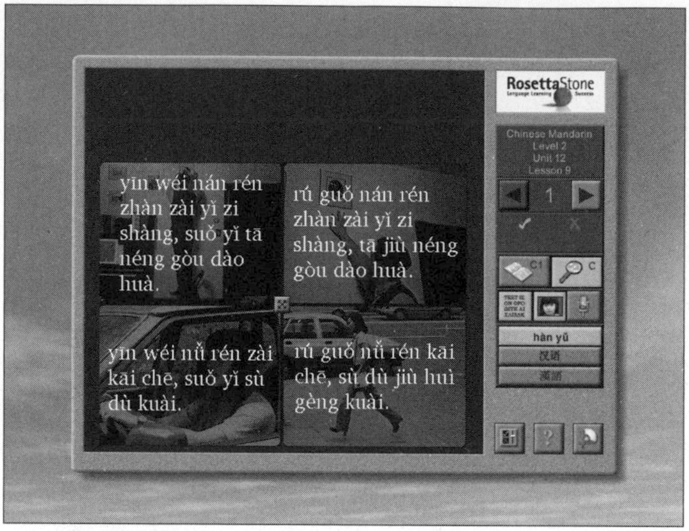

Figure 5-2: Rosetta Stone immerses you into a new language through various exercises.

Tooting Your Own Horn

Learning to play an instrument is much like learning a foreign language. You can't just read about it; you have to hear and try it yourself, listening and correcting as you go along. Well, I have good news: You can turn your Mac into an interactive music teacher with the right software.

Learning to play music is more than just banging away on drums or a keyboard. To understand the science behind music, buy a program called Math & Music (`www.wildridge.com`), shown in Figure 5-3. This unique course explains the physics behind sound — how vibrating strings relate to harmony and how ratios define the musical scale.

To learn how to read music and chords, buy Practica Musica (`www.ars-nova.com`), which can help train your ear to recognizing different notes while practicing writing your own music at the same time.

After you understand how music works and how to read it, you might be anxious to start making music of your own. If you want to learn to play the guitar, buy GuitarVision (`www2.guitarvision.com`), which works with iTunes to help you learn the exact chords, notes, and finger positioning to play many of your favorite songs stored in iTunes.

Or you might try learning to tickle the ivories with PianoWizard (`www.pianowizard.com`), which uses video games to help you play your favorite songs, in genres from classical to pop. If you're a teenager, you can play and hear your favorite music while annoying your parents at the same time.

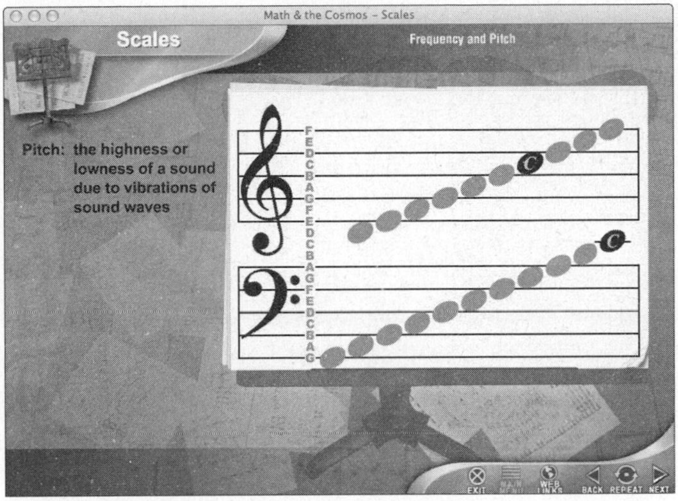

Figure 5-3: The Math & Music program uses sound and graphics to teach music.

To learn the guitar, bass, or piano, look at eMedia's (`www.emediamusic.com`) software tutorials. If you don't want to spend any money, play with the free copy of GarageBand that comes with every Mac.

With GarageBand, you can learn music, play an instrument, record your tunes, and mix them to produce the perfect song. Think of your Mac as a production studio, music teacher, and recording engineer that can help you write and record your own unique song.

Getting Touchy-Feely with Your Keyboard

No more poking along on the computer keyboard with your index fingers. You *know* people are looking at you funny. Even your six-year-old types better than you do. To finally start getting the hang of your keyboard, check out one of the most popular typing tutorials, Mavis Beacon Teaches Typing (available from `www.broderbund.com`), which has been used in schools and employment agencies for years. This program combines typing lessons with arcade games to make learning fun. (Now if bosses would only use arcade games to make working in an office fun, we'd be all set.)

Another popular typing program is Ten Thumbs Typing Tutorial (`www.tenthumbstypingtutor.com`), shown in Figure 5-4. In addition to providing the usual drills and games to teach typing, the program also works with iTunes by letting you type lyrics from your favorite songs. For greater flexibility, practice typing lyrics from different types of songs, or else if you only type lyrics from rap music, you might get really good at typing four-letter words and nothing else.

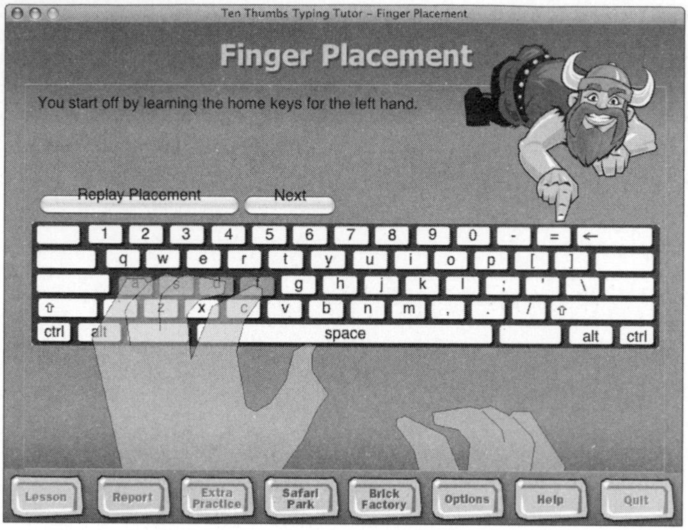

Figure 5-4: Ten Thumbs Typing Tutorial uses colorful graphics to make typing fun.

For a free typing tutorial, grab a copy of Letter Invaders (`www.fooledya.com/games/letters`), which is based on the ancient arcade game Space Invaders. With this typing tutorial, letters fall from above, and you have to type them correctly to destroy them. You can even learn something about programming while you're becoming a real typist by downloading the source code so that you can see exactly how the program works. (You can even modify and improve it yourself, if you already know what you're doing.)

Taking Your Grey Matter to the Gym

The brain is like a muscle. (The only difference is that it's not as easy for guys to attract women on the beach by showing off their brains.) The more you use it, the stronger it gets, so to help keep your brain strong, visit Custom Solution of Maryland (`www.customsolutionsofmaryland.50megs.com`) and browse through the site's various free programs, such as

- **Auto Flash:** Lets you create and display flash cards for any subject.
- **Brain Tease:** Provides brainteasers to keep your mind sharp and active.
- **eBook Library:** Lets you read electronic books to practice and learn speed reading.
- **Math Practice:** Lets you play simple games with algebra and Roman numerals.
- **Mimic:** Practice memory skills using music.
- **SAT Vocab Prep:** Learn new words to increase your vocabulary.

- **Speak N Spell:** Practice your spelling.
- **TickerType:** Learn to type.

To find all sorts of educational software for you or your children go online shopping at Academic Superstore (`www.academicsuperstore.com`). With so many different ways to keep yourself amused while learning, you'll never have an excuse for not learning something new today.

Playing Hooky with Your Hobby

Almost everyone has a hobby that they'd rather be doing instead of work. Although hobbies can be fun, they often have tedious or repetitive actions that can suck up your time and make you feel like you're at a job. To keep such necessary, tedious actions from stopping you from fully enjoying your hobby, load the right program and make your Mac help you speed up and simplify your hobby more than ever.

If you enjoy scrapbooking, combining photographs, memorabilia, and journaling into a book to keep track of your memories, you might want to digitize the whole process. Grab your favorite digital photographs and place them in a digital scrapbook using iScrapbook (available at `www.chronosnet.com`) or iRemember (`www.macscrapbook.com`). Best of all, both programs can yank pictures out of iPhoto so you can take advantage of all the hard work you spent organizing pictures in iPhoto.

Not only can digital scrapbooks store your memories, but they allow you to share them with others in ways that physical scrapbooks cannot. You can e-mail them or print them up after embellishing them with fancy borders and graphics.

The most likely people who might want to share your memories are your relatives. To help you keep track of your relatives and your family tree, you can use MacFamilyTree (available at `www.onlymac.de`), Family (`www.saltatory.com`), or Reunion (`http://leisterpro.com`). By making it easy to track family names, photographs, birthdates, and locations, you can track your relatives wherever they go (and avoid them if necessary).

If you enjoy working with needlepoint, you might want to create your own designs with Stitch Painter (`www.cochenille.com`). Coin collectors might want to grab a copy of Numismatist's Notebook (available at `www.tabberer.com/sandyknoll`), and comic book collectors might want a copy of ComicBookLover (`www.bitcartel.com`). If you're the outdoor type who enjoys planting, try using PlanGarden (`www.plangarden.com`) to choose the best plants for your area.

Want to design your dream house or need to remodel your current house? You can draw up your own plans by using Interiors (`www.microspot.com`). To help pay for your new house or remodeling project, try Lotto Sorcerer (`www.satoripublishing.com/LS`) to help you win your state's lottery. Lotto Sorcerer predicts the numbers most likely to appear, based on the fact that it's impossible to create truly random numbers, so some numbers will always have a slightly greater chance of getting picked than others.

No matter what your hobby or interests are, there's likely a program that can help you enjoy your hobby even more.

Bring on the Games!

Historians might someday chronicle the computer's role in increasing business productivity and communication, but everyone really knows that the computer's greatest contribution to society has been to help people play games. Four popular types of video games are

- Computerized versions of traditional board games like chess and backgammon
- Strategy games that emphasize planning and thinking
- Arcade games that emphasize eye-hand coordination
- Multiplayer, online virtual worlds

REMEMBER

Some games combine multiple elements, such as a multiplayer game that emphasizes arcade-style play, or a multiplayer game that lets people play bridge or poker online.

Some video games can be educational, such as teaching you how to manage a business, whereas other video games can be nostalgic, such as ancient arcade video games like Pac-Man or Space Invaders. Still other video games can provide an emotional outlet so you can blast away aliens, soldiers, and other fictional computer-generated images and vent your frustration on an imaginary image rather than on a living creature within your reach. If you just want to play video games, you can turn your Mac into the ultimate entertainment center.

Playing strategically

Strategy games are more complicated board games. Unlike arcade-style games where reflexes determine your success, strategy games rely on planning and thinking to win. Aspyr (`www.aspyr.com`) provides several popular strategy games.

Aspyr also sells Sid Meier's Civilization game, which lets you control an entire civilization. Using trade, politics, and outright war, you can expand your civilization at the expense of others and try to take over the world without having to get elected to political office first to do it.

If you've ever dreamed about running your own TV station, play TV Station Manager (available from Winter Wolves at `www.winterwolves.com`), where you control the programming of an independent TV station and try to boost ratings. If you think there's too much garbage on TV these days, see whether you can make your TV station profitable offering quality entertainment. Like most real TV stations, you might find that trashy TV shows really are more profitable in the long run.

The same company, Winter Wolves, also provides Soccer Manager and Boxing Manager. In Soccer Manager, you manage a soccer game and choose different players to control a soccer team. In Boxing Manager, you pick a boxer and manage him through fights. Manage your boxer correctly, and he can work his way up to the championship. Manage him poorly, and he'll wind up flat on his back on the canvas.

Sports Interactive Games (`www.sigames.com`) offers Out of the Park Baseball and NHL Eastside Hockey manager, where you can pretend to manage a professional sports team and guide them to victory. See if you can win a baseball championship without any of your players relying on banned performance-enhancing drugs. Take your hockey team to the top while trying to keep the front teeth of all your players intact. The challenges can be endless.

One popular series of strategy games is the Tycoon series, such as Roller Coaster Tycoon (where you design and manage an amusement park) and Zoo Tycoon (where you design and manage a zoo). These Tycoon games let you fantasize about how you could make your local zoo or amusement park more exciting and profitable if only given the chance. Add a death-defying roller coaster to your amusement park and see how sales of milk shakes from a nearby concession stand might go down. Add an exotic animal to your zoo and see how much additional revenue you can generate without exploiting the animal in the process.

If the idea of being a manager sounds too tame for you, consider destroying entire civilizations at the touch of a button with DefCon (`www.ambrosiasw.com`), a game in which you play the role of a general in control of a nuclear arsenal. (See Figure 5-5.) Launch nuclear missiles at your enemies and see how much faster you can destroy the planet by using atomic weapons rather than diplomacy.

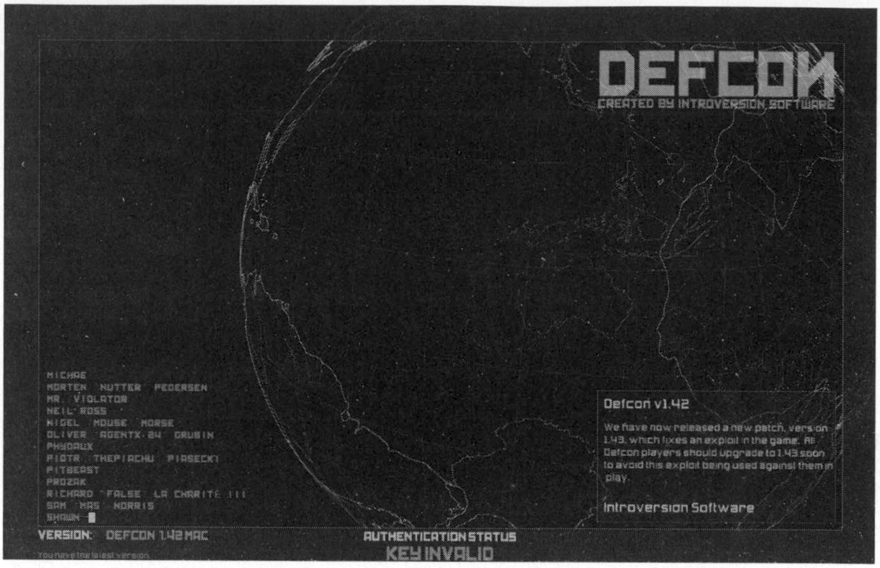

Figure 5-5: DefCon lets you conquer the world by blowing it up with thermonuclear weapons.

In case you'd rather save the planet than destroy it (which pretty much rules out any chance you might have for becoming a dictator), play Global Warming (available at `www.midoritech.com`). By playing the game, you can see how your actions can help save the planet both in the make-believe world of your Mac and in the real world around you.

Rather than play a strategy game that you've never heard of, you might prefer playing a game that you already know how to play. If you like Stratego, buy WebStratego (`www.metaforge.net`), which lets you play against people from all over the world through the Internet. If you like playing Risk, try taking over the world with a computer version called Lux Delux (`http://sillysoft.net`).

One of the more unique strategy games is called Bridge Construction Set (`www.garagegames.com`), where you try to design a bridge that can hold up a train. Design the bridge correctly, and the train crosses safely. Design the bridge poorly, and the train crashes into the river below. By teaching you how to build a bridge, this game indirectly teaches physics at the same time.

Head on down to the arcade

Long before video games appeared in coin-operated arcades, people used to play pinball. Although pinball machines have faded into obscurity, that doesn't mean you can't still play them on your Mac. (It's just that tilting your Mac won't help boost your score any.)

For an electronic version of a pinball game, visit LittleWing Pinball (`www.littlewingpinball.com`). These pinball games let you tilt, bump, rattle, and shake a virtual pinball machine to achieve the best score.

Pinball machines may be ancient history for today's generation of kids. Instead, they might prefer arcade games that originated with Pong, Space Invaders, Asteroids, and Pac-Man. The goal of these games was simple: Use your reflexes to stay alive as long as possible.

For a free Pac-Man clone, download a copy of Pac the Man X (`www.mcsebi.com`). If you remember playing Frogger, trying to navigate a frog across a busy highway without getting squished, you can relive your childhood by playing the Christmas Super Frog (`www.koingosw.com`), which is like Frogger but with a Christmas theme. If you remember trying to save cities from nuclear missiles with Missile Command, you can download a free Missile Command clone (`http://iskub.sippan.se/missile`) and see whether you still have what it takes to protect the world from a nuclear holocaust.

Growing beyond the primitive two-dimensional graphics of the early arcade games, the latest computer arcade games now embrace three-dimensional graphics for use in first-person shooter games and sports simulations.

Video game accessories

You can play most games by using the keyboard and the mouse. However, arcade-style video games can be much clumsier to play. Trying to fly an F-16 jet fighter simulator using the keyboard can seem unnatural and confusing, so that's why many companies sell special game-playing accessories such as joysticks, steering wheels, and even special mice designed to put more controls at your fingertips than a traditional mouse.

If you want to play a flight simulator or a first-person shooter game, you'll probably want a joystick. If you want to play a racing simulator, you'll probably want a steering wheel and pedals. For optimum graphics, you should get a Mac with a separate graphics card inside, included in most iMacs, MacBook Pros, and Mac Pros. (The Mac Mini, MacBook, and some iMacs don't use a separate graphics card, which means games can run slower or choppier.)

Some popular companies that make game-playing accessories include TrustMaster (`www.thrustmaster.com`), CH Products (`www.chproducts.com`), and Logitech (`www.logitech.com`). With the right joystick or steering wheel, you can immerse yourself in your favorite video game and leave the real world behind (until, of course, someone from the real world reminds you to pay your electricity bill).

First-person shooter games typically give you the view of a soldier running through a maze or rough terrain, blasting away targets and trying to avoid getting shot at in return. For a free first-person shooter game, grab a copy of AssaultCube (`http://assault.cubers.net`), which lets you play with others to roam around buildings and gun each other down.

For a historical first-person shooter game, play Call of Duty (`www.aspyr.com`), which puts you in the middle of various World War Two battles to see whether you can survive. If you'd rather play a flight simulator and dogfight other planes, buy a copy of OSX Skyfighters 1945 (`www.donsgames.com`) and strap yourself into the virtual cockpit of a P-51, Fw-190, Hellcat, or Japanese Zero and see if you can become an ace.

If the idea of killing even virtual enemies makes you squeamish, try to win a battle of wits and skill by playing a sports simulation game instead. Play GL Golf (`http://nuclearnova.com`) and practice your putting and golf strokes without having to get any fresh air outside to do it. If playing 18 holes sounds too exhausting, conquer a miniature golf course by playing Wacky Mini Golf (`www.danlabgames.com`) and try conquering those pesky windmills blocking the putting green instead. If you're ready, take on Tiger Woods in Tiger Woods PGA Tour (`www.aspyr.com`) and see whether your golf skills can match up with the masters.

In case golf doesn't get your adrenaline pumping, jump into a race car and run your opponents off the track in Jammin' Racer (`www.danlabgames.com`). For a more realistic racing simulation, grab a free copy of VDrift (`http://vdrift.net`), which lets you simulate racing on tracks in Detroit, Le Mans, Monaco, and Barcelona, as shown in Figure 5-6. For a motocross simulation, download a free copy of X-Moto (`http://xmoto.sourceforge.net`) and take out your road rage on animated opponents.

To play football without getting beat up on the playing field, try PlayMaker Football (`http://playmaker.com`). To play table tennis and test your mean serve on virtual opponents, try Table Tennis Pro (`www.grassgames.com`). For a snowboarding simulation, buy Slope Rider (`www.monteboyd.com`). If you'd rather control a penguin sliding down a snow-covered slope, try the free Tux Racer (`http://tuxracer.sourceforge.net`) game instead.

No matter what type of game you want, you can find one that runs on your Mac. If you want to play a game that runs only on Windows, install a copy of Windows on your Mac by using Boot Camp (see Book V, Chapter 4) and turn your Mac into a game-playing PC. With the ability to play games designed for both Windows and the Mac, you actually have a greater variety of games to play than anyone running a Windows computer. With the libraries of Windows and Mac games to choose from, your only limitation is finding the time to play all the games you want.

Writing your own games

If you enjoy playing games, you might like creating your own games even better. Although writing your own game might seem scary, you can get a lot of help by buying various tools to make game creation easier.

To create simple games, buy the Mac Game Creator Toolkit (`http://members.aol.com/AlStaff/macgamecreator.html`), which provides several different programs for creating old-fashion, text-based games (similar to the old Zork style games where you type commands to explore an area such as GO WEST or KILL TROLL).

You can also buy Animation Engine and Revolution (`www.runrev.com`) to create simple 2-D graphics such as card games or board games. If you want to get a bit more sophisticated, you'll have to learn a programming language, such as C++.

Although you can create an entire game from scratch by using any programming language, such as C++, even the professionals don't do that. To speed up game development, the professionals use a game engine, which basically contains commands for animating objects on the screen. By using a game engine, programmers can focus on just writing the commands to make their game work rather than be forced to write commands to display and manipulate graphics on the screen as well.

Some popular game engines include the Torque Game Engine (`www.garagegames.com`), Unity Game Engine (`www.unity3d.com`), and the PTK Game Engine (`www.phelios.com`). By combining these game engines with the C++ programming language, you can create games that rival the professionals.

Playing multiplayer, online role-playing games

After a while, playing even the most exciting game by yourself can get boring, which is why many people prefer playing games online to compete against others. Such an online experience can give people a sense of community, even if they never meet. One of the most popular of these online role-playing games is the World of Warcraft (`www.worldofwarcraft.com`), a fantasy virtual world that lets you create a cartoon character called an *avatar* and roam around bartering, negotiating, and attacking people or mythical creatures with a sword or a magic spell. With over eight million players, no session of World of Warcraft will ever be the same.

Although some people prefer fantasy, others prefer science fiction. If you'd rather use lasers rather than sword and conquer universes rather than castles, join EVE Online (`www.eve-online.com`) and roam through outer space, shooting at spaceships, trading with other planets, and negotiating with aliens (who might not be any more bizarre than the people you normally associate with at work). By playing EVE Online, you can take over a galaxy and let mere mortals on this planet remain ignorant of your true accomplishments and abilities.

Figure 5-6: VDrift lets you drive a race car through the world's toughest courses.

If living in a virtual world of fantasy and science fiction doesn't appeal to you, you might prefer Second Life (`http://secondlife.com`), which puts you inside a virtual world similar to the real world. The only difference is that inside this virtual world, you can experiment with different ways of living that you might never do in real life like playing different genders or acting aggressive (if you're normally shy) or making yourself ugly (if you're normally attractive). Second Life also offers a special Teen Life area just so teenagers can explore within a safe environment with other teenagers. (Now you just have to worry about the danger of meeting other teenagers.) In both Second Life and Teen Life, you create a character (an avatar) and roam around interacting with others. You can buy virtual land, run a business, or just meet new people without the fear of real-life rejection.

For more games, visit Mac Games and More (`www.macgamesandmore.com`). With the right game running on your Mac, you need never be bored again.

Book VI

Time-Saving Tips with a Mac

The 5th Wave By Rich Tennant

"Why can't you just bring your iPod like everyone else?"

Contents at a Glance

Chapter 1: Protecting Your Data 643
Chapter 2: Managing Your Time with iCal 659
Chapter 3: Storing Contact Information in the Address Book 679
Chapter 4: Using Dashboard 693
Chapter 5: Automating your Mac 705

Chapter 1: Protecting Your Data

In This Chapter

- Understanding backup options
- Using Time Machine
- Working with data-recovery programs
- Encrypting your data

Backing up data is something that most people routinely ignore, like changing the oil in their car on a regular basis. The only time most people think about backing up their data is after they've already lost something important, such as a business presentation. Of course, by that time, it's already too late.

Backing up your data might not sound as exciting as playing video games or browsing the Internet, but it should be a part of your routine every day. If you can't risk losing your data, you can't risk not taking the time to back it up.

Understanding Different Backup Options

The simplest and most practical solution for backing up your data is to make duplicate copies of every important file. Although this seems simple in theory, you must make sure to copy your files periodically, such as at the end of every day. If you forget to copy your files, your backup copies could become woefully outdated, which can make them nearly useless.

Another issue with backing up data concerns storing and retrieving it. If you store duplicates of your important files on your hard drive, you have to make sure you don't accidentally use those backup files instead of the original files (and then accidentally copy the obsolete original files over the backup copies that are actually more current).

To back up your files, consider using more than one method, because the more backup copies you have of your critical files, the more likely it is that you'll never lose your data no matter what might happen to your Mac.

REMEMBER

To reduce the amount of storage space needed to store copies of your files, you can archive and compress your files into a ZIP or DMG file. (See Book I, Chapter 6 for more information about creating ZIP and DMG files.)

Using your hard drive

The simplest way to back up your files is to create and store duplicate copies of your files in another part of your hard drive. This method has the advantage of not requiring that you buy any new equipment. The huge disadvantage of this option is that your hard drive might fail and wipe out both your original data and any backup files you have stored.

Another problem is that the more data you need to back up, the more space both your original and backup files will gobble up, until eventually you might run out of room on your hard drive. For these reasons, using your hard drive to store backup copies of files is suitable for backing up a handful of files, but it's impractical for backing up large amounts of data.

Backing up to CDs/DVDs

Every Mac can write to CDs, and most Macs can also write to DVDs. As a result, storing backups on CDs or DVDs is a popular option because CDs and DVDs are easy to store and are pretty durable. The biggest drawback of CDs and DVDs is their limited storage capacities. CDs can store up to 700MB of data, and DVDs can store 4.7GB of data, with the newest DVDs capable of storing up to 8.5GB of data.

If you need to backup only word processor or spreadsheet files, a single CD should be sufficient. However, music, video, and digital photographs take up more space, which means that you might need to use several CDs to completely back up all your files of those types.

DVDs can store much more data than CDs, but even they can be limited when you're backing up hard drives that contain several gigabytes worth of files. The more discs you need to back up your files, the harder it can be to keep track of all the discs that make a complete backup of your data.

Storing data on multiple discs can be slow and tedious, which means you might not back up your data as often as you should. Eventually, this means your backup files are too far out of date to be useful, which defeats the purpose of backing up your data in the first place.

If you can comfortably fit your most crucial files on a CD or DVD, this can be a simple and fast backup option, but if your data exceeds the storage limits of a single CD or DVD, using multiple discs can be too cumbersome, so you should probably rely on another backup method.

Storing backups on USB flash drives

The low-cost and high-storage capacities of USB flash drives make them an attractive alternative to using CDs for backing up your most crucial files. USB flash drives offer ease of use because you can plug them into any open USB port in a Mac and move them to another Mac.

The biggest drawback of USB flash drives is their limited storage capacities, which range from 256MB to 16GB or sometimes more. As a result, USB flash drives are most convenient for carrying your most critical files but not necessarily for backing up all your important files. In contrast to the hassles of writing (or *burning*) data to a CD or DVD, saving files to a USB flash drive is as simple as saving a file in another part of your hard drive.

USB flash drives are small and easy to carry, so many people store their most critical files on USB flash drives that they take with them. However, if you lose your USB flash drive, anyone who finds your USB flash drive can peek at your files. If you can't afford to have strangers peeking at your files, consider buying a special USB flash drive that offers encryption to protect your files from anyone who doesn't have your password.

Backing up with external hard drives

To prevent the loss of all your data if your hard drive should suddenly die, you can use external hard drives that connect to your Mac through a USB or FireWire port.

Both USB (Universal Serial Bus) and FireWire ports are used for connecting peripheral to a computer. USB ports are more commonly used for connecting a mouse or digital camera, whereas FireWire ports are often used for connecting video camcorders or other computers together. FireWire ports tend to transfer data slightly faster than USB ports.

The main advantage of external hard drives is that copying large files is much faster and more convenient than copying the same files to a USB flash drive or CD/DVD. In addition, external hard drives are easy to unplug from one Mac and plug into a second Mac. Because of their low cost, fast copying speed, and ease of moving and plugging into any Mac, external hard drives are the most popular choice for backing up files.

Perhaps the biggest drawback of external hard drive is that they can't protect against a catastrophe near your computer, such as a fire burning down your house or a flood soaking your computer desk and office. If a disaster wipes out the entire area around your computer, your external hard drive will likely get wiped out in the process as well.

You can treat an external hard drive as just another place to copy your files, but for greater convenience, you should use a special backup program. Backup programs can be set to run according to a schedule (for example, to back up your files every night at 6:00 pm).

If the files haven't changed since the last time you backed them up, the backup program saves time by skipping over those files rather than copying the same files to the external hard drive all over again. To retrieve files, you could just copy the files from your external hard drive back on your original hard drive, but watch out! If you changed a file on your original hard drive, copying the backup copy could actually wipe out the most recent changes and restore an old file to your hard drive, which probably isn't what you want.

To keep you from accidentally wiping out new files with older versions of that same file, backup programs always compare the time and date a file was last modified to make sure you always have copies of the latest file. To try a free backup program for use with an external hard drive, grab a free copy of SilverKeeper (`www.lacie.com/silverkeeper`), PsyncX (`http://psyncx.sourceforge.net`), Carbon Copy Cloner (`www.bombich.com`), or SuperDuper (`www.shirt-pocket.com`).

Storing backups off-site

In the old days, corporations used to back up data to tapes (which resemble oversized audio cassette tapes) and ship them to another location. Such off-site storage protects the data because even if a disaster wiped out both your computer and any backup systems nearby, such as external hard drives, it's unlikely that it would also wipe out the off-site storage area. Off-site storage virtually guarantees that you'll never lose your data.

Although off-site storage can get expensive, many low-cost (and even free) off-site storage options are available for Mac users. One simple way to create off-site storage is to open a free e-mail account (such as with Yahoo!) and e-mail yourself your important files. Now you can always retrieve your important files from anywhere in the world that offers Internet access.

Many companies sell off-site storage space for a monthly fee. However, to entice you to try their services, they often provide a limited amount of free space that you can use for an unlimited period of time at no cost whatsoever. To get your free off-site storage space, sign up with one or more of the following off-site data backup sites:

- **XDrive (**`www.xdrive.com`**):** Free 5GB of storage space
- **MediaMax (**`www.mediamax.com`**):** Free 25GB of storage space
- **Mozy (**`http://mozy.com`**):** Free 2GB of storage space
- **ElephantDrive (**`www.elephantdrive.com`**):** Free 1GB of storage space

Going Back to the Past with Time Machine

One problem with traditional backup programs is that they store only the latest versions of your files. Normally, this is exactly what you want, but what if you want to see an earlier version of a letter you wrote two weeks ago? Unless you kept a copy of your backups you made two weeks ago, trying to find files created on certain dates in the past is nearly impossible.

Fortunately, that type of problem is trivial for Apple's new backup program, Time Machine. Unlike traditional backup programs that copy and store the latest versions of files, Time Machine takes snapshots of your Mac hard drive so that you can view the exact condition of your Mac hard drive two weeks ago, two months ago, or even two years ago.

By seeing the exact condition of what your Mac hard drive looked like in the past, you can see exactly what all your files looked like at that time. After you find a specific file version from the past, you can copy and paste it into the present.

Setting up Time Machine

To use Time Machine, you need an external hard drive that connects to your Mac through a USB or FireWire cable.

To set up Time Machine to work with your Mac and external hard drive, follow these steps:

1. **Connect the external hard drive to your Mac.**
2. **Click the Apple menu and choose System Preferences.**

   A System Preferences window appears.
3. **Click the Time Machine icon under the System category.**

   The Time Machine pane appears, as shown in Figure 1-1.
4. **Click the On button.**
5. **Click the Choose Backup Disk button.**

   A dialog appears, listing all available external hard drives you can use, as shown in Figure 1-2.

Figure 1-1: To set up Time Machine, you need to turn it on and choose an external drive to use.

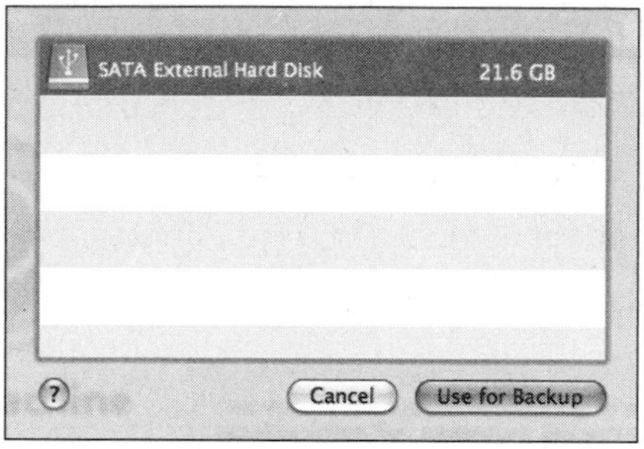

Figure 1-2: You must choose an external hard drive to use with Time Machine.

6. **Click an external hard drive and click the Use for Backup button.**

   The Time Machine pane appears again, listing your chosen external hard drive, as shown in Figure 1-3.

7. **Click the Close button of the System Preferences window.**

REMEMBER

Time Machine automatically backs up your hard drive every hour for the past 24 hours, every day for the past month, and every week until you run out of room on your external hard drive. When your external hard drive runs out of room, Time Machine starts deleting the oldest files to make room for the newer ones.

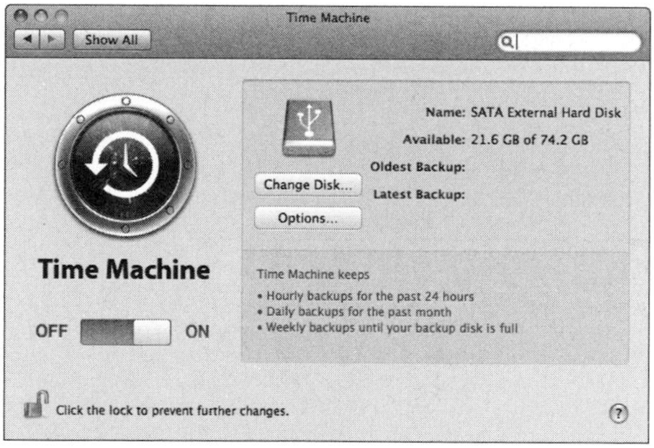

Figure 1-3: The Time Machine pane can show how much free space remains on your external hard drive.

Defining files to skip

To save space and to avoid copying files you don't want or care about anyway, you can identify certain files and folders that you want Time Machine to ignore. For example, you might not want to back up your Applications folder if you already have all your programs stored on separate DVDs anyway.

To tell Time Machine which files or folders to skip, follow these steps:

1. **Click the Apple menu and choose System Preferences.**

   A System Preferences window appears.

2. **Click the Time Machine icon under the System category.**

   A Time Machine window appears (refer to Figure 1-1).

3. **Click Options.**

   The Do Not Back Up dialog appears, as shown in Figure 1-4.

4. **Click the plus sign (+) button.**

   The dialog that appears lists your folders and files, as shown in Figure 1-5. You might need to click a folder to view specific files.

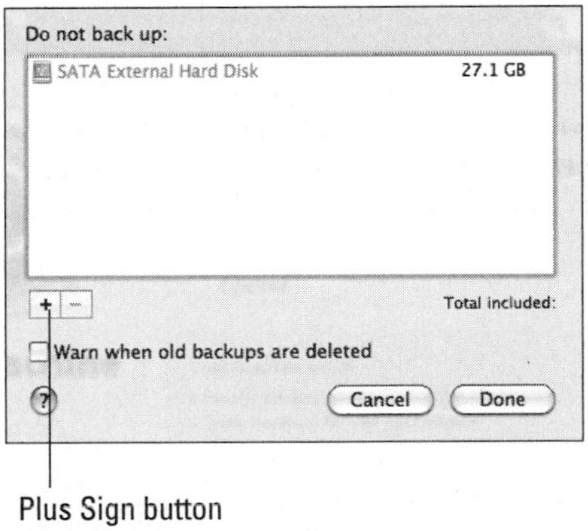

Figure 1-4: The Do Not Back Up dialog lets you specify which files, folders, and volumes Time Machine will ignore.

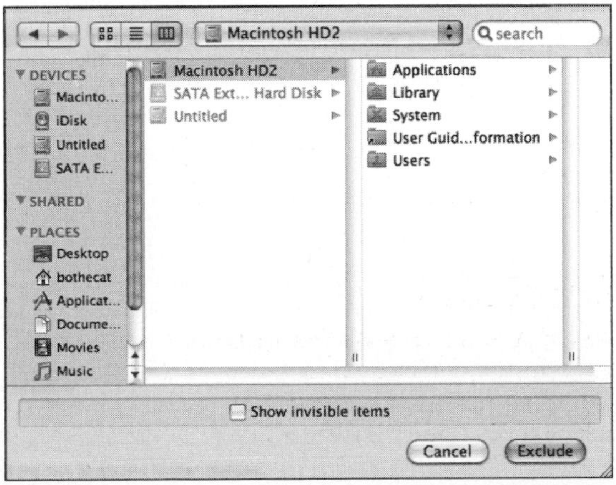

Figure 1-5: You can select a volume, folder or file that Time Machine will skip over.

5. **Click a file or folder that you want Time Machine to ignore.**

   You can select multiple drives, files and folders by holding down the ⌘ key and clicking the ones you want.

6. **Click the Exclude button.**

   The Do Not Back Up dialog appears again (refer to Figure 1-4).

7. **(Optional) Select or deselect the Warn When Old Backups Are Deleted check box.**

   If this check box is selected, Time Machine won't delete any of your old backups without displaying a dialog requesting your approval.

8. **Click Done.**

   The Time Machine pane appears again.

9. **Click the Close button of the System Preferences window.**

Retrieving files and folders

After you've configured Time Machine to back up your Mac, you can use Time Machine to view multiple windows, with each window representing a previous condition of your Mac. So, for example, if you want to retrieve a folder or file from three weeks ago, locate the Finder in Time Machine that represents your Mac three weeks ago. Then you can copy the folder or file and paste it in the Finder.

To retrieve folders or files from Time Machine, follow these steps:

1. **Click the Time Machine icon in the Dock.**

   The Time Machine screen appears, as shown in Figure 1-6. (If the Time Machine icon doesn't appear in the Dock, you have to double-click the Time Machine icon in the Applications folder.)

2. **Choose one of the following ways to pick a Finder from the past:**

   - *Click a Finder.* Each time you click a window, Time Machine moves the entire group of windows forward or backward.
   - *Move the pointer to the Time Machine timeline.* The timeline bars expand to display a specific date. To choose a specific date, click it.

3. **Select the file or folders you want to retrieve.**

   If you select a file and press ⌘+Y to choose the Quick Look command, you can view the contents of your selected file just to make sure you really want to retrieve it.

4. **Click the Restore button in the bottom-right corner of the screen.**

   Time Machine displays the current Finder with your selected items retrieved.

5. **Click Cancel to exit Time Machine.**

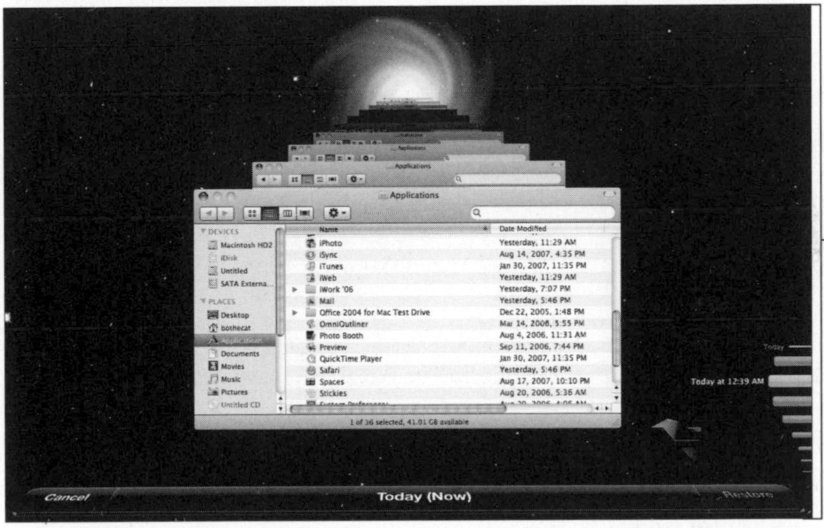

Timeline

Figure 1-6: Time Machine displays all previous backups as a series of cascading windows.

Working with Data-Recovery Programs

You can lose files in a variety of ways:

- **Accidentally deleted from the hard drive:** The most common way to lose a file is by accidentally deleting it. If you try to recover your lost file through a backup program such as Time Machine, you might be shocked to find that your backup program can recover only your file from the previous hour. So if you spent the last 45 minutes changing a file and accidentally deleted it, your backup program might hold the file from only an hour ago, but it won't contain any of the changes you made in the last 45 minutes.
- **Hardware failure:** Another way to lose a file is through a hardware failure, such as your hard drive mangling portions of its disk surface and wrecking any files stored there. Such a failure can go unnoticed because

the hard drive still works. As a result, your backup program will copy and save these mangled versions of your file. The moment you discover your file is corrupted, you'll also find that your backup program has been diligently copying and saving the same corrupted version of your file.

- **Deleted from removable media:** A third way you can lose data is by deleting it from removable media such as a USB flash drive or digital camera flash memory card (such as a Compact Flash or Secure Digital card). Most likely, your backup programs protect only your hard drive files, not any removable storage devices, which means you could take twenty priceless pictures of your daughter's wedding, only to delete all those pictures by mistake. Because your backup program might never have saved those files, you can't recover them at all.

In all three situations, backup programs can't help you, so you might need to rely on special data-recovery programs instead. Data-recovery programs work by taking advantage of the way computers store and organize files by physically placing them in certain areas, such as in one area of a hard drive.

To keep track of where each file is stored, computers maintain a directory that tells the computer the names of every file and the exact physical location where file is stored. When different programs, such as word processors or spreadsheets, need to find and open a file, these programs first look at this directory so they know where to find a file.

When you delete a file, the computer simply removes that file's name from the directory. However, your file still physically exists on the disk surface, but the computer can't find it again. So data-recovery programs basically ignore the directory listing of a disk and search for a file by examining every part of the entire storage device to find your missing files.

If you didn't add any files since you last deleted the file you want to retrieve, a data-recovery program will likely retrieve your entire file again. If you saved and modified files since you last deleted a particular file, there's a good chance any new or modified files might have written over the area that contains your deleted file. In this case, your chances of recovering the entire file intact drops rapidly over time.

If a hardware failure corrupts a file, it might mean that all or part of your file gets wiped out for good. However, in many cases, a hardware failure won't physically destroy all or part of a file. Instead, a hardware failure might physically scramble a file, much like throwing a pile of clothes all over the room. In this case, the file still physically exists, but the directory of the disk won't know where all the parts of the file have been scattered. So, to the computer, your files have effectively disappeared.

The art of computer forensics

Most anything you store on your Mac can be recovered, given enough time and money. When most people lose data, they're thankful when a data-recovery program can retrieve their files. However, in the criminal world, people may want to delete files so that nobody can ever find them again to hide evidence. To retrieve such deleted files, law enforcement agencies rely on something called computer forensics.

The basic idea behind computer forensics is to make an exact copy of a hard drive and then try to piece together the deleted files on that copy of the original hard drive. Some criminals have lit hard drives on fire, poured acid on them, and sliced them apart with a buzz saw — and law enforcement agencies can still manage to read and recover the files from the slivers of hard drive fragments that contain the magnetic traces of the original files.

The good news is that if you can't recover a file yourself by using a data-recovery program, you can often hire a professional service that can recover your data for you. The bad news is that if you have any information on your hard drive that you want to keep secret, there will always be a way to find and recover your data no matter how much you try to destroy it.

A data-recovery program can piece together such scattered files by examining the physical surface of a disk, gathering up file fragments, and putting them back together again like Humpty Dumpty. Depending on how badly corrupted a file might be, collecting file fragments and putting them back together again can recover an entire file or just part of a file, but sometimes recovering part of a file can be better than losing the whole file.

Even if you format and erase your entire hard drive, your files may still physically remain on the hard drive, making it possible to recover those files.

Some popular data-recovery programs include:

- **FileSalvage and CameraSalvage (**`www.subrosasoft.com`**):** FileSalvage retrieves deleted and corrupted files; CameraSalvage recovers deleted files from flash memory cards.
- **Stellar Phoenix Macintosh and Stellar Phoenix Photo Recovery (**`www.stellarinfo.com`**):** Stellar Phoenix Macintosh retrieves deleted and corrupted files. Stellar Phoenix Photo Recovery recovers deleted files from flash memory cards.
- **Klix (**`www.joesoft.com`**):** Specialized program for recovering lost digital images stored on flash memory cards like Secure Digital or Compact Flash cards.

- **Data Rescue II** (www.prosofteng.com): This program recovers and retrieves data from a hard drive that your Mac can no longer access due to a hard disk failure.
- **Mac Data Recovery** (www.datarecoverymac.com)**:** This program specializes in recovering files from corrupted or reformatted hard drives.

One data-recovery program might be able to retrieve files that a second data-recovery program cannot.

Encrypting with FileVault

Sometimes your biggest threat isn't from hardware failure or accidentally deleting your data, but from the prying eyes of others who want to peek at your data. To protect your data, you can take one or more of the following steps:

- Physically lock your Mac behind closed doors (armed guards optional).
- Make sure everyone using your Mac has his or her own separate account (see Book I, Chapter 7 for more information about creating accounts).
- Encrypt your files by using the Mac's built-in encryption program called FileVault.

Encryption physically scrambles your files so that even if people can access your files, they can't open or edit them unless they know the correct password. Encryption can't stop someone from copying your files, but it can stop someone from using your files. When you use FileVault, your Mac encrypts your entire home folder that contains your folders such as Documents, Music, and Pictures.

FileVault uses an encryption algorithm called Advanced Encryption Standard (AES), which is the latest American government standard for scrambling data that even national governments with supercomputers can't crack.

Setting up FileVault

FileVault scrambles your files so that no one lacking your password can read their contents. When you type in a password, you can access your files and use them normally, but as soon as you close a file, FileVault scrambles it once more. FileVault works in the background so that you never even see it working.

WARNING! FileVault uses your *login* password to encrypt your data. For added safety, FileVault lets you set a second password, called a *master* password, that can decrypt any encrypted files stored on your Mac. If you forget your login password and your master password, your data will be encrypted forever with no hope of unscrambling and retrieving it ever again.

To turn on FileVault, follow these steps:

1. **Click the Apple menu and choose System Preferences.**

   A System Preferences window appears.

2. **Click on the Security icon under the Personal category.**

   The Security pane appears.

3. **Click the FileVault tab.**

   The FileVault pane appears, as shown in Figure 1-7.

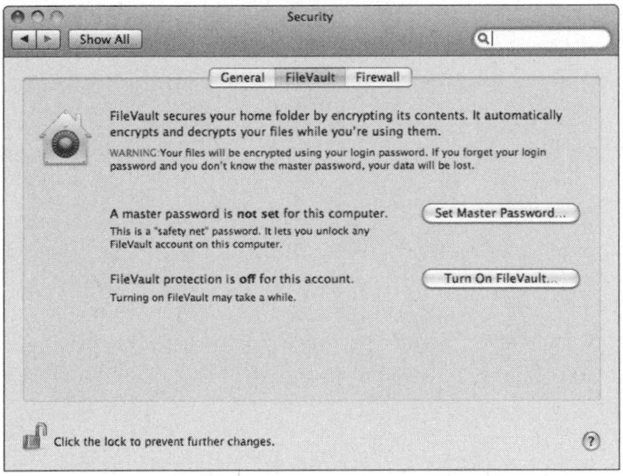

Figure 1-7: The FileVault pane lets you turn on FileVault and set a password.

4. **Click the Set Master Password button.**

   A dialog appears, asking for a password as shown in Figure 1-8.

5. **Type your master password and a hint and then click OK.**
6. **Click the Turn On FileVault button.**

   A dialog appears, asking for your login password.

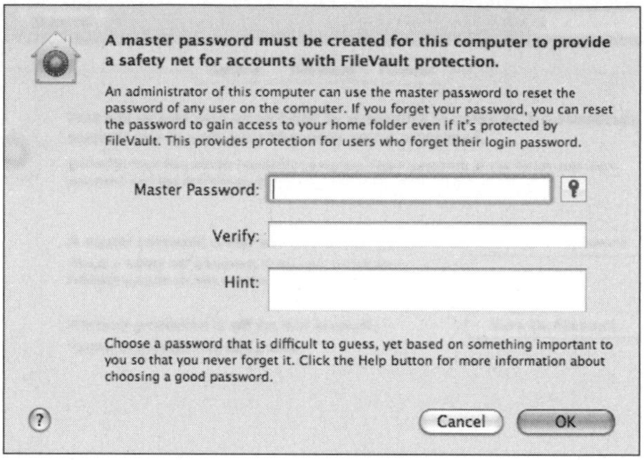

Figure 1-8: Choose a master password that's hard to guess but easy to remember.

7. **Type your login password and click OK.**

   A warning dialog appears, telling you how FileVault can prevent Time Machine from retrieving your old files again as shown in Figure 1-9.

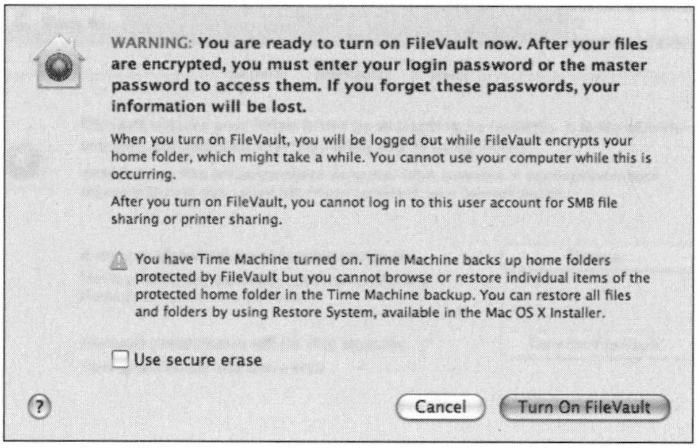

Figure 1-9: A warning dialog appears to let you know the consequences of using FileVault.

8. **Click Turn On FileVault.**

   A window appears to let you know that FileVault is encrypting your home folder. (Be patient. This can take a while. When FileVault is done encrypting, your Mac displays a dialog asking that you log into your account.)

REMEMBER

When FileVault is turned on, your Mac might run slower because it needs to take time to decrypt and encrypt files as you open and close them.

Turning off FileVault

In case you turned FileVault on and later change your mind, you can always turn FileVault of again by following these steps:

1. **Click the Apple menu and choose System Preferences.**

   A System Preferences window appears.

2. **Click the Security icon under the Personal category.**

   The Security pane appears.

3. **Click the FileVault tab.**

   The FileVault pane appears, as shown in Figure 1-10.

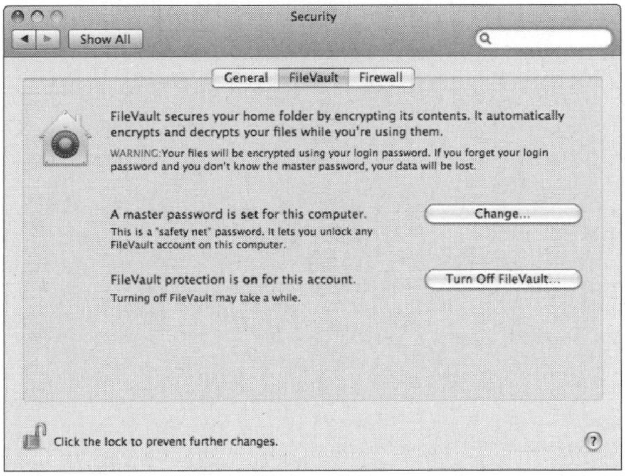

Figure 1-10: When FileVault is turned on, the Turn Off FileVault button appears.

4. **(Optional) Click Change if you want to change your master password.**

5. **Click the Turn Off FileVault button.**

   A dialog asks for your password.

6. **Type your login password and click OK.**

   A dialog appears, informing you that you are about to turn off FileVault, as shown in Figure 1-11.

7. **Click the Turn Off FileVault button.**

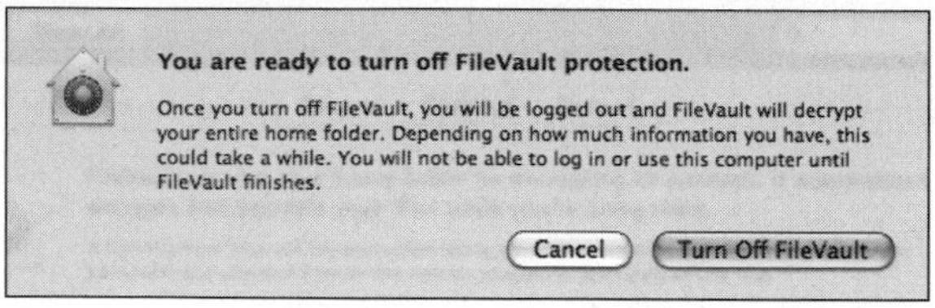

Figure 1-11: A dialog informs you if you turn off FileVault, it might take some time to decrypt your home folder.

Chapter 2: Managing Your Time with iCal

In This Chapter

- Understanding the iCal window
- Using calendars
- Creating and storing events
- Finding events
- Storing To Do lists
- Sharing calendars
- Printing, saving, and exporting calendars

The iCal program lets you track appointments and tasks that you need to do. To help separate your different appointments, such as personal and business appointments, you can create separate calendars so that you can see which days you'll be busy for work and which days you'll be busy for your personal schedule.

Using calendars might seem simple, but they can be a powerful tool to organize your schedule, track your time, and help you plan your goals. The more efficiently you can use your time, the more you'll get done and the faster you can reach your goals. Given these incentives, it only makes sense to invest a little time in discovering how your Mac can save you a lot of time in the long run.

Understanding iCal

The iCal window displays the following items, as shown in Figure 2-1:

- **Calendar List:** Displays all calendars that contain related appointments such as Home or Work-related events
- **Mini-Month:** Displays the dates for an entire month so you can see which day a specific date falls on, such as Tuesday or Saturday
- **Events:** Shows events scheduled in Day, Week, or Month views
- **To Do list:** Displays tasks that you need to accomplish

I go into more detail about each of these items in the following sections.

Figure 2-1: The iCal window provides different ways to view times and dates.

> **REMEMBER:** Any scheduled activity, such as a doctor's appointment, a business meeting, or your daughter's soccer practice, is called an *event.*

Working with the Calendar List

The iCal program initially includes a Home and Work calendar, but you can always create or rename additional calendars. You might want an additional calendar for a specific work or home-related project, or you might need a separate calendar to help you track all of your children's scheduled activities.

The Calendar List displays all the different calendars you've created, as well as the Home and Work calendars provided by iCal. The Calendar List has two uses:

- ✦ To select a calendar to view (which appears in the middle pane of the iCal window)
- ✦ To hide or display events stored on a particular calendar

When you want to store an event, you must first choose which calendar to use. The main reason to have separate calendars is to organize and sort your various events into calendar types. For example, the provided iCal Home calendar is for storing personal events, and the Work calendar is for storing business-related events.

By selecting or deselecting the check box next to each calendar in the Calendar List, you can selectively view specific events, such as only business events. Or you can view both business and personal events together.

The following sections give you the lowdown on managing your calendars in iCal.

Creating a new calendar

Although iCal provides a Home and Work calendar, you might need to create additional calendars for other purposes. To create a new calendar, follow these steps:

1. **Double-click the iCal icon in the Applications folder to load iCal.**
2. **Choose File⇨New Calendar or right-click in the Calendar List and when a pop-up menu appears, choose New Calendar.**

   An Untitled calendar appears in the Calendar List, as shown in Figure 2-2.
3. **Type a descriptive name for your calendar and press Return.**

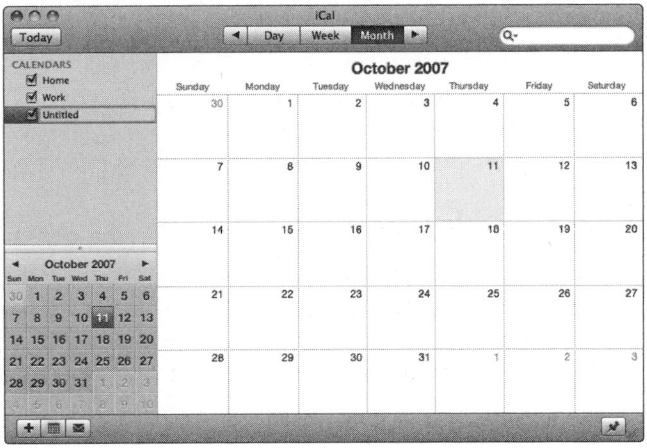

Figure 2-2: A new calendar appears without a name.

Creating a new calendar group

Rather than create a bunch of separate calendars, you might want to organize multiple calendars in a group. For example, if you had a calendar to schedule events for your son and daughter, you could put both of those calendars into a group called Family.

Grouping not only helps you see the relationships between calendars, but it also lets you hide grouped calendars to avoid cluttering up the Calendar List. When you hide a calendar group, you also hide all calendars stored within that group.

A calendar group can't store events; it simply stores one or more calendars.

To create a calendar group, follow these steps:

1. **Double-click the iCal icon in the Applications folder to load iCal.**
2. **Choose File⇨New Calendar Group or right-click in the Calendar List.**
3. **From the pop-up menu that appears, choose New Group.**

   A calendar group appears in the Calendar List with a triangle to its left, which you click to hide or show any grouped calendars.
4. **Type a descriptive name for your group and press Return.**

Adding a new calendar to a group

After you've created a group, you can add new calendars to the group by following these steps:

1. **In the Calendar List, click the group name to which you want to add a new calendar.**
2. **Choose File⇨New Calendar.**

   A new calendar appears indented under the group.
3. **Type a descriptive name for your new calendar and press Return.**

Moving an existing calendar to a group

If you have an existing calendar that you want to move into a group, follow these steps:

1. **Move the cursor over a calendar, in the Calendar List, that you want to move into a group.**
2. **Hold down the mouse button, drag the mouse over the group where you want to move the calendar, and release the mouse button.**

   Your existing calendar now appears indented under the group.

Moving a calendar out of a group

In case you don't want a calendar in a group, you can move it out of a group by following these steps:

1. **Move the cursor over a calendar, in the Calendar List, that appears indented under a group.**

2. **Hold down the mouse button, drag the mouse over the CALENDARS title, and release the mouse button.**

Your existing calendar now appears outside of any groups.

Moving a calendar or group

To help organize your calendars and groups, you might want to rearrange their order in the Calendar List by following these steps:

1. **Move the cursor over the calendar or group you want to move.**

2. **Hold down the mouse button and drag the mouse up or down.**

A thick horizontal line appears where your calendar or group will appear in the Calendar List, as shown in Figure 2-3.

Figure 2-3: A horizontal line shows where your calendar or group will appear when you release the mouse button.

3. **Release the mouse button when you're happy with the new location of your calendar or group.**

Renaming and deleting calendars and groups

At any time, you can rename a calendar or group. The name of a calendar or group is for your own benefit and has no effect on the way iCal works. To rename a calendar or group, just double-click a calendar or group name, which highlights that name. Type a new name and press Return.

If you find that you no longer need a particular calendar or group, click the one you want to delete and choose Edit➪Delete. If you have any events stored on a calendar, a dialog appears, asking whether you really want to delete that calendar or group. Click Delete. If you delete a calendar or group by mistake, choose Edit➪Undo or press ⌘+Z.

When you delete a calendar, you also delete any events stored on that calendar. When you delete a group, you delete all calendars stored in that group along with all events stored on those calendars. Make sure you really want to delete a calendar or group of calendars.

Using the Mini-Month

The Mini-Month is a miniature view of the current month that lets you see which days fall on specific dates. You can also use the Mini-Month display to switch to a different day or week within the Day or Week view displayed in the right pane of the iCal window. You can hide or show the Mini-Month by choosing View➪Show/Hide Mini Months or by clicking the View/Hide Mini-Month icon that appears in the bottom-left corner of the iCal window.

Creating and Modifying Events

An event is anything that gobbles up time, usually starting at a predictable time and (you hope!) ending at an equally predictable time. Some common types of events are meetings, appointments with clients, times when you need to pick someone up (such as at the airport), or recreational time such as a Saturday night date. If you know a particular event will occur on a specific day and time, you can store that event in an iCal calendar so that you won't forget or schedule something else in that same time period.

Viewing events

The iCal program shows all the events you've scheduled for that day, week, or month. To change the time frame of your displayed events, click the Day, Week, or Month button. Figure 2-4 shows each of the views available.

Creating an event

To store an event, you need to decide which calendar to store the event on, what date and time to schedule the event, and how long you think the event will last. To create an event, follow these steps:

1. **In the Calendar List, click a calendar in which you want to store the event.**
2. **Click the Day, Week, or Month button at the top of the iCal window.**

   If you click either the Day or Week button, you can define the starting and ending times for your event. If you choose the Month button, you can create an event but cannot define the start and ending time.

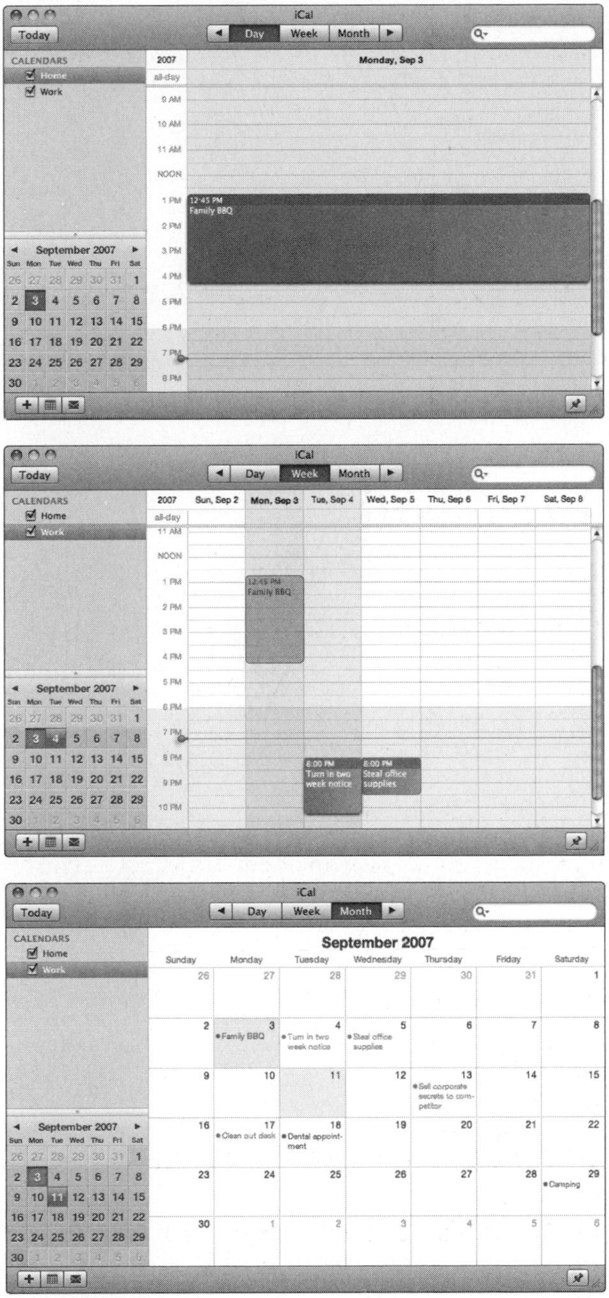

Figure 2-4: The three different time frames to view events.

3. **Double-click a time (in the Day or Week view) or day (in the Month) view where you want to place an event.**

   A New Event color-coded box appears, as shown in Figure 2-5.

4. **Type a description of your event and press Return.**

If you're in the Day or Week view, you can define the start and end time of an event by moving the mouse cursor to the top or bottom of an event until it turns into a two-way pointing arrow. Hold down the mouse button and move it up or down to define your start and end times in 15-minute increments.

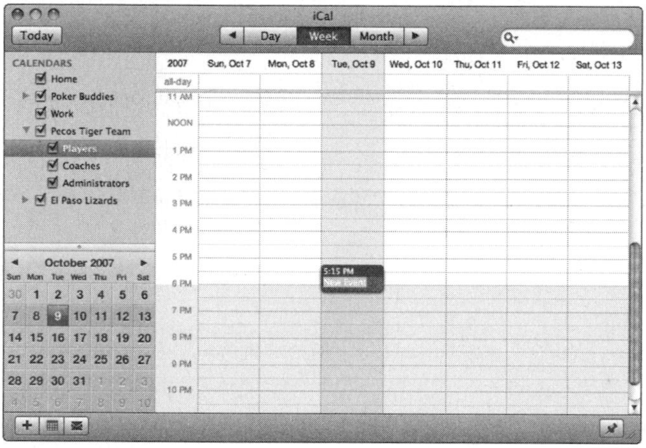

Figure 2-5: A new event appears as a color-coded box.

Moving an event

In case you stored an event at the wrong date or time, you can always move it to a new date and time by following these steps:

1. **Move the cursor over the middle of the event box.**
2. **Hold down the mouse button and drag the cursor to a new time or date.**

   The event moves with the cursor.

3. **Release the mouse button when you're happy with the new date and time of the event.**

Duplicating an event

If a particular event occurs more than once, you could type the event multiple times, but why spend all that effort? Instead, you can create an event and duplicate it so you can move the duplicate to another date. To duplicate an event, just click it and choose Edit⇨Duplicate or press ⌘+D. When the duplicate appears, move the cursor over it, drag the event to a new date, and release the mouse button.

Editing an event

Editing an event lets modify an event by changing the time, the date, or its description. You can also add features to an event such as setting an alarm or automatically opening a file.

Changing the description of an event

Each time you create an event, you need to type in a description of that event. To modify this description, follow these steps:

1. **Click the event you want to modify and choose Edit⇨Edit Event or press ⌘+E.**

   An edit dialog appears, as shown in Figure 2-6.

2. **Click in the event description (in Figure 2-6, this is simply New Event).**

   A text box appears around the event description.

3. **Use the arrow and Delete keys to edit the current event description and type any new text. Click Done when you're finished.**

   REMEMBER: If you click the Location field, you can type a location where an event takes place.

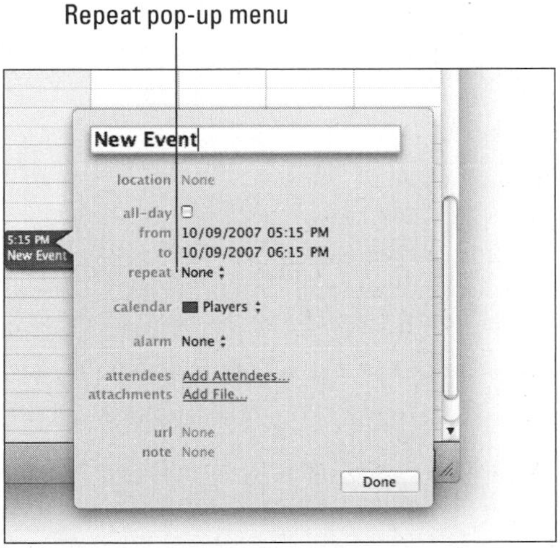

Figure 2-6: The edit dialog lets you modify different parts of an event.

Creating a recurring event

For an event that occurs regularly, such as every Monday or every month, you can create an event once and tell iCal to display that event on a recurring basis. To create a recurring event, follow these steps:

1. **Create an event as described in the "Creating an event" section, earlier in this chapter.**
2. **Choose Edit➪Edit Event or press ⌘+E.**

   An edit dialog appears (refer to Figure 2-6).
3. **Click the Repeat pop-up menu and choose an option such as Every day or Every month.**
4. **(Optional) In the Repeat pop-up menu, click Custom.**

   A dialog appears, as shown in Figure 2-7, letting you define specific days for the recurring event, such as every week on Monday and Thursday. Click OK when you're done creating a custom recurring event.
5. **In the edit dialog, click Done.**

   The iCal program automatically displays your recurring event throughout the rest of the calendar until you modify the event.

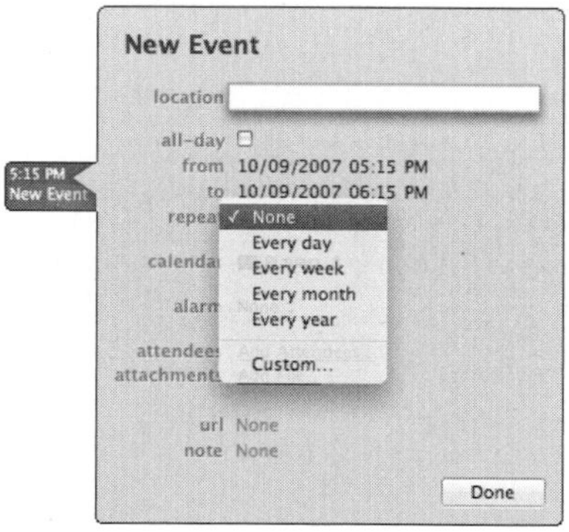

Figure 2-7: The Custom option lets you define multiple days for your event to occur.

Setting an alarm for an event

Scheduling an event is useless if you forget about it. That's why the iCal program gives you the option of setting an alarm that can notify you of upcoming events. To set an alarm, you need to decide how you want the alarm to notify you, such as displaying a message on the screen.

To set an alarm for an event, follow these steps:

1. **Click an event that you want to set an alarm.**
2. **Choose Edit➪Edit Event or press ⌘+E.**

   An edit dialog appears (refer to Figure 2-6).

3. **Click the Alarm pop-up menu.**

   You can choose the following options:

   - *None:* Removes any alarms you have already set for the event.
   - *Message:* Displays a message on the screen to alert you of an event.
   - *Message with Sound:* Displays a message on the screen and plays a sound to alert you of an event.
   - *Email:* Sends an e-mail message to yourself.
   - *Open File:* Loads and displays a file, such as a report that you can review for an upcoming meeting.
   - *Run Script:* Runs an AppleScript file that can control your Mac.

4. **Click in the time pop-up menu to define when you want the alarm to trigger, such as 15 minutes or 1 hour before the event.**
5. **(Optional) Depending on the alarm type you chose, you might have other pop-up menus that appear to let you choose how to use your alarm. Adjust the settings as desired.**
6. **Click Done.**

Moving an event to another calendar

You can always move an event from one calendar to another, such as your Work to Home calendar. To move an event to another calendar, follow these steps:

1. **Click an event that you want to modify.**
2. **Choose Edit⇨Edit Event or press ⌘+E.**

   An edit dialog appears (refer to Figure 2-6).

3. **Click in the Calendar pop-up menu and choose the calendar name in which you want the event to appear.**
4. **Click Done.**

Adding information to an event

To prepare for an event, you can also store information about that event's location, attendees, any important files related to the event (such as a presentation), a Web site address, and any additional notes you want to jot down.

To add information to an event, follow these steps:

1. **Click an event that you want to modify.**
2. **Choose Edit⇨Edit Event or press ⌘+E.**

   An edit dialog appears (refer to Figure 2-6).

3. Choose one or more of the following:

- *Location:* Fill in the Location field to remind yourself where an event will take place.
- *Attendees:* Click in the Attendees field to type the names of people associated with an event.
- *Attachments:* Click the Add link to attach a file to an event, such as a business presentation that you'll need to give at the event.
- *URL:* Click and type a Web site address that's relevant to your meeting, such as a competitor's Web site that you want to talk about during the event.
- *Note:* Click and type any additional notes about your event.

4. Click Done.

Deleting an event

When you no longer need to remind yourself of an event, you can delete it. To delete an event,, just click it and choose Edit⇨Delete. If you delete an event by mistake, press ⌘+Z or choose Edit⇨Undo to retrieve your event.

Finding Events

Storing events is only as useful as the ability to view upcoming events again so you can prepare for them. To help you find and view events, iCal offers several different methods that include using colors to identify different types of events to letting you search for a specific event by name.

Color-coding events

To help identify which events belong to which calendars, you can assign a color to every calendar in your Calendar List. So if you assign the color blue to your Home calendar and the color red to your Work calendar, you can quickly identify which events on your calendar are Home-related (the blue ones) or Work-related (the red ones).

To assign a color to a calendar, click a calendar in the Calendar List and choose File⇨Get Info or press ⌘+I. In the Info dialog that appears (see Figure 2-8), just click the color pop-up menu, click on a color, and click OK. All events stored on that calendar now appear in the color you chose.

REMEMBER

Use contrasting colors for multiple calendars to make it easy to tell which events belong to which calendar.

Figure 2-8: The Info dialog lets you edit a calendar's name and assign it a color.

Selectively hiding events

Normally, iCal displays all events, color-coding them so that you can tell which events belong to which calendars. However, if you have too many events, you might find that mixing Home and Work events can seem too confusing. If you want to see only events stored on a specific calendar (such as Home or Work calendars), you can hide events stored on other calendars.

To hide events stored on other calendars, deselect the check box of any of those calendars in the Calendar List. To view events stored on calendars, make sure a check mark appears in the check box of that calendar, as shown in Figure 2-9.

Checking for today's events

Probably the most important events you need to worry about are the ones you've scheduled for today. To see all events scheduled for today, click the Day or Week button at the top of the iCal window and then choose View➪Go to Today.

TIP: Another quick way to review any upcoming events for today is to use the Calendar widget in Dashboard. To display today's events in the Calendar widget, click the current date (which appears in the left pane) of the Calendar widget until the events pane appears, as shown in Figure 2-10. (For more information about Dashboard, see Book VI, Chapter 4.)

Checking events for a specific date

Sometimes you might need to know whether you have any events scheduled on a certain date. To check a specific date, click the Day or Week button at the top of the iCal window and then choose View➪Go to Date.

REMEMBER: The Month view can show you the events scheduled for a particular date, but the Day and Week views can show you the specific times of your events for that day.

Figure 2-9: Hiding a calendar hides all events stored on that calendar.

Searching for an event

If you scheduled an event several days ago, you might forget the exact date of that event. To help you find a specific event, iCal lets you search for it by typing all or part of the information stored in that event, such as the event name, the attendee names, or any notes you have stored about an event.

To search for an event, follow these steps:

1. **Click in the Spotlight text box in the upper-right corner of the iCal window.**
2. **Type as much text as you can remember about the event you want to find, such as an attendee's name or the location of the event.**

   The iCal program displays a list of events that match the text you typed. The list appears below the calendar, as shown in Figure 2-11.

Figure 2-10: The Calendar widget can show you today's upcoming scheduled events.

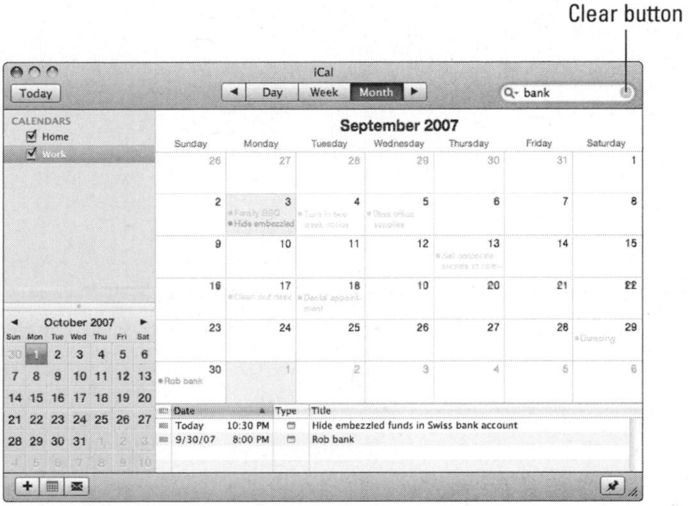

Figure 2-11: Spotlight can help you search and find events.

3. **Double-click an event that Spotlight found.**

   Your chosen event appears.

4. **Click the Clear button in the Spotlight text box to remove the list of matching events from the bottom of the iCal window (or choose View➪Hide Search Results).**

Making a To Do List

A To Do list typically contains goals or reminders of important tasks that you want to accomplish usually by a specific date or time. By reviewing your To Do list every day, you can stay focused on achieving the goals that are most important to you so that you don't waste time accomplishing tasks that won't get you any closer to your goals.

Viewing and hiding the To Do list

You can view your To Do list and then hide it to make more room for viewing your events. To show the To Do list, choose View➪Show To Do List. The To Do list appears on the right side of the iCal window.

To hide the To Do list from view, choose View➪Hide To Do List. This tucks the To Do list out of sight once more. By default, iCal hides the To Do list.

REMEMBER

Another way to hide or display the To Do list is to click the pushpin icon at the bottom-right corner of the iCal window.

Adding tasks to the To Do list

When you add a task to your To Do list, you must assign it to a calendar so that it appears color-coded, like an event. By color-coding your To Do tasks, you can identify which tasks might be Work-related and which might be related to any other calendars you might have created.

To add a task to the To Do list, follow these steps:

1. **Choose View⇨Show To Do List. (Skip this step if the To Do list is already visible.)**
2. **Click a calendar that you want to assign a task to, such as the Work or Home calendar.**
3. **Double-click in any blank space in the To Do list.**

   A blank To Do task appears, color coded to match the calendar you chose in Step 2.
4. **Type a description of your task and press Return.**

   Your chosen task appears in the To Do list.

Setting due dates for your To Do list tasks

It's a good idea to place due dates on your To Do list tasks so that way you'll have a deadline, which can spur you into taking action to achieve your goal. If you don't put a due date on a task, it's much easier to fool yourself into thinking you're working toward your goals when you're really not.

To assign a due date to a To Do task, follow these steps:

1. **Click a task in the To Do List.**
2. **Choose Edit⇨Edit To Do (or press ⌘+E).**

   An edit dialog appears, as shown in Figure 2-12.
3. Select the Due Date check box. When you select the Due Date check box, a date appears so that you can type a month, day, and year for the due date; then click Done.

Prioritizing your To Do list

Not all tasks are equally important. To prioritize your tasks, click the prioritize button that appears to the right of a task in the To Do list. A pop-up menu appears, from which you can choose None, Low, Medium, or High, as shown in Figure 2-13. Then click the To Do pop-up menu (the gray button at the top of the To Do window that contains the text "To Do Items by Priority") and choose Sort By Priority, as shown in Figure 2-13. This option puts your High priority tasks at the top of your To Do List.

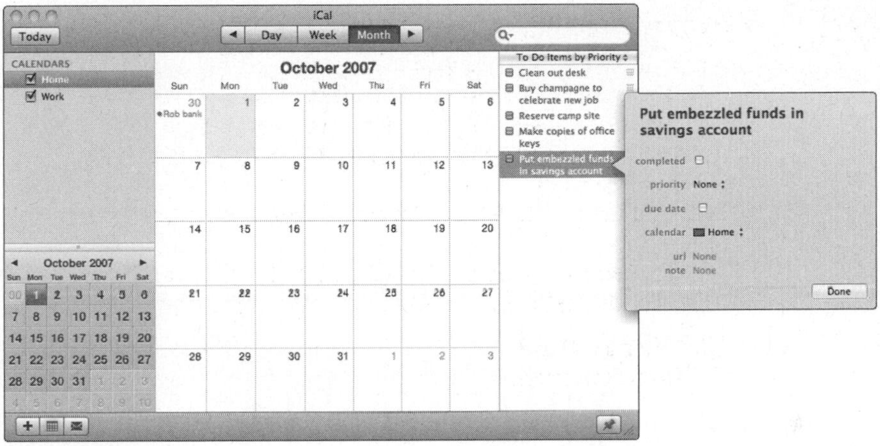

Figure 2-12: The edit dialog lets you modify a To Do task.

Completing, editing, and deleting To Do tasks

Completing tasks can give you a sense of accomplishment. Rather than delete a completed task, you can mark it as complete instead. To mark a task as complete, select the check box that appears to the left of a task in the To Do list.

After you've created a task, you can always edit it later to correct any misspellings or to modify a task. To edit a To Do task, follow these steps:

1. **Double-click a task.**

   An edit dialog appears (refer to Figure 2-12).

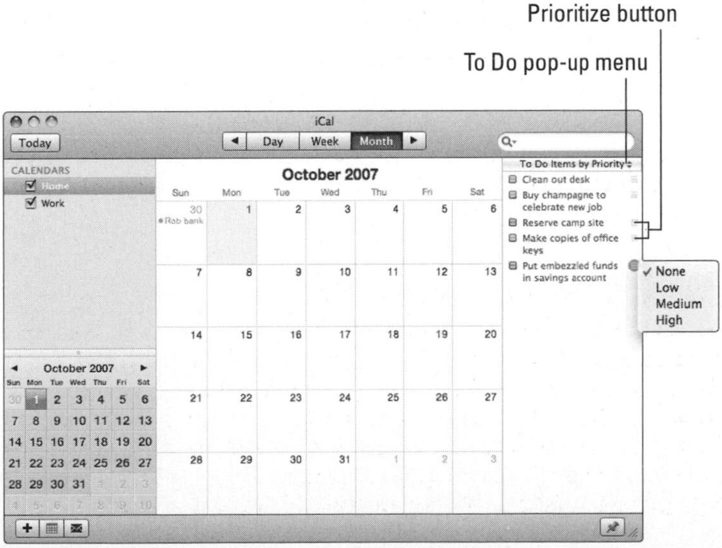

Figure 2-13: If you sort tasks by priority, you can see the most important tasks on your To Do list.

2. **Click in the top text box and type a new description of your task, or use the arrow and Delete key to edit the existing text.**
3. **Click Done.**

When you're done with a task, you'll eventually want to delete it to avoid cluttering up your To Do List. To delete a task, click the task and choose Edit⇨Delete. If you accidentally delete a task, you can retrieve it by pressing ⌘+Z or choosing Edit⇨Undo.

Managing iCal Files

The iCal program stores files in a special file format called iCalendar (which uses the `.ics` file extension). Because the iCalendar file format is considered a standard for storing calendar information, you can share your calendar files with any program that recognizes the iCalendar format, including Microsoft Outlook.

Exporting iCal data

To share your calendars with other programs (even those running on other operating systems such as Windows or Linux), you need to export your iCal file by following these steps:

1. **Choose File⇨Export.**

   A dialog appears, giving you a chance to choose a filename and location to store your iCal data, as shown in Figure 2-14.
2. **Click in the Save As text box and type a name for your file.**
3. **Click the drive and folder where you want to save your exported file.**
4. **Click Export.**

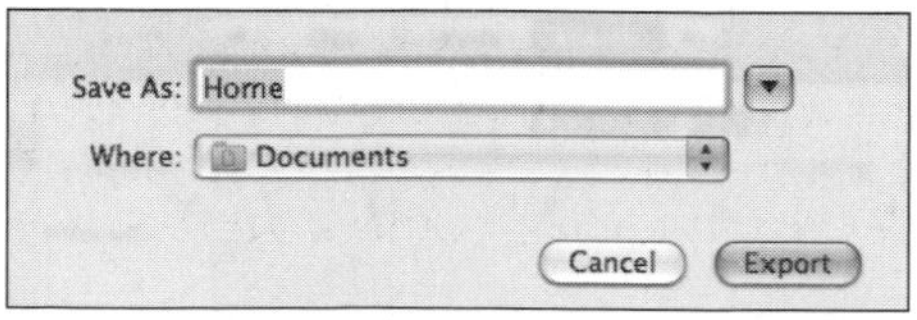

Figure 2-14: To export your calendars, you need to specify a name for your exported file and a location to store it.

Importing iCal data

If you have calendar information stored in another program, you have to save that data as an iCal file or in a vCal file. If you've been using Microsoft Entourage, you can save your Entourage calendar information as a separate file.

After you've saved calendar data from another program, you can import that file into iCal by following these steps:

1. **Choose File➪Import.**

   An Import dialog appears, asking you to define what type of file format you want to import into iCal.

2. **Click a radio button to define the file format, such as Import an iCal File, and click Import.**

   An Import dialog appears, displaying three options for importing iCal, vCal, or Entourage data.

3. **Click the drive and folder that contains the file you want to import.**
4. **Click the file you want to import and click Import.**

   The iCal program imports your chosen file.

Backing up iCal data and restoring a backup file

Because iCal can store all your upcoming events (appointments, meetings, and so on), disaster could strike if your hard drive fails and wipes out your iCal data. For that reason, you should always keep a backup copy of your iCal data. To do so, follow these steps:

1. **Choose File➪Back Up iCal.**

   The Save dialog appears.

2. **Click in the Save As text box and type a descriptive name for your iCal backup file.**
3. **Click the drive and folder where you want to save your iCal backup file.**
4. **Click Save.**

TIP: It's a good idea to save your iCal backup file on a separate drive, such as an external hard drive. That way if your Mac hard drive fails, you won't lose both your original iCal data and your backup file at the same time. For more details on backing up files, see Chapter 1 of this minibook.

To retrieve your schedule from a backup file that you created earlier, choose File➪Restore iCal. In the Open dialog that appears, click the drive and folder where you saved your backup iCal file. Then click Open. A dialog appears, asking whether you want to replace your current iCal data with the contents of the backup file. Click Restore, and your backup data now appears in iCal.

Printing an iCal file

Even if you have a laptop, you can't always have your computer with you, so you might want to print your calendar in the Day, Week, or Month view. That way you can review it during the day and make sure you're sticking to your schedule.

To print a calendar, follow these steps:

1. **Choose File⇨Print.**

   A Print dialog appears, as shown in Figure 2-15.

2. **Click the View pop-up menu and choose Day, Week, or Month.**

3. **(Optional) Change any other settings, such as the paper size or time range that you want to view.**

4. **Click Continue.**

   Another Print dialog appears.

6. **Click the Printer pop-up menu, choose a printer, and click Print.**

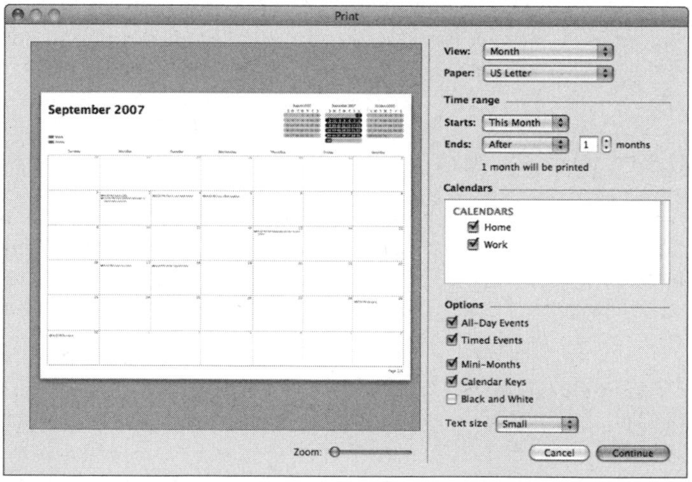

Figure 2-15: The Print dialog shows you how your calendar will appear on paper.

Chapter 3: Storing Contact Information in the Address Book

In This Chapter

- **Storing names in Address Book**
- **Organizing names in groups**
- **Managing your Address Book**

Most people write down important names and contact information in an address book, but your Mac comes with an electronic version called (surprise!) the Address Book. Besides storing names and contact information, the Address Book also connects with other programs so that you can click someone's e-mail address and immediately write and send a message to that person.

The Mac Address Book also lets you search through stored names and print them as mailing labels or lists, which is impossible to do with a paper address book. So the next time you need to store names and contact information, you'll find it's much easier to store this data in the Address Book on your Mac.

Storing Names

The Address Book acts like a giant Rolodex file that can hold names and contact information including e-mail addresses, telephone numbers, and postal addresses in separate windows referred to as *cards*. When you save information about a person on a card, you can find that information again.

Designing a template

Each time you add a name, the Address Book displays blank fields, with each field representing information to fill in about that person, such as company, first and last name, title, and e-mail address. You might not want or need to store all that information about everyone, so you can define the Address Book template to list only the fields you want to use, such as name and e-mail address. To modify the Address Book template, follow these steps:

1. **Start the Address Book program by clicking the Address Book icon in the Dock.**

   If the Address Book icon doesn't appear in the Dock, you have to double-click the Address Book icon inside the Applications folder.

2. **Choose Address Book⇨Preferences.**

   A Preferences window appears.

3. **Click the Template icon.**

   The Template window appears, as shown in Figure 3-1.

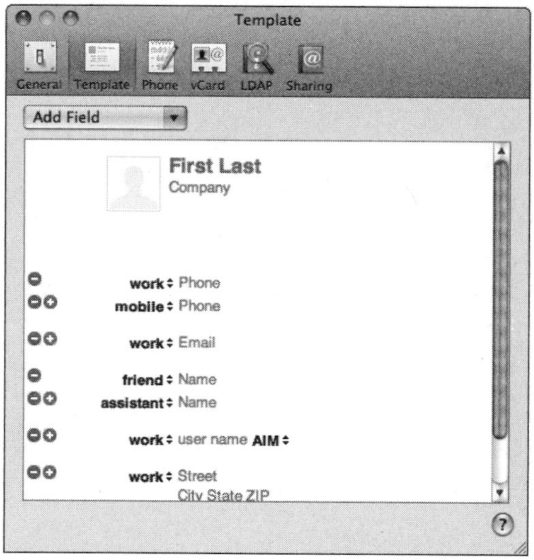

Figure 3-1: The Template window shows all the fields that you can store.

4. **Find a field you don't want to store and click the minus sign to the left of the field to remove it, repeating this for every field you want to remove.**

5. **Click in the Add Field menu and choose a field to add, such as URL or Birthday (see Figure 3-2), repeating this for each field you want to add.**

6. **(Optional) Click the Phone icon to make the Phone window appear, as shown in Figure 3-3.**

7. **Click in the Formats pop-up menu, choose the way you want your phone numbers to appear, and click the Close button of the Phone window.**

8. **Click the Close button of the Template window.**

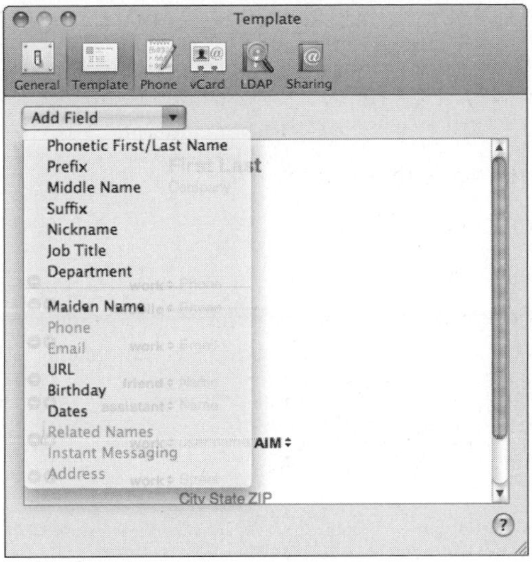

Figure 3-2: The Add Field menu provides additional fields you can add to a template.

The template defines only the fields you know you want to use for storing names you'll save in the Address Book. You can always add fields to individual cards later.

Figure 3-3: The Phone window defines a specific format for displaying telephone numbers.

Storing names

After you've defined a template for your Address Book, the next step is to store actual names and contact information. To add a name, follow these steps:

1. **Choose File⇨New Card.**

   The Address Book window displays a blank card for you to fill in, as shown in Figure 3-4.

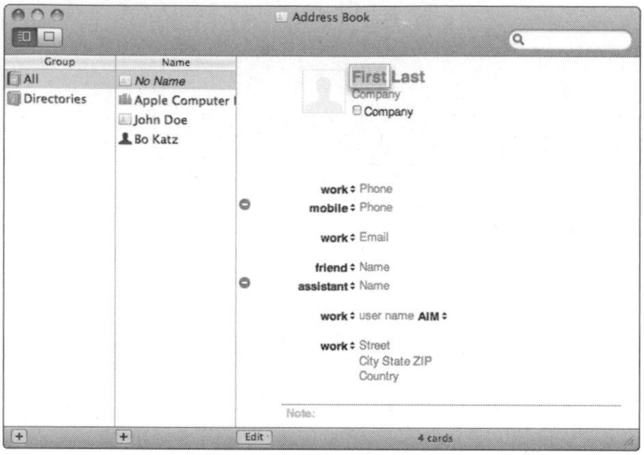

Figure 3-4: Adding a new name means filling out a blank card.

2. **Click in the fields, such as Name or Telephone Number, and enter the information you want to save.**

   You don't need to fill in every field.

3. **Click the Edit button at the bottom of the Address Book window to save your new card.**

Displaying companies and people

You have two ways to display a person's card: by the person's name or by company name. To help you differentiate between company and people names, the Address Book displays different icons to the left of each name, as shown in Figure 3-5.

REMEMBER

One card, identified by the My Card icon, always represents your own information. To define a different card to represent you, click that card and choose Card➪Make This My Card. To view your card at any time, choose Card➪Go to My Card.

When you create a new card, the Address Book assumes that you want to display that card by a person's name. To make a card appear in the Address Book by company name instead, click the card and choose Card➪Mark as a Company. Your chosen card now displays a company name and icon. To change a company back into a person's name, choose Card➪Mark as a Person.

Editing a card

Information on cards will need to change whenever people change their address or company. To keep this information up to date, you can edit a card by following these steps:

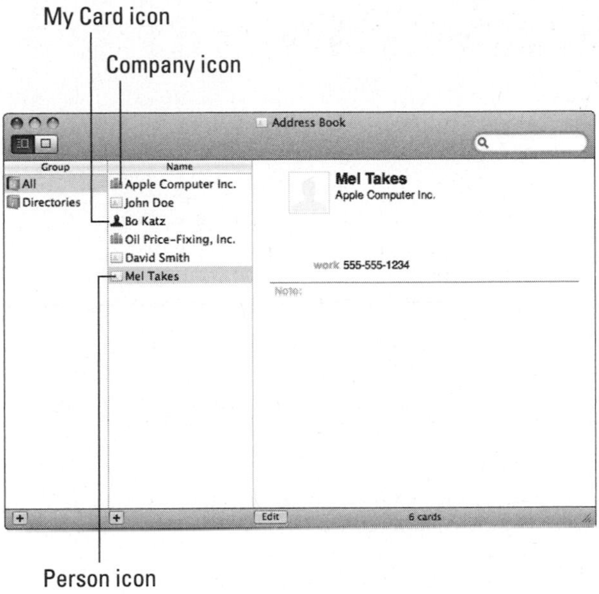

Figure 3-5: Icons identify companies and people.

1. **Click the All group under the Group category in the Address Book window and then click the name you want to edit.**

   You might need to scroll down if you have a long list of stored names.

2. **Click the Edit button near the bottom of the Address Book window.**

3. **Click in the field in which you want to type or edit information, such as an e-mail address or phone number.**

4. **(Optional) Choose Card⇨Add Field to choose a field to add on a card, as shown in Figure 3-6.**

   After you add a field to a card, you need to type information into that field.

5. **Click the Edit button again.**

   Address Book saves your data.

Adding pictures to a name

To help yourself remember certain people or companies, you can include a picture, either a photograph of that person or a symbolic image that reminds you about that person (such as a cartoon devil's face for a particularly troublesome client). To add a picture to a card, follow these steps:

1. **Click the name for which you want to include a picture.**

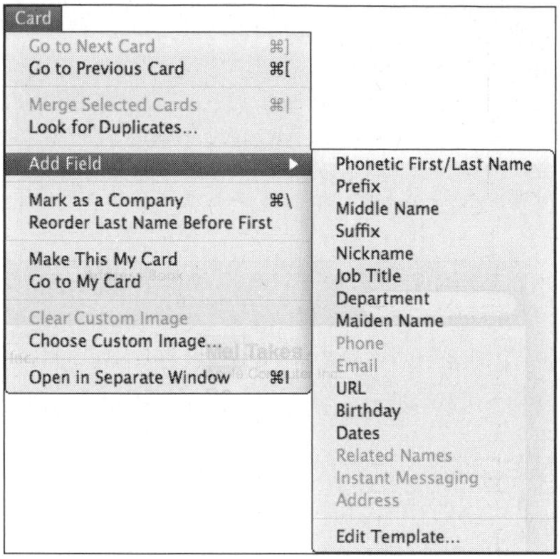

Figure 3-6: The Add Field submenu lets you add a new field that appears only on the currently displayed card.

2. **Choose Card⇨Choose Custom Image.**

   A dialog appears, as shown in Figure 3-7, allowing you to take a picture by using the built-in iSight camera or to choose a picture file stored on your hard drive.

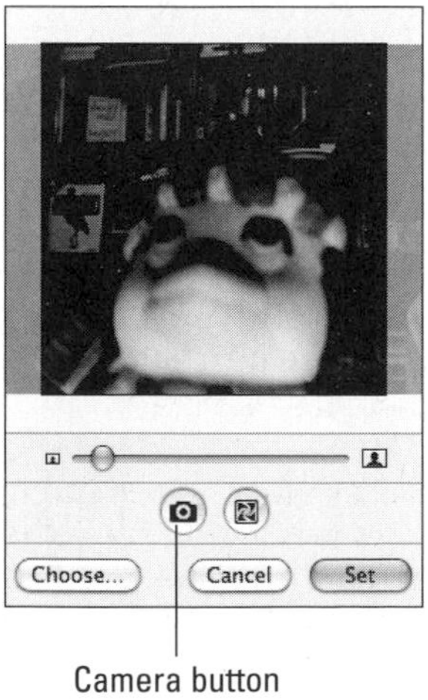

Figure 3-7: You can add a picture to a card by choosing a picture file or taking a picture through the iSight camera.

3. **Click the Camera button to take a picture or click the Choose button to select a picture file.**
4. **Click the Set button when you're happy with your chosen image.**

Searching names

The more names you store in your Address Book, the harder it can be to find the name you want. Rather than scrolling through and searching for names yourself, you can search for specific names by following these steps:

1. **Click in the Spotlight text box in the upper-right corner of the Address Book window.**
2. **Type a word or phrase that you want to find, such as a person's name or company that person works for.**

   The Address Book displays a list of cards that match the text you typed.
3. **Click a name to display all the information about that person or company.**

Deleting a name

Periodically, you should browse through your Address Book and prune the names of people you don't need to save any more. To delete a name from your Address Book, just click the name and choose Edit➪Delete Card. If you accidentally delete a name, press ⌘+Z or choose Edit➪Undo to restore it.

TIP

If you hold down the ⌘ key, you can click and choose multiple names to delete. If you hold down the Shift key, you can click two names and select those two names and all names in between as well.

Creating Groups

To help you find all the names you've stored, the Address Book program lets you organize your list of names into groups, such as for your co-workers, friends, family members, political party associates, and so on. For greater convenience, you can even store the same name in multiple groups. Although you don't have to use groups, this feature can help you manage your list of important names and contact information.

REMEMBER

Your Address Book initially contains two groups: All and Directories. The All group automatically stores all names you've saved in the Address Book. The Directories group contains a list of names of everyone connected to a local area network. If you're using a Mac at home without a local area network, the Directories group will be empty.

Creating a group

You can create as many groups as you want, but each time you create a new group, you have to add names to that group. To create a new group,, just choose File➪New Group. When the decidedly generic "Group Name" appears in the Address Book window, type a more descriptive name in its place and press Return.

A new group will, of course, initially be empty until you start adding names to it. To add names to a group, follow these steps:

1. **Click the All folder in the Group column to see all the names stored in your Address Book.**
2. **Move the cursor over a name, hold down the mouse button, and drag the cursor over the group name where you want to store your names.**

   If you hold down the ⌘ key, you can click and choose multiple names. If you hold down the Shift key, you can click two noncontiguous names to select those two names and all names in between as well.
3. **Release the mouse button when the group name appears highlighted.**

   Your chosen name now appears in your newly created group and in the All group.

Creating a group from a selection of names

If you already have a group of names you want to organize, you can create a new group and store those names at the same time. To create a new group from a selection of names, follow these steps:

1. **Click the All folder in the Group column to see all the names stored in your Address Book.**
2. **Hold down the ⌘ key and click each name you want to store in a group.**

   You can select a range of names by holding down the Shift key and clicking two noncontiguous names. Doing so selects those two names and all names in between.
3. **Choose File⇨New Group from Selection.**

   A group called plain old "Group Name" appears under the Group category in the Address Book window.
4. **Type a more descriptive name for your group and press Return.**

   Your group now contains the names you selected in Step 2.

Adding names automatically with Smart Groups

Adding names manually or selecting them for a group is fine, but what if you frequently add and delete names? Doing all this manually can get old. To more easily keep your group's names accurate and up to date, you can use the Smart Group feature instead.

With a Smart Group, you define the types of names you want to store, such as names of everyone who works at a certain company. Then the Smart Group automatically adds and removes any names you add to or remove from your Address Book.

To create a Smart Group, follow these steps:

1. **Choose File⇨New Smart Group.**

   A dialog appears, asking for a name and rule for storing names in the group automatically, as shown in Figure 3-8. A *rule* lets you store names based on certain criteria. For example, you might want to store the names of all people who work for Apple and live in Texas.

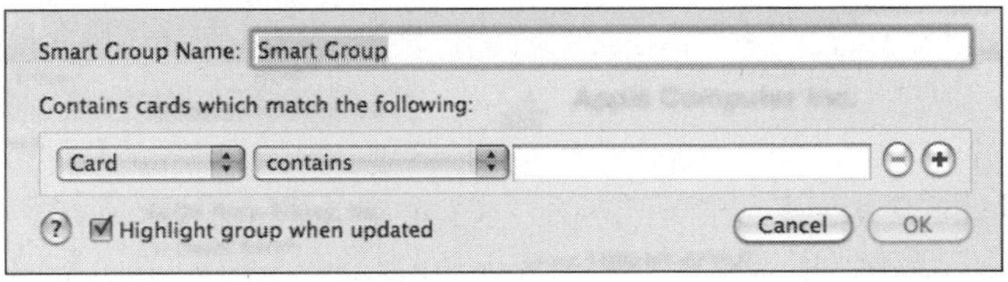

Figure 3-8: A dialog appears for defining a name and rule for creating a Smart Group.

2. **Click in the Smart Group Name text box and type a descriptive name for your Smart Group.**
3. **Click in the first pop-up menu and choose the criteria for including a name in your Smart Group, such as Company or City, as shown in Figure 3-9.**

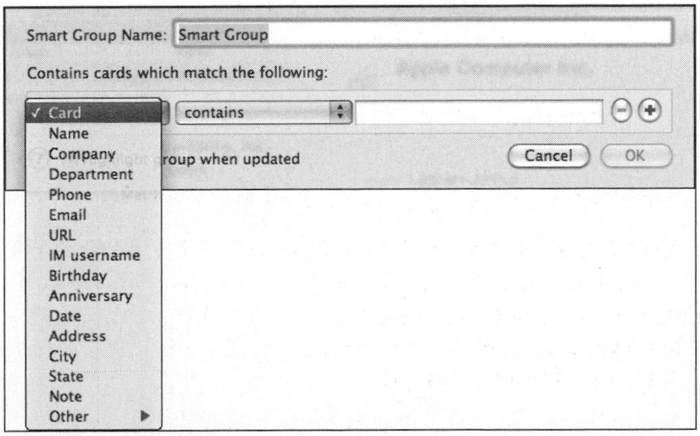

Figure 3-9: The first pop-up menu defines the criteria for storing names in your Smart Group.

4. **Click in the second pop-up menu and choose how to use your criteria defined in Step 3, such as "contains" or "was updated after."**
5. **Click in the text box and type a word or phrase for your criteria to use.**

   For example, if you want to create a Smart Group that stores only names of people who work at Apple, your entire Smart Group rule might look like "Company contains Apple," as shown in Figure 3-10.

Figure 3-10: A fully defined rule describes the types of names to add in a Smart Group automatically.

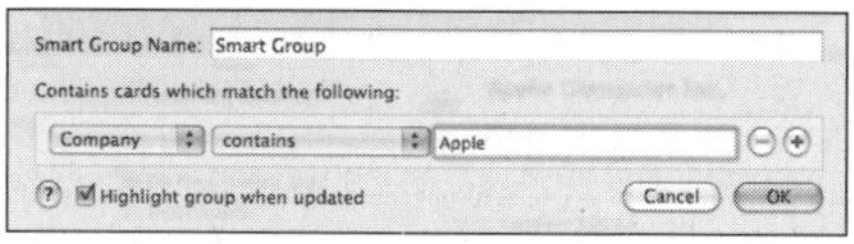

6. **(Optional) Click the plus sign to the right of the text box to create any additional rules.**

   If you create any additional rules and then decide you don't want them, you can always remove them by clicking the minus sign that appears near the rule.
7. **Click OK.**

Creating a Smart Group from search results

Defining the criteria for automatically storing names into a Smart Group can be cumbersome because you aren't quite sure whether your defined criteria will work exactly the way you want. As an alternative, you can use Spotlight to search for the types of names you want to store and then create a Smart Group based on your Spotlight search results. By doing this, you can see exactly which types of names appear in your Smart Group.

To create a Smart Group from Spotlight search results, follow these steps:

1. **Click in the Spotlight text box in the upper-right corner of the Address Book window, type the text you want to find, such as the name of a company or part of an e-mail address, and press Return.**

   The middle pane of Address Book shows the names found by the text you typed into Spotlight.

2. **Choose File⇨New Smart Group from Current Search.**

   A Smart Group appears in the Group category, using the text you typed as the group name.

Deleting a Group

If you've created a group and no longer need it, you can delete it. When you delete a group, you delete only the group folder, but you do not delete any names stored in that group. To delete a group, click the group and then choose Edit⇨Delete Group.

Managing Your Address Book Files

Eventually, your Address Book can hold so many important names and contact information that you can't afford to risk losing this information. One way to preserve your contact information is to print your entire Address Book. Another way is to store copies of your Address Book in other locations so that you always have access to your important names and contact information, even if your Mac's hard drive gets wiped out.

Printing your Address Book

The Address Book lets you print all or some of your contact information in different formats, such as mailing labels or cards that you can carry with you. To print your Address Book, follow these steps:

1. **Use one of the following methods to select the names you want to print:**
   - ✦ Click one name.
   - ✦ Hold down the ⌘ key and click multiple names.
   - ✦ Hold down the Shift key, click a name, and then click another name elsewhere in the list. Selecting these two names highlights them both, along with all names in between.
   - ✦ To print all names stored in a group, click the group name, and then choose Edit⇨Select All or press ⌘+A.
2. **Choose File⇨Print.**

   A Print dialog appears.
3. **Expand the Print dialog by clicking the down arrow that appears to the right of the Printer pop-up menu.**

   You see before you the expanded Print dialog, as shown in Figure 3-11.

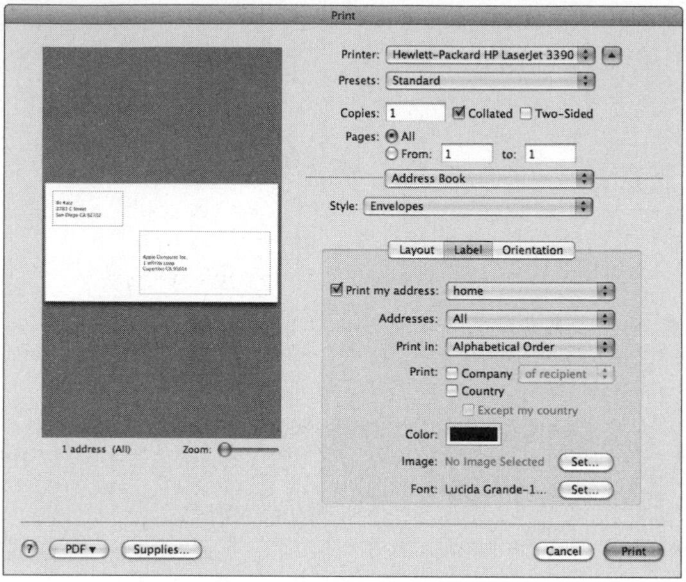

Figure 3-11: The expanded Print dialog lets you choose how to print your selected names.

4. **Click in the Printer pop-up menu and choose a printer to use.**
5. **Click in the Styles pop-up menu and choose one of the following:**
   - *Mailing Labels:* Prints names and addresses on different types of mailing labels.
   - *Envelopes:* Prints names and addresses on envelopes fed into your printer.
   - *Lists:* Prints your Address Book in a long list.
   - *Pocket Address Book:* Prints your Address Book in a condensed form suitable for carrying with you.

   REMEMBER

   Depending on the style you choose in this step, you might need to pick additional options, such as defining the specific size of your mailing labels or choosing whether to print names in alphabetical order.
6. **Click Print.**

Exporting your Address Book

Sometimes you might need to share your contact information with others. To save one or more names from your Address Book into a file that other programs and people can use, you export your data to a vCard or archive format. A vCard is a standard format that many programs use to store contact information. By storing your data as a vCard, you can copy information to another program and computer, such as a Windows PC running Outlook.

If you need to share contact information with another Mac user, you can save your Address Book data as an archive file or as a vCard file.

To export names from your Address Book, follow these steps:

1. **Select the names you want to export by using one of the following methods:**
   - Click one name.
   - Hold down the ⌘ key and click multiple names.
   - Hold down the Shift key, click a name, and then click another name elsewhere in the list. Selecting these two names highlights them both, along with all names in between.
   - To print all names stored in a group, click the group name and then choose Edit⇨Select All or press ⌘+A.
2. **Choose File⇨Export.**

   A submenu appears.
3. **Choose Export vCard or Address Book Archive.**

   A Save dialog appears, asking for a name for your exported data and a location.
4. **In the Save dialog, click in the Save As text box and type a descriptive name for your file.**
5. **Click in the Where pop-up menu and choose a folder in which to store your file.**
6. **Click the Save button.**

REMEMBER

When exporting data for use in another program, you might lose some information, such as a person's picture or notes you've written down about that person.

Importing data into your Address Book

Other people might have important contact information that you want. To allow you to import this information, they need to export and save the data in one of four file formats:

- **vCards:** Standard file format used to store contact information and used by programs on different types of computers
- **LDIF:** Standard data interchange file format that stands for LDAP Data Interchange Format

- **Text File:** Ordinary ASCII text file format that all computers can understand
- **Address Book Archive:** Standard Address Book file format, useful for transferring data between Macs using Address Book

To import data into your Address Book, follow these steps:

1. **Choose File⇨Import.**

   A submenu appears, as shown in Figure 3-12.

Figure 3-12: The Import submenu lets you specify a file type.

2. **Choose vCards, LDIF, Text File, or Address Book Archive.**

   An Import dialog appears.

3. **Click the file you want to import and click Open.**

   The Address Book displays your newly imported names.

Chapter 4: Using Dashboard

In This Chapter

- Viewing Dashboard widgets
- Adding and removing widgets
- Finding and installing more widgets

Many programs cram so many features that each succeeding program version gets more bloated and harder to use. If you just want to perform a simple task, such as adding a few numbers together, you probably don't need to load a complicated program like a spreadsheet. Instead, you'd be better off using a much simpler program specifically designed to solve a single task.

That's the idea behind Dashboard. Dashboard provides you with quick access to a collection of small, single-task programs called widgets. Some typical widgets display a calendar, weather forecasts for your city, a calculator, stock market quotes, and movie times for your neighborhood movie theaters.

Widgets are designed to simplify your life, and Dashboard is the program that helps you display, manage, and hide widgets. By using Dashboard, you can be more productive without having to learn an entirely new program to do so.

Getting to Know Your Dashboard Widgets

To view your widgets, you open Dashboard by pressing the F12 key or clicking the Dashboard icon on the Dock. When you're done using a widget, you close it (and the Dashboard) the same way: by pressing F12.

As soon as you open Dashboard, you see several widgets pop into view, as shown in Figure 4-1. The default widgets that appear are the calendar, clock, calculator, and weather widgets.

The calendar widget lets you view dates for different months and years. The clock widget displays the current time in a big clock, which can be easier to read than the tiny time display in the right end of the menu bar. The calculator widget acts like a typical four-function calculator, and the weather widget offers forecasts for different cities.

By opening Dashboard, you can check the weather, punch some numbers into the calculator, check the time, or verify which day a particular date falls on. After you've used a widget, you can hide Dashboard and all its widgets out of sight once more.

Many widgets, including the weather forecasting widget, rely on an Internet connection to work. If you aren't connected to the Internet when you display such a widget, the widget can't display the latest information.

Moving a widget

If you don't like the position of your widgets on the screen, you can always move them to a new location. To move a widget, just click it and drag it to its new position.

Customizing a widget

Some widgets always appear the same way, such as the Calculator widget. Other widgets let you customize them to change their appearance or the type of data it displays. To customize a widget, follow these steps:

1. **Press the F12 key to open Dashboard and display all your widgets.**
2. **Move the mouse over a widget you want to customize.**

   If you can customize the widget, an *i* button (the Information button) appears in the widget's bottom-right corner, as shown in Figure 4-2.

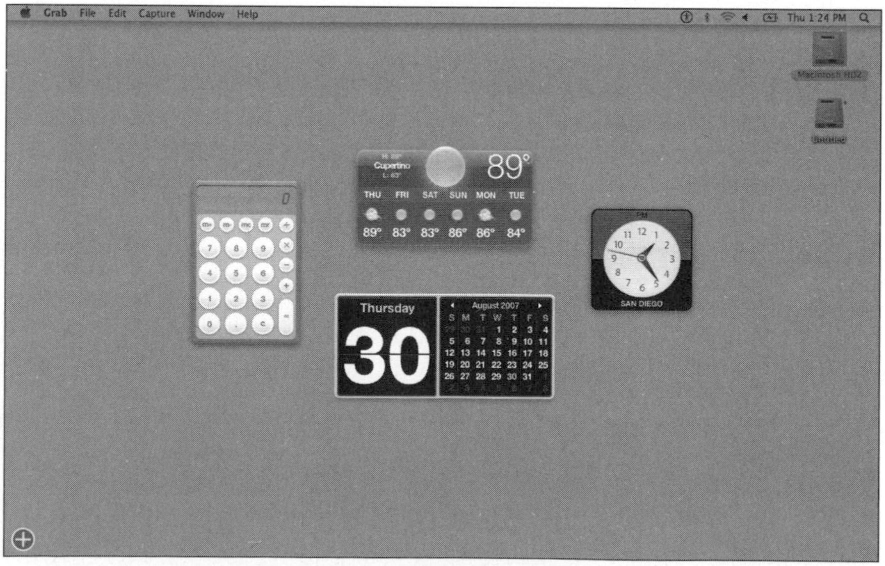

Figure 4-1: Dashboard displays widgets that appear over any programs currently running.

Figure 4-2: An Information button lets you know you can customize a widget.

3. **Click the Information button.**

   The widget spins around and displays various options you can change, as shown in Figure 4-3.

Figure 4-3: A widget with an Information button displays options you can modify.

4. **Make any changes to the widget and click Done.**

   The widget spins around again and displays your changes.

Customizing the Dashboard shortcut key

By default, every Mac uses the F12 function key to open and close Dashboard. If you want to change this (or any other shortcut key, for that matter — just click a different shortcut in Step 4 if desired), you can do so by following these steps:

1. **Click the Apple menu and choose Preferences.**

   A Preferences window appears.

2. **Click the Keyboard & Mouse icon under the Hardware category.**

   The Keyboard & Mouse window appears.

3. **Click the Keyboard Shortcuts button.**

   A list of keyboard shortcuts appears, as shown in Figure 4-4.

4. **Double-click the Dashboard shortcut.**

   The Dashboard shortcut key appears highlighted.

5. **Press the new shortcut key you want to use.**

   Your new shortcut key appears in the Keyboard Shortcuts column.

6. **Click the Close button of the Keyboard & Mouse window.**

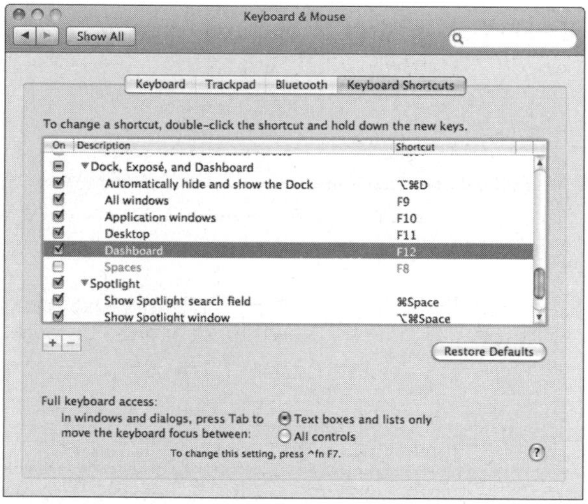

Figure 4-4: The list of Keyboard Shortcuts shows which keys have been assigned to specific tasks.

Adding and Removing Widgets

When you open Dashboard, you'll see several widgets, even if you actually want to use just one widget. In case you don't want to see a particular widget, you can have to remove it from Dashboard. (Don't worry; you can always put it back on Dashboard again.)

Removing a widget from Dashboard

When you remove a widget from Dashboard, you don't physically delete the widget. Instead, you just tuck the widget in storage where you can retrieve it again later. To remove a widget from Dashboard, follow these steps:

1. **Press F12 to open Dashboard and display all your widgets.**

2. **Click the plus sign button that appears inside a circle in the bottom-left corner of the screen.**

   Dashboard displays Close buttons on the upper-left corner of every widget on the screen as shown in Figure 4-5.

If you move the pointer over the widget you want to remove and hold down the Option key, a Close button appears in the upper-right corner of just that one widget.

3. **Click the Close button of the widget you want to remove.**

   Your chosen widget disappears.

4. **Press F12 or click anywhere on the screen except on another widget to close Dashboard.**

Removing a widget doesn't delete that widget from your computer; it just keeps that widget from popping up every time you open Dashboard.

Making a widget appear in Dashboard

When you open Dashboard, you see only a handful of all possible widgets in Dashboard's library of widgets. (You can always download additional widgets off the Internet if you want.)

Table 4-1 lists all of Dashboard's available widgets that you can choose to display every time you open Dashboard, as shown in Figure 4-6.

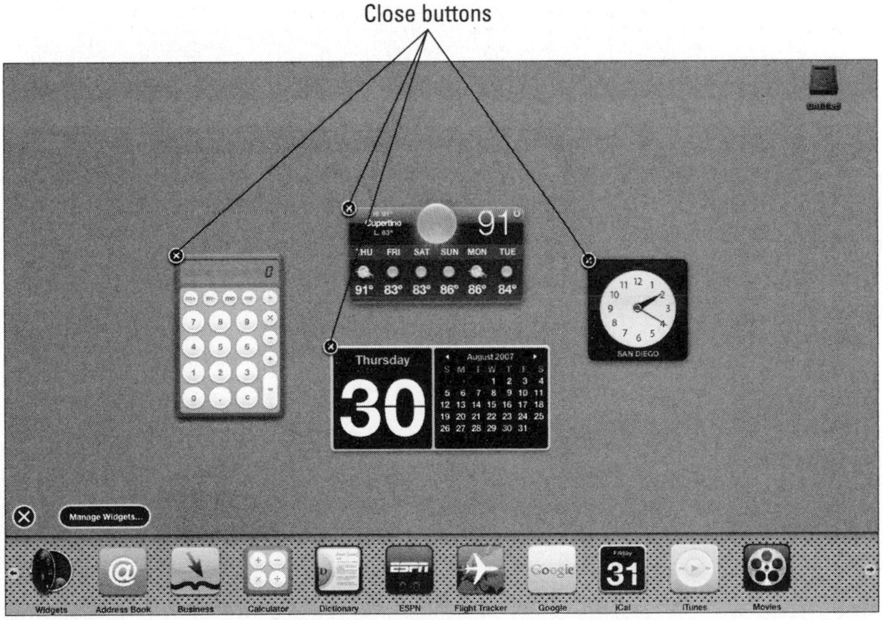

Figure 4-5: Close buttons let you remove any widgets you no longer want to see.

Table 4-1 Dashboard's Library of Widgets

Widget	*What It Does*
Address Book	Lets you search for names stored in your Address Book
Business	Displays a Yellow Pages directory for looking up business names and phone numbers
Calculator	Displays a four-function calculator
Dictionary	Displays a dictionary and thesaurus for looking up words
ESPN	Displays sports news and scores
Flight Tracker	Tracks airline flights
Google	Displays a text box to send a query to Google and display the results in Safari
iCal	Displays a calendar and any appointments stored within iCal
iTunes	Lets you Pause, Play, Rewind, or Fast Forward a song currently playing in iTunes
Movies	Displays which movies are playing at which times at a certain ZIP code
People	Displays a White Pages directory that lets you search for a person's name and address to find his or her telephone number
Ski Report	Displays the temperature and snow depth at your favorite ski resort
Stickies	Displays color-coded windows for jotting down notes
Stocks	Displays stock quotes
Tile Game	Displays a picture tile game in which you slide tiles to recreate a picture
Translation	Translates words from one language to another, such as Japanese to French
Unit Converter	Converts measurement units, such as inches to centimeters
Weather	Displays a weather forecast for your area
Web Clip	Displays parts of a Web page that you've clipped from Safari (see Book III, Chapter 1 for more information about creating Web Clips)
World Clock	Displays the current time

To add a widget to Dashboard, follow these steps:

1. **Press F12 to open Dashboard.**

   All your widgets pop up on the screen.

2. **Click the plus sign button that appears inside a circle in the bottom-left corner of the screen.**

   Dashboard displays its list of widgets at the bottom of the screen (refer to Figure 4-5).

3. **Click a widget that you want to display in Dashboard, such as ESPN or Stocks.**

   Your chosen widget appears on the screen.

4. **Move the cursor over the widget, hold down the mouse button, and drag the cursor to move the widget on the screen where you want it to appear. Release the mouse button.**

5. **Press F12 or click anywhere on the screen except over a widget.**

   All your widgets disappear. The next time you open Dashboard, your newly added widgets appear on the screen.

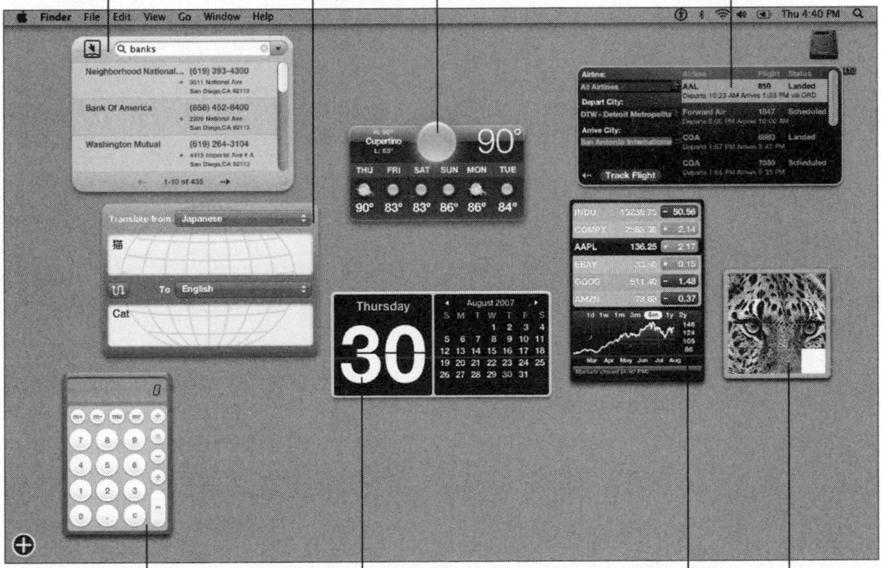

Figure 4-6: Dashboard widgets can display a wide variety of information.

Finding New Widgets

Dashboard comes with a library of widgets, but people are always creating more, which they often store on Apple's Web site. To find the latest widgets, follow these steps:

1. **Visit Apple's Web site (`www.apple.com/downloads/dashboard`) using your favorite browser (such as Safari).**

   The widget download page appears, listing the most popular widgets.

2. **Scroll down the Web page until you see the Widget Browser, shown in Figure 4-7.**

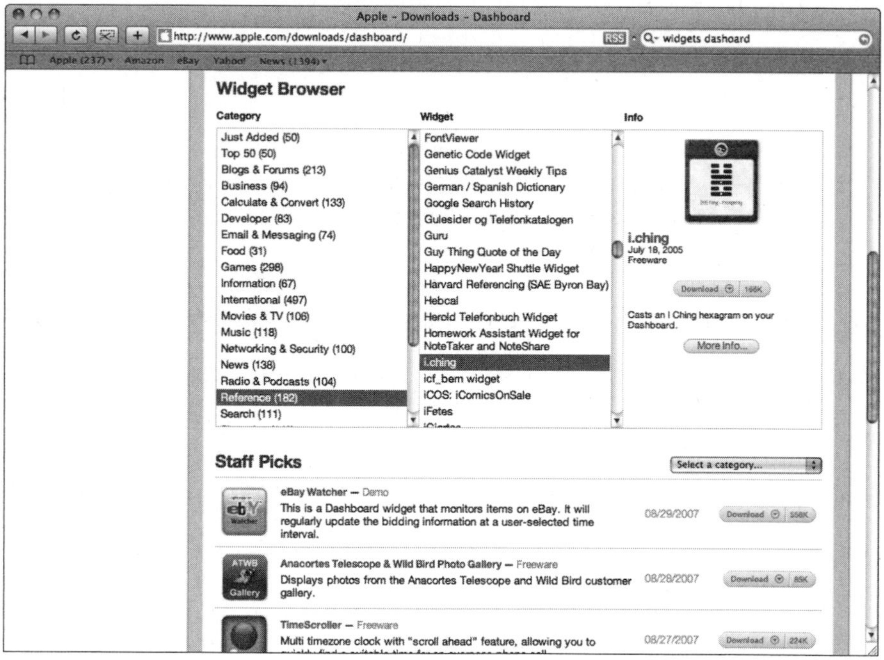

Figure 4-7: Apple's Web site organizes widgets by category.

3. **Click a category such as Business, Food, or Games.**

   A list of available widgets appears in the middle pane.

4. **Click a widget in the middle pane.**

   The right pane displays details about that particular widget.

5. **Click the Download button of a widget that you want to download.**

   Your Mac downloads your chosen widget and displays a dialog, asking whether you want to install your newly downloaded widget in Dashboard, as shown in Figure 4-8.

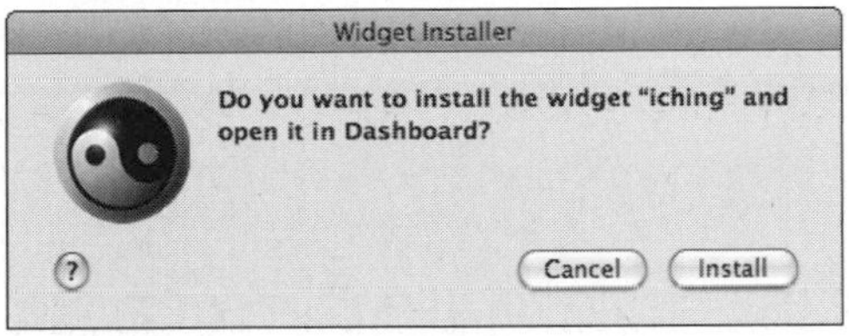

Figure 4-8: After you download a widget, you can install it in Dashboard right away.

6. **Click the Install button.**

   Dashboard appears and displays your widget on the screen. You might want to move it to a new location.

Disabling and Deleting Widgets from Dashboard

If you keep installing new widgets, eventually your list of available widgets can get crowded and overwhelming. To reduce the number of available widgets, you can disable or delete them.

Disabling a widget hides it from view but keeps it stored on your hard drive in case you change your mind and later decide to display it after all. Deleting a widget physically removes it from your hard drive.

You can't delete the original set of widgets that come with Dashboard. You can delete only widgets that you've downloaded and installed on Dashboard. (See the previous "Finding New Widgets" section for more about downloading new widgets.)

Disabling a widget

To disable a widget and temporarily remove it from view, follow these steps:

1. **Press F12 to open Dashboard.**

   Your widgets appear on the screen.

2. **Click the plus sign that appears in a circle in the bottom-left corner of the screen.**

   A Manage Widgets button appears.

3. **Click the Manage Widgets button.**

   A list of installed widgets appears, as shown in Figure 4-9.

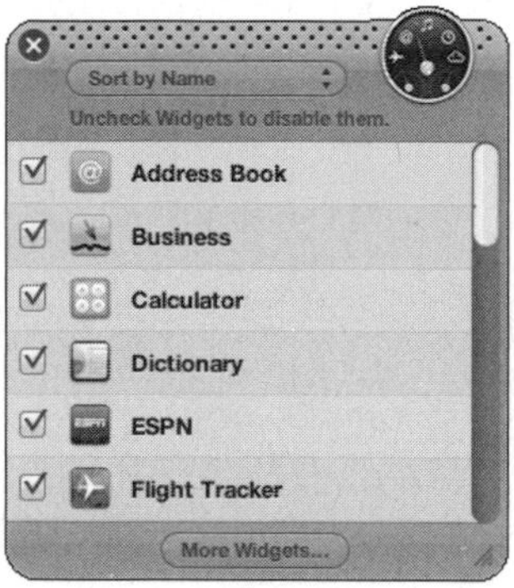

Figure 4-9: A window lists all installed widgets with a check box next to each one.

4. **Select or deselect a check box in front of a widget.**

   If its check box is deselected, the widget is disabled and won't be available for display through Dashboard. (If a widget is already displayed through Dashboard, deselecting its check box prevents the widget from appearing anymore.)

5. **Click the Close button of the Manage Widgets window.**

6. **Press F12 or click anywhere on the screen except over a widget to exit the Dashboard.**

Deleting a widget

You cannot delete any widgets that came with Dashboard, but you can delete any widgets that you downloaded and installed (see the "Finding New Widgets" section, earlier in this chapter, for more about downloading additional widgets). To delete a widget, follow these steps:

1. **Press F12 to open Dashboard.**

   Your widgets appear on the screen.

2. **Click the plus sign that appears in a circle in the bottom-left corner of the screen.**

   A Manage Widgets button appears.

3. **Click the Manage Widgets button.**

   A list of installed widgets appears (refer to Figure 4-9).

4. **Click the minus sign that appears to the right of a widget you want to delete.**

   A dialog appears, asking whether you really want to move the widget to the Trash, as shown in Figure 4-10.

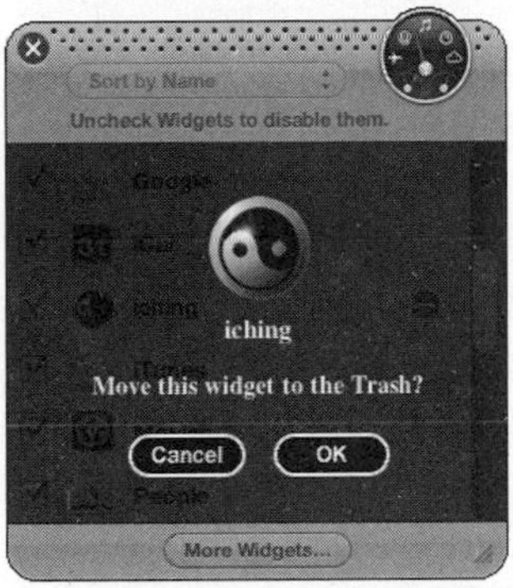

Figure 4-10: A dialog appears if you try to delete a widget.

5. **Click the Close button of the Manage Widgets window.**
6. **Press F12 or click anywhere on the screen except over a widget to exit the Dashboard.**

If you have an idea for a cool widget, you can try creating one yourself by using the free Dashcode program. (You might need to install Dashcode off your Mac OS X 10.5 installation disc, or you can download Dashcode off Apple's Web site at `www.apple.com/macosx/developer`.) Dashcode provides templates to help you create a widget. Who knows? With a little bit of creativity and a little help from Dashcode, you could create the next widget that appears on Apple's Web site one day.

Chapter 5: Automating Your Mac

In This Chapter

- Getting to know Automator
- Understanding actions
- Exploring sample Automator workflows
- Creating Automator programs

Computers are supposed to make your life easier, but too often, they complicate life unnecessarily. Many times you might need to perform a repetitive task, such as renaming a batch of digital photographs every time you copy them off your digital camera. Although such a task is trivial, it's also tedious and time consuming.

Fortunately, your Mac can carry some of these burdens for you automatically through a feature called Automator. With Automator, you can program your Mac to perform specific tasks that you don't want to do yourself.

Understanding Automator

Automator lets you choose from a library of predefined tasks, called *actions,* which tell specific programs on your Mac what to do. By stringing these actions together, you can create simple programs that can, for example, retrieve a Web page and read the text out loud, or rename groups of files automatically.

Automator organizes its library of actions into the categories:

- **Calendar:** Adds, deletes, or retrieves items from iCal.
- **Contacts:** Finds and retrieves names from the Address Book.
- **Files & Folder:** Manipulates items within the Finder.
- **Fonts:** Adds, retrieves, and deletes fonts from the Font Book.
- **Internet:** Retrieves Web pages from the Internet using Safari.
- **Mail:** Finds and retrieves messages from Mail.

- **Movies:** Plays, converts, or retrieves images using iDVD, DVD Player, and QuickTime Player.
- **Music:** Manipulates songs in iTunes and on an iPod.
- **PDF:** Renames, searches, converts, and retrieves data from PDF files.
- **Photos:** Manipulates digital photographs.
- **Presentations:** Plays and displays slides in a Keynote presentation.
- **Text:** Manipulates text within the TextEdit program.
- **Utilities:** Provides a variety of tasks for burning CDs/DVDs and running or quitting programs. Also contains the Watch Me Do task, which lets you record mouse and keyboard actions.
- **Other:** Provides tasks for manipulating Keynote and other programs that work with Automator, such as Omni Outliner.

Actions need to accept input. So, for example, if you create an action that retrieves a Web page off the Internet, its input would be a specific Web site address, such as `www.dummies.com`. You can also make an action more flexible, such as by having it ask a user for input or retrieve input from another action.

After an action receives input, it does something with that input, such as renaming files a certain way or running a program. Many actions also create some form of output, which can be used by another action as input. Figure 5-1 shows two simple actions. The first action, Get Specified Text, retrieves a chunk of text. The second action, Speak Text, uses a computer-synthesized voice to read the text.

Actions link together based on compatible input and output. An action that produces text as output can link to another action that accepts text as input. However, an action that produces text as output won't link properly to another action that accepts a PDF file as input. The output from one action must always be compatible with the input of another action. If the output and input of two actions aren't compatible, Automator won't display the connecting input and output links between actions.

When using Automator, you'll need to understand the Automator user interface. The left pane displays Automator's library of actions. By clicking on a library, the middle pane lists specific actions stored in that library.

Clicking on an action displays a brief description in the bottom left corner of the Automator window. The right pane is where you drag and drop actions to link actions together and form a complete Automator program. The specific order that you arrange actions to create your program is called a *workflow.*

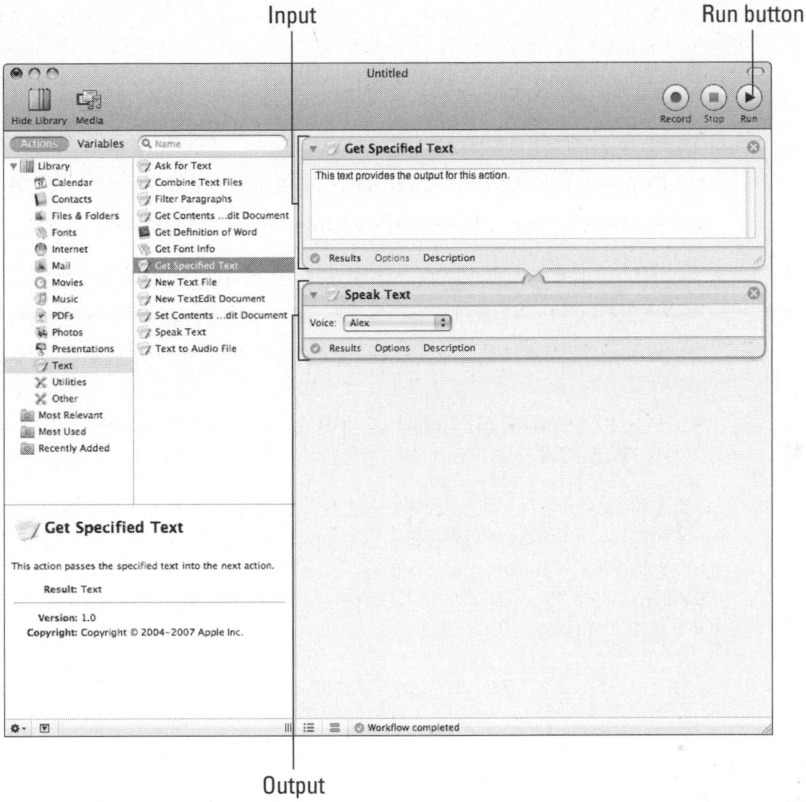

Figure 5-1: Actions link together when one action creates output that another action uses as input.

Understanding Actions

To create a workflow, you need to arrange actions together. However, even though Automator provides many different types of actions, not every action can link together. To help you understand the variety of actions available, actions typically work with one of four types of objects:

- ✦ Files and folders
- ✦ Music (audio) files
- ✦ Digital photographs
- ✦ Text

To work on different objects such as text or digital photographs, each type of action automates a specific type of program on your Mac, such as the Finder, iTunes, iPhoto, Safari, iCal, or TextEdit program.

Actions either retrieve data or process the data that another action retrieved. Actions can retrieve data by asking the user when the workflow runs. This method gives the workflow the flexibility to work with different types of data, but it adds the inconvenience of not running completely automatically without user intervention.

A second way actions can retrieve data is by having you specify exactly what type of data the action should use, such as a specific file. This method lets your workflow run without any intervention from you, but you lose the flexibility of working with different data unless you modify the action within Automator.

Some examples of actions that retrieve data are as follows:

- **Find Sources in iTunes:** Lets you define which songs or playlists to use and outputs the song or playlist.
- **Get Specified URLs:** Retrieves a Web page from a specific URL, such as `www.dummies.com` or `www.whitehouse.gov`, and outputs the Web page.
- **Ask for Text:** Displays a dialog so the user can enter an answer and outputs this answer.
- **Get Specified Finder Items:** Retrieves the name of a file or folder and outputs the name of a file or folder.

Actions that retrieve data must then pass that data to another action that actually processes that data. Some actions that process data then create output for another action to use. Other actions simply accept input and then do something with that input, such as playing a specific song in iTunes or rotating a digital photograph.

The following are some examples of actions that process data:

- **Play iTunes Playlist:** Accepts a playlist name and starts playing the songs in that playlist.
- **Get Text from Webpage:** Accepts a Web page, retrieves the text off that Web page, and outputs this text.
- **Speak Text:** Accepts text and reads this text in a computer-synthesized voice.
- **Rename Finder Items:** Accepts the name of a file or folder and changes that name.

Eventually, every workflow needs to end with an action that does something to data. In the preceding list, the Get Text from Webpage action accepts a Web page as input and sends the text of that Web page out as output. You can't end a workflow with this particular action because it doesn't do anything useful that you can see or hear. However, you can retrieve text from the first Web page on Apple's Web site and link the Get Text from Webpage action to the Speak Text action, which reads all text from Apple's Web page, as shown in Figure 5-2.

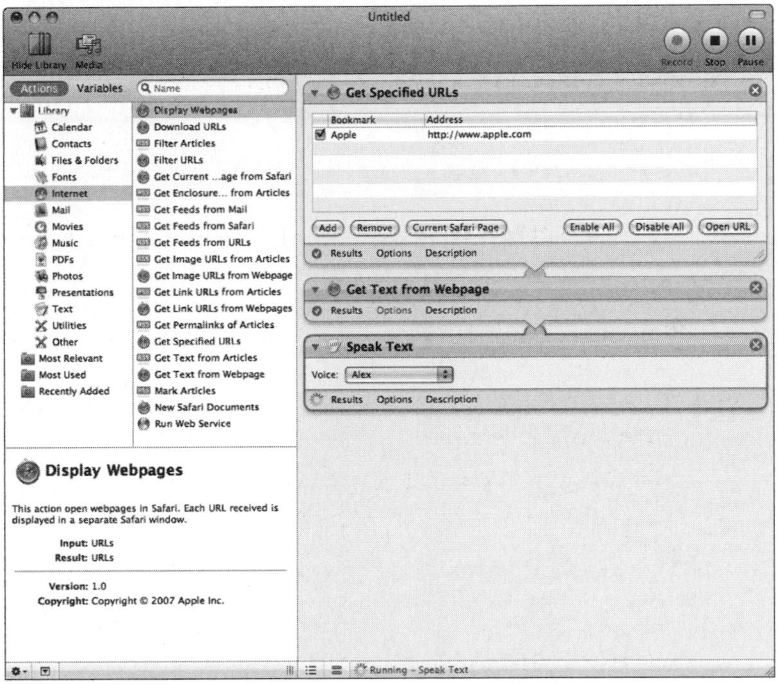

Figure 5-2: An action that processes data can output that data to an action that actually does something with that data.

Creating a workflow

The first step to creating a workflow is to pick an action that retrieves data. To help you get started, you can have Automator create an initial action, or a *starting point action,* for your workflow by following these steps:

1. **Double-click the Automator icon in the Applications folder to load Automator. (If Automator is already running, choose File⇨New.)**

   A dialog appears, letting you choose the type of data you want to manipulate, such as files, music, photos, or text, as shown in Figure 5-3.

2. **Click an icon such as Files & Folders or Text.**

   A list of options appears, as shown in Figure 5-4.

   REMEMBER

   If you click the Custom icon, Automator displays its window without any starting point action at all.

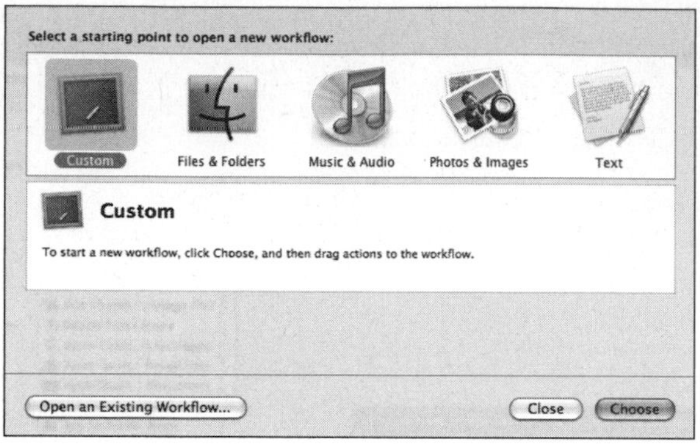

Figure 5-3: Automator provides a variety of starting points for creating a workflow.

3. **Select the different options for your chosen starting point and click Choose.**

   The Automator window appears and displays your first action, as shown in Figure 5-5.

The Get Content From pop-up menu lets you define where to retrieve data, such as from a specific iTunes playlist or from a dialog asking the user to type in text. The second pop-up menu offers variations on the choice you picked from the Get Content From pop-up menu, such as asking you to type in text right now or asking the user for text when the workflow runs.

A starting point action displays pop-up menus or other ways to choose different options for retrieving data. In comparison, if you place an action that processes data as your first action in a workflow, that action won't display any choices at all, because it expects to receive data from another action.

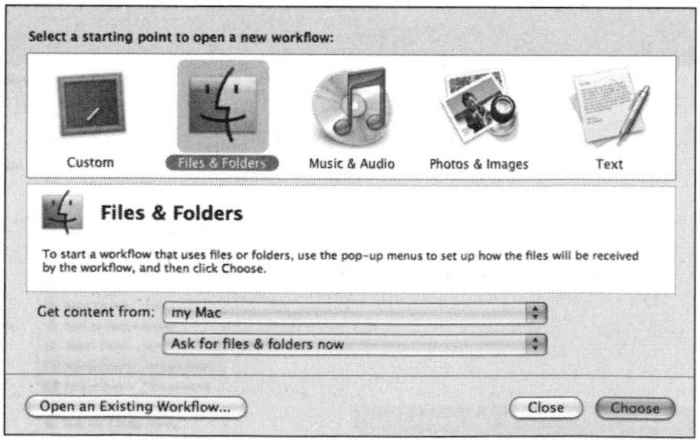

Figure 5-4: Every starting point action needs to know where to find data.

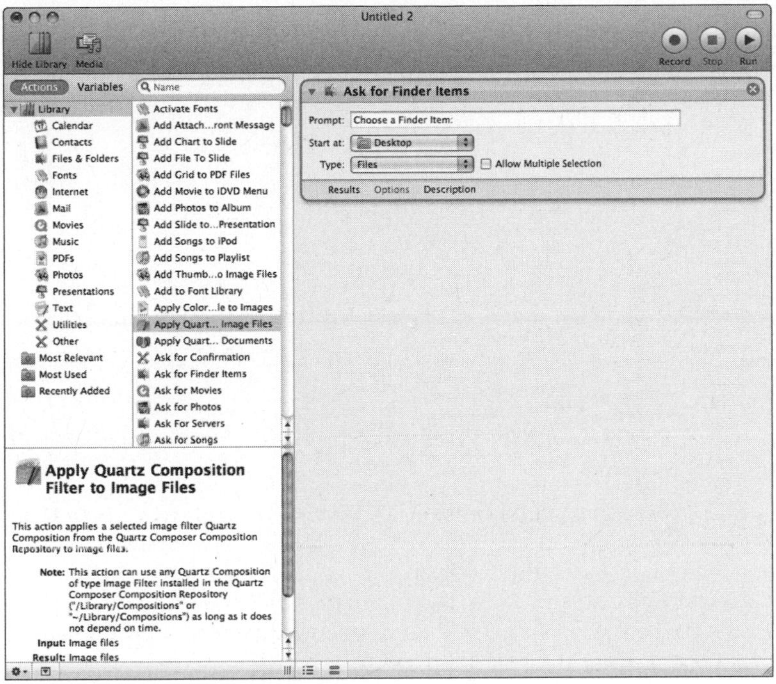

Figure 5-5: The first action typically lists options for retrieving data.

The first action in a workflow must give you choices for defining where to find specific data. If an action doesn't give you choices for defining how to get data, you can't use that action as the first action of your workflow.

Adding, rearranging, and deleting actions

After you select an action that starts your workflow by retrieving data, you need one or more actions that process that data. To add an action to a workflow, follow these steps:

1. **Click a library in the left pane of the Automator window, which contains the action you want to choose.**

   (If you need an action that works with Text, click the Text library. If you need an action that involves the Internet, click the Internet library.) A list of actions, stored in your chosen library, appears in the middle pane of the Automator window.

   Click Library to view all available actions listed in alphabetical order.

2. **Move the cursor over an action you want to use in the middle pane, hold down the mouse button, and drag the cursor over the right pane of the Automator window, underneath or above another action.**
3. **Release the mouse button.**

In case you placed an action in the wrong location, you can move an action to a new location by dragging it with the mouse or clicking the action and choosing Action➪Move Up (or Move Down).

To delete an action, click its Close button. If you delete an action by mistake, press ⌘+Z or choose Edit➪Undo.

Running and testing a workflow

After you've arranged multiple actions into a workflow, you can test your workflow to make sure it actually works the way you want. To run a workflow, you have two choices:

- ✦ Click the Run button or choose Workflow➪Run.
- ✦ Choose Workflow➪Step.

If you run a workflow, Automator runs through every step in your workflow. If you choose Workflow➪Step, Automator runs one action at a time. To run each additional action, you have to choose Workflow➪Step.

The main reason for using the Step command is to en sure that each action is doing exactly what you want at each step of your workflow. If an action can't run for some reason, Automator displays an error message as shown in Figure 5-6.

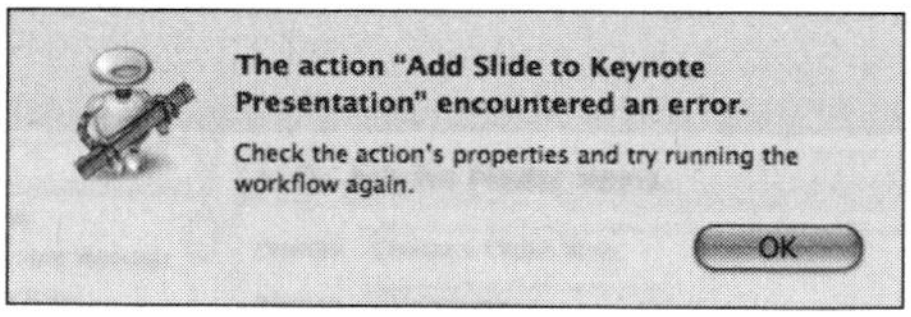

Figure 5-6: If an action can't run because it's not receiving the proper input, an error message appears.

To fix problems with your workflow, you might need to delete the faulty action and replace it with another one, or you might need to add another action that outputs the proper data that the other action can accept as input.

Saving a workflow

For any file in any program you work on, remember this motto: Save early and save often! To save a workflow, follow these steps:

1. **Choose File⇨Save.**

   A Save As dialog appears.

2. **Click in the Save As text box and type a descriptive name for your file.**
3. **Click in the Where pop-up menu and choose a folder in which to store your file.**
4. **Click Save.**

Opening a saved workflow

After you've saved a workflow, you can open it again by following these steps:

1. **Double-click the Automator icon in the Applications folder to load Automator if it's not already open.**
2. **Click Open an Existing Workflow. (You can also choose File⇨Open to open an existing workflow.)**

   An Open dialog appears.

3. **Click the workflow file you want to open and click Open.**

Creating Example Workflows

Trying to piece together actions to create a workflow can get frustrating if you don't know how different actions might work. To create your own workflows more easily, study the following examples that manipulate text, digital photographs, and files.

REMEMBER: As you can see by browsing through Automator's libraries, there are dozens of other types of actions that involve different types of programs such as iCal or Address Book. Just experiment with creating workflows out of different actions, and you'll gradually discover more ways to control your Mac than you ever thought possible.

Playing with text

The following workflow consists of three actions, as shown in Figure 5-7:

- **Get Specified URLs:** Asks for a URL (such as `www.cnn.com`) and retrieves the Web page from that site.
- **Get Text from Articles:** Retrieves the text of RSS feeds.

- **New TextEdit Document:** Displays the text of the RSS feeds in a TextEdit document that you can read or print.

REMEMBER

RSS feeds are summarized headings and text that describe new content on a Web page. By reviewing RSS feeds from a Web site, people can decide whether they want to visit that Web site to read the complete article.

To create this workflow, follow these steps:

1. **Double-click the Automator icon in the Applications folder to load Automator.**

   A dialog appears (refer to Figure 5-1).

2. **Choose Custom⇨Choose.**

   The Automator window appears.

3. **Click the Internet library in the left pane of the Automator window.**
4. **Move the cursor over the Get Specified URLs action, hold down the mouse button, and drag the cursor over the right pane of the Automator window.**
5. **Release the mouse button.**

   The Get Specified URLs action appears as shown in Figure 5-8.

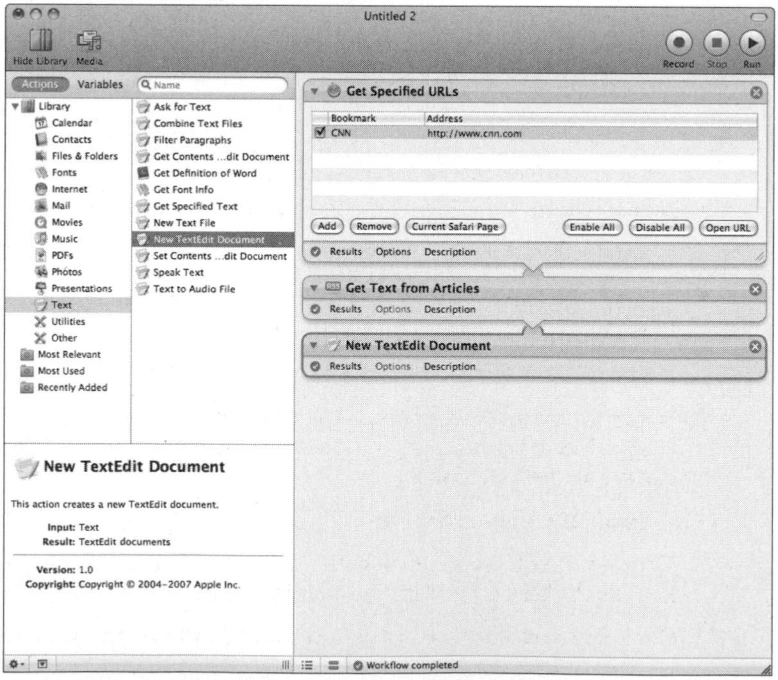

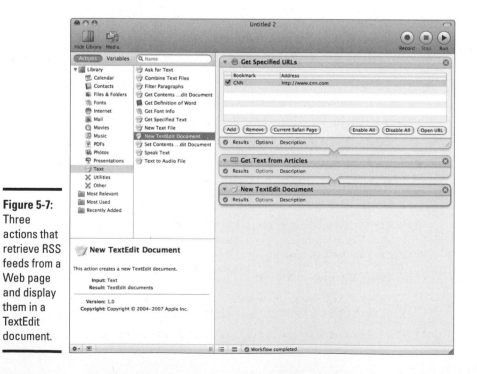

Figure 5-7: Three actions that retrieve RSS feeds from a Web page and display them in a TextEdit document.

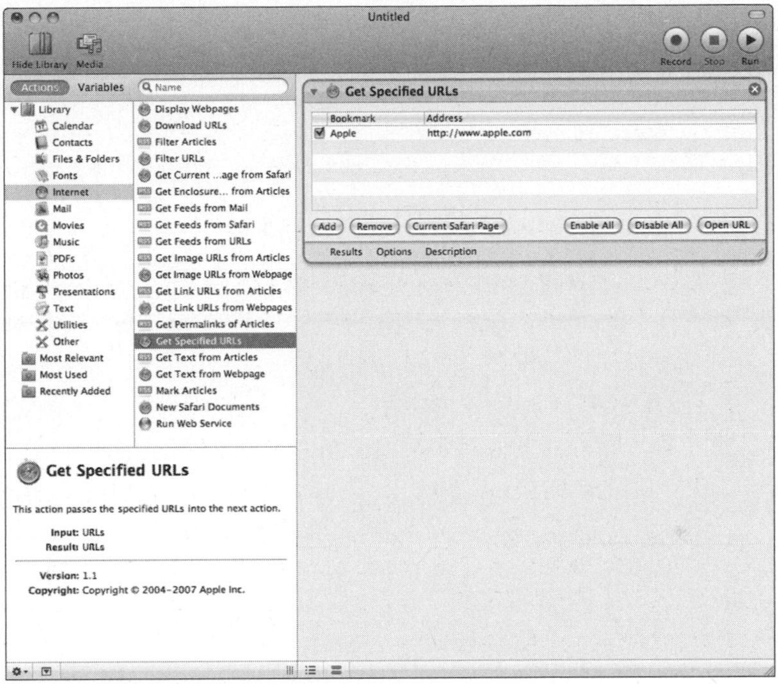

Figure 5-8: The Get Specified URLs action lets you define a specific Web site that contains RSS feeds.

6. **Double-click Apple under the Bookmark category.**

   Automator highlights Apple.

7. **Type** CNN **(or the name of any Web site that offers RSS feeds) under the Bookmark category.**

   This replaces "Apple" with "CNN."

8. **Double-click the `http://www.apple.com` address.**

   Automator highlights the entire URL address.

9. **Type** http://www.cnn.com **under the Address category and press Return.**

   This replaces "http://www.apple.com" with "http://www.cnn.com."

10. **Move the cursor over the Get Text from Articles action, hold down the mouse button, and drag the cursor underneath the Get Specified URLs action in the right pane.**

11. **Release the mouse button.**

    The Get Text from Articles action appears directly underneath the Get Specified URLs action and connects the two actions together.

12. **Click the Text library in the left pane of the Automator window.**

13. **Move the cursor over the New TextEdit Document action, hold down the mouse button, and drag the cursor underneath the Get Text from Articles action.**

14. **Release the mouse button.**

    All three actions appear connected in a workflow.

15. **Click the Run button or choose Workflow⇨Run.**

    A TextEdit document appears, containing the text from the RSS feeds taken from the CNN Web site, as shown in Figure 5-9.

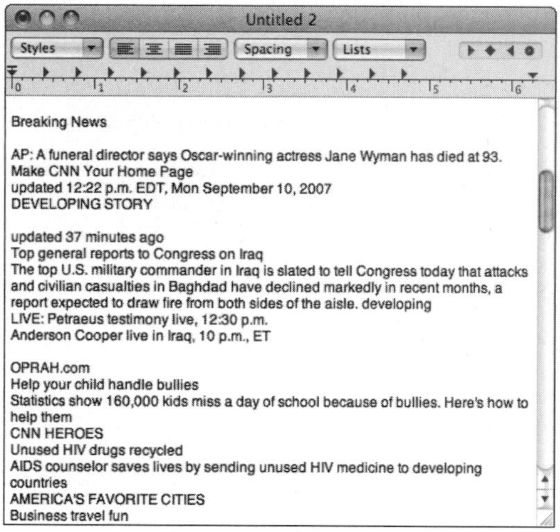

Figure 5-9: Your workflow yanks RSS feed text off the CNN Web page and stores it in a TextEdit document.

16. **Choose TextEdit⇨Quit TextEdit.**

    A dialog appears, asking whether you want to save your workflow.

17. **Click Save or Don't Save.**

    If you click Save, you need to give your workflow a descriptive name.

Playing with digital photography

The following workflow consists of three actions, as shown in Figure 5-10:

REMEMBER

- **Take Video Snapshot:** Captures and saves your picture using the built-in iSight camera.

  If your Mac doesn't have a built-in iSight camera, you can also plug in a USB webcam or a video camcorder through a FireWire cable.

  Flip Images: Flips an image horizontally or vertically.

  Open Images in Preview: Displays your flipped image in a window.

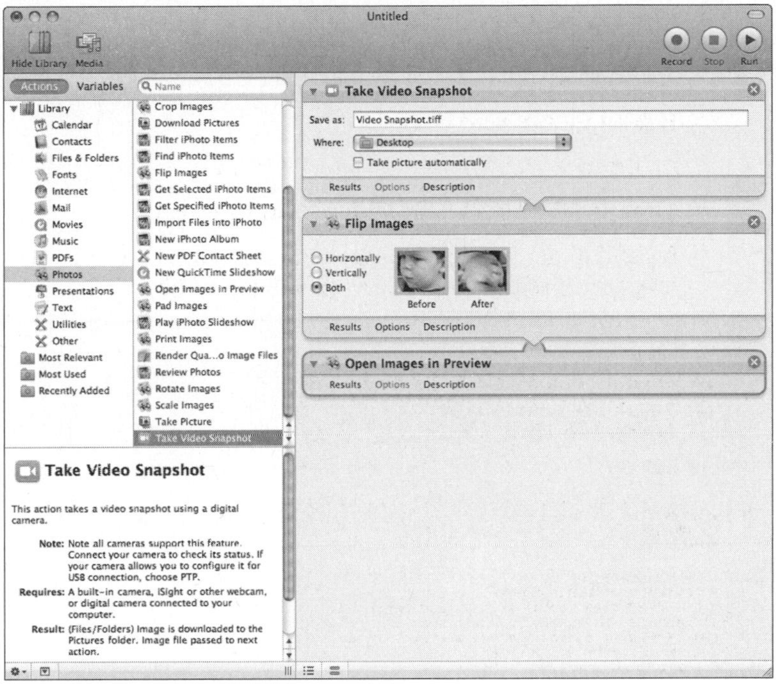

Figure 5-10: Three actions that take your picture, flip it upside-down, and then display it on the screen.

Here are the steps to build the workflow:

1. **Double-click the Automator icon in the Applications folder to load Automator.**

   A dialog appears (refer to Figure 5-1).

2. **Click Photos & Images.**

   Two pop-up menus appear, as shown in Figure 5-11.

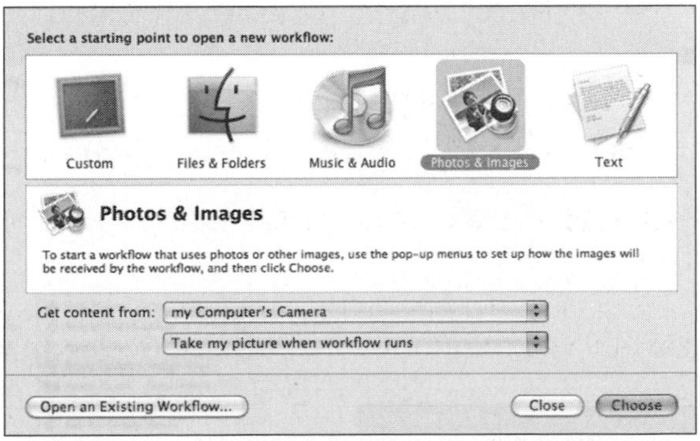

Figure 5-11: With a starting point action, you must define the data to retrieve.

3. **Click in the Get Content From pop-up menu and choose My Computer's Camera.**
4. **Click in the second pop-up menu and choose Take My Picture When Workflow Runs.**
5. **Click the Choose button.**

   The Automator window displays the Take Video Snapshot action.

   Instead of clicking Photos & Images in step 2, you can click Custom in Step 2 to add the Take Video Snapshot action into the workflow manually from the Photos library.
6. **Click the Photos library in the left pane.**
7. **Move the cursor over the Flip Images action, hold down the mouse button, and drag the cursor underneath the Take Video Snapshot action.**

   A dialog appears, asking whether you want to make copies of your pictures before flipping them.
8. **Click Don't Add.**

   The Flip Images action appears underneath the Take Video Snapshot action.
9. **Click the Both radio button in the Flip Images action.**
10. **Move the cursor over the Open Images in Preview action, hold down the mouse button, and drag the cursor underneath the Flip Images action.**
11. **Click the Run button.**

    Your workflow takes your picture and displays the flipped picture in a Preview window.

Playing with files

The following workflow consists of three actions, as shown in Figure 5-12:

- **Get Specified Finder Items:** Selects a file or folder on your hard drive.
- **Copy Finder Items:** Copies a file or folder to an existing folder on your hard drive.
- **Rename Finder Items:** Lets you specify how to rename a file using the date or time to help identify a file.

These steps create the example workflow:

1. **Double-click the Automator icon in the Applications folder to load Automator.**

   A dialog appears (refer to Figure 5-1).

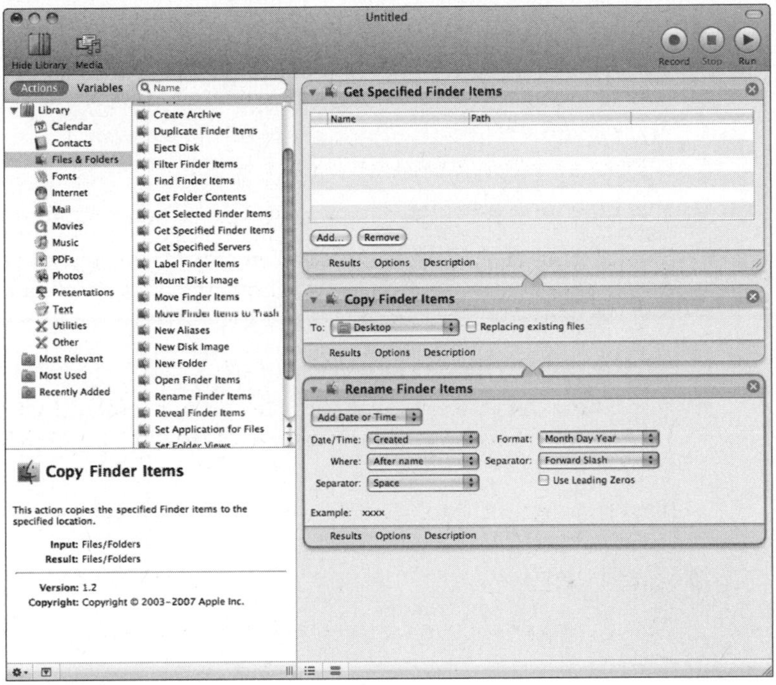

Figure 5-12: Three actions that take a file, copy the file to the Desktop, and then rename that copy of the file.

2. Click Files & Folders.

Two pop-up menus appear, as shown in Figure 5-13. The first pop-up menu reads My Mac, and the one below it reads Ask for Files & Folders Now.

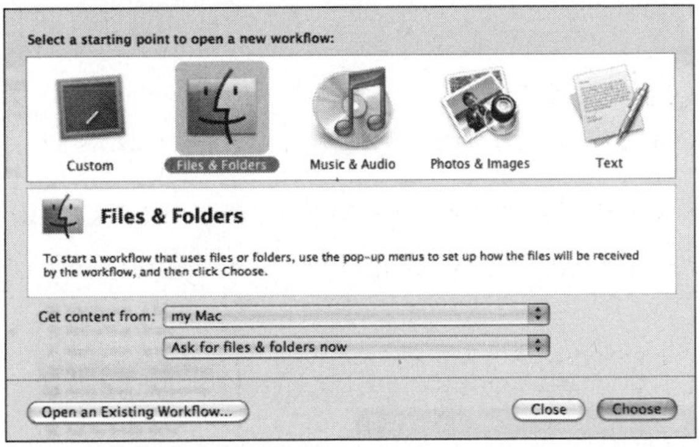

Figure 5-13: Clicking Files & Folders displays two pop-up menus.

3. Click the Choose button.

The Automator window appears and displays an Open dialog so you can choose a file.

4. **Click a file inside your Documents folder and click Add.**
5. **Click the Files & Folders library in the left pane.**
6. **Move the cursor over the Copy Finder Items action, hold down the mouse button, and drag the cursor underneath the New Folder action.**
7. **Move the cursor over the Rename Finder Items action, hold down the mouse button, and drag the cursor underneath the Copy Finder Items action.**

   The Rename Finder Items action displays a variety of pop-up menu options, as shown in Figure 5-14.

8. **Click in the different pop-up menus and choose one or more options.**
9. **Click the Run button.**

   Automator copies a file and displays the renamed copy of your file on your Desktop. (You might have to press F11 to view your Desktop to see your file.)

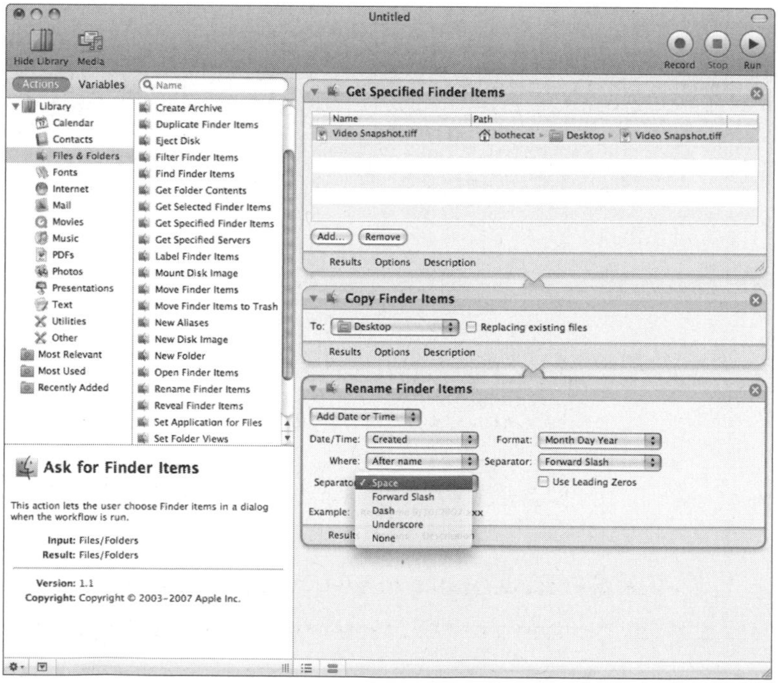

Figure 5-14: The Rename Finder Items action displays pop-up menus for defining how to name a file.

Making your Mac imitate you with the Watch Me Do action

Most actions represent specific tasks that various programs can do, such as setting an event (appointment) in iCal or playing a song in iTunes. To give you greater flexibility with your tasks, Automator also includes a unique Watch Me Do action stored in the Utilities library.

The Watch Me Do action records your mouse or keyboard commands and plays them back. This ability to record mouse clicks and keystrokes is similar to the macro feature found in many programs. So, for example, if you record your mouse clicking the Safari icon on the Dock and then opening the Applications folder to double-click the Calculator icon, the Watch Me Do action performs these actions every time it runs.

To record mouse or keyboard commands in a Watch Me Do action, follow these steps:

1. **Click the Record button or choose Workflow⇨Record.**

   Your Desktop appears along with an Automator Recording window, as shown in Figure 5-15.

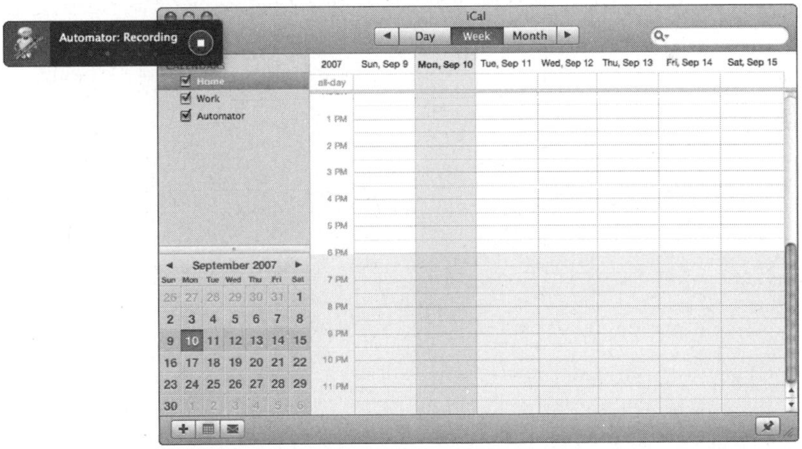

Figure 5-15: The Automator Recording window lets you know that it's recording mouse and keyboard activity.

2. **Click the mouse button or type anything that you want to record.**
3. **Click the Stop button in the Automator Recording window.**

   Automator lists the mouse and keyboard commands you recorded in a Watch Me Do action, as shown in Figure 5-16.

4. **Click the Run button or choose Workflow⇨Run to see the Watch Me Do action replay your recorded mouse and keystroke commands.**

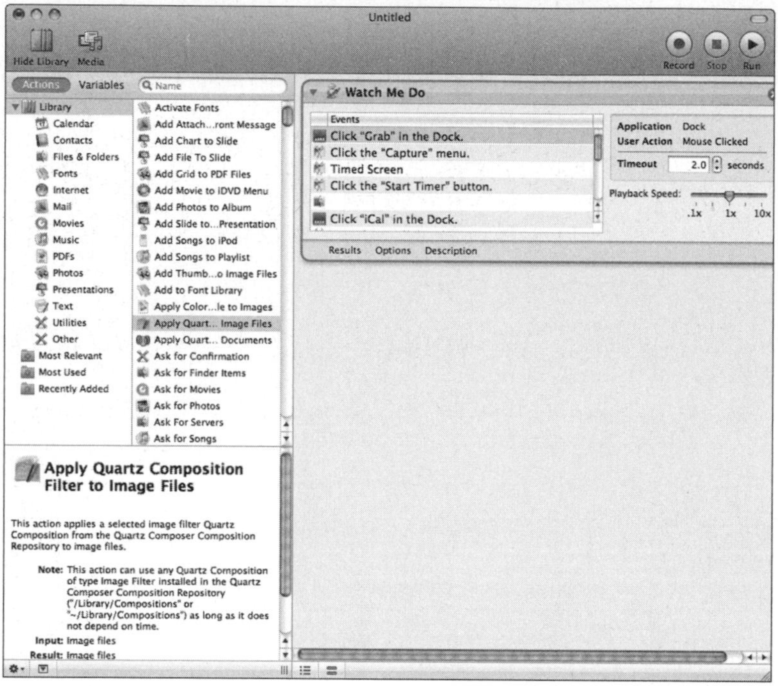

Figure 5-16: The Watch Me Do action contains a list of your recorded mouse and keyboard commands.

Book VII

Mac Networking

"Your mail program looks fine. I don't know why you're not receiving any personal e-mails. Have you explored the possibility that you may not have any friends?"

Contents at a Glance

Chapter 1: Networking Your Macs 725
Chapter 2: Sharing Files and Resources on a Network 739
Chapter 3: Bluetooth Wireless Networking 751

Chapter 1: Networking Your Macs

In This Chapter

- Creating a wired network
- Creating a wireless network
- Setting up an Airport Extreme base station
- Connecting to a mobile phone or PDA

If you have multiple computers in the same place, you may find it convenient to connect your Mac to a network. A *network* allows multiple computers to share files. Although you could copy a file on a USB flash drive, plug it into another computer, and copy the files on to that second computer, such an approach (dubbed *sneaker net*) is slow and clumsy. However, when multiple computers connect to a network, they can share files almost as quickly and easily as copying a file from one folder to another.

Creating a Wired Network

The simplest wired network just connects two computers together using either a FireWire cable or a cable that conforms to a networking cable standard called *Ethernet.* Every Mac has a FireWire port and an Ethernet port, so if you plug a FireWire cable or Ethernet cable into the FireWire or Ethernet ports of two Macs, you'll have a simple network, as shown in Figure 1-1.

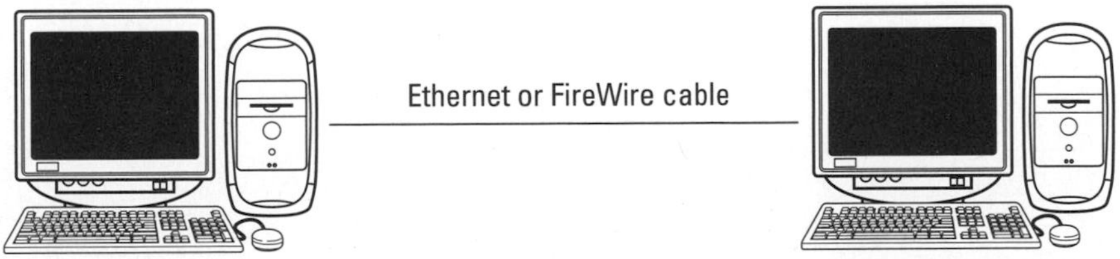

Figure 1-1: A simple network connects two Macs through a FireWire cable or an Ethernet cable.

Ethernet cables are often identified by the speeds that they can send data. The earliest Ethernet cables were called Category 3 (or Cat 3) cables and could transfer data at 10 megabits per second (Mbps). The next generation of Ethernet cables was called Category 5 (Cat 5) cables, which could transfer data at 100 Mbps. (A slightly improved version of the Cat 5 cable is called Cat5e cable.) The current Ethernet cable standard is now Category 6 (Cat 6) cables, which can transfer data at 1,000 Mbps.

Connecting two computers can be convenient for sharing files, but most networks typically consist of multiple computers connected together. Such a large network of multiple computers allows different computers to share files with each other.

Because it's physically impossible to connect more than two computers together through a single cable, networks typically use something called a *hub.* Each computer connects to the hub, which indirectly connects each computer to every other computer also connected to the hub, as shown in Figure 1-2.

An improved variation of a hub is called a *switch.* Physically, a hub and a switch both connect multiple computers in a single point (as shown in Figure 1-2).

With a hub, a network acts like one massive hallway that every computer shares. If a bunch of computers are transferring data at the same time, the shared network can get crowded with data flowing everywhere, slowing the transfer of data throughout the network.

With a switch, the switch directs data between two computers, which is like having a traffic cop directing traffic as opposed to letting cars fight each other on a road. As a result, a switch can ensure that data transfers quickly regardless of how much data the other computers on the network are transferring at the time.

A variation of a switch is called a *router,* which often adds a firewall. Because routers cost nearly the same as ordinary hubs and switches, most wired networks rely on routers. So if you want to create a wired network of computers, you just need

- ✦ Two or more computers
- ✦ A network switch
- ✦ Enough cables to connect each computer to the network switch

The speed of a wired network depends entirely on the slowest speed of the components used in your network. If you plan on using Cat 6 cables in your network, make sure your network switch is designed for Cat 6 cables. If not, you'll have the fastest Ethernet cables connected to a slow network switch, which will run only as fast as the slowest part of your network.

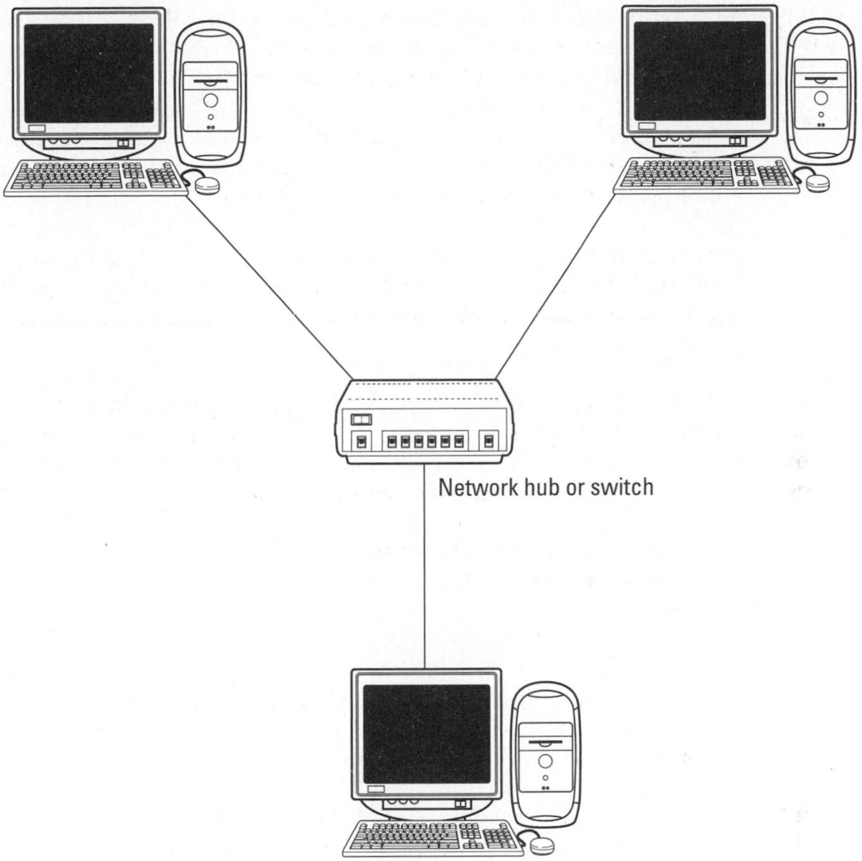

Figure 1-2: A hub or switch allows multiple computers to connect together in a network.

Creating a Wireless Network

Because wired networks can be so inflexible, more people are setting up wireless networks instead. Essentially a wireless network is no different than a wired network, except (no surprise here) that there are no wires and wireless networks tend to be a bit slower and have problems with interference of the wireless signals from one part of a building to another.

Due to physical obstacles, wireless networks don't always reach certain parts of a room or building, creating "dead spots" where you can't connect wirelessly. Walls or furniture can disrupt the wireless signals.

All you need is a device called an *access point,* which can plug into your existing wired network. This access point broadcasts a signal that other computers can receive, creating a wireless connection to the network, as shown in Figure 1-3. You can even sit outside of a building and access a wireless network from the comfort of a lawn chair.

Not all wireless networks are alike. The earliest wireless networks followed a technical specification called 802.11b or 802.11a. Newer wireless equipment followed a faster wireless standard called 802.11g, and now the latest standard (at the time of this writing) is called 802.11n. When setting up a wireless network, make sure your wireless access point uses the same wireless standard as the wireless adapter plugged into each of your computers. In case all this technical jargon about 802.11 standards has your head swimming, just buy Apple's Airport or Airport Extreme, which is guaranteed to work with all the latest Mac computer models. (The Airport Extreme is the faster wireless access point that uses the 802.11n standard.)

At the time of this writing, the Airport Extreme base station uses a draft version of the 802.11n wireless standard, which means 802.11n wireless adapters sold by other companies might not work correctly with Apple's Airport Extreme.

The hazards of wireless networking

To access a wired network, someone must physically connect a computer to the network using a cable. However, connecting to a wireless network can be done from another room, outside a building, or even across the street. As a result, wireless networks can be much less secure because a wireless network essentially shoves dozens of cables out the window, so anyone can walk by and connect into the network.

The practice of connecting to unsecured wireless networks is known as *war driving* (also war flying, war walking, or war boating, depending on how you move around). The basic idea behind war driving is to drive around a city and keep track of which areas offer an unsecured wireless network. After getting connected to an unsecured wireless network, an intruder can wipe out files or interfere with the network.

When creating a wireless network, you have to rely on a variety of security measures. The simplest security measure is to use a password that locks people out who don't know the password. For further protection, you can also use encryption.

Encryption scrambles the data sent to and from the wireless network. Without encryption, anyone can intercept information sent through a wireless network (including passwords). Still another security measure involves configuring your wireless network to let only specific computers connect to the wireless network. By doing this, an intruder can steal your password and still not gain access to the wireless network unless he or she can also gain access to one of the wireless network's approved computers.

Ultimately, wireless networking requires more security measures simply because it offers potential intruders the ability to access the network without physically being in the same building. Wireless networks can be as safe as wired networks, but you might need to go through a lot of extra precautions just to make sure every part of your wireless network is as secure as possible.

TIP

For more information about wireless networking, pick up a copy of *AirPort and Mac Wireless Networks For Dummies,* by Michael E. Cohen (Wiley Publishing).

Setting Up an Airport Extreme Base Station

Although you can use any wireless access point to create a wireless network of Mac computers, it's probably easier (albeit more expensive) just to buy Apple's Airport Extreme base station instead. The Airport Extreme base station includes Ethernet ports along with wireless capability. That way you can connect computers to your network using both cables and wireless technology, essentially allowing your network to connect as many computers as possible (as long as they can access the wireless signals, that is).

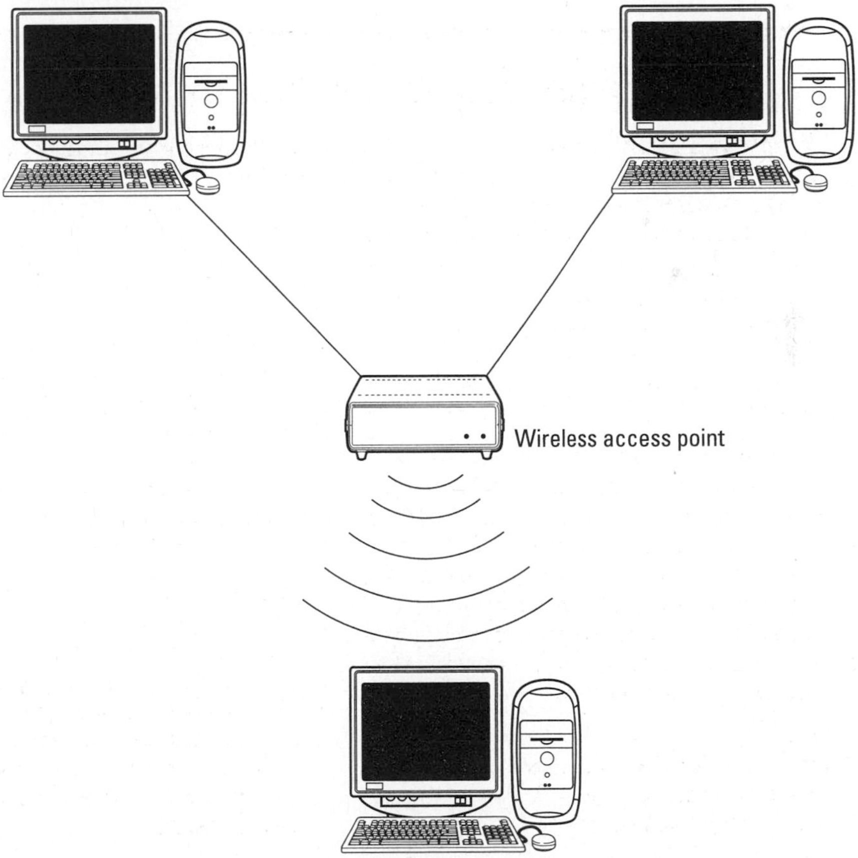

Figure 1-3: A wireless access point extends the reach of a wired network.

Before you can use the Airport Extreme base station, you must configure it first by following these steps:

1. **Run the Airport Utility program. (You might have to install the latest version of this program from the CD that comes with the Airport Extreme base station.)**

   A dialog appears, as shown in Figure 1-4.

2. **Enter a descriptive name for your wireless network into the Wireless Network Name text box.**

   This name is purely for your own use. You could type **jlKVdj%Kfj+** if you wanted, and your Mac would be perfectly happy with this name.

3. **Enter a descriptive name for your Airport base station into the Base Station Name text box.**

   This name is useful for identifying the base station, especially if you have two or more base stations hooked up to the same network.

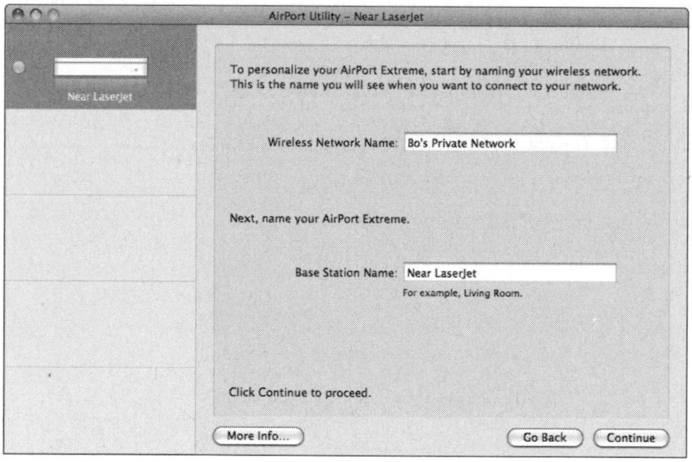

Figure 1-4: A dialog lets you choose a descriptive name for your Airport Extreme base station.

4. **Click Continue.**

   Another dialog appears, as shown in Figure 1-5.

5. **Choose a location from the Country pop-up menu.**

   Californians like me would choose the U.S. of A.

6. **Select the 802.11n (802.11b/g compatible) radio button.**

   If you know for a fact that your network uses the 802.11a standard, select the 802.11n (802.11a compatible) radio button instead.

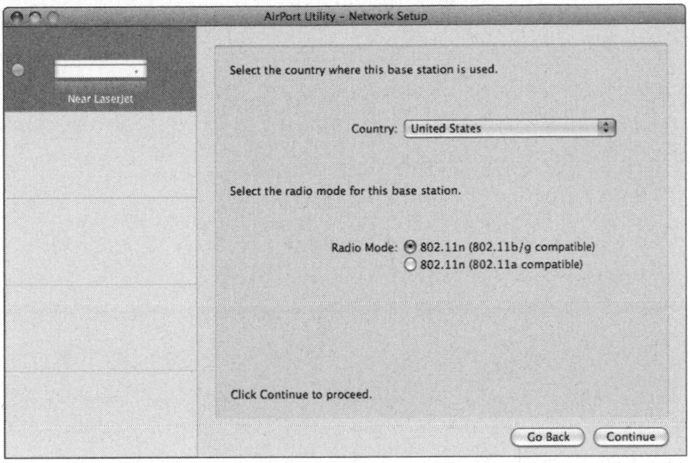

Figure 1-5: A dialog lets you choose a location and wireless standard to use.

7. **Click Continue.**

   Another dialog appears, as shown in Figure 1-6.

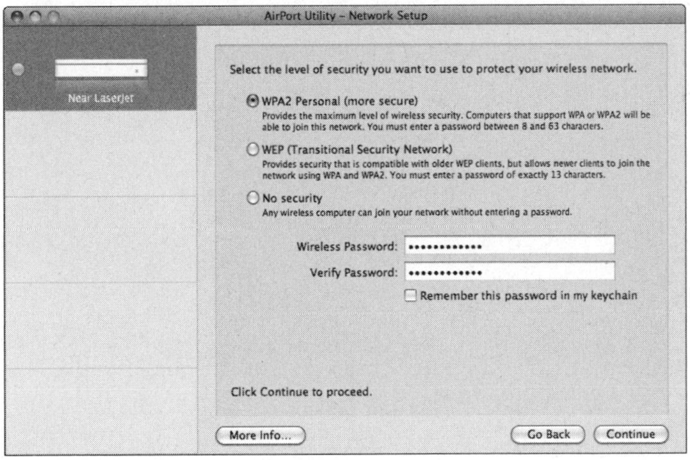

Figure 1-6: You can choose an encryption standard for scrambling your wireless network's signals.

8. **Select one of the following radio buttons:**

   - *WPA2:* Wi-Fi Protected Access, which provides the strongest and most secure encryption.
   - *WEP:* Wireless Encryption Protocol, an older encryption standard that can be easily broken by marginally determined intruders.
   - *No security:* Allows anyone to access the wireless network.

9. **Click in the Wireless Password text box and type a password.**

   This password will be needed if you want to change any settings to your Airport Extreme base station. (If you chose WEP in Step 8, you have slightly different password format restrictions compared with WPA2.)

10. **Click in the Verify Password text box and type your password a second time.**

11. **Click Continue.**

    Another dialog appears, as shown in Figure 1-7.

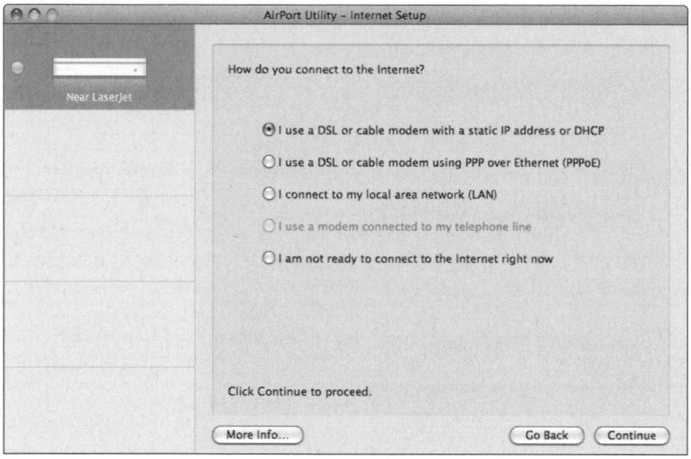

Figure 1-7: The dialog lets you define how to connect to the Internet.

12. **Select the radio button that defines how your network connects to the Internet.**

    If you aren't sure, don't select any radio button. The Airport base station will attempt to determine your Internet connection by itself.

13. **Click Continue.**

    Another dialog appears, as shown in Figure 1-8.

14. **Make sure the Using DHCP option is chosen in the Configure IPv4 pop-up menu and click Continue. (Unless you know the specific settings to type, use DHCP.)**

    Another dialog appears, as shown in Figure 1-9.

    DHCP stands for Dynamic Host Configuration Protocol, which essentially means your Mac can usually figure out the proper settings to use so you don't have to type them in manually. Configuring makes sure your Mac can connect to the Internet.

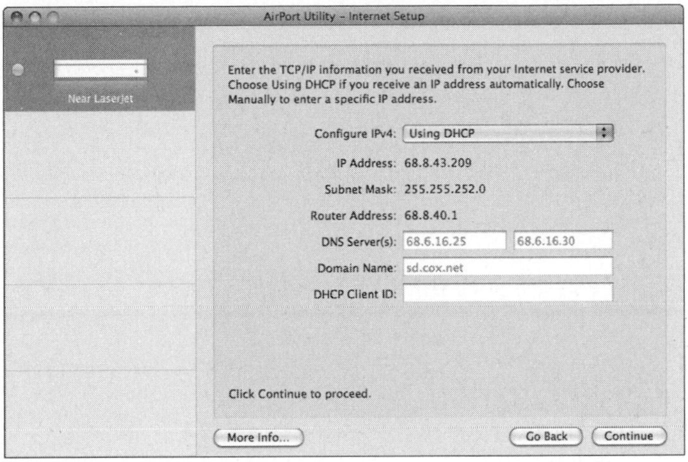

Figure 1-8: The dialog lets you define how to connect to the Internet.

If you don't plug an external hard drive into the USB port of the Airport Extreme base station, you can skip Steps 15 and 16. A Secure Shared Disk is an external hard drive plugged into the USB port of the Airport Extreme base station, which requires a password to access.

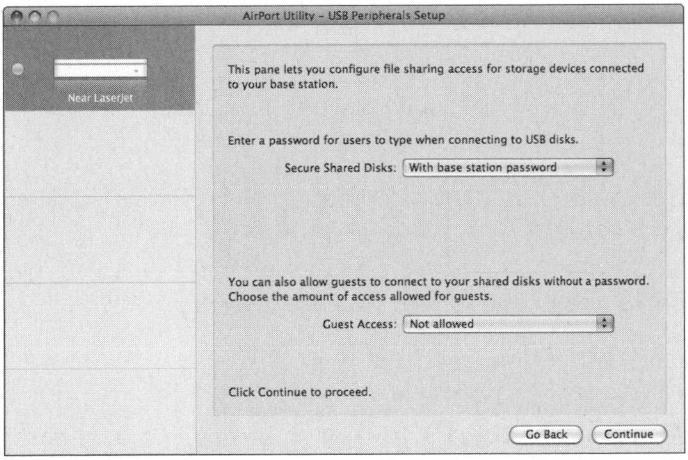

Figure 1-9: The dialog lets you set a password and access for an external hard drive.

15. **(Optional) Click in the Secure Shared Disks pop-up menu and choose one of the following:**

    - With a Disk Password: Uses the password needed to access your Mac.
    - *With a Base Station Password:* Uses the password defined for the Airport Extreme base station.

16. **Click in the Guest Access pop-up menu and choose one of the following:**
    - *Not Allowed:* Guest accounts can't access the external hard drive plugged into the USB port of your Airport Extreme base station.
    - *Read Only:* Guest accounts can read but not save or modify files stored on the external hard drive plugged into the USB port of your Airport Extreme base station.
    - *Read and Write:* Guest accounts can modify, erase, and save files stored on the external hard drive plugged into the USB port of your Airport Extreme base station.
17. **Click Continue.**

    Another dialog appears, as shown in Figure 1-10.

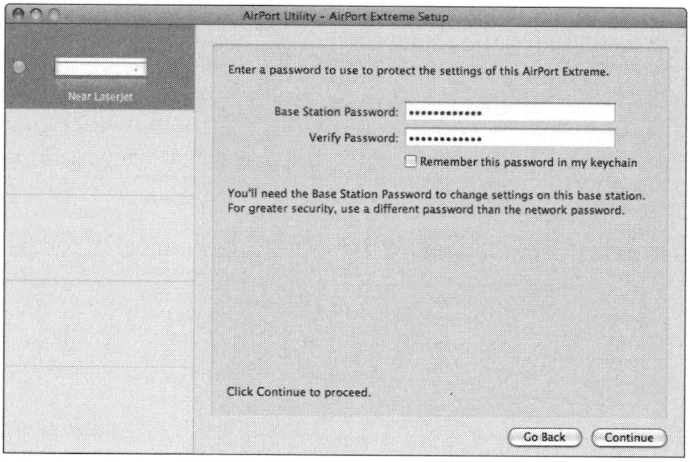

Figure 1-10: The dialog lets you define a password for protecting the settings of the Airport Extreme base station.

18. **Click in the Base Station Password text box and type a password.**

    The password you define here is used to protect the settings of the Airport Extreme base station so unauthorized users can't mess it up. (Of course, authorized users can still mess it up if they don't know what they're doing.)
19. **Click in the Verify Password text box and retype your password.**
20. **Click Continue.**

    Another dialog appears, listing all the settings you've defined.
21. **Click Update if you approve of all the displayed settings. (Or click Go Back until you see a window where you can change a setting.)**
22. **Click Done.**
23. **Choose Airport Utility⇨Quit Airport Utility.**

After you've physically connected your wired network or configured your wireless network, you must still configure your Mac to work on that network by sharing files and printers, which is the topic of Book VII, Chapter 2.

Connecting a Phone or PDA to a Mac

Many people store names and contact information in their mobile phones or personal digital assistant (PDA) handheld devices. However, such mobile, handheld devices create two main problems. First, if you already store names, contact information, and appointments using iCal and Address Book on your Mac, you probably don't want to retype this information into your mobile device. Second, if you lose your mobile phone or PDA, you could wind up losing all of your important contact information.

To prevent both of these problems, your Mac comes with a program called iSync. By using iSync, you can connect and transfer data back and forth between your Mac and many handheld devices such as a mobile phone or PDA. Now you can type in a name on your mobile phone, type an appointment on your Mac using Address Book, and iSync smashes all this information together and stores your updated schedule on both your mobile phone and your Mac.

Besides sharing contact information and appointments between your Mac and a handheld device, iSync also lets you transfer files from your Mac to your handheld device. If you need to read some important documents, transfer them from your Mac and store them on your PDA so you can read them in an airport terminal, while waiting in line at the supermarket, or any time you're away from your Mac.

The iSync program can work with a wide variety of mobile phones and Palm PDAs. For a complete list of devices compatible with iSync, visit Apple's Web site (`www.apple.com/macosx/features/isync/devices.html`). If you have a Windows Mobile, a Blackberry, or an older Palm OS device, you'll need to buy a Missing Sync program for your particular device from Mark/Space (`www.markspace.com`), which will allow you to synchronize your data with a Mac.

The three basic steps for using iSync are

1. **Add your handheld device to your Mac's iSync Devices list.**

   This links the handheld device to your Mac. The idea here is to keep your handheld device from trying to synchronize with multiple Macs, which could prevent contact information and appointments from being synchronized correctly. You need to add a handheld device to your Mac only once.

2. Connect the handheld device with your Mac.

   Handheld devices connect either through a USB cable or Bluetooth wireless connection.

3. Decide what to transfer or synchronize between your Mac and the handheld device.

   Lets you specify whether to synchronize and transfer names and contact information, appointments, or files such as word processor or spreadsheet files.

Adding a handheld device to your Mac

Before you can use iSync to synchronize data between your Mac and your handheld device, you need to add the handheld device to iSync. If you have a Palm OS device, choose Devices⇨Enable Palm OS Syncing. (You'll need to follow additional instructions specific to getting a Palm OS device to work with a Mac, which will appear on the screen after you choose this Enable Palm OS Syncing command.)

If you have a handheld device that connects using Bluetooth or a USB cable, choose Devices⇨Add Device (or press ⌘+N) as shown in Figure 1-11.

Figure 1-11: The Devices menu in iSync provides commands for adding a handheld device to your Mac.

REMEMBER

In case you want to synchronize your handheld device with another computer, you must first remove the device from the iSync Devices list on your Mac by following these steps:

1. **Load iSync by double-clicking the iSync icon in the Applications folder.**
2. **In the iSync window, click the icon for the handheld device that you want to remove.**
3. **Choose Devices⇨Remove Device.**

Synchronizing a handheld device with your Mac

After you've added a handheld device to the iSync Devices list so your Mac can recognize it, you can synchronize and transfer data between your Mac and a handheld device by following these steps:

1. **Connect your handheld device (mobile phone or PDA) to your Mac. (If you have a Bluetooth handheld device, just place it near your Mac.)**
2. **Load iSync.**

   The iSync window appears, displaying an icon for your handheld device, as shown in Figure 1-12.

Figure 1-12: The iSync window displays icons of all the handheld devices.

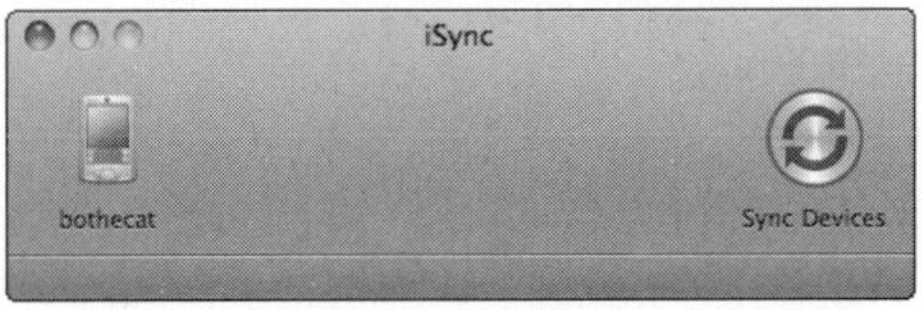

3. **Click the icon of the handheld device that you want to synchronize.**

   The iSync window expands to display additional options, as shown in Figure 1-13.
4. **Choose your options for synchronizing data and click the Sync Devices icon or choose Devices➪Sync Devices.**

Resetting a handheld device with your Mac

Synchronizing your handheld device with your Mac can keep your crucial contact and appointment information stored in two locations. However, sometimes the data on your handheld device might get hopelessly outdated if you don't use it for a long time, or it can get scrambled if someone accidentally uses (plays) with your handheld device.

If this happens, the only accurate information might be on your Mac, so you can reset your handheld device, essentially wiping the handheld device clean and loading it with the data on your Mac instead. To reset your handheld device, follow these steps:

1. **Connect your handheld device (mobile phone or PDA) to your Mac. (If you have a Bluetooth handheld device, just place it near your Mac.)**

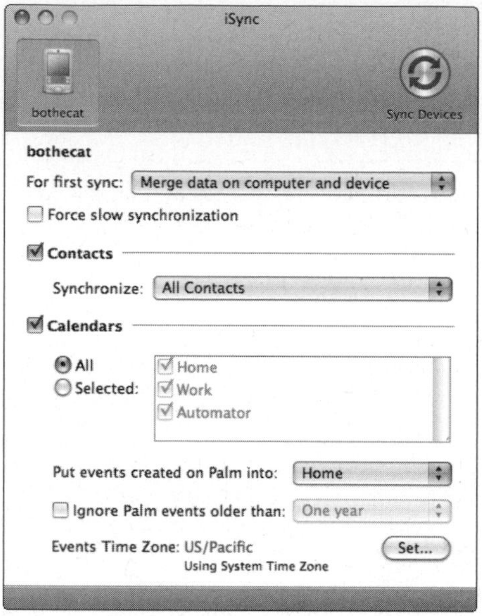

Figure 1-13: The iSync window displays synchronization options for your chosen handheld device.

2. **Load iSync.**

   The iSync window appears, displaying an icon for your handheld device (refer to Figure 1-12).

3. **Click the icon of the handheld device that you want to reset.**

   WARNING!

   Resetting wipes out all data currently stored on your handheld device, so make sure you don't need any of this data.

4. **Choose Devices⇨Reset Device (or Reset All Devices to reset all handheld devices added to your Mac).**

Chapter 2: Sharing Files and Resources on a Network

In This Chapter

- Sharing files
- Sharing printers
- Sharing an Internet connection

Physically connecting multiple computers through cables or wireless adapters might create a network, but for greater flexibility, use the network so all computers can share files and equipment with other computers connected to the network. By sharing over a network, everyone can benefit, and the benefits can range from swapping files quickly and easily to sharing a single printer instead of having to buy a printer for every computer.

Although networks allow others to share your files, nobody on a network can rummage through your Mac without your permission, just as nobody should enter your house until you invite them in. Ideally, a network should allow you to share files and equipment over a network without risking the loss of crucial files on your own computer.

Sharing Files

Sharing files makes it easy for different people to work on a project. Without a network, you could give someone a copy of a file, but then you might suddenly have three different versions of the same file, and nobody would know which file contains the most accurate information.

Even worse, two or more files could each contain different parts of the most updated information, so now you have the problem of finding this updated portion of each file and merging it into a single file again. Obviously, worrying about multiple copies of the same file wastes time, so networks allow everyone to work on a single file and keep one copy of that file stored in one location.

When your Mac is connected to a network, you have the option of sharing one or more folders with everyone else on the network. To share folders, you need to define different permission levels, which allow or restrict what users can do with a folder:

- **Read & Write:** Other users have the ability to retrieve, delete, and modify files in the shared folder.
- **Read Only:** Other users can copy and open files, but they cannot modify or delete them.
- **Write Only:** Other users can only store files in the folder; they cannot copy or open any files already stored in that folder.
- **No Access:** Blocks everyone (or just certain users) from accessing files on your Mac at all.

To share files, you need to decide which folders to share, who can access that folder, and what access level (Read & Write, Read Only, Write Only, or No Access) you want others to have in accessing your shared folder.

You don't have to share folders. If you don't share folders, you can still use a network by accessing files shared by other network users.

Turning on file sharing

To turn on file sharing, follow these steps:

1. **Choose ⇨System Preferences.**

   The System Preferences window appears.

2. **Click the Sharing icon under the Internet & Network category.**

   The Sharing pane appears, as shown in Figure 2-1.

3. **Select the File Sharing check box in the leftmost column.**
4. **Click the plus sign button underneath the Shared Folders column.**

   A dialog appears, displaying all the drives and folders on your Mac, as shown in Figure 2-2.

5. **Click a folder, such as the Public folder, which contains the Drop Box folder.**

   The Drop Box folder is a special folder that allows others to store or drop files in, but it doesn't allow anyone (except you) to view and retrieve files back out again. A Drop Box folder essentially acts like a mailbox that lets others drop letters (files) in but won't let them peek inside to read any letters (files) inside.

6. **Click Add.**
7. **Repeat Steps 4–6 for each additional folder you want to share over the network.**

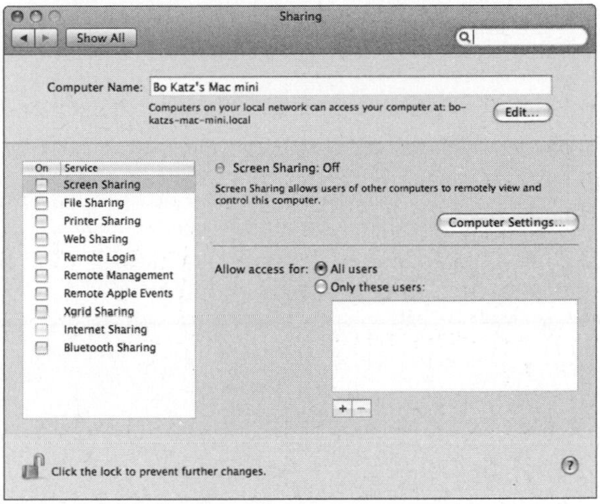

Figure 2-1: The Sharing pane lets you turn on file sharing and choose folders to share.

8. **Click the Close button of the System Preferences window.**

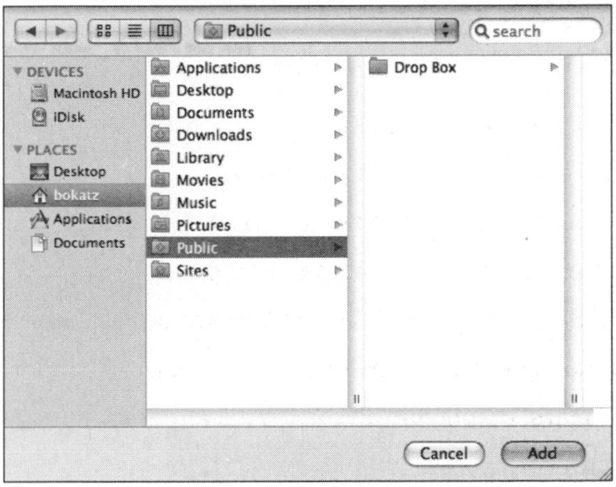

Figure 2-2: The Public folder contains a special Drop Box folder.

File sharing works only as long as a computer is not turned off or in sleep mode. If you share a folder and your Mac goes into sleep mode, other people on the network won't be able to access your shared folder until your Mac wakes up again.

Defining user access to shared folders

After you've defined one or more folders to share, you can also define the type of access people can have with your shared folders, such as giving certain people the ability to open and modify files while stopping other people from accessing your shared files at all.

When defining access to shared folders, you can define access for three types of network users:

- **Yourself:** Give yourself Read & Write access or else you won't be able to modify any files in your own shared folders.
- **Everyone:** Allows others to access your shared folders as guests without requiring a password.
- **Names of specific network users:** Allows you to give individuals access to your shared folders by name and password.

If you trust everyone on a network, you can give everyone Read & Write privileges to your shared folders. However, it's probably best to give everyone Read privileges and give only certain people Read & Write privileges.

Defining access privileges for guests

To define access privileges for guests, follow these steps:

1. **Choose ⇨System Preferences.**

   The System Preferences window appears.
2. **Click the Sharing icon under the Internet & Network category.**

   The Sharing pane appears.
3. **Click a folder in the Shared Folders list.**

   The Users list enumerates all the people allowed to access this particular shared folder, as shown in Figure 2-3. By default, every shared folder lists your name with Read & Write privileges.
4. **Click the Everyone (the guest account) entry to call up its pop-up menu and choose an access option, such as Read & Write, Read Only, Write Only, or No Access.**
5. **Repeat Steps 3 and 4 for each additional shared folder you want to configure.**
6. **Click the Close button of the System Preferences window.**

Giving individuals access to shared folders

When you define the guest account (Everyone) for a shared folder, anyone on the network can access your files based on the access level you've defined for the guest account (Read Only, Write Only, and so on). Because you might want to give certain people greater access to your files, you can create individual accounts and passwords for accessing a shared folder.

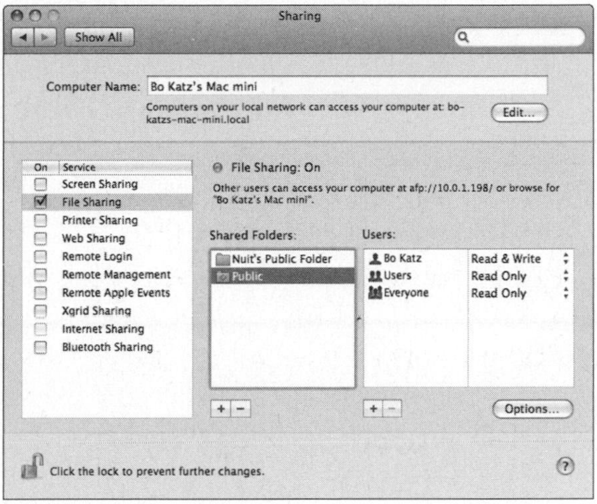

Figure 2-3: Each shared folder displays a list of users who can access that folder.

To define a username and password to access a shared folder, follow these steps:

1. **Choose ⇨System Preferences.**

   The System Preferences window appears.

2. **Click the Sharing icon under the Internet & Network category.**

   The Sharing pane appears.

3. **Click on a folder in the Shared Folders list.**

   The Users list enumerates all the people allowed to access this particular shared folder (refer to Figure 2-3).

4. **Click the plus sign button under the Users list.**

   A dialog appears, as shown in Figure 2-4, and it lets you choose the name of a person stored in your Address Book or create a new user altogether.

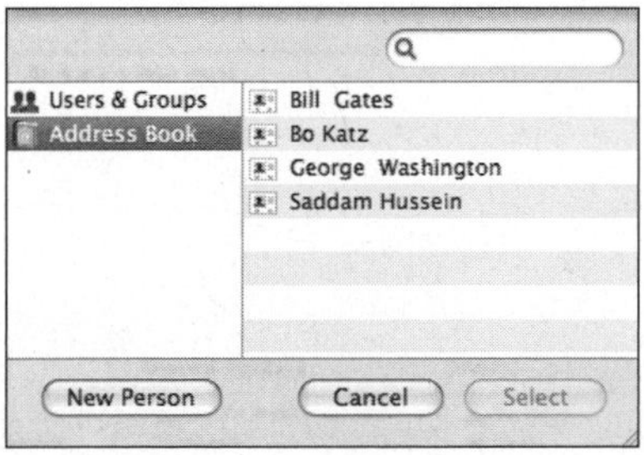

Figure 2-4: A dialog lets you create a new user who can access your shared folder.

5. **Click New Person.**

   A New Person dialog appears. Here you can type a username and password, as shown in Figure 2-5.

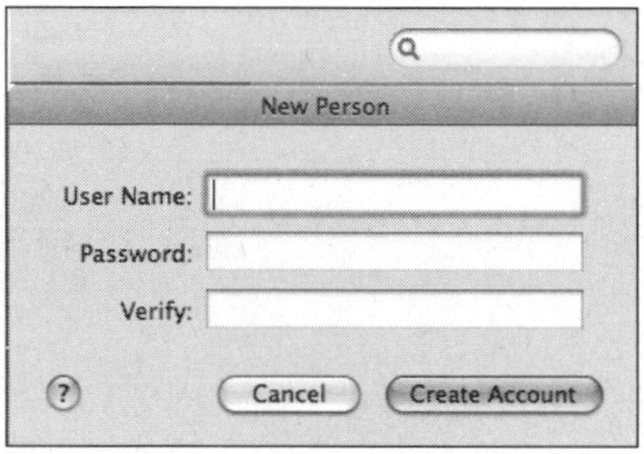

Figure 2-5: The New Person dialog lets you define a new user and password for accessing a shared folder.

6. **Enter a name in the User Name text box.**

   The name can be an actual person or just a made up name like "Superman" or "John Doe".

7. **Enter a password in the Password text box.**
8. **Reenter the password in the Verify text box.**
9. **Click the Create Account button.**

   Your new account name appears in the Users & Group category, as shown in Figure 2-6.

10. **Click the name of your new account, in the Users & Groups category, and click Select.**

    Your chosen account name appears in the Users box.

11. **Click the pop-up menu that appears to the right of the name you just added to the Users box and choose Read & Write, Read Only, or Write Only.**
12. **Click the Close button of the System Preferences window.**

Removing accounts from shared folders

If you've created an account for others to use for accessing your shared folders, you might later change your mind and want to change their access privileges (such as changing their access from Read & Write to Read Only), or perhaps you'll just delete their account altogether.

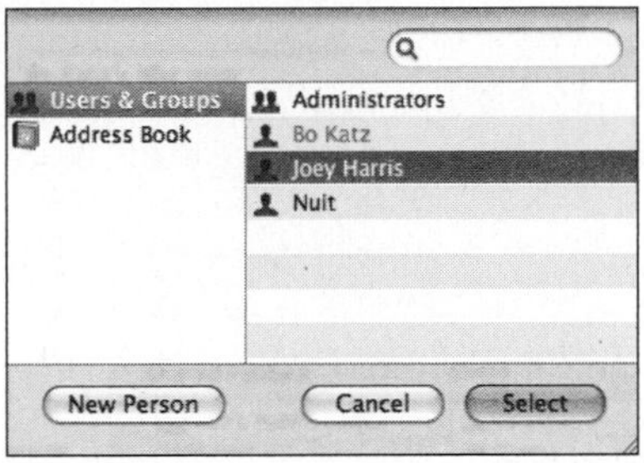

Figure 2-6: New network account names appear in the Users & Groups category.

To delete an account from a shared folder, follow these steps:

1. **Choose ⇨System Preferences.**

   The System Preferences window appears.

2. **Click the Sharing icon under the Internet & Network category.**

   The Sharing pane appears.

3. **Click a folder in the Shared Folders list.**

   The Users list box lists all the people allowed to access this particular shared folder (refer to Figure 2-3).

4. **Click a name that you want to delete in the Users list box.**

5. **Click the minus sign button under the Users list box.**

   A dialog appears, asking whether you want to keep the account from accessing your shared folder.

6. **Click OK.**

7. **Click the Close button of the System Preferences window.**

Accessing shared folders

Although you can share your folders with others on a network, others might want to share their folders with you. To access a shared folder on someone else's computer, follow these steps:

1. **Click the Finder icon in the Dock.**

   The Finder appears.

2. **Choose Go⇨Network.**

   A Network window appears, listing all the computers that offer shared folders as shown in Figure 2-7.

3. **Double-click the computer you want to access.**

   Another Network window appears, listing all the shared folders you can access.

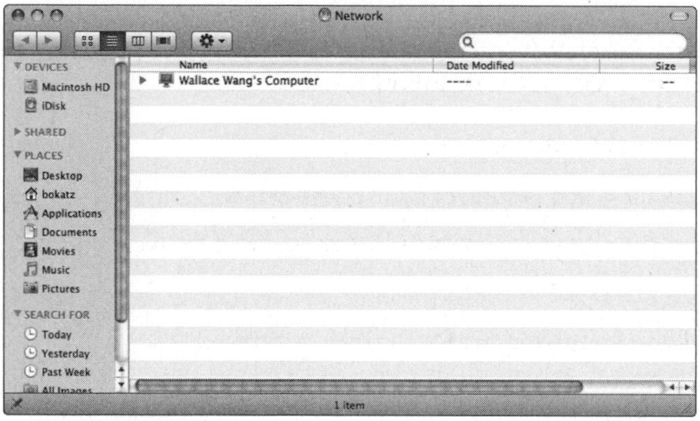

Figure 2-7: The Network window lets you connect to other computers.

4. **Click the Connect As button to display a dialog as shown in Figure 2-8.**

Figure 2-8: The Connect as dialog lets you access a shared folder with an account name and password.

5. **Select the Registered User (or Guest) radio button.**

   If you select the Guest radio button, skip to Step 8.

6. **Click in the Name text box and type the account name to use for accessing that shared folder.**

   The account name is the name that the computer's user created in the earlier section, "Giving individuals access to shared folders."

7. **Click in the Password text box and type a password.**

8. **Click Connect.**

   Depending on the access you have to the shared folder (Read Only, Read & Write, and so on), you might be able to copy, open, modify, or delete files.

TIP

Another way to access a shared folder is to type a shared folder's AFP (Apple Filing Protocol) address into the Safari browser address text box where you normally type a Web site address like `www.cbsnews.com`. To find a computer's AFP address, follow these steps:

1. **Choose ⇨System Preferences.**

   The System Preferences window appears.

2. **Click the Sharing icon under the Internet & Network category.**

   The Sharing pane appears.

3. **Click File Sharing under the Service category.**

   Directly underneath the File Sharing: On text is the AFP address of that particular Mac, such as afp://10/0/1/197, as shown in Figure 2-9.

4. **Click the Close button of the System Preferences window.**

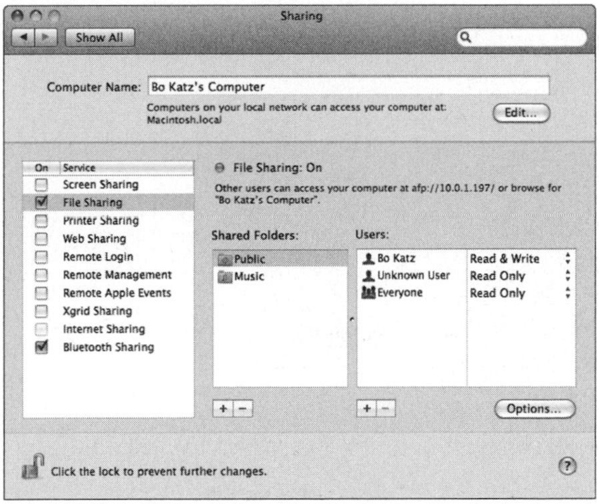

Figure 2-9: The AFP address appears in the Sharing window.

Sharing Printers

If you want computers on a network to print, you could buy a separate printer for each computer. However, this solution would be expensive and would gobble up space. Another alternative is to connect a printer directly to one computer, and configure that one computer to share its printer with any computer connected to the same network. To share a printer with other computers on a network, follow these steps:

1. **Choose⇨System Preferences.**

   The System Preferences window appears.

2. **Click the Sharing icon under the Internet & Network category.**

   The Sharing pane appears.

3. **Select the Printer Sharing check box.**

   A list of printers physically connected to your Mac appears, as shown in Figure 2-10.

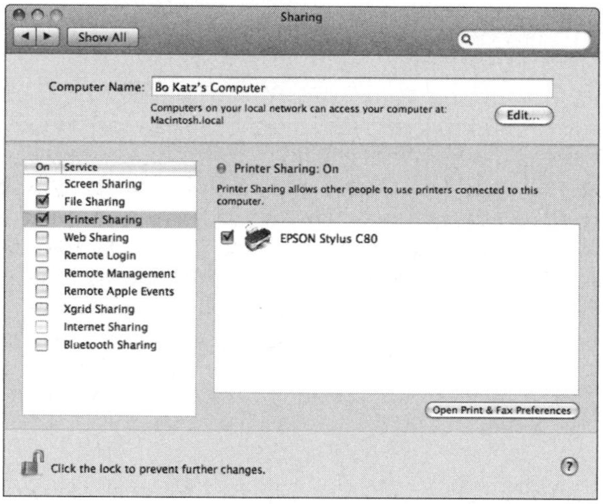

Figure 2-10: Each physically connected printer appears with a check box in the Sharing window.

4. **Select or deselect the check boxes of the printers you want to share.**
5. **Click the Close button of the Sharing window.**

REMEMBER

When you want to print, a Print dialog appears. If you click the Printer pop-up menu and choose Add Printer, a window appears, listing all the available printers connected directly to your Mac (USB) or shared over the network (Bonjour or Bonjour Shared), as shown in Figure 2-11.

TECHNICAL STUFF

Bonjour is a networking standard developed by Apple, which is used by most printers to connect to other computers through Ethernet cables (wired networks) or through wireless connections (802.11a/b/g/n). Since Apple released Bonjour as an open source standard, other companies have been able to use it, which means Windows users can even download the free Bonjour for Windows program so Windows PCs can access shared printers on a network.

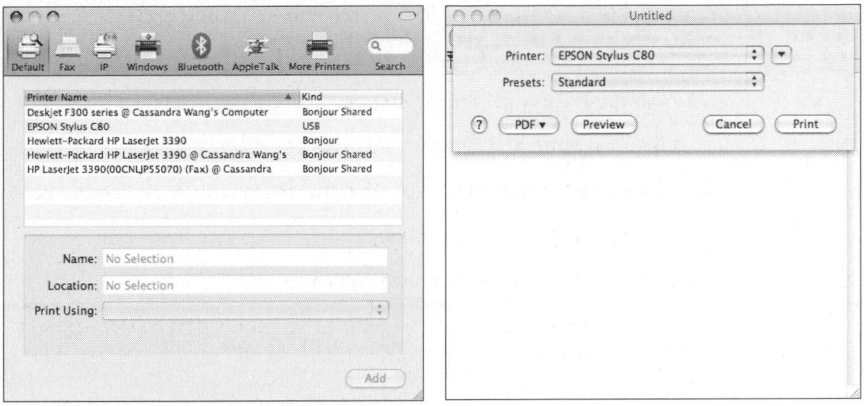

Figure 2-11: A Printer window lists all available printers you can use over a network.

Sharing an Internet Connection

Sharing an Internet connection lets one Mac access the Internet through another Mac. For example, one laptop Mac might have access to the Internet through a wireless connection, but a second, older laptop Mac might not have a wireless adapter (such as an Airport Extreme card) and would therefore lack access the Internet. However, with Internet Sharing turned on, the second Mac can access the Internet through the first Mac.

To share an Internet connection, follow these steps:

1. **Choose ⇨System Preferences.**

   A System Preferences window appears.

2. **Click the Sharing icon under the Internet & Network category.**

   The Sharing pane appears.

3. **Click the Internet Sharing option in the list box on the left.**

   Internet Sharing options appear, as shown in Figure 2-12.

4. **Choose one of the following from the Share Your Connection From pop-up menu:**

   - *Built-in Ethernet:* Your Mac is connected to another computer through Ethernet cables.
   - *Built-in FireWire:* Your Mac is connected to another computer through a FireWire cable.
   - *AirPort:* Your Mac and the second computer share an Airport wireless connection.
   - *Bluetooth:* Your Mac and the second computer share a Bluetooth wireless connection.

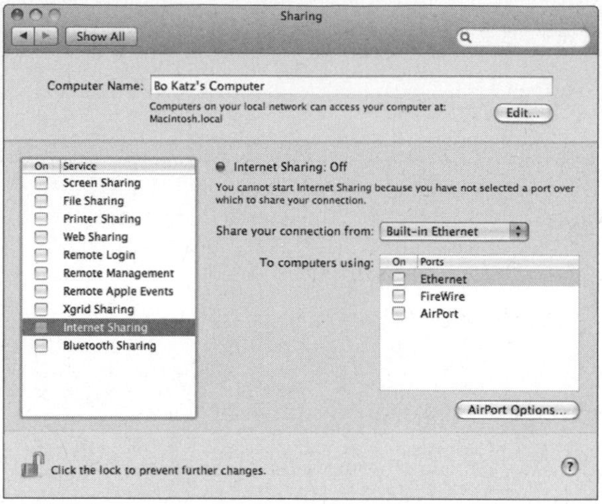

Figure 2-12: To turn on Internet Sharing, you must define how to share your Internet connection.

5. **Select one or more check boxes in the To Computers Using list box, such as Ethernet or FireWire.**
6. **Select the Internet Sharing check box.**

   A dialog appears, asking whether you're sure you want to turn on Internet sharing, as shown in Figure 2-13.

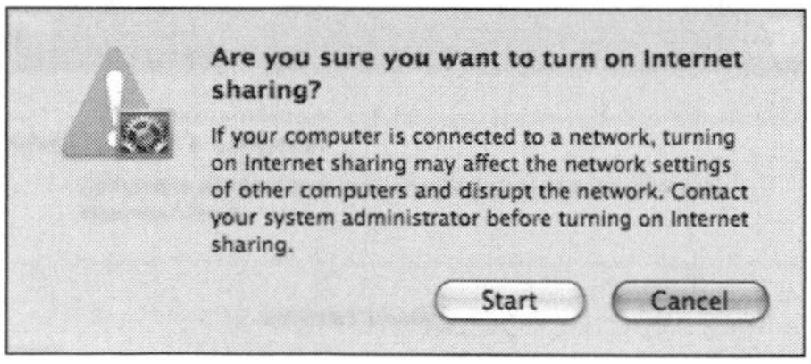

Figure 2-13: A dialog warns that turning on Internet sharing could affect network performance.

7. **Click Start.**
8. **Click the Close button on the System Preferences window.**

   The second computer, connected to your Mac through Ethernet, FireWire, AirPort, or Bluetooth, can now access the Internet.

Chapter 3: Bluetooth Wireless Networking

In This Chapter

- Identifying Bluetooth capabilities
- Configuring Bluetooth
- Pairing devices
- Sharing through Bluetooth

Bluetooth is the name of a wireless technology standard designed primarily for connecting devices within a short distance of one another, unlike networks where one computer can be in one room and another computer in another room on another floor of the building.

Many handheld devices, such as mobile phones and handheld computers, use Bluetooth, but you can use Bluetooth to connect two or more Macs in what's called a *personal area network* (PAN). Because of its short-range nature, Bluetooth is handy for connecting devices for short periods of time and for transferring small files, unlike networks that are meant to connect computers on a more permanent basis.

Bluetooth can connect devices up to 30 feet (10 meters) away, although any obstacles such as walls can limit the range of a Bluetooth device.

Identifying Bluetooth Capabilities

Not every Mac has Bluetooth capabilities. If you have a newer Mac, chances are good you have Bluetooth capability, but if you have an older Mac, you probably don't have Bluetooth capability built-in. In that case, you'll need to buy a Bluetooth adapter that plugs into a USB port or fits inside your Mac.

To determine if your Mac has Bluetooth capability, follow these steps:

1. **Click the Apple menu and choose System Preferences.**

   A System Preferences window appears.

2. **Look for a Bluetooth icon under the Hardware category.**

   If you see a Bluetooth icon, your Mac has Bluetooth capability. If you don't see a Bluetooth icon, your Mac doesn't have Bluetooth capability.

Configuring Bluetooth

After you determine that your Mac has Bluetooth capability (either built-in or added through a Bluetooth adapter), you might want to take time to configure how Bluetooth works on your Mac. For example, you might not want to allow other computers to browse your hard drive through Bluetooth without your knowledge. Otherwise, it's possible for someone to access your computer from across the room using Bluetooth, and you would never know it.

To configure how Bluetooth works on your Mac, follow these steps:

1. **Choose ⇨System Preferences.**

   The System Preferences window appears.

2. **Click the Sharing icon under the Internet & Networking category.**

   The Sharing pane appears.

3. **Select the Bluetooth Sharing check box.**

   A list of Bluetooth options appears, as shown in Figure 3-1.

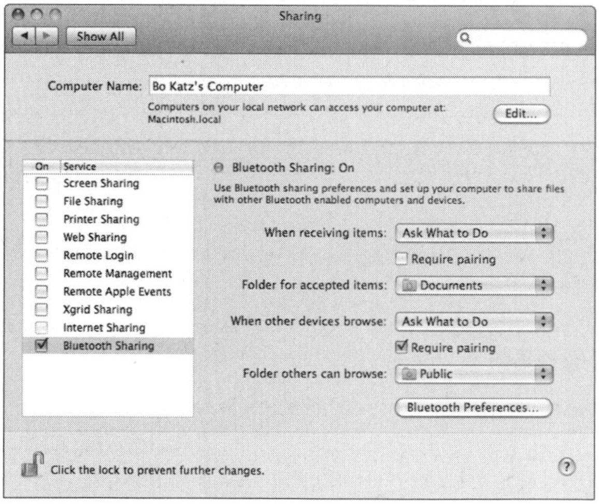

Figure 3-1: The Sharing window lists options for Bluetooth sharing.

4. **Choose one of the following from the When Receiving Items pop-up menu:**

   - *Accept and Save:* Automatically saves any files sent to you through Bluetooth. (Not recommended because someone can send you a malicious program such as a virus or Trojan Horse that could wipe out your files when opened.)

- *Accept and Open:* Automatically saves and opens any files sent to you through Bluetooth. (Not recommended because this — like the previous option — could automatically run a malicious program sent to your Mac through Bluetooth.)
- *Ask What to Do:* Displays a dialog that gives you the option of accepting or rejecting a file sent to you through Bluetooth.
- *Never Allow:* Always blocks anyone from sending you files through Bluetooth.

5. **Select or deselect the Require Pairing check box.**

   If selected, this check box won't let anyone send files to you until you "pair" that other computer with your own. Pairing links another device specifically to your Mac, which is commonly used to link Bluetooth keyboards, mice, and the Apple Remote to a specific Mac. The next section, "Pairing a Device," explains how to pair a Bluetooth device with your Mac.

6. **Choose either Documents or Other from the Folder for Accepted Items pop-up menu.**

   If you choose Other, an Open dialog appears, letting you click a folder where you want to store any files sent to you through Bluetooth.

7. **Choose one of the following from the When Other Devices Browse pop-up menu:**

   - *Always Allow:* Automatically gives another Bluetooth device full access to the contents of your Mac. (Not recommended, because this allows others to mess up your files accidentally or deliberately.)
   - *Ask What to Do:* Displays a dialog that gives you the option of accepting or rejecting another device trying to access your Mac through Bluetooth.
   - *Never Allow:* Always blocks anyone from browsing through your Mac using Bluetooth.

8. **Select or deselect the Require Pairing check box.**

   Generally, you want pairing because pairing lets you selectively choose which devices can access your Mac through Bluetooth.

9. **Choose either Public or Other from the Folder Others Can Browse pop-up menu.**

   If you choose Other, an Open dialog appears, letting you click a folder that you can share.

10. **Click the Close button of the System Preferences window.**

Pairing a Device

Pairing lets you determine ahead of time which Bluetooth-enabled devices can connect to your Mac. By using pairing, you can keep total strangers from trying to access your Mac without your knowledge. For additional security, you can also require that paired devices use a password (also called a *passkey*) that further verifies that a specific device is allowed to connect to your Mac.

Pairing with your Mac

To pair a device with your Mac, follow these steps:

1. **Choose ⌘⇨System Preferences.**

   The System Preferences window appears.

2. **Click the Bluetooth icon under the Hardware category.**

   The Bluetooth pane appears, as shown in Figure 3-2.

3. **Click the Set Up New Device button.**

   The Bluetooth Setup Assistant window appears.

4. **Click Continue.**

   Another Bluetooth Setup Assistant dialog appears, asking what type of device you want to connect to your Mac, as shown in Figure 3-3.

Figure 3-2: The Bluetooth pane lets you pair a device with your Mac.

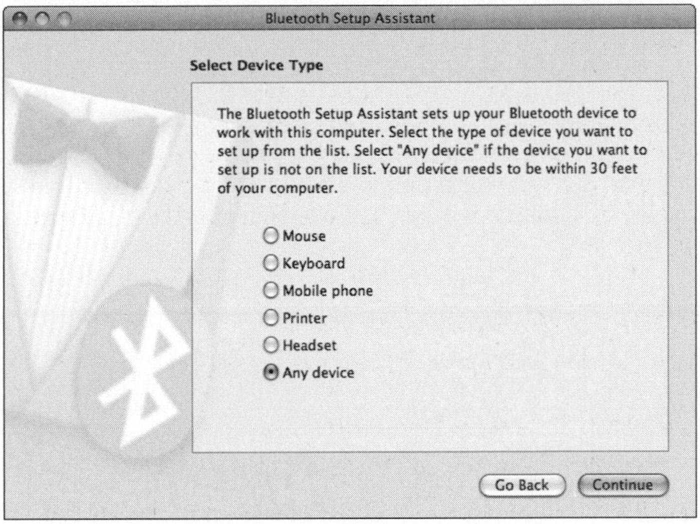

Figure 3-3: The Bluetooth Setup Assistant dialog lets you define the type of Bluetooth device to pair with your Mac.

5. **Select the radio button that identifies the type of device you want to pair with your Mac, such as a Keyboard or Mobile phone.**

   If you want to pair another computer with your Mac, select the Any Device radio button.

6. **Click Continue.**

   Another Bluetooth Setup Assistant pane appears, listing all the Bluetooth enabled devices found within range of your Mac, as shown in Figure 3-4.

7. **Select a device and then click Continue.**

   Another Bluetooth Setup Assistant pane appears that informs you about how the Setup Assistant is trying to gather information about the Bluetooth-enabled device you chose in Step 5.

8. **Click Continue.**

   Another Bluetooth Setup Assistant pane appears, displaying a passkey you can use to link with the other Bluetooth device, as shown in Figure 3-5.

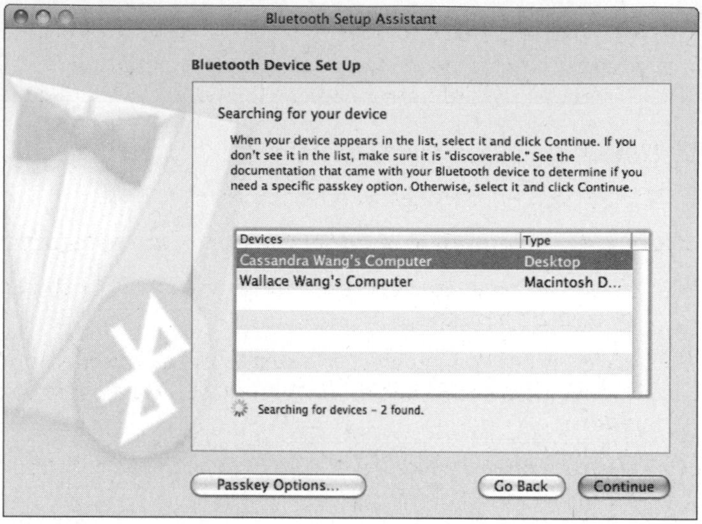

Figure 3-4: The Bluetooth dialog lists all Bluetooth-enabled devices that you can pair with your Mac.

Figure 3-5: The Bluetooth dialog offers to define a passkey for linking another device to your Mac.

9. **Type the passkey on the other device that you want to pair with your Mac.**

   The Bluetooth Setup Assistant window informs you that the pairing has succeeded.

10. **Click Quit.**

Removing a paired device from your Mac

After you've paired a device with your Mac, you might want to remove it later. To remove a paired device from your Mac, follow these steps:

1. **Choose ⌘⇨System Preferences.**

   The System Preferences window appears.

2. **Click the Bluetooth icon under the Hardware category.**

   A Bluetooth pane appears, as shown in Figure 3-6, listing all devices paired with your Mac.

3. **Click to select the device you want to unlink from your Mac and then click the minus sign button in the bottom-left corner of the Bluetooth window.**

   A dialog appears, warning you that if you disconnect this device, it will no longer be available to your Mac.

4. **Click Remove.**

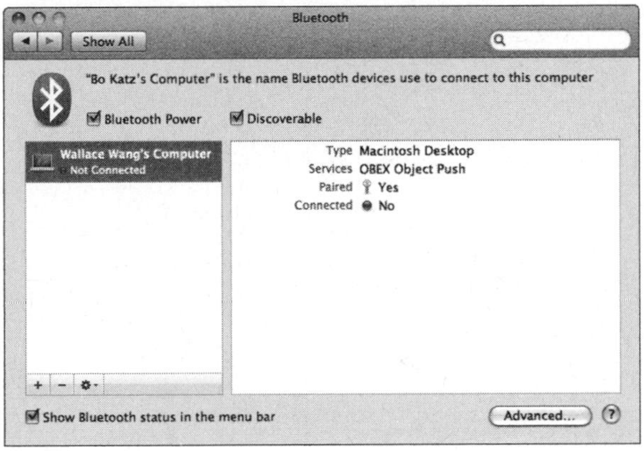

Figure 3-6: The Bluetooth pane shows you all paired devices on a Mac.

Sharing through Bluetooth

Because Bluetooth lets you create a simple, short-range network between Mac computers, you can use a Bluetooth network to share files or even an Internet connection with others. Such a simple network isn't meant to share massive numbers of files or an Internet connection for a long-term basis, but it is handy for quick file copying or browsing a Web page.

The speed of ordinary networks connected through Ethernet cables is 10, 100, or 1,000 megabits per second (Mbps), whereas the maximum speed of a Bluetooth network is only 1 Mbps.

Sharing files

When you need to copy a file from one computer to another, you can set up a Bluetooth connection. Sharing files through Bluetooth allows you to transfer files to another computer without the hassle of using connecting cables or mutually compatible removable storage devices like Compact Flash cards or USB flash drives.

To share files through Bluetooth, follow these steps:

1. **Click the Finder icon in the Dock.**

   The Finder appears.

2. **Choose Go➪Utilities.**

   The contents of the Utilities folder appear.

3. **Double-click the Bluetooth File Exchange icon.**

   A Select File to Send window appears, as shown in Figure 3-7.

4. **Select a file.**

   To select multiple files, hold down the ⌘ key and click each file you want to send.

5. **Click Send.**

   A Send File window appears, listing all Bluetooth-enabled devices near your Mac, as shown in Figure 3-8.

6. **Select a Bluetooth-enabled device and click Send.**

   If you choose another Mac computer to receive your files, a dialog might appear on the receiving Mac, asking the user to accept or decline the file transfer, as shown in Figure 3-9.

If the receiving Mac has been configured to Accept and Save or Accept and Open transferred files, you won't see the dialog in Figure 3-9. The dialog in Figure 3-9 appears only if the user has selected Ask What to Do (the default option) when configuring their Bluetooth settings.

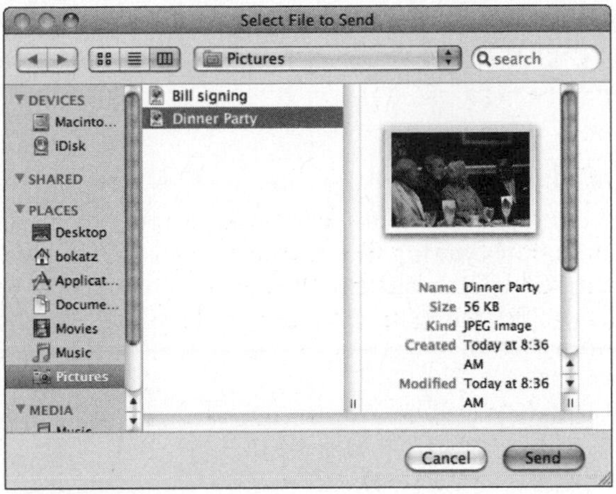

Figure 3-7: The Select File to Send window lets you choose a file to send over a Bluetooth connection.

Figure 3-8: The Send File window lets you choose a Bluetooth-enabled device to receive your file.

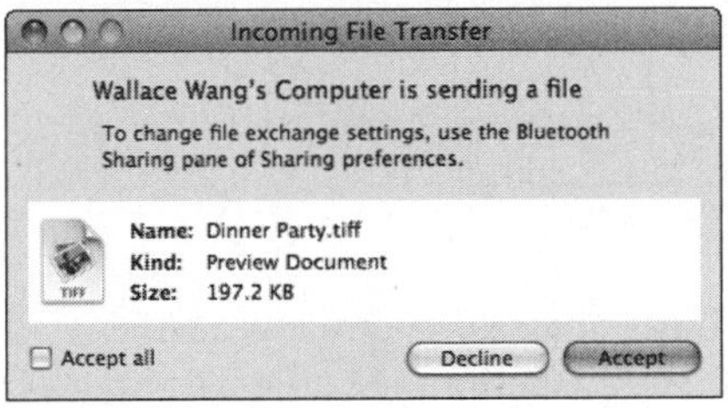

Figure 3-9: The receiving Mac can accept or decline a file transfer.

Sharing an Internet connection

Sharing a Bluetooth Internet connection is great for letting someone browse Web sites or retrieve e-mail through your Internet connection, but you won't be able to use Bluetooth for video conferencing or hosting a Web site, due to the slower Bluetooth data transfer speeds.

To share an Internet connection, follow these steps:

1. **Choose ⇨System Preferences.**

   The System Preferences window appears.

2. **Click the Sharing icon under the Internet & Network category.**

   The Sharing pane appears.

3. **Click Bluetooth Sharing.**

   A list of options for configuring Bluetooth sharing appears (refer to Figure 3-1).

4. **Click Bluetooth Preferences.**

   A Bluetooth window appears (refer to Figure 3-2).

5. **Click the Advanced button.**

   A dialog appears, as shown in Figure 3-10.

6. **Select the Share My Internet connection with Other Bluetooth Devices check box.**

7. **Click OK.**

   At this point, follow the steps in the earlier "Pairing with your Mac" section to use the Bluetooth Assistant to link your Mac to a Bluetooth-enabled device. After you finish linking another device to your Mac, you'll be able to share your Internet connection. Pairing keeps other computers from trying to access the Internet through your Mac.

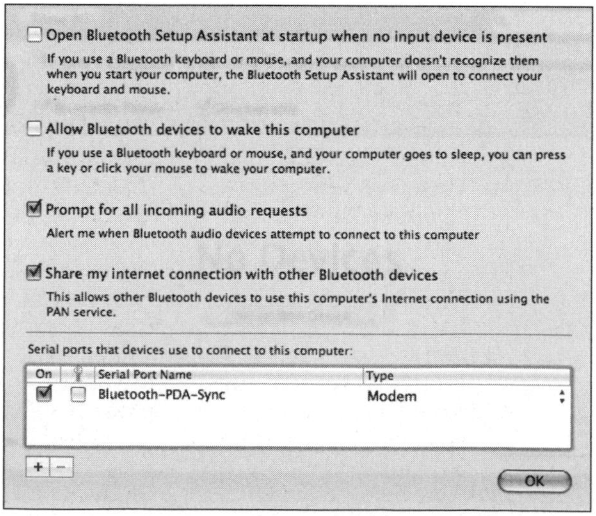
Open Bluetooth Setup Assistant at startup when no input device is present
If you use a Bluetooth keyboard or mouse, and your computer doesn't recognize them when you start your computer, the Bluetooth Setup Assistant will open to connect your keyboard and mouse.
Allow Bluetooth devices to wake this computer
If you use a Bluetooth keyboard or mouse, and your computer goes to sleep, you can press a key or click your mouse to wake your computer.
Prompt for all incoming audio requests
Alert me when Bluetooth audio devices attempt to connect to this computer
Share my internet connection with other Bluetooth devices
This allows other Bluetooth devices to use this computer's Internet connection using the PAN service.
Serial ports that devices use to connect to this computer:
On
Serial Port Name
Type
Bluetooth-PDA-Sync
Modem
OK

Figure 3-10: A dialog displays options for sharing Bluetooth connections.

Index

Numbers

4th Dimension database, 594
68000 processors, 11

A

AAC (Advanced Audio Coding) format, 185–186
AbiWord word processor, 79, 572–573
About Me Web pages, 446
About This Mac window, 12–13, 615
Academic Superstore site, 633
access levels, 740
access points, 727, 729
accessibility features
  hearing limitations, 155–156
  keyboard limitations, 156–157
  mouse limitations, 157–159
  overview, 153
  speech capabilities, 164–166
  vision limitations, 153–159
  voice recognition, 160–164
accessories, game-playing, 637
Account Summary dialog, Mail, 295–296
accounts
  creating, 147–149
  deleting, 151–152
  e-mail, 292
  Guest
    defining parental controls, 348–353
    overview, 347
  Managed with Parental Controls, 345–347, 353–354
  overview, 145–146, 344–345
  setting up, 16
  switching between, 149–151
  types of, 146–147
Accounts pane, iChat Preferences pane, 333
Accounts preferences pane, 147, 149–151
Acrobat Reader program, 288
Action transitions, Keynote, 528
actions, Automator
  adding, 711–712
  deleting, 711–712
  overview, 705–709
  rearranging, 711–712
  running, 712
  Watch Me Do action, 721–722
  workflows
    creating, 709–711
    opening saved, 713
    saving, 713
    testing, 712
activating Spaces, 70
active programs, 56
Activity Monitor program, 171–172
Add Arrange Region button, GarageBand window, 471–472
Add Bookmark dialog, 270–271
Add Buddy dialog, iChat, 321–322
Add button, Buddy List window, 322–323
Add Column After option, Numbers Table menu, 544
Add Column Before option, Numbers Table menu, 544
Add Field menu, Address Book, 680–681, 683–684
Add Row Above option, Numbers Table menu, 544
Add Row Below option, Numbers Table menu, 544
Add to Existing Event radio button, iMovies, 404–405
Add To Sidebar check box, Save As dialog, 120, 122
Address Book
  adding e-mail address to, 308–309
  groups, 685–689
  managing files, 689–692
  names
    adding pictures to, 683–684
    deleting, 685
    designing templates, 679–681
    displaying companies and people, 682
    editing cards, 682–683
    searching, 685
    storing, 681–682
  overview, 679
Address Book Archive format, 692
Address Book check box, Speech Commands subtab, 163
Address Book widget, Dashboard, 698
Address Panel, Mail, 309
addresses
  e-mail, 308–310
  Web site, 265, 361–362
Adjust play, iTunes, 188
Adjust window, iPhoto, 395
Administer Printers restrictions, 348
Administrator accounts, 146–147, 344
Adobe Acrobat Reader program, 578
Adobe Dreamweaver, 79
Adobe Flash, 224, 598, 610–611
Adobe Illustrator, 609–610
Adobe Photoshop, 598, 608–609
Adobe Photoshop Elements, 79, 389

Adobe Photoshop Lightroom program, 609
Adobe SoundBooth, 79
Advanced Audio Coding (AAC) format, 185–186
Advanced Encryption Standard (AES), 118, 654
Advanced window, iTunes, 203
advertiser-sponsored Web site hosts, 360–362
AES (Advanced Encryption Standard), 118, 654
AFP (Apple Filing Protocol), 747
AfterTheMac wireless adapters, 258
AIFF (Audio Interchange File Format), 184
AIM (AOL Instant Messenger), 319
Airport Extreme base stations, 258–259, 728–735
Airport Extreme card, 258
Airport Utility dialog, 730–734
Alarm pop-up menu, iCal edit dialog, 669
alarms, iCal event, 668–669
Album view, iTunes, 191–193
albums, iPhoto, 386–389
Albums option, Front Row Music menu, 252
alert sounds, 140, 155–156
alias icons, 62–64, 88
align left text justification, Pages, 488
align right text justification, Pages, 488
All group, Address Book, 685
Allow All Incoming Connections radio button, Firewall pane, 341
Allow Anyone privacy level, iChat, 333
Allow Only Essential Services radio button, Firewall pane, 341
Allow People in My Buddy List privacy level, iChat, 333
Allow Power Button to Sleep the Computer check box, Energy Saver dialog, 20
Allow Specific People privacy level, iChat, 333
Always open in column view check box, Options window, 104
anchor points, 222, 277, 605
Animation Engine and Revolution program, 639
animation, graphics, 587
Anime Studio program, 610
Announce the Time check box, Date & Time preferences pane, 138
Any pop-up menu, New Smart Folder window, 121–122
AOL Instant Messenger (AIM), 319
appearance, 135–137
Apple Aperture program, 609
Apple Filing Protocol (AFP), 747
Apple Lossless format, 184
Apple menu, 33–34, 74–75
Apple Remote, 239–243
Apple TV, 253
Application menu, 33–34
Application Specific Items check box, Speech Commands subtab, 163
Application Support folder, 89–90
Application Switcher, 66
Application Switching check box, Speech Commands subtab, 163
applications, 241–242. *See also* programs
Applications folder, 60, 80, 93, 96
AppZapper uninstaller program, 91
Aqua user interface, 26
arcade games, 636–639
Arrange By pop-up menu, Options window, 103
Arrange By submenu, Finder View menu, 101
Arrow button, Save As dialog, 106–107
arrow keys, 31, 71
arrows
  on icons, 63–64
  scroll, 41
Artists option, Front Row Music menu, 252
Artwork column, Track Editor pane, 480
ASCII (Text) files, 576
Aspect Ratio pop-up menu, iMovies New Project dialog, 407
Aspyr strategy games, 634–635
AssaultCube game, 638
attachments, e-mail, 298–299, 307–308
Attachments field, iCal edit dialog, 670
Attendees field, iCal edit dialog, 670
Audacity open source program, 79
audio. *See also* GarageBand; Smart Playlists, iTunes
  burning audio CDs, 202–204
  file formats, 183–186
  iMovie video clips, 418–419
  iTunes
    converting CDs into digital files, 188–190
    deleting playlists, 202
    importing digital audio files, 190–191
    listening to CDs, 186–188
    overview, 186
    playing digital audio files, 194–195
    playlists, 196–197
    searching for songs, 195
    sorting digital audio files, 191–194
  listening to in Front Row, 246–247
  overview, 183

streaming, 288
tracks in DVD Player, 236
audio chats, 325, 328–329
Audio Interchange File Format (AIFF), 184
Audio tab
Magic iDVD window, 428
Media Browser, 520–521
audiobooks, 253–254
Audio/Video Interleaved format, 224
Audit My PC site, 343
Auto Flash program, 632
automatic log in, 148–149
Automatically Setup Account check box, Mails New Account dialog, 293–294
Automator
actions
adding, rearranging, and deleting, 711–712
creating workflows, 709–711
opening saved workflows, 713
overview, 707–709
running and testing workflows, 712
saving workflows, 713
overview, 705–707
workflows
digital photography, 716–718
files, 718–720
text, 713–716
Watch Me Do action, 721–722
Average Quick Formula, Numbers, 550

B

Back button, Safari, 276–277
Back command, Go menu, 98–99
Background Color button, Pages Format Bar, 487
background images, Desktop, 129–130
backups
CDs and DVDs, 644
data-recovery programs, 651–654
external hard drives, 645–646
FileVault, 654–658
hard drives, 644
iCal data, 677–678
off-site, 646
overview, 643
Time Machine
defining files to skip, 648–650
overview, 646–647
retrieving files and folders, 650–651
setting up, 647–648
USB flash drives, 644–645
balance, sound, 139
Base Station Password text box, Airport Utility dialog, 734
BBC language lessons, 628
Bcc (Blind carbon copy) field, Mail Message window, 299–300
Bento database, 594
Berlitz language course, 629
Blank Web pages, 447
Blind carbon copy (Bcc) field, Mail Message window, 299–300
Block Everyone privacy level, iChat, 333
Block Specific People privacy level, iChat, 333
Blog Web pages, 447
blue tabs, text boxes, 499
Bluetooth wireless networks
configuring, 752–753
identifying capabilities, 751
pairing devices, 754–756
removing paired devices, 757
sharing through
files, 758–759
Internet connection, 759–760
overview, 757–758
Blu-ray discs, 223–224
Bold icon, Pages Format Bar, 487
Bonjour networking standard, 748
bookmarks
video, 231–233
Web browser
adding, 270–271
deleting, 271–272
importing and exporting, 274–276
moving, 272–273
overview, 268–276
storing in folders, 273–274
using, 274
books, iPhoto, 399–400
Boot Camp
amount of free space, 615
choosing operating system with, 619–620
hardware capabilities, 615
overview, 614
Windows streaming audio programs, 288
booting up, 15–16, 167–170, 240–241
bouncing junk e-mail, 355–356
box, scroll, 41
Boxing Manager game, 635
Brain Tease program, 632
Bridge Construction Set game, 636
broadband connections, 257–258
Broderbund Kid Pix open source program, 79
Bronze-ranked programs, CrossOver Mac, 624
browsers, 291
browsing
Internet. *See also* bookmarks, Web browser
defining home page, 264–265
overview, 264
searching for Web sites, 267
searching previously viewed sites, 267–268
with SnapBack, 276–277
tabbed browsing, 277–279

browsing *(continued)*
visiting Web sites, 265–266
Web Clips, 279–281
iPhoto Library Events, 375–376
Buddi open source program, 79
Buddy List window, iChat, 322
buddy lists, iChat, 321–325
Buddy names submenu, iChat, 324
Build In transitions, Keynote, 528
Build Inspector pane, Keynote, 529–530
Build Out transitions, Keynote, 528
built-in Desktop images, 129–130
Bullet Point text boxes, Keynote, 518
Burn CDs and DVDs restrictions, 348
Burn Folders, 125–127
Burn option, Magic iDVD window, 429
burning
audio CDs, 202–204
files and folders to CD/DVD, 125–127
GarageBand music, 476
iDVD projects to DVD, 440
photos, 398
video straight to DVD with iDVD, 425–426
business reports, 594
Business widget, Dashboard, 698
buttons, iDVD project, 438

C

cable modems, 262
cables, security, 335
Calculator widget, Dashboard, 698
Calendar category, Automator, 705
Calendar widget, Dashboard, 671
calendars
iCal
adding to groups, 662
Calendar List, 660–664
creating, 661
moving, 663
moving existing to groups, 662
moving out of groups, 662–663
renaming, 663–664
renaming and deleting, 663–664
iPhoto, 399–400
Call of Duty game, 638
camera angles, video, 236
cameras, digital video, 403–405
CameraSalvage program, 653
Camino open source program, 79
Cancel option, Close dialog, 39
Canvas X program, 609–610
capturing images, 213–216
Carbon copy (Cc) field, Mail Message window, 299–300
Carbon Copy Cloner program, 646
card readers, 212
cards
Address Book, 679
iPhoto, 399–400
Cat 6 cables, 726
cathode-ray tubes (CRT), 132
Cc (Carbon copy) field, Mail Message window, 299–300
CDs
audio
burning, 202–204
converting into digital files, 188–190
in Front Row, 250–251
listening to in iTunes, 186–188
backing up to, 644
booting from, 169–170
burning to, 125–127
jammed, 174
saving GarageBand music to, 476
saving iPhoto images to, 398
cell references, 550, 583
cells
Numbers table, 536, 542, 553–556
spreadsheet, 582
Cells Inspector window, Numbers, 548–549, 554–556
cellular phones, 735–738
Celtx word processor, 79, 574
Center option, System Preferences window, 131
center text justification, Pages, 488
chapters, DVD, 230
character styles, Pages, 491–493
Chart button, Numbers, 585
Chart Inspector window, Numbers, 557–558
Chart Wizard button, Microsoft Excel, 585
charts
Numbers, 536, 538, 540–541, 556–559
spreadsheet, 585–586
chats. *See* instant messaging
Check for New Mail pop-up menu, Mail General pane, 305
Check Spelling pop-up menu, Mail Composing pane, 303
Choose Backup Disk button, Time Machine pane, 647–648
Christmas Super Frog game, 637
Circular selection tools, image-editing programs, 219
ClamXav open source program, 79
Clean Up Selection, Finder View menu, 101
click-and-drag method, 112
clicking, with mouse, 26–27

clip art images, 599
Clipping Indicator icon, Pages text boxes, 498
clips, video. *See* iMovie; videos
Clock icon, iMovies, 414
Clock preferences pane, 138
Clone Stamping Tool, 221–222
Close buttons
 Dashboard widgets, 696–697
 windows, 38
closed captioning, DVD Player, 235–236
closing documents, 73
closing windows, 38–39
Coda Web page designing program, 367
code, HTML, 365–366
Color It! program, 608
Color Picker window, OS X, 519–520
colors
 color-coding iCal events, 670–671
 coloring pixels, 603
 icon arrangement by, 102
 image, 219–220, 394–395
 Keynote presentation, 518
 Keynote text, 519–520
 presentation program text, 587
 removal, Instant Alpha, 505–506, 526
 user interface, 136–137
Colors pop-up menu, Display preferences pane, 135
columns
 Numbers tables, 544–546
 page formatting, 571
Columns field, Exposé & Spaces window, 69, 72
Columns view, Finder, 99, 103–104
ComicBookLover program, 633
Command key, 31–32
commands, 30, 34–35, 50–52
Commands subtab, Speech Recognition preferences pane, 162–163
Comma-Separated Values (CSV) format, 562, 595
commercial software, 78
compact discs. *See* CDs
compact Flash Type I and Type II, 208
compatibility
 office suite, 589
 word processor, 571
Composers option, Front Row Music menu, 252
Composing pane, Mail Preferences pane, 303
Compress command, File menu, 115
Compress option, GarageBand Send Song to iTunes dialog, 476
compressed files, 87, 184–186
Compressed option, Image Format pop-up menu, 116
computers
 forensics, 653
 identifying parts of, 13–14
 models, 9–11
 overview, 1–5
 pairing Apple Remotes with, 242–243
 processors, 11–13
configuration, Bluetooth, 752–753
Connect as dialog, 746–747
connections, Internet
 dial-up access, 261–263
 Ethernet connection, 257–258
 overview, 257
 wireless access, 258–261
consumer version Web page designing programs, 367
Contact Sheet print style, 396
Contacts category, Automator, 705
Content pane, 350
Content restrictions, 348
Content Slider, Numbers, 561
Continuous play, iTunes, 188
Contrast adjustments, iPhoto, 395
conversion
 file formats, 578–579
 graphics files, 611–612
 programs, digital video file format, 225
Copy Finder Items action, Automator, 718
copying
 files or folders, 108, 111–113
 Pages formatting styles, 495
 text, 568
Corel Painter X program, 608
costs
 .MAC, 369–370
 laptop, 10
 office suites, 589
 Web site hosting services, 362
Count Quick Formula, Numbers, 550
Cover Flow view
 Finder, 99, 104–105
 iTunes, 191, 193–194
crashed programs, 74–75
Create a Partition for Windows box, Boot Camp Assistant window, 617
Create button, Mails New Account dialog, 293–294
Create New Event radio button, iMovies, 404–405
Create Project dialog, iDVD, 430–431
Create Project option, Magic iDVD window, 429
cropping images, 390–391
CrossOver Mac, 624–625
CRT (cathode-ray tubes), 132
crunching numbers, 581
CSV (Comma-Separated Values) format, 562, 595
Currency category, Excel Format Cells dialog, 585
Currency icon, Numbers Format bar, 548
custom image dialog, 684

Custom option, iCal edit dialog, 668
Custom Solution of Maryland site, 632–633
customization
  accounts
    creating, 147–149
    deleting, 151–152
    overview, 145–146
    switching between, 149–151
    types of, 146–147
  Dashboard widget, 694–695
  date and time, 137–139
  Desktop, 129–132
  display and appearance, 135–137
  DVD Player, 236–238
  iWeb Web page parts
    deleting objects, 454
    moving object, 451
    overview, 451
    rearranging object, 453–454
    resizing object, 452
    working with text, 454–456
  overview, 129
  picking printer, 144–145
  saving energy, 142–143
  screen saver, 132–135
  sounds, 139–142
cutting text, 568
Cyberduck FTP client program, 368, 458

D

Dashboard widgets
  adding, 697–699
  customizing, 694–695
  deleting, 702–703
  disabling, 701–702
  finding new, 700–701
  moving, 694
  overview, 29, 693–694
  removing, 696–697
  shortcut key, 695–696
  Web Clips, 279–281
Dashcode program, 703
data, 30
data protection. *See* backups
Data Rescue II program, 654
data sharing, Boot Camp, 622
databases, 594
data-recovery programs, 651–654
Date & Time preferences, 137–139
Date Created option, Arrange By pop-up menu, 101, 103
Date Modified option, Arrange By pop-up menu, 101, 103
date, sorting iPhoto Library Events by, 380
Day button, iCal, 664–666, 671
Decimal icon, Numbers Format bar, 548
Decrease decimal places icon, Numbers Format bar, 548
dedicated Web page designers, 367–368
default file formats, 578–579
default image retrieval programs, 210–211
default operating system, 619
default printers, 145
default themes, Keynote presentations, 511–512
default widgets, Dashboard, 693
DefCon games, 635
Delete keys, 30–31, 485–486, 569
Delete the Home Folder radio button, delete user account dialog, 152
deleting
  accounts, 151–152
  Address Book
    groups, 689
    information from, 310
    names, 685
  alias icons, 64
  Automator actions, 711–712
  Dashboard widgets, 702–703
  e-mail messages, 310–311
  filenames, 110
  files and folders, 108, 127–128, 651
  iCal
    To Do tasks, 675–676
    events, 670
  iMovie
    projects, 411–412
    video clips, 410–411
  iPhoto pictures, albums, and folders, 389
  iTunes playlists, 202
  Keynote slides, 516–518
  mailbox folders, 314
  names and groups in iChat buddy list, 324–325
  Numbers elements, 540–541, 545, 556, 559, 561
  Pages text, 485–486
  Photo Booth pictures, 214–215
  printers, 144–145
  program icons, 86
  smart mailboxes, 316
  songs from iTunes playlists, 197
  styles from Styles Drawer, 495
  text, 569
  user setting files, 89–90
  video bookmarks, 232–233
  video clips, 234–235
  Web browser elements, 271–272, 279
  Web Clips, 281
  Web page objects, 454
  Web pages, 448
Description text box, Incoming Mail Server dialog, 294
Desktop folder, 96
Desktop preferences pane, 130–132
desktop publishing programs. *See* Pages
Desktops
  changing, 129–132
  configuring Spaces, 69–70
  creating, 69
  icons, 44–45

moving windows to different, 70–71
number of available, 72
overview, 68
removing program icons from, 87–88
switching, 71–72
turning off Spaces, 72–73
Device category, Finder Sidebar, 94–95
device icons, DMG, 85
Devices category, Finder window Sidebar, 49, 94
Devices menu, iSync, 736
DHCP (Dynamic Host Configuration Protocol), 258, 732
dialogs, 35, 106–108
dial-up Internet access, 261–263
Dictionary widget, Dashboard, 698
digital audio files
converting CDs into, 188–190
in Front Row, 246–247, 251–252
importing to iTunes, 190–191
playing, 194–195
saving GarageBand music as, 476
sorting, 191–194
digital editors, 217
digital image file formats, 209
digital photography, 205–209, 609, 716–718. *See also* images
digital scrapbooks, 633
digital video cameras, 403–405
Digital Video Disc (DVD) format, 223–224
digital video files, 224–226, 405–406, 420
direct message text chats, 327
Direct Selection tool, vector-editing programs, 605–607
Directories group, Address Book, 685
Disable Remote Control Infrared Receiver check box, System pane, 339
disabling
Dashboard widgets, 701–702
screen savers, 134–135
Disc Burning item, System Profiler window, 14
disc formats, video, 223–224
disc image (DMG) files, 83–85, 114–118, 440
Disc Setup category, DVD Player, 237
disconnecting drives, 95
disk maintenance, 175–179
Disk Utility program, 116–118, 168, 175–179
DiskWarrior program, 168
display, computer, 18, 135–137
DivX player, 224
DMG (disc image) files, 83–85, 114–118, 440
Do Not Back Up dialog, Time Machine, 649–650
Do Not Change the Home Folder radio button, delete user account dialog, 152
.doc format, 575–576
Dock
force quitting through, 75
icons, 45–48
minimizing windows, 39
removing program icons from, 87–88
restrictions, 348
storing files and folders in, 123–125
switching between programs, 65
Docs & Spreadsheets office suite, 591–592
document files, 59
document icons, 59–62
document templates, Pages, 481–484
document windows, 65
documents, 73. *See also* Pages; word processing
Documents folder, 61, 93, 96
documents list, icon shortcut menu, 65
.docx format, 575–576
domain names, 265, 364
Don't Save option, Close dialog, 39
dots under icons, 56, 65
Double Mat print style, 397
double-clicking, 26–27, 59–62
Down control, Apple Remote, 239
downloading
files, 289–290
images off Web sites, 215–216
software, 83
video players, 225
widgets, 700–701
Downloads folder, 96
Downloads window, Safari, 289–290
Drag Media Here to Create a New Project pane, iMovies, 407
dragging
icons to Dock, 57
with mouse, 26–27
Dragon Burn program, 127
drawing
file formats, 612
versus painting, 597–599
programs, 608–611
vector editing
Direct Selection tool, 605–607
drawing lines, 607–608
overview, 604
Selection tool, 604–605
Dreamweaver Web designing program, 368
drivers, printer, 144
Drop Box folder, 740
Drop Photos Here drop well, Magic iDVD window, 428
DSL modems, 262
Ducking feature, GarageBand, 478
due dates, iCal, 674
duplicate files, 643–644
duplicating iCal events, 666–667

DVD (Digital Video Disc) format, 223–224
DVD option, Front Row menu, 245
DVD Player
audio tracks, 236
closed captioning, 235–236
controlling with Apple Remote, 242
creating video clips, 233–235
customizing, 236–238
DVD and Title menus, 229
full screen and window modes, 226–228
overview, 226
placing bookmarks in video, 231–233
skipping through video, 229–230
viewing different camera angles, 236
viewing frames in steps and slow motion, 230
DVD/CD master option, Image Format pop-up menu, 117
DVDs. *See also* DVD Player; iDVD
backing up to, 644
booting from, 169–170
burning to, 125–127
jammed, 174
playing in Front Row, 246
saving iPhoto images to, 398
Dynamic Host Configuration Protocol (DHCP), 258, 732

E

EazyDraw program, 610
eBook Library program, 632
Edit button
Address Book, 683
iPhoto, 390
edit dialog, iCal, 667–669
Edit Drop Zones button, iDVD project window, 433
Edit Keywords dialog, iPhoto, 385
Edit Mask button
Keynote Format menu, 525
Pages Format menu, 503
Edit menu commands, 34, 111
editing
audio in GarageBand
arranging tracks by regions, 471–473
joining track, 469–470
modifying key and tempo, 473–474
moving tracks, 470–471
overview, 468
splitting track, 468–469
cards in Address Book, 682–683
To Do tasks, 675–676
documents, 578
events, 667–670
images
adding visual effects, 393–394
controlling colors, 394–395
cropping, 390–391
fixing, 393
overview, 216–222, 389
rotating, 389–390
straightening, 392
iMovie video clips
adjusting size, 413–415
audio files, 418–419
overview, 412
rearranging order, 412–413
titles, 415–417
transitions, 417–418
Numbers charts, 558
Pages text, 485–486
pictures and movies in Keynote, 523–527
video footage, 402
educational programs
languages, 627–630
mental skills, 632–633
music, 630–631
typing, 631–632
effects, Keynote, 527–530
Effects window, iPhoto, 394
Eject button, Finder, 95
Eject Disk option, DVD menu, 246
Eject key, 29–30
ElephantDrive site, 646
elliptical selection tools, raster-editing programs, 600–601
e-mail
.MAC accounts, 369
backing up to accounts, 646
deleting messages, 310–311
filters, 357
iPhoto images, 397–398
junk, 354–357
number of accounts, 363
organizing
mailbox folders, 313–314
overview, 311–318
rules, 316–318
searching, 311
smart mailboxes, 314–316
sorting, 311–312
overview, 291
reading, 306–307
retrieving, 305–306
sending Web pages by, 285–286
setting up account, 291–296
storage space, 364
storing addresses, 308–310
viewing and saving file attachments, 307–308
writing
creating new, 296
e-mail stationery, 300–302
file attachments, 298–299
forwarding messages, 297–298
messages to multiple recipients, 299–300
overview, 296
replying to messages, 297
spell and grammar checking, 303–305
Email option, Alarm pop-up menu, 669

eMedias software tutorials, 631
emptying Trash, 87–88, 128, 311
Enable Access for Assistive Devices check box, Seeing preferences pane, 154–155
Enable Fast User Switching check box, Accounts preferences pane, 150
Enable Spaces check box, Exposé & Spaces window, 69
Encapsulated PostScript (EPS) files, 612
Enclosing Folder command, Go menu, 99
encryption
  FileVault, 148, 346, 654–658
  USB flash drive, 645
  wireless network, 728
Encryption pop-up menu, New Image from Folder dialog, 118
End key, 31
Energy Saver dialog, 19–21
Energy Saver preferences pane, 142–143
Enhance button, iPhoto window, 393
entertainment
  educational programs
    languages, 627–630
    mental skills, 632–633
    music, 630–631
    typing, 631–632
  games
    arcade, 636–639
    online role-playing, 639–640
    strategy, 634–636
  hobbies, 633–634
  overview, 627
Envelopes option, Address Book Styles pop-up menu, 690
Episode Artwork box, Track Editor pane, 480
EPS (Encapsulated PostScript) files, 612
Eraser tools, raster-editing programs, 602
erasing
  Photo Booth pictures, 214–215
  pixels, 602–603
ergonomic input devices, 166
error messages, 266, 712
Escape key, 29–30, 245
ESPN widget, Dashboard, 698
Ethernet cables, 725–726
Ethernet Internet connections, 257–258
EVE Online game, 639
Event Library, iMovie, 401–406
Event name text box, iPhoto, 376
Events category, iPhoto sidebar, 380–381
events, iCal
  adding information to, 669–670
  changing description of, 667
  checking for specific date, 671–672
  checking for today's, 671
  color-coding, 670–671
  creating, 664–666
  deleting, 670
  duplicating, 666–667
  moving, 666, 669
  overview, 660, 664
  recurring, 667–668
  searching for, 672–673
  selectively hiding, 671
  setting alarm for, 668–669
  viewing, 664
Events, iPhoto Library
  browsing through, 375–376
  creating, 375
  merging, 377–378
  moving pictures from one to another, 379
  naming, 376–377
  overview, 375
  sorting, 380–381
  splitting, 378
  viewing pictures stored in, 381–383
Exchange accounts, 291
exiting folders, 98
expanded dialogs, 35
Export As dialog, Safari, 283–284
Export Movie dialog, iMovies, 420
Export to Disk dialog, GarageBand, 476
exporting
  Address Book, 690–691
  iCal data, 676
  Keynote presentations, 532–534
  Numbers spreadsheets, 562–563
  Pages documents, 507–508
  Web bookmarks, 274–276
Exposé & Spaces icon, System Preferences window, 69
Exposé & Spaces window, 69–70, 72–73
Exposé feature, 42–44, 66–67
Exposure adjustments, iPhoto, 395
extensions, Web site address, 265
external hard drives, 645–646
Eyedropper tools, raster-editing programs, 604

F

Facebook networking site, 362
Family program, 633
family tree programs, 633
Fast User Switching, 149–151
fast-forwarding DVDs, 229
fee-based Web site hosting services, 363–364
feedback, GarageBand, 467
Fetch FTP client, 368
ffmpegX program, 225
file attachments, e-mail, 298–299, 307–308
file compression, 643
file extensions, 109–110

file formats
  audio, 183–186
  digital image, 209
  graphic, 611–612
  presentation, 596
  spreadsheet, 595
  word processing
    converting, 578–579
    Microsoft Word, 575–576
    Open Document files, 577
    Portable Document Format files, 577–578
    Rich Text Format files, 576
    Text files, 576
    Web page files, 577
File menu commands, 34
file sharing
  accessing shared folders, 745–747
  defining user access
    giving access, 742–744
    guest privileges, 742
    overview, 741–742
    removing accounts, 744
  overview, 739–740
  through Bluetooth, 758–759
  turning on, 740–741
  Word Processor, 572
File Transfer Protocol (FTP), 368, 458
FileMaker database, 594
filenames, 109–110
files
  .MAC storage for, 369–370
  archiving, 114–118
  burning to CD/DVD, 125–127
  Cover Flow, 104–105
  deleting, 127–128
  delivery services, 298
  DMG, 83–85
  downloading, 289–290
  Finder, 94–99
  manipulating
    copying, 111–113
    moving, 113–114
    overview, 108–109
    renaming, 109–111
  overview, 93
  retrieving with Time Machine, 650–651
  saving Web pages as, 283–284
  searching
    overview, 118
    Smart Folders, 119–123
    Spotlight, 118–119
  size limit of e-mail accounts, 298
  storing in Dock, 123–125
  transfer limitations, 363
  workflows, 718–720
Files & Folder category, Automator, 705, 719–720
FileSalvage program, 653
FileVault encryption, 148, 346, 654–658
FileVault tab, Security pane, 655–657
Fill Screen option, System Preferences window, 131
filtering junk e-mail, 356–357
Final Draft word processor, 79, 574
Find feature, Safari, 281–282
Finder
  Columns view, 103–104
  Cover Flow view, 104–105
  creating folders, 105–108
  downloading DMG files, 84
  hard drive free space, 615
  Icon view, 100–102
  icons, 48–50
  List view, 102
  navigating, 97–99
  overview, 44–45, 94–97
  selecting items in, 100
  stationery images in, 301–302
  using in program installation, 81–82
finding
  events, 670–673
  new Dashboard widgets, 700–701
Firefox Web browser, 79
Firewall pane, Security window, 340–341
firewalls, 327, 342–343
FireWire, 170, 645, 725–726
firmware, 16, 614
first time use dialogs, 85–86
Fit to Screen option, System Preferences window, 131
fixing images, iPhoto, 393
FLAC (Free Lossless Audio Codec) formats, 184
flash memory cards, 94–95, 206–208, 212–213
Flash program, 610–611
Flash video format, 224, 533
flashing screens, 155
Flight Tracker widget, Dashboard, 698
Flip Images action, Automator, 716, 718
Flip4Mac program, 224, 287
folders
  archiving, 114–118
  burning to CD/DVD, 125–127
  deleting, 127–128
  Finder
    Columns view, 103–104
    Cover Flow view, 104–105
    creating folders, 105–108
    Icon view, 100–102
    List view, 102
    navigating, 97–99
    overview, 94–97
    selecting items in, 100
  iPhoto image, 386–389
  mailbox, 313–314
  manipulating
    copying, 111–113
    moving, 113–114
    overview, 108–109
    renaming, 109–111
  overview, 93
  retrieving with Time Machine, 650–651
  shared
    accessing, 745–747
    defining user access, 741–744
    overview, 739–740
    turning on file sharing, 740–741
  storing in Dock, 123–125
  storing Web bookmarks in, 273–274
Font icon, Numbers Format bar, 549

Font pop-up menu, Pages Format Bar, 486
Font size icon, Numbers Format bar, 549
Font Size pop-up menu, Pages Format Bar, 486
Font submenu, iWeb Format menu, 455
Fonts category, Automator, 705
Fonts icon, Keynote toolbar, 519
fonts, Keynote, 518–519
Fonts window, OS X, 519
For New Documents category, Keynote General Preferences pane, 512
force quits, 74–75, 171
force shutdowns, 22
foreign language programs, 627–630
forensics, computer, 653
Format bar
  Numbers, 548–549
  Pages, 486–487
Format button, Numbers Format bar, 554–555
Format Cells dialog, Microsoft Excel, 584
formatting
  Keynote text, 518–520
  Numbers tables, 546–549, 553–556
  Pages styles, 491–495
  Pages text, 486–487
  spreadsheet text and numbers, 584–585
  word processor text and pages, 569–571
Formula Editor, Numbers, 551
formulas
  Numbers, 537–538, 549–553
  spreadsheet, 581, 583–584
FortuneCity Web site hosting service, 361
Forward button, Safari, 276
Forward command, Go menu, 99
forwarding e-mail messages, 297–298
frames, video, 230
Free Lossless Audio Codec (FLAC) formats, 184
free Web site hosts, 360–362
freeware software, 78
Freeway Web page design program, 367
Front Row
  accessing, 244–245
  Apple Remote, 239–243
  movies and videos, 245–250
  music and sounds, 250–254
  overview, 239
  viewing pictures, 254
Front Window check box, Speech Commands subtab, 163
frozen programs, 74–75, 171–174
FTP (File Transfer Protocol), 368, 458
full screen mode, DVD Player, 227–228, 237
function keys, 29–30, 70
functions
  Numbers, 552–553
  spreadsheet, 584
Fusion program, 288, 620–622

G

game engines, 639
games
  arcade, 636–639
  online role-playing, 639–640
  strategy, 634–636
  writing, 639
GarageBand
  editing audio
    arranging tracks by regions, 471–473
    joining track, 469–470
    modifying key and tempo, 473–474
    moving tracks, 470–471
    overview, 468
    splitting track, 468–469
  overview, 459
  recording audio
    overview, 459
    real instruments, 466–468
    software instruments, 463–466
    through Magic GarageBand, 460–462
  recording podcasts, 477–480
  saving music, 474–476
General category, DVD Player, 237
General options, Security window, 243
General pane
  Mail Preferences window, 305–306
  Safari Preferences window, 264
General Preferences pane, Keynote, 511–512
Genre pop-up menu, iTunes Info pane, 199
Genres option, Front Row Music menu, 252
Geocities site, 361
Get Content From pop-up menu, Automator, 710
Get Specified Finder Items action, Automator, 718
Get Specified URLs actions, Automator, 713–715
Get Text from Articles actions, Automator, 713
GIF (Graphics Interchange Format) files, 611
GL Golf game, 638
Global Speakable Items check box, Commands subtab, 163
Global Warming game, 636
Gold-ranked programs, CrossOver Mac, 624
golf games, 638
Google Docs & Spreadsheets office suite, 591–592
Google Pages site, 361
Google widget, Dashboard, 698
grammar checking, e-mail, 303–305

graphic effects, Keynote, 528–530
graphic file formats, 611–612
graphics. *See also* images
  displaying in presentation programs, 587–588
  Web page, 444–445, 449–450
graphics cards, 14
Graphics Interchange Format (GIF) files, 611
GraphicsConverter program, 608
Graphics/Displays item, System Profiler window, 14
green plus signs, 113, 377–378
group text chats, 328
grouping, Keynote slides, 516–518
groups
  Address Book, 685–689
  iChat buddy list, 322–325
Guest Access pop-up menu, Airport Utility dialog, 734
Guest accounts
  creating, 344–345, 347
  defined, 146
  defining parental controls, 348–353
GuitarVision program, 630

H

hackers, 335
HackerWatch site, 343
HandBrake program, 225
handheld devices, 735–738
hard drives
  alias icons on, 63
  backing up, 644
  deleting files from, 89
  folders in, 95–96
  identifying free space on, 615
  maintenance, 175–179
  problems with, 168
  Sleep mode, 18
hardware controls on function keys, 29–30
hardware failure, 651–652
HD DVD (High-Definition Digital Versatile Disc) format, 223–224
headless Macs, 9
headphones, 140–141
hearing limitations, correcting, 155–156
Hearing preferences pane, 155
Help menu, Finder menu bar, 50–51
help system, 50–53
hiding
  To Do lists, 673
  Dock, 48
  events selectively, 671
hierarchy, folder, 96–97
High Definition category, DVD Player, 237
High-Definition Digital Versatile Disc (HD DVD) format, 223–224
Highlight Color pop-up menu, Appearance preferences pane, 137
highlighting options, Front Row, 244
Highlights adjustments, iPhoto, 395
History menu, Safari, 267–269
hobbies, 633–634
Home calendar, iCal, 660
Home key, 31
home pages, 264–265
Honorable Mention-ranked programs, CrossOver Mac, 624
hosting options, Web site, 360
hosts, Web, 360–364
hot corners, 133–135
HTML (HyperText Markup Language), 283, 365–366, 445, 533
http (HyperText Transfer Protocol), 265
hubs, 726–727
hung up programs, 171–174
Hybrid Image option, Image Format pop-up menu, 117
Hyperlink submenu, iWeb Insert menu, 456
hyperlinks, 443, 455–456
HyperText Markup Language (HTML), 283, 365–366, 445, 533
HyperText Transfer Protocol (http), 265

I

ibooks, 10
iCal
  Calendar List item, 660–664
  To Do lists, 673–676
  events
    adding information to, 669–670
    changing description of, 667
    checking for specific date, 671–672
    checking for today's, 671
    color-coding, 670–671
    creating, 664–666
    creating recurring, 667–668
    deleting, 670
    duplicating, 666–667
    moving, 666
    moving to another calendar, 669
    searching for, 672–673
    selectively hiding, 671
    setting alarm for, 668–669
    viewing, 664
  managing files, 676–678
  Mini-Month, 664
  overview, 659–660
iCal widget, Dashboard, 698
iChat
  accepting or blocking invitations, 330–334
  chatting
    audio chats, 328–329
    overview, 325–330
    text chats, 326–328
    video chats, 329–330
  overview, 319

setting up accounts
organizing buddy list, 322–325
overview, 319–321
storing names in buddy list, 321–322
Icon view, Finder, 99–102
icons
Address Book, 682–683
in Apple Menu Bar, 33–34
arranging in Finder Icon view, 100
book, 4–5
Desktop, 44–45
Dock, 45–48, 57–59
Finder, 48–50
folder, 102
overview, 44
program, 81–82, 87–88
starting programs with
alias icons, 62–64
document icons, 61–62
overview, 59–60
program icons, 60
iDraw program, 610
iDVD
burning video straight to DVD, 425–426
creating DVDs with Magic iDVD, 427–429
overview, 425
using iPhoto pictures in, 399
working with projects
adding options to title menu, 433–438
adding photos to title menu theme, 432–433
defining opening content, 439
moving and deleting buttons, 438
overview, 430–432
saving, 440–441
Illustrator program alternatives, 609–610
iMacs, 10
Image Capture program, 210–213
Image Format pop-up menu, New Image from Folder dialog, 116–117
images. *See also* iPhoto
adding to names in Address Book, 683–684
adding to Web pages, 457
capturing, 213–216
digital photography, 205–209
editing, 216–222
GarageBand podcast, 479–480
iDVD project title menu theme, 432–433
in Keynote presentations, 521–527
modifying in e-mail stationery design, 301–302
Numbers, 536, 560
overview, 205
Pages, 501–506
selecting, 599–600
transferring to Mac, 209–213
viewing in Front Row, 254
Images format, 533
IMAP (Internet Message Access Protocol) e-mail accounts, 291
iMovie
adding videos to Keynote presentations, 522–523
editing video clips
adjusting size, 413–415
audio files, 418–419
overview, 412
rearranging order, 412–413
titles, 415–417
transitions, 417–418
importing video into Event Library, 403–406
overview, 401–403
Project Library
creating projects, 406–407
deleting project, 411–412
deleting video clips, 410–411
overview, 406
printing project, 412
selecting video clips, 408–410
saving videos, 419–423
Import Bookmarks dialog, 275–276
Import dialog
iCal, 677
iMovie, 403–404
iTunes, 191
Import Photos dialog, iPhoto, 374
Import submenu, Address Book, 692
importing
data into Address Book, 691–692
iCal data, 677
pictures to iPhoto, 373–375
video into iMovie Event Library, 403–406
Web bookmarks, 274–276
Importing pane, iTunes Preferences window, 188–190
inactivity time, 18
Incoming Mail Server dialog, Mail, 294
incoming server names, 292
Increase decimal places icon, Numbers Format bar, 548
Indent marker, Pages window, 490
indented slides, 516–517
Info dialog, iCal, 670–671
Info pane, iTunes, 198
Info window, 110–111
Information button, Dashboard widgets, 695
input, Automator actions, 706–707
Input preferences pane, 141–142
Insert Function dialog, Numbers, 552–553
Inspector dialog, Numbers, 584
Inspector window, Pages, 501
Install icon, 81–82

installation
software
from CD/DVD, 80–83
off Internet, 83–86
overview, 80
Windows, 616–618
Installation & Setup Guide, 616–617
installer programs, 82–83
Instant Alpha feature, 505–506, 525–527
Instant Calculations, Numbers, 551–552
instant messaging
accepting or blocking invitations, 330–334
chatting
audio chats, 328–329
overview, 325–330
text chats, 326–328
video chats, 329–330
overview, 319
setting up iChat accounts
organizing buddy list, 322–325
overview, 319–321
storing names in buddy list, 321–322
instruments, Magic GarageBand window
making music with, 463–468
overview, 461–462
Intaglio program, 610
Intel processors, 11–13, 77, 615
interface, user. *See* user interface
Interiors program, 634
Internet. *See also* bookmarks, Web browser
browsing
defining home page, 264–265
overview, 264
searching for Web sites, 267
searching previously viewed sites, 267–268
with SnapBack, 276–277
for software, 77–78
tabbed browsing, 277–279
visiting Web sites, 265–266
Web Clips, 279–281
connections
dial-up access, 261–263
Ethernet connection, 257–258
overview, 257
sharing, 749–750, 759–760
wireless access, 258–261
downloading files, 288–290
overview, 257–290
saving Web pages, 283–286
searching for text on Web pages, 281–282
viewing and playing multimedia files, 286–288
Internet category, Automator, 705
Internet Connect program, 263
Internet Message Access Protocol (IMAP) e-mail accounts, 291
Internet Service Providers (ISPs), 257
invitations, iChat, 330–334
iPhoto
adding pictures to Keynote presentations, 521–522
choosing photo for Desktop, 130–131
controlling with Apple Remote, 242
editing pictures
adding visual effects, 393–394
controlling colors, 394–395
cropping, 390–391
fixing, 393
overview, 389
rotating, 389–390
straightening, 392
importing pictures, 373–375
Library Events
browsing through, 375–376
creating, 375
merging, 377–378
moving pictures from one to another, 379
naming, 376–377
overview, 375
sorting, 380–381
splitting, 378
organizing pictures
adding keywords, 385–386
deleting pictures, albums, and folders, 389
naming, 383–384
overview, 381–389
rating, 384–385
storing in albums and folders, 386–388
viewing stored pictures, 381–383
overview, 373
retrieving images using, 210–211
sharing pictures, 396–400
iPod format, 533
iPod presentations, 590
iRemember program, 633
iScrapbook program, 633
iSight video cameras, 213, 329
ISP Web site hosts, 362–363
ISPs (Internet Service Providers), 257
iSync program, 735–736
Italic icon, Pages Format Bar, 487
iTunes
controlling with Apple Remote, 242
converting CDs into digital files, 188–190
deleting playlists, 202
importing digital audio files, 190–191
listening to CDs, 186–188
overview, 186
playing digital audio files, 194–195
playlists, 196–197
saving GarageBand music in, 475–476
saving iMovie videos for, 421
searching for songs, 195

Smart Playlists
defining rules, 199–202
editing, 202
overview, 197
tagging songs, 198–199
sorting digital audio files, 191–194
iTunes Preferences window, 188–189
iTunes Top Movies option, Front Row Movies menu, 247
iTunes widget, Dashboard, 698
iWeb
creating Web sites, 445–448
customizing Web page parts
deleting objects, 454
graphics, 457–458
moving object, 451
overview, 451
rearranging object, 453–454
resizing object, 452
working with text, 454–456
designing Web pages, 449–451
overview, 368–369, 443
publishing Web pages, 458
using iPhoto pictures in, 399
Web page parts, 443–445
iWork program, 573

J

Jam Packs, 460
jammed CDs/DVDs, 174
Jammin' Racer game, 638
jingles, GarageBand, 478–479
joining tracks, GarageBand, 469–470
JPEG (Joint Photographic Experts Group) files, 209, 611–612
jumping
between folders, 98
to video bookmarks, 232
junk e-mail, 313, 354–357
justification, Pages text, 488

K

Keep in Dock option, icon shortcut menu, 57–58
key alert, spoken commands, 161–162
Key pop-up menu, GarageBand window, 474–475
Keyboard preferences pane, 156–157
Keyboard Shortcuts button, Keyboard & Mouse window, 695–696
keyboards
arrow keys, 31
correcting limitations, 156–157
function keys, 29–30
laptop, 10
modifier keys, 31–33
numeric keys, 31
overview, 27–28
typewriter keys, 30
Keynote
adding media files, 520–523
changing presentation views, 512–514
controlling with Apple Remote, 241–242
creating presentations, 509–510
editing pictures and movies, 523–527
exporting presentations, 532–534
overview, 509
rehearsing presentations, 531–532
slides
adding, 514–515
deleting, 516
editing text on slide, 518
formatting text, 518–520
grouping, 516–518
manipulating text, 518
overview, 514–520
rearranging, 515–516
themes, 510–512
transitions and effects, 527–530
viewing presentations, 531
keys, modifying GarageBand tracks by, 473–474
keystrokes
shortcuts, 32–33
Word Processor, 568
Keyword Is pop-up menu, Speech Recognition preferences pane, 162
keywords, iPhoto images, 385–386
kilobit values, 184–185
Kind option, Arrange By pop-up menu, 102, 104
Kind pop-up menu, New Smart Folder window, 121–122
Klix program, 653
Known not to work ranked programs, CrossOver Mac, 624

L

Label option, Arrange By pop-up menu, 102, 104
language programs, 627–630
laptop computers, 10, 142
Lasso tools, image-editing programs, 219, 601–602
LCD Mode pop-up menu, GarageBand window, 473–474
LDIF format, 691
learning programs
languages, 627–630
mental skills, 632–633
music, 630–631
typing, 631–632
Left Margin marker, Pages window, 489
Letter Invaders typing tutorial, 632
Letter Star word processor, 573–574
libraries
Automator, 711
iMovie, 401–406

Library Events, iPhoto
browsing through, 375–376
creating, 375
merging, 377–378
moving pictures, 379
naming, 376–377
overview, 375
sorting, 380–381
splitting, 378
viewing pictures stored in, 381–383
Library folder, 96
Library of Widgets, Dashboard, 698
License Agreement window, 84
Light Table view, Keynote, 512, 514
line spacing
Pages text, 487–488
word processors, 570
Line tool, vector-editing programs, 608
Lineform program, 610
lines, drawing, 607–608
Link pane, iWeb, 456
linked text boxes, Pages, 498–500
links. *See* hyperlinks
list styles, Pages, 491, 493
List view
Finder, 99, 102
iTunes, 191, 192
Listen Continuously with Keyword radio button, Speech Recognition preferences pane, 162
Listen Only while Key Is Pressed radio button, Speech Recognition preferences pane, 162
listening keys, 161–162
Lists option, Address Book Styles pop-up menu, 690
Location field, iCal edit dialog, 670
log files, 353
log in, automatic, 148–149
Login Options, Accounts preferences pane, 149–150
login passwords, 655
Logs pane, Parental Controls, 353–354
Loop Browser, GarageBand, 478–479
lossless audio files, 184
lossy audio files, 184–186
lottery programs, 634
Lotto Sorcerer program, 634
Lux Delux game, 636

M

.Mac, 319, 369–370
Mac Data Recovery program, 654
Mac Game Creator Toolkit, 639
Mac Help window, Finder, 52–53
Mac Mini computers, 11
Mac OS X CD/DVD, 169
Mac OS X operating system, 16, 77
Mac Pro computers, 11
MacBook computers, 10
MacFamilyTree program, 633
Macintosh computers
identifying parts of, 13–14
models, 9–11
overview, 1–5
pairing Apple Remotes with, 242–243
processors, 11–13
MacLink Plus file-conversion program, 579
Magic Eraser tool, raster-editing programs, 602
Magic GarageBand, 460–462
Magic iDVD, iDVD, 425, 427–429
Magic Wand tool, 602
Magnetic Lasso tools, 219, 601
magnifying Dock, 47–48
Mail & iChat pane, 351
Mail & iChat restrictions, 348
Mail category, Automator, 705
Mail Photo dialog, iPhoto, 397–398
Mail program, 79, 291–292
mailbox folders, 313–314
mailboxes, smart, 314–316
Mailing Labels option, Address Book Styles pop-up menu, 690
maintenance
frozen or hung up programs, 171–174
hard drive, 175–179
overview, 167
preventative, 179–180
removing jammed CDs/DVDs, 174
startup troubles, 167–170
Male or Female Voice track, GarageBand window, 477
malware, 335
Manage Widgets button, Dashboard, 702–703
Managed with Parental Controls accounts, 146, 344–347, 353–354
margins, Pages text, 487–491
Mariner Write word processor, 573
MarinerPak office suite, 594–595
marquees, 219, 601
masking pictures
Keynote, 524–525
Pages, 503–504
master passwords, 655–656
Math & Music program, 630
Math Practice program, 632
Mavis Beacon Teaches Typing program, 631
Maximum Quick Formula, Numbers, 550
Media Browser
GarageBand, 479–480
iMovie, 423
iMovies, 423
Pages, 484
Media button
iDVD project window, 432
iWeb window, 449, 457–458
media files, Keynote, 520–523

Media icon
Keynote window toolbar, 520–522
Numbers Sheet pane, 560
Pages toolbar, 484, 502
MediaMax site, 646
megapixels, 205–206
Mellel word processor, 573
memory cards, flash, 206–208
memory requirements, Boot Camp, 623
Memory Sticks, 208
mental skills programs, 632–633
Menu Bar check box, Speech Recognition Commands subtab, 163
menu bars, 33–34, 227
Menu control, Apple Remote, 240–242
menulets, Spaces, 33–34, 70, 72
menus
DVD and Title, 229
Finder, 106
Front Row, 244–245
iDVD project, 433–438
Numbers pop-up, 555–556
using to copy files or folders, 111
merging iPhoto Library Events, 377–378
Mesa spreadsheet program, 589
Message option, Alarm pop-up menu, 669
Message with Sound option, Alarm pop-up menu, 669
messaging. *See* instant messaging
metronomes, 468
mice, 26–27, 41, 111–113, 157–159
Micro SD cards, 208
Microphone Calibration dialog, 161
microphones, 141
Microsoft Excel files, 562
Microsoft Office, 78–79, 589–590, 595
Microsoft PowerPoint file format, 596
Microsoft Windows
Boot Camp
choosing operating system with, 619–620
identifying amount of free space, 615
identifying hardware capabilities, 615
overview, 614
CrossOver Mac, 624–625
installing, 616–618
overview, 613
virtual machines, 620–623
Microsoft Word
alternatives to, 79, 572–573
file formats, 507–508, 575–576
overview, 571–572
Mimic program, 632
Mini SD cards, 208
minimizing windows, 39–40
Mini-Month item, iCal, 664
Minimum Quick Formula, Numbers, 550
minus sign icon, Print & Fax preferences pane, 144
Missile Command clone game, 637
Missing Sync program, 735
mix CDs, 202
mobile phones, 735–738
modems, 262–263
modifier keys, 31–33
Montage word processor, 574
Month button, iCal, 664–666, 671
motocross simulation game, 638
Mouse & Trackpad preferences pane, 158–159
Mouse Keys feature, 158–159
mouses, 26–27, 41, 111–113, 157–159
Move corners, Number tables, 542–543
Move to Trash option, alias icon shortcut menu, 64
Movie Magic Screenwriter word processor, 574
Movie menu option, iDVD, 436
Movie Web pages, 446
movies. *See* videos
Movies category, Automator, 706
Movies folder, 96
Movies Folder option, Front Row Movies menu, 247
Movies, iDVD projects, 430
Movies option, Front Row menu, 245
Movies tab, Media Browser, 457, 522
Movies widget, Dashboard, 698
Moving Picture Expert Group (MPEG) format, 224–225
Mozy site, 646
MP3 (MPEG-1 Audio Layer 3) format, 185–186
MPEG (Moving Picture Expert Group) format, 224–225
MPEG StreamClip program, 225
MPEG-1 Audio Layer 3 (MP3) format, 185–186
MPEG-4 files, 420
multimedia files, 286–288
multiplayer games, 639–640
multiple recipients, e-mail, 299–300
music. *See* audio; GarageBand; iTunes
Music and Sound Effects button, iMovies toolbar, 418–419
Music category, Automator, 706
Music folder, 96
Music menu, Front Row, 246, 249–251
music programs, 630–631
music videos, 248–250
musical genres, Magic GarageBand window, 461
Musical Typing keyboard, 464

My Albums Web pages, 446
My Rating submenu, iPhoto Photos menu, 384–385
My Status submenu, iChat, 331–332
My Submenu button, iDVD projects, 438
MySpace networking site, 362

N

Name & Extension text box, Info window, 110–111
Name option, Arrange By pop-up menu, 101, 103
names
  Address Book
    adding pictures to, 683–684
    deleting, 685
    designing templates, 679–681
    displaying companies and people, 682
    editing cards, 682–683
    searching, 685
    storing, 681–682
  file, 109–110
  folder, 107–108, 109–110
  group, 686
  in iChat buddy lists, 322–325
  iPhoto images, 383–384
  iPhoto Library Events, 376–377
  Numbers sheets, tables, and charts, 542
navigating Finder, 97–99
Navigator view, Keynote, 512
NcFTP Client program, 368
NeoOffice program, 78, 592–594
Network Diagnostics dialog, Safari Web browser, 259–261
Network window, 745–746
networks
  Airport Extreme base stations, 729–735
  Bluetooth
    configuring, 752–753
    overview, 751
    pairing devices, 754–756
    removing paired devices, 757
    sharing through, 757–760
  connecting handheld devices, 735–738
  file sharing
    accessing shared folders, 745–747
    defining user access, 741–744
    overview, 739–740
    removing accounts, 744–745
    turning on file sharing, 740–741
  overview, 725
  printer sharing, 747–749
  sharing Internet connections, 749–750
  wired, 725–727
  wireless, 727–729
New Account dialog, 147–148, 293
New Album dialog, iPhoto, 386–387
New Album From Selection dialog, iPhoto, 387
New Folder dialog, Finder, 107
New Image from Folder dialog, Disk Utility, 116–118
New Mail Sound pop-up menu, General pane, 305
New Mailbox dialog, Mail, 313
New Message window, Mail, 296
New Paragraph Style dialog, Pages, 495
New Person dialog, 744
New Project dialog
  GarageBand, 463–464, 466
  iMovies, 406–407
New Site dialog, iWeb, 446
New Smart Album dialog, iPhoto, 388
New Smart Folder window, 121
New Smart Mailbox dialog, Mail, 315–316
New TextEdit Document actions, Automator, 714–716
New Video Clip dialog, 232–233
Next control, Apple Remote, 239
Nisus word processors, 573
No Access permission level, 740
No security radio button, Airport Utility dialog, 731
None option, Alarm pop-up menu, 669
non-removable devices, 94
Norton AntiVirus program, 79
Note field, iCal edit dialog, 670
Num Lock key, 31
Numbers
  adding pictures, 560
  adding text boxes, 559–560
  creating spreadsheets, 538–539
  deleting text boxes, shapes and pictures, 561
  designing tables, 542–547
  making charts, 556–559
  overview, 535
  sharing spreadsheets, 561–563
  spreadsheet parts, 535–538
  typing data into tables
    deleting data in cells, 556
    formatting data entry cells, 553–556
    formatting numbers and text, 547–549
    overview, 547–556
    typing formulas, 549–553
  working with sheets, 539–542
Numbers category, Excel Format Cells dialog, 584
numbers, spreadsheet, 582–585
numeric keys, 31, 71

Numismatist's Notebook program, 633
Nvu open source program, 79, 367

O

objects, vector graphic
moving with Selection tool, 604–605
reshaping with Direct Selection tool, 605–607
resizing with Selection tool, 604–605
.odf (Open Document) files, 577
Office, Microsoft, 78–79, 589–590, 595
office suites
file formats, 595–596
Google Docs & Spreadsheets, 591–592
MarinerPak, 594–595
Microsoft Office, 589–590
NeoOffice, 592–594
OpenOffice, 592–594
overview, 581
presentation programs, 586–589
RagTime, 594
spreadsheets
charts, 585–586
formatting text and numbers, 584–585
formulas, 583–584
overview, 581–582
parts of, 582–583
ThinkFree Office, 590–591
Office, ThinkFree, 590–591
off-site backup options, 646
offsite storage sites, 369–370
Ogg Vorbis format, 185–186
OmniGraffle program, 609
On CD Insert pop-up menu, Importing pane, 189
OneStep DVD, iDVD, 425–426
online role-playing games, 639–640
Open dialog, iMovies, 405–406
Open Document (.odf) files, 577
Open Document Spreadsheets format, 595
Open File option, Alarm pop-up menu, 669
Open Images in Preview action, Automator, 716
open source programs, 78–80, 572
Open VoiceOver Utility button, Seeing preferences pane, 154
OpenDocument format, 596
opening content, iDVD projects, 430
OpenOffice office suite, 79, 592–594
operating systems, 16, 619–620. *See also* Windows operating system
operators, Numbers formula, 550
Optimization pop-up menu, Energy Saver dialog, 19, 143
Option key, 113
Optional before Commands option, Keyword Is pop-up menu, 162
options, iDVD project title menus, 433–438
Options pane, iTunes, 199
Options tab, Energy Saver dialog, 20–21
Options window, Finder, 103
OSX Skyfighters 1945 game, 638
Other category, Automator, 706
outgoing connections, blocking, 342
Outgoing Mail Server dialog, Mail, 295
outgoing server names, 292
Outline view, Keynote, 512–513
output, Automator actions, 706–707
Output preferences pane, 140–141

P

Pac the Man X game, 637
Page Down key, 31
Page Layout templates, Pages, 481–483, 485
Page Source files, 283–284
Page Up key, 31
Pages
digital photographs, 501–506
document templates, 481–484
exporting documents, 507–508
pages
formatting in word processors, 570–571
Pages
formatting styles, 491–495
overview, 481
spell checking, 506–507
text
editing, 485–486
formatting, 486–487
overview, 485
spacing and margins, 487–491
text boxes
creating, 496
linked, 498–500
moving, 497
overview, 496
resizing, 497–498
wrapping text around, 500–501
pages
Web. *See* Web pages
Paint Brush tool, 603–604
Paint Bucket tool, 603–604
Paintbrush open source program, 79
painting
versus drawing, 597–599
file formats, 611–612
overview, 597
programs, 608–611
raster editing

painting *(continued)*
erasing pixels, 602–603
Magic Wand tool, 602
overview, 599–600
Paint Brush and Paint Bucket tools, 603–604
selecting areas, 600–601
selecting entire pictures, 600
selecting irregular shapes, 601–602
pairing
Apple Remotes with Macs, 242–243
Bluetooth devices, 754–756
Palm OS devices, 736
PAN (personal area network), 751
Paper Size pop-up menu, iPhoto Print dialog, 397
paragraph
margins, 570
styles, 491–492
Parallels program, 288, 620–621
Parental Controls
defining for Guest accounts, 348–353
DVD Player, 237
Managed Accounts with, 345–347
monitoring Managed accounts, 353–354
overview, 146, 344
Partition button, Boot Camp Assistant window, 617–618
partitions, hard drive, 614, 616–618, 620
passkeys. *See* passwords
Password dialog, 337–338
Password pane, Accounts window, 336–337
passwords
account, 336–339
account restrictions, 348
e-mail account, 292
FileVault, 654–655
initial account setup, 16
ISP, 263
paired device, 754
requests for when installing software, 81
wireless network, 728
pasting Pages formatting styles, 495
PDAs (personal digital assistants), 735–738
PDF (Portable Document Format) files
exporting Numbers spreadsheets to, 562
exporting Pages documents to, 507–508
overview, 577–578
saving Keynote presentations as, 533
storing vector graphics as, 612
viewing online, 288
PDF category, Automator, 706
Pen tool, vector-editing programs, 608
Pencil tool, vector-editing programs, 607
People widget, Dashboard, 698
Percentage icon, Numbers Format bar, 548
permissions
disk, 178–179
shared folders, 740
personal area network (PAN), 751
personal digital assistants (PDAs), 735–738
Phone window, Address Book, 680–681
phones, 735–738
Photo Booth program, 213–215
Photo Browser window, iPhoto, 301–302
photographs. *See* images; iPhoto
photography, digital, 205–209
PhotoLine 32 program, 217, 608
Photos & Images option, Automator window, 717–718
Photos button, iDVD project window, 432
Photos category, Automator, 706
Photos category, iPhoto sidebar, 382
Photos tab, Media Browser, 457, 502, 521–522, 560
Photos Web pages, 446
Photoshop Elements program, 217, 608
Photoshop program, 217, 368, 608–609
PhotoStudio program, 608
PhotoStudio X digital editor, 217
PianoWizard program, 630
pictures. *See* images; iPhoto
Pictures Folder, 96, 131
Pimsleur language course, 629
pinball games, 636–637
Pixel digital editor, 217
pixels, 135, 205, 216–217, 597
Pixen digital editor, 217
placeholder text and graphics, Web page, 449–450, 483–484
Places category, Finder window Sidebar, 49
Plain Text file format, 507–508
PlanGarden program, 633
Play Feedback When Volume Is Changed option, Sound preferences pane, 140
Play Front Row Sound Effects option, Sound preferences pane, 140
Play User Interface Sound Effects option, Sound preferences pane, 140
playlists, iTunes, 196–197
Playlists option, Front Row Music menu, 252
PlayMaker Football game, 638
Play/Pause control, Apple Remote, 240

plus sign icon
New Smart Folder window, 121–122
Print & Fax preferences pane, 144
PNG (Portable Network Graphics), 611
Pocket Address Book option, Address Book Styles pop-up menu, 690
podcasts, 252–253, 447, 477–480
Point Selection tool, vector-editing programs, 606
pointer, mouse, 158–159
Polygonal Lasso tool, raster-editing programs, 601
POP (Post Office Protocol) e-mail accounts, 291
pop-up menus, Numbers, 555–556
portable edition, ThinkFree Show presentation program, 590
Portable Network Graphics (PNG), 611
Post Office Protocol (POP) e-mail accounts, 291
power button, 15
Powerbook laptops, 10
Power-Glide courses, 629
PowerPC processors, 11–12, 615
PowerPoint format, 533
Practica Musica program, 630
preferences, DVD Player, 237–238
Preferences folder, 89–90
Preferred Speed pop-up menu, iTunes Advanced window, 203
presentation programs. *See also* Keynote
displaying graphics, 587–588
displaying text, 586–587
file formats, 596
rearranging slides, 588–589
transitions, 588
Presentations category, Automator, 706
Presets pop-up menu, iPhoto Print dialog, 397
preventative maintenance, 179–180
Preview button, iMovies Print dialog, 412
Preview pane, Mail, 306–307
Preview program, 288
Preview window
iChat video chat, 329–330
iDVD, 428–429
for screen savers, 132
Previous control, Apple Remote, 239
Previously Viewed category, DVD Player, 237
prices
.MAC, 369–370
laptop, 10
office suites, 589
Web site hosting services, 362
primitives, 598, 604
Print & Fax preferences pane, 144–145
Print dialog
Address Book, 689–690
iCal, 678
iMovies, 412
iPhoto, 396–397
Numbers, 561
Safari, 284–285
Print Size pop-up menu, iPhoto Print dialog, 397
Print view, Numbers, 561–562
Printer pop-up menu, iPhoto Print dialog, 397
printers, 144–145, 747–749
printing
Address Book, 689–690
iCal files, 678
iMovie projects, 412
iPhoto images, 396–397
spreadsheets, 561–562
Web pages, 284–285
privacy levels, iChat, 332–334
processors, Macintosh, 11–13
Product Quick Formula, Numbers, 550
program files, 59
program icons, 59–60, 80–82, 86–88
programming, game, 639
programs. *See also individual programs by name*
active, 56
browsing for on Internet, 78
controlling with Apple Remote, 241–242
default image retrieval, 210–211
delays in Boot Camp, 622
deleting settings, 86
display of, 35–36
e-mail, 291–292
overview, 55
quitting, 73–75
running from Dock, 55–59
shutting down frozen or hung up, 171–174
Spaces
configuring, 69–70
moving windows to different Desktops, 70–71
number of available Desktops, 72
overview, 68
switching Desktops, 71–72
turning off, 72–73
turning on and creating Desktops, 69
starting with icons
alias icons, 62–64
document icons, 61–62
overview, 59–60
program icons, 60
switching between, 64–68
uninstaller, 91
Project Library, iMovie
creating projects, 406–407
defined, 402–403
deleting
projects, 411–412
video clips, 410–411
overview, 406
printing project, 412
selecting video clips, 408–410
Project window, Magic GarageBand, 462

projects, iDVD
adding options to title menu, 433–438
adding photos to title menu theme, 432–433
defining opening content, 439
moving and deleting buttons, 438
overview, 430–432
saving, 440–441
proofreading, 305, 507
protection, data. *See* backups
PsyncX program, 646
Public folder, 96
Publish All to .Mac option, iWeb, 458
Publish to iTunes dialog, iMovies, 421
Publish to .Mac option, iWeb, 458
pull-down menus, 32
Put the Computer to Sleep When It Is Inactive For slider, Energy Saver dialog, 19, 143
Put the Display to Sleep When the Computer Is Inactive For slider, Energy Saver dialog, 19, 143
Put the Hard Disk(s) to Sleep When Possible check box, Energy Saver dialog, 19, 143

Q

Quick Formulas, Numbers, 550
Quick Look command
File menu, 108–109
Time Machine, 650
Quick Look window, Mail, 308
Quicken program, 79
QuickTime format, 224, 532
QuickTime Player program, 224–225
quitting programs, 73–75

R

race car games, 638
RagTime office suite, 594
Random play, iTunes, 187
RapidWeaver Web page designing program, 367
RAR files, 87
raster images
defined, 597
erasing pixels, 602–603
file formats, 611–612
Magic Wand tool, 602
overview, 599–600
Paint Brush and Paint Bucket tools, 603–604
selecting areas, 600–601
selecting entire picture, 600
selecting irregular shapes, 601–602
RAT (Remote Access Trojan), 342
rating iPhoto images, 384–385
RAW file format, 209, 612
RBroser FTP client program, 368
Read & Write permission level, 740
Read Only permission level, 740
reading e-mail, 306–307
read-only discs, 125
Read-only option, Image Format pop-up menu, 116
Read-Write option, Image Format pop-up menu, 116
Real Player program, 224, 286–287
RealVideo format, 224
Recent Folders command, Go menu, 98
recording audio
overview, 459
podcasts, 477–480
real instruments, 466–468
software instruments, 463–466
through Magic GarageBand, 460–462
Recording window, Automator, 721
Rectangular selection tools, image-editing programs, 219, 600–601
recurring events, iCal, 667–668
red-eye removal tools, 220, 393
Reduce Noise adjustments, iPhoto, 395
regions, arranging GarageBand tracks by, 471–473
registration, domain name, 364
rehearsing Keynote presentations, 531–532
reinstalling operating systems, 169
relational databases, 592
remember icons, book, 4
remodeling programs, 634
Remote Access Trojan (RAT), 342
removable drives, 94–95
removable media, deleting files from, 652
removal, flash memory card, 212–213
Remove From Dock option, icon shortcut menu, 59
Remove History Items pop-up menu, Safari General pane, 268–269
Rename Finder Items action, Automator, 718, 720
replying to e-mail messages, 297
reports, business, 594
Require Pairing check box, Sharing pane, 753
Required 15 Seconds after Last Command option, Keyword Is pop-up menu, 162

Required 30 Seconds after Last Command option, Keyword Is pop-up menu, 162
Required before Each Command option, Keyword Is pop-up menu, 162
resetting handheld devices, 737–738
reshaping objects, Direct Selection tool, 605–607
Resize Columns to Fit Content option, Numbers Table menu, 545
Resize corners, Number tables, 542–544
resizing
  Dock, 46–47
  Numbers charts, 559
  Numbers rows and columns, 545–546
  objects with Selection tool, 604–605
  windows, 38
resolution
  digital photo, 205–207
  screen, 135–136
  vector graphics, 598
Resolutions list, Display preferences pane, 135
Restart Automatically after a Power Failure check box, Energy Saver dialog, 20
restarting computer, 23
restoring iCal backup files, 677–678
Resume Playing option, DVD menu, 246
Retouch button, iPhoto, 393
retrieving files or folders
  with Time Machine, 650–651
  from Trash, 128
Return key, 30
Reunion program, 633
reusing flash memory cards, 206
rewinding DVDs, 229
rewritable discs, 125
Rich Text Format (RTF) files, 507–508, 576
Right Margin marker, Pages window, 490
right mouse buttons, 27
ripping music, iTunes, 186–188
role-playing games, 639–640
Rosetta program, 12
Rosetta Stone language course, 629
rotating images, iPhoto, 389–390
routers, 258–259, 340, 726
Rows field, Exposé & Spaces window, 69, 72
rows, Numbers tables, 544–546
RSS feeds, 713–716
RTF (Rich Text Format) files, 507–508, 576
ruler, Pages window, 489–490
rules, e-mail, 316–318
Rules window, Mail, 317–318
Run Script option, iCal Alarm pop-up menu, 669
running programs, 56, 65

S

Safari Web browser, 79, 264
Safe Mode, 168
SAT Vocab Prep program, 632
Saturation adjustments, iPhoto, 395
Save As dialog, 106–108, 120, 122
Save button, Mail, 308
Save Disc Image As dialog, iDVD window, 440
Save option, Close dialog, 39
Save the Home Folder in a Disk Image radio button, user account deletion dialog, 152
Save VIDEO_TS Folder As dialog, iDVD window, 441
saving
  e-mail file attachments, 307–308
  files, 73–74
  GarageBand music, 474–476
  iDVD projects, 440–441
  iMovie videos, 419–423
  iPhoto images to CD or DVD, 398
  Pages formatting styles, 495
  Web pages, 283–286, 366–367
Scalable Vector Graphics (SVG) files, 612
scrapbooks, digital, 633
screen
  flashes, 155
  resolution, 135–136
screen savers, 132–135
Script formatting word processors, 574–575
scrolling, 27, 41, 105
SEA files, 87
search engines, 267
Search For category, Finder window Sidebar, 49, 122
Search text box, Help menu, 50–51
searching
  Address Book names, 685
  files
    overview, 118
    Smart Folders, 119–123
    Spotlight, 118–119
  iCal events, 672–673
  iTunes songs, 195
  through e-mail, 311
  Web page text, 281–282
  Web sites, 267–268
Second Life game, 640
Secure Digital flash memory cards, 208
Secure Empty Trash, Finder, 128
Secure Shared Disks pop-up menu, Airport Utility dialog, 733
security. *See also* accounts; backups
  cables, 335
  downloading, 289
  firewalls, 340–343
  junk e-mail, 354–357
  overview, 335
  passwords, 336–339

security.*(continued)*
physical, 335–336
slots, 335
wireless Internet, 261
wireless networking, 728
Security pane, iChat, 333–334
Security window, 243
Seeing preferences pane, 154
Select File to Send window, 758–759
Select Invert command, raster-editing programs, 600
selecting
pictures for albums in iPhoto, 387
raster images
areas of, 600–601
entire picture, 600
irregular shapes, 601–602
with Magic Wand tool, 602
overview, 599
Selection tool, vector grapics-editing programs, 604–605
Selective play, iTunes, 187
selectively hiding events, iCal, 671
Send File window, 758–759
Send Song to iTunes dialog, GarageBand, 475–476
servers, 360
Set access for Specific Services and Applications radio button, Firewall pane, 341
Set Alert Options dialog, 165
Set Key dialog, 165
Settings For pop-up menu, Energy Saver dialog, 19
Setup Assistant program, 16
Shadows adjustments, iPhoto, 395
Shape tools, vector-editing program toolbox, 608
Share Your Connection From pop-up menu, Sharing pane, 749
Shared category, Finder window Sidebar, 49
shared folders
accessing, 745–747
defining user access
giving access, 742–744
guest privileges, 742
overview, 741–742
removing accounts, 744
overview, 739–740
turning on file sharing, 740–741
Shared Folders list, Sharing pane, 742
shareware software, 78
sharing Numbers spreadsheets, 561–563
Sharing pane, 740–742
Sharpness adjustments, iPhoto, 395
SheepShaver program, 77
Sheet pane, Numbers, 539–540
sheets, Numbers, 535–536, 538–542, 558
Shields Up! site, 343
Shift key, 100, 168
shooter games, 638
shortcut keys
Dashboard, 695–696
digital-editing programs, 217
Spaces, 70
word processor, 568
shortcut menus, icon, 57–58
shortcuts, keystroke, 32–33
Shorten file format, 184
shortened names, iChat buddy list, 324
SHOUTcast program, 288
Show All Bookmarks window, 271–273
Show Battery Status in the Menu Bar check box, Energy Saver dialog, 21
Show Date and Time in Menu Bar check box, Date & Time preferences pane, 138
Show icons check box, Options window, 104
Show Map command, iDVD window, 439
Show preview column check box, Options window, 104
Show Spaces in Menu Bar check box, Exposé & Spaces window, 70
Show Track window, GarageBand, 464–465
Show Universal Access Status in the Menu Bar check box, Seeing preferences pane, 155
Show Video Effects window, iChat, 329–330
Show View Options, Finder View menu, 103
shows, TV, in Front Row, 247–248
shrinking windows, 43
Shuffle Songs option, Front Row Music menu, 252
shutting down
computer, 22
programs, 73–74, 171–174
Sid Meier's Civilization game, 635
Sidebar, Finder, 49, 94–95, 123
SilverKeeper program, 646
Silver-ranked programs, CrossOver Mac, 624
Simple Border print style, 396
Simple Finder restrictions, 348
Simple Mat print style, 397
single-clicking, 26
SIT files, 87
Sites folder, 96
Size option, Icon view Arrange By submenu, 101, 103
Size to Export radio button, Export Movie dialog, 420
Size to Publish radio button, iMovies YouTube dialog, 422–423
Ski Report widget, Dashboard, 698
skimming iMovie videos, 408–409

skipping through videos, DVD Player, 229–230
Sleep mode, 17–21, 240
Slide Inspector, Keynote, 527
Slide Only view, Keynote, 512–513
sliders, Numbers, 553–555
slides, Keynote
adding, 514–515
deleting, 516
grouping, 516–518
overview, 509, 514
rearranging, 515–516
slideshows
Front Row, 254
iDVD, 430, 434–436
presentation programs, 586–589
Slope Rider game, 638
Slow Keys feature, 156–157
slow motion, DVD Player, 230
Smart Albums, iPhoto, 388
Smart Folders, 64, 119–123
Smart Groups, Address Book, 686–689
smart mailboxes, 314–316
Smart Playlists, iTunes
defining rules, 199–202
editing, 202
overview, 196–197
tagging songs, 198–199
SnapBack feature, 276–277
Soccer Manager game, 635
social networking Web sites, 362
software
finding, 77–80
firewall programs, 342
installing
from CD/DVD, 80–83
off Internet, 83–86
overview, 80
overview, 77
problems, 16
programs, 11–12
uninstalling
overview, 86–87
program icons, 87–88
user setting files, 89–91
software instruments, 460, 463–466
songs, iTunes playlist, 196–197
Songs option, Front Row Music menu, 252
Sort Buddies submenu, iChat, 323–324
sorting
e-mail, 311–312
iPhoto Library Events, 380–381
Sound Effects preferences pane, 139–140
sounds, 139–142, 520–521
Spaces feature
configuring, 69–70
moving windows to different Desktops, 70–71
number of available Desktops, 72
overview, 68
switching Desktops, 71–72
turning off, 72–73
turning on and creating Desktops, 69
spacing, Pages text, 487–491
Spam filters, 357
Speak N Spell program, 633
speech
capabilities, 164–166
recording, 477–478
Speech Recognition preferences pane, 160–163
speed
dial-up connection, 262
flash memory card, 207
wireless standard, 258–259
spell checking
e-mail, 303–305
Pages documents, 506–507
Spelling and Grammar dialog
Mail, 304–305
Pages, 506–507
spelling, on search engines, 267
splitting
iPhoto Library Events, 378
tracks, GarageBand, 468–469
Sports Interactive Games, 635
sports simulation games, 638
Spotlight feature
Address Book window, 685, 688
Finder, 62, 88
iCal, 672–673
iTunes, 195
Mail, 311
overview, 118–121
spreadsheets. *See also* Numbers
charts, 585–586
file formats, 595
formatting text and numbers, 584–585
formulas, 583–584
overview, 581–582
parts of, 582–583
spyware, 342
Stacks, Dock, 124–125
Standard accounts, 146, 344
Standard print style, iPhoto Print dialog, 396
standards, wireless, 728
StarOffice office suite, 593
star-ratings, photos, 384–385
Start from Beginning option, DVD menus, 246
Start Screen Sharing button, iChat, 326
starting point action, Automator, 709–711
startup, 15–16, 167–170
Startup Disk window, 619–620
stationery, e-mail, 300–302
status, iChat, 331–332
Stellar Phoenix Macintosh program, 653
Stellar Phoenix Photo Recovery program, 653
Step command, Automator, 712
steppers, Numbers, 553–555
stepping through videos, DVD Player, 230
Stickies widget, Dashboard, 698
Sticky Keys, 156–157

Stitch Painter program, 633
Stocks widget, Dashboard, 698
storage capacity, flash memory card, 206–207
storage space, Web site, 363
storing files and folders in Dock, 123–125
straightening images, 392
strategy games, 634–636
streaming audio, 185, 288
Stretch to Fill Screen option, System Preferences window, 131
student edition, Microsoft Office, 572
StuffIt Expander program, 87
Style icon, Numbers Format bar, 549
Style pop-up menu, Pages Format Bar, 486
Styles Drawer, Pages, 494
styles, Pages formatting, 491–495
Styles pane, Numbers window, 547
Styles pop-up menu, Address Book Print dialog, 690
submenus, iDVD, 430, 438
subtitles, DVD, 235–236
Sum Quick Formula, Numbers, 550
SuperDuper program, 646
SVG (Scalable Vector Graphics) files, 612
switches, 726–727
switching
  Desktops, 71–72
  between programs, 64–68
Symantec Security Check site, 343
symbol guide, keystroke commands, 33
synchronizing handheld devices, 737
System folder, 96
System pane, Security window, 338–339
System Preferences window
  Energy Saver icon, 18–19
  Exposé & Spaces icon, 69–70, 72–73
  Keyboard & Mouse icon, 26
System Profiler window, 13–14
System restrictions, 348

T

Tab key, 30
tabbed browsing, 277–279
Table Inspector pane, Numbers, 546
Table Tennis Pro game, 638
Tables icon, Numbers Sheet pane, 540–541
tables, Numbers
  defined, 536–537
  designing, 542–547
  overview, 540–541
  typing data into
    deleting data in cells, 556
    formatting data entry cells, 553–556
    formulas, 549–553
    numbers and text, 547–549
    overview, 547
Tagged Image File Format (TIFF), 209, 611
Take Video Snapshot action, Automator, 716
Target Disk Mode button, Startup Disk window, 620
tasks, iCal To Do, 674–676
technical stuff icons, book, 4
Teen Life game, 640
telephone modems, 262
television shows, in Front Row, 246–249
temperature adjustments, iPhoto, 395
Template window, Address Book, 680
templates
  Address Book, 679–681
  Numbers, 539
  Pages document, 481–484
tempo, modifying GarageBand tracks by, 473–474
temporary styles, Pages, 495
Ten Thumbs Typing Tutorial program, 631
Terminal window, 172–174, 179–180
text
  Automator workflows, 713–716
  iDVD, 430, 436–437
  Keynote, 518–520
  Pages
    editing, 485–486
    formatting, 486–487
    overview, 485
    spacing and margins, 487–491
  presentation programs, 586–587
  spreadsheet, 584–585
  Web page, 281–282, 444, 449, 454–456
  word processors
    adding, 567–568
    copying, 568
    cutting, 568
    deleting, 569
    formatting, 569–570
  wrapping around Pages text boxes, 500–501
Text (ASCII) files, 576
text boxes
  Numbers, 536, 559–560
  Pages
    creating, 496
    linked, 498–500
    moving, 497
    overview, 485, 496
    resizing, 497–498
    wrapping text around, 500–501
  Web page, 454–455
Text category, Automator, 706
text chats, 325–328
Text Color button, Pages Format Bar, 487
Text color icon, Numbers Format bar, 549
text editors, 366
text effects, Keynote, 528–530
Text File format, 692

Text Inspector window, Pages, 490–491
text justification, Pages, 487
text labels, spreadsheet, 582–583
Text Size drop-down menu, Options window, 104
Text to Speech preferences pane, 164–165
TextEdit program, 571
Theatrical Trailers option, Front Row Movies menu, 247
Theme button, iWeb window, 450
Theme list, New Site dialog, 446
themes
Keynote presentation, 511
Web site, 446–447, 450–451
Themes pop-up menu
iDVD project window, 431
Magic iDVD window, 427
ThinkFree Office office suite, 590–591
thumbnail images
Exposé, 43, 66–67
iMovie video, 402, 404, 412
Thunderbird open source program, 79
TickerType program, 633
TIFF (Tagged Image File Format), 209, 611
Tiger Woods PGA Tour game, 638
Tile Game widget, Dashboard, 698
Tile option, System Preferences window, 131
Time Limits account restrictions, 348, 352
Time Machine
defining files to skip, 648–650
overview, 646–647
retrieving files and folders, 650–651
setting up, 647–648
time settings, 137–139
Time Zone preferences pane, 138
timeline, Time Machine, 650
timers, Keynote slideshow, 532
timing screen savers, 133
Tint adjustments, iPhoto, 395
Tip icons, book, 4
title bars, window, 38
Title menus, DVD, 229
title menus, iDVD project, 430, 433–438
Title text boxes
iPhoto, 383–384
Keynote, 518
titles
iMovie video clip, 415–417
sorting iPhoto Library Events by, 380
To Do lists, iCal
adding tasks to, 674
completing tasks, 675–676
deleting tasks, 675–676
editing tasks, 675–676
hiding, 673
prioritizing, 674–675
setting due dates for, 674
viewing, 673
To field, Mail Message window, 299
Toast Titanium burning program, 127
toaster screen saver, 133
toolbars, 42
toolbox, raster-editing program, 599–600
Toon Boom Studio program, 610
Track Editor pane, GarageBand, 479–480
Track Info pane, GarageBand, 467–468
trackpads, 10
tracks, GarageBand, 468–473
transitions
iMovie video clip, 417–418
Keynote, 510, 527–528
presentation, 588
Translation widget, Dashboard, 698
Transmit FTP Client program, 368
transparent images, 505–506, 525–527
Transparent Language course, 629
Trash, 87–88, 127–128, 310–311
trial periods, software, 78
triangle symbols, folders, 102–103
Trim Clip pane, iMovies, 414–415
Tripod Web hosting service, 361
troubleshooting
CDs and DVDs, 169, 174
frozen or hung up programs, 171–174
hard drive, 175–179
overview, 167
preventative maintenance, 179–180
startup troubles, 167–170
Turn Off FileVault button, Security pane, 657
Turn On FileVault Protection check box, New Account dialog, 148
Tux Racer game, 638
TuxPaint program, 79, 609
TV shows, in Front Row, 246–249
TV Station Manager game, 635
Tycoon series games, 635
typewriter keys, 30
typing programs, 631–632
typing, right to left, 571

U

Underline icon, Pages Format Bar, 487
Unforgettable Languages course, 629
UniLang language Web site, 628
uninstalling software
overview, 86–87
program icons, 87–88
user setting files, 89–91

Unit Converter widget, Dashboard, 698
Universal Access preferences pane, 153–159
universal binaries, 11–12
universal file formats, 577
unlinking text boxes, Pages, 500
Untested ranked programs, CrossOver Mac, 624
Up control, Apple Remote, 239
uploading
  defined, 288
  Web pages, 368
URL field, iCal edit dialog, 670
USB flash drives, 644–645
USB ports, 645
Use Ambient Noise Reduction check box, Input preferences pane, 142
Use Secure Virtual Memory check box, System pane, 339
Use Theme radio button, Keynote General Preferences pane, 512
user access, shared folders, 741–744
user accounts, 344
user interface
  changing color of, 136–137
  dialogs, 35
  help system, 50–53
  icons
    Desktop, 44–45
    Dock, 45–48
    Finder, 48–50
    overview, 44
  keyboard parts
    arrow keys, 31
    function keys, 29–30
    modifier keys, 31–33
    numeric keys, 31
    overview, 27–28
    typewriter keys, 30
  menu bar, 33–34
  menu commands, 34
  mouse parts, 26–27
  overview, 25–26
  windows
    closing, 38–39
    manipulating with Exposé, 42–44
    minimizing, 39–40
    moving with title bar, 38
    overview, 35–37
    resizing, 38
    scrolling through, 41
    toolbar button, 42
    zooming, 40
user setting files, 89–91
usernames, 292
Users folder, 96
Utilities category, Automator, 706
Utilities folder, Go menu, 115–116

V

vCard format, 690–691
VCD (Video Compact Disc) format, 223–224
VDrift game, 638
vector graphics
  Direct Selection tool, 605–607
  drawing lines, 607–608
  file formats, 612
  overview, 598
  Selection tool, 604–605
verification, disk and disk permission, 175–179
Verify Disk option, Disk Utility program, 175–176
Verify Disk Permissions, Disk Utility program, 175
video cameras, digital, 403–405
video chats, 325, 329–330
Video Clips window, 235
Video Compact Disc (VCD) format, 223–224
video games, 623, 634, 637
VIDEO_TS folder, 440–441
videos. *See also* iMovie
  adding to Web page, 457–458
  digital video formats, 224–225
  DVD Player
    choosing audio tracks, 236
    closed captioning, 235–236
    creating video clips, 233–235
    customizing, 236–238
    DVD and Title menus, 229
    full screen and window modes, 226–228
    overview, 226
    placing bookmarks in video, 231–233
    skipping through video, 229–230
    viewing different camera angles, 236
    viewing frames in steps and slow motion, 230
  in Keynote presentations, 522–527
  online posting, 369
  overview, 223
  playing digital video files, 225–226
  playing in Front Row, 245–250
  in presentation programs, 587
  video disc formats, 223–224
  watching Internet, 286–287
video-sharing, 421–423
views, Keynote presentation, 512–514
virtual machines, 620–623
virtualization programs, 620–623
vision limitations, correcting, 153–159
visual effects, iPhoto, 393–394
VLC media player, 224–225
voice recognition, 160–164
VoiceOver feature, 153–154
volume, 139, 155–156
Volume slider, iTunes, 187

W

Wacky Mini Golf game, 638
Wake for Ethernet Network Administrator Access check box, Energy Saver dialog, 20
Wake When the Modem Detects a Ring check box, Energy Saver dialog, 20
waking up computers, 17
war driving, 728
warning dialog, FileVault, 656
warning icons, 4
Watch Me Do action, Automator, 721–722
Waveform audio format (WAV), 184
Weather widget, Dashboard, 698
Web archives, 283–284
Web Clip widget, Dashboard, 279–281, 698
Web pages
  adding new, 447–448
  creating, 365–368
  designing, 449–451
  parts of, 443–445
  saving, 283–286
  searching for text on, 281–282
  uploading, 368
Web sites. *See also* iWeb
  capturing pictures from, 215–216
  creating Web pages, 365–368
  hosting options, 360
  overview, 359
  searching for, 267–268
  types of, 360–364
  uploading Web pages, 368
  using .Mac, 369–370
  visiting, 265–266
WebStratego game, 636
Week button, iCal, 664–666, 671
Welcome Web pages, 446
WEP radio button, Airport Utility dialog, 731
When Other Devices Browse pop-up menu, Sharing pane, 753
When Receiving Items pop-up menu, Sharing pane, 752–753
Widget Browser, Apple Web page, 700
widgets
  adding, 697–699
  customizing, 694–695
  deleting, 702–703
  disabling, 701–702
  finding new, 700–701
  moving, 694
  overview, 693–694
  removing, 696–697
  shortcut key, 695–696
window mode, DVD Player, 228
windows
  closing, 38–39
  manipulating with Exposé, 42–44
  minimizing, 39–40
  moving to different Desktops, 70–71
  moving with title bar, 38
  overview, 35–37
  resizing, 38
  scrolling through, 41
  switching between programs, 67–68
  toolbar button, 42
  turning browser tabs into, 278–279
  zooming, 40
Windows category, DVD Player, 237
Windows Media Player, 286–287
Windows Media Video format, 224
Windows operating system
  Boot Camp
    choosing operating system with, 619–620
    determining free space, 615
    hardware capabilities, 615
    overview, 614
  CrossOver Mac, 624–625
  installing, 616–618
  overview, 613
  virtual machines, 620–623
Windows program icons, 621
Winter Wolves game, 635
wired networks, 725–727
wireless Internet access, 258–261
wireless keyboards, 241
wireless mice, 241
Wireless Network Name text box, Airport Utility dialog, 730
wireless networks
  Bluetooth
    configuring, 752–753
    identifying capabilities, 751
    pairing devices, 754–756
    removing paired devices, 757
    sharing through, 757–760
  overview, 727–729
word processing. *See also names of specific word processing programs*
  copying or cutting text, 568
  creating documents and adding text, 567–568
  deleting text, 569
  file formats, 575–579
  formatting text, 569–570
  overview, 567
  page formatting, 570–571
  specialized word processors, 573–575
  TextEdit program, 571
Word Processing templates, Pages, 481–483, 485
word processors, 571–575. *See also names of specific word processing programs*

Word program
  alternatives to, 79, 572–573
  file formats, 507–508, 575–576
  overview, 571–572
Work calendar, iCal, 660
workflows, Automator
  creating, 709–711
  defined, 706
  digital photography, 716–718
  files, 718–720
  opening, 713
  saving, 713
  testing, 712
  text, 713–716
  Watch Me Do action, 721–722
World Clock widget, Dashboard, 698
World of Warcraft game, 639
WPA2 radio button, Airport Utility dialog, 731
Wrap Inspector, Pages, 501
Write Only permission level, 740
writing games, 639

X

xD Picture Cards, 208
XDrive site, 646
X-Moto game, 638

Y

YouTube, 421–423

Z

ZIP files, 87, 114–115
zipper icons, 115
Zoom buttons, windows, 40
Zoom feature, Seeing preferences pane, 154
Z-Write word processor, 574